Refiguring
ENGLISH
STUDIES

Refiguring English Studies provides a forum for scholarship on English Studies as a discipline, a profession, and a vocation. To that end, the series publishes historical work that considers the ways in which English Studies has constructed itself and its objects of study; investigations of the relationships among its constituent parts as conceived in both disciplinary and institutional terms; and examinations of the role the discipline has played or should play in the larger society and public policy. In addition, the series seeks to feature studies which, by their form or focus, challenge our notions about how the written "work" of English can or should be done; and to feature writings which represent the professional lives of the discipline's members in both traditional and nontraditional settings. The series also includes scholarship that considers the discipline's possible futures or that draws upon work in other disciplines to shed light on developments in English Studies.

Other volumes in the series:

The American Poetry Wax Museum

REALITY EFFECTS, 1940–1990

Jed Rasula
Queen's University

Refiguring English Studies
Stephen M. North, Series Editor
SUNY at Albany

National Council of Teachers of English
1111 W. Kenyon Road, Urbana, Illinois 61801-1096

Staff Editor: Michael Greer

Interior Design: Doug Burnett

Cover Design: Doug Burnett

NCTE Stock Number: 01372-3050 (hardcover) 01380-3050 (softcover)

"Speeches to a City No Larger Than the Reach of a Single Voice," by Bob Perelman, first appeared in THE FIRST WORLD (The Figures, 1985). Excerpt reprinted by permission.

"Inspection," by Ed Dorn, reprinted by permission of the author.

"Child on Top of a Greenhouse," copyright 1946 by Editorial Publications, Inc. from THE COLLECTED POEMS OF THEODORE ROETHKE by Theodore Roethke. Used by permission of Doubleday, a division of Bantam Doubleday Dell Publishing Group, Inc.

"I Know a Man," by Robert Creeley, from THE COLLECTED POEMS OF ROBERT CREELEY, 1945–1975, copyright 1982 by The Regents of the University of California. Reprinted by permission.

Library of Congress Cataloging-in-Publication Data

Rasula, Jed.
      The American poetry wax museum : reality effects, 1940-1990 / Jed Rasula.
         p. cm. — (Refiguring English studies, ISSN 1073-9637)
         Includes bibliographical references (p.) and index.
         ISBN 0-8141-0137-2 (hardcover). — ISBN 0-8141-01380 (pbk.)
         1. American poetry—20th century—History and criticism—Theory, etc. 2. Poetry—Authorship—Social aspects—United States—History—20th century. 3. Authors and publishers—United States—History—20th century. 4. Authors and readers—United States—History—20th century. 5. Poetry—Publishing—United States—History—20th century. 6. Canon (Literature) I. Title. II. Series.
PS323.5.R37 1995
811'.5409—dc20
                                          95-23878
                                               CIP

CONTENTS

ACKNOWLEDGMENTS

I've had the good fortune to be a member of the editorial board of *Sulfur* for the past ten years, to which I have contributed numerous commentaries on contemporary poetry. Two pieces in particular, focusing on the servility of the renewing establishment and of poets themselves ("Part of Nature—Part of Us" and "Literacy Effects"), provided the polemical incentive to undertake the documentation assembled here. "Literacy Effects" was first presented as a talk at the *Sulfur* conference at Eastern Michigan University in March, 1988. Portions of other chapters were initially tested out as conference papers at annual meetings of the American Comparative Literature Association and the Modern Language Association. "Poetry's Voice-Over," which became part of Chapter One, has been dramatically expanded as a study in mythopoiesis for *Sound States*, edited by Adalaide Morris (University of North Carolina Press). In 1987 Robert von Hallberg solicited my response to an exchange between Jerome McGann and Charles Altieri for the volume *Politics and Poetic Value*, and I thank the University of Chicago Press for permission to absorb that contribution, "The Politics Of, the Politics In," into Chapter Four. Part of Chapter Five appeared in *American Literary History*, and I thank the editor, Gordon Hutner, and Oxford University Press for permission to reprint. Finally, I must sadly acknowledge that my title comes from a short polemic published in that most extraordinary poetry magazine *Temblor*, so ably and ingeniously edited by Lee Hickman, who, if AIDS had not intervened, I could have counted on to be an impeccable and stern reader of *The American Poetry Wax Museum*. My small polemic was reprinted (with some corrections) in the fugitive and indispensable *Jimmy and Lucy's House of "K"*, for which I thank Andrew Schelling and Benjamin Friedlander.

Essential financial support—vital to the documentary research on which this book is based—was provided by the Advisory Research Committee of Queen's University. Subsequently, a grant from the Social Sciences and Humanities Research Council of Canada awarded for a different project inadvertently came to the aid of this one in the last stages of preparation for publication.

While this book is not related to my dissertation, much of the conceptual frame was developed during doctoral studies in the History of Consciousness Program at U.C. Santa Cruz in 1986–87, and I particularly want to thank Hayden White, Jim Clifford, Donna Haraway, Tom Vogler, and Shelly Errington. The Rasula girls, Sonja and Hilda, along with Suzi Wong, have made the long circuit from Santa Cruz and Los Angeles to Canada a migration of love. For general encouragement and/or productive conversations that were vital along the way, I'm pleased to thank Jerry McGann, Marjorie Perloff, Mary Ann Caws, Paul Mann, Nate Mackey, Don Byrd, Charles Bernstein, Clayton and Caryl Eshleman, Jerry and Diane Rothenberg, Andrew Schelling, Steve McCaffery, Mark West, Stephen Pender, and Chris Keep. Frank Burke, Charles Acland, Annette Burfoot, and Mary Carpenter of the Queen's Cultural Studies Group were of invaluable stimulus during a crucial period of composition. My research assistants Sophie McCall, David Cuthbert, and Shannon Chace-Hall endured my puzzling requests with good cheer. I also thank Robert Bertholf and the staff of the Poetry/Rare Books Collection at the Capen Library, SUNY Buffalo, for lucid guidance when I most needed it. Steve North's editorial prompting enabled me to see a definitive shape emerge from a maelstrom of a manuscript, and the anonymous readers for the press stimulated crucial second thoughts that made focusing on a final revision particularly rewarding. Michael Greer's navigation of the manuscript through the final shoals of preparation for the press was a nautical feat which I was lucky to witness, and made everything appear simpler than it really was.

Finally, I would like to dedicate this book to the memory of Mike Erwin, my first companion in the venture, and adventure, of poetry. Completing this book twenty years after a memorable autumn we spent travelling far and wide visiting and interviewing poets together has made me feel, all over again, the acute loss of his charmed existence.

CHAPTER ONE

The Wax Museum

POLEMICAL PREFACE: THE AMERICAN POETRY WAX MUSEUM

On Fisherman's Wharf in San Francisco you can visit the Ripley's Believe It Or Not and the Guinness World Record museums. Since the city was immortalized (as the "San Francisco Renaissance") by the premier reading of "Howl" in the Beat debut at the Six Gallery in 1955, it's a bit surprising not to find a corresponding museum dedicated to poetry. If there were, it would be an American Poetry Wax Museum, operated by the MLA and subsidized by the nationwide consortium of Associated Writing Programs. Special galleries would be dedicated to corporate benefactors, including *The New York Times Book Review, The New Yorker, Poetry* and *American Poetry Review.* Strolling through the exhibits the familiar figures would appear with uncanny verisimilitude—Dickinson, Eliot, Stevens, Frost, Plath—posed in that peculiarly arrested stance only waxen figures have. On the audio headset's guided tour you'd hear the sounds of the poet's voices, and the lip-sync problem would be only mildly disturbing. It might even seem natural that the poems emanate from a voice-over provided by the venue itself.

Do poets really want a waxen shrine, an air-conditioned immortality? Robert Bly used to have a parodic Waxworks feature in *The Fifties* and *The Sixties*. John Ashbery's shadow-sparring with his numerous critical champions for the past two decades has offered one of the more exotic spectacles in the American scene, fretting "this pornographic masterpiece, / Variegated, polluted skyscraper to which all gazes are drawn," and asking in response to the idolators of the high sublime: "What need for purists when the demotic is built to last, / To outlast us, and no dialect hears us?" (*Wave*, 17). Ashbery is only one of a number of poets taken under the custodial wing of the covering cherub, but they all have good cause to write out of a profound terror: they share the same creative panic that inspired Poe's story "The Premature Burial," and drove Albert Fearnaught to patent a Grave Signal Coffin in 1882 in order to placate the public's dread of waking up in a mausoleum.

Is the convenience of the guided tour worth the trouble? After all, there's no real official culture in the United States save for the mirage of that provisional medium, the Required Reading List. But, driven by the fear that there is no culture but consumerism, the culture brokers artificially tone up the tradition by exposing literature to the critical equivalent of ultraviolet sun lamps. There may be something to be said for the apparition of the well-tanned muse; but the superimposed stencil of the bathing suit is distracting. To pretend to a "tradition" not much more than a century old is premature. It's still under contention whether Pound and Stevens can belong to the same tradition. This is to admit, really, that we have no tradition. At best, we might hope to sort out bad habits from original idioms, parasitic attachments from paradoxical aspirations. To invoke "tradition" as if it were an established consensus is hyperbolic at best, and at its worst is predatory philistinism. To insist prematurely on an established lineage is to foreclose on the very energies that seem unavoidably American: the ability (or need) to work in the open, to persist in (or despite, as in Keats's "negative capability") a nagging uncertainty.

The culture brokers can never rest easy as long as there is the slightest uncertainty as to what the culture consists of—unless, that is, they mount a surrogate version in wax. Since (white) America has no ancient culture, nothing conveniently delimited by the ravages of time, cultural watchdogs instinctively fall back on a vigilante temperance morality. Unfortunately, poets themselves have often complied with critical anxieties. It's not enough to recognize that there's "too much" published poetry, as conventional wisdom has it; there is a groundswell of verbal toxic waste. And the Wax Museum is no substitute for a waste management policy. The Wax Museum pretends that simple cutbacks will do the job. The politics of exclusion masquerading as either the New America or the Great Tradition is not a pretty sight. On the other hand, poets on the dole claiming divine right to handouts aren't an appetizing prospect either.

The most painful truth about recent decades of American poetry is this: the lyric voice has contributed to a mode of subjectivity as distinctly American as self-help primers, television game shows, and video arcades. Poets and critics alike are quick to bemoan the fact that poetry is in contention for leisure time. But assuming that poetry is somehow an authentic leisure activity (as opposed to the electronic allures) sidesteps the issue, which has to do with the *economy of attention*. Contemporary American poems tend to be written out of the same reflex that exposes a roll of film on impulse snapshots, a conviction that poetry is good, per se, and that *being a poet* is best of all. Such misplaced assurance does nothing but add a little more wax to the effigy in the Museum.

The notion of leisure time is bankrupt, along with the naïvete of "good intentions." Poetry suffers from a hedonism of literacy, which takes the beauty of its image to be sufficient assurance that evil is always done elsewhere. But one needn't be the originator of evil to recognize one's place in the circuitry that transmits it. What can leisure time be when the political condition is Standby Alert? In a bizarre symbiosis of poet and critic, the *acceptable* American poem has entered a new phase of nostalgia—not a longing for the vanished past, but an ardor for the future to be past as well, so the Wax Museum can be complete, and each spawning striving talent relieved of the terrible need to live in order to have something to write about. Is the fundamentalist hankering after a nuclear Armageddon all that different?

While the American Poetry Wax Museum may be a fanciful illustration, it's not idly conjured. The canon-building anthologies operate in a dignified precinct which is tacitly equivalent to the sanctuary space of the museum—a kind of Arnoldian shrine. I have deliberately sullied the solemnity of the occasion by suggesting that the suitable museum for American poetry is wax, bringing a mass culture medium into contrapuntal relation with a purportedly highbrow practice. In 1980 Don Byrd remarked that "poetry is well on its way to ranking with tatting, restoring antiques, and pitching horseshoes as a harmless pastime," adding that harmlessness had made poetry fashionable. "The number of poets is staggering. For the first time we begin to have a democratic poetry. . . . We offer cradle to grave opportunities for self-expression." But this proliferation demands appraisal, moving Byrd to ask: "Can a democratic poet express anything but himself or herself, and, if not, does 'poetic' self-expression constitute poetry?" ("Meter" 180). The present book is a study of the canonizing assumptions (and compulsions) that have fabricated an image of American poetry since World War II, foremost of which is the enshrinement of the self-expressive subject. Much of what follows oscillates between documentary and polemic in an attempt to preserve the tensions that underlie the field of American poetry and which are typically subdued by anthologists and glossed over by commentators. It is a field of productive tensions, in my view, which are foreclosed prematurely by denials that they exist. In a subject plump with disinformation at almost every level, much more remains to be done than I attempt here. So I offer in this chapter a theoretical scaffolding intended not simply to contextualize the other chapters, but as an invitation to other poets and critics to consider what it means to assemble and police a national canon of poetry.

WAX

> For once the Muse's help will we implore,
> And she shall lodge us, wafted on her wings,
> Above the press and danger of the Crowd,
> Upon some Showman's platform: what a hell

For eyes and ears! what anarchy and din
Barbarian and infernal! . . .
—All moveables of wonder from all parts,
Are here, Albinos, painted Indians, Dwarfs,
The Horse of Knowledge, and the learned Pig,
The Stone-eater, the Man that swallows fire,
Giants, Ventriloquists, the Invisible Girl,
The Bust that speaks, and moves its goggling eyes,
The Wax-work, Clock-work, all the marvellous craft
Of Modern Merlins, wild Beasts, Puppet-shows,
All out-o'-th'-way, far-fetch'd, perverted things,
All freaks of Nature, all Promethean thoughts
Of man; his dulness, madness, and their feats,
All jumbled up together to make up
This Parliament of Monsters.

(Wordsworth, *The Prelude* VII: 656-661, 680-692)

In *The Place of the Stage* Steven Mullaney provides a stimulating account of how literature can occupy a marginal social position that nevertheless embodies the centralizing labor of national destiny. He traces a continuum between civic ceremony and high ritual at the center, to theatrical production, public address, and carnivalesque festivities as they shade over to the periphery (of public awareness, cultural status, and spatial location). Focusing exclusively on sixteenth-century London, Mullaney makes it clear that the drama of display has tantalizing implications for modern museums, collections, and anthologies: "The rhythm is one of exhibition, followed by exclusion or effacement." The sacrificial ancestry of exhibition links display with ritual purgation: "'Exhibition' once referred to the unveiling of a sacrificial offering—to the exposure of a victim, placed on public view for a time preliminary to the final rites that would, after a full and even indulgent display, remove the victim from that view" (74). It's hyperbolic to equate valued paintings with sacrificial victims, of course, but this historical perspective is a necessary compensation for the self-congratulatory spirit of reverence, adulation, and charity that goes by the name of "art appreciation."

Memory and commemoration are contingent on dismemberment, violation—an equation almost formulaically rehearsed in the history of wax displays. Waxworks have traditionally collapsed extremities of human experience into a single configuration. Deriving from traditions of votive offerings, wax modelling was favored in both elite and popular cultures by the seventeenth century (Jordanova 35). Wax effigies of royalty were displayed in their funeral processions, reinforcing the structural distinction between the king's two bodies. Death masks were a customary post-mortem affair for dignitaries. And in revolutionary Paris the two functions merged, when Marie Grosholtz (the young woman who famously became Madame Tussaud) made death masks from the heads of Marie Antoinette and Louis XVI, straight from the guillotine, from which she reportedly fashioned full wax replicas. This particular king and queen embodied the extremes of royal dignity and criminal aberration, features that were to set the parameters for Madame Tussaud's Wax Museum in London in the early nineteenth century. The criminal glamour associated with deposed royalty began to accrue, in wax, to common criminals as well. Virtually all the nineteenth-century waxworks made a point of juxtaposing high and low, court and dungeon, dignity and infamy.[1]

Waxworks pandered to the taste for spectacle, although the mores of the period necessitated cunning presentational strategies. In Wharton's *The Age of Innocence*, a woman of dubious character is referred to as having been "'with Living Wax-Works, touring New England. After the police broke *that* up, they say she lived—'. . ."

---

[1] In *Monstrous Imagination* Marie-Hélène Huet points out an inviting symmetry between Tussaud's wax casts and the infamous criminals Burke and Hare, who procured top quality corpses to sell to medical schools by suffocating living victims. "Unlike Burke, whose smothering caused death, Madame Tussaud, using her plaster casts, brought her famous victims back from death to an illusion of life" (205). As Huet points out, the symmetry was reinforced when, after their apprehension and execution, Burke and Hare themselves became prime exhibits in wax in Tussaud's Chamber of Horrors. Huet goes on to mention Conan Doyle's insistence that Sherlock Holmes's digs be on the same street where Tussaud's Wax Museum had won renown: "The bachelor of crime and the mother of the Chamber of Horrors may be said to have created for the beholder a fictional phrenology of art, a space of investigation halfway between the monstrous womb and the 'detective's rooms,' between the executioner's gaze and the drug-addicted private eye" (217–18).

(36). Waxworks lead straight to the damnation in perpetuity implied by the suspended sentence. The infamies of the "resurrectionist trade" in the eighteenth century had spurred the use of wax models for medical instruction, and these became the basis of nineteenth-century exhibits of dubious character. To cite a typical example, the Cosmorama Rooms in London advertised a "Female Figure formed from the Venus de Medicis," fabricated in wax to reveal the internal organs, "thus affording to those who delight in the contemplation of the sublime productions of Nature an opportunity of doing so without witnessing the disgusting process of the dissection of a natural subject" (Altick 339). Such exhibits were prevalent even as late as the turn of the century in "anatomical museums" which "displayed such exhibits as 'models of genitalia and other parts of the body designed to show the signs of Veneral Disease'" (L. Hall 58). These venues were eventually reanimated in flesh, in the form of *tableaux vivantes* in which actors posed in scenes from famous paintings, operas, and episodes from antiquity. The Coal Hole, for instance, offered "Mme. Pauline and her talented company of female artistes," whose customary *déshabille* made it necessary for the establishment to forbid admission to ladies (Altick 349). Tussaud's, of course, operated at a level above the Coal Hole, but it still had its Chamber of Horrors. Even some of the figures displayed in Tussaud's main promenade were in questionable taste. A writer in *Punch* complained in 1849 that "it is of ill Consequence that there should be a Murderers' Corner, wherein a Villain may look to have his Figure put more certainly than a Poet can to a Statue in the Abbey" (Altick 337).[2] Poets' aspirations didn't need to be confined to Westminster, however, for

---

[2] Wax exhibits continue to be the favored medium for displaying torment. There is a "Blacks in Wax" museum in Baltimore, which documents the inhumanity of the Middle Passage and the slave trade. There is also a "London Dungeon" museum devoted to barbarities of torture (boiling water, flogging, being drawn and quartered, branding, and the rack), along with displays of "early medicine," plague victims, and leprosy. For those in need of an incomparable festival atmosphere, the color brochure advertises "evenings with a difference": "Our amazing, atmospheric premises are available for private bookings, from small cocktail parties, to large Charity or private Balls."

Madame Tussaud had taken note of their wax appeal as early as 1819, when Shakespeare represented "Literature" and "Drama" was depicted by Kemble in the role of Coriolanus. By 1830 Byron and Scott had joined the collection (Cottrell 117, 124), motivating an American viewer to complain that "Shakespeare is represented as a modern dandy, 'who cultivates his hair'; and Byron as a Greek, with a belt around the waist containing a whole arsenal of arms" (Altick 336).

American impresario P. T. Barnum sensed that the heterogeneous format of the wax museum was ideally suited to the democratic hodgepodge of the United States, and tried unsuccessfully to buy Tussaud's. An equally curious American response is that of the author of *The Confidence-Man* (in which the riverboat "Fidèle" is virtually a floating museum for human types in transit). Shortly after completing the novel, Melville went to Europe where, on March 27, 1857, in the museum adjoining the Pitti Palace in Florence, he took stock of Gaetano Zumbo's wax tableaux illustrating in fifteen compartments the depredations of the plague. "Terrible cases & wilderness of rooms of them," Melville noted in his journal, "Death & scythe— pointing— tossed skeletons & tools. horrible humiliation." But Melville's imagination doted on the horrors, itemizing the "intricacy of heaps," putrid corpses, "slime & ooze of corruption." His summary comment: "Moralist, this Sicilian" (*Journey* 220–21).[3] By some law of arcane reciprocity, the Italian semiotician Umberto Eco came to Melville's homeland a century later and found the U.S. summed up (not so morally) as the choice and final destination of the waxwork impulse. "The whole of the United States is spangled with wax museums," Eco discovered, ferreting out seven wax versions of the Last Supper between San Francisco and Los Angeles—a veritable New World resurrectionist trade (*Travels* 12, 16). The perennial American dialectic between old and new, between fantasy and reality, is embodied most hauntingly in wax. "Hop o' My Thumb and Fidel Castro now belong forever to the same ontological area," Eco noted, diagnosing that "constant in the average American imagi-

---

[3] Zumbo's wax "Teatri della Vanità" still exists, and can be viewed in vivid color in the Italian edition of the art journal *FMR* 7 (Ottobre 1982).

nation and taste, for which the past must be preserved and celebrated in full-scale authentic copy; a philosophy of immortality as duplication" (14, 6).

Eco's insight illuminates much of our homespun variety of the repetition compulsion. Driven by a taste for novelty, Americans seem intent on celebrating as sublimely original only those achievements that are servile imitations. It's a cultural anxiety familiar to scholars of colonial and early American literature and art, but I think we find the same compulsions on view in the American Poetry Wax Museum. Commenting on the state of humanistic education for a symposium in 1950, Cleanth Brooks exasperatedly cited Tussaud's to get a point across:

> [T]he study of literature ought not to be merely a tour through a kind of refined Madame Tussaud's. And, with all reverence speaking, the study of literature is too often merely such a tour, with the professor himself the only live figure among the exhibits, and sometimes, yielding to the morgue-like atmosphere, actually becoming himself only a livelier-looking wax effigy. ("Quick" 5)

In subsequent chapters we'll examine the canonization of American forms of poetic derivation; but for the moment it will suffice to point out that the spectre of English verse, from the metaphysicals to Yeats and Auden, animates postwar poetry in a spectacularly ghoulish way, as if the American poet were little more than a wax mannequin outfitted with British couture.

Freud linked the "uncanny" with the phenomenon of doubles, the repetition compulsion, the return of the repressed, premature burial, and the disturbing realism of wax figures. In the sepulchral plenitude of the Anglo-American poetic canon, the doubling is compulsive, the repetition uncannily artificial. This mimicry has traditionally secured official sanction, a recent instance being Helen Vendler's *Harvard Book of Contemporary American Poetry* (the *Faber Book* in England), in the introduction to which she appeals to this sense of poetic doubling, "like a snake doubling back on itself at each motion." Poetry, she says, "looks—and looks again," and each poem "is, in Wallace Stevens's phrase, 'one last look at the ducks'" (2–3). I see in this compulsory reiteration of sovereign moments something that amounts to a definition of poetry as commodity form. It is a systematic displacement of the *double take* by the repetition compulsion, of cognition by re-cognition; a circling back around the already familiar in order to certify familiarity as authority and ownership.[4] Adorno thought such an aesthetic the death of art: "when something becomes too familiar it stops making sense." And I think we can see Stevens's second look at the ducks as the esthete's decadent thrill at *controlled estrangement*, which Adorno called the false allure of "the illusion of intelligibility" that surrounds such moments like a halo (*Aesthetic* 262). In his view, the aesthetic resonance of the uncanny was altogether more powerful because unanticipated and undirected: "Estrangement from the world is a moment of art"—a posture of non-repetition fulminating in America in Emerson's phrase, "this new yet unapproachable America," which culminates an epiphany in his essay "Experience" advancing the radical proposition that *life has no memory* (485).

For two centuries the United States has represented "the new" for the rest of the world. In our time we have a litany of exhortations to "Make it New" in Pound's adamant credo: from Roosevelt's "New Deal" and the Communist organ *The New Masses* to the New Criticism, and most recently Ron Silliman's "New Sentence." But always we're dogged by the sense that the new isn't necessarily real, that reality is somehow more palpably felt in the endowment of antiquity. In the terms Robert Creeley memorably

---

[4] An exemplary demonstration of an uncanny encounter with the spectral double as a condition of property value is Henry James's late tale "The Jolly Corner." The uncanny, Anthony Vidler points out, "might be characterized as the quintessential bourgeois kind of fear: one carefully bounded by the limits of real material security and the pleasure principle afforded by a terror that was, artistically at least, kept well under control" (4). Vidler's project in *The Architectural Uncanny* is to retrieve the concept from this domestication, reintroduce it into public space, and thereby repoliticize the uncanny as the sign of "a yet unfinished history that pits the homely, the domestic, the nostalgic, against their ever-threatening, always invading, and often subversive 'opposites'" (13).

conveys, recounting a question put to another poet at a public reading: "Was that a real poem, or did you make it up yourself?" (*Essays* 577). So too, in his journey into hyperreality, Eco discovered that "the American imagination demands the real thing and, to attain it, must fabricate the absolute fake: where the boundaries between game and illusion are blurred, the art museum is contaminated by the freak show, and falsehood is enjoyed in a situation of 'fullness,' of *horror vacui*" (*Travels* 8). Eco discovered in America what Henry James found in London in the *donée* of his tale "The Real Thing," namely "the perverse and cruel law in virtue of which the real thing could be so much less precious than the unreal . . ." (258).

To approach the wax museum is to apprehend the spirit of Zeno's paradox; this is also the point of reversal—of Eco's hyperreality and Baudrillard's simulacra—when the real starts chasing the copy. While Eco uncharacteristically has not done his homework, and so fails to recognize that the art museum has always been "contaminated" by the freak show of the waxworks and the ethnographic exhibit, he correctly locates the American paradox in a devotion to *authentic fakes*. Eco sees this as a museological syndrome, but Baudrillard came prepared to see America itself as a land overrun by the museum without walls. "The museum, instead of being circumscribed in a geometrical location, is now everywhere, like a dimension of life itself," he wrote in *Simulations*: "We are all become living specimens . . ." (15–16).

By "we" Baudrillard means Europeans, for he sees Americans alleviated from the self-reflection necessary for such awareness. "Here in the U.S., culture is not that delicious panacea which we Europeans consume in a sacramental mental space . . ." (*America* 100). Culture is not *imagined*, I take him to mean, but *lived*, inhabited as a second nature. "In this sense, for us the whole of America is a desert. Culture exists there in a wild state: it sacrifices all intellect, all aesthetics in a process of literal transcription into the real" (99). Baudrillard calls this "the zero degree of culture, or unculture" (78). By "literal transcription" he means what Americans call "know-how," the "can do" military spirit. The European discovers in America "the perfect simulacrum—that of the immanence and material transcription of all values" (28). But because Americans are themselves "simulation in its most developed state, they have no language in which to describe it, since they themselves are the model" (29). So the "charm and power of American (un)culture derive precisely from the sudden and unprecedented materialization of models" (79). Despite his up-to-the-minute jargon, Baudrillard's American tour permits him to revisit preestablished rhetorical *topoi*, European time versus American space. "Ours is a crisis of historical ideals facing up to the impossibility of their realization. Theirs is the crisis of an achieved utopia, confronted with the problem of its duration and permanence" (77). As a result, "We live in negativity and contradiction; they live in paradox (for a realized utopia is a paradoxical idea)" (79).

For Baudrillard, Americans are exotic zoological specimens from which he feels no real immunity because America represents a return of the *expressed*. Europe inaugurated modern industrial techniques which were perfected by Taylorism and Fordism in America, then transformed from modes of production into modes of consumption, finally returning to Europeans as a society of the spectacle, the implosion of the masses in the seductive zones of the simulacra, as hyperreality, as prelude to an empire of signs, land of the totem cult of personality, and other arcane deliberations. One thing is certain: museums were not invented in America; nor were anthologies. The packaging of art and poetry into articulated regencies of the showcase is a European development with which Americans have struggled mightily not to free themselves but to cultivate themselves as the most eligible of specimens, driven by a compulsive need to have their duplicates authenticated.

CONDITIONS OF DISPLAY

Museums are modern institutions, but they perpetuate an old impulse to gather and compare exotica. They are ostensibly vestigial remains of the Renaissance cabinets of curiosity, but with a difference that reveals them to be altogether distinct in kind. Museums are driven by the inventory, the taxonomic compulsion to sort and measure—a *motivated* taxonomy, deriving from the military need for a "disciplinary apparatus" (Hooper-Greenhill 190). Museums are also like factories—or "counter-institutions to the factory," as Philip Fisher puts it, explaining: "As objects become more short-lived and geared to an ongoing series of inventions and improvements that produced, as one side effect, obsolescence, the museum became ever more skilled at preservation; that is, at keeping selected things in a state that would never deteriorate or change" (*Making* 29). Consider how many exhibits are subtitled "Continuity and Change" and the sense of Fisher's comparison becomes evident. The museum is a pedagogic institution as well, though what it teaches is aesthetic aptitude as a requisite in the social transition from production to consumption. Culture consumption in America is not class specific; or, to be more precise, conversance with poetry or jazz is not contingent on having "means." What *is* necessary is enlistment in the evaluative procedures that mint cultural capital as a by-product, foremost of which is recognition.[5] The museum, like the factory, is not merely a "mode" of production but a site prompting membership.

Museums and factories alike are integrated into a corporate continuum predicated on surplus capital—in Veblen's terms, conspicuous wealth. In the United States the grand municipal museums are the endowments of robber barons. These museums developed as public emblems of moral restraint, reassurance that unprincipled business practices could yield benevolent cultural institutions. The museum was thus associated with civic virtue, both on the part of the wealthy patrons and as a corresponding duty of self-enlightenment on the part of the middle classes. The museum becomes the sanctuary of priceless things, validating the corresponding scale of wealth outside—a medium that measures monetary value by defining its quarantined objects as "priceless." They are also ways of recuperating the image of wealth as corporate benefaction of culture under the sign of nationalism.

---

[5] Bourdieu's elucidation of the form of what he calls "social capital" seems to me even more pertinent, at least in America, to the form of cultural capital: "Exchange transforms the things exchanged into signs of recognition and, through the mutual recognition of group membership which it implies, re-produces the group" ("The Forms of Capital" 250).

As Fisher elaborates, "The modern factory system expands during the same period as both the political nationalism and the democratization of access that dominate the historical period from the Enlightenment to the present" (29). The burden of nationalism as an achieved or implemented ideology falls very heavily on those institutions that sustain the myth, or narrate the tale, of an enabling past. The dominant mode of production may be the factory, but factories are notoriously unconcerned with anything but the immediate future. So the burden of the past falls on such antiquarian enterprises as the museum, the anthology, and the classroom. As derivatives of Renaissance cabinets of curiosity—collections of marvels, oddities, and treasures—the taxonomic organization of such collections into museums is late, coinciding with the rise of nationalist rhetorics, so that the very principle of order is felt to be congruent with national identity.[6] (The inventory impulse is itself formalized in the American polity as a census of the population.) It is one thing for a nation to commemorate its own destiny by erecting monuments and statues of heroes; it is quite another to implicate collections of heterogeneous cultural effluvia in this procedure of self-validation.

Some things are more enterprising agents of cultural nationalism than others. Works of art—musical, pictorial, literary—prove to be utterly pliable. The institution puts into operation a system of equivalences involving a qualitative link between a purportedly universal enterprise and a distinctly national goal. If the "human family" can be equated with the beneficence of the American institution hosting the exhibit, the American host becomes inseparable from the

---

[6] My formulation may appear to be at odds with Foucault's familiar account of the demise of the classical *episteme*. But I would emphasize that Foucault analyzes the lapse of an ancient epistemological regime, leading up to the nineteenth century, when "the epistemological field became fragmented, or rather exploded in different directions" (*Order* 346). My account presumes such an explosion, and I further attribute to the rise of nation-states an urgency that has as much to do with regaining epistemological security as it does with political freedom and patriotic pride. Nations become the patrons of the evolving institutions of the new epistemic grids (the discursive sponsorship of unities in Foucault's "archive" in *The Archaeology of Knowledge*), institutions long familiar in the demarcation of disciplines in universities (see Peter Manicas, *A History and Philosophy of the Social Sciences*).

dignity of the premise. "Corporate" sponsorship is hardly restricted to the activities of Exxon, Firestone, or IBM as hosts of blockbuster exhibitions at the Met. The corporate endeavor in its distinctly modern manifestation begins with the *nation* as a strategy of retrospective incorporation, which is located in such symbol factories as the Met and the National Gallery. If Civilization can be thought of as a broadcast network, with History as the feature presentation, then the nation is clearly the host or sponsor. Lest this analogy seem frivolous, one might recall the legacy of archaeological competition in the eighteenth and nineteenth centuries between Britain and France, in which national rivalry was engaged not only in diplomacy and on the battlefield, but in the archaeological excavation of Mesopotamian and Egyptian civilizations.

The "invention of tradition" extends not only into the remote past, but up to the present as well. Eric Hobsbawm sees national traditions as secularized variants of the religious calendar, in which "nationalism became a substitute for social cohesion through a national church, a royal family or other cohesive traditions, or collective group self-presentations, a new secular religion"—a substitute especially relevant to the emerging middle class, "or rather that large intermediate mass which so signally lacked other forms of cohesion" ("Traditions" 303). Hobsbawm is alert to a specifically American inflection of this process, noting that Americans are not merely citizens of a nation and custodians of an invented tradition, but avatars of American*ism*, which is a condition exceeding the scope of political allegiance (280). Where other nations acknowledge certain behavior as unpatriotic, Americans see an almost metaphysical disavowal, something "un-American," a violation of allegedly universal values. This puts enormous pressure on the individual, a pressure not so much to conform as to embody and exemplify, in personal character, the charmed circle of "perfect individualism" which, in Whitman's words, "deepest tinges and gives character to the idea of the aggregate" (479).

Etienne Balibar, discussing the ideology of the nation state, stresses the interdependence of nationality and individuality. "The history of nations," he says, "is always already presented to us in the form of a narrative which attributes to these entities the continuity of a subject" (86). An institutionally mediated solidarity requires "the projection of individual existence into the weft of a collective narrative" (93) and "must at one and the same time be a mass phenomenon and a phenomenon of individuation . . ." (94). Not only does this necessitate prospective acts of identification, but retrospective acts of recognition. Ronald Reagan's ready store of memories involving experiences he never had must be seen as an act of nation building, not a personal pathology—evoked most elegantly in Balibar's epigraph (from Derrida), ". . . a 'past' that has never been present, and which never will be" (86). The paramount requirement of the nation form is the conscription of individuals as agents, not so much as willing agents but agents whose (rational or irrational) self-interest reiterates that of the state as it simulates on a grand scale "the continuity of a subject." In other words, individual subjects must ceaselessly reinscribe the pattern of continuity as they constitute a *holomovement of individuation*. The burden of interiority in the West is the task of making collectivity real; the individual subject is prevailed upon to *realize* the collective will, a hegemonic assignment that Nietzsche took to be an encroachment of "herd" mentality on the individual creative impulse. The collective "universal" of the nation state is literally invisible and inscrutable except in symbols like the flag and the provisional coalescence of sentiment around public occasions of patriotism like the national anthem. The abstraction of the universal demands periodic reincarnation. Even poetry can serve as a signifier of patriotic gallantry, inasmuch as the recitation of its history (as in *The Continuity of American Poetry*) affirms in a nationalist narrative the developmental energies prodigiously evident in the careers of "major" poets. Little wonder, then, that what is canonized is not so much particular poets, but rather the *construction of subjectivity* as such, particularly a subjectivity exemplifying an upward and outward spiral of manifest destiny.

The subscription of individual allegiance to the essentially anonymous sodality of nationhood is what typifies modernity, creating "that remarkable confidence of community in anonymity which is the hallmark of modern nations" (Anderson 40). It is against the backdrop of this anonymity that cultural forms become testaments to individuality. The museum, the anthology, the "greatest hits" package inscribe the numinous order of individuation on an otherwise inscrutable collectivity. The collectivized generality of modern nation states requires individuation so that the pragmatic features of "belonging" may become legible. As any politician knows, bland declarations about the superiority of a nation are ineffective as political slogans unless they are linked with the salient detail—George Bush's "thousand points of light," for instance. The museum collection and the anthology reify the unique, which is transcribed into an image of the collective benevolence of the host. The social medium that most conspicuously qualifies as host is the nation.

What I've been saying will seem intuitively implausible, in that the great museums are obviously international—the Louvre, the Tate, the Met. This is in part because collections of art across territorial boundaries were often established before nation states developed, and art museums are the geographical heirs of these collecting traditions. It also marks the permeability of national borders to the flow of capital assets. The "host" effect, however, works along a metonymic chain that is finalized by nationality. For instance, one of Hitler's priorities in occupying France was to appropriate the works of the Louvre for the ennoblement of Germany. Hitler, like any conqueror, was more than willing to subjugate a populace while putting its art on a pedestal. Artworks signify different nationalities, but not in the mode of conflict, art being pledged by European aesthetics to "universal" characteristics. Flemish paintings in the National Gallery in Washington D.C. obviously denote the Netherlands, but since the Gallery is American these same works *connote* the national host.

"Culture" is unrecognizable except within the confines of that political showcase or exhibition hall, the State. Since the nation state is the explicit medium of collectivity, it is difficult to conceive of cultural performance in collective terms (it being nearly impossible to conflate national purpose with specific private endeavors). Culture therefore becomes a parallel world, a zone that signifies the collective; but it achieves this generality by individual means—a realm that preserves in its own way the ancient doctrine of correspondences, "multum in parvo" and "as above, so below." The category of culture, then, signifies the productive activity of self-entitlement on the part of the patron or sponsor. From the state's point of view, the notable work is individuated, obliged to be *exemplary* so that its surplus aura can generate prestige for the host. There are always two things on display: the show and the sponsor, and Erik Barnouw's work on the role of the sponsor in American mass media illuminates the extent to which "content" is actually filler, a kind of stuffing or internal padding carried along by the structural armature of the host.

Culture, under these circumstances, ceases to resemble the lived milieu that we associate with indigenous peoples, or with the aristocratic societies of royalty and privilege. The debate about the status of culture in a democratic society is too vast to revisit here; but Hannah Arendt's basic formulation is useful. She contends that "culture" and "society" were synonymous when society was understood to consist of people of rank. In the modern democratizing regimes of nation states the notion of society has expanded to include the population at large. Society consists of all the classes, not just the elite. This expanded application of "society" is obviously bound to affect the term "culture" as well, which can no longer be associated with a particular class. Hence the proliferation of categories—high and mass cultures, middlebrow, "counterculture" and even "subculture."

The recent "culture wars" have notably been a debate about distinguishing public from private life, and this is where the positions taken by the different factions are curiously intertwined. The political right, concerned about obscenity, declares that art is thoroughly public: art is inseparable from the issue of display. But the display mentality of the right has been traditionally nourished by its affiliations with wealth and property, so that what's on display as art is really private property beneficently on loan to some exhibiting institution.[7] Part of the censorial impulse, then, derives from a privi-

---

[7] Debora Silverman's scintillating analysis of power, prestige, and art exhibitions in the Reagan administration provides a thorough and commendable overview of the *mentalité* involved. See *Selling Culture: Bloomingdale's, Diana Vreeland, and the New Aristocracy of Taste in Reagan's America.*

leged class's inherited sense that "culture" is specific to its own needs—privileged above all by not being obliged to distinguish public from private. As for the political left, the defense of transgressive art usually hinges on a notion of artistic autonomy, which is but a variant of the class interest concerns of the right. (I'm not aware of anybody attempting to defend Serrano's "Piss Christ" out of a conviction that a majority of the population should be exposed to it.) Thus, both ends of the spectrum converge on the issue of art as special interest, even if the debates are conducted in the name of that vast abstraction, "the public." In any case, the debate is grounded in a view that there are two separate public realms, one of which is paradoxically private. Culture (or the humanities) is an essentially private or inner realm, a "life of the mind," while the ostensibly "worldly" spheres of politics and business are conspicuously ceded to the motives of *private* profit. The dominant political ideology, shared by the left and the right, views the humanities as incompetently capitalistic. A common way of putting it is to speak of artists as impractical or unrealistic; so they are nurtured, supported, capitalized—but also in some measure incarcerated. The humanities are a harem culture.

So where do museums and anthologies fit in? Anything on display is part of harem culture; anything, that is, promised as private gratifications on public view. The gallery of paintings coordinates a dialectical interplay of public and private, as the viewer wanders through public space communing (the word suggests plurality) with the works; these itineraries of devotional attention are private, ideally introspective—even when you come across a group of schoolchildren, the docent is telling them in so many words to look into their own hearts or souls or sensibilities to find out the meaning of the work that seems to be in such plain view ("what does it mean to *you*?"). Do all these accumulated intimate moments add up to culture, however, just because they take place in public? Undoubtedly some public purpose is served by the museum, or by any other host institution; but is the same purpose shared by the artwork? Is the museum purposive in the same way as the artist? Obviously not, since the work is not painted in the museum; the poem is not written for the anthology. These display formats forcibly detach the works

from their previous contexts and rehabilitate them for the comportment appropriate to their new homes.

In Philip Fisher's apt formulation, the museum "resocializes"
the objects adopted as its contents. "The museum swamps, particulates,
and reassembles the artifactual, instrumental, and symbolic object
realms of the past and in the process it silences or effaces, or, as we
might say, 'forgets' large areas of meaning and use" (93). What is "forgotten" is really in some sense what is unknowable because of the constraints imposed by the host. Or, to put this in terms of Fisher's equation of the museum with the factory: the exhibit produces certain kinds
of objects and results, using whatever raw material it has access to. The
mystique of the museum is that some precious object, Rembrandt's
"Nightwatch," has by force of its own radiance summoned protecting
walls around itself. But, considering the long foreground of art plunder
that precedes the modern institution of the museum, it's clear that art
works are hostages, or captives of a narratological adventure which it is
the instituted purpose of the museum to consecrate. The museum
declares a nomenclature of appraisal that places an obligation on the
viewer to undertake a corresponding journey of rehabilitation. This is
not Rilke's archaic torso of Apollo that I have in mind, reproaching the
viewer with the brutal line "Du mußt dein Leben ändern" (you must
change your life); quite the contrary, the museum reassures you that
whatever changes are in the offing are regulated by the institution itself,
and you are to adapt to them in the mode of aesthetic acquiescence lux-
uriating in the primal lure of artistic achievements arrayed before you.

This narrative conducts the viewer to the appointed end of
nationalism through the public relations medium of the "universal."
Again, Fisher's perspective is helpful:

> The museum, as it develops in European culture as a result
> of the Enlightenment, is part of the universalizing zeal of
> Western culture, of which the intellectual project of
> anthropology is an arm. Behind the façade of a curiosity
> about difference, the Enlightenment project of universaliza-
> tion chips away from isolated systems just those fragments
> that can smoothly appear within the widest but still
> ordered cultural totality. (95)

The verb is colorful but precise: the discrete works are always chipped fragmentarily from another context—hence the stress on organic form, harmonic interaction, and formal resolution in aesthetics. T. S. Eliot's famous passage in "Tradition and the Individual Talent" is a thesis of concordances redeemable from the rubble. The "universal" is constituted by a heap of fragments that are reconstituted as contributing features of a new domain. Generic categories like "art" and "poetry" are the tools by which the fractures between the assembled fragments are airbrushed away.

The issue is readily grasped by considering another mode of exhibition, the ethnographic display:

> The artfulness of the ethnographic object is an art of excision, of detachment, an art of the excerpt. Where does the object begin and where does it end? This I see as an essentially surgical issue. . . . Perhaps we should speak not of the ethnographic object but of the ethnographic fragment. Like the ruin, the ethnographic fragment is informed by a poetics of detachment. Detachment refers not only to the physical act of producing fragments, but also to the detached attitude that makes that fragmentation and its appreciation possible. . . . A history of the poetics of the fragment is yet to be written, for fragments are not simply a necessity of which we make a virtue, a vicissitude of history, or a response to limitations on our ability to bring the world indoors. We make fragments. (Kirshenblatt-Gimblett 388)

And, I'd add, we make fragments fit together. That is the art of the display, not only in exhibitions but in film, television, sound recordings, even public events. Fragmentation is necessary for subsequent reengagement and synthesis. There is nothing untoward about this, of course, since mental acts and physical procedures rely on a sequentiation of parts. But there is a damaging conflation of functions in the art of display; as James Clifford stresses, "The *making* of meaning in museum classification and display is mystified as adequate *representation*. The time and order of the collection erase the concrete social labor of its making" (220). The museum does not display its own productive activity, but represents the arrangement of its objects as happily congealed in the explanatory framework that appears to emanate naturally from them. An exemplary artwork or ethnographic object tacitly gives expert testimony to the taste and insight of its host. There are contexts of accident and contexts of purpose, and the power of the collection derives from its ability to purge accidental (metonymic) traces from the object. This involves more than stripping and cleansing; the emergent purposive context is a supplement that must appear inevitable. The spatial context is overshadowed by, or subsumed within, a narrative of temporal rejuvenation. The vanished time of an object's original context dissolves, as the museum time machine cultivates a more capacious time in which objects attain a gregarious conviviality with objects from other times. Ultimately, Pollock and Rubens inhabit the same temporality, which is called "timeless" but is in fact the historical *durée* of the museum.

The narrative of progress installed in displays of science and technology proved contagious in the nineteenth century, providing the model which cultural exhibits were compelled to duplicate. Eurocentric racism and imperialism benefitted enormously from this tendency to reconstruct the cultural past as a totality endowed with evolutionary character. In her study of early modern anthropology, Margaret Hogden sees this restructuring as a way of retaining the old hierarchical orders by transposing their rationale from a spatial to a temporal grid (435). In the process, not only could cultural others be rendered historically tardy and even delinquent, but the rhetoric of self-assurance could be levied on living Western artists as a tacit imperative. The arts were thus regulated diachronically (and cross-culturally) across time, and synchronically as "the modern" came to signify the apex of history. This impossible (and implausible) burden is imposed on the literary chronicle, which is now under orders, as it were, to integrate new figures as a vindication of the logic of progress, while retaining traditional figures without marking them as correspondingly obsolete.

All the small times and micronarratives fade in the presence of the grand time of the institution, the federated array. "The collection replaces history with *classification*, with order beyond the realm of temporality," Susan Stewart argues (151). This is the solace of the museum: its agility at handling the medium of time, its ability to recuperate lost time. Things on display are liberated from time, saved for eternity. The ravages of history that are seen progressively destroying the contextual worlds of periodized things are converted, by the museum and the collection, into a positive force of production. The blurred quotidian incites discursive energy, and the exhibition retards the erasure in explanatory captions; the prized objects emerge purified by an isolation that detaches them from the confusing heterogeneity of their natal states. The collection sanitizes things of their metonymic associations so that a new order can prevail—the taxonomic initiative of the collection itself. What is especially fascinating here is the way in which the labor of gathering is transfigured into the play of an aggregate. The collection becomes the sign of collectivity; the display case and the aesthetic isolation of the pedestal certify the community value of belonging.

The precondition for this new beginning is an act of violent separation, an act of plunder and excision. The principle—if violation can be regarded as principled—is taxonomic. The inventory displaces invention as the means of production: "Once the object is completely severed from its origin, it is possible to generate a new series, to start again within a context that is framed by the selectivity of the collector" (Stewart 152). The rationale of the museum is "preservation," a term that obscures the predatory role of the institution in procuring objects in need of preservation in the first place. So objects in the museum appear like migrants or survivors of natural catastrophe. Their neighbors didn't survive the flood—such is the implication—but they did, and need a new home, a metropolitan hub.[8] As in a vortex, the powerful suction of a center draws all

---

[8] My fantasia is inspired in part by Manuel De Landa's fanciful "robot historian," whose view of humans would necessarily conflict with ours. "The robot would stress the fact that when clockworks once represented the dominant technology on the planet, people imagined the world around them as a similar system of cogs and wheels. . . . The robot historian of course would hardly be bothered by the fact that it was a human who put the first motor together: for the role of humans would be seen as little more than that of industrious insects pollinating an independent species of machine-flowers that simply did not possess its own reproductive organs during a segment of its evolution" (3).

peripheral objects toward it, without exception. Many will be destroyed in the process, but at that legendary calm at the eye of the storm a few will be preserved, and in their continued preservation they will remain securely under the watchful eye. It is within the unique element of calm—that sanctuary stillness enforced literally at gunpoint in art museums—that a peace that passeth understanding suffuses the objects (the plunder) with a new vitality, a throbbing inertia. In such environs, a "narrative of luck" reinforces the sanctity, seeming part of a divine dispensation as much as evidence of human labor (Stewart 165). The "work" manifest in the museum is legible primarily as donation or gift, reinforcing the view that the objects are survivors of a catastrophe, and that the institution is charitable in its shelter of the needy.

It should be apparent by now that the museum is a machine, a social force like a factory, with exceptional powers. In "Teddy Bear Patriarchy," Donna Haraway examines natural history museums as sites of production, engineering, in particular, "technologies of enforced meaning, or realist representation" (30). Realism in this account is an ideological production in which culture readjusts nature so as to produce the "natural history" that best serves its narrative needs. Taxidermy was the key technique, which Haraway describes as "the production of an organized craft for eliciting unambiguous experience of organic perfection" (34). The intricate knottiness of this formula suggests as well the teleology of poetry on display in the taxidermic preparations of anthologies. The "organic perfection" so elaborately exhibited in *Understanding Poetry*, for instance, is concordant with Haraway's stipulation that "organic" meanings are technologically enforced by a doctrine of the real. She does not mention the extent to which literary realism developed as a charitable institution, a civic obligation to provide fastidious documentation of public malfeasance—Zola's miners in *Germinal* or Frank Norris's railroad monopolies in *The Octopus*. Insofar as the act of representation comes to be associated with a particular method— realism—there is likely to be an aura of benevolence. Display environments like natural history museums disguise the forcible trauma of separation and detachment, conjuring through the medium of realism a rebirthing clinic: "Realistic art at its most deeply magical issues in revelation" (Haraway 34). Amidst all the transients of the collection—those disjecta of natural or historical turbulence, now eligible for rehabilitation to a promised land—the act of representation takes on the character of guided supervision (or, to use the suitably forceful term, *surveillance*). Culture is a category that signifies the productive activity of self-entitlement on the part of the exhibitor: culture, that is, can consist entirely of the labor of others (aliens in time or space), but the act of controlled display *acculturates* the ambient array into a synthetic vehicle for the host.

There is a twofold repatriation involved here: the museum produces everything strange as familiar and necessary and at the same time converts everything familiar into the strange and contingent. We visit the museum to find ourselves strangers. In the most literal sense, a trip to the Met secures as "our" heritage the Benin bronzes, rococco furniture, samurai armor, haystacks by Monet, and Hellenic as well as Gupta statuary—a "juxtaposition of dead visions," Valéry called it, "with each thing jealously competing for the glance that will give it life" (203). What is ostensibly on view is a global juggling of styles for "universal" consideration as art. The hidden labor is that of the viewer, who is free to pick and choose among the discrete objects on display for personal affinities, but who is otherwise trapped in the museum like a fly in a spiderweb. Trapped, I mean, by the explanatory grid, by the fact that the museum is a loudspeaker directing mental traffic. The anxiety generated in such a space hardly affects the objects, which are inanimate and hence immune. The brunt of the anxiety of belonging, of fitting in, is projected onto the viewer; and that anxiety follows the visitor home.

In 1985 the Beauborg mounted an immense exhibit, "Les Immatériaux," curated by Jean-François Lyotard, in pursuit of the chimera of the postmodern. John Rajchman, in his review of the occasion, defined the force of the terminological shift as follows: "The great question of modernism was: what is art? Now it is replaced by the postmodern question: who are we in all of this?" (112). The choice of pronoun is judicious: it is no longer an issue of personal identity, but of plurality. It's a question that might seem remote from

the concerns of postwar American poetry, which has worn a trench
around the first person singular in its ritual peregrinations. Critical
devotees of lyric solipsism have persistently pecked and sniffed at
contemporary poetry as if to ask: who are we in all this? The question
Rajchman heard at Beauborg, *posed* in the exhibit as an urgency
imposed by technoscience, "need not have a single answer," in his
view, since "'we' are not a single entity which technoscience alien-
ates or realizes" (114). Rajchman's escape clause consists of the "new
heterogeneous languages" invented under the sign of postmodernism.
But postmodern heterogeneity, semiotic slippage, decentering and
reinvention of identity are emphatically *not* among those features
which typify the poetry that is critically certified and anthologized
today. The anthologies remain hierarchically motivated, dedicated to
preserving the dream of autonomous agency and experiential authenticity. This "voice that is great within us" is not Rajchman's sign of
plurality, but a unitary compulsion that leads to what Lyotard sees as
totalitarian. "The danger [Lyotard] sees in technoscience," Rajchman
explains, "is not an alienation of our supposedly natural identity. . .it
is the 'totalitarian' possibility that there exists only *one* artificial
identity that submits us to centralized control" (114). Our "natural"
anxiety is thus a dual anxiety of incorporation: the trauma of finding
ourselves included against our will; but also of needing to find out
how to be included in the corporative dream of culture.[9]

In subsequent chapters my concern will be in part to document
this anxiety, because the most significant poetic activities of the postwar era have emerged as group affairs. New Criticism, the Beats, and,
lately, the language poets initially gained impetus as collaborative
enclaves; after achieving success the members have invariably sought
to disassociate themselves from perceived group attributes. At issue
here, for the moment, is a larger pattern of social collectivization facili-

---

[9] Like the "double discourse of the natural and the technological
that...makes up the American body-machine complex" which Mark Seltzer
documents in *Bodies and Machines*, the reciprocity of nature and artifice
excites a special *frisson*, a "thrill and panic of agency at once extended and
suspended"—which was, for nineteenth-century passengers, the experience
of a train ride (4, 18).

tated by cultural sites like the museum. In *Uncommon Cultures* Jim Collins defines the postmodern as a disengagement from globalizing explanation: "'culture' no longer can be conceived as a Grand Hotel, as a totalizable system that somehow orchestrates all cultural production and reception according to one master system" (xiii). The diaspora created by all the energy released from this cognitive Hilton is intimidating. "Rather than isolatable anxieties of influence, the struggles texts engage in to 'clear a space' for themselves within specific semiotic environments are the direct result of an all-pervasive anxiety of *confluence* that affects all cultural production" (6). If the anxiety of influence is what prevails in the individual ego of the poet struggling with predecessors, the new trauma is collective identity, laboring under the anxiety of confluence, worried whether the voice that is great within us has gotten *into* us by ventriloquial misadventure.

THE CULTURE CURE

André Malraux's influential thesis of the museum without walls has become pervasive in ways he was not prepared to realize. As Philip Fisher insists, the "universalizing zeal" of the Enlightenment *creates* fragments and ruins which then become pliable in its projects of rehabilitation (95). Insofar as the "universal" is instantiated globally, each thing and any place—no matter how far afield—becomes continuous with the space of the museum.[10] For Malraux, a museum

---

[10] A slightly different approach to the same problem can be found in Marc Shell's *Children of the Earth*, which pursues the apparently divergent spectres of universalism and particularism only to find them linked in a dialectical kinship: "In the 1990s, half a century after two world wars, the veneration accorded to universalism is as disturbing in its political implications as the particularist nationalism that universalism pretends to eschew but actually merely defines by polar opposition. After all, the ideal of universal brotherhood—'All human beings are brothers; none are others'—offers no specifically human mediation between species and family, that is, recognizes no being that is both 'other' and 'human' besides such partly domesticated borderline creatures, defining kin and kind, as pets, animal nurse mothers, and godmen. And so it makes virtually inevitable the slide away from the purportedly humane ideal" (193–94).

without walls meant a museum of unrestricted access; but postmodern proliferation of simulacra and codes makes the museum a source of unrestricted production. For Rajchman, the museum is "no longer a space or sanctuary apart from things, but a mirror of their infinite reiteration" (108). Even everyday life is susceptible to the pressures of the exhibition. Frank O'Hara is the exemplary chronicler of the shift from a museum with to one without walls, as his poems track his passage from the physical plant as such—the Museum of Modern Art, where he was a curator—through the streets of Manhattan, which manifest themselves as a rotating exhibit to which his poems contribute the placards. Indeed, O'Hara's poems are like those paths of crumbs Hans leaves as he and Gretel go into the forest, ways of clandestinely marking a possible return. The museum, exceeding its allotted bounds, contaminates the whole of culture, remaking it in its own image. When the museum is pervasive, when the museal is everywhere, we find ourselves estranged anew as living specimens. What Guy Debord called "the society of the spectacle" marks the endpoint of this tranformation. Ethnographic exhibitions like those chronicled by Barbara Kirshenblatt-Gimblett initiate the production of the quotidian as spectacle: "Once the seal of the quotidian is pierced, life is experienced as if represented" (410). What does this condition feel like?

Walter Benjamin's meditation on ruins in his *Trauerspiel* consigns to German Baroque tragedy the chore of labeling catastrophe, reanimating decay in the mournful medium of the placard in a pathology exhibit. Ruins are runes for Benjamin, who sees in the Baroque not only historical desolation but a debacle of language as well: allegory is energized by its flaunting of words broken off from their meanings, become objects in their own right. In the postmodern society of the spectacle (which Benjamin prophesied fragmentarily but did not live to see, except in the laboratory of the Third Reich), the passion of the commodity turns into a global rebus, as if the museum's captions had become free-floating pockets of signification, semiotic succubi in search of placeholders. This properly postmodern condition was not altogether obscure to certain of Benjamin's contemporaries. Wyndham Lewis, for instance, concocted memorably grotesque satirical fabrications in *The Apes of God*, a *roman à clef* that scandalized because its originals (the Sitwells) seemed summoned into existence solely as decoys to attract the plutonic fury of Lewis's sentences. In order to get this effect, Lewis had to depict his social milieu as if everything had already been adapted to the exhibitionary constellation. In the Prologue, Lady Fredigonde Follett is described as a trapezoidal figure, a Mayan pyramid, as she has her hair done by a maid, after which "[p]osterity for the moment held no further interest for her—one museum was much the same as another" (27). Later in the novel Mr. Zagreus is presented in the manner of an inventory sheet, as if he were a porcelain plate in an exhibit, requiring pedigree:

> This highbrow-sub-sheik of the slum had been the triste-est Tristan tricked out in the dirtiest second-hand operatic wardrobe — the shoddiest Don Giovanni — the most ludicrous Young Lochinvar — the most squalid Sorel, he had been the most unprepossessing sham Ratnerskolnikoff without the glamour of poverty of the Russian (because of his healthy business sense) — he had been the Judas without the kiss (for no fairly intelligent Christ would ever trust him) with a grim apocryphal lech for a Magdelen — he was the Childe Harold without the Byron collar, and worse, sans genius — the Childe Roland without the Dark Tower, or corpse-like Adolphe, a Manfred or a Zara, risen again, but who could only half-live —*the eternal imitation-person* in a word, whose ambition led him to burgle all the books of Western romance to steal their heroes' expensive outfits for his musty shop — the split-man of another tale. (153–54, my emphasis)

All of Lewis's creatures (a term he prefered to "character") are subjected to a comparable stucco of attributes, gratuitous in the conventional world of sentimental realism, but indispensible in a world defenseless against the museum without walls. It's a world that drove Berryman to the desperate antics of his Henry poems (another "split-man"), and gave Lowell's introspections such a vivid public patina. "Help, saw me in two, / put me on the shelf!" Lowell exclaims in "Child's Song": "Sometimes the little muddler / can't stand itself!" in the completed rhyme (*Union* 22). The clockwork universe of the old gods running down—"beginning in wisdom, dying in doubt" (46)—is that civic plaza of *For the Union Dead*, a world in which the poet-chronicler is merely another stupefied fragment, a bit of marble remorselessly drilled from the statuary of *Life Studies*. In "Home After Three Months Away" (in the asylum), the manic-depressive condition has been transformed from a state of subjectivity to objectivity: "Cured, I am frizzled, stale and small" Lowell ends the poem, in which it's hard to resist hearing "cured" as a verb applied to meat (*Life* 84).

The "cure" in Lowell's poem sounds more like a curse, associated as it is with ego deflation, which in the dragstrip of American identities can also be construed as cultural deprivation. The American relation to Europe has predominantly been driven by fantasies of recuperation, a European sojourn being a culture cure for those stricken by the malady of "America."[11] The appetite for European models is gluttonous: even such "characteristically" American poetry as Ginsberg's is only one part American (via Whitman), and three parts European (via Blake, Smart, and the Bible). "Howl," in fact, incorporates the most salient features of the wax milieu: criminality, sexuality, insanity, and ethnography. It's a profoundly pathological work, but at the same time obsessively American in affirming a (home-grown) culture cure in the "saxophone cry that shivered the cities down to the last radio / with the absolute heart of the poem of life butchered out of their own bodies good to eat a thousand years" (16).

---

[11] Baudrillard's take on America does not make our condition as vapid as it often sounds: his is, after all, a diagnostic treatment, and he itemizes real pathologies: "Protect everything, detect everything, contain everything— obsessional society. Save time. Save Energy, Save money. Save our souls— phobic society. Low tar. Low energy. Low calories. Low sex. Low speed— anorexic society" (*America* 40). In a later work he extends the critique: "Freud thought he was bringing the plague to the USA, but the USA has victoriously resisted the psychoanalytical frost by real deep freezing, by mental and sexual refrigeration. They have countered the black magic of the Unconscious with the white magic of 'doing your own thing,' air conditioning, sterilization, mental frigidity and the cold media of information" (*Cool Memories* 69).

American poetry is not a pragmatically demonstrable state of affairs, but a social "imaginary," something that exists only in display. Poems have rarely circulated in America as cultural items, as *pragmata* of daily life. They appear, when they do, as exotic species, nurtured with devotion. So poems are not intrinsically distinct from museum specimens, curiosities in need of explanation, of reassuring placement. As *specimens* they are also suggestive of pathological conditions—and nothing seemed more natural, in recent decades, than for prominent poets to succumb to mania and suicide. Poetry as such, regardless of authorship, comes under scrutiny as an exotic genus in need of rehabilitation. The dominant modern institutions, according to Michel de Certeau in *The Practice of Everyday Life*, are colonization, psychiatry, and pedagogy, which focus and bring into line the renegade tendencies of the masses, the unconscious, and the child, respectively. The society of the spectacle engineers these elements into a coherent ideological motif, that of the nation, which is therefore less a polity than a fantasy. The fantasy is certified in its purity as a hegemonic "voice" at that point when individual members of the society or group appear to spontaneously exhibit the rules of order, the principles of cohesion, and reiterate in almost ritual fashion a miraculous unity of individual utterance and collective sentiment. This is the birth of the poetry workshop.

The poet in America (or anywhere else, for that matter) is born into a nursery, a school, and an "exhibitionary complex" as Tony Bennett calls it—"a set of cultural technologies concerned to organize a voluntarily self-regulating citizenry" (126). The poet, like other performers, occupies that threshold between seeing and being seen, between being one of "them" and one of "us"—a controller of aesthetic traffic in "a self-monitoring system of looks" (133). The 1901 Pan-American Exposition offered a "Short Sermon to Sightseers," instructing them: "Please remember when you get inside the gates you are part of the show" (Neil Harris 59). The exhibitionary space tacitly arraigns viewers, testing their probity and suggesting that the items on view can be a way of opening a hidden door into themselves. The exhibit, and the anthology, are formalized lesson plans for micronarratives of self-instruction. Paul Bourget, visiting the Columbian Exposition in the late nineteenth century, was startled by the difference in American demeanor: where a general levity and carnival atmosphere dominated pavilions in France, Americans wandered about "with a sort of blank avidity, as if they were walking in the midst of a colossal lesson in things" (Neil Harris 62). Another Frenchman was equally appalled at the spectre of the modern museum: Paul Valéry embodies the epicurean dismay at finding primary objects of pleasure constrained in a public service role—art as instructional media, aesthetic utility. Assaulted by the museum's "wax-floored solitude, savoring of temple and drawing room, of cemetery and school," he felt "lost in a turmoil of frozen beings" all demanding, "in vain, the abolition of all the others" (203, 202). The artworks, subordinated to explanatory protocols, contend among themselves as "units of incompatable pleasure," resulting in "an abuse of space that does violence to the eyesight" (204). Valéry finds in this an impoverishment by superabundance, a paradoxical condition encouraging either superficiality or a misguided erudition, in which case "the immense museum is . . . saddled with a limitless library. Aphrodite is transformed into a dossier" (205). He realized, ruefully, that it was above all the institution of patronage that prevails. Surveying the museum, Valéry admitted "I cannot but think of the bank at a casino, which wins every time" (205). The primary category on view in the museum is the unique and impervious power of the institution itself. So the great metropolitan museums attain an uncanny legislative power, as sites of commemoration, because they "remember" the whole astonishing scope of human culture. If the European museum is like a pacemaker for the ailing heart of a moribund culture,[12] the American museum (and anthology) is a steroid for canon building.

---

[12] The display format as a site of European rehabilitation is given a sobering countenance by Thomas Pynchon in *Gravity's Rainbow*, in which he uses the museum/mausoleum complex as narrative armature, guiding his characters through such mortuary grids as the Hell Museum, City Paranoiac, Happyville, Racketednstadt, Zwölfkinder, and The White Visitation. What Pynchon facilitates with all this paraphernalia of host institutions is an afterimage of those

While the "carceral archipelago" and the "exhibitionary complex" developed contemporaneously, the latter requires institutions "not of confinement but of exhibition" (Bennett 124, 123). The exhibitionary complex is instrumental in organizing consent, effecting voluntaristic unanimity by remote promptings. The exhibit, reified into the enshrined venue of the museum, is a prototype version of hypertext, training populations in the art of reassembling fragmentary evidence into coherent narratives. The museum is a transitional education in the negotiation of hyperspace, the solipsistic euphoria of simulated connectedness. It need not be carceral because its inmates are self-regulating. The museum begins with the goal of character building and ends up in the zone of interactive technologies, the task now being that of "building a person" in the cyborg world. When Friedrich Kittler characterizes the book of poetry as "the first medium in the modern sense," I think not only of "McLuhan's law, according to which the content of a medium is always another medium" (115), but of the spiritualists' *medium*, also known as the "control." My concern, in elaborating this thesis of a poetry wax museum, is to suggest that the seemingly autonomous "voices and visions" of poets themselves have been underwritten by custodial sponsors who have surreptitiously turned down the volume on certain voices, and simulated a voice-over for certain others. Nothing defines the situation more succinctly than the police phrase *protective custody*.

The Renaissance cabinet of curiosity, the *Wunderkammer*, a motley consortium of crazy things, evolves into that eminently modern institution the museum, a taxonomy of protective spaces. Treasured objects are immunized against worldly contamination in the retreat into the museum, like the souls gathered in the mountain

---

"celibate machines" that proliferate in the interwar years in forms Hal Foster calls "Armor Fou." The metallic epidermis, followed by the creation of artificial organs, makes resurrection a starkly dehumanized material value. Rey Chow, writing on "Benjamin's Love Affair with Death," describes the female antitype to these fantasies of rejuvenated bachelor machines: "The figure of woman . . . is the ultimate figure of death. The beauty of woman is the surreal beauty of an organ which is severed, embellished, and only thus 'enlivened'" (85).

sanatorium in Thomas Mann's *The Magic Mountain.* In "Museums: The Hidden Agenda" Neil Harris traces the transition from unassuming heap to corrective institution:

> Rather than serve simply as a receptive vessel in which could be poured the accumulated knowledge, wealth, and loot of a newly managed world, in response to these anxieties the museum also became a corrective, an asylum, a source of transcendent values meant to restore some older rhythms of nature and history to a fast-paced, urbanizing, mechanized society. Museums could be organized as settings to promote integration and solidarity, between social and economic classes, between humanity and nature, between mankind and time, or between human beings and the act of creation. (137)

The use of the museum, in Harris's view, is conciliatory. The carceral space merges imperceptibly with the bargaining table to produce this peculiarly modern ambience of things that are carefully preserved and, at the same time, ruthlessly interrogated. Things on display comply with the explanatory voice-over in a show of "integration and solidarity." "In the drama of the specimen," Barbara Kirshenblatt-Gimblett says, "the curator was a ventriloquist whose task it was to make the object speak" (398). It's a carnival trick, a sleight of speech, by which one voice substitutes for another, in a masquerade of autonomy. Anthologists and critics are often experts at this, assembling a retinue of texts into a show that celebrates the uniqueness of the poems while deftly speaking for them, through them, and in spite of them.

Recent assaults on the canon have suffered from a fundamental misrecognition which is derived from, and encouraged by, canonical rhetoric itself: that is, the conflation of voice and voice-over. Critics of the canon have gullibly accepted the rhetoric of pluralism, the nationalist claim that "we" are represented by canonical writers and, indeed, that they speak "for" us. In this way canonical writers are as likely to suffer a presumptuously colonizing appropriation as those on the periphery. bell hooks's mimicry of the imperial imagination can also apply to the curatorial gaze:

> *No need to hear your voice when I can talk about you bet-*
> *ter than you can speak about yourself. No need to hear*
> *your voice. Only tell me about your pain. I want to know*
> *your story. And then I will tell it back to you in a new way.*
> *Tell it back to you in such a way that it has become mine,*
> *my own. Re-writing you I write myself anew. I am still*
> *author, authority. I am still colonizer, the speaking subject*
> *and you are now at the center of my talk.* (343, ital. in orig-
> inal)

The difference between the colonial agent and the curator of the
national archive is simply in the pronouns: the curator says "we"
and "ours" instead of "my" and "mine."

In the display cocoon of the anthology, the animation of
poetic reputations continues to be a resurrectionist trade, in which
the editor administers a few drops from a prefatory elixir that brings
the stillborn poetry stunningly, if momentarily, to life, like the application of vitalium and resurrectine to the corpses in *Locus Solus*:

> [These] two new substances, each of them inactive without
> the other, [released] a powerful current of electricity at that
> moment, which penetrated the brain and overcame its
> cadaveric rigidity, endowing the subject with an impres-
> sive artificial life. As a consequence of a curious awaken-
> ing of memory, the latter would at once reproduce, with
> strict exactitude, every slightest action performed by him
> during certain outstanding minutes of his life; then, with-
> out any break, he would indefinitely repeat the same
> unvarying series of deeds and gestures which he had cho-
> sen once and for all. The illusion of life was absolute:
> mobility of expression, the continual working of the lungs,
> speech, various actions, walking—nothing was missing.
> (Roussel 118)

In the American Poetry Wax Museum, the waxen bards are servomechanisms of cultural prestige. The wax figure is in a state of
arrest, ecstatic arrest, since that is the form adopted by technologies
in the nation-building pressures of the nineteenth century (also the
premium age of wax exhibits). The canonical author lugubriously

resembles the cadavers animated by "resurrectine" in Roussel's *Locus Solus* or the rigor-mortized cyclist in Jarry's *Supermale*. Ecstasy, in these mechanistic scenarios, is *techne en-theos*, the tool swarming with godly energy. Curatorial ventriloquism animates the objects on display and reanimates the spectator as the privileged witness of the curative properties of the aesthetic clinic.

VOICE–OVER

> MACROB. "But if I am to be kept as a static souvenir of myself, in this celestial waxworks, how can I in future will anything?"
>
> BAILIFF. "Ah! the willing must occur during your terrestrial life. There is no more willing here! . . . I am placed here to expound the laws of this new existence when called upon to do so and to pass you in if I find you have reached the proper point of crystallization. I consider you personally to have turned out extremely well Macrob and that you are ripe for an eternity of yourself."
>
> (Wyndham Lewis, *The Childermass* 232–33)

There is a bookish distinction we customarily maintain between primary and secondary works, or creative text and critical commentary. If we hadn't already been goaded into questioning its validity by theoretical *agents provocateurs* (Barthes, Derrida), the complex multimedia environment we inhabit offers a reproachful reminder about the archaic posture implied by the scriptural model. Would it make a difference—and would that difference be audible rather than legible—to invoke another model? Instead of text and commentary, then, consider the format of exhibition and soundtrack. A display in one medium, the visual, is attended and articulated by a performance in another medium, the audial. The museumgoer, touring the galleries with a headset, views the paintings by audio-prompter, a supervisory commentary uttered directly into the inner ear. To which event do we accord primacy—visual or auditory? Are the paintings really "seen" if the viewer's gaze is being choreo-graphed by a taped voice-over? Is it possible that the paintings on view are actually little more than a cartoonized canonical sequence of visual supports for the authority of the voice-over?

John Rajchman was stimulated by the Beaubourg exhibit to recognize a paradigm shift from modern to postmodern, involving a shift in focus from the status of art to the perplexing question "Who are we in all this?"—where "all this" was not just the exhibited clut-ter of computer terminals and high-tech hardware, but the manifest proliferation of such material in the everyday environment outside the museum. Going to the Beaubourg, we return home to find our-selves still in the exhibit. The question of who "we" are, then, must take account of these drastically altered circumstances for identify-ing ourselves in the reflecting medium of culture. In the interface zones of what Scott Bukatman calls "terminal identity," our sense of self is attenuated *and* sensitized, deprived *and* enhanced. In Rajch-man's view "instead of anxiety, we have melancholy and mania, tropes of a postmodern condition, 'subjectivity' in a culture which can no longer place the human subject at its center" (112). In the neopuritan atmosphere of postwar American poetry the capitaliza-tion of the speaking subject becomes an obsessional neurosis, a han-kering for a capitol to serve as F.D.I.C. of cultural capital. It is also the great preoccupation of anthologists, as they continue to deny, in every way they can, the advent of the decentered subject.

In *The Puritan Origins of the American Self*, Sacvan Bercov-itch documents the extraordinary Puritan investment in selfhood as a defining American preoccupation. It's a paradoxical obsession, of course, since the very name "puritan" denotes a self-abnegation. Read-ing Puritan tracts, Bercovitch notes that "every aspect of style betrays a consuming involvement with 'me' and 'mine' that resists disintegra-tion. We cannot help but feel that the Puritans' urge for self-denial stems from the very subjectivism of their outlook, that their humility is coextensive with personal assertion" (18). The complex agonies of Puritan selfhood result in a compulsion to use the material of degrada-tion to surmount degradation, to cancel every citation of self with denial of self, in a language which renders the personal pronoun incessant and central. The flamboyant hedonism of the Beats, the compulsive exhibitionism of the Confessional poets, and the mundane self-preoccupations of workshop poetry have indelibly marked post-war American poetry as a late (or more accurately *decadent*) efflores-cence of the Puritan ego. Studies of contemporary poetry compulsive-ly reiterate this in their titles: *Escape from the Self* (Malkoff), *Self and Sensibility in Contemporary American Poetry* (Altieri), *The Still Per-formance: Writing, Self, and Interconnection in Five Postmodern American Poets* (McCorkle), *Introspection and Contemporary Poetry* (Williamson), *What I Cannot Say: Self, Word and World in Whitman, Stevens, and Merwin* (Byers), *Discovering Ourselves in Whitman: The Contemporary American Long Poem* (Gardner). The prevalent associa-tion of the poem with the "voice of the poet," anchoring the language of poetry in the language of subjectivity, is obviously pertinent for advocates of "self-expression"; but it is equally the case in any discus-sion of the vatic role of poetry, and the rhetoric of the high sublime. No matter how de- or transpersonalized the poetic "voice" may appear, the voice remains a calculus of the speaking subject. In fact, inasmuch as we talk about poetry we assume poetry to be talking about us. If poetry seems piloted by the capital "I," talk about poetry is invariably a discourse of "we." Fiction and poetry are joint stock part-ners in a cultural monologue plurally uttered, on the topic of some-thing called "the self." So when we talk about poetry it tends to be about the "poetry of the self," which always seems peculiarly to take the plural form, as in Helen Vendler's *Part of Nature, Part of Us.* We are now engulfed in evidence of a superstition that a humanoid unit called The Self has its natural corollary in an aesthetic unit, The Poem. The institutionalization of this superstition perpetrates a sys-tem in which the poet's voice is represented and displaced by the voice-over of critical commentary.

"Voice" is the medium delegated to poetry as the primal signa-ture of selfhood. So pervasive is this equation of poetry with voice that scholars indiscriminately apply the concept of voice throughout the entire range of poetic traditions, without regard for oral or written dis-tinctions. However, a conscientous discrimination of traditions would indicate that even in the seemingly prior or archaic circumstances of oral epic recitation "the voice" is far from being a spontaneous natural instrument. Voice is a technical construct; and as Jerome Rothenberg has sought to demonstrate in his anthology *Technicians of the Sacred* and elsewhere, the "primitive" is complex, and in human communities a "natural" condition is achieved only by means of a skilled technoculture. To dream of a centered, autonomous voice as the innate sign of selfhood is assuredly ancient—the concept of divinity seems inseparable from it, in Greco-Hebraic cultures—but it may be only in our past half-century that poets have submitted to a vast delusion that voice is simple and *precedes* technical intervention.

This naive conviction is motivated by the most prestigious precedent, however, including that of Descartes, intent on stripping away intrusive cultural and metaphysical baggage in order to settle on, and thus define, a putative inmost core of the cogitative ego. I bring up the Cartesian ego, encased in the Enlightenment technology of Kant's faculties, in order to emphasize the wizardry of the construct—for Descartes's "method" is indeed a technical, albeit mental, construct (and poems continue to be voice-loops prerecorded by the Kantian faculties[13]). The hypothesis of rational self-interest which underwrites the Cartesian as well as the Kantian projects is obviously askew. Despite this, what is notable is the degree to which poetry is still inspected for evidence of rational self-interest. This compulsion seems to me to persist because poetry has been inseparable from the *voice of reason* since the Romantic sublime, which is concurrent with and thus responsive to Enlightenment claims for rationality as anchorage of identity. Yet the Romantic sublime also sustains the legacy of bardic rapture, in which poetic voice is the emblem of dispossession and shamanic derangement. Here, the charisma of poetry activates

---

[13] Poetry since the eighteenth century has been the exercise of the Kantian faculties. Poems are engines for affirming space, time, causality, and the unity of consciousness, registering Understanding as cognition, pleasure and pain as Judgment, will and desire as Reason: the Faculties, those blind mice (Anschauung, Einbildungskraft, Verstand, Vernunft) who persevere in their orthodontic regulation (straightening and ordering, sometimes involving extractions) of raw sensory experience. Experience of the sort that constitutes subjectivity is the electromagnetic energy required for animating Cartesian puppetry (subjectivity doesn't include batteries).

voice as a law unto itself. The poet's voice has long been our cultural paradigm for a voice that compels assent by imputing to all who hear it an agreement about its priority. The poet's honeyed voice is a benchmark of the irresistible, the voice one cannot help but attend to. The poet's voice, complicit with a cultural voice-over, is intimately bonded to a sense of helplessness, or ecstatic inertia. Stunned with gratitude, we gape openmouthed at the sound of a voice, a voice ringing in our ears in the museum headset: the voice of the other implanted directly in our heads, a technical effect, a voice-over.

Poetry is a receptacle of the most archaic associations of the linguistic function, which makes it seem inept if not simply irrelevant today. But poetry lingers on, as a low-tech material base for high theory. The "linguistic turn" in the human sciences has ironically accentuated and valorized the very contingencies that made poetry appear fallible. Poetry now has to struggle with multiple legacies, as it occupies the epistemological status of a debased medium, classical rhetoric, while at the same time signifying the dignity and impunity of the more exalted functions of "literature."[14] The parameters of poetry's voice-over are now beyond reckoning, since every

---

[14] The chorus of complaints about poetry's "marginalization" overlooks a long and highly relevant history, of which I offer a sketch here. Poetry is marginalized because of its intimacy with the problem of language. I don't mean that poetry makes us feel language problematically (though that may be the case), but that a modern crisis of language has fallen largely into the domain of poetry. In antiquity poetry and rhetoric were technical arts, human augmentations of Nature. Literature in the modern sense didn't exist. "Litteratura" meant for the Romans what "grammatike" had meant for the Greeks: letters, or reading and writing. In the Christian era *litteratura* was secular writing, as distinguished from *scriptura*, or sacred writing. The language arts in the secular curriculum constituted the Trivium, consisting of grammar, dialectic, and rhetoric. Poetry was free to migrate back and forth between rhetoric and grammar, between figures and letters. In antiquity and through much of the Renaissance, poetry was only incidentally linked with rhetoric. Poetry led a perfectly nomadic existence, distinguished only by its technical features, not by any supposition of essence. It could come in handy as a pedogogic aid, but only when exemplifying the use of figures, the rules of grammar, or the art of dialectic. Poetry could illustrate, but it didn't have to be epistemologically responsible for its illustrations. Dante's grand poem was only a Commedia; Shakespeare's plays were transient entertainments. Petrus Ramus' sixteenth century attack on rhetoric inadvertently implicated poetry. By insisting that invention and arrangement belonged to logic, as functions of

reason, Ramus pared rhetoric down to a single element, stylistics. In this respect poetry and rhetoric were united, having as their identifying feature the use of figures or tropes. Ramism set the stage for Bacon's "Great Instauration" in which the division of knowledge aligned poetry with history and philosophy—poetry being the fanciful idiom of a freeplay not bound by worldly responsibilities. Nonetheless, in Bacon's apportionment of learning, the intimation is there that poetry *must* have some role to play. Even idle fancies can be recruited for their socioscientific instrumentality. Despite Bacon, it's not until the eighteenth century that we find a modern sense of literature as a "body of writing" (to use Wellek's definition) as distinct from the humanizing characteristics of a literary culture. With this we pass from *letters* as the humanist medium of civil education, to *literature* as a nationalizing institution of acculturation (or in specifically Althusserian terms, an Ideological State Apparatus). Rhetoric, after its Ramist disemboweling, had virtually disappeared as a topic, lingering on tropologically in verse. It's important to realize here that in the developing scientific culture it is not poetry as such which is spurious, but rhetoric. By the time the pedagogic traces of rhetoric have dissipated, poetry simply persists as a sort of surrogate rhetoric—which is to say, something of possible interest in its own right, but afflicted with the shadow of obsolescence that follows the demise of rhetoric. By the nineteenth century, poetry is a residue of the dark ages before the rise of the novel, something for antiquarian tastes, or at best a recipe book for homilies and epithets, lending a metrical buzz to devotional reading.

In 1957 Donald Davie pondered the implications of Malraux's museum without walls in two radio broadcasts on "The Poet in the Imaginary Museum." He sees an ambiguous legacy, with poetry positioned *inside* the museum of international modernism, but left *outside* it at the same time by virtue of the parochial constraints of the medium; poems are written in *a* language, whereas paintings are inscribed in *the* medium of the art (50). The result is a divided consciousness in which "the modern poet must always, as it were, peep round from behind his poem, to advise the reader—if by no more than a lifted eyebrow or a sidelong glance—that the poem is not to be trusted all the way, that there are modes of experience or ways of saying things which the poet is aware of though his poem on its own account is not" (55). What Davie might have added is that modern poetry is not only exposed as an incomplete gesture, but falls far short in fact of cultural aspirations for a universal code. Rhetoric is not the only spectre haunting poetry. Concurrent with Bacon and the development of the Royal Academy, there are those singular speculations on language which result in the universal-language schemes of John Wilkins, Leibniz, and many others. Mathematics, of course, is eventually elected as a universal idiom of the sciences, but the obligation to repeal Babel becomes one more spectre for poetry to contend with. It is this pressure that Wordsworth begins to respond to in *The Prelude*, in which "the growth of the mind" is conveniently the *poet's*, not the scientist's. And while Wordsworth has clearly prevailed over Erasmus Darwin (despite Elizabeth Sewell's persuasive effort to subsume them both into an orphic tradition), the lineage of science has proven more culturally pervasive in its implementation of universal language schemes, at least in terms of computing and information technologies.

definition of poetry necessarily excludes something which returns, in the mobility of our communications environment, like the unforeseen siren call of an unacknowledged Muse, depositing a new litter of poems in its wake. The voice returns to us in an environment of disconnections, amputations, in a prodigal prosthetic congress, in which the "power" and "authority" of the voice can no longer be traced to a plausible speaker.

The swarm of voices clinging like bees to the media web arouses different connotations of language for us than it did for Hesiod, visited by the Heliconian Muses. Instead of oracles we now have artificial intelligence, an heir of cybernetics.[15] Cognitive science has modeled language on neurology, and language in turn has become a paradigm of codes and systems. Poetry, meanwhile, seems like raw industrial sewage from the immense transformations required here: language macroprocessors flit about weightlessly in the superconductive environs of cognitive science and the hyperspace of critical theory, while the diesel-driven bigrigs of poetry still chug along the interstates, belching smoke. Poetry is dirty language. Polarized between the rhetoric of the airwaves and the logic of instrumental reason in the administered society, the only solution provisionally available is not generic but intonational. Authority is tonal, a persuasive intimacy in the imperative mode.

In our media environment (an environment, to be precise, inseparable from its media), the frantic mobility of voices amounts to a vast spectacle of dissociative turbulence. The voice-over vicariously attaches some remnant of the body to the spin cycle of information and control, which can masquerade as entertainment, news, politics, and even education. The voice-over itself acts as a gentle summons, an intimate command. It calls out to us from the other room to return to the monitor, to stay tuned to a specific transmitting channel. Rick Altman

---

[15] This formulation may be misleading, inasmuch as there is a terminological shift that redirects attention from the cybernetic promise of a human/tool interface to the extrahuman mentation of high-tech "brains." Writes J. David Bolter: "Unfortunately, the elegant name of cybernetics, created from the Greek word for governor but smacking perhaps of the antiquated technology of the war years . . . gave way to 'artificial intelligence'" (193).

has made the pregnant observation that much of the time television sets are on in the U.S. they're not being watched, but heard or rather overheard from other rooms (42). Such use of the medium potentially converts all television voices into voice-over, since the voice hails from an unseen speaker and applies to a (temporarily) unseen image or situation. The domestic confidentiality of the voice-over itself, however, is effaced by the universality of the voice-over function. We're cocooned in a surrogate multiplicity; the voices we've become accustomed to are utopian, belonging nowhere, regionless, without accent, rendering neutrality enticing and anonymity exemplary.

If the oral rhetoric of print culture aspired to do the police in different voices (from Dickens to Eliot), the compulsion today is to homogenize the proliferation of voices—and internalize the police. We have yet to reckon with the punitive role of the voice-over. Excessive preoccupation with the reign of the visual—the centrality of the panopticon as brute enforcer—has if anything played along with the powerbrokers of the scopic regime. The ruler's eyes ("His eyes are empty rectangles, shaped / Like slightly curved sticks of chewing gum. He witnesses. / But we are the witnesses") have swollen into the grotesque choral aggregate of the panopticon. Strolling along an aisle in the American Poetry Wax Museum, your perplexity is prompted by a voice-over:

> . . . You get thrown to one side
> Into a kind of broom closet as the argument continues car-
>   olling
> Ideas from the novel of which this is the unsuccessful
> Stage adaptation. Too much, perhaps, gets lost.
> What about arriving after sunset on the beach of a
> Dank but extremely beautiful island to hear the speeches
> Of the invisible natives, whose punishment is speech?

> (Ashbery, *Houseboat Days* 14)

Whoever "you" are there is something hypnotic about the lure of the carceral voice. From silent film through radio days and into the postwar supplementation of voice with its televisual component, the voice-over has been consistently pitched in the imperative. This is not surprising, given that during this same period the military technology systems environment developed its "command-control" structures of feedback and adaptive self-correction.

The pathos of signification at the present time is a mourning for the sign, a mourning for the innocent, natural, uncoerced sign that precedes what Herbert Schiller has called the "corporate takeover of public expression." "The corporate 'voice' now constitutes the national symbolic environment," he writes, noting that the ominous significance inheres not so much in the specific claims expressed by any given corporations, but "the organic process by which the corporate 'voice' is generalized across the entire range of cultural expression" (44).[16] After the corporate voice-over becomes generically indistinguishable from public discourse, any act of communication is a form of bereavement, insofar as it is the active reminder of how we perpetuate our own captivity. To speak is to perform a duet with the corporate voice-over, and any attempt to struggle or resist simply strengthens the bonds that constrain us, since the bonds are nothing less than our own words.

Captured, and enraptured, by mediaspeak, we settle into the dismayed inertia of the mammal mesmerized by headlights bearing fatally down. So we mourn the signs that would protest the kidnapping of our means of expression, *as if* there were in fact "means of expression" not already overtaken (and underwritten) by preemptive voice-over and reinforced scopically by an image-track. In scholarly discourse this lament has been ingeniously displaced; instead of protesting an erosion of the right to language as such, we have developed a pathological awareness of the "arbitrariness of the sign." The situation is curious: what more eloquent elision of the real topic could be imagined? The systematicity with which the sign has been

---

[16] Colloquial expressions claimed as corporate slogans—like "Just do it!" and "You deserve a break today"—become a form of private property that is not off-limits to the public at large. Quite the reverse: the public is enticed to adopt the corporate slogan as if it were native, "part of nature, part of us" in Wallace Stevens's line. The "language of the tribe" is thus broadcast by sound and image back to the population, but only after being run through a corporate vocoder.

revoked—privatized for corporate purposes—is rendered as an arbitrariness of the sign itself. In other words, an historical determinant of late capitalism as it impinges on language is misdiagnosed as a congenital defect of language as such.

The voice-over of the concept stipulated by Aristotle and reaffirmed by Kant continues in the compulsion to hear individual voices as components of a larger and more "universal" voice. The unity of consciousness, initially conceived as a matter of ethical dignity, then as superior intellect, eventually appears in the cyborg as unlimited circuitry in a techno-human system. Such a biotechnical mind is no longer congruent with a voice, so the specificity of the speaking subject gives way to the ventriloquial mimicry prevalent today. Poetic "license" is deflated when voice is licensed for commercial applications, carrying language along with it as the effluvia that accompanies image protocols as they efficiently transcode populations and bodies into spectacles of need, fanning "the desire to reproduce the given as a plenitude of possibility" (Agger 55).

The printed page is no longer the sole medium of writing: electrical pulsations on a monitor dissolve print fixity into print fluidity, which is an oxymoron. Ever since Hesiod's encounter with the Muses, the poet has been conceived of as the Muses' medium, the raw material instrument through which the poem is transmitted. The poet is also a "control," in the mediumistic sense (at a seance the control is the person transmitting spirit voices), a proxy for phantoms. There is a final, more contemporary sense of control, which Norbert Wiener derived from the Greek word for steersman: cybernetics.[17] So, in that founding myth of poetic inspiration, Hesiod—putting his voice at the disposal of

---

[17] "Cybernetics" refers to that interdisciplinary complex of research into communication and control in animals and machines culminating in a series of famous conferences sponsored by the Macy Foundation from 1942 into the 1950s. Until the term was adopted as the title of the 1949 Macy conference (after the publication of Wiener's *Cybernetics* had secured it for general use), the topic had been called "Feedback Mechanisms and Circular Causal Systems" or "Teleological Mechanisms" (H. Foerster xix–xx). The principle of feedback crucial to cybernetics was developed in the petroleum industry in the 1930s and refined in military weapon systems during World War II (Parsegian 14).

the Muses—converts poetry into cybernetics. As a theory of control in systems behavior, cybernetics has always been positioned at the prosthetic interface, that juncture at which the tool may become an extension of the person, or the person an extension of the tool.

Culturally, the images that stir our imagination cluster around the cyborg (cybernetic organism) and related styles of adapting flesh to heroic interpenetrations of information and control. Poets would hardly seem to figure in such fantasies, but as I've suggested, Hesiod sets the scene for the poetic cyborg, collapsing material instrumentality and spiritual possession into a single apparatus. The cyborg is our figure for this ambiguous medium, in which the cybernetic compulsion to balance an equation involving information and control requires a human icon, if only as solace to the pre-cyborgian users of such systems. The Muses were user-friendly: the *Theogony* was successfully transmitted through Hesiod without evaporating him. But the cyborg has sinister connotations (whether we think of *Terminator* or *RoboCop*): the medium, human organism, may be consumed in the process, surviving in the recombinant cyborg only in a state of suspended animation.[18]

---

[18] During the Beaubourg exhibit Lyotard, as curator, gave a talk on "Matter and Time," in which he speculated on the consequences of technological anthropomorphism, or the extension of our perceptual capabilities through tools. He concluded that these systems would deliver a blow to human narcissism comparable to the Copernican decentering (earth is not the center of the cosmos), the Darwinian delay (humans are not primary but evolved), and the Freudian dethroning (consciousness is not the master of meaning). The consequence of technoscience is that mind, or the rational, is not exclusively human but increasingly a function of technical hardware and software systems. Lyotard was confronting the habitat of dispossession we have evolved into a global network of electronic memory systems abstracted from human agency, become "nobody's memory" (64). The poetry of the future will be commemorated in holographic simulations, perhaps, but the poetry of our recent past has often inspired the grandiose claim—consecrated morbidly in wax—that it's everybody's memory, "part of nature, part of us." The anthologist assumes the curatorial task of providing the collective voice-over for the exhibit, a task which Lyotard calls "tele-graphy" or inscription-at-a-distance (76). Gathered together under cover of a single volume, anthologized poems are susceptible to the estranging intimacy legislated by telegraphic motivations which, in effect, constitute an inscription-by-proximity: the wax figure embodies, above all, the wax modeller's art.

The figure of the poet as cyborg I want to evoke as the image of suspended animation is most effectively suggested by a scene from a film. In Chris Marker's documentary meditation *Sans Soleil* we see a mannequin in a men's clothing department of a Tokyo department store fabricated to resemble John F. Kennedy, outfitted with a tape-loop from the famous inauguration speech: "Ask not what your country can do for you, ask what you can do for your country." (The Muses appear here as a female choral accompaniment, a supra-voice-over, seconding the emotion in a Tokyo Motown motif.) For some time now we've been citizens of a Cybernation, occupying a mental homeless shelter that harbors Dan Rather, Roseanne Barr, and Bullwinkle. If Loony Tunes return as *tour de force* of the American sublime (as in Ashbery's "Daffy Duck in Hollywood"), it's altogether relevant to compare Pound's "news that stays news" with network news and the way the voice of the "anchor" underwrites the braille of the daily Real.

The imperative voice-over can follow many orders of authority.

> Odd, how easy the news-like
> voice comes over and says,
> "I am the agenda,
> for reasons which must remain
> unconscious as cars acting out
> the look of a secure self
> whose national habits
> have been dictated by the ineffable
> mouth of a pre-fabricated history."
>
> (Perelman, *Captive Audience* 47)

The voices we hear as the soundtrack of public life no longer remember, nor do they display, their paths to and from actual bodies. Instead, they are equations of infantile laminar flow; free-floating tourniquets marking the interface between anxiety and authority. We hanker after the reassuring sound of a voice, no longer attending to what it says, and untroubled by its disembodiment. We're scared less by dark than by quiet. After the Second World War the Swiss philosopher Max Picard wrote: "By taking it away from silence we have made language an orphan. The tongue we speak today is no longer a mother-tongue but rather an orphaned tongue" (41). An orphanage is the institution of surrogate parenthood. In the Wax Museum we can see poetry in its orphanage, where mute icons of imaginative authority are sheltered along with the voices just out of their reach.

If it is the fate of a former American president to be a design element in a fashion display, what about those *unacknowledged* legislators, Shelley's poet governors (or cyberneticians)? So we return to Pound, Frost, H. D., Lowell, Olson, Plath, and others in the Wax Museum, posed in that peculiarly arrested stance only wax figures have. Possibly there could be recordings of the poets' voices, but the lip-sync problem would accentuate the very pathology the exhibit would be designed to conceal: namely, the fact that the poets (being dead) can't speak for themselves. The waxen effigies would have to be laboriously outfitted with vocal prostheses, in order to achieve even a semblance of autonomy. So it's likely the custodians would opt for the more congenial and cost-effective strategy of the voice-over. Think of students, then, along with their phantom companion the "general reader," wandering into the great Hall of English Literature wearing their headsets. You can see, by the awkwardness of their postures, the difficulty they have negotiating the space as they stand before *The Waste Land*, for instance, and after the resounding final "shantih" the Brooks/Warren baritone swells into their ears[19]: "*The Waste Land* is a poem totally concerned with the breakup of a

---

[19] The voice I have in mind is that of Westbrook Van Voorhis, narrator of the Fox Movietone series "The March of Time" which dominated the 1930s and reached its zenith during World War II. Van Voorhis was officially known as "The Voice of Time," but acquired the colloquial moniker "The Voice of God" (Kozloff 29). Baritone authority was ideologically coded into the technical features of broadcasting equipment. Public distaste for female announcers was quite pronounced in the early days of radio, the explanations for which range from the supposition of a natural inferiority in women's voices to technical deficiencies in the transmitters (McKay). As Amy Lawrence puts it: "Evidently the 'problem' of the woman's voice is always a tangle of technological and economic exigencies, each suffused with ideological assumptions about woman's 'place'" (32).

civilization—not, to be sure, the physical breakup, with buildings crashing into the street or government offices burning, but a spiritual breakup . . ." (*Understanding Poetry* 306). The poet's own voice is explicitly relegated to the role of talking head, voice-over for a civilization "gone in the teeth" as Pound (another fabricator of wasteland voices) put it. As talking head, of course, the poet is subservient to a scripted series of episodes which have the *production value* of conviviality, spontaneity, and confidentiality—with quality control guaranteed by the efficiency experts in the writing programs and workshops.

Regardless of *Understanding Poetry*, the contemporary media environment is so saturated with voice-overs that we're hard pressed to imagine a naive one-on-one encounter with a poem. Film subtitles, prerecorded sales pitches, audience sampling calls at dinnertime, canned laughter, public address systems, intercoms, overdubs in the music we listen to, Muzak, lip-sync, karaoke, newscasters voicing-over catastrophe footage, and sportscasters reviewing instant replay all converge in a congestion of voices. It's not surprising that one of the most popular recent television shows is *Murphy Brown*, about network newscasters—those talking heads whose drone overdubs the society of the spectacle—starring the daughter of a ventriloquist who spent his career doing voice-over for his lap dummy. Murphy herself is a cue-card for a generation; her angst and trials of identity serve to reconnect a demographically targeted audience with its hippie youth, its yuppie success, and its politically correct maturity. Murphy's identity crises, the continuous substance of the program, are legislated as prototypes for her audience. The subtext for audience and Murphy both is the necessary priority of identity, or subjectivity. The comic premise is selfhood beset by technical malfunction (sentimentally coded as lifestyle choices). And the tacit message of Murphy's attachment to Motown is that subjectivity requires an aesthetic (poetic) support: self-consciousness is a voice-activated technology.

Meanwhile poets, patiently laboring under a vast cultural misconception, imagine that authenticity is conflatable with subjectivity, not realizing that subjectivity is simply the most acutely engineered of all our technologies—voice-activated, setting in motion a replay of cultural "memories" which are generic and thus belong to nobody.[20] These memories are more effective for being customized, like those photographically provided for the "replicants" in Ridley Scott's *Blade Runner*—or injected as a neocortex "vacation" for Arnold Schwarzenegger in *Total Recall*—for whom the prefab snapshot enables a reverie of intimacy that cannot be contradicted by experience because there's no longer a distinction between the subject and the semiotic cue. The sign, or the word, signals a "past" that is accessible in the present, trained on the present, and has it so thoroughly in its sights that the memory traces are *dedicated* to a present that would be destabilized by the foreground of a lived past. The replicants savor their simulated past just as, now, poets are compelled to nurture a simulated present, convulsively tuning in to the solace of "immediacy." The simulacrum is the primal scene; and in poetry the compulsion is to retrieve the present in a medium (print) that facilitates fantasies of the unmediated. Voice has been nominated as the icon of this fantasy, but the wish-fulfilling association of voice with the speaking subject's authenticity (phonocentrism) has exacted a price: poets have lost touch with the archaic parables of voice-over, which instruct us in the ways in which inspiration always divests us of that security we so desperately crave as the sign of an empowerment we forever wish was ours alone, not a sport of the gods or a bewitchment of the muses. Because so much contemporary verse practice has courted the equation subjectivity = authenticity, we've become estranged from what Shklovsky referred to as "forwarding [or baring] the device"[21] —which is itself the classic modernist formula for estrangement. As Donald Wesling suggests, "modernity must both despise and require the device" (3). So poetry has been traumatized by any intimation that "the voice that is great

---

[20] "What queer lives we've had even for poets!" wrote Lowell to Berryman in 1962. "There seems something generic about it, and determined beyond anything we could do" (quoted in Hamilton 298).

[21] Conversely, much recent vanguard practice has so relentlessly bared its devices that this gesture, too, now serves as a generic epiphany of recognition for the initiated.

within us" has gotten into us by forces beyond our control. The device that is great within us, then, is the swollen sum of our erasures. Do we really want to talk about poetry if "talk" just adds a little more putty to the shrine, from which the bodiless voice of an oracle (a voice whose mobility is the essence of its diffuse authority, its omnipresence in the personal mode evidence of its pervasively intimate command) emanates straight to the center of subjectivity, securing postural rectitude? To begin to talk about poetry today, we can't afford not to wonder: Who is the lap-dummy for poetry's voice-over, with its "universal" voice of inspiration and its uncanny ability to write prescriptions for just what we think we always wanted?

CODA: IN THE GREENHOUSE

The waxen shrine, not surprisingly, hasn't been a *topos* in the image bank of American poetry; and Wordsworth's Parliament of Monsters with its waxworks and freaks of nature has been set aside in favor of another sort of exhibit, traditional to the American scene: "Nature."[22] Theodore Roethke's reputation rests on his breakthrough volume of autobiographical archetypes, *The Lost Son*, published the same year as *Pisan Cantos*, when Ezra Pound was in what he called "the bughouse." The opening sequence (the working title of which was "News of the Root") recalls the father's extensive greenhouses in a poetic repossession of "Cuttings," "Root Cellar," "Forcing House," and others that are among the most widely anthologized of postwar American poems. The greenhouse has a notable affinity with the museum: both are showcases of exotica, posed as normality. Roethke's is a world where vegetative miracles gasp into existence, where "small cells bulge," "sucking and sobbing," swelling "with steam and stench," orchids sway "adder-mouthed," where "even the dirt kept breathing a small breath." These lines are from the first four

---

[22] A conspicuous exception is Albert Goldbarth, whose poetry rivals garage sales, flea markets, "junktique shops" and "dustclumped auctionhouse[s]," and constitutes a veritable Wunderkammer of Americana. (*Popular Culture* 27).

poems in *The Lost Son*, a sequence which manifests human life only at its end, in "Frau Bauman, Frau Schmidt, and Frau Schwartze," where the "ancient leathery crones" are muse benefactors to the lost child, "their snuff-laden breath blowing lightly over me in my first sleep."

If this greenhouse/museum world is a poetic sanctuary, as it clearly is in Roethke's mythopoeisis, the poem of greatest interest is the most literally autobiographical, "Child on Top of a Greenhouse":

> The wind billowing out the seat of my britches,
> My feet crackling splinters of glass and dried putty,
> The half-grown chrysanthemums staring up like accusers,
> Up through the streaked glass, flashing with sunlight,
> A few white clouds all rushing eastward,
> A line of elms plunging and tossing like horses,
> And everyone, everyone pointing up and shouting!

> (*Collected Poems* 43)

Even during a first reading it's hard not to see Roethke's colossal desire for poetic approval and fame, to be on top of the world (even, in the conceit of the fourth line, above the sun), rousing a snort of approval from trees and humans alike. In a letter to Kenneth Burke, Roethke stressed the danger involved: "being up on top of this greenhouse was something that even the most foolhardy older kids condemned . . ." (*Letters* 119). Foolhardy or not, the image the poem offers is a silhouetted boy, an image of transgression but also of escape, release from the dark entanglements cultivated so carefully down below in the moist warmth of biopoetic humus. The poem's prescience resonates for us now in part because Roethke achieved the eminence the poem yearns for. The figure looms, clumsy and colossal, atop the greenhouse (but it remains a boy: later we'll look into the sustaining myth of the American poet as juvenile exception, "the figure of youth as virile poet" as Wallace Stevens had it). The greenhouse, a place of primal striving and fertility, strangely emerges as a place compelling the fantasy of escape, but why?

Greenhouses are controlled environments, sites of artificially induced vegetal animation. So they impose limits on life; to be in the greenhouse is to be housed in a cell of approval, cocooned in expectations. But the greenhouse also resonates with fears of being buried alive, trapped in a museum, or shut up in a corrective institution; the greenhouse may be but a quaint emblem and analogy for the wax exhibit. Theodor Adorno remarks that "museum and mausoleum are connected by more than phonetic association. Museums are like the family sepulchres of works of art" (*Prisms* 175). "In the halls of the Museum," Robert Duncan writes, "all that we meant to remember . . . falls into that fame that silences what we were" (*Ground Work I* 60). That anthologies can also be a funerary medium was lamented by Donald Davidson, one of the original Fugitives, who remarked in 1957 that the "admission of modern poetry to the textbooks of school and college classes may be, in a sense, as much an entombment as a triumph" (quoted in Hubbell 235). Davidson hearkened back to a mythic era when lines of poetry dropped from the lips of educated gentlemen like manna for the conversational sublime; but even for those less disposed to such nostalgia, the carceral apparatus of the anthology and the textbook is unmistakable. Yet, eerily, the mausoleum of the Muses is also a site of reproduction, in which Sylvia Plath heard herself resonating with the echoes of her canonization, haunted in life by the approaching sterilization of fame. Plath's "Barren Woman" begins "Empty, I echo to the least footfall, / Museum without statues . . ." (157). And Laura Riding's "Echoes" assemble the moiré of an uncanny curriculum: "Let us seem to speak / Or they will think us dead, revive us. / Nod brightly, Hour. / Rescue us from rescue" (75). These are the sounds poets make as their advancing reputations gleam in the eyes of their custodians.

Suitably, the most celebrated poetic event of the past decade, James Merrill's *The Changing Light at Sandover*, is preoccupied with the status of the greenhouse as successor to Atlantis (121), sacred to "God B" (for Biology). "GOD B IS NOT / ONLY HISTORY BUT EARTH ITSELF   HE IS THE GREENHOUSE" (187). At the same time, God B's provenance extends astrally: "THE SUN & ITS / WHOLE SYSTEM IS OF THE GREENHOUSE" (199). The greenhouse custodian, the Romantic sublime, is a subaltern in Merrill's poem: "NATURE IS A FORCE AT ONCE FECUND & LAZY. . . / WHO IN A SENSE KEEPS THE GREENHOUSE / GREEN IF UNTIDY" (228). In Merrill's cosmic panorama divine energies are revealed as the transitory productions of subordinate gods. *The Changing Light at Sandover* is in fact Macrobius's fifth-century dream rewritten for the late twentieth century. A condition of the revelation is that poetry, too, be reassessed in terms of its limits, dislodged from its vices and habits by the ouija board interlocutors and informants, whose news for poetry includes the claim that "THE REVEALD MONOTHEISM OF TODAY IS LANGUAGE" (239). Merrill's is a poem befitting an age anxious about the old sources of solace—poetic form, thematic integrity, and the transcendental ego; a poem (really a masque) appropriate to the benumbing realization Larry Levis describes as "a loss more profound than the loss of political goals or partisan feelings. Part of what got lost is the possibility of wholly believing in the grand fiction of Romantic alienation and individuation" (477). For many, this gives way to the greatest fear of all: the loss of poetry.

The institutional priorities of the greenhouse exact concessions, the most mortifying of which is that a poetry isolated and artificially nourished in order to shield it from antipoetic predators becomes a lifeless poetry, its dignity purchased at the expense of vitality.[23] The terms of preservation are also those of extinction. Roethke's greenhouse reappears in another guise, in a motif developed by Karl Shapiro in one of his audacious forays of the 1950s into the subject, "Is Poetry an American Art?" "I believe that American poetry is a European translation which has never really taken root with us and never will," Shapiro maintained, proposing that "Ours is a hothouse poetry, kept alive by artificial respiration and fluorescent light" (*Children* 45). Midway through the essay the greenhouse is refigured as a pottery studio:

---

[23] "The museum was the most suitable place for reproducing in the individual withdrawal from facticity and the consolation of being elevated to a more dignified world . . ." (Marcuse 131).

> For poetry is—let us admit it—a minor art of America, like
> pottery. Our poetry becomes more and more ceramic as the
> decades roll by. And outside the pot shop the boys with
> their hammers and rocks peer in at the window. . . . Per-
> haps we should teach our children that once upon a time
> there was a thing called poetry, that it was very beautiful,
> and that people tried to bring it to our shores in boats but it
> died. And a few people couldn't live without it, so they
> went back to the Old World to see it. And others built elab-
> orate greenhouses, called English Departments, where they
> kept it breathing. And they watered it with the most expen-
> sive electricity, but it didn't like it here and died anyhow.
> And some fractious students lost their tempers and began
> to smash the greenhouse windows. And then everybody
> started reading prose. (59, 62)

This was not, it turns out, the end of the tale (broken windows never
melted wax). When everybody started reading prose it soon became
apparent that much of the prose was about poetry, and about the
pleasurable acoustic of shattering glass. And those boys outside the
pot shop? They're still wondering, like the poets half-in, half-out of
Donald Davie's "imaginary museum," how to tell the inside from the
outside after their hammers and rocks summoned them from the
enticement of transparency into the enigma of reflections ("Mirror
makers know the secret—one does not make a mirror to resemble a
person, one brings a person to the mirror" [Spicer 55]). "This is
where grammatical terror opens a distance between you and yourself
in order to insert the mirror," Rosmarie Waldrop writes in her spirited ventriloquism of Wittgenstein in *The Reproduction of Profiles*
(73). "Our lord of the mirror. I closed my eyes, afraid to resemble";
"As if my body were only layers on layers of windowpane" (62, 65).
"At some point," Davie says of his "Poet in the Imaginary Museum,"
"there must always be a flaw in the mirror, a deliberately contrived
maladjustment between content and form . . . . The illusion must, if
only for an instant, be broken; the convention at some point must be
deliberately transgressed" (55). Like the climax of Orson Welles's
film *The Lady from Shanghai*, every presentation is spooked by its
medium, its smoke and mirrors; but in the circuit from waxwork to

greenhouse to pot shop, by way of what Spicer called "the English Department of the spirit," the sidelong glance sometimes reveals an opening, and in the blink of an eye the arrested pose of the wax figurine might even appear to move.

> One day you look at the mirror and it's open
> and inside the place where the eyes were
> is a long road gray as water
> and on it someone is running away
> a little figure in a long pale coat
> and you can't move you can't tell
> it's too late for that
> who was it you ask

> (Merwin, *Writings* 107)

CHAPTER TWO

The Age of "The Age of"

Part One: From the Age of Criticism to the Age of Sociology

WHAT THE WOMAN LIVED

It has been standard practice to narrate the vicissitudes of modern poetry with a ritualistic recitation of familiar names in an epic of trials and conquests. In other words, a Theogony or an Odyssey—prototypes invited, after all, by Pound, as literary matchmaker and later unwitting star of the technicolor melodrama of his own fate. Kenner's *The Pound Era* is the necessary and inevitable portrait of the age, in a way that couldn't possibly be attempted by assigning the starring role to Frost or Stevens. In the romance of modernism, slum pediatrics may seem a glorious calling for a poet; even clerical work in a bank, indemnity reports and the contractual details of trade publishing at Faber appear less dispiriting than the fate of university teaching allotted to the next generation. And those who lived truly public and literary lives, like Yeats and Pound, seem positively drenched in ambrosia. Pound's later years in the "bughouse" seem fitting penance, in retrospect, for such a charmed life. The problem with the heroic postures involved in such a frieze, aside from the hieratic implications, is the gradual erasure of a lived, human dimension.

The antics and agonies of the celebrated confessional generation might be seen, in part, as a desperate flailing of mortals deceived by their predecessors as to the divinity of the poetic calling. The biographies of Berryman, Schwartz, Lowell, Olson, Ginsberg, O'Hara and even Duncan are tales of lives lived in a comparable literary dominion; not as grandiose as the modernists, perhaps (excepting Ginsberg), but psychologically more intense, more cramped and conflicted. But these lives are misleading insofar as they perpetuate our compulsive need for lives of poets to be exemplary, either positively or negatively. Many poets, however, lead *interested* rather than interesting lives. Rilke may be paradigmatic in this respect: a minimum of biographical import made for a maximum of poetic impact. I want to develop here a sense of poetry in America as a matrix of lives lived, not a Jurassic Park of spectacular behemoths. The efficient medium to hand—one which grazes on the public/private interface of the administrative environment of poetry at mid-century—is epistolary. The letters of Louise Bogan are useful in that she was a fastidious observer, knew or had significant contact with many of the more famous personnel of the poetry world, and was generationally situated so as to have a dual perspective on both the modernist and the subsequent generations.[1]

Born in 1897, Bogan's contemporaries included Jean Toomer and e.e. cummings (1894), F. Scott Fitzgerald and John Dos Passos (1896), William Faulkner (1897), Ernest Hemingway, Léonie Adams, Allen Tate and Hart Crane (1899). This was a generation poised as young adults to catch *The Waste Land* head-on, as an astonishing disfiguration of poetry from a near contemporary—as a challenge to be personally met, worked through. (The next generation missed that initial impact, and took its Eliot more like an obligatory if intoxicating medicine: Eberhart, Warren, Kunitz, Rexroth, and, in England,

---

[1] Unless otherwise indicated, subsequent citations from Bogan are from her letters, *What the Woman Lived: Selected Letters of Louise Bogan, 1920–1970.*

Auden and Empson.) It is illuminating to find Bogan describing herself, responding to a request for biographical details, as born "ten years before Auden, Isherwood, and L. MacNeice, and about two thousand after Sappho" (189).

At forty Bogan described herself as "never . . . a member of a 'lost generation.' I was the highly charged and neurotically inclined product of an extraordinary childhood and an unfortunate early marriage" (6, *n*2). Bogan emerged a widow with a three-year-old child in 1920. She was on the editorial board of the poetry magazine *The Measure*, and was acting editor in 1924–25. During this time she was close to a circle of anthropologists who wrote poetry, including Margaret Mead, Ruth Benedict, and Edward Sapir. In 1925 she married Raymond Holden, who was managing editor of *The New Yorker* from 1929–32, but they separated in 1933. She had amicable, and amorous, relations with a number of men, being closest to Rolfe Humphries, Edmund Wilson, Morton Dauwen Zabel (editor of *Poetry*), and Theodore Roethke. "My, how the women married to literary men hate me!" she wrote after a weekend with Wilson in 1937. "They positively fry in their own juices, while I am in the room, and wig-wag frantic signals to the poor males, who are only trying to be nice . . . " (167). She had an affair with Roethke, ten years her junior, in 1935, about which she wrote to Edmund Wilson "I, myself, have been made to bloom like a Persian rose-bush, by the enormous love-making of a cross between a Brandenburger and a Pomeranian . . . 26 years old and a frightful tank. We have poured rivers of liquor down our throats, these last three days, and, in between, have indulged in such bearish and St. Bernardish antics as I have never before experienced" (84). She was bold, loved her liquor ("Influences: I think alcohol comes in here" [190]), and seems to have been chronically insecure about the calibre of her own poetry, but was perceptive and meticulous in her treatment of the writing of others. Her life consisted of literary work, reviewing and translating and serving on committees, none of it particularly lucrative. It was the literary life available to members of her generation, for whom academe was rarely in the cards.

Bogan had a lifelong mistrust of academia. "This cozening by academic friends will ruin her," she wrote regarding Léonie Adams (the friends were Warren and Tate [39]). Her skepticism persisted, and in 1958 she clarified to a *New Yorker* reader, querying her severe treatment of John Hollander, that "since I am a formalist myself, I could not very well attribute formalism to others as a fault! I was writing, in the piece you mention, about empty, academic formalism, which *is* a fault, in any language or period" (314). She was a perennial judge of applications for Guggenheim Fellowships from 1944 on, but by 1963 was wearying of the predictability of the applicants. "I struggle with the Guggenheim stuff," she wrote. "Academics and beats; beats and academics. Pretty poor stuff" (327, *n*1). This was, she saw, becoming a formulaic substitute for more serious matters. She had eclectic tastes and a spirited nature, so her evaluation of poets runs the gamut in unaffiliated and unpredictable ways.

"Our time," she observed in 1928, "just loves poems about the internal organs of the body, the mechanisms of sex, abortion, fecal processes, etc. It's like looking inside the hood of an automobile, or watching the shafts and gears and sprockets in a factory" (42). Bogan wasn't repelled by any of this, just disinterested. Her greatest and abiding enthusiasm in poetry understandably turned out to be Rilke, whose work she discovered in 1935. At this point her close friend Rolfe Humphries had signed on as a Communist Party member, and while their friendship remained intact their letters are a dossier of constant bickering. In 1936 she responds to a Humphries proposal that "an organization of writers for the defense of culture seems to me to be a rather tendentious scheme. If culture is going to be overthrown, it will be, in any case. No puny organization of writers is going to stop it." Besides, she goes on, "Why ask for the world without ruins? Why ask for a world in which art never changes or fails or is partially erased? The Fascists burn the books, and the Communists bar the heterodox, and what difference is there between the two?"(125).[2] The similarity would not become apparent to

---

[2] Later the same year she wrote for Humphries a parodic review of her own work as she conceived it might be received in *New Masses*: "Miss Bogan seems to have written some more punk, operatic, prima-donnaish poetry, in which she shows off to a remarkable degree, airing her outmoded, and, we fear by now, rather antiquated charms and sex-agonies in the most futile

Humphries and companions for several years to come, when Stalin signed his mutual non-aggression pact with Hitler in 1940. "I wish people would stop being sentimental about [revolution], and writing about it as though it might appear by the waving of a wand," she told Humphries. "I think there is no doubt this generation should be swabbed off the board," adding that "it would be a good thing if everyone were compelled to shut up for about five years" (127).[3]

Bogan was an early and continual admirer of Auden ("I really think he's the works" [144]), though she was quick to diagnose the features of an Auden cult that sprouted during the thirties. After a visit to Bennington she noted that one of the faculty members "now goes for . . . Auden as she once went for fur-trimmed suits from Altman's" (131). Responding in 1940 to May Sarton, who would subsequently become a regular correspondent, Bogan speculated on a "distrust of form and emotion," even a "hatred shown toward lyric poetry," to

---

way imaginable. Far better if Miss B. had confined herself to writing articles on hay, grain and mash for *The Breeder's Gazette*. She has a poem on Italy that makes no mention of either Mussolini or Fascism." (133) Humphries had his own parody of the prevalent idiom to offer Edmund Wilson in 1944: "I think what I want to do next is a Great American Symphonic Poem in 4 movements—The Rivers (Adagio) The Forests (Andante ma no troppo) The Cities (Allegro) and The Air and the Seas (Cornuto) The whole thing will be entitled 'The American Corn,' published, but seriously, by Simon and Schuster in an edition of 1 0000000000000 copies. Dedicated to Paul Engle, Wm. Rose Benét, R. Davenport, J. D. Adams, and R. Norton. Maybe also A. MacLeish and R. Hillyer, B. DeVoto, V. S. Brooks, and the Sainted Memory of S. V. Benét, saint and martyr" (*Poets*, 188). Engle was at that point director of the Creative Writing Program at the University of Iowa—the first of its kind, and grandaddy of all subsequent MFA programs; MacLeish was Librarian of Congress, Director of the Office of Facts and Figures (a war propaganda agency), and later Assistant Secretary of State; and Hillyer was an editor at *Saturday Review* and leader of the notorious attack on the Bollingen Prize awarded to Pound in 1949.

[3] They didn't, of course, but continued in partisan crescendo for several years, even when they were not fellow travellers. *New Republic* presented nine poets under the headline "Social Symbolists" on July 13, 1938, selected by Selden Rodman and including Cowley, MacLeish, Gregory, Rukeyser, Fearing, Agee, and Schwartz, of whom only one was actually affiliated with the Communist Party. That this gathering is left unmentioned by Cary Nelson in *Repression and Recovery* indicates the sheer abundance of material pertinent to an ongoing *recovery*. Nor does Nelson ever mention Rolfe Humphries, by the way.

which Auden had unwittingly contributed. "Auden, I think, is a man of genius, but he, too, has been protected and swaddled against any reality but the fashionable kind" (207). Malcolm Cowley, to her surprise, sent her an Auden book to review for *New Republic* in 1935. "In the old days it would have gone to Allen Tate," she remarked, "and Allen would have said, 'In fusing the basis of the intellect out of the microscopic dualisms concurrent in the derivative dichotomies so uselessly prevalent, and notwithstanding the disuses fallen upon the gentility . . . '" (106). Tate had been a friend since the twenties, but as her parody shows, Bogan was dubious of scholastic doubletalk. In 1929 she remarked of Yvor Winters, "He is *such* a serious, learned, conscientious boy, so passionately for style and dignity in writing, and for ethics and humanism in life. . . . He cannot write a review without dragging in special pleading for the restitution of metaphysical birthright to modern American writers. I have seen him, at a very gay dinner party, when all the other guests were making themselves wreaths out of the centerpieces, almost come to fisticuffs . . . over Gerard Manley Hopkins!" (48). In 1940 she characterizes a young poet as having "been through the regular mill: sitting at Ransom's feet at Kenyon, and hearing Allen at Benfolly, and knowing Auden and everything . . . " (204). The follies of careerism always roused her scorn, even when friends were involved.

In 1938 she was pondering the two large collected editions of Jeffers and Williams, observing how advantageously such a volume showed off the latter's work, and how efficiently Jeffers' monotony was revealed. Williams "has absolutely no sense of drama, and I might do a piece, putting him against Jeffers, who has too much" (179). She was amenable to Frost's poetry but deplored the man; was passionate about Moore's work; and while she valued *Harmonium* thought that Stevens's later style suffered from preciousness.[4]

---

[4] She reports an extraordinary anecdote in 1935 about Stevens getting drunk in Key West, duking it out with Hemingway, then barging in on Dos Passos only to be disappointed: "'So you're Dos Passos,' said S., 'and here I find you, playing cheap things on the phonograph and surrounded by women in pajamas. I thought you were a cripple and a man of culture! Women in pajamas!' and he stormed out of there." She seems to have gotten the story from

Among her own peers in that decade some were assembled in a comment to Zabel about the effects of her own work on them: "I want
[the last poem in *The Sleeping Fury*, 1937] set in italics, to give M.
Rukeyser, K. Patchen, S. Burnshaw, H. Gregory, and M. Zaturenska
something *really* to worry about" (145). All but Burnshaw would
continue to loom on her literary horizon well into the fifties, and
both Bogan and Humphries were among those outraged by *A History
of American Poetry, 1900–1940* (1946), since the authors, Gregory
and Zaturenska, had always struck them as the worst in sycophantic
fawning and poetry careerism.[5] Those who would do the real worrying were poets of the next generation: the Schwartz-Jarrell-Berryman
circle was especially in awe of Bogan's vehemance, smarting at every
phrase. She roasted *In Dreams Begin Responsibilities* with a withering parts-list of Schwartz's sources: "The Kafka-Auden-Isherwood
Dog, a monocle and some ice cream from W. Stevens, playing cards
from Eliot, and Anglo-Saxon monosyllables from Molly Bloom"
(*Alphabet* 353–54).[6] While she admired Lowell, she was dismissive
of Berryman and Jarrell, suspicious perhaps of their literary politick-
ing, as was Rolfe Humphries who referred disparagingly in 1951 to
this "new generation . . . as advertised by itself, R. Jarrell, Ciardi,
Schwartz, etc." (225). By the end of the war Bogan was established
not only as a reviewer, but an authority on the state of American

---

Dos Passos himself, who characterized Stevens as "a disappointed man, who
doesn't dare to live the life of an artist, preferring the existence of an insurance broker, so that he tends to idealize men of letters" (121).

[5] They are both there in the famous photograph taken for *Life* in the Gotham
Book Mart, as part of the Sitwell's publicity campaign during their American visit in November 1948. Auden, Eberhart, Moore, Spender and Benét are
the senior poets on hand, mingled with their (slight) juniors José Garcia
Villa, Charles Henri Ford, Schwartz and Jarrell. Tennessee Williams and
Gore Vidal are also in the picture. Lowell, like Rolfe Humphries and Bogan,
had been invited but declined. John Berryman was ecstatic to have been
included, but left the room when the photo was posed because he was disconcerted by Benét "sitting there like a mummy" and Jarrell "blazing . . .
with ambition" (Mariani 214–15, and Eileen Simpson 168–69).

[6] Schwartz found Bogan's review "favorable enough, I suppose, but from
beginning to end it is full of mistakes which show how poorly she read the
book," as he urged his publisher, James Laughlin, to write a "disinterested"
complaint to *The Nation* (Schwartz, *Letters* 45–46).

poetry, as reflected in her *Achievement in American Poetry* of 1951, and her frequent invitations to panels and other forums of authoritative commentary.[7]

The cloistered environment of committee members haggling over professional awards and fellowships was a regular feature of Bogan's life from the 1930s until her death in 1970. She approached these situations with integrity, it appears—though she was keenly aware of the nature of literary politics, noting after Roethke won the Pulitzer in 1954 that "Ted has made a point of knowing all the right people *everywhere*, since the start of his career" (287). She chose the twenty-one-year-old Robert Lowell for the Glascock Prize at Mount Holyoke College. Judging entries for the Hopwood Memorial Prize the next year she noted that they "were uniformly Yeats-or-Auden soaked" (191). She was instrumental in securing two prizes for Marianne Moore, the Harriet Monroe Memorial Award for 1944 ("She should have received every prize in America, long ago, including the Pulitzer and anything the Am. Acad. of A. and Letters had to hand out" [236]), and the Bollingen Prize in 1952, when she had to fend off Auden's choice of "R. Jarrell, of all people" as she put it (276). Far and away the most notable and controversial committee Bogan sat on was the one convened by Allen Tate at the Library of Congress in 1948, which gave the Bollingen to Pound.

The postwar years found Bogan entering her fifties and in a retrospective mood. She published a succinct survey, *Achievement in American Poetry 1900–1950*, in which she noted that the generation following the modernists "though generally far more informed and better equipped then their elders, found themselves functioning in a period of absorption, rather than in one of energetic projection" (102). Commenting, obliquely, on her own generation, or Auden's, or both: "A stiffening of method becomes evident; a drying out of emotion takes place. A growth of self-consciousness points to a return of skep-

---

[7] In 1954 she was gratified by the "great and unexpected" invitation to survey "the contemporary situation in American poetry" for the *Times Literary Supplement*, a task, she noted, that would formerly have gone to Conrad Aiken (289).

ticism and relative timidity" (102–03). Turning to the actual present, midcentury, there's no ambiguity in what she sees: "At present, this tendency toward expertness and control—toward conscious manipulation of texture, conscious heightening of tension, and conscious distillation of meaning—is accompanied by what seems to be a complete exhaustion of experimentalism" (103). She had by this point weathered enough changes of fashion to recognize that neither formalism nor experimentalism, neither activism nor asceticism, in and of themselves guaranteed results. So, while she was clearly a member of the poetic establishment—a permanent consultant to granting agencies, regular reviewer in the most influential journals, and confidante of a considerable number of major poets and critics—she was too much an individualist to bother about party lines. Highbrow though her cultural tastes were, she could speculate on the value of a broader historical view. Amid the furor of the highbrow/lowbrow debates she professes "I have thought that 'popular art'—so-called—should be brought into some relation with the more formal arts. An anthology of poetry, which included 'popular songs,' ballads, etc., along with 'serious' and formal poetry (the two kinds of expression being printed without any lines of demarcation between) would, it seems to me, be extremely interesting and valuable" (252). Nearly half a century later, this remains a project in limbo. In 1952 she could proclaim Wilbur "the finest talent among the American young," yet two years later stingingly observe after an Academy of Arts and Letters board meeting that "R. Wilbur gets the Rome Fellowship, of course. Such goings on!" (278, 288). At the same time, she got along well with Kenneth Rexroth and spent an enjoyable evening with his Beat entourage in San Francisco just weeks after the famous Six Gallery reading in October 1955. "[L]ast night there was a party for the *young* (mostly), here. They are simply *bouncing* with life, have read everything, and have a pet genius, whose name I can't spell, but who is a French-Canadian. . . . (He charms cats, which is a good sign.) This 'pet genius' thing is not a good sign; but Hart Crane was one, in the East, years ago, was he not?" The pet genius, of course, was Kerouac. Bogan had something startling of her own to tell the energetic lads: "The young write *old-fashioned* free-verse, and were rather shocked when I told them that 'the modern' was now the official style, and should be *revolted* against" (302). This is a bit disingenuous, as Bogan had been making this point for at least a decade. In a 1944 *New Yorker* review of Robert Penn Warren she acclaimed the fruits of the Audenesque mode of vernacular formalism: "This style is now a supple instrument," she wrote, but "too early to say [whether it is] capable of endurance and growth" (*Alphabet* 407). While "the folk line and the line of bourgeois literature can be counted on to keep flourishing: it is formal poetry that now needs critics and friends" (407–08).

Bogan committed herself to both roles, as friend *and* critic of the new formalism in the postwar years. She wrote appreciative reviews of formalist practice in Shapiro, Lowell, Wilbur, Bishop, Hecht, Merwin, and Barbara Howes; but she was discriminating, and even scornful of formalism gone "bloodless" (Jarrell [*Alphabet* 301]) and overburdened with "tricks" (Viereck [*Alphabet* 233]), or in an extreme case like Berryman's *Dream Songs*, achieved at the expense of "heartless ingenuity [and] desperate artificiality" (*Alphabet* 54). "At the moment," she wrote in 1958—appraising John Hollander's tendency to "technical cliché" and "triviality and emptiness of subject"—"after a resetting of poetic conventions that has taken twenty years, gifted young poets, almost without exception, write in form. It is a pity that most of them turn out to be dull" (*Alphabet* 442). In 1953 she published an appreciation of "The Pleasures of Formal Poetry" in the *Quarterly Review of Literature*, but that did not impede her receptiveness to "Experimentalists of a New Generation" in 1957, when she noted the Beat/Black Mountain activists bringing "renewed vigor to the American experimental line, which, until this recent outburst of energy, had almost entirely disappeared in affectation and artificiality" (*Alphabet* 129). While she was cautionary on the matter of form ("Once form has been smashed, it has been smashed for good. . . . It is never enough to smash form; form must be continually refreshed and renewed"), she was optimistic that this "renewed poetic liveliness . . . may lead into renewed poetic life" (*Alphabet* 130). She may be the only observer of the scene at that point who made unbiased comments about *both The New Poets of England and America* and *The New American Poetry*.

Bogan's range of interests afforded her a unique insight into the phenomenon of confessionalism as well, noting that St. Augustine and Rousseau (the "classic confessors") were not poets, and that "the kind of confession that is good for the soul requires not the condensation of poetry but the discursiveness of prose." Whitman's posture of confession was likewise "independent of metre and rhyme," and Bogan observes that the confessional impulse in Yeats and Rilke resulted in prose, even while they continued writing lyric poetry "of striking formal beauty." She judiciously accommodates to her notion of formalism the relevant criteria of classical rhetoric: "even as [Shapiro] inveighs against the pretensions of falseness of form and celebrates poetry as pure play," she says of *The Bourgeois Poet*, "[he] is skilfully manipulating a set of binding and intensifying devices that keep on adding unity to his composition—simile and metaphor, image and symbol, repetition and parallelism, exhortation and peroration" (*Alphabet* 370).

The issue of form for Bogan was ultimately bound up with poetic legacy in a broad historical sense. "The Pleasures of Formal Poetry" is almost exclusively concerned with Greek prosody and French symbolist practice; and Valéry was a major presence for her, as he was for Allen Tate and many others around World War II. Rilke embodied the best of "formalist" solutions, since he ranged from the most inimitable metrical concentration in the *Neue Gedichte* and the *Sonnets* to an equally adept free verse in the *Duino Elegies*. Rilke's spiritual preoccupations were enticing to Bogan's sensibility, but more than that, she saw this as intrinsic to the calling of poetry as such. The devotional ambiance of the Beats, along with their Dionysian pep, earned her respect. She might remain dubious about the cultural side-effects of the hang-loose attitude, but unlike many of her peers she did not view the interest in Zen and jazz and hipster bohemianism as lifestyle fads. She was always quick to note a tendency of formalism to become fussy, for the villanelle and sestina to devolve into the fetishistic furniture of style. The technicalities of formalism, she shrewdly observed, derived from a fear of emotion; "young poets today [1953], I have found, are particularly terrified of the Sublime" (*Alphabet* 158). "In modern poetry, this larger emotion is rare indeed; the whole emotional set of the period is against it. The minor Gothic shudder, on the other hand, appears with fair regularity" (*Alphabet* 300). That the Sublime was proximate to madness she had no doubt: "that McClure guy, who writes out of a 'peyote depression,' may yet connect with the sacred fire in no uncertain way," she wrote to a friend (336).[8]

In the lengthy chronicle that follows, much will involve an enlargement of sites and contests previewed here by way of Louise Bogan: the emergence of the New Criticism, the wagers of experimentalism and social commitment, the spectacle of poetry careerism and the management of reputations, the conflict between conformity and individualism, the clash between academic and Beat, cooked and raw, and again and again the postural antinomies of form and whatever seems to defy it. I have not sought here to rehabilitate Bogan's verse, but to create a clearing for the casual epistolary intimacy, ardor, and deliberation of her voice to be heard. I have done so because her life overlaps the period I will discuss; because she paid attention to many of the issues I'll be dealing with; and above all because she is a figure who engages our awareness of what Cary Nelson calls "the social meaning of a life lived on poetry's behalf" (*Repression* 246).

POETRY AND GENERAL CULTURE

The dominant condition circumscribing American poetry in the second half of the twentieth century is its subsistence in administrative environments. From the New Criticism of the 1940s to the rise of the Associated Writing Programs of the 1970s, American poets could be sure of one thing: regardless of whether they had access to a general public, there was at least the solace that certain bureaucratic

---

[8] "It's easy to be stuffy," she goes on, "but it's the pompous paranoids that are the worst. Charles Olson, for example, who calls himself Maximus, and states that HE IS THE ONLY MAN WHO UNDERSTANDS MELVILLE. . . ." The letter is dated Thanksgiving, 1962.

precincts privileged poems as the raw material, the data, of administration. Before chronicling the vicissitudes of reputation and the
packaging of careers in Part Two of this chapter, it will be useful to
look at the construction of the institutional venue that legislated the
production and reception of poetry at mid-century: the New Criticism. Since there are numerous discussions of the critical vocabulary
and pedagogic consequences of New Criticism, my focus is on the
oddly neglected fact that New Criticism was in effect a public relations firm that pioneered and then successfully promulgated a certain brand of poetry. Insofar as a canon of modern American poetry
has seemed self-evident to so many critics and anthologists, the New
Criticism succeeded.

    "What a true old bore that Ransom is!" Louise Bogan
exclaimed on reading *The New Criticism* in June 1941. "His greatest
feats are his diagrams: the round one wherein the affect slides down
from ten minutes past, to half-past, on the dial, when hit from the
outside by the stimulus (the *attitude*, not the *affect*: excuse me!), is
enough to make a cat laugh." Beneath the laughter, though, was the
rueful realization that scholasticism was closing in on modern poetry with a vengeance. "The Schools are all around poetry; the same
old methods of mediaeval university teaching are beginning to creep
back, and all over, the teaching of Mods" (*Letters* 219). The same
year Conrad Aiken commented privately that "I think the Tate-to-
Blackmur-to Winters-to-Brooks (Cleanth)-to-Ransom roundelay is
becoming a menace, and with widening rings, and ought to be dealt
with, but they're tough babies" (*Letters* 253). Rolfe Humphries, writing to a correspondent in 1956, splenetically asked "Who . . . give[s]
a good goddamn what Cleanth Brooks says in refutation of Yvor
Winters' rebuttal of John Crowe Ransom's attack on Kenneth Burke's
analysis of Allen Tate's logistics" (244). Critics (not necessarily the
founding New Critics themselves) gained in stature, "dragging the
muse from the sublime to the meticulous," as Peter Viereck complained (*Archer* 232).

    Why should poets have been anxious about the esoteric doc-
trines of a coterie of literary theorists? New Criticism has long been a
routine feature of the history of literary studies in academe; but the

focus has been too exclusively on its pedagogic and theoretical role, with little regard for the fact that the New Criticism was a key agent in the emerging power structure of the postwar poetry establishment. The doctrinal aspects of the New Criticism have overshadowed the pragmatic relation of its theories to the development of poetry. The New Critics were intent on making the exegesis of poetic tradition serve the future of poetry as they conceived it. So the "Tate-to-Blackmur-to-Winters" roundelay was a "menace" to poets not included in their campaign for poetry.

The New Critics were, by and large, practicing poets, often autodidactic, and endowed with the high Modernist legacy of cultural elitism. They were ambitious and strategically resourceful, establishing a publishing matrix that lodged itself in university curricula for decades, controlling the tenor of American poetry while dictating the terms of its reception. The New Criticism remains the most successful American literary movement of the century, though it's not generally recognized in quite those terms. New Criticism has received much documentary commentary in recent years, largely because the vexing business of "theory" has spurred scholars like Gerald Graff, among others, to review the history of the profession— the profession being the teaching of literature at the post-compulsory level. This academic self-scrutiny, unfortunately, has made New Criticism appear internal to scholarly life in America, and less a matter of general culture. Edward Said, for instance, says that "until the advent of American and English New Criticism, the job of a critic was an appreciation of work as much for the general reader as for other critics" (*World* 144). New Criticism, in Said's view, effected the break between the general public and the scholarly or professional enclave. For the New Critics, however, the boundary that needed patrolling was not between the ivory tower and the village green, but between high and other (not necessarily "low") culture. Said ignores the fact that the New Critics were not simply trying to overthrow the prevailing philological bias in academia, but to gain academic credit for belles lettres. In a sense, the phenomenon of New Criticism was not an insurgence within the academy; it was also a reproach from the plane of "general culture" directed *at* the academy from outside.

Austin Warren admitted to Blackmur's biographer that "he thought me an academic and a pedant; I thought him an autodidact and hence a charlatan" (Fraser 29). Of those most closely associated with the original wave of New Critics, only Austin Warren and Yvor Winters held a Ph.D. Cleanth Brooks had a Master's and was a Rhodes Scholar, as was Robert Penn Warren. Ransom and Tate had Bachelor's degrees, while Burke and Blackmur were genuinely untutored in the literal sense of the word. Among the New Critics, then, we have a range of interests, from the polymathic Burke at one extreme of eclecticism and catholicity, to the more recognizably "narrow" professionalism of Brooks's close readings.

In the matter of a general literary culture, a salient feature of writings by the New Critics is that they were almost exclusively published by commercial trade presses. It is now almost unheard of for scholarly books to appear outside the university press domain, particularly works of literary criticism. Richard Poirier's *The Renewal of Literature*, Northrop Frye's *The Great Code* and *Words With Power*, Elaine Showalter's anthology *The New Feminist Criticism*, and the occasional title by Hugh Kenner are among the rare exceptions. Even the ubiquitous Fredric Jameson has published only with scholarly presses, unless we count Routledge, which has become in effect an unaffiliated academic press catering to a scholarly market grown so large that the traditional academic publishers can no longer satisfy demand. Works of scholarship were routinely published by university presses before World War II, of course; so part of what distinguished the New Critics as aspirants to academic sinecure was their alliance with a different publishing network. The activity is impressive and really needs to be itemized for full impact, author by author. R. P. Blackmur: *The Double Agent* and *The Expense of Greatness* (Arrow Editions, 1935 and 1940), *Language as Gesture* and *The Lion and the Honeycomb* (Harcourt, 1952 and 1955), *Form and Value in Modern Poetry* (Doubleday, 1957); Cleanth Brooks: *The Well Wrought Urn* (Reynal & Hitchcock, 1947) and, with Wimsatt, *Literary Criticism: A Short History* (Knopf, 1957); Kenneth Burke: *Counter-Statement* (Harcourt, 1931), *A Grammar of Motives* and *A Rhetoric of Motives* (Prentice-Hall, 1945 and 1950); John Crowe Ransom: *The*

World's Body (Scribner's, 1938), *The New Criticism* (New Directions, 1941); Allen Tate: *Reactionary Essays on Poetry and Ideas* (Scribner's, 1936), *Reason in Madness* (Putnam, 1941), *On the Limits of Poetry* (Swallow, 1948), *"The Hovering Fly" and Other Essays* (Cummington Press, 1948), *The Forlorn Demon* (Regnery, 1953), *The Man of Letters in the Modern World* (Meridian, 1955), *Collected Essays* (Swallow, 1959); Robert Penn Warren: *Selected Essays* (Random, 1958); Yvor Winters: *Primitivism and Decadence* (Arrow, 1937), *Maule's Curse* and *The Anatomy of Nonsense* (New Directions, 1938 and 1943), *In Defense of Reason* and *The Function of Criticism* (Swallow, 1947 and 1957); *On Modern Poets* (World, 1957). Copious as this is, I've omitted nonliterary works like Ransom's *God Without Thunder* and Burke's *Permanence and Change*, as well as titles published after the peak of New Critical hegemony in the 1950s. The critical works of Eliot, Richards and Empson, each allied with the New Critics, were also issued by trade publishers. Only W. K. Wimsatt and Austin Warren conducted their careers in the customary scholarly pattern, publishing under university imprints, as was also largely the case with Brooks, whose highly regarded debut in close reading, *Modern Poetry and the Tradition*, was issued by the University of North Carolina Press in 1939. Tate, Ransom, and Winters, arguably the theoretical core of New Criticism, never published with university presses, and Burke stuck with the trades apart from *The Philosophy of Literary Form* (LSU, 1941)—until, of course, California began reissuing his earlier titles late in his career.[9]

---

[9] The phenomenon of critical works released by commercial houses was not restricted to New Criticism. The New Critics forged alliances with other intellectuals, some of whom were scholars, in quarterlies that appealed to a general public from a distinctly scholastic vantage—namely, *The Kenyon Review, The Sewanee Review, The Southern Review, Accent,* and *The Partisan Review.* The *Partisan* originated as "A Bi-Monthly of Revolutionary Literature Published by the John Reed Club of New York" in 1934, but after its gradual disengagement from Marxism in the wake of Stalin's purges and the approach of war, the *Partisan* regulars were general intellectuals, publishing like the New Critics with the trades, but, unlike them, not affiliated with academia. The conspicuous exception was Lionel Trilling, a professor at Columbia, whose publications were all commercial, from his biography of Matthew Arnold in 1939 to *The Liberal Imagination, The Opposing Self* and *Beyond Culture.* While the other quarterlies published work by budding young professors, however, *Partisan Review* (aided no doubt by its New

Despite all this publishing activity, the New Critics had an obviously limited appeal. They wrote as "men of letters," and generally disdained comment on all but the most austere literary topics. They held the values of a cultural elite, openly opposing the *administrative* elitism of professional scholarship. Their audience was restricted to "serious" readers, obviously, above all to those readers whose sensibilities were *made* serious by the New Criticism. The New Criticism commanded the respect of a younger generation of poets, students, and scholars. Ransom was the same age as T. S. Eliot, a decade older than Burke (b. 1897), Tate (b. 1899), Austin Warren (b. 1899), and Winters (b. 1900). Robert Penn Warren (b. 1905), Blackmur (b. 1904) and Brooks (b. 1906) were of the generation of Trilling (b. 1905) and Auden (b. 1907). The poets who rose to prominence during World War II were of a generation receptive to the determination and authority of the New Critics, whose triumph was just then becoming certain. David Perkins speaks of John Berryman as "having internalized the New Criticism as a superego" (397). As Lowell recalled, "When I was twenty and learning to write, Allen Tate, Eliot, Blackmur, and Winters, and all those people were very much news. You waited for their essays, and when a good critical essay came out it had the excitement of a new imaginative work" (*Prose* 237). While Berryman was skeptical, by 1948, as to how beneficial criticism in general had been, he acknowledged that "[o]ne or two extraordinary things, like Robert Lowell's poetry, were helped into existence by some of this criticism," adding that "undoubtedly the general conscience of literate poets improved" ("Response" 860). The New Criticism consolidated its reputation among poets and in academe by the journals it controlled: *The Southern Review, The Kenyon Review, The Sewanee Review*, along with other journals sympathetic to the New Critics or the poets they sponsored, *Partisan Review* and *The Hudson Review*.

York location) was a conduit for independent intellectuals to develop careers in the public eye. Such *Partisan* regulars as Philip Rahv, William Barrett, Alfred Kazin and Irving Howe fit the profile, while others who ended up as professors conducted their writing along the trade publisher avenue, including Richard Chase, Frances Fergusson, and Leslie Fiedler.

Ransom, Tate, and Warren had been members (along with Laura Riding) of the Fugitive group at Vanderbilt in the aftermath of *The Waste Land*. The subsequent evolution of the group into the Southern agrarian political position of *I'll Take My Stand* (1930) is well documented. The important thing about this foreground is that the New Criticism developed as a *specifically* literary concern in large part because literature was the area in which the key theorists felt they could have an impact. This, too, carried an attractive message for a younger generation disillusioned by the end of the 1930s with the prospect of a "committed" poetry. The New Critics demonstrated the value of an insulated textuality, and were able to appear persuasive in part because of the precedent they set in social commentary. Having asserted a forceful political claim in 1930, their turn to literary theory seemed less like an abdication than a realistic assessment of the areas of potential efficacy.

New Criticism discovered the ideal corollary of utopian regionalism in the figure of the "text itself," a phantom object as scintillating in 1940 as *écriture* would be in Paris in 1970. If New Criticism has been repeatedly castigated for its antipolitical aestheticism, its polemical value has to be situated. The emphasis on formalism was a strategic assault on the prevailing bias in the humanities in the early part of the century, which was a philologically disposed historical scholarship. Textual editing, the history of ideas, influence studies, biographical and period monographs were the defining activities of English professors. What the New Critics saw in all this was a hermeneutic impoverishment, in which actual poems were merely bibliographic minutiae of a pseudoscientific historicism. For Ransom and the others, it was unpardonable that the professors were mute in the presence of the poem; or, to be precise, that lack of anything to say of the poem *qua* poem was camouflaged by a litany of extratextual data. There was another concern as well, in that the New Critics held their poetic practice in equilibrium with their critical work, and felt criticism as such was no impediment to poetry.

Conventional scholarship, on the other hand—with its connotations of archival myopia—was deemed too pure and rigorous to admit of any moonlighting. Yvor Winters' chairman at Stanford bluntly informed him that scholarship and poetry did not mix, and that poetry published by professors was a disgrace to the department (Graff, *Professing* 153–54). In any event, the doctrinal insistence on the autonomy of the poetic object was relatively short-lived, as reflected by revisions of Brooks and Warren's influential *Understanding Poetry*. The practice of close reading was never as myopically insulated from extratextual reality as we now pretend it was; and this chimerical retrospection reflects, in part, the triumph of New Criticism's polemic against historicism and philology.[10] The important point is that the success of New Criticism, in the end, was not the result of brilliant maneuvering or bold leadership alone; rather, it signifies the adaptability of basic New Critical tenets to the emerging liberal values of the society (values to which Ransom and Tate, at least, were not sympathetic).

Terry Eagleton has remarked it "ironic" that New Criticism canonized modernism by subjecting it to a reification symptomatic of everything the modernists themselves opposed: "the very social order against which such poetry was a protest was rife with such 'reifications,' transforming people, processes and institutions into 'things'" (49). While Eagleton's point is clever, and to some extent accurate, it contributes to a misperception of New Criticism as essentially distinct from a poetic project. In canonizing modernism, the New Critics *also*

---

[10] Geoffrey Hartman's evaluation of the continuing viability of close reading elegantly captures its pertinence to more recently popular theoretical enthusiasms: "Close reading...survives to this day as a presentational device that keeps the text central without overobjectifying it. Quotations become fragments as well as illustrations; they are extracts representing the work but also free the reader's imagination toward multivocal options, the making of meaning and a precarious linguistics of transmission." This ingenious repatriation of New Critical protocols to reader-response criticism, Bakhtinian heterology, and *Tel Quel* intertextuality is then made to accomodate a Rortyan pragmatist liberalism: "To read Empson and Richards—or, in America, Burke and Blackmur—is to find oneself in the presence of an intelligence that will not give up personal testimony for a stricter language of proofs. Theirs remains an open-ended discourse: impressions are erected into contingent truths rather than laws" ("English as Something Else" 42). This may have been the case for Burke and Blackmur, but not for the more centrally positioned authoritarian figures like Ransom, Tate, and Brooks. The precedents they set were dictatorial, even as they could pretend not to be doctrinal.

set the criteria (and developed the "talent," like a sports franchise) for what would follow. We need to bear in mind that the initial militancy of New Criticism against academic scholasticism was the work of poet-critics. Lionel Trilling's perspective in 1942 is judicious: "What the partisans of the so-called New Criticism revolted against was the scientific notion of the fact as transferred in a literal way to the study of literature. They wished to restore autonomy to the work of art, to see it as the agent of power rather than as the object of knowledge" (*Liberal Imagination* 183).[11] Who but a group of practicing poets would want to press for a view of poetry as an agent of power? This attitude is consistent with those of Pound, Yeats, and Eliot, as well as Olson, Duncan, and Ginsberg. That we fail to mention Ransom and Tate in this lineage, when speaking of poetics, is symptomatic of the thoroughness with which New Criticism has itself been isolated as an aspect of pedagogic history. However, it is an isolation clearly attributable to the New Critics themselves, inasmuch as they developed, within their institutional matrix, the kind of projects germane to that environment—scholarly quarterlies, symposia, and the summer institute—and so in the long run identified their commitment to poetry with institutional custodianship rather than with the poets themselves.

---

[11] This essay, "The Sense of the Past," originally appeared in *Partisan Review*. It begins as a critique of New Critics' neglect of a sense of the past, but rather than harping on this—Trilling was, after all, informally allied with them at this point—he uses the occasion to suggest not only the plausability but the inevitability of a developed historical sensibility. His premise is that the historical sense is unavoidable, something we can't elect to do without; so we adapt ourselves to it conscientiously or else submit to its ideological preformulations. "The refinement of our historical sense," Trilling recommends, "chiefly means that we keep it properly complicated" (*Liberal Imagination* 188). In a particularly ingenious move, Trilling points out that historians engage their data as compact, representative samplings, or "abstractions." "But in pursuing our purpose, in making our abstractions, we must be aware of what we are doing; we ought to have it fully in mind that our abstraction is not perfectly equivalent to the infinite complication of events from which we have abstracted" (188–89). The ingenuity at work here displaces the brunt of the critique from New Criticism to historicism, which Trilling uses as a reflective surface to display back to the New Critics the deficiencies of their methodical scrutiny of the "poem itself," which is equivalent in "abstraction" to the historian's "actual event." In his conclusion Trilling advocates a Nietzschean amalgamation of historicism and formalism (197).

The initial impetus had been to lay claim to a space that could accommodate poetic practice with critical intelligence, uniting them in a larger project to retrieve culture from a homelessness imposed by technocratic instrumentalism. The New Critics were uniformly opposed to science, or what they mistook for science. "For the first time in human history we have pure science, which is pure prose, and that means that we have pushed language to the point where it is the perfect instrument for science," Ransom wrote in 1942. "The consequence is that literature, with its imaginative order of knowing, is homeless. It has to make up its own occasions, and it becomes factitious and technical in a degree that was never known before" ("'Brooks-MacLeish' Thesis" 41). As the New Critics busied themselves with identifying various conceptual fallacies, they succumbed to their own fallacious notion that science dealt strictly with hard facts, in a language cleansed of ambiguities, and in the process they ended up producing a critical vocabulary that mirrored what they scorned. It is peculiar that not only the New Critics but even their successors overlooked the enormous status of paradox in modern physics and mathematics, from Bertrand Russell and Gödel's Proof to the Copenhagen Interpretation. That an intensive effort to theorize paradox for literature could proceed in ignorance of these matters constitutes a more resounding condemnation of New Criticism than anything that has been laid at their door from within literary studies. As different lines of poetry developed after the war, the major difference may be between those who followed the New Critics in a serene ignorance of all but strictly high cultural matters, and those whose work was informed in significant ways by science. This is surely a qualitative distinction between, say, Lowell and Berryman, and Olson's fascination with Riemann and Whitehead, or Duncan claiming *Scientific American* as a poet's bible.

THE COUP OF NEW CRITICISM

In a symposium cosponsored by the *Southern* and the *Kenyon* reviews in 1940, on "Literature and the Professors," Ransom forecast the coming revolution. After years of haranguing the incumbent historicism, Ransom played a rhetorical trump by suggesting that his adversaries "have done well. They have done so well, in fact, that the job is about finished, and they must look for another job, like the victims of technological unemployment; or, to see them under a more dignified figure, as the entrepreneurs, they must look for another field for their capital investments" ("Strategy" 226). Damnation through praise was never more effective; but of course by this point Ransom may have felt he had the coin of the new realm firmly in hand, and subsequent capital investments and theoretical mortgages were going to have to be secured with loans from Criticism, Inc. In his estimate, "the future of the professorship of literature is immense . . . because I judge that the revolution will presently occur, rather peacefully and in the course of nature, and the professors start in upon a new order of studies: the speculative or critical ones" (227). It's instructive to consider the rhetoric of appeasement offered here in the wake of the Munich Accord: Ransom, like Hitler, was extending an amicable accord to enemies whose strength he was shrewdly calculating as inferior to his own. The more confrontational rhetoric he could leave to his associates.

Ransom had not always been so conciliatory. Retaining the Greek sense of critic (*krites*=judge), he reproached scholars for "compiling the data of literature" without committing themselves to "literary judgment" (*Essays* 94). The pervasiveness of "close reading" in English programs in the postwar years obscured the implications of *commitment* in the practice of critical judgment. Formalism as *criticism*, then, was not an indiscriminate immersion in the depoliticized viscera of a neutered lyric, but a judgmental excursion in practical criticism—in theory, if not always in practice.[12] Early successes by New Critics left their opponents feeling violated, in fact, because their assessments could be merciless. Romantic and Victorian poetry, in particular, took some time to be rehabilitated after New Critical

---

[12] By 1950, after the procedures had been thoroughly institutionalized, Allen Tate would concede without protest Malcolm Cowley's remark that the New Critics "have surrendered or abnegated a very large part of their duty as critics" because "the New Criticism on the whole has been applied to an accepted canon" (Haydn 88).

excoriations. The New Critics succeeded in part because their dogmatism was openly partisan; they invaded the academy like guerilla
fighters, with a keener grasp of the features of the ambient ground
(the textures of the poems themselves), thus possessing a greater
mobility than their opponents, who were encumbered with the baggage of historical scholarship. Like guerrilla forces, the New Critics
were heavily outnumbered, yet managed somehow to effect a *coup
d'etat* in record time. Before founding *The Kenyon Review*, Ransom
consulted with Tate: "I have an idea that we could really found criticism if we got together on it," he wrote, because "the professors are
in an awful dither trying to reform themselves and there's a big
stroke possible for a small group that knows what it wants in giving
them ideas and definitions and showing the way" (Graff, *Professing*
157). The "small group," once in power, became notorious for the
pontifical aura of its pronouncements.

The gist of what Grant Webster has called "Tory Formalism"
manifested itself in an ecclesiastical vocabulary that denounced the
"heresy of paraphrase" (Brooks), the "intentional fallacy" and the
"affective fallacy" (Wimsatt and Beardsley). To put it this way is to
overstress the doctrinal impulse, which manifested itself most
severely after the Second World War. Significantly, it was *Poetry* that
published the two-part "Guide to the New Criticism," a terminological primer which was revised and issued as a booklet in 1951. This
"Guide" called Ransom "a John the Baptist and leading theorist of
the school," judiciously adding that he "has recently tempered his
enthusiasm" (Elton 5). Both Ransom and Tate viewed warily the
institutional success of New Criticism. Ransom had always referred
to "the professors" as distinct in kind from himself and his confeder-
ates, and when they took up his cause he was, not surprisingly, disposed to criticize the "doctrinal satisfactions" of these "cold-blooded
critics" who were, after all, his followers (Janssen 175).[13]

---

[13] In "Why Critics Don't Go Mad" (1952) Ransom conjured the spectre of
the critical muse, "the Great Scholar" who "causes me to be apprehensive
that my kind of criticism may be so partial as to belittle the poem, for he
will know it at once, and it will be painful to see him register his embarrassment. Is he the figment of a bad conscience?" (*Poems and Essays* 151).

Tate likewise downplayed the spectre of group cohesion: "It began as *explication du* [sic] *texte*, and from there people went in many different directions."[14] To William Barrett's suggestion that "there have been New Critics, but no such thing as *the* New Criticism," Tate responded: "I think that's a very good way to put it, and to put an end to the question: What is It?" Historically, he noted, the New Critics came together out of a common engagement with literature, "and out of that serious engagement certain personal friendships were formed. We all got to know one another. It was inevitable that we became personal friends, with resulting interactions of influence. That's about all the New Criticism comes to." "It developed out of a pedagogy," Tate said, because that circle of friends congregated in an academic setting—first at Vanderbilt, later at Kenyon, LSU, Princeton, and the Indiana School of Letters. He admitted the truth of Malcolm Cowley's charge that the consequence of the New Critical reactionary disposition was "to separate an intelligent sector of the American public from political interest." He conceded the triviality of some of "the disciples." But Tate was adamant in resisting any notion that New Criticism was driven by a party line, insisting that even to enquire about critical proprieties was to succumb to unwarranted political claims: "It seems to me that to ask a literary critic in the modern world to find out what critical system is suited to a democratic society is to put him in a party line at once, because

---

[14] The passages cited in this paragraph are from a fascinating document, a transcribed debate in response to Robert Gorham Davis's concerted attack on New Criticism, "The New Criticism and the Democratic Tradition" (*The American Scholar* [Winter 1949–1950]). On August 22, 1950, the journal's editor, Hiram Haydn, convened a group consisting of himself, Davis, William Barrett, Malcolm Cowley, Kenneth Burke and Allen Tate, publishing the transcript in consecutive issues of *The American Scholar*. My citations above are, in order, from pages 97, 98, 88, 227, 221, 87. The proceedings read in part like a ghoulish persecution of the offending Davis; all the more so when we recall that this was just at the onset of the McCarthy hysteria, and then notice Hiram Haydn saying "I think it would be very helpful if he [Davis] would name names and re-define what he means by the New Criticism" (Haydn 91). As the conversation procedes, the participants run into an inordinate amount of difficulty dealing with Davis's offending text: years of "close reading" had not prepared them to reach any consensus as to what might constitute the text as such!

nobody knows what criticism is relevant to a democratic society."
Furthermore, Tate added, "I like a lot of free play."

The extraordinary success of the New Criticism during and
after the war meant that the strictures and procedures of the core
passed out of their hands, migrating into that "general culture"
which they had attempted to set standards for, but primarily settling
in the academy. Whether inside or outside, it was, as Randall Jarrell
infamously called it, "The Age of Criticism." (*Kenyon* editor Ransom
had *also* written an essay on "An Age of Criticism" for *New Republic*
[March 31, 1952].) Jarrell's piece, written for *The Kenyon Review* in
1951, speculated that the editors "may think it an unkind tactless
piece more or less directed at them, among many others—as it is"
(*Letters* 270).[15] Jarrell of course spent his life teaching (in some eight
institutions), but like Tate and Blackmur was not a "PhD man" and
fancied he could set himself apart from "the professors." "The Age of
Criticism" makes a direct though oddly affectionate assault on what
had become the institutionalized New Criticism. Jarrell wryly noted
that close reading as technical exercise had been substituted for
reading as pedestrian exercise; to the question "Have you read" a
given poem, he testified, people reply "Well, not really—I've *read* it,
but I've never read a thorough analysis of it, or really gone through it
systematically" (*Age* 73). Certainly he delivers the most menacing
blow by pointing out that "New critic is but old scholar writ large, as
a general thing" (75). Denouncing the pretensions of institutional

---

15 Jarrell couldn't complete the essay in time for the *Kenyon* deadline, and
ended up publishing it in the *Partisan* instead, the following year. It was of
course as a prize student of Ransom and Tate that Jarrell could occupy with
impunity this critical position. I don't mean to suggest collusion, but Jarrell
had been privileged from an early age to exercise his critical wit in the prestigious quarterlies controlled by the New Critics, and had developed a reputation for being merciless in his treatment of other poets. "The poet who gets
a going-over by Mr. Jarrell," Malcolm Cowley complained in a revealing
analogy, "is like the scared Negro at a county fair who sticks his head
through a sheet while people throw baseballs at it . . ." (quoted in Mary Jarrell's editorial comment in Jarrell's *Letters* 41). Not until Robert Bly's
reviews in *The Fifties* and *The Sixties* would there be another poet as handy
with the critical whip; but of course Bly had to create his own magazine to
air his views.

success, Jarrell favored a return to criticism proper, involving both judgment and (in moderation) explication, handled with a mixture of boldness and humility. "Remember that you can never be more than the staircase to the monument," he concluded in a direct appeal to critics. "At your best you make people see what they might never have seen without you; but they must always forget you in what they see" (86). Criticism is a *service profession*, a handmaiden to the stars, which are properly literary and ennobling. "Once, talking to a young critic, I said as a self-evident thing, 'Of course, criticism's necessarily secondary to the works of art it's about.' He looked at me as if I had kicked him, and said, 'Oh, that's not *so!*' (I had kicked him, I realized)" (84). One might imagine this exchange taking place, not in 1952, but in 1980, against a backdrop of Barthes and Foucault on the death of the author. Jarrell professed a kind of innocent amazement at the critics' temerity, but he caught the issue: "critics are already like conductors, and give you *their* 'Lear,' *their* 'Confidence Man,' *their* 'Turn of the Screw.' It's beginning to frighten me a little; do we really *want* it to be an Age of Criticism?" (85). Forty years later it's still an age of criticism, whether we want it to be or not.

In 1984 William Cain found it necessary, in his study of a climate then inebriated by continental theory, to elaborate at some length the position of New Criticism. "The New Criticism appears powerless, lacking in supporters," he wrote. "No one speaks on behalf of the New Criticism as such today, and it mostly figures in critical discourse as the embodiment of foolish ideas and misconceived techniques." This is even more the case today, as New Criticism is routinely slotted into a vernacular history of ideas (conversational references to "New Criticism" constituting a truly pervasive gesture of acknowledgement-as-disavowal). Cain goes on:

> But the truth is that the New Criticism survives and is prospering, and it seems to be powerless only because its power is so pervasive that we are ordinarily not even aware of it. So deeply ingrained in English studies are New Critical attitudes, values, and emphases that we do not even perceive them as the legacy of a particular movement. On the contrary: we feel them to be the natural and definitive conditions for criticism in general. It is not simply that the

> New Criticism has become institutionalized, but that it has
> gained acceptance as the institution itself. It has been
> transformed into "criticism," the essence of what we do as
> teachers and critics, the ground or given upon which
> everything else is based. (105)

Edward Said has been equally insistent that New Criticism has
passed into the climate of pedagogic thought as such, accurately
characterizing the influx of continental theory as "the new New Criticism" (*World* 159).[16] John Guillory has recently argued that New
Criticism made the notion of *difficulty* glamorous (*Capital* 168–69),
underscoring the subsequent inevitability of imported critical theory:
where the New Critics generated credibility for their methods by
making poetry appear difficult and then lucidly decoding its intimi-
dations, critical theory rendered criticism itself arduous. For the generation of academics saturated by covert New Critical pedagogy in
the secondary schools, the esoteric perplexities of John Donne or
Gerard Manley Hopkins seemed positively lucid compared to Kristeva's *Revolution in Poetic Language*, Barthes' *S/Z*, Derrida's *Dissemi-
nation*, Lacan's *Écrits*, and Adorno's *Negative Dialectics*. Pride of
place in the scholarly consolidation of difficulty thereby passed from
poetry to criticism.

The New Critics are worthy of scrutiny along lines suggested
by Bruno Latour's "metrology": Latour's paradigm suggests, most
persuasively, why the lyric was the privileged object of analysis. Put
simply, the operational tools of the critic need to appear more
refined as well as more extensive than the rhetorical and conceptual
parameters of a given text. The critic cannot go out into the world—

---

[16] Said astutely recognizes the disfigurations produced by enthusiasm for
the new: "A new canon means also a new past or a new history and, less
happily, a new parochialism. Any reader of modern French criticism will be
astounded to realize that Kenneth Burke, in whose huge output many of the
issues and methods currently engaging the French were first discussed, is
unknown" (*World* 143–44). A correction is required: any reader of modern
French criticism who has *also* bothered to become informed about American
precursors of "theory," like Burke. I have taught Burke to graduate students
who had never even heard of him, but who were "naturally" aware of Lacan,
Barthes, Derrida, Kristeva and numerous other French theorists.

the total context—of poetry, since that would be to expose critical doxology to an unmanageable heterogeneity. So, New Criticism made itself into a laboratory in Latour's sense, and in so doing required the most compact yet microscopically robust specimens it could find. Metaphysical and modernist poems were ideal. Following Latour's corollary, these kinds of poems—or, to be precise, the laboratory conclusions they supported—could then be returned to the outside as the paradigm of what "poetry" in general should be. The sociological consequences are plentiful and easy to see: anthologies of the 1950s are filled with specimens for New Critical analysis, spontaneously mimicking the "treated" specimens released from the lab. Once their methods of close reading as applied to the lyric had gained general approval, the New Critics no longer needed to control the poetic environment; it had become self-regulating in compliance with prevailing feedback principles.

AUTHORITY

Tate's declared preference for latitude in criticism ("I like a lot of free play") was made at precisely the time when he converted to Catholicism. "The covert Christianity of much American New Criticism," Geoffrey Hartman has reflected, "escaped analysis" ("English" 43). I don't propose such analysis here, since it's sufficient to defer to Hartman's observation, in *Criticism in the Wilderness*, that the theory of meaning promoted by New Criticism "acted as an unacknowledged theological restraint. The end of literary studies was not knowledge but rather a state of grace" (285–86). René Wellek, an avowed champion, has admitted that "ultimately poetry with several of the New Critics turns out to be, if not religion, then a preparation for religion" (156). Karl Shapiro complained bitterly that "literary criticism hardly exists in our time; what we really have is culture criticism or theology ill concealed. The critic today uses literature only as a vehicle for ideas . . . " (*Defense* 8). The close textual analysis favored by the New Critics could celebrate tensional "conflict structures" like irony, paradox, and wit because they could be held in check at the level of the poem.[17]   What was otherwise socially unbearable could be ideologically resolved by the functional stasis of symbolic structure. Admiration for the ritual resolutions of sublimated ideological contradictions in the poem was reinforced, extratextually, by theological doctrine and ecclesiastic ritual, which proposed to resolve similar antinomies according to a criterion of *belief.*

The New Critical position, as formulated by Ransom in 1933, adopted Eliot's famous pronouncement in *For Lancelot Andrewes* (1929): In politics, royalism; in religion, Anglo-Catholic; in literature, classical. "I am astonished upon discovering how comprehensively this formula covers the kingdom of the aesthetic life as it is organized by the social tradition," Ransom enthuses. "I am so grateful that it is with hesitation I pick a little quarrel with the terms. I would covet a program going something like this: In manners, aristocratic; in religion, ritualistic; in art, traditional" (*Essays* 66). Ransom would not leave the final import of his platform to inference, so he clarified it by suggesting that "the word for our generation in these matters is 'formal,' and it might even bear the pointed qualification, 'and reactionary.'" The vital components, then, were formalism, Christianity, regionalism; but these all need to be seen as rejoinders to alternatives, because New Criticism was antithetical (or "reactionary," to use Ransom's term) in all of its intellectual formulations. In 1880 Matthew Arnold had predicted that "most of what now passes with us for religion and philosophy will be replaced by poetry" (340). The ritualistic disposition Ransom spoke of could accommodate poetry and religion

---

[17] Conflict, it must be emphasized, was internalized by New Criticism as a principle of form. Geoffrey Harpham in *The Ascetic Imperative* thinks it a "paradox [that] New Criticism's promotion of formal unity . . . concentrated almost exclusively on species of disunity—irony, tension, ambiguity, and paradox . . ." (250). But that is precisely the point: paradox within reverberates to the challenge of paradox without. The New Criticism was a mystery religion of sorts, to be initiated in which required some threshold of enigma. Harpham is much closer to the essence of New Criticism when he addresses the sacerdotal aspect of formalism in general: "The formalist critic," he says, "stands between the reader and his desire for meaning, insisting on the obstacles or barriers between text, author, and world. . . . At its most rigorous, formalism insists, in fact, precisely on the systematic invalidity of the reader's response . . ." (251).

as aspects of the same rage for order. As for the "aristocratic" demeanor, this could be adapted to the high calling of poetry and the nearly sacramental practice of criticism as a forum for judgment. The fundamental tenet of the New Critical worldview is the degeneracy of the modern age; so its impulse to formalism is necessarily conservative. Allen Tate published *Reactionary Essays on Poetry and Ideas* in 1936, timed significantly to oppose that decade's enthusiasm for communism and the dream of a proletarian literature.[18] (To the end of his life Tate never failed to register his distaste, given the opportunity, for "fellow travellers.")

The archetypal New Critical response to Eliot's famous line "these fragments I have shored against my ruins" was to substitute *forms* for "fragments." The New Critics foreclosed on the collage legacy implicit in Eliot's practice—subsequently taken up instead in the vocabulary of "energy," "action," "process" in Abstract Expressionism and open form poetics—by fetishing the poem as a drama of "tensegrity" (the term Buckminster Fuller applied to his geodesic dome). As the New Critics became the custodians of tradition, their authority was wielded in a somewhat duplicitous way, since their stress on formalism exonerated them from charges of overt censorship. The proscription of specific content is readily seen as censorious, whereas formalism is a clandestine but quite effective mode of censorship in its own right. It is against this subtle maneuver of the New Criticism that we need to hear Creeley's dictum that form is an extension of content, for it reminds us that the new visions of Beat and Black Mountain poetics could not be advanced in the rectilinear metrics of the reigning academic style: a different content required, first, a demolition of old forms.

As New Criticism evolved into a widespread pedagogic practice, the immobilization of the text itself was increasingly subjected to the display logic of the "exhibitionary complex." However much

---

[18] *Reactionary Essays* consists mainly of essays on poets—Donne, Dickinson, Hart Crane, John Peale Bishop, E. A. Robinson, Eliot, Pound, MacLeish—with a look at Elizabethan satire, and some pieces on the Old South.

Ransom himself complained about the fetishism implicit in Brooks's well-wrought urn, the outcome was to quarantine The Poem in an artificial environment in which it was celebrated for triumphs that were meaningless because nothing was contested except the internal order of the poetic object itself. Poetic tension and worldly conflict were presumed to be homologous, but this was only one assumption among many. In his valuable study of literary ideology, *The Critical Twilight*, John Fekete sees, as potentially "Ransom's most important methodological insight," the dialectic of necessity and contingency as transferred from the quotidian to the texture of the poem. Such an insight "could lead to a social and historical view of a unified reality within which art and science could be located according to their division of labor as forms of social consciousness." Unfortunately,

> The New Critical science replaces the real world with its own ideological-metaphysical categories (for example, a core of constancy, or the fullness of the world's body) that are then assumed to *be* the reality and are duly investigated with rigorous precision. In this fashion, the work of art is insulated and fetishized, and the problem of historical relation to the world is reduced to the problem of cognition of preconstituted objectivity. (101)

In other words, having isolated the poem in the first place in compliance with the stipulations of methodical explication, the critic reads this isolation into the character of the object as such. The poem is methodologically prefigured as unique, and the whole environment of reading is forced to comply with the configuration of its autonomy.

Fekete underscores Adorno's point, in "On Lyric Poetry and Society," that the demand for lyric purity is social in nature. The New Critics' sense of "paradox" is decidedly *not* that of Adorno, who speaks of "[t]he paradox specific to the lyric work [as] a subjectivity that turns into objectivity"—so objectified because lyric expression is contingent on "the priority of linguistic form" (*Notes* 43). It is, in short, a struggle *in* language for the *right to*—and the *rights of*—language as such; and language is necessarily social in the end. So Adorno views lyric as "always the subjective expression of a social antagonism" (45). The key term is *expression*, pointedly sub-

stituted for the Marxist doctrine of *reflection*. Adorno wants to preserve lyric as a site of struggle, and to see it as mere reflective surface
is to relinquish it to hegemonic rule. He focuses instead on lyric as
the occasion for witnessing the dialectic in action, in which the
polarities of subject and object are rendered fluid and susceptible to
intermingling.[19] The New Critics, by insulating the poem from linguistic heterodoxy, end up procuring it in the very image of that
debased Marxist thesis of "reflection" which they scorned. Insofar as
they admitted a dialectical principle at all, it was in the image of
"tradition."[20]

Fekete, applying Frankfurt school materialism, calculates the
cost of "preconstituted objectivity" in New Criticism in terms of
reification and alienated labor. "In other words," he writes, "the
structure of alienated reality is accepted even at its surface as being
permanently unchangeable. The project of humanizing our concrete
existence is ruled out; it is argued that we can humanize only our
thought, symbolically, by way of 'compensation.'" Consequently, the
verbal icon "subordinates the realm of aesthetic humanism to the reified categories of neocapitalist production relations" (91). The "cry
of the self" in the lyric is taken to be a cry of authenticity, rather than

---

[19] In a passage that recapitulates his essay, Adorno writes: "Classical philosophy once formulated a truth now disdained by scientific logic: subject
and object are not rigid and isolated poles but can be defined only in the
process in which they distinguish themselves from one another and change.
The lyric is the aesthetic test of that dialectical philosophical proposition. In
the lyric poem the subject, through its identification with language, negates
both its opposition to society as something merely monadological and its
mere functioning within a wholly socialized society [*vergesellschaftete
Gesellschaft*]. But the more the latter's ascendancy over the subject increases, the more precarious the situation of the lyric becomes" (*Notes* 44).

[20] Stephen Fredman characterizes Eliot's "Tradition and the Individual Talent" as advancing a "cubist view" in which "tradition is spatialized as revis-
able collage." "No one will deny," he writes, "that traditions change, but to
speak of tradition spatially as a 'form,' as though it were a modernist work of
art, is truly preposterous" (12). However, one might at least credit Eliot with
being *ambitiously* preposterous. His concern to behold tradition as a simultaneity is an impractical recommendation, of course, but one that intimates his
subsequent religious conversion, since the requirement his sense of tradition
involves is individually unmanageable (except in the case of illumination) and
must be deeded to a supervising institution like the Church of England.

the registration of alienated labor. Fekete sees Ransom pioneering the integration of New Criticism to the dominant postwar liberal pluralism by "mak[ing] peace with the prevailing rationality, and prepar[ing] the theoretical ground for the literary technicism corresponding to the Keynesian technicism that was concurrently transforming social life" (85). "Works of art (or religious exercises) are thus viewed as 'compensatory concretions' to help us 'manage as we are' . . . " (91). What Ransom arrives at is an ideology of "functional equilibrium" (97). In terms of sociological functionalism, the stress is on adjustment rather than conflict, compensation rather than critical interchange.

Without saying it in so many words, Fekete has essentially described the loss for poetry of its having been inoculated by New Criticism against the virus of the real. He enables us to diagnose that "manic power" of the poets most obviously beneficiaries of the New Critical support structure—Lowell, Schwartz, Jarrell, Berryman, Roethke, Plath—as a desperate attempt to strike clear of the pedagogic greenhouse in which they found themselves at once nourished and trapped. Their poems could thrive like exotic botanical monsters under the devotional scrutiny of so many close readings, but there was always the quarantine, the constraint, to endure. These poets could feel themselves impinged upon, psychologically, as providers of raw material for the refinements of critical productivity. The New Criticism was like a monetary exchange, converting the currencies of poetry and criticism back and forth, under T. S. Eliot's papal guidance. William Carlos Williams notoriously declared that *The Waste Land* ruined poetry by deeding it to the professors; but Karl Shapiro put it more accurately: "it was a poem that made poetry and criticism one and the same thing" (*Defense* 159).

Much of Jarrell's 1952 essay "The Age of Criticism" duplicates charges (and mimics the strategies) made by New Critics attacking their scholastic adversaries fifteen years earlier. By developing an institutionally self-effacing jargon of authority, the New Criticism competed for scientific credibility in a humanities milieu that starkly juxtaposed English with psychology and sociology. Jarrell recognized this apparent career move as a rhetoric of intimidation: by using "a style which insists upon their superiority to the society that disregards them, [English professors] both protect themselves and punish their society" (*Age* 77). The isolationist impulse behind close reading was an asceticism of the elite. The New Critics, Blackmur reflected in 1948, "were internal free-lancers—without adequate relation to the society of which they expressed the substance more and more as an *aesthetic* experience" (Response 865). Demonstration of aesthetic integrity became a surrogate authoritarianism, elevating the critic to sacerdotal status. But the success of New Criticism was in the notably secular domain of the universities, in many ways at the center of the administered society which had motivated the original New Critics-cum-Fugitive repudiation. Success, that is, meant that control and supervision began to pass from the hands of Ransom, Tate, and their fellows, as the humanistic ministry gave way to the liberal administration.

LIBERAL ADMINISTRATION

In 1940 Allen Tate, assessing "The Present Function of Criticism," recklessly declared, "the tradition of free ideas is as dead in the United States as it is in Germany" (*Essays* 237). He lashed out at the pretences of "positivism" in literary studies, associating it with pragmatism and instrumentalism as "the expression of a middle-class culture—a culture that we have achieved in America with so little consciousness of any other culture that we often say that a class description of it is beside the point" (239). At the time, Tate could sustain the fantasy that this *modus operandi* was about to be rendered dysfunctional by the war. It was reasonable to suppose, of course, that global conflict would change everything, yet what Tate failed to anticipate was that it would change everything into a postwar variety of American capitalism. But here's his prognosis:

> Could the outlook be worse for the future of criticism? In
> the United States we face the censorship of the pressure-
> group. We have a tradition of irresponsible interpretation
> of patriotic necessity. We are entering a period in which
> we shall pay dearly for having turned our public education
> over to the professional "educationists" and the sociolo-
> gists. These men have taught the present generation that
> the least thing about man is his intelligence, if he have it at
> all; the greatest thing, his adjustment to Society (not to a
> good society): a mechanical society in which we were to be
> conditioned for the realization of a *bourgeois* paradise of
> gadgets and of the consumption, not of the fruits of the
> earth, but of commodities. Happily this degraded version
> of the myth of reason has been discredited by the course of
> what the liberal mind calls "world events." . . . (237)

Tate was an advocate of literature as *gnosis* (another major essay of
1940 is "Literature as Knowledge"), which he always contrasted with
"information," the congenital business of historical scholarship deni-
grated by the New Critics. The implications of Tate's critical gnosticism, it turns out, lead to some revealing parallels with Adorno,
Williams, and Olson.

In 1938 Ransom had published *The World's Body* in which
he insisted on the "ontology" or quiddity of the poem as an event in
the world—neither an information transmitter nor a private sanctuary. A decade earlier William Carlos Williams had written *The
Embodiment of Knowledge* (not published until 1974), exploring the
facticity of words as incarnate media. For Williams, meaning is manifestation rather than message. This is widely recognized of Williams
("no ideas but in things"), but less so in the case of Ransom and Tate.
Ransom, in "Criticism, Inc.," holds that "[t]he poet perpetuates in his
poem an order of existence which in actual life is constantly crum-
bling beneath his touch. His poem celebrates the object which is real,
individual, and qualitatively infinite. He knows that his practical
interests will reduce this living object to a mere utility." To this
Coleridgean complex of the infinite inhering in the particular, "[t]he
critic should find in the poem a total poetic or individual object
which tends to be universalized, but is not permitted to suffer this

fate" (*Essays* 105). Ransom's position is remarkably similar to that put forward later by Adorno: "immersion in what has taken individual form elevates the lyric poem to the status of something universal by making manifest something not distorted, not grasped, not yet subsumed" (Adorno, *Notes* 38). Likewise, Williams urges "a return to the category of the whole," making it clear that the *whole* will necessarily entail everything we ever thought was trivial. "Every man so far, has been misled by the childish error of searching for an 'absolute' in a special category. Without exception, no one has been able to escape it. Perhaps the practicing artist has come nearest" (*Embodiment* 127). In Ransom's more narrowly literary position the business of the poem is to resist the logic of paraphrase—the prosthetic readjustment of the poem into a prose "equivalent"—as well as the logic of coercive generalization.

Despite his famous pronouncement that Auschwitz spelled the doom of poetry, Adorno recognized that poetry would persist; and in "On Lyric Poetry and Society" (1957) he described the infernal dialectic whereby "[t]he lyric work hopes to attain universality through unrestrained individuation" (*Notes* 38). Adorno was acutely aware of mass culture as the medium of generalized (and generic) exchange, yet he held out hope for the value of radical specificity. The lyric urge, however, represented a dangerous invitation to the artist to succumb to the saccharine absolute of "false universality" represented in commodity culture as the "profoundly particular." In the lyric, the celebrated particular could readily slide over into consumer fetishism. Tate, like Adorno, feared the chimera of universality, recognizing that it was perpetuated most insistently by the mass media promise of enhanced communication. In a seminal address of 1952, "The Man of Letters in the Modern World," Tate distinguishes between communication and communion. Communication, in this view, is a dehumanizing utility, resulting from "the victory of the secularized society of means without ends" (*Essays* 388). In the form of "mass communication" the informational model serves only the carceral will; communication is control. Tate longs to dispel the secular bewitchment of mass communication for a different, sacred, sort of mass. "The battle is now between the dehumanized society of secularism, which imitates Descartes' mechanized nature, and the eternal society of the communion of the human spirit" (381). Communion, contrasted with the control ethos of communications technologies, is participation. "Communication that is not also communion is incomplete. We *use* communication; we *participate* in communion" (385). Tate is very clear about the fact that the mass "audience" of the media is an abstraction, not a concrete referent: he cites Coleridge to suggest the fallacy of presuming "communication" with a hypothetical "'multitudinous Public, shaped into personal unity by the magic of abstraction'" (387). The error, in Tate's view, is to regard literature as a form of communication, for that is to condemn it in advance to the ineffectual pantomime of the mass media, which substitute control for communion.

There is a political subtext which Tate makes explicit by referring to "the melancholy portrait of the man who stands before you" (the essay was originally a public lecture), a literary man, who like all literary men in the modern world is incapable of "affect[ing] the operation of the power-state." The politician, on the other hand, all too easily intervenes in worldly matters, only to increase the secularized divorce of ends from means. This is a "double retreat from the moral center, of the man of action and the man of letters, that we have completed in our time" (382). Tate's vindication of the man of letters is "a fearful lesson," simple though it may be: "What modern literature has taught us is not merely that the man of letters has not participated fully in the action of society; it has taught us that nobody else has either" (384). The chimera of communication substitutes private gratification for social communion, abstracting what is *common* in its compulsive celebration of the unique, the "one of a kind" and the "once in a lifetime" offer. Tate insists that "literature has never communicated," that it "cannot *communicate*: from this point of view we see the work of literature as a participation in communion. Participation leads naturally to the idea of the common experience" (388). Politics presumably addresses the public welfare, the commonwealth; and Tate's formulations are intended to combat the fact that modern politics has too easily served special interests—a point that cannot be separated from the mystique of "communications" which have converted the entire public order to the rule of special interests.

By 1952 Tate had long been associated with "reactionary" positions in poetry, politics (where a clarification is needed: he voted FDR and New Deal), and pedagogy; and even the arch formality of his title, "The Man of Letters in the Modern World," betrays his association with the literary ministry of his friend T. S. Eliot. But Tate had also managed a rapprochment with Williams (who for decades had "despised" Tate for his associations—not only with Eliot but Ransom and the academic crowd in general[21]), and his fully articulated position here puts him into unlikely proximity to Charles Olson, whom Williams had honored in *The Autobiography* by citing two full pages from "Projective Verse." The point of convection between Olson and Tate is the simultaneity of their concerns. Olson's first two Maximus poems were written in 1950, but there wasn't a third until the summer of 1952, when Tate was reading his lecture in Paris at the Congress for Cultural Freedom. There is a passage in "The Man of Letters" that captures the gist of Olson's "present shame of, / the wondership stolen by, / ownership" in "Letter 3" (*Maximus* 13):

> A society of means without ends, in the age of technology, so multiplies the means, in the lack of anything better to do, that it may have to scrap the machines as it makes them; until our descendants will have to dig themselves out of one rubbish heap after another and stand upon it, in order to make more rubbish to make more standing-room. The surface of nature will then be literally as well as morally concealed from the eyes of men. (386)

A few years later, Samuel Beckett could have adopted this as an epigraph to *Endgame* (in which Hamm and Clov in the dustbins would be Ransom and Tate).

---

[21] They met in 1946 at a conference in Utah. "At Salt Lake Allen Tate, whom I had always despised, and who in his turn had always considered me of the lunatic fringe, and I learned mutually to respect, even to like each other," wrote Williams in his *Autobiography* (312).

The alliances forged among poets, and among literary figures in general, are not necessarily based on agreement; nor, when there is agreement, is it likely to stick. The longstanding *professional* association of Tate with Ransom and the New Critics has overshadowed his other associations: he was a close friend of Hart Crane's and spent several years in the 1920s in Europe, where he met Eliot, Hemingway, Stein, Fitzgerald, and others. Despite this, Tate was fabricated into a puppet of the New Criticism much as Olson was identified with Black Mountain.[22] In the shorthand versions of literary history, which are so often written out laboriously in longhand without any further research, it has become much too convenient to repeat the same old story about an oppressive New Critical hegemony, with Ransom as ward boss, pulling the strings of a literary community grown so sterile that only the uncouth eruptions of Ginsberg and the Beats could topple the suffocating monumentality of it all. As we'll see, there *was* in fact a hegemonic literary establishment, and New Criticism certainly did have something to do with it, but like any establishment it operated primarily through the inertial media of mimicry and routinization—to the increasing dismay of its founders, in the case of New Criticism.

Tate had the misfortune to live to see his early ambitions realized: New Criticism was a success, and poets became public figures. But he was not sanguine about the professionalization of New Criticism, and had nothing but revulsion for Ginsberg and the Beats. He was elitist to the end (but it needs to be borne in mind that the hipster ethos was elitist in its own way). Douglas Bush, in his Presi-

---

[22] A valiant attempt at recontextualization appeared too late for me to make significant use of here, though it largely corroborates what I've been saying: in *Hart Crane and Allen Tate: Janus-Faced Modernism*, Langdon Hammer contends that Tate and his fellow "reactionary modernists did not defend an old cultural order, but . . . they struggled to legitimate a new one; and to this end they struggled both alongside and against other modern authors, other readings of the modern" (5). Tate's advocacy of modernism, as Hammer shows, is situated along a fault line between "Modernism" and modernity. As Tate wrote in an unpublished letter which Hammer quotes (referring to Pound, Eliot, Yeats and Joyce), "Theirs is the right kind of modernism, which by opposing everything modern is reactionary" (xii).

dential Address to the MLA in 1948, retaliated against the ascendancy of New Criticism, singling out Ransom and Tate as prime offenders. "The critics, some of whom are poets, have bemoaned the failure of belief, the loss of traditional values, the aggressive nihilism of the scientific positivists, but they themselves have been doing all they could to create a moral vacuum" (21). The vacuum was the result of an elitist withdrawal—"the new criticism . . . assumes that literature exists for the diversion of a few sophisticates" (19)—and Bush asserts that "[i]t is only in our time that the effort seems to have been generally abandoned, that cultural divisions have been accepted as unbridgeable, and that poets and critics have decided to write for one another" (20). But it is really, after all, a chicken and egg question, despite (or maybe because of) the frequency with which it recurs: Who flinched, or withdrew the challenge, or stepped aside, or abdicated the social contract first—the general public, or the intelligentsia?[23] As I've already indicated, Tate was less interested in resolving the problem than in accepting some of the blame.[24] Tate was agonized over the fact that modern society had no real place for the arts—that, indeed, the "man of letters" in the modern world was an anomaly—or that such place as

---

[23] The *durability* of the fantasy of some cognitive intimacy between the elite and the preterite is its most notable aspect. This (along with the apocalyptic implications of mass culture) is usefully surveyed by Patrick Brantlinger in *Bread and Circuses.* Interestingly, Ransom and Tate are not mentioned; nor indeed is New Criticism as such.

[24] In "The Obscurity of the Poet" Jarrell put the blame on the general public, which he noted had not singled out poetry for evasion but was in fact averse to reading as such. Not only are poems too imposing, he quipped; "so, too, are *Treasure Island, Peter Rabbit,* pornographic novels—any book whatsoever" (*Age* 19). As for the middlebrow critics, Jarrell saw through their pretenses instantly: "When a person says accusingly that he can't understand Eliot, his tone implies that most of his happiest hours are spent at the fireside among worn copies of the *Agamemnon, Phèdre,* and the Symbolic Books of William Blake; and it is melancholy to find, as one commonly will, that for months at a time he can be found pushing eagerly through the pages of *Gone With the Wind* or *Forever Amber* . . . " (9–10). By employing the masculine pronoun, of course, Jarrell glosses over the issue of gendered readership, which is more pertinent to his analysis than he is willing to admit.

there was, as in the university, was prescriptively functionalist. *Every* site of deliberate and conscientious activity, he felt, had become a space of withdrawal.

So, in symposia at Vanderbilt and Harvard in 1950 and 1951, Tate felt compelled to ask "Is Literary Criticism Possible?" "Literary criticism, like the Kingdom of God on earth, is perpetually necessary and, in the very nature of its middle position between imagination and philosophy, perpetually impossible," he concluded. "It is of the nature of man and of criticism to occupy the intolerable position. Like man's, the intolerable position of criticism has its own glory. It is the only position that it is ever likely to have" (*Essays* 487). John Fekete, tracing a similar accomodationist itinerary in Ransom during the 1950s, would see this as a resignation to the dominant ideology. But the real concession is that of Jarrell, for whom there *is* a Promised Land and its name is Poetry. Tate, on the other hand, was unwilling to consign criticism to a secondary role because he was not prepared to concede that *any* conscientious act of imagination, reason, or faith was subordinate. That he refused to assign a role to criticism (as well as to poetry) is attributable to his anti-instrumentalism. But New Criticism had become English department functionalism—the antithesis of everything Tate valued—and he was not happy with the result. He was certainly dismayed by the fact that, as Peter Viereck later put it, "[t]he real mischief of the 1950s came from the *nouveaux* New Critics, the sacred calves of the graduate schools . . . [t]rained seals of jargon . . . " (*Archer* 232).

Tate had resisted the prescriptive urgencies in the utilitarian rhetoric of Marxism in the 1930s, and he consistently applied the same criteria to New Critical pedagogy in the 1940s and beyond. The irony is that, because of his personal contacts and achievements, he was by default a functionalist middle manager, all the time supposing he maintained his integrity in proper gentlemanly fashion by being fiercely loyal to his friends. Mary Jarrell, in an editorial note for her edition of Randall's letters, characterizes Tate as

> ... continually serving as a fellow or chancellor or adviser
> in the literary establishment. A fountain of gossip about lit-
> erary politics, awards, and reputations, he had access to per-
> sons of influence in academe, Madison Avenue, and Wash-
> ington, and he used it unstintingly to advance younger writ-
> ers such as Hart Crane, Lowell, Taylor, and Jarrell. (13)

Thinking to preserve the integrity of poetry by controlling the institutions of its reception, Tate became an unwitting yet all too culpa-
ble facilitator of the age of sociology, in which "[t]he lyric passes
into psychology; the epic into the novel; the novel into sociology; literature into literary criticism . . . " (Byrd, "Meter" 181). And he
ended up being among the most forceful and adept power players in
literary politics—signalled by his role in awarding the Bollingen
Prize, under the auspices of the Library of Congress in 1949, to Ezra
Pound.

THE POUND AFFAIR

By the time Ezra Pound was apprehended by American authorities
in Rapallo, Italy in 1945, he was an accident waiting to happen. A
few months shy of sixty, Pound had spent several decades in isolated pursuit of cultural absolutism, relentlessly examining historical
documents pertinent to a global civilization. It is a long way from
the snapshot suddenness of the haiku "In a Station of the Metro" to
the genuine "rag bag" *The Cantos* had become, some thirty years
later. But in a sense there was little difference: Pound approached
the awesome scale of world civilization with the same assurance as
he had glancing at the metro crowd, confident that a valid overview
could be achieved if the technical means were available. He developed the snapshot ethos of the imagist haiku into the poetic principle "dichten = condensare," writing as condensation. For Pound,
the entire cultural order, including politics, economics, education,
religion, and of course literature, was in need of rectification.
Pound's urgency manifested itself in his commitment to Italian fascism and his willingness to broadcast his views on radio, spon-

sored by the fascist authorities. When he was seized in 1945, then, he was an elderly, overworked autodidact with a stupefying self-confidence and—most importantly—a nearly unparalleled sensitivity to language.

He was a hero to many, like Eliot, a beneficiary of Pound's generosity and his impeccable literary insights. A younger generation held him in awe for his prescient support of, and influence on, Eliot, Yeats, Joyce, Hemingway, Frost, H. D., Lewis, and many others. He had written some of the most celebrated poems of his time; but he had also been writing *The Cantos*. Pound, in short, was a living legend who for some time had been writing less than legendary poetry—such, at least, was the consensus in 1945. The horrors of his incarceration, and the heroism of his composition of *The Pisan Cantos* during captivity, have been monumentalized in *The Pound Era* by Hugh Kenner, a rare work of scholarship that merits comparison with Frank Capra's sentimental masterpiece *It's a Wonderful Life*. *The Pisan Cantos* became the subject of the most notorious literary controversy of the postwar period in American letters, but Pound himself embodied controversy years before his book was published. When he was incarcerated at St. Elizabeth's, all too symbolically proximate to the nation's capital, Pound was news that stayed news in the worst way. Yet, because he was a clearinghouse for all the divergent avenues by which poetry in English had become modernized (and not strictly those associated with modern*ism*), he was impossible to avoid: the simple mechanics of conceptual travel required a layover at Pound Central.

If he had faltered under physical duress in 1945–46, by the time *The Pisan Cantos* appeared it was evident that Pound's mental quickness was hardly impaired, despite the official diagnosis that he was incurably insane—a point which a myriad of visitors realized. Lowell, Berryman, Olson and Duncan are just a few of those who flocked to St. Elizabeth's, where he held court. He was still surging on adrenalin, his confidence in the correctness of his views absolutely unimpaired, as Charles Olson was revolted to discover. But Olson persisted, driven by a diagnostic curiosity, and found Pound impetuous, "the nerves turning like a wild speed-machine . . . . His mind bursts from the lags he sees around him" (*Pound* 97). Despite, or maybe because of, his monomania, Olson felt "he does not seem to have inhabited his own experience. It is almost as though he converted too fast" (99). Perhaps someday the similarity between Pound and Charlie Parker will be recognized, and a dual portrait might be written about these paragons of the prophetic depravity of cognitive fast-forward—a dystopic view to balance the more buoyant account of passion and discipline in W. T. Lhamon's *Deliberate Speed.*

The first literary incident was in 1946, shortly after federal attorneys suspended treason charges against Pound on the grounds of insanity. The *Anthology of Famous English and American Poetry* edited by William Rose Benét and Conrad Aiken was due to be reprinted by Random House when the management decided to drop Pound from the collection on the basis of his political beliefs. Aiken was alarmed, and finally another Random House author, W. H. Auden, decisively intervened by announcing his intention to change publishers if Pound was purged from the anthology (Carpenter, *Auden* 363).[25] Another controversy (less public) unfolded in early 1949. Rolfe Humphries had been asked by James Laughlin to write an introduction to Pound's *Selected Poems* which was scheduled for New Directions. John Berryman had made the initial selection and written an introduction that had proven unsatisfactory. Humphries ran into trouble, however, by insisting on making some mention of Pound's political beliefs. From February through April there was a steady exchange of letters between Humphries, Laughlin, Pound and his wife Dorothy. The Pounds objected to Humphries's use of the term "anti-Semitism." Pound believed that it did not belong "in a permanent introduction" because it dealt "with temporary irritations, not with literature at all" (Humphries 213). He told Laughlin "there will be no allusion to jews or to mental condition or the whole deal is off" (218). A steady round of haggling resulted in

---

[25] Random House president Bennett Cerf was forced to admit a "mistake" had been made. Interestingly, Cerf reported in his column for *Saturday Review* (March 16, 1946), in an omen of what was to come, that he'd received 140 letters in favor of Pound's exclusion, and 142 against.

Humphries's withdrawal from the project, objecting to the prospect of a *supervised* introduction. He also saw it as a disservice to Pound himself, and told him so: "if in what I write as introduction there's not a single word of disagreement with you on any point, the job is going to look like the most fatuous and hypocritical kind of blurb-writing," he wrote on April fifth, "not the considered opinion of a guy who tries to be honest, and admires the *Personae* and *Cantos* over and above disagreements that he nevertheless thinks he has a right to and must express" (221). Pound's final response, to Laughlin, was that Humphries was "[n]uts about free speech. He can free speech anywhere, save in permanent form, in an introduction, where it is irrelevant" (222).[26] In the end the book was issued without any introduction.

It was during these negotiations that the notorious affair involving the Bollingen Prize unfolded. *The Pisan Cantos* was published in 1948, and the prize was awarded, under the auspices of the Library of Congress, in February 1949. This was the first (and, to date, the last) literary award ever associated with the U.S. government. It came about in the following way. Archibald MacLeish had been Librarian of Congress in 1943, and appointed Allen Tate to the position of consultant in poetry. Tate proposed that the Library establish a body of Fellows in American Letters, constituting a board of advisors in literary matters. The recommendation was adopted, and subsequently each poetry consultant automatically went on to become a Fellow. After Tate, the consultants were Robert Penn War-

---

[26] Lest Pound be seen solely in the posture of whitewashing his career for posterity, we might bring Stanley Fish to his defense. "'Free speech,' argues Fish, "is just the name we give to verbal behavior that serves the substantive agendas we wish to advance; and we give our preferred verbal behaviors *that* name when we can, when we have the power to do so, because in the rhetoric of American life, the label 'free speech' is the one you want your favorites to wear. Free speech, in short, is not an independent value but a political prize . . . " (*Free Speech* 102). As Pound clearly recognized, Humphries's insistence on free speech would not make Pound himself appear to be among anybody's "favorites." What's more, Pound maintains allegiance to eternal verities in such a way as to make clear his own sense (which Fish would dispute) that politics are strictly local and can be sloughed off by force of will.

ren, Louise Bogan, Karl Shapiro, Robert Lowell, and Léonie Adams who held the office during 1948–49. In addition to these six, the other Fellows in office to deliberate on the Bollingen Prize were Conrad Aiken, W. H. Auden, T. S. Eliot, Theodore Spencer, Katherine Anne Porter, Willard Thorp, Paul Green, and Katherine Garrison Chapin. Chapin was the wife of Francis Biddle, who, as Attorney General, had indicted Pound (in absentia) for high treason in 1943.[27] The decision to award a prize in poetry was made possible by the Bollingen Foundation, but the initiative was Tate's.

The Bollingen Foundation was named after C. G. Jung's house in Switzerland, and was a trust established largely with Mellon capital (of Pittsburgh aluminum) to facilitate translation and publication of the writings of Jung and his Eranos circle. The earliest titles in the Bollingen series were under the imprint of Pantheon Books, and later the series went to Princeton University Press where it remains today. As a charitable foundation, however, Bollingen did much more than publish books. Grants were given to writers; much money went to the Modern Poetry Association of Chicago to support *Poetry* magazine; and in 1946 the Library of Congress was granted funds to undertake a sizeable project to record poets reading their works. With the precedent of this kind of support, Tate naturally thought of the Bollingen Foundation as a funding source for the poetry prize, and met with success. It was Luther Evans, Librarian of Congress in 1948, who named it the Bollingen Prize in honor of its benefactor. The stage was set, then, in November 1948, for the Fellows to convene to deliberate the recipient of the award.

First place ballots went predominately to *The Pisan Cantos*, with a few for *Paterson*, but in the end Pound prevailed. Karl

---

[27] E. Fuller Torrey speculates that "her inclusion was probably an attempt to further embarrass the Department of Justice by associating her with the award" (235). I've not seen any evidence to support this, however. Chapin was a poet herself, and frequently involved with the Library of Congress in official and semi-official capacities. In 1962, during the National Poetry Festival, she was one of the official speakers, along with several of her former Fellows from the Bollingen committee. By the time the final vote was cast, incidentally, Theodore Spencer was dead, and Paul Green abstained.

Shapiro was the only dissenter. T. S. Eliot had recently won the Nobel Prize, and Shapiro admits to stargazing as his incentive for attending (*Reports* 41). Louise Bogan was likewise enthralled, and a bit disconcerted to see the Possum sharpening his pencil with a penknife during the meeting.[28] The Eliot charisma was uppermost in so many people's minds that, after the award began generating controversy, it was rumored that Eliot had personally compelled the others to vote for Pound. In April 1949 Shapiro declared in print that "[t]he presence of Mr. Eliot at the meeting . . . perhaps inhibited open discussion," particularly on the subject of anti-Semitism. But he usefully added that, for the time being, "few poets anywhere are in a position to say what they really think of Pound's work" ("Question" 519). A journalist reviewing the affair ten years later was assured by Eliot that "[t]he award to Pound had already been put forward and discussed amongst some of the members of the Committee, before I arrived in America that year." Pound himself imagined it was Lowell who had been the prime mover (Loftus 352). In fact, Tate appears to have been as decisive as any single Fellow, but the choice was never a matter of contention. All the Fellows were aware of the inevitable controversy that would ensue, and that awareness is sufficient indication of their resolve.

"Pound, in Mental Clinic, Wins Prize for Poetry Penned in Treason Cell" blazed the *New York Times* headline, sparking confrontation in scores of journals, magazines, and newspapers. The public debate raged for a few years, resurrecting aspects of prewar disputes about politics and art. Pound himself disparagingly referred to it as the "Bubble-Gum" prize, "Bollingen's bid for immortality" (Carpenter, *Serious* 793). The flashpoint was Robert Hillyer's bilious assault in *Saturday Review*, which ignited an out-

---

[28] They sat together at lunch, about which Bogan breathlessly informed a correspondent: "We talked, during the end of the entrée, and *through* the coffee and ice-cream! Of form, and Youth's fear of form; of rhythm (we got it back to the heart-beat and the breath) . . . " (*Letters* 265). Shapiro had a less satisfactory time of it, and in his autobiography he reports in some detail the solicitousness with which the other Fellows treated him as the resident Jew (*Reports* 41–43).

pouring of support and outrage in equal proportion.[29] The first of
Hillyer's articles was "Treason's Strange Fruit" in the June 11 (1949)
issue (deploying the title of Billie Holiday's 1939 song about lynch-
ing), followed a week later by "Poetry's New Priesthood," an indict-
ment of New Criticism for having fostered the atmosphere sanctioning the award. Linking Pound's fascism with what he mistakenly
took to be the Nazi sympathies of Jung's circle (a charge he was later
forced to retract), Hillyer concocted a fantastic paranoid scenario in
which a cabal consisting of the Library of Congress Fellows, the
New Critics and their quarterlies, aluminum tycoon Paul Mellon
and the Bollingen Foundation was undertaking "the mystical and
cultural preparation for a new authoritarianism" (McGuire 214). In
the ensuing wrangle, the magazines controlled by or disposed to the
New Criticism supported the award: *Poetry, Sewanee Review, Hudson Review*, along with *New Republic, The Nation*, and *Harper's*.
But the bulk of opinion was anti-Pound, and various postures of
denunciation emanated from a broad spectrum of publications, from
Masses and Mainstream to *Catholic World, Partisan Review,
Atlantic*, and *Time*. The general consensus was that the government
had been compromised, and Congress promptly put an end to
involvement by the Library of Congress (the Bollingen Prize being
subsequently taken up by Yale University). Dr. Fredric Wertham,
leading crusader against the derelictions of comic books, used the
occasion to denounce the psychiatric diagnosis of insanity that kept
Pound from standing trial.[30] In short, the Pound question provided

---

[29] The denunciation Hillyer drew from his articles surely left him smarting. In
1960, after the heyday of the New Critics was past, he must have fancied he had
the last word in a curt dismissal of modern poetry: "Though the symbolism of
T. S. Eliot's poetry and the incoherence of Ezra Pound's *Cantos* have served as
damaging models for younger men, the more nearly complete sterilization and
confusion of recent American poetry were accomplished by the New Criticism
(most of whose adherents now deprecate the term)" (*Pursuit* 193).

[30] Wertham was a psychiatrist and self-appointed crusader tilting at the
windmills of popular culture, most flamboyantly in his book *Seduction of
the Innocent*. For an account of Wertham's determination to link comic books
with a rise in juvenile delinquency, and the ambiguous role played by the
"Classic Comics" series in particular, see Rasula, "Nietzsche in the Nursery."

a forum for many people to air opinions on issues tangentially related to the award itself.

In his contribution to *Partisan Review*'s "The Question of the Pound Award," Robert Gorham Davis suggested that the prize signified the triumph of the New Criticism. "What confronts us in the Pound case is a complex of ideas dominant in American criticism during the forties, and made so largely by the talents and critical activities of some of the judges, of Eliot, Auden, Tate and Warren. The judges were judging themselves along with Pound, their master" (513). Eliot had dedicated *The Waste Land* to Pound, "*il miglior fabbro*," but none of the others thought of themselves as disciples in any sense, and issued a statement denying that they constituted a clan of devotees (a statement to which MacLeish and Williams were also signatories). But Davis was broadly correct in recognizing that the judges were nearly all initiates in, and dedicated to, the cause of Anglo-American literary modernism, and that the New Criticism was in some sense the management firm on the home front that had packaged this largely expatriate enterprise. Davis outlined a "complex of ideas . . . promoted with tactical skill" in an account that recapitulated the background of New Criticism and delineated its ideological position crudely but accurately:

> It asserts that living language, literary sensibility and poetic values are supported by the traditional, the Catholic, the regional, the mythic, the aristocratic, and by a sense of the tragic, of transcendental absolutes, of sin and grace. Language and sensibility and values are destroyed by rationalism, liberalism, positivism, progressivism, equalitarianism, Shelleyanism, sociology, and the ideology of the Enlightenment. This has been made explicit by Eliot in *After Strange Gods* and *The Idea of a Christian Society*; by the Southern regionalists, including Tate and Warren in much that they have written since their first manifesto, *I'll Take My Stand*; and by Auden in the Herod-as-liberal speech in *A Christmas Oratorio* and in the various reviews urging liberals and reformers to go jump in the lake. (514)

The New Critics invariably represented their concerns in terms of tradition, which could rather ominously take on all the sarcophagal attributes of "the firm" in the corporate sense. Tate indicated that he, at least, had voted for the *career* rather than the book itself, which he conceded was lacking "coherent form." Responding to the charge that a critical emphasis on form had predisposed the judges to subordinate political considerations, he insisted this was absurd precisely because the *Cantos* were formally chaotic. Tate plainly stated that his vote was an honorary gesture for one who "had done more than any other living man to regenerate the language, if not the imaginative forms, of English verse" ("Remarks" 667). The separation of politics from art, Tate held, was impracticable: "We cannot choose the aesthetic or the practical; art or life. It is never either-or; it is both-and. We as a society have got to take them indissolubly together" (668). Tate was in effect rehearsing his subsequent position for "The Man of Letters in the Modern World" by balancing Pound's criminality with that of the "monism of the statesman who imagines that what he says is scarcely said in language at all, that it exists apart from the medium, in something indefinite like 'practicality.' If we [poets] do not look after the medium," he added, "nobody else will" (668).

Tate's position leaves the question dangling at "both-and," which was indefensible for Shapiro, who later called the award "an act of intellectual arrogance which has no parallel in literary history" (*Defense* 29). It was a win-win proposition: "Thus, the intellectual critic has it both ways: he can dictate to society about its ills and he can regard a poem as a pure exercise of language, at his convenience." But this was to misconstrue the "arrogance" of Tate, for whom there was no question of mere convenience, because Tate and many of his associates were genuine wasteland personalities, haunted by Eliot's spectre of collapsing order, and convinced that the corporate liberal humanist tendency in American life was the ruin of culture, the end of sensibility, and a supreme violence to the imagination. The Fellows' rebuttal to *Saturday Review* was that Pound's fascism had aroused a corresponding authoritarianism with "standard-brand positive Americanism as a test for literary worth" (13). Collectively signed, the Fellows' statement (and this phrasing in particular) sounds uncannily like the voice of Tate. Tate was arrogant all right, but with the arrogance of desperation. Tate's acolyte Lowell inherited the haughtiness (which was politely called pride) along with many of his opinions.[31] Tate had dismissed the political arguments by saying that Pound's convictions were childish and could thus wield no influence. In 1961 Lowell took the same line: "He had no political effect whatsoever and was quite eccentric and impractical." He then went on to claim fascism and other problematic views as a *positive* attribute of Pound's work: "he'd be a very Parnassan poet without them . . . they made him more human and more to do with life, more to do with the times. They served him. Taking what interested him in these things gave a kind of realism and life to his poetry that it wouldn't have had otherwise" (*Prose* 252). It seems that Lowell later took Pound's precedent to heart as the tacit justification for his own egregious violation of privacy in the poems of *The Dolphin* and *For Lizzie and Harriet*.

Responses to the Bollingen fiasco were permeated with imprudence, as if Pound's own precipitous temperament infected the disputes, and few surmounted the residual crudity of the form-content distinction. Those who attempted a more nuanced appraisal, primarily associated with *Partisan Review*, were motivated by political opportunism as they scrambled to reposition themselves in the new cold war ideology.[32] As Robert Casillo observes, "Having condemned Pound for his beliefs, placing him 'beyond the bounds of our intellectual life,' the liberal critics largely ignored him and thus ironically paved the way for his more recent cultural rehabilitation

---

[31] Lowell's relation to Tate has been overlooked, largely because Tate's stature as poet does little service to the customary sequencing of major figures, in which Lowell is seen to "succeed" the likes of Pound, Eliot, and Frost. To trace the extent of Lowell's dependency on Tate is to threaten his work with a considerable down-scaling, of course; but the derivations are there, especially in Lowell's attitudes about, and judgments on, poetry and other poets.

[32] Marjorie Perloff has analyzed the duplicitous rhetoric of *Partisan* adherents, who were rigorously isolationist in 1940 but were quite prepared to condemn Pound, in 1949, for having advocated similar views. The sore point was the issue of anti-Semitism; but as Perloff notes, the Jewish Partisans of 1940 said nothing about the pogroms, and only seemed to remember their Jewishness when the Bollingen affair provided them with an excuse for righteousness. See "Fascism, Anti-Semitism, Isolationism."

as a poet of ideas" (11). The incident aroused much public debate by commentators who clearly knew nothing about Pound's (or any modern) poetry, nor did they care to learn. But the affair had deeper implications for the poetry community, since it became one of those things about which poets necessarily had views. Delmore Schwartz, hosting a party in the summer of 1949, defiantly bellowed to Lowell, Empson, and other guests that the jury had been rigged by Eliot as an anti-Semitic conspiracy (Atlas 274). Surely many similar incidents of distemper went unrecorded. Pound's case incited numerous poets to write articles, editorials, letters to editors, moving some to write more substantial pieces of self-scrutiny. Olson wrote "Grandpa, Goodbye" in 1948 in the wake of his visits to Pound at St. Elizabeth's, and William Carlos Williams urged him to get it published: "Why not try John Crowe Ransom? Partisan Review. (Shove it FAR up their asses) They ought to print it but they won't" (Olson, *Pound* 138).[33] Despite having been on the jury, Lowell did not participate in the public debates, because in the summer of 1949 he suffered the first of his many manic episodes resulting in police detention and hospitalization; but one wonders to what extent that was *his* way of

---

[33] Williams's disdain for the "professors" persisted, despite positive reviews of *Paterson*. But Williams's poetics were not taken seriously on their own merit. That he represented extraliterary values to the postwar's new formalists can be discerned in a comment by Richard Wilbur: "A selection of Williams's poems might be made which would be our best Baedeker to the possibilities of sense-experience in the city world" (*Sewanee Review* 58.1 [Winter 1950]: 140). Symptomatic of the anomalous position occupied by Williams at this time are two erroneous comments from relatively recent books surveying that seething cold war terrain. Grant Webster, assessing *Partisan Review* in the postwar years, comments that, "[a]lthough it generally does not publish much by any one poet, it publishes one or two things by the new poets of the time—W. C. Williams, Karl Shapiro, Richard Wilbur, Elizabeth Bishop, John Berryman, Theodore Roethke, Frank O'Hara, W. D. Snodgrass, Daniel Hoffman—so that a reader will at least have heard of them" (221). Webster is a literary scholar who should have known Williams's career better than to regard him as a "new poet" of the 1940s. The historian John Patrick Diggins may perhaps be excused for the same misattribution of chronology. "The fifties may be called the 'placid decade' but out of it came a galaxy of implacable poets," he writes, footnoting the declaration with a list of some twenty poets, culminating with "William Carlos Williams, who, though starting earlier, wrote his first poem in the forties" (243).

lending support to his mentor, acting out incarceration and manic euphoria in his own terms. Three poets who published more extensive commentary were Archibald MacLeish, Peter Viereck, and Karl Shapiro, and a review of their positions will help clarify the unfolding matrix of postwar American liberal culture in which Pound and the Bollingen affair need to be placed.

Nobody at the time was disposed to see, as we now can, the *unwitting* epic dimension provided for the poem by circumstances beyond the poet's control; and *The Pisan Cantos* in particular are an object lesson in the right person being in the right place at the right time—if only to dramatize the perils of being colossally wrong. The formal disorder Tate noted turned out not to be an impediment when it came to awarding a prize; but, when the committee was dominated by a New Critical sensibility purportedly disposed to the virtues of symmetry and autonomy, why not? John Paul Russo notes an equivocation between form and substance in the matter of New Critical allegiance: "The principal modernist themes are alienation, cultural anarchy, the grotesque, fright, despair, and nothingness; not balance, wholeness, synthesis." Consequently, for the New Critics, "fidelity to their method, wherever it led, proved stronger than their desire for closure as stated in their theory. They were willing to take the cure of history as mediated by the great texts of modernism" (221). Nowhere is the cure of history more evident than in *The Cantos*, which propose themselves as nothing less than a scientific laboratory in which the petri dishes of culture are sampled for traces of that civilizing vaccine meant to allay the periodic depredations of history. If the New Critics hankered after decorum, it was to be the decorum of the millenium, when push came to shove, not the baubles of lyric decoration that provided the rosary beads of interpretive method.

Archibald MacLeish, a poet of Pound's own generation, has long been known for his dictum "A poem should not mean / But be" from the "Ars Poetica" of *Streets in the Moon* (1926). The sentiment concurs with Williams's objectivism—as well as that of Oppen, Reznikoff, Zukofsky—but it has been primarily associated with New Criticism. Another epithet from the poem is more appropriate to the

New Critics' (and his own) defense of Pound: "A poem should be equal to: / Not true" (*Poems* 107). In addition to being Librarian of Congress throughout much of World War II, MacLeish was also Director of the Office of Facts and Figures, and from 1944–45 Assistant Secretary of State. He had written a controversial pamphlet in 1940, *The Irresponsibles*, attacking the prevalent American mood of nonintervention in the European war. Charging the world crisis to a triumph of force over form, he blamed intellectuals and (without being explicit) the pioneers of artistic modernism for the "cynical brutality" of "*the repudiation of the forms*" (*Time* 108–09). MacLeish distinguished two types of "irresponsibles," the writer and the scholar: "Where the modern scholar escapes from the adult judgments of the mind by taking the disinterested man of science as his model, the modern writer escapes by imitation of the artist" (118). These types are recognizably the historical and philological scholars on the one hand, and the New Critics as formalist esthetes. When the outcry over the Bollingen erupted, however, MacLeish promptly sided with the Fellows, becoming a signatory to their *Case Against the Saturday Review of Literature*.[34] In 1950 he published a booklet that recapitulated the debate in the form of a dialogue, attempting "to expose the actual issues of what should have been a great debate" (*Opinion* n. p.).

There are two speakers in *Poetry and Opinion*, Mr. Saturday and Mr. Bollingen. The former complains of overreaction to his con-

---

[34] MacLeish later said that he would have opposed the nomination of Pound for the award if it had happened during his term as Librarian of Congress. But he also explained that his subsequent involvement was motivated by the concern "to clear Pound of any involvement in that procedure. That wasn't his idea. It was something that Allen Tate and some others thought would be a bright idea" (*Reflections* 65). It was MacLeish who organized Pound's release from St. Elizabeth's in 1958—a testament to fortitude, inasmuch as Pound had pointedly slandered MacLeish in his radio broadcasts during the war. Late in his life, though, Pound sent a letter of apology, "the most disturbing letter I've ever gotten," says MacLeish, because "Pound was the kind of man who should never apologize!" (66). Frost has often been credited with Pound's release, largely on the strength of his affadavit to the District Court of Washington, D. C., citing "the disgrace of our letting Ezra Pound come to his end where he is" (*Poetry and Prose* 439). But it was in fact MacLeish who mobilized Frost, Hemingway, and Eliot, whose collective stature was more than any presiding judge could overlook.

demnation of the prize: "There is no question here of the suppression of a book of poems but of the apotheosis of a book of poems" (*Opinion* 17). But he proceeds to persecute the book for its author's opinions, about which Mr. Bollingen has to clarify the terms of debate, pointing out that Mr. Saturday's objections presume a social theory of poetry. "Only by demonstrating that it is the *function of poetry itself* to communicate right ideas about these things, can you argue that wrong ideas invalidate the poetry" (35). MacLeish is clearly on the Bollingen side, but takes pains to dignify the opposition by contextualizing the issues in terms of the defenses of (and attacks on) poetry going back through Shelley and Sidney to Aristotle and Plato. (The tacit subtext here is that the anti-Poundians didn't have a sufficient historical sense to know where to go for ammunition.) He replicates New Critical party line by conceding that Pound's volatile opinions must be accounted for, but that they need only be justified *in* the poem, not in themselves (36)—a position paralleling Lowell's argument that even pernicious notions "humanize" the persona of the text. MacLeish also reiterates the New Critics' adherence to the poetic vision of modernism as the critique of "tragic disorder" in civilization (45), insisting in the end that "the loyalty [in *The Cantos*] is not to dogmas of fascism but to the poet's vision of a tragic disorder which lies far deeper in our lives and in our time" (48).[35] What MacLeish achieved with this pamphlet was a repositioning of the whole debate in a broader historical context, restoring it to the tradition of poetic "defense" rhetoric, and articu-

---

[35] Casillo's summary of MacLeish is supercilious in its cleverness: "He . . . praises Pound's poem for its compelling 'image' of the true incoherence of the modern world. Thus, thanks to the fallacy of imitative form, MacLeish transforms incoherence into a mimetic virtue, while covertly introducing extrinsic criteria in order to justify Pound" (338, n.30). MacLeish, on the contrary, elucidates the position one is obliged to take in order to *avoid* the fallacy of mimetic formalism: it is, in his view, the Platonic one, which cuts the formalist ground from under the defense of poets by appealing to a more exalted criteria of form (the world of Ideas, or archetypal forms), so that their political infractions stand all the more starkly revealed. As Plato realized, of course, the result would be the expulsion from the republic not merely of political undesirables but of poets and even poetry as such.

lating the point of conflict as one involving a larger conflict than the war recently concluded.[36]

Peter Viereck, Pulitzer poet of 1949, a political scientist and staunch conservative (*Conservatism Revisited: The Revolt Against Revolt* appeared in 1949), was among the more vociferous critics of the Bollingen decision. He made ample use of various periodicals to advance his arguments in the aftermath of the award, and was still hammering away four years later in his pamphlet *Dream and Responsibility*. Viereck held that the modernist vanguard, as represented by Pound and Eliot, had been dishonored by such followers as the New Critics. "They have frozen [Pound's] dynamic experimental zest, which three decades ago was still doing more good than harm, into a static Alexandrian school," Viereck wrote, apparently oblivious to the fact that the New Critics had sanctioned the post-

---

[36] This is precisely the distinction overlooked by Gerald Graff in his commentary on *Poetry and Opinion*. He usefully notes that MacLeish discriminates between "opinion" as referring to "dogmatic mass ideologies" and "intuition": "Thus fascism is an 'opinion'; the view that civilization is 'a vast disorder,' etc., is an 'intuition'" (*Poetic Statement* 175). MacLeish honors *The Pisan Cantos* as being in the service of such an intuition, and therefore extricates the poem from charges that it is contaminated by Pound's opinions (which MacLeish does not deny are held by the poet). What Graff fails to recognize is that this distinction is itself in accord with MacLeish's rhetorical strategy in the pamphlet, which is to expand the temporal parameters of the debate. With such an expanded framework in mind, then, opinions are local, intuitions durable; and to consider the issues in light of Plato, as MacLeish recommends, is to see that Socrates in the dialogues is the voice of intuition contending with a steady succession of opinions advanced by his interlocutors. This is not to make Pound out to be a socratic hero (much as he too courted the hemlock), but to make the quite rudimentary observation that, for all his (self-diagnosed) reprehensible enthusiasm for Mussolini, Pound did *not* view fascism as the crowning achievement of civilization, nor as a utopian solution to historical vagaries. Pound was too much of a neoplatonist to mistake a specific form of political power for the heavenly city. The problem of Pound's culpability is compounded by the fact that theorizing fascist aesthetics is often disoriented by the sheer scale of political malevolence with which the twentieth century has been marked. The arts, in such discussions, too readily become a synecdoche for political responsibility in a time when it is unclear how power is actually exercised. So the putatively mimetic basis of the arts implicates poets as (if not more) effectively than politicians and scientists when it comes to allocating political blame.

modernist return to formalism which he himself championed. Scornful of "sectarian literary patronage systems," Viereck saw Pound as "the keystone of this school of criticism," shrewdly adding, "If he goes out of fashion, then the whole structure becomes shaky" (*Dream* 21). This much, at least, Viereck got right. The Pound award was integral to the hegemony of New Criticism, which had triumphed in the academy with its methodology, but which had further cards to play in its self-appointed role as the steward of contemporary poetry, a poetry that would perforce continue to pledge allegiance to Europe, and for that reason could never concede final eminence to Williams, who had been the only other viable contender for the Bollingen.

Where most of those roused to fury in 1949 by the Bollingen controversy soon let bygones be bygones, Viereck held onto it as a touchstone of his poetics. As late as 1987 he returned to the scene of the crime in the appendix, "Form in Poetry," to his poetry collection *Archer in the Marrow*: "Is modern poetry," he puns there, "a tale told by an Eliot, full of Pound and fury, signifying Williams?" (228). While he adds nothing to his copious earlier commentary, he does reflect on the personal significance of the award to his career as a poet. "It was as if potential dissenters were being given an object lesson," he says of Pound's defenders. Viereck testifies to having been specifically warned by one "influential editor" who, "while privately agreeing, said I must stop criticizing what he called 'the Pound-Eliot-Tate establishment,' or I would 'no longer be publishable'" (235). In fact, Viereck's literary stock did wane during the 1950s, for reasons unmistakably related to the hegemony of Eliot and his epigones. But he survived all the intervening vicissitudes, characterizing the free verse that dominated the sixties and seventies as an "indispensable garbage disposal unit" (231), and in 1993 spurning the New Formalism as "an equal menace to creativity . . . a dead mechanical form, artificial rather than based on the human biology of walking, breathing, feeling" ("Anti-Form" 302).

The Poundian lineage in American poetry turned out to be a fault line, and the Bollingen incident was its first seismic event. As long as Eliot was the Great Eminence of Anglo-American letters, he tolerated little lattitude in the matter of Pound, whose reputation

was insured by the Bank of Eliot like an FDIC security deposit. The
New Criticism became in effect the talent and booking agency for the
Pound-Eliot cadre, and the Bollingen fiasco showed how ably its
adherents could also serve as spin doctors. A manifestly political
event, the crime of high treason, was absorbed into the carceral apparatus of pedagogy at a time when heuristic protocol meant that
Pound's poetry, not his life, would serve the curriculum. The volatility of the life was less threatening to the United States government
than it was to the critical pedagogy of the recently ascendent New
Criticism. At stake was not a preservation of the form/content distinction, as Robert Casillo argues in *The Genealogy of Demons*—the
New Critics were not simply defending form against the predations
of a suspect content. The defense of Pound actually had little to do
with Pound himself, and operated on another level than the textual
issues that preoccupied critics of the award. What was crucial was
the preservation of the administrative security system that had
assumed custodial control of poetry (not just Pound's poetry) as
surely as the man was impounded in a mental asylum.

Not surprisingly, the agency that took custody of the reputation was the literary establishment which, having succeeded in setting
the theoretical countenance of literary study, had further superinten-
dence work to do on the poetry that would serve it as The Right Stuff.
Pound, the man, was "saved" as an accidental by-product of that
generic value, Poetry. In a world in which the particulars of poetry
would matter as little as the specific contents of packaged foods, the
symbolic value of "poetry" was more important than poems (and,
except in equally symbolic instances, poets). Pound was "saved" for
poetry in the double sense Hegel celebrated in the word *Aufhebung*:
preserved and cancelled simultaneously. Close readings of his poetry
were encouraged literally at the expense of any corresponding scrutiny of the career; and this, in turn, forestalled for many decades a proper reckoning of the literary cost of the corporate-sector appropriation
and packaging of that grand chimera of our time, "modernism."[37]

---

[37] In the rush to probe the putative fascist tendencies of modernism, it's
important to heed Russell Berman's warning that "if one were to endeavor to

MacLeish's compulsion to view the Bollingen dispute as archetypal was foreshadowed by Karl Shapiro before the *Pisan Cantos* were even published. Shapiro's fourth volume of poetry, *Trial of a Poet and Other Poems* (1947), culminates in the oratorical polylogue of the title poem. Shapiro's choice of multiple speakers, like MacLeish's dialogue, suggests the extent to which Pound made poets aware of their own conflicted responses to the issues he stirred up. In "Trial of a Poet" the personae are Poet, Public Officer, Doctor, Priest, and a Chorus of Poets. The Priest responds as one who has lost the sacraments to Matthew Arnold's culture priests, complaining of the Chorus of Poets that they "see the glazed mosaic of a saint" when they gaze on the prisoner poet (70). The priest also sees the work of modernism spawning "art-monsters," "demented fragmented masterpieces / Founded on a strong nostalgia for savage crudities" (62). The Nazi phrase "degenerate art" (*Entartete Kunst*) would have served to vilify modernity as "the festival / Of *Dada*, evil form / Of evil content" (78). The Public Officer likewise reviles modernism as the "blasphemy of natural form" and "the treason of forms and anti-style" (62). Poundians are "writers of pornography and free verse," and at the end the Officer melodramatically curses, "Hence, loathed experimentalist!" (79). Fittingly, the Poets in chorus echo the twenties Bohemian wasteland mentality: "We live in crisis," they croon,

---

set the poetics of the modernist authors attracted to fascism in some resonance with their political proclivities, then the resulting model (or models) would not be adequate as accounts of modernism in general." Consequently, "the proper question for literary critical inquiry has to do with the extent to which the political imagination of the author or the text (which may be extraordinarily eccentric when measured against the standard of the established political power) contributes to the construction of an aesthetic project and, in particular, one that can be labeled characteristically modernist" (104). That Pound was "extraordinarily eccentric"—in his radio broadcasts and in his poetry—there can be no doubt. Berman's book compels reexamination of any easy alignment (as well as any convenient separation) of political ideology and aesthetic form; but it's interesting to note that the features he sees constituting "fascist modernism" in German writers like Ernst Jünger are precisely applicable to Pound: teleological iteration manifested in a bias toward cyclical history (the dynastic fluctuations in China, for Pound), spectacle (the collagist display-case method of *The Cantos*), and a penchant for the pseudodocumentary (105–06).

"We breathe crisis, and do not see the end of crisis. / Let the liars smooth our arts, / Let the liars versify / In true iamb, falling trochee, / Elegant choriamb and brittle brittanic" (63). Of course Jarrell, Lowell, and Shapiro himself were achieving success precisely for rehabilitating the "true iamb" in a poetic Restoration billed as the progressive culmination of revolutionary modernism.

The Doctor is the most poignant figure; Shapiro was evidently well aware of the delicate moral dilemma faced by the psychiatrists whose evaluations of Pound would "save" him from hanging as a traitor—but also save the country from such an awkward martyrdom of a major poet—by condemning him to an old age cohabited with lunatics. The Doctor is able to see Pound vacillating between inconsequence and criminality, with no middle ground:

> Out of his new-found phrases and dead footnotes
> He wove a critique of life, a bad world history,
> With a Cloud-Cuckoo-Land for his heroes
> And a hell in minute detail for the rest.
> I think we must find the bridge between
> This harmless sublimation and his consummate crime. (61)

(The pinions for such a bridge, as it happened, were not even attempted until more than thirty years later, by such scholars as Massimo Bacigalupo, Robert Casillo, and Tim Redman.) Finally, in a scene strikingly evocative of Raymond Roussel's reanimation of cadavers with "resurrectine" in *Locus Solus*, the Doctor stirs the torpid poet into volubility in a marvellous collage of disjointed phrases from Thomas Love Peacock's essay "The Four Ages of Poetry" (which occasioned Shelley's famous "Defense"). The Poet eventually becomes lucid, reviews the positions taken by the players, and condemns himself "to be known hereafter as a dull poet and the lapdog of his age" (78). This is the only part of "Trial of a Poet" that rings false, as Shapiro's personal invective is ventriloquized into the poet's voice, admitting aesthetic transgression where Pound himself, in the end, specified the tragic moral flaw of unwonted pride.

Unlike other poets, Shapiro was uniquely positioned to feel tainted by Pound, not only as a member of the Bollingen committee but as a Jew—he would stridently title a 1958 collection *Poems of a*

Jew in defiance of the genteel WASP literary establishment he had come to despise. He chose not to reprint "Trial" in his *Collected Poems* in 1978, but in his 1962 book *In Defense of Ignorance* he returned to the Pound issue to ponder the fate of "The Scapegoat of Modern Poetry." The essay is vitriolic, and Shapiro confesses having written it "with a feeling of lassitude and distaste." But the incentive emanates from his Bollingen tenure, when "[o]ne of the judges . . . informed me sanctimoniously that the award to Pound was a great act of piety, a remark which I am still puzzling about after all these years" (83). "Scapegoat" is a kind of dramatic monologue in which Shapiro histrionically resists every appeal Pound had been represented as offering. "Pound has never really stopped being archaic," he says—which is not inherently offensive—but then underscores his attitude: "Pound sentimentalizing over usury in Quakerish English is almost too painful to read" (71). Shapiro's main point is virtually identical to Gertrude Stein's remark that Pound was a "village explainer." "He is, in fact, a well-known American type," Shapiro clarified, "the provincial overexposed to the guidebook" (62). "We recognize in Pound that peculiar buffoonery of the frontier American, the intellectual dandyism of the tourist abroad, and the enormous wasted energy of the crank" (85). So how is Pound made out to be a scapegoat? Shapiro concludes that he was a pawn in Eliot's game. Shapiro had been the one, after all, to lend credence to the suspicion that Eliot had commandeered the Bollingen committee, and a dozen years later—amid pervasive evidence of the durability of the Eliot establishment—felt confirmed in his assessment. In *In Defense of Ignorance*, the essay on Pound is preceded by a comparably scathing treatment of Eliot, "The Death of Literary Judgment."

The eagerness of Shapiro and Viereck to have done with the business of Pound, prolonged over many decades, is symptomatic of a period profoundly ambiguous about history, literature, and their conjunctive apparition, literary history. We can pinpoint the postwar decade as the precise moment when literary modernism was recuperated for pedagogic practice, which is to say, when the modernist affront was domesticated. The much-noted fixation on paradox associated with New Criticism might well apply to the brutal paradox that the demographic success of modernism was also a moment of dispossession—a "profound paradox of culture" Bruce Robbins calls it, "both oppositional cutting edge and professional ground. Modernism in this sense seems to define a predicament from which we have yet to extricate ourselves with any great success—*the* predicament, perhaps, of intellectuals at the present time" (*Vocations* 63). Robbins's "present time" is 1993, and thus the quandary he evokes is well on to being half a century old; a paradox, then, of shocking durability. The real shock of "the shock of the new" is that the shock never wore off: *something* about modernism is always a shocker, whether it's nihilism, fascism, colonialism, sexism, or as Robbins indicates, *professionalism*. What disturbed Viereck and Shapiro about Pound, Eliot, and the New Criticism was the cultural *Gesellschaft* they established; the fact that, for all the posturing of rugged individualism, dark nights of the soul, and aesthetic autonomy, it added up to another country club, as if all the talk of kulchur finally boiled down to a *cult*.

Yet, for all their dismay at the New Critical-modernist triumph, history has proven their "success" less paradoxical than bonechilling to contemplate. In the inner sanctum of the canonization of modernism—for which I take the Bollingen prize as a foreshadowing synecdoche—what we find is an image befitting the nuclear age, an image of explosive intensities neatly contained by experts, the poem as atomic sedative. The final paradox: a toxic salvation. Despite their rag-tag quality, *The Cantos* clearly advanced an image of the eternal city, organic and holistic, immunized against the vicissitudes and squalor of history. When Pound professed to be writing a poem that "included" history, his agrarian sympathizers would have understood this as, in effect, a containment policy: poetry subsuming the chaotic contingencies of history to a more durable transtemporal order, of which poetic structure was the exemplary paradigm.[38] However, as Jerome McGann has elucidated, anyone braving the dark heart of *The Cantos* must confront the fact that the

---

[38] Interestingly, MacLeish later expanded his dictum about a poem being rather than meaning, specifying that poems do not "designate" their particulars but "contain" them (Russo 204).

poem conjures up a crisis of conscience from which the reader is no more exempt than Pound was; and that his poem including history is pledged to a horrifying reciprocity *with* and within history, in which poem, poet, and reader are contained. "If the *Cantos* could speak," says McGann, "part of what it would say is 'I myself am hell'; and if it could be read, its readers would have to find ways of repeating those words" ("*Cantos*" 13). Pound succeeded—in many contradictory ways, as McGann demonstrates—in "creating a style which made its own poem subject to its own structure of judgment" (22, *n*31). That we have grown accustomed to the structure of its judgment is not so clear; we still have to reckon the aesthetic *frisson* of Pound's manner and method as an insidious enactment of fascist "structures" of belief. But in recognizing Pound's fabled intensities (*The Cantos* are thoroughly porous to what, in Wordsworth, are insignias of scarcity, those "spots of time") we have an opportunity to draw near to the lingering—and in some cases swelling—residues of a fascist sensibility, the gist of which should not be preemptively associated with the extremity signified by anti-Semitism, but with that ongoing carceral disgruntlement felt in modern administered societies.

Pound's incarceration had been written into *The Pisan Cantos* (themselves penned in confinement), most memorably in the image of perceptual stasis: "But in the caged panther's eyes: / 'Nothing. Nothing that you can do . . . '" (*Cantos* 530). The poet's ongoing captivity in the decade after the Bollingen affair is rich with connotation. Life in a mental asylum proved no obstacle to the network of correspondence and consultation that Pound had coveted from Rapallo, and it only seemed to increase in the more centralized location of the nation's capital. The caged panther's eyes grew progressively "furious from perception," as he infamously put it in *Rock-Drill* (606), in a context implicating Hitler as perceptual model, made explicit finally in *Thrones* ("Adolf furious from perception" [541]). Pound's fury (the "speed" Olson noted) became paradigmatic as a form of arrest: his physical detention, coupled with his frenzied escalation of contacts, is an exemplary image of the "carceral continuum" elaborated by Foucault. I mean this not only in the sense in which Foucault names the carceral as the most suitable bonding agent within the modern episteme of social adjustment—the "carceral network" as the grand instrument of normalization—but also with reference to the panopticon. "The carceral texture of society is the apparatus of punishment that conforms most completely to the new economy of power and the instrument for the formation of knowledge that this very economy needs. Its panoptic functioning enables it to play this double role" (*Discipline* 304–05). The panopticon is of course Bentham's prison design for supervisory omnipotence. The image of Pound, however, offers an instructive reversal: in the asylum, the poet's perceptual fury scans the world as if *he* were the cognitive center of panoptic epistemology. As a lone crank in an Italian coastal town, Pound was the classic autodidactic loner; but institutionalized and technically relieved of responsibility for his own affairs (his wife became his legal guardian), Pound is empowered in ways foreclosed to him otherwise. He becomes, in short, the very image of the command-control technocrat operating from within a maximum security module.[39]

Cultural authority, as Bourdieu has elaborated, derives from the power to define categories of taste and not from anything specific to the contents. This was more or less openly acknowledged in Hillyer's attacks on the award, in that he objected not only to *The Pisan Cantos* (the "content" chosen to exemplify the category of superior poetry), but the legislative power of the New Criticism as a cultural network capable of defining poetry so that Pound and poets like him would be structurally advantaged to exemplify the art. Hillyer and others, that is, were alarmed at the spectre of an emergent "monopoly of credibility" (Larson 17). As I've suggested, the ultimate appeal

---

[39] In a brief essay intended to supplement Foucault's account of disciplinary regimes, Gilles Deleuze notes that we've lately come to inhabit regimes of "control." "Control is short-term and rapid rates of turnover, but also continuous and without limit, while discipline was of long duration, infinite and discontinuous. Man is no longer man enclosed, but man in debt" ("Postscript" 6). This enigmatic but penetrating assertion uncannily affirms Pound's longstanding preoccupation with banking, credit, and usury. If Pound and Eliot were figures to whom fellow poets and enthusiasts of modernism in general were indebted, this also suggests that New Criticism devised ways to service that debt in the emerging society of "control."

made by Pound's defenders was on behalf of his expertise, his special authority in the technical domain of versification. It was an appeal that succeeded, not because of the power and authority of the judges (which is what opponents of the award were preoccupied with), but because the culture of expertise and systems efficiency was becoming pervasive. The great irony—and I use the term in deliberate mimicry of its terminological eminence under the regime of New Criticism—is that so many of Pound's supporters deplored the emergence of just such a social order.

In the wake of the Bollingen controversy—buffered by his own impertinence—Pound looked on from St. Elizabeth's at the unfolding Communist witch hunts with approval. Here, too, he seems an uncanny simulation of his nation's disposition: despite fascist sentiments during the war, little adjustment was required for him to be aligned with official American postwar policy. We might even suggest that Pound, (re-)entering the American cultural scene as a systems efficiency expert and assuming his proper (carceral) role, merits comparison to the Nazi rocket scientists conscripted for the American space weapons program.[40] In the cold war viral atmosphere, the surgical location and expulsion of hitherto invisible threats from within had the effect of commandeering particular prestige for the managerial class (and in the 1950s introspection would be deeded to the culture of expertise, with psychoanalysis and sociology becoming the privileged mediums of self-awareness). The fluid state dynamic of historical turbulence would increasingly be subordinated to the static model of a stable social order administering change as a function of technical efficiency. As Andrew Ross documents in *No Respect*, the State Department's containment policy regarding the spread of communism was matched by comparable

---

[40] Confronting a euphoric/hysteric groundswell of denunciations of deconstruction as "nihilistic" in the wake of disclosures about Paul de Man's shadowy past, Derrida promptly noted that the charge of "nihilism" was *also* endemic in Nazi anti-intellectualist rhetoric. He adds that this might be attested to by the "many intellectuals and teachers who came from Germany to take up residence in the United States after the war—not all of whom fled Nazism!" "An enormous amount of work remains to be done," he adds, "on what might be called the American memory or 'crypt' of Nazism" (214).

cultural strategies, the "discursive climate" in both instances acceding to the medical paradigm of the *cordon sanitaire*. The role of intellectuals was "to issue the national culture with a clean bill of health . . . " (51). The problem of cultural hygiene emerged most vividly for poetry around the Bollingen controversy, if for no other reason than the fact that Pound had been certified as mentally diseased, so the award itself tainted the literary merit system with an unsanitary aura. Pound threatened the emerging expert culture with a rupture of the carceral continuum that privileged expertise. The "professionals" had obviously faltered on two counts: the psychiatrists, it was feared, had produced a diagnosis advantageous to Pound as prospective defendant in a treason case; and the literary professionals had likewise misjudged as qualitatively superior a book of ravings.

In the end the administrative gestures were only a charade of remorse, an obligatory protest at defilements presumed to have already passed into "history." The technical fact of Pound's incarceration served to mask the greater dynamic of containment that unfolded not only around him, but around all poets, even those like Allen Tate who imagined themselves acting out of personal initiative. Thinking to preserve the integrity of poetry by controlling the institutions of its propagation, Tate became an unwitting factotum of the age of sociology, ending up as one of the most forceful and adept insiders and power players in literary politics—as in his role in awarding Pound the Bollingen Prize—and an object lesson, for us, in the hazard of dreaming that the utopia one imagines will take a form other than that prepared for it in advance by the institutions one happens to inhabit.

THE AGE OF SOCIOLOGY

An introspective compulsion began to infuse American life soon after the war, particularly in the aftermath of the use of nuclear weapons on Japan. By 1950 introspection would be deeded to the managerial temperament, and sociology would become the privileged medium of self-awareness. The penchant for time-capsule thinking—edible history diachronic sentiment—is characteristic of the mid-century, so it's appropriate to begin in that mode with a quick synopsis of salient images from Pound's trial to the Bollingen incident. Self-scrutiny attended the readjustment of the war economy to postwar consumer prosperity, and a return to domestic life for millions of displaced personnel. Accordingly, the Oscar-winning best picture for 1946 was *The Best Years of Our Lives*, a dystopic panorama of soldiers returning home to find their futures pawned off and the American way of life mutilated (already the dark side of the street had permeated cinematic style to such an extent that French critics, seeing their first Hollywood films since before the war, coined the term *film noir*). Archetypal scenes of beginnings and ends were reflected by two 1946 bestsellers, Dr. Spock's *Common Sense Book of Baby and Child Care* and John Hersey's *Hiroshima*.

In 1947 Marlon Brando and Montgomery Clift enrolled in the first classes offered by Lee Strasberg in method acting at the Actor's Studio in New York (and *A Streetcar Named Desire*, the play that would launch Brando's movie career in a few years, opened on Broadway in December). Jackie Robinson, breaking the color line, was signed by the Brooklyn Dodgers. In February, Charlie Parker was released from the asylum at Camarillo and returned rejuvenated to the music business, cutting the Dial and Savoy recordings (mostly with the young Miles Davis as sideman) that accelerated jazz into bop. In July there was a UFO panic, and sightings were reported in thirty-five states and Canada. The Truman Doctrine was launched to stop the spread of Communism in the Balkans; and Bernard Baruch coined the term "cold war."

The next year, 1948, was the first season for the fledgling television industry. The intrinsic fascism of the military mind was belabored in Mailer's bestselling *The Naked and the Dead*, while Dale Carnegie, prewar advocate of managerial hucksterism, offered up a new round of advice in *How to Stop Worrying and Start Living*. Some key scientific vistas to a new world were also published in 1948: the first volume of the famous Kinsey report on *Sexual Behavior in the Human Male*, and Norbert Wiener's *Cybernetics*. At Black

Mountain College in North Carolina, aided by students and fellow faculty members (including John Cage, Merce Cunningham, and Willem de Kooning), Buckminster Fuller built his first geodesic dome. Jackson Pollock was starting to do action paintings. Harry Truman was zigzagging the country's railway lines in the Truman Special, campaigning for the presidency (and his inauguration was the nation's first important televised spectacle). At the same time Neal Cassady and Jack Kerouac were speeding along the highways in a hectic lifestyle campaign, the nature of which wouldn't be made public until *On the Road* appeared in 1957. Charles Olson was pondering a long poem on the theme of the West (and snagged a Guggenheim for the research). The rise of the "wild West" ethos, which was to dominate film and television for over a decade, was embodied by John Wayne in two 1948 roles, in Howard Hawks's *Red River* and John Ford's *Fort Apache* (reprised in *She Wore a Yellow Ribbon* [1949] and *Rio Grande* [1950]).

Richard Nixon's House Unamerican Affairs Committee was very active during this period, and Louis Zukofsky's college pal Whittaker Chambers became prominent for his accusations that Alger Hiss had led a secret Communist cell in the 1930s. Hollywood, under the leadership of Actors' Guild President Ronald Reagan, began purging reds; and in early 1950 Senator Joe McCarthy brandished his stage prop, the infamous list of alleged subversives. From St. Elizabeth's, Pound looked on at the Communist witch hunt with approval. The year Pound was awarded the Bollingen for *The Pisan Cantos* the Nobel Prize went to Faulkner (the second American in a row—in 1948 it had gone to Eliot—international recognition of a literary supremacy commensurate with political supremacy), and Arthur Miller won a Pulitzer for *Death of a Salesman*. NATO was created in April 1949. *Billboard* inaugurated the new music chart category of "rhythm and blues" to replace what had formerly been "race records." In September Billy Graham's first Crusade for Christ was launched in Los Angeles, perfectly timed (unwittingly) to coincide with the first successful detonation of a Soviet nuclear bomb.

It was a turbulent transition, resulting in yet another overseas war (in Korea). But the overwhelming feature of American life was the perpetuation in peacetime of xenophobic wartime vigilance, of which the anticommunist fervor was only the most conspicuous means of self-regulation. The fluid state dynamic of historical turbulence would increasingly be subordinated to the static model of a stable social order administering change as a function of technical adjustment. The domestic scene was homogenized in part as a security measure against (equally homogenized) "threats" from abroad. But the U.S. did not need to become a security police state, because the existing corporate institutions were becoming far more effective regulators, facilitating compliance of a sort that could mimic freedom by making economic "necessity" appear voluntary. Domestic culture became, in Henri Lefebvre's phrase, "the bureaucratic society of controlled consumption," in which "publicity is the poetry of Modernity, the reason and pretext for all successful displays. It takes possession of art, literature, all available signifiers and vacant signifieds; it is art and literature, it gleans the leavings of the Festival to recondition them for its own ends . . . " (107).

The most damaging aspect of the liberal consensus in the arts was the concession of priority to administrative protocols. The deeper issue behind the academization of poets was the dramatically escalated administration of everyday life—or of "culture" in several senses, high, low, and middlebrow. Popular culture was increasingly susceptible to marketing and management skills: less and less was it a matter of the hard sell, the hoodwink—which orients itself to *caveat emptor*, setting its sights on a single victory—more and more a matter of structuring ongoing assent. This was installment plan culture (reinforced by television's seriality, which consolidated narrative on the installment plan), with deferred payment as incentive, promising continual elevations in standard of living. Installment credit in the U.S. rose from $4 billion to $43 billion between 1954 and 1960 (Jezer 126). What this implied for consumers was an increased sense of long-range planning, and the development of management skills in the home (Home Economics classes rose to prominence in high schools), skills that were formerly perceived as corporate and institutional. The household was being retooled, developed into an industrial worksite in which everyday life and "leisure time" were calibrated with corporate enterprise. Advertising had made this appeal throughout the twentieth century, but it was not really implemented until the postwar years, when domestic prosperity, easy consumer credit, and the mass media triumph of television gathered everyone into the grid of technological sentience. Culturally, what had the greatest impact was incontrovertible evidence that the desires of the nation were in harmony to a degree previously unthinkable. Sitcoms like *Father Knows Best, Leave It To Beaver* and *The Donna Reed Show* mesmerized viewers because they affirmed the unanimity of thought, lifestyle, and ambitions of a middle class revealed through the new medium to be much larger than had been previously realized. In some sense, the fabled conformism of the fifties grew out of the disclosure that people were *already* conforming without having known how extensive their conformity was. Since the mass media was highly selective in its images of everyday life and the kind of people who typified the norm, it was possible for this spectacle of the average to appear even more pervasive than it was. It was very hard to infer that the nation harbored millions of nonwhites, for instance, or women who weren't suburban mothers. "Across the political spectrum," writes Jackson Lears, "celebrants and doubters alike accepted the same basic assumption that postwar America was a homogeneous mass-consumption society. The very terms of the discussion promoted the primacy of consumption as a category of understanding" (47). What was at hand was the formation of a hegemonic bloc in Gramsci's sense, in which the interests of the American middle class were presumed to represent not only the aspirations of all Americans, but of "humanity" as well.

In this middlebrow milieu, it proved impossible to mention culture without explaining it, as if culture were some esoteric new invention like the garbage disposal. We might call this "The Age of Explanation." Americans wanted to know a great deal. Science offered intriguing technical explanations for phenomena ranging from electrons to the solar system; business mentality gauged everything in terms of cost, investment, overhead, percentages, yield— technical terms that implied the world of finance was instrinsically sounder than it had been in the Great Depression. But sociology mesmerized because it sought to explain the unexplainable. Why do we live the way we do? How do we agree and disagree? What is conflict? The general topic headings in the huge textbook, *Theories of Society,* edited by Talcott Parsons, Edward Shils and others in 1961, indicates the concerns: "Differentiation and Variation in Social Structures," "Personality and the Social System," "Culture and the Social System," and "Social Change." In the era of technoscience supremacy, with nuclear weapons and computers the most conspicuous triumphs, the sciences had acquired a dignity and authority which carried over into the "social sciences."

If the resident humanists of the universities and the upper middlebrow journals like *Saturday Review* could tell people what to read, social scientists could go one better, explaining *why* they read. The result was an increasing administration of both high and low from the middle, as few understood better than Theodor Adorno. From the vantage of the legislative middle, "[t]he seriousness of high art is destroyed in speculation about its efficacy," while "the seriousness of the lower perishes with the civilizational constraints imposed on the rebellious resistance inherent within it as long as social control was not yet total" (*Culture* 85). In Bakhtin's now more familiar terms, the festive, carnivalesque energies of popular culture were smothered by adminstrative rationality: Mardi Gras became, instead, the Main Street four o'clock parade in Disneyland. And as for such high cultural activities as poetry, they were ceaselessly beleaguered by the instrumentalist demand to explain themselves. Poetry fared well in the age of sociology because New Critical pedagogy constituted a veritable explanation industry, reassuringly in the hands of "qualified experts." The romance of technical efficiency was affirmed as poems were explicated in terms of their formidible metrical apparatus; and the sociological demand to know how and why poetry fit into society was satisfied by appealing to a simple functionalism, in which poems were compensatory mechanisms absorbing the traumas of history.

As Adorno shrewdly realized, rationalized administration not only injects into culture extrinsic standards and norms, but, in its refusal to enter into the creative spirit, paradoxically ends up creating its own irrationality. "Such expansion of administrative competence into a region, the idea of which contradicts every kind of average generality inherent to the concept of administrative norms, is itself irrational . . . " (*Culture* 98). Adorno's point is simply illustrated, bearing in mind that, for him, culture is "the perennial claim of the particular over the general." The critic purports to celebrate the unique qualities of a poem, but does so only by appealing to generic formulae which are taken as the extrinsic measure or *rationale* of the poem's achievement. Adorno credits his formulation of this paradox to Eduard Steuermann (the great pianist, incidentally, and student of Busoni), who said that "the more that is done for culture, the worse it fares." "This paradox could be developed as follows," says Adorno: "culture suffers damage when it is planned and administrated; when it is left to itself, however, everything cultural threatens not only to lose its possibility of effect, but its very existence as well" (94).

There are problems inherent in Adorno's repudiation of mass culture (epitomized by jazz, which he mistakenly took to be *mass* rather than authentically *popular* culture as such), which I will pass over here in view of the fact that my topic, being poetry, is "high" in every sense Adorno intended; and also because he offers useful provocations about administration rationality and the cult of the expert. "Culture long ago evolved into its own contradiction, the congealed content of educational privilege; for that reason it now takes its place within the material production process as an administrated supplement to it" (*Culture* 109). As long as artists are formally *trained* in a given medium, then, this educational privilege establishes them in an administrative, albeit sacerdotal, relation to their art. By "administered supplement" Adorno presumably means that the material exigencies of capitalism do not include (high) culture at the core, but at the periphery, so the resident explainers or "experts" have the social role of *injecting* this peripheral activity into the mainstream, which means justifying it by appealing not to its intrinsic qualities but with reference to the absorbent social middle. Since poetry is inimical to the middlebrow comforts secured by consumer society, the ground of justification had to be shifted to the poet, whose life could be construed as heroic or colorful. At the same time, the *advocate* of high culture, submitting to such appeals in the effort to explain the "relevance" of the art, attains prominence precisely as an "expert," which is an approved social role fully accommodated to instrumental reason, systems efficiency, and the world of administrative priorities.

The result for poetry is that it ceases to be recognizable as such unless it makes a conspicuous show of *humanization*, which I would define as the mechanization of humanism in a technocentric society placing premium value on "the human" as abstract universal. When Robert Duncan speaks of such poetry as "chickening out" on God and the universe, his complaint is that the appeal to psychology and sociology as justification of the arts demeans the entire poetic legacy, denying or belittling those archaic biological and cosmological provocations which precede the modern liberal state. Adorno, alert everywhere to paradox, to the unresolvable contradictions of capitalism, noted that "[f]ew things have contributed so greatly to dehumanization as has the universal human belief that products of the mind are justified only in so far as they exist for men," adding that "the belief itself bears witness to the dominance of manipulative rationality" (*Prisms* 182). While I am wary of his apparently unironic declaration that this posture of humanism is a "universal human belief," Adorno's understanding of dehumanization is useful. Going against the generally Luddite disposition of Romantic modernism, Adorno's critique of Enlightenment recognizes that *mechanization* is only a metaphor, a convenient denial of the fact that the universalization of criteria for "humanity" historically precedes, and in fact provides a preliminary coding of, nineteenth-century industrialism. It is not machines that strip us of our humanity, but the very notion of *humanity* that dehumanizes.

Driven by similar concerns, Lionel Trilling defined the task of art as an emancipation from culture—culture, that is, understood in Adorno's sense as the consolidated repertoire of instrumental rationality, configured as the unique provenance of "man." Trilling, like Adorno, realized that the problem involves paradox. Liberalism's goal, as he saw it, was to maximize happiness for the greatest number of people. Yet this salutary ambition is constantly thwarted by its method, or rather its belief in method as such. Liberalism, allied with positive rational planning, constrains the passional and empathetic nature of its agents by *centralizing* emotion. This was the basic position outlined in the preface to *The Liberal Imagination* in 1950.

> So far as liberalism is active and positive, so far, that is, as it moves toward organization, it tends to select the emotions and qualities that are most susceptible of organization. As it carries out its active and positive ends it unconsciously limits its view of the world to what it can deal with, and it unconsciously tends to develop theories and principles, particularly in relation to the nature of the human mind, that justify its limitation. Its characteristic paradox appears again, and in another form, for in the very interests of its great primal act of imagination by which it establishes its essence and existence—in the interests, that is, of its vision of a general enlargement and freedom and rational direction of human life— it drifts toward a denial of the emotions and the imagination. And in the very interest of affirming its confidence in the power of the mind, it inclines to constrict and make mechanical its conception of the nature of mind. (xiii–xiv)

Trilling saw the predation of instrumental reason necessitating a reevaluation of politics, inasmuch as he tacitly credited Adorno's perspective that dehumanization could not be legislated from above, but must be secured as an inclination or ambition that seems innate to individuals. The individualizing pressure of conformity—the pressure exerted by the mass on the individual to be self-regulating—makes humanism into a kind of bootstrapping operation in which each person gravitates to generic human norms, but perceives this pilgrim's progress in terms of *individuation*. It is an irony nicely compressed in the command "Be yourself!" So Trilling came to regard culture as the realm in which politics was played out most effectively in the mode of self-regulation: " . . . it is no longer possible to think of politics except as the politics of culture, the organization of human life toward some end or other, toward the modification of sentiments, which is to say the quality of human life" (xi).

Trilling's critique of the liberal imagination is invaluable here because of its applicability to anthologists' ontologies, since the liberal credo is *the* rationale which has guided and consistently narrowed the parameters of poetry on display in anthologies, tending "to select the emotions and qualities that are most susceptible of organization," which entails (whether "unconsciously," as Trilling claims for liberalism, or not) a tendency to rely on "theories and principles . . . that justify its limitation." The coercive universalism implicit in certain overcoded phrases is evidence of this: "part of nature, part of us," "the cry of the human," and "the voice that is great within us." Wallace Stevens's compliance in coining so many of these epithets should be remembered less for any ambition to speak for others, but as a tic that pervades his writing, since his poetic persona tends to the regal plural of the first person singular. In Stevens the process of notating advances on a central self is always a peeling away. He has been mistakenly identified with the orbic cumulus of Emerson, for whom all things are eventually resolved in the self, where the more likely ancestor would be Thoreau, compulsively paring off senseless clutter, the paraphernalia of society as well as the crust of personal habit. Stevens's most Thoreauvian formula is that accumulation is progressive deterioration, memorably in "The World is Larger in Summer" (the second part of the late poem "Two Illustrations That the World is What You Make of It"). Yet this impulse is also Stevens's figure of nemesis, the "anti-master man, floribund ascetic" in "Landscape with Boat":

> . . . Nabob
> Of bones, he rejected, he denied, to arrive
> At the neutral centre, the ominous element,
> The single-colored, colorless, primitive.

> (*Palm* 176)

Stevens began as a Cubist-inspired experimentalist, who would appear to have advanced beyond his early irreverence; but in fact he continued to be a genuine experimentalist insofar as he adhered to a notion of the propositional imagination. "The Man with the Blue Guitar" is an exercise in repeating a basic premise with the genera-

tive sympathies of "suppose, suppose." In the exercise of "imagination as value" (the title of an essay in *The Necessary Angel*), "Poetry
is the imagination of life" (65). But such imagination involves not
the meticulous elaboration of a portrait, an image of verisimilitude,
but the perpetual donning of masks, replication of gestures and postures, entailing a ceaseless sloughing off which *devolves* the false
totality hovering chimerically out of reach. So Stevens approvingly
cites Simone Weil, who "says that decreation is making pass from
the created to the uncreated, but that destruction is making pass
from the created to nothingness." For Stevens, the value of imagination is to help us adhere to the incentives of decreation (which—he
might have added, but didn't—are in several senses *re*creation).
"Modern reality is a reality of decreation," he goes on, "in which our
revelations are not the revelations of belief, but the precious portents
of our own powers" (*Angel* 174–75).

Trilling spoke of "mind" where Stevens favored "imagination," but both were preoccupied with keeping access routes open to
"the precious portents." Trilling himself was never comfortable with
poetry, and insofar as he clarifies his belief in literature as a counter-
force or check on the liberal imagination, this is understandable: "To
the carrying out of the job of criticizing the liberal imagination, literature has a unique relevance . . . because literature is the human activity that takes the fullest and most precise account of variousness, possibility, complexity, and difficulty" (xv). The prose arts, ranging from
fiction to essay and jeremiad, consolidated a fuller account for
Trilling. It was for similar reasons that Karl Shapiro became more
involved in writing criticism than poetry during the heyday of liberalism, and after denouncing antipoetry as well as poetry found a personal solution in the prose poem. Shapiro criticized the reigning
modernist mode as "a poetry of reference," dependent on "predigest-
ed cultural contents"—a labor which rendered poets themselves
"hostages of convention" (*Children* 38, 47, 58). In fact, Shapiro's
repudiation of such conventions unwittingly illuminates the problem
specific to his generation of postwar poets, who were formalists (if
not altogether "hostages"), yet who were attached to, and ultimately
preyed upon, by the Romantic doctrine of poetic exceptionalism. It is

as if metrical conservatism demanded somewhere a manifestation of poetry's excesses, a demand met by the personal violence of alcoholism, sexual predation, and nervous breakdowns. For his part, Trilling was never disposed to credit imaginative autonomy: "Trilling did not interpret the relation between artist and society in terms so favourable to the artist that society could only be construed as barbarism and the artist as a tragic hero" (Donoghue 176). One might add that the role of artist as tragic hero is scripted by the society as a way of disenfranchising its renegades while at the same time preserving them, as it were, for an internal audit.

Trilling's persistent concern was to preserve literature as a site of engagement, as a kind of exemplary *trouble*. So he famously complained that teaching modern literature innoculated the disturbance that was modernism; and he generalized that "American literature as an academic subject is not so much a *subject* as an *object* of study: it does not, as a literature should, put the scrutinizer of it under scrutiny but, instead, leaves its students with a too-comfortable sense of complete comprehension" (*Liberal Imagination* 292). It was this administrative serenity that irked Trilling in 1950 and has continued to plague pedagogy ever since. Students are not often given affirmation that the meddlesome quality of a literary work should be preserved, let alone drawn out; rather, they are taught to "appreciate" literature, which easily translates into a directive to keep complaints private and squelch discomfort; or, in more authoritarian circumstances, given to understand that whatever they think can and may be used against them, and that it is better by far to recapitulate what has been sanctioned. Acceding to the wisdom of the professionals has tainted literature as much as anything else in public life, with the result that a poem is viewed with as much distrust as a complex plumbing fixture: in the unfortunate event that you have to deal with it at all, you call in a professional; and professors of literature are called upon, esoterically, to undertake a sort of cognitive plumbing (in, it might be added, the rarely used executive washroom in a remote upper story of the building). The dilemma, as Bruce Robbins has clarified, is less attributable to professionalism as such than what professionalism signifies. In his account, occupational ambiguity begins with "the contradiction between, on the one hand, an intellectual and political ideal of wholeness which gets called 'the intellectual,' and on the other hand a real, necessarily partial place within the division of labor, a place which is called 'the professional'" (*Vocations* 62).[41]

The Liberal Imagination refuses both the truculent heroism of the alienated intellectual and the serene confidence in a benevolently American way of life. Trilling saw these as alternatives of ideology, whereas what he wanted was a literature of "ideas." The conservative and the reactionary impulses, he writes in a much-quoted phrase from the preface, are only "irritable mental gestures which seek to resemble ideas" (ix). In the final essay, "The Meaning of a Literary Idea," Trilling spoke out against the mystique of anti-intellectualism he saw pervading modern fiction, and argued for a renewed respect for intellect. "[T]o call ourselves the people of the idea is to flatter ourselves," however. "We are rather the people of ideology," which Trilling defined as "the habit or ritual of showing respect for certain formulas to which, for various reasons having to do with emotional safety, we have very strong ties . . . " (286). Ideological respect for some formulas, of course, translates into disrespect for others, as Andrew Ross has shown in his study of intellectual attitudes toward (and in) popular culture, *No Respect*.[42] Cultur-

---

[41] Stanley Fish draws on Magali Larson's *The Rise of Professionalism* to draw a corollary to the effect that "the ideology of anti-professionalism—of essential and independent values chosen freely by an independent self—is nothing more or less than the ideology of professionalism taking itself seriously" (*Doing What Comes Naturally* 245). What Fish derives from Larson is her thesis that modern professionalism incorporates into itself the humanist dream of self-fashioning. "'Career,' she concludes in a powerful aphorism, 'is a pattern of organization of the self,' which is another way of saying that the self of the professional is constituted and legitimized by the very structures—social and institutional—from which it is supposedly aloof'" (244).

[42] Ross peculiarly makes little mention of Trilling, and in one instance misleadingly aligns him with "liberal imagination" as if Trilling were a proponent of it. Ross advocates, instead, a "liberatory imagination," which would go beyond the liberal guarantee of "autonomous rights and privileges already achieved and possessed," to guaranteeing the continued pursuit of unforseen rights, particularly rights that have no claim to "universal" status (*No Respect* 177).

al authority, as Ross understands it (following Bourdieu), is marked by the power to define categories of taste and evaluation, rather than from anything specific to the contents of those categories (61). From the perspective of the hegemonic primacy accorded consumerism, a poet like Pound all too clearly signifies the *unconsumable*, thereby invalidating the rationale by which poets like Hillyer assume a social role for poetry, a role congruent with the functionalist paradigm that dominated that "age of sociology." The problem was the credibility of the system, and *system* must be understood here as a functional equilibrium stipulated by the founding political documents of the United States and the recently emergent administrative organization of social welfare that, with the Marshall Plan, made Americanism seem like a viably global application.

The climate of opinions about general culture that made the New Criticism such a pervasive pedagogical influence needs to be seen against the backdrop of sociological functionalism. "By the 1950s sociological functionalism was increasingly regarded not simply as one of many sociological approaches but *the* sociological method," writes one historian of sociology (Swingewood 231). Another points out that "[f]unctionalism was a theoretical superstructure erected on the solid, institutionalized, academic sociology . . . reconciled to the existing social order at a time when the United States was not witnessing any major ideological confrontations and the social world seemed perfectly stabilized" (Szacki 502).[43] Functionalism has

---

[43] The spectre of mass culture in the fifties—which was the sociological topic most insistently posed for intellectuals and artists—is given a terse synopsis by Lhamon in *Deliberate Speed*: "By drawing in and suffocating any folk culture surviving outside its value systems, middle-class culture had *in theory* resolved all tensions. This was the nightmare of left and liberal intellectuals in the fifties and early sixties—from Daniel Bell to David Riesman, C. Wright Mills to Herbert Marcuse. These writers described the various processes by which they said the middle class expanded with its repressive tolerance (Marcuse) inhibiting any agency of change (Mills), creating henceforth a crowd that was lonely (Riesman) but sufficiently satisfied (Packard) or desublimated (Marcuse) that it would not, could not, think to challenge the dominant ideology (Bell). All these writers considered the large center of society in one way or another as insufficient, deeply uninviting, and largely unchangeable. And they called it Mass Culture" (139).

been associated with Talcott Parsons and Robert K. Merton, but that obscures both its lineage and extent. Emile Durkheim, for instance, advanced a model of social institutions promoting solidarity; and Radcliffe-Brown underlined the potential of structural and systemic analysis. Parsons emphasized the functional integration of parts to social wholes in a normative order, in what is the most pervasive of functionalist concepts. Social order facilitates adaptive mechanisms of integration and consensus; but one conspicuous problem with functionalism is that voluntarism is assimilated to the requirements of the social system. There is thus little sense of what has lately been popularized as "oppositionality," since in the functionalist view individual behavior is mainly a matter of compliance in varying degrees. This results in a somewhat inertial concept of the subject, which motivated later attempts to overcome the stasis of functionalism in the symbolic interactionism pioneered by George Mead (who died in 1931, but whose theories had a delayed effect). C. Wright Mills, one of the more colorful sociologists of the 1950s, developed conflict theory as a means of overcoming the simple functionalist polarity of adjustment versus maladjustment.

The appeal of functionalism, to a considerable extent, was its emphasis on wholes. A sociological holism with subliminal appeal to biological organicism, functionalism construed its object (society) in much the same terms that New Criticism denoted the poem as a well wrought urn. T. S. Eliot's famous paradigm of tradition as a spatial order absorbed the potential for change into the internal dynamics of a closed system—poetic innovation as functionalist homeostasis. In the postwar decade of liberal humanist hegemony, the spatial model was reinforced by the containment hypothesis dictating U.S. foreign policy—a model that led Arthur Schlesinger, for instance, to posit a "vital center" in which political will conveniently found itself reflected in corporate management. *The Vital Center*, published in 1949, "became the bible of the new liberals" (Guilbaut 245, n. 80). The static implications of the spatial paradigm not only ended up obfuscating the problem of social change, but tacitly lent credence to the internal structures of bureaucratic hierarchy. In the 1950s, this led to the cult of the efficiency expert, the systems engineer, and the prestige of expertise in general. Serge Guilbaut in fact uses *The Vital Center* to illuminate the way in which abstract expressionism in the arts consolidated the authority of a caste of "experts," in which the populist affiliations of the artists were subordinated to the interpretive intervention of credentialed handlers. Much the same protocol dominated literary matters, as the New Critics vindicated "difficulty," thereby setting themselves apart as the technical experts best qualified to supervise the internal equilibrium of that highly sophisticated machine, the poem. The professionals also allayed anxieties about poetry. "What is the fear of poetry?" asked Muriel Rukeyser in 1949. "To a great extent it is a fear produced by a mask, by the protective structure society builds around each conflict" (44).

In the 1950s the *cordon sanitaire* hospitalized poetry, which turned increasingly to the satisfactions of the recluse, the numbed enumeration of saving graces in a liturgy of damage control. Nothing more was expected, in fact, than that poets might continue to produce raw data for the managerial class assigned to look after it. Awards continued; careers advanced like lines on fever charts; and the literary establishment briefly achieved the sublime self-deception that the unofficial self-portrait of the age was in the hands of a few gifted individuals, whose compulsively personal revelations were conveniently homologous with the pluralist dimensions of a collective will. But the truth was that poets were, collectively, the boy in the bubble; and however gratifying their own minute gestures of metrical self-assembly seemed inside the concave shell of the poetry world, viewed from outside it looked very much like a supine comatose patient, whose lifeline was past medical repair and thus strictly a matter of interest to the sociologists. "He was found by the Bureau of Statistics to be / One against whom there was no official complaint," Auden wrote, as if for a monument to his adopted land. "Was he free? Was he happy? The question is absurd: / Had anything been wrong, we should certainly have heard" (201).

Part Two: "The Age Demanded..."

"The age demanded an image / Of its accelerated grimace" wrote Pound in "Hugh Selwyn Mauberley," lamenting the decline of cultural standards. "The 'age demanded' chiefly a mould in plaster, / Made with no loss of time . . . ." I've already proposed a further debasement in the form of the wax exhibit; my purpose in the rest of this chapter is to chronicle the installation of the official postwar exhibit of the American Poetry Wax Museum, beginning with the reconfiguration of modernism after the war, continuing through the era of fifties conformity, and culminating in the famous battle of the anthologies of 1960 which resulted in a stalemate that continues to mark the world of American poetry as we near the century's end.

THE AGE OF AUDEN

In 1943, at age sixty-four, Wallace Stevens gave a lecture at Mount Holyoke called "The Figure of the Youth as a Virile Poet." Having written "Notes Toward a Supreme Fiction" the previous year, Stevens was at the height of his powers, experiencing an imaginative rejuvenation as he approached retirement. For a senior poet in the full flush of what Hermann Broch has usefully named *Alterstil* or the "style of old age," this was a meditation in the rhetorical mode of chiasmus. To recapitulate the gist of Stevens's talk: as virility seasons into maturity, so senescence reawakens juvenile powers. Stevens almost seems to be rebuking his juniors by pointing out that his work is more youthfully virile than theirs could possibly be; for he is nowhere disposed to identify the youth as virile poet in any terms other than those of the imagination, where it is a "figure," not a person. But for the juniors themselves, who had to write and develop under the shadows of the vast primeval creatures of modernism, the imagination could be a treacherous resource.

James Breslin has described the atmosphere for young poets after the war as being poisoned by "the most suffocating presences of all—canonized revolutionaries" (*Modern* 2). The situation was even worse, for these canonical figures were publishing some of their best work: Eliot's *Four Quartets*, Pound's *Pisan Cantos*, H. D.'s *Trilogy*, Williams's *Paterson*, and 300 of the 534 pages of Stevens's *Collected Poems* appeared in *Parts of a World* (1942), *Transport to Summer* (1947) and *The Auroras of Autumn* (1950). Frost, Cummings, Moore, and Jeffers continued to be productive. In fact, with Yeats dead before the war, and David Jones and Basil Bunting not much heeded, the situation was acute for younger Americans because all the eminent senior poets writing in English were, for the first time, American. (Auden was still in his thirties at war's end: despite his prewar eminence, he was in fact Roethke's contemporary, and Roethke was still thought of as one of the "younger" poets when he won the Pulitzer in 1954. If Auden appeared "senior" by 1945, it was attributable to the longevity of his public exposure, not to mention the lustre of being English and thus culturally ancient by birthright.) The situation in 1948 prompted John Berryman's comment that "The young poets lately . . . have had not fathers but grandfathers" (*Freedom* 299). The "fathers" in poetic abeyance in Berryman's account included Tate, Van Doren, Warren, Winters, Léonie Adams, and Louise Bogan. Berryman's formulation alludes to the genealogical opportunism that characterizes his generation. Imitation of grandparents is less troubling than mimicry of the parent, but it was imitation all the same.

After 1960, when it was clear that Charles Olson could not be conveniently ignored, it became fashionable to dismiss or belittle him as a derivative poet, overly indebted to Pound and Williams. These views have remained commonplace among those who were never bothered by the nearly undissolved saccharine lumps of Yeats and Auden in Schwartz, Berryman, Roethke, and other success stories of the postwar years. The issue of literary genealogies is complicated by the anxiety of influence—or *anxieties* of influence more numerous than Harold Bloom reckoned with—and the reception of young poets is invariably guided by a sense of how their work appears to confirm yet also advance the recent past. The shamelessly derivative poets along with the disturbingly original ones tend to be ignored, while those who attract the most attention are those whose originality is obvious but whose derivations seem just subtle enough to make critics look good by pointing them out.

So what was it that made that generation's imitations seem like a plausible advance on the esteemed but awkwardly active modernist grandparents? In my view, it was not the maturity of the Berryman generation that proved appealing, but their comportment as juniors. It was *cute*, even if that was a term that would never enter the critical vocabulary. "I am not a little boy" ends Berryman's frequently anthologized "The Ball Poem"—a desperate, almost incredulous assertion. The early style of Berryman and Roethke was a kind of doggy panting for attention and approval, in the blatantly derivative rhythms and rhymes (and even image patterns) of Yeats and Auden. It's dismaying to contemplate the success of such barefaced poetic subservience. In the essay referred to above, Berryman noted that, "By 1935 . . . the Auden climate had set in strongly," and poetry became "ominous, flat, and social; elliptical and indistinctly allusive; casual in tone and form, frightening in import" (297). Cleverly designed to emphasize those aspects of Auden that Berryman himself had taken pains to avoid, this is nevertheless a decent evocation. But it overlooks the most salient feature of all, which is the *juvenility* of the Auden generation.

It was Auden who vindicated adolescent restlessness by dignifying it as a legitimate style in the 1930s. As with any style, there is a corresponding *pose.* This is the era Wyndham Lewis named in a pamphlet as *The Doom of Youth*: when the whole world has become a nursery, he said, the privileges of youthful liberty and independence are squelched. At the same time, the rest of society adopts a posture of subservience to those youthful fads and fashions which become the authorizing signatures of the whole culture. The great vanguard scandals of modernist writing in English were *The Waste Land* and *Ulysses*, but the affront could not be attributed to callous youth or juvenile adventurism, since the authors were well into their thirties. These works defined revolt as *monumentality*, rendering Anglo-American modernism distinct from the sputter and sizzle of the continental avant-garde, dada, and futurism. The portentous tone of *The Waste Land* galvanized Eliot's own generation because of the amplitude of its aesthetic soundings—the "police" Eliot did in different voices—and because the reverence accorded the filchings from Dante and Shakespeare outweighed the irreverence of the music hall and cockney pub allusions; but for the generation born to experience the Great War at a distance, in their adolescence, *The Waste Land* was not high lament but high camp. The flippant posturing of the Bright Young Things—Waugh, Auden—was a bad boy attitude adopted in elite circles for the choreographed "scandal" of the matrons and public school administrators. The combat weariness and desperation of the previous generation gave way, by the end of the 1920s, to a voguish petulance. This is what so enchanted those Americans who, looking with dismay at the broad representational canvases being unfurled not only in *New Masses* and Dos Passos's *U.S.A.* but in *The Cantos*, leaped at the new lyric wit as an excuse for not having to strain their modest aspirations, relieved at the permission to write poems and not obliged to write *the poem*.

The designated American counterpart to Auden in the 1930s was Delmore Schwartz. The frenzy of acclaim that greeted his first book has mystified many, but I think it can be explained by reference to the increasing juvenility of the culture, which had a desperate need for a boy poet to capture the public imagination. After all, this was the moment when slim Frank Sinatra became the idol of the bobby-soxers, the first inkling of the gigantic youth market that would be increasingly courted in the postwar years. Schwartz's metier, it turned out, was not poetry but the short story and the review-essay; and, significantly, one of his better pieces is a *Partisan Review* article from 1952, "Masterpieces as Cartoons," on the Classics Illustrated comic book series. As Schwartz's talent dissipated (widely observed from the publication of his second book of poetry, *Genesis*, in 1943, until his death in 1966), his early poems were canonized in the anthologies as a sentimental vestige of the "promise" his career had once, briefly, represented, but chiefly because it was not his alone but the promise of a generation.[44]

Schwartz's generation—which included Berryman, Jarrell, Lowell, Shapiro, Ciardi, Garrigue, Viereck (to cite only those who rose to early prominence)—was coincident with the last flush of youthful exuberance before World War II, the last generation eligible to be considered prodigal. James Hillman's account of the *puer* complex in archetypal psychology is germane to the American poets: "Eternal Becoming never realized in Being; possibility and promise only" (27).[45] Consequences of this ithyphallic promise are hyperac-

---

[44] The clamor for attention on the part of the Beats in the fifties is undeniable, but it's distinct in kind from that of the Schwartz generation. The Beats were not aiming for approval from the academy, or from the literary establishment (or, if they were, which is unlikely, their attempts were so roundabout and furtive as to seem inept). The Beats were in fact a genuine underground, not by snubbing their noses at academia but by refraining from the customary subservience of literary careerism. Ginsberg's rise to prominence may be attributed to the clarity of his literary affiliations. That is, as junior aspirant his "grandfather" models were obligingly evident. In fact, inasmuch as these consisted of Blake, Smart, and Whitman, Ginsberg's patrimony was, at the time "Howl" appeared, hovering on the brink of canonization. The intimacy of association proved to be such that, with each passing decade, the ascent in status of Blake and Whitman in particular ensured a corresponding eminence to Ginsberg. It may not be too much to suggest that, by giving contemporary voice to the rhythms and concerns of Blake, Smart, and Whitman, Ginsberg actually advanced their fame along with his own.

[45] This is more clearly applicable to Schwartz than it is to Lowell, of course. But Lowell's successive *personae* can be gleaned within Hillman's expansive version of the puer complex: "The single archetype tends to merge in one: the Hero, the Divine Child, the figures of Eros, the King's Son, the Son of the Great Mother, the Psychopompos, Mercury-Hermes, Trickster, and the Messiah. In him we see a mercurial range of these 'personalities': narcissistic, inspired, effeminate, phallic, inquisitive, inventive, pensive, passive, fiery, and capricious" (23). The masculine bias of Hillman's characterization is intentional, since the puer is the antipsychological figure *par excellence*. Psychology, he says, "requires time, femininity of soul, and the entanglement of relationships" (26). The peculiarly American pathology of puer-poets is convincingly confirmed in Hillman's etiology of the puer's incestuous relationship with the Great Mother. The puer is characteristically disinterested in a relationship with a woman "unless it be some magical puella or some mother-figure who can admiringly reflect and not disturb this exclusive hermaphroditic unity of oneself with one's archetypal essence" (25). The biographies of Schwartz, Lowell, and Berryman make this point painfully lucid.

tivity, impatience, an inability to adapt—hence "no development; development means devolution, and loss and fall and restriction of possibilities" (25)—and no strategies of "indirection . . . timing and patience" (24). Puer's struggles magnify the demeanor of the pantheon; the puer is the figure of buoyant eternity, the figure for whom everything is already achieved, and there is no need to develop or adapt: the characteristic compulsion is to shoot straight to the zenith, burn incandescently and pass on. "Hungering for eternal experience makes one a consumer of profane events," Hillman says. "Thus when the puer spirit falls into the public arena it hurries history along" (26). However, "by refusing history, by pushing it all down into the unconscious in order to fly above it, he is forced to repeat history unconsciously" (28). Schwartz and Lowell in particular sanctified poetry's reposession of the *puer aeternus*, preparing the field for the eventual arrival of Dylan Thomas, that immense Bachanalian epiphany of the profound infant. Paul Christensen imagines that "[w]hat seems to have awakened the *puer* myth to sudden vitality at midcentury was the appearance of Dylan Thomas in America in 1950—whose performances and themes were the *puer* myth in essence" ("Innocence" 161). But I see Thomas as the final flowering, the affirmative apparition from abroad that confirmed, for Americans, the wager of poetic juvenility. Thomas *concluded* a venture inaugurated by Auden.

Auden's was the preeminent example of the figure of youth as virile poet succeeding as public relations gambit. But his influence extended far beyond this, largely because of the incidental fact of his choosing American residence in 1939. The magnetism of T. S. Eliot as archdeacon of New Criticism extended to his poetic reputation as ace among modernist poets. Equally influential in poetry and criticism, Eliot's majesty also spanned the Atlantic, so that by the time Yeats died and the war was underway Eliot was *the* premier living poet of not one, but two, literary traditions. When Auden moved to New York he came with the intent to stay, taking up citizenship and immersing himself thoroughly in the literary life of his adopted country. Yet Auden, unlike Eliot, never succeeded in crossing the ocean: his poetry made little accomodation to American verse idioms, and reciprocally there was never any serious attempt to integrate Auden's work into the anthologies or histories of American poetry. In a sense there was no need to, since his influence was so pervasive it's as if he cloned himself into scores of poets publishing under other names and being anthologized in his place. By the time Richard Howard published *Alone With America* in 1969, it made sense that this book about American poetry since 1950 should be dedicated to both Ezra Pound and W. H. Auden.

Auden apparently determined to take up permanent residence in the United States when he and Christopher Isherwood were passing through New York in July 1938, after their trip to China. They returned together the following January, and a few months later Auden met Chester Kallman, who became his life companion, and who clearly substantiated for Auden the wisdom of coming to America. Despite his later seasonal residences in Ischia and in Austria, and his election as Professor of Poetry at Oxford in 1956, he maintained a New York residence until 1972. Auden arrived with an established reputation, although his stature was not what it was in England. But the prospects were apparent: Richard Eberhart thought "Auden's coming to America may prove to be as significant as Eliot's leaving it" (Carpenter, *Auden* 254). He was in fact readily taken up as an available master, teaching and lecturing at numerous colleges and literary clubs, and becoming a frequent consultant on committees and bursaries. In this capacity he is best known for his role in the 1949 Bollingen Prize award to Pound, and for his prescient selection of poets for the Yale Younger Poets series, including W. S. Merwin, John Ashbery, Adrienne Rich, Daniel Hoffman, James Wright, and John Hollander.

Auden's choice of Yale Younger Poets in the early and mid-1950s did much to sanction formalism as the mode of the period. But Auden himself had been a staunch advocate all along, declaring for instance in 1945 that every poem should "attempt to solve one new technical problem for oneself, of metric, diction, genre, etc." (Carpenter 339). By force of personal authority and conspicuous example, Auden led the postwar return to an emphasis on metrics. Obviously the New Critics' disposition to formalism was enormously significant, but theirs was a pedagogic and scholastic advocacy, whereas Auden was a living and inspiring poet (in contrast to Tate and Ransom, whose poems appear to have inspired nobody). "[H]e was the influence when I was young," said Louis Simpson. "He was the tone that everyone was imitating" (*Company* 248). But it was more than the tone; or rather, the tone seemed inseparable from the versified pluckiness of the Auden couplet, making for "a fascinating poetry of deflated affirmation" (Perkins 149). Auden's Phi Beta Kappa poem for the 1946 Harvard commencement ends with a perfect example of deflated affirmation:

> If thou must choose
> Between the chances, choose the odd:
> Read *The New Yorker*, trust in God;
> And take short views. (263)

Responding to a *Paris Review* interviewer in 1985, John Ashbery (who wrote his senior thesis at Harvard on Auden in 1949) commented, "It's odd to be asked today what I saw in Auden. Forty years ago when I first began to read modern poetry no one would have asked—he was *the* modern poet" (185). The key word here is *modern*. To David Perkins, Auden was a revelation even as late as 1950 when he was first exposed to him in college: "It struck me as the first poetry I had read that simply took the modern world for granted, as though it were entirely natural for poetry to speak of golf balls, gasworks, stockbrokers, bureaucratized work, and the like" (148). Auden pioneered a twofold reaction to high modernism when it was at its peak in the late 1920s, laying claim to the historic contingencies of the moment in an idiom that flamboyantly rescuscitated pre-modern versification for postmodern effect.

In the long run Auden turned out to be an occasional poet in the precise sense of the term; that is, writing *to the occasion* was a thematic challenge commensurate with the technical challenge of the verse form. He was in that sense the ideal figure to commemorate the feel of postwar education for Harvard's graduating class of 1946. "Under Which Lyre"—a loose re-setting of the Homeric Ode to Hermes (*Collected Poems* 259–63)—chronicles the changing ethos of higher education at that unique moment when enrollments were bulging due to the G. I. Bill, and the New Criticism and poetic modernism had become curricular orthodoxy.

> Encamped upon the college plain
> Raw veterans already train
>   As freshman forces;
> Instructors with sarcastic tongue
> Shepherd the battle-weary young
>   Through basic courses. . . .

in which

> . . . nerves that steeled themselves to slaughter
> Are shot to pieces by the shorter
>   Poems of Donne.

The patronage of Apollo is derided in the poem, since "Unable to invent the lyre, / [he] Creates with simulated fire / Official art." Yet Auden oddly also attributes to Apollo the demotic forces of mass culture:

> His radio Homers all day long
> In over-Whitmanated song
>   That does not scan,
> With adjectives laid end to end,
> Extol the doughnut and commend
>   The Common Man.

Auden maps the emerging scenarios of American verse and ridicules them all—academic, populist, and avant-garde:

> Lone scholars, sniping from the walls
> Of learned periodicals,
>   Our facts defend,
> Our intellectual marines,
> Landing in little magazines,
>   Capture a trend.

Such wit, not being native to American poetry in the first place, seemed thrillingly intimidating at the time. So Auden's exhortation to "take short views" can be seen as an imperious admonition (at least in its consequences for American poets) rather than an offhand clever cap to a commencement address.

It's beyond my purpose here to probe Auden's personal motivations: that his precepts had an enormous impact on the direction of postwar American poetry surely reflects the desires of his audience as much as it does his personal initiative. In any case, Auden's *tastes* permeated the mood of the times. The "age of anxiety" which he promptly named in his poem of 1947 was existentialist, psychoanalytic, and increasingly timid about its formerly strident political convictions. David Antin, with characteristic flair, belittled the Auden charisma in a sketch that is at once funny, insulting, and by no means inaccurate:

> It's hard to understand why versified Kierkegaard should appear fundamentally different from versified Marx. No matter what Auden says it's still chatter. The difference between the Auden of 1930 and 1940 is merely that people are saying a few different things at the same cocktail party. The only "position" one can attribute to Auden is a mild contraposto, one hand in his pocket, the other holding the martini. Which is what is modern about his work. It is modern because he has a modern role to play. The scene is always some kind of party, "Auden" is the main character, and the name of the play is "The Ridiculous Man." Original Sin, The Oedipus Complex, the Decline of the West, the Class Struggle, the Origin of the Species are the lyrics of a musical. There are no changes of opinion, because there are no opinions, just lyrics; there are no changes in style—even at a cocktail party a man may place one finger in the air as he moves to a high point. ("Approaching" 105)

Antin, born in 1932, speaks as one immune from the Auden appeal, much as Auden's own generation felt free to distance themselves from the Fisher King enthusiasms of the Eliot generation. But Karl Shapiro, whose generation was most susceptible to Auden, came to a similar estimation, viewing Auden's contemporaneity as finally superficial, and regarding him as as "one of those creatures flung over the time barrier by a nineteenth-century time machine" (*Defense* 116). Shapiro went on to argue that "one can understand Auden best by seeing him in the role of curator of the tradition of English poetry. One of the reasons Auden fled England must have been his fear of being recognized as a traditional English poet to the manner born. He has Poet Laureate written all over him" (119). Auden's move into conservatism in his later years took him increasingly out of the orbit of poetry's benchmarks; but no matter, his first decade in America was enough to make his influence pervasive and indelible.[46] At a time when there was an evident need to consolidate a sense of tradition—which in American cultural life meant a justification of the new political superiority of the United States in world affairs— Auden was *the* indisputably "major" poet on hand who was willing to offer guidance. The American modernists had all notoriously sought to found an American art on a European basis, exporting themselves and their art in the process; but it was Auden who was prepared to reverse the trend, demonstrating to Americans how to import a poetry culture, much as horticulturalists imported French vine stock to get the California wine industry going. The sense of tradition he elucidated turned out to be British, so that the result of Auden's presence for American poetry was yet another twist in the "Atlantic double-cross" so aptly named by Robert Weisbuch.

Karl Shapiro's debts to Auden were considerable, and the second volume of his autobiography, *Reports of My Death*, concludes with a pilgrimage to Auden's grave. But in 1960, in a testier mood, he was disposed to summary judgment. "Thus the master of the Middle Style, the poet who will probably give his name to our age of moral expediency and intellectual retreat—the age of Auden." "The retreat of Auden is the retreat from poetry to psychology," he explained, "an almost total sacrifice of the poetic motive to the rational motive" (*Defense* 141, 116). That's one way of putting it, since Auden's passion for crossword puzzles epitomizes the problem-solving attitude, as does his conviction that poetry solves strictly formal

---

[46] It was not until the late 1940s that the Auden influence began to be reassessed. Delmore Schwartz noted then that "[m]any good poets have been spoiled by the belief that they had to rush into print with a new book every year . . . [and] the example of Auden has intensified the natural desire to appear in print very often . . . " (*Essays* 26). At the same time, Kenneth Rexroth, prefacing his anthology *New British Poets*, remarked, "Looking back, it seems today that the Auden circle was more a merchandising cooperative than a literary school" (*Letters* 8).

problems at best. But the most illuminating comment on Auden may be by a formalist of quite another persuasion, Robert Duncan. "I'm not building a psyche; I'm building a poetry," he declared, corroborating Shapiro's sense that Auden's was a retreat from poetry to psychology. Duncan was disposed to see the distinction as involving a choice of quests, in which he favored the poetic over the psychological quest. He contrasts his own poetic quest with, if not Auden himself, the Auden imitators and heirs: "The ones who were in the Age of Auden (and for much of the time that I was in the Age of Olson, the Age of Auden was still going on) did not read that as a quest; that was something else. I don't know what it was, but it makes for such a division of poets that they glare at each other as if one came from cannibal Africa and the other one from the Victorian parlor . . . " ("Interview" 528, 519). Poetry undertaken in the spirit of the quest is not likely to take on the demeanor of moral expediency and intellectual retreat. And, in fact, Olson, Duncan, and many others with similar convictions about poetry were often described by the poets of the more Audensian persuasion as arrogant, presumptuous, bombastic, derivative, and a host of other epithets. Auden became infamously known as the poet who declared the ineptitude of his calling when he said that poetry makes nothing happen. Duncan, on the other hand, advocated a poetry in tune with holistic thinking, in which the concern of the poet is always with "*what is happening.*"

The contrast has been conventionally figured as one between energy and artifact, or "process and thing" as Stanley Kunitz put it in a review of the scene for *Harper's* in 1960. These terms of contrast are misleading, inasmuch as they derive from subsequent antagonisms between Beats and academics. In the immediate postwar years, the dynamic verve of tension, irony, and paradox as celebrated by the New Critics made the well-proportioned object seem for most poets paradigmatic of energy as such; for others, it was more like revving the engine in the garage rather than taking the car out on the road. The new pedagogic appreciation of the metaphysical poets made much of American poetry of the 1930s and into the '40s look flaccid and formally inept. "American poetry of the forties, which I grew up in, seemed to me pretty wooden. I mean, it was like living in a packing crate, and I knew I had to get out of that," W. S. Merwin said ("Art" 68). Merwin's career pattern is typical: the concentration of formal verse seemed to be a solution in 1950, just as the liberation of free verse would be for him by 1960.

Louis Simpson, looking back in 1972, saw the return to forms as a sign of enervation: "In the postwar years poets, like everyone else, seemed exhausted. Many poets were content to write in traditional forms, taking their ideas from the critics. . . . There were not men living in those days, not even poets, but masks, *personae*, aspects of the New Criticism" (*Air* 157, 165). While it may be true of mediocre poets, Simpson's perspective fails to account for the energized excitement, the sense of renewal, which greeted the early work of Lowell, Shapiro, and others. When F. O. Matthiessen edited *The Oxford Book of American Verse* in 1950 (one of the few American anthologies to include Auden), it was not an empty gesture to conclude the volume with Schwartz, Shapiro, Jarrell, and Lowell: they were the hinges of the door opening to a bold future. In fact, there seemed virtually no risk involved in selecting these young poets as a capstone to an authoritative anthology. So Simpson's wraiths of the New Criticism were more substantial than he lets on. The formal absolutism of the early Lowell won admiration because of its militancy: a conceptual brutality, coupled with pounding metrical schemes, seemed an authentic fulfillment of the New Critics' dreams for a poetry powerful enough to succeed modernism. Lowell later acknowledged the artifice, and the constraints: "When I wrote," he said, commenting on his first two books, "most good American poetry was a symbol hanging like a gun in an armory. . . . I had a mechanical, gristly, alliterative style that did not charm much, unless . . . something slipped" (*Prose* 286).[47] Lowell's choice of words suggests something mechanical, and Robert Bly was later ruthless in satirizing the mechanistic attitude of the dominant forties mode:

---

[47] Lowell's tendency to attribute the cogency of poems to their "charm" is telling here; and it's an infectious term for his primary idolator, Helen Vendler, as well, appearing in each of the first three sentences of her introduction to *The Harvard Book of Contemporary American Poetry*. In a seventeen page introduction, incidentally, Lowell is significantly promoted, appraised, or approvingly cited in twelve pages.

> The poem is conceived as a clock that one sets going. This
> idea encourages the poet to construct automated and flaw-
> less machines. Such poems have thousands of intricately
> moving parts, dozens of iambic belts and pulleys, precision
> trippers that rhyme at the right moment, lights flashing
> alternately red and green, steam valves that whistle like
> birds. This is the admired poem. . . . Robert Lowell in *Lord
> Weary's Castle* constructed machines of such magnitude
> that he found it impossible to stop them. Like the automat-
> ed, chain-reacting tool of the sorcerer's apprentice, the
> poems will not obey. The references to Mary or Jesus that
> end several of them are last-minute expedients, artistically
> dishonest and resembling a pile of cloths thrown into a
> machine to stop it. (*American Poetry* 16)

The metrical automata of the fittingly named *Lord Weary's Castle*
came to seem for many, including Lowell himself, attenuated, unin-
volved, and a bit precious like Hawthorne's Owen Warland in "The
Artist of the Beautiful" who vainly endeavors "to spiritualize
machinery." Nevertheless, a dozen titles from that volume continue
to be among the most heavily favored poems in anthologies, and the
book itself established Lowell as the heir apparent to the modernist
titans.

Lowell's seemingly meteoric rise to fame was only the public
manifestation of what was, in fact, one of the most assiduously cultivated of poetic destinies. It is not at all to downplay Lowell's innate
gift to point out that his success was in effect a committee fabrica-
tion. His teachers had been Richard Eberhart, John Crowe Ransom,
and Allen Tate; Randall Jarrell had been his college roommate; other
friends included the already acclaimed Delmore Schwartz, and such
ambitious peers as Berryman and Roethke. When *Lord Weary's Castle* was published, Jarrell—who had by then gotten a reputation as
the most ferocious and accomplished reviewer of the period—
acclaimed the book in *The Nation* in the strongest possible terms: "A
few of these poems, I believe, will be read as long as men remember
English" (Hamilton 122). In April 1947 Lowell hit the beneficence
jackpot, with a Pulitzer, a Guggenheim fellowship, an award from
the American Academy of Arts and Letters, and in June he became

Consultant in Poetry at the Library of Congress (he had just turned
thirty in March). Throughout his public life, Lowell was beset with
manic-depressive crises, undergoing repeated institutionalization, a
pattern that would doom other careers but which, in his case, was
less a problem because of the extensive support of his allies. It might
not be too much to suggest that Lowell was a perenially broken man
whose personal integrity was held together by the collective will of
his admirers. I put it this way not to denigrate Lowell, but to emphasize the solidarity of the push that buoyed him up as the unofficial
laureate of his time.

Lowell's glamour can be discerned in part by the attitude of
poets outside his inner circle. During this time, of course, Pound
was holding court in St. Elizabeth's, receiving numerous visitors,
Lowell among them. At Pound's instigation, Charles Olson attempted "an impromptu epistolary common front called the Committee of
Correspondence" to "'fight the fake' and 'promote the serious'"—
one of his contacts being John Berryman, who didn't take the bait.
"Olson's jazzed-up tone put Berryman off," according to Paul Mariani (*Dream* 183). In fact, Berryman had already signed on to the sure
thing as represented by Lowell. Theodore Roethke, ten years Lowell's senior, would, like Olson, find himself in an uphill struggle for
recognition. In 1947 he proposed to a correspondent, "I still say we
could function more efficiently as a Michigan mob (Seager, Roethke,
Jackson, Dick Humphreys) on occasion—as those southerners do.
Boy, do they stick together,—as you no doubt have noticed" (*Letters*
132). The "southerners," of course, were the New Critics and their
poetic champion elect, Robert Lowell. (That Lowell had abandoned
his family *alma mater*, Harvard, for Kenyon College, was tantamount to a blood pledge, a cult initiation.) Roethke maintained a
guarded friendship with Lowell, but distrusted his association with
a literary mafia: "All those greenhouse [poems] and the nutty suburban ones came back from Ransom, from *Poetry*, etc.," he wrote
William Carlos Williams—certainly the person to grant a sympathetic hearing on the subject of exclusion. "What the hell. But as an old
pro, I suppose I should realize that the better you get, the more
you'll get kicked in the ass. I do think the conceptual boys are too

much in the saddle: anything observed or simple or sensuous or personal is suspect right now" (*Letters* 111). The power of the Lowell mystique was so intense that Frank O'Hara, in 1962, and Allen Ginsberg, in 1977, felt sullied by the occasion of doing public readings with Lowell. Robert Duncan had the misfortune to be shunned at the last minute by *The Kenyon Review* because of Ransom's inopportune awareness of his homosexuality;[48] but Duncan later recognized the incident as good fortune instead: "So I was *out*, just read out, out, at a point when I would have been *in* at the wrong place. . . . I'm glad I wasn't in there; I would have been read not as an advertisement [for homosexuality, as Ransom feared] but a conformist of the first water" ("Interview" 524).

One of Duncan's earliest publications in the "official" literary world would be in Auden's *Criterion Book of Contemporary American Verse* in 1956. Duncan had been in contact with Auden by the end of the war, and had proposed to write an essay on homoerotic patterns in his poetry, the prospect of which led Auden to appeal to the younger poet to consider the consequences. "As you may know," he wrote, "I earn a good part of my livelihood by teaching, and in that

---

[48] The poem in question was "An African Elegy," which had been held back from one issue because of space constraints, and bumped a second time to make way for Wallace Stevens's "Esthétique du Mal." By that time, Ransom had seen Duncan's essay on "The Homosexual in Society" in Dwight Macdonald's magazine *Politics* (August 1944). "Originally I thought your poem very brilliant," Ransom wrote the young poet, "and it occurred to me that Africa was a fine symbol of whatever was dark in the mind." "I didn't think the particular darkness was defined," he added, though in light of Duncan's essay he was now disposed to see the poem as "an obvious homosexual advertisement" (*Letters* 318, 319). Looking at the poem, it's hard to substantiate Ransom's concerns. "An African Elegy" toys with Conradian stereotypes of darkest Africa to intimate profound distress, but in the text this is associated most explicitly with Virginia Woolf's recent suicide. The only hint of homosexual affiliation I can find is the figure of Death, who regards Orpheus as "my lover like a hound of great purity / disturbing the shadow and flesh of the jungle" (*First Decade* 14). In any case, Ransom appealed to Duncan's sense of tact, suggesting that the "homosexualists" should "sublimate their problem, [and] let the delicacy and subtlety of their sensibility come out in the innocent regions of life and literature . . . ." A reprint of Duncan's essay, along with the poet's own running commentary dating from 1959, appeared in *Jimmy and Lucy's House of "K"* 3 (January 1985): 51–69.

profession one is particularly vulnerable"—vulnerable, that is, to exposure as a homosexual (Faas, *Duncan* 195). Auden's sexual preference was hardly top secret; and it's likely, given the tenor of Ransom's homophobic response to Duncan, that the New Critical nexus was wary of Auden in the end for this reason. But Auden's circumspection set a precedent for many gay poets—O'Hara, Ashbery, Merrill in particular—in contrast to which Ginsberg's open homosexuality could be seen as a transgression of that code, among others. The Lowell circle, of course, was what one might call flagrantly heterosexual. The Age of Auden in America, given sexual mores, would never quite signify what Lowell—as man or as paradigm—could. So when *Life* magazine published a photo-spread of the new poetic star, Hollywood agents were quick to inquire whether Lowell had ever done any acting. As it happened, he was already starring in his best role: the figure of the youth as virile poet.

THE AGE OF ANXIETY

In 1935, Robert Frost responded to *The Amherst Student*'s felicitations on his sixtieth birthday by noting that "sixty is only a pretty good age [but] not advanced enough" (*Poetry and Prose* 343). He then punned his age into a world historical condition: "Fortunately we don't need to know how bad the age is. There is something one can always be doing without reference to how good or how bad the age is" (344). This is blatantly apolitical, considering "the age," but patently Emersonian: "We haven't to get a team together before we can play," Frost added. But in the matter of certifying literary success, teamwork would appear to be all. That, at least, is what the spectre of the New Critics' version of modern poetry implied. To many, the New Criticism brought stability to the volatile spirit of modernism. It was a kind of cleanup operation, this corporate packaging of a still fluid and murky legacy. James Breslin, in a handy formulation that spans both the Auden and the Lowell camps, suggests that "[w]hen the postwar period was not calling itself 'the age of anxiety,' it was calling itself (somewhat anxiously) 'the age of criticism'" (*Mod-*

ern 15). The anxieties specific to poetry were twofold, expressed as a concern about poetry's role in society: poets (and intellectuals generally) were stranded between the unpalatable options of the ivy tower and the monster midway. To enter academe was to submit to the maw of Criticism, Inc.; but the prospects for poetic populism were dim, associated as they were with Carl Sandburg, Vachel Lindsay, and Stephen Vincent Benét. Such apprehensions were of course inseparable from the question of the arts as such, yet under the sway of New Criticism and the sympathetic quarterlies, solicitude for the arts in the 1940s was often discussed *as* a question of poetry. Poetry was a flagship for the art fleet. The incommensurability between cultural activities and what were felt to be social needs was signified by what poets did, or what poems expressed. "[T]here is a new literary tendency [which] may be explained (in the sense of diagnosis) as a consequence of inadequate relation between culture and society," noted R. P. Blackmur, asking, "Why does Robert Lowell call his verse *Lord Weary's Castle*, Randall Jarrell his *The Losses*, John Berryman his *The Dispossessed*?" ("State" 862).

Henry Wells, writing on "The Usable Past in Poetry" for *American Quarterly* in 1949, spoke of this "inadequate relation" as a sociological problem of "adjustment":

> Urgent problems in adjustment between the artistic heritage and the creative artist have in the present century confronted writers and workers in all the arts. The root of the difficulty can be simply stated: At the very time when our data on the past have prodigiously increased, the rapid movement in industrial civilization sweeps us farther and farther away from what appears our rightful and often hard-won heritage. The general public, lacking higher education, is largely untouched by works leaning the most consciously upon the past; the creative artists and the scholars have thus tended to form an elite even more exclusive than its nearest parallel in the thought of the Renaissance. (235)

Wells's attitude is notably free of the common complaint that popular culture and mass media were degrading a pristine cultural heritage: he recognizes that the problem is systemic, inseparable from the entire social cycle of "progress" as economic productivity. The enlargement of the present, in terms of media exposure and available consumer goods, automatically deflates the scale of the past.

The more pervasive attitude, however—one which would be increasingly pronounced during the fifties—is typified by a contributor to the 1950 centenary symposium at the University of Wisconsin assessing the state of the humanities: "Art must cease being considered as a commodity provided by mysteriously endowed specialists for the delectation of an equally exclusive body of patrons and must become an activity in which all participate. Then art can become an instrument of social therapy as potent as security and health" (Chermayeff 141–42). The obvious damage sustained by the arts in the face of this demand continues up to the present, since it attributes an unreasonably recuperative potential to the cultural sphere, ultimately implicating the arts in the correction of every conceivable social problem. A position midway between Chermayeff's and Wells's is that of Blackmur, responding to a 1948 *Partisan Review* questionnaire on "The State of American Writing." "If American middlebrow culture has grown stronger in this decade," he suggests, "I would suppose it was because the bulk of people cannot see themselves reflected in the adventures of the elite . . . . The middlebrow does not want to be dragged through the adventures of his culture; he wants to enjoy it, to escape from it" (862). These three responses to the cultural dilemma of democracy leave the arts in a thoroughly conflicted space. An art that faithfully documents grim reality is unpalatable to the masses, whose tastes are escapist; but when the public repudiates such art, it's the artists themselves who are made out to be elitist. The problem, then as now, lies in the myth of a general public in the first place, which is arrived at by confusing *audience* with *population*, a confusion predicated on the modern phenomenon of mass education, and socially naturalized by the capitalist propensity to see consumerism as a human universal. Prefacing his 1938 *Collected Poems*, e. e. cummings rankled at the tyranny of this "strictly scientific parlourgame of real unreality" in which "mrsandmr collective foetus" pursue their "undream of anaesthetized impersons, or a cosmic comfortstation, or a transcendentally sterilized lookiesoundiefeelietastiesmellie" (461). For a neoromantic like cummings, the *only* role for the arts was to preserve the integrity of the individual in the face of universal imprecations to collective identity, whether appealed to in the name of democracy, communism, or fascism.[49]

In 1941 Delmore Schwartz had set forth his position on the alleged isolation of poetry in terms conspicuously similar to those cited above by Wells: "The fundamental isolation of the modern poet began not with the poet and his way of life; but rather with the whole way of life of modern society. It was not so much the poet as it was poetry, culture, sensibility, imagination, that were isolated" (*Essays* 7). Schwartz fails to follow his reasoning through to the next step, which is to notice that his terms ("sensibility," "imagination") have themselves been compromised, so one is left wondering how the poet's "way of life" can be distinguished from the values which make it distinct in the first place. A few years later, after the war, such tautologies would be more difficult to maintain. Blackmur professed uncertainty on the *Partisan*'s question regarding poetry's diminished audience, cautioning that "I am not sure we have not merely returned, for the kind of court poetry we write, to the audience which preceded the era of universal education" (865). The postwar education boom gradually confronted critics with the fact that

---

[49] "The very thought of being oneself in an epoch of interchangeable selves must appear supremely ridiculous," he reflected in his Charles Eliot Norton lectures at Harvard in 1952 (*i* 23–24). Confronting the perplexing tautologies of his homeland ("This is a free country because compulsory education" [*i* 67]), cummings railed against a nation overrun by "a fanatical religion of irreligion, conceived by sterile intellect and nurtured by omnipotent non-imagination. From this gruesome apotheosis of mediocrity in the name of perfectibility, this implacable salvation of all through the assassination of each, this reasoned enormity of spiritual suicide, I turn to a complementary—and if possible even more monstrous—phenomenon. That phenomenon is a spiritually impotent pseudocommunity enslaved by perpetual obscenities of mental concupiscence; an omnivorous social hypocrisy, vomiting vitalities of idealism while grovelling before the materialization of its own deathwish . . . " (*i* 103). Such vehement denunciations are not often associated with cummings as author of benign and frolicsome poems about spring. Those spouting the recent rallying cry "to reclaim a legacy" conveniently forget that much in that "legacy" is, like cummings, at least as seditious as any of the current academic "nihilists" they scorn.

the arts were not efficient delivery systems for humanist values. Teaching Shakespeare, Milton, and Arnold did not ennoble the mind and humanize the sensibility, except haphazardly. High culture could not, apparently, be transmitted through universal education. The G. I. college graduate still preferred *Gunsmoke* to *The Iliad.* Where Schwartz had seen society abandoning the cultured sensibility and thus isolating the poet, Shapiro was later to see that poets were imperiled by being thoroughly integrated into emergent middlebrow culture. Poets, adopted by the schools, became social insiders rather than cultural outcasts. Schwartz himself, like Shapiro, was a beneficiary of this pedagogic embrace. In 1958 he would reflect, "I feel no doubt whatever that the paradoxical character of my own experience is typical in every way of most if not all the poets of my own generation . . . . I was asked to do many things because I was a poet: the one thing I was not asked to do very often was to write poetry" (*Essays* 38). Schwartz's formulation cut to the quick of the dilemma confronting postwar poets, which was finding themselves inhabiting an anomalous celebrity, valued (paid, cozened) as poets in a society for which poetry itself held no interest.

The poets who would be much acclaimed, understandably, were those who demonstrated a feverish self-interest. Americans might not care for poetry, but were always ready to be mesmerized by egotism, self-aggrandizement, and raw ambition.[50] Prestige was attainable for poets not on the merits of their work but on the extremities of their behavior. This is hyperbolic, however, and a bit anachronistic, more applicable to the peak of confessional poetry in 1960 than to the late forties. Still, Lowell's literary triumph became, in *Life,* a cult of

---

[50] This is nowhere more evident than in the biographies of Berryman, Schwartz, Rexroth and Olson, all of which succeed as biographies of public figures, but which fail to give any corresponding sense of what the poets' passion for poetry might be. The task of the literary biographer, apparently, is to document the public side of private manias; but since poetry has no public side to speak of—other than the clumsy register of literary prizes and publishing contracts—these biographies tend to expose the poet as frantic lunatic, posturing and declaiming about nothing at all. No matter how well written, though, reading a poet's biography without concurrently reading the work is like watching television with the volume turned off.

celebrity, paving the way for subsequent mass media profiles of poets, culminating in the orgy of attention to the Beats, since they made much better copy than any of their literary predecessors. Lionel Trilling, responding to the *Partisan* questionnaire, excoriated the opportunism underlying this middlebrow solicitation of the arts:

> In such a situation we see the operation of intellect-pres-
> tige and sensibility-prestige, which are quite consonant
> with the other prestige notions of our civilization, the
> belief that there is an absolute, high-priced cultural best
> which can be acquired in cheap imitation. The result of
> this is the diminution of the common fund of middling
> responses to life, the depletion of the general stock of ordi-
> nary good sense and direct feeling. (888)

It's difficult now to see how one might distinguish "ordinary" good sense and its "common fund of middling responses" from middle-brow mentality as such, which spread by means of such appeals. Trilling, like so many highbrow critics of the time, was anxious to hold out the spectre of a more authentic model of the average with which to chastise the demonstrable *mediocracy* around him. Like others of his generation, Trilling had also passed through the Communist euphoria of the 1930s, and he was not willing to abandon the masses to middlebrow entrepreneurs. On this particular occasion, he resorts to calling the middlebrow attitude "Stalinist" rather than the more conventional "Philistine," because "Stalinism becomes endemic in the American middle class as soon as that class begins to think; it is a cultural Stalinism, independent of any political belief . . . " (889). Leslie Fiedler, who, like Trilling, was a *Partisan* regular, testified that "[o]ur generation is haunted by the memory of the profane mystique which created that drab memorial, [Communism, which] was at once a self-sacrifice and a self-assertion"—in other words, a new puritanism (871). "The proper anguish of our generation of writers," Fiedler continued, "is compounded chiefly of that social guilt and the uneasiness I spoke of above at having to reinvent the whole vocabulary of ethical responsibility, that stubbornly insists, despite ingenuity and patience, in resembling what our fathers spoke in churches we have foresworn . . . " (872).

The age of anxiety—which in Auden's poem of that title was linked to the development of a Christian consciousness ("We would rather be ruined than changed, / We would rather die in our dread / Than climb the cross of the moment / And let our illusions die" [407])—is here disclosed as political guilt arising from political disappointment. Many of the thirties poets who had momentarily achieved a binocular vision, resolving politics and poetry into a single view, now had only poetry (or "culture") left to hang on to. The emerging postwar aesthetic was clearly susceptible to charges of political nostalgia. William Arrowsmith, in the new journal *The Hudson Review*, criticized the *Partisan* crowd for universalizing the peculiarities of their own experience. Naming Schwartz, Berryman, Fiedler, Jarrell and Hardwick as "the core of what seems to be a definable group," he writes:

> What this group shares in common has been stated often enough: their age, their common experience of alienation and disillusion, as well as standards somewhat similar; their work is—"urban, alienated, skeptical, self-indulgent." While I cannot share PR's obvious enthusiasm for these writers, nor find real quarrel with the sensibility of the group (often honest and always desperate), I do deplore PR's tendency to employ the marginal experience of these writers as a norm—the tendency, that is, to make the Stalinist adventure and subsequent disillusion one step in an artistic *cursus honorum*, to accentuate the necessity of alienation, and even to equate intellectuality with neurosis. (533)

Arrowsmith here summarizes the gist of postwar leftist wariness at a moment when such critiques, in other hands (in Senate subcommittee hearings), would be escalated into political persecution. Blackmur caught the mood as well: "It is as if one's private hysteria were the matrix for public disorder," he wrote in 1948. "It is as if we believed the only possible unity and enterprise were those of crisis—against any enemy, for survival. We have a secular world stricken with the mood of religious war" ("State" 861).

What is surprising in retrospect about the various statements for *Partisan Review* is the omission of any reference to nuclear weapons or the holocaust. This is, I think, a peculiarity of the American literary establishment of that period, which was preoccupied with periodization: "If the twenties were Eliot's decade," Berryman wrote for the *Partisan* questionnaire, "and the thirties Auden's, this has been simply the decade of Survival" (856). Berryman mentions genocide in passing, but makes it clear that the real concern is that "[e]verybody lost years." This would account in part for the determination of soldier-poets like Wilbur and Hecht and Shapiro to buckle down to their poetry, after demobilization, with a resolution not unlike that of the small businessman turning his attention from combat logistics to the debit ledger. Both poet and businessman had to make up for lost time, in part to compensate for the advantages secured by their competitors, the ones who hadn't lost years to the war. And both would feel themselves pitted against a pervasive, if largely unknown, malevolence.

Lowell, Berryman, Schwartz, and Roethke were among the poets who avoided military service, advancing their careers on behalf of "poetry," a cause as abstract and potent as patriotism. Later, Shapiro would reflect that his generation was massively implicated in the professionalization of the poet's role in middle-brow culture, and traced the lineage, noting that "Williams is fighting for the existence of poetry (while Eliot and Pound fought for the 'uses' of poetry)" (*Defense* 144). Roethke, as dedicated to poetry careerism as anyone, was nonetheless driven by the sense that something more was at stake. "I think I've got hold of a really big theme," he wrote to Kenneth Burke as he made his breakthrough in the greenhouse poems, "it's got everything, involves just about every neurosis, obsession, fundamental itch or what have you. . . . It may take me five years or longer; but when I get done Eliot will be nothing: a mere *litterateur*. He ain't much more, anyway" (*Letters* 150). In light of the forces that would erupt with the Beats in the fifties, and through the deep image and confessional strains of the sixties, Roethke's sense that he was pioneering something was justified. "I know that poems that run back into the unconscious and depend upon associational rightness have a hard time breaking in on readers who are conditioned by the purely literary kind of thing," he wrote Burke in 1946. In the conviction that progress succeeded only as regress—that, in alchemical terms, the way up is the way down—Roethke specified that "by back I mean down into the consciousness of the race itself not just the quandries of adolescence, damn it." Artistic maturity, for Roethke, was clearly a *man's* job: "It's always seemed to me that many of these blood-thinkers or intuitives aren't or weren't tough enough. They just fart around with the setting sun like Wordsworth or if they do get down in the subliminal depths they get punchy or scared and bring nothing back from the snake-pit (or hen-house)" (*Letters* 116).

Ten years later, after Roethke had won a Pulitzer and the gaming table of polite verse had been overturned by the Beat scuffle, the scholar Robert Langbaum could redescribe "nature poetry" in terms not only more familiar to us now, but germane to broader tendencies in world poetry. "Our nature philosophy has been made not only by Darwin but by Freud and Frazer," Langbaum wrote. "It connects not only man's body but his mind and culture to the primeval ooze; and you cannot convey that sense of nature in poems about the cultivated countryside of England or New England" (331). As if to insist on the geographical fact, Roethke, like Bly and Wright later, was rooted in the midwest. Because "the new nature poetry is really about that concept by which living unconsciousness has come to be understood as a form of consciousness," Langbaum went on, "[t]he new concept of the unconscious . . . has extended mind to the very borderline between animate and inanimate nature. For it has connected the substratum of our minds with the minds of the very lowest reaches of animal life, thus reanimating all of nature and making nature poetry possible again" (332). In 1948 Roethke had patiently explained to Babette Deutsch that the protagonist of his poems was "hunting, like a primitive, for some animistic suggestion, some clue to existence from the sub-human. These he sees and yet does not see: they are almost tail-flicks, from another world . . . . In a sense he goes in and out of rationality; he hangs in the balance between the human and the animal" (*Letters* 140).

This was a return, not a turn, to the "nature" of Emerson and Thoreau; trusting to "the divine animal who carries us through this world" in Emerson's image (*Essays* 460); abiding with Thoreau's "wish to speak a word for Nature, for absolute freedom and wildness" in "Walking" (294); of Whitman's conviction that "the soggy clods shall become lovers and lamps" ("Song of Myself" #30); carried forward in the theistic brutalities of Jeffers, and only emerging with the sense of a *tradition*—as opposed to Roethke's claims for an audacious personal journey—in McClure and Snyder, among the Beats, and then Bly as the Barnum of wildness ("the more form a poem has—I mean living form—the closer it comes to the wild animal" [*American Poetry* 293]).[51] In the age of anxiety, with Auden at the helm and Lowell as the figure of youth as virile poet, the spirit of transcendentalism was probably as far from the center of poetic preoccupations as it had ever been, even in the pastoral heyday of the "fireside" poets. Poets are always busy discerning lineage, so it's not too difficult to see that the age of anxiety was also the age of Criticism, Inc., meaning that the only legacy capable of arousing a requisite anxiety was modernism. If there was a poetic unconscious in 1949, it was not Nature, but the international vanguard that constituted a more ample modernism than anything admitted by the Anglo-American New Critical canon.

---

[51] Despite his posturing as poetry's maverick, Bly's poetic conservatism comes to the fore in *News of the Universe*, his 1980 anthology for Sierra Club, which includes Jarrell, Bishop, Eberhart, Wright, Haines, Wilbur, Snyder, Levertov, Stafford, Kinnell, John Logan, Robert Francis, Robert Mezey, Mary Oliver, and Wendell Berry. Not that the specific poems selected don't work in Bly's context, but the commercialism inherent in the choice of names literally foreclosed the possibility of presenting poets of the 1960s and '70s more demonstrably allied with the ecological values *News of the Universe* purported to represent. I think particularly of Howard McCord, James Koller, John Brandi, Drummond Hadley, Keith Wilson, John Oliver Simon, Zig Knoll, Andrea Wyatt, Gretel Ehrlich—most of them published by small west coast presses like Capricorn, Oyez, Four Seasons, Coyote, Kayak, Black Sparrow, and Wingbow. As it was, Bly's only concession to the unorthodox was to dedicate *News of the Universe* to Kenneth Rexroth.

MODERNISM: AFTER THE REVOLUTION OF THE WORD

In *Partisan Review*'s questionnaire on "The State of American Writing, 1948," one of seven questions addressed experimentalism: "It is the general opinion that, unlike the twenties, this is not a period of experiment in language and form," the editors asserted, asking, "Does present writing base itself on the earlier experimentation, in the sense that it has creatively assimilated it, or can it be said that the earlier experimentation came to a dead end?" (855). In his response, Blackmur felt the time was unpropitious: "Experiment in language requires more of a culture safely assumed than we seem to possess," he noted, and "when a writer is responsible for much more of the substance of his culture than the profession is accustomed to, he will tend to submit as much as possible to the controlling aspect of executive form" (863). Put simply, reactionary politics lead to formalism. This presumes an isomorphism of social fact and personal will; but this presumption had been questioned by Schwartz and Jarrell at the beginning of the decade. Commenting on Eliot's famous justification of modernist complexity in the arts ("Our civilization comprehends great variety and complexity, and this variety and complexity, playing upon a refined sensibility, must produce various and complex results"), Schwartz criticized the superficiality of the equation:

> I think he is identifying the surface of our civilization with the surface of our poetry. But the complexity of modern life, the disorder of the traffic on a business street or the variety of reference in the daily newspaper is far from being the same thing as the difficulties of syntax, tone, diction, metaphor, and allusion which face the reader in the modern poem. If one is the product of the other, the causal sequence involves a number of factors on different levels, and to imply, as I think Mr. Eliot does, that there is a simple causal relationship between the disorder of modern life and the difficulty of modern poetry is merely to engender misunderstanding by oversimplification. (*Essays* 4)

Schwartz's concerns were justified, of course, but the solutions of his generation are in retrospect puerile; it was all too easy for poets to return to premodern metrics by appealing to a logic as simple as Jarrell exposed it to be in 1942: "External formlessness, internal disorganization: these are justified either as the disorganization necessary to express a disorganized age or as new and more complex forms of organization" (*Kipling* 80). As the decade progressed, fewer and fewer poets would entertain the prospect of "more complex forms of organization," reverting instead to models of complexity derived from metaphysical poets as annotated by the critics. When Olson made an attempt to speak of composition by field in 1950—explicitly engaging the complexities of that prospect by invoking Whitehead and Heisenberg—he was derided because the antiscientific temperament of the literary world disallowed such analogies, and could see in "field" only a naive recapitulation of the modernist law of homology: disorder within reflects disorder without.

Charles Bernstein, following the lead of poets like Antin and Rothenberg, laments the official version of a "gutted modernism":

> Many of the New Critics, like Vendler, constructed their own partisan map of High Modernism, purged of the more formally radical and avant-garde directions not only among excluded poets but, significantly, within the poets canonized. It is this type of gutted modernism, which frequently transforms itself into outright antimodernism, that may lead some critics to cede "modernism" as a project to its most politically and aesthetically conservative commentators and consequently to suggest that the avant-garde and modernism are antithetical. (*Poetics* 94)

While the admonition is welcome, Bernstein, like many others, disregards the afterimage of bohemian ineptitude lingering from the thirties, which was a powerful incentive to ambitious poets like Lowell, Schwartz, Jarrell and their peers to pursue a poetry of rigor, in forms that would reflect their determination as much as demonstrate their prowess. The general response to the *Partisan* question on experimentalism was not conceptual but sociological. "The experimentalism of the twenties as it has survived in a thin academy of revolt seems a tyranny of the Interesting as perilous as the tyranny of Subject Matter in the thirties," wrote Leslie Fiedler (872). Robert Gorham Davis concurred: "Nor do these young writers who would have been the bohemians, the avant-gardists, the radicals and little magaziners of the twenties and thirties constitute a dissident faction in the colleges, fighting against academic conservatism. With the emphasis on textual explication, on absolute values, on individual ethics and on the complete autonomy of art, the new critics and the old guard have formed a nearly solid front" (867). In short, the new professionalism—of critics in academe and of their retinue of formalist poets (also increasingly academicized)—was masquerading as the postwar's vanguard. Clement Greenberg noted the trend: "It seems to me that the most pervasive event in American letters over the last ten years is the stabilization of the avant-garde, accompanied by its growing acceptance by official and commercial culture," he observed. "The avant-garde has been professionalized, so to speak, organized into a field for careers . . . " (876). Greenberg's remarks were specific to the visual arts, and were less applicable to poetry. Mina Loy, Bob Brown, Eugene Jolas, and Louis Zukofsky—to cite figures who might conceivably have represented the core of a postmodernist vanguard in the 1940s—were never mentioned.

Even the attempts by certain *Partisan* respondents to vindicate the cause of experiment fail to address the general indifference to (or ignorance of) such figures. "Experimental," after all, was a term likely to be associated with Pound and Eliot, with Stein, but certainly with a *moment* a quarter century past. Lionel Trilling noted the opprobrium attached to the term itself: "Nowadays we are inclined to equate experiment in literature with the complicated apparatus of scientific experiment . . . for us the preeminently experimental is the contrivance of mechanical devices of form." But in his view, this was a red herring: preoccupation with form, he said, has desensitized us to *style*: "There is in English what might be called a permanent experiment, which is the effort to get the language of poetry back to a certain hard, immediate actuality, what we are likely to think of as the tone of good common speech" (891). This view effectively synthesized a tradition that would run from Wordsworth and Whitman to Pound, Eliot, and Williams, and would be reaffirmed by Olson and Ginsberg in a few years; and it's useful to the extent that it removes the speech impulse from the onus of its specifically modernist associations in the Poundian litany of Dos and Don'ts—at the expense, however, of grounding the poetic vanguard in presumptions that have come under suspicion as *logocentrism.*

Possibly the most authoritative response to the *Partisan* question was by Wallace Stevens, who with characteristic tendentiousness proclaimed that "[p]oetry is nothing if it is not experiment in language." Yet, having declared himself firmly on the side of experiment, he then offered an equivocation: " . . . central experiment is one of the constants of the spirit which is inherent in a true record of experience," he specified. "But experiment for the sake of experiment has no such significance. Our present experience of life is too violent to be congenial to experiment in either sense. There is also the consideration that the present time succeeds a time of experiment" (884). With this, we're back in the domain sketched out by Blackmur's argument—namely, experiment is a cultural prerogative, and is inadmissable at the present cultural moment. Not only was Stevens as senior poet an eminent authority on the matter, but he was living proof of the veracity of his own argument, having proceeded from the experimentalism of *Harmonium* and the Cubist perspectivalism of *The Man With the Blue Guitar* to the neoromantic sublime of his recent grand long poems, "Notes Toward a Supreme Fiction," "Esthétique du Mal," "Credences of Summer," and "The Auroras of Autumn." Stevens could have been equally explicit about his own experience, while offering general recommendations, if he had qualified his sense of the experimental a bit differently; it might have been helpful, in 1949, for younger poets to hear testimony that experiment was as much a personal as a cultural necessity, that *Harmonium* was as necessary a prologue to *Transport to Summer* as *The Waste Land* was to *Four Quartets.* As it was, however, Stevens's dicta implied that such benefits were specific to his generation, uniquely privileged to develop and then renounce them.

Younger poets were disposed to agree with Stevens in any event. The incentive to dismiss experiment did not originate in a repudiation of modernism itself, but in a dismissal of its perpetuation as habit for the next generation(s). James Laughlin's *New Directions* annual, started in 1936, turned out to be a showcase for an increasingly hapless and anemic variety of experimentalist posturing. At the same time, *New Directions* was lending credibility to what would become the postwar bastion of literary conservatism. Laughlin was publishing books by leading New Critics, *Maule's Curse* and *The Anatomy of Nonsense* by Yvor Winters (1938 and 1943) and *The New Criticism* by John Crowe Ransom (1941). Laughlin's publishing interests had arisen at Pound's behest, and the "new" directions he subsidized always reflected the accidents of personal contact as much as any distinct vision. Pound put Laughlin onto Williams and Henry Miller; Djuna Barnes' *Nightwood* came by way of Eliot; Dylan Thomas via Sitwell, and so on. Delmore Schwartz sent Laughlin poems after the first *New Directions* annual appeared, and became the first of Laughlin's actual "discoveries." Schwartz worked for the publisher for a time, and introduced Laughlin to the work of Berryman and Jarrell, who were published in New Directions chapbooks in the early forties. Jarrell, who was never one to conceal his convictions, blasted the *New Directions* annuals in 1942, not long after he'd appeared in one of Laughlin's *Five Young Poets* chapbooks: "Nowadays, seeing people being conscientiously experimental together has the brown period smell of the Masonic ceremonies in *War and Peace*; even Mr. Laughlin and the few Constant Experimenters know that something has happened to experiment—so *New Directions*, especially the experimental sections, gets more conventional every year" (*Kipling* 87). This was an overstatement, perhaps, but not by much. And to judge from the contents of the annual over the years, Laughlin himself seems to have agreed. Zukofsky, for instance, appeared in the first three numbers (1936–38) but never again. Insofar as New Directions is rightly heralded as *the* firm most closely affiliated with high modernism—and an invaluable lifeline for subsequent generations of poets who have insisted on the modernist legacy in a broad and eclectic sense (Rexroth, Snyder, Olson, Duncan, Oppen, Creeley, Rothenberg, Antin, Gustaf Sobin, Susan Howe, Rosmarie Waldrop, and Michael Palmer)—it is nevertheless misleading to trace in it any purist lineage. It is, for instance, disconcerting to review volumes of the annual and consistently find work by poets presumed to be enemies of the Pound-Williams line: Elizabeth Bishop, John Berryman, John Malcolm Brinnin, Richard Eberhart, Peter Viereck, and May Swenson were among the most frequent contributors in the thirties and forties. Of those more likely to be associated with the Pound impetus only Rexroth, Niedecker, and Charles Henri Ford appeared as often. In 1940 and 1941 the annual featured "A Little Anthology of Contemporary Poetry" set apart from the rest of the contents, and while most of the poets are long forgotten, the names familiar today are Berryman, Brinnin, Josephine Miles, Weldon Kees, and astonishingly Oscar Williams and Gene Derwood.[52] By 1950, Jean Garrigue, William Jay Smith, Anthony Hecht, Daniel Hoffman, and Richard Wilbur had all appeared in *New Directions*.

Apart from *New Directions*, traces of the vanguard had grown very faint after the war. It was not until 1953, so far as I can discern, that the demise of the vanguard was prominently noted as problematic. Reviewing the poetry scene for *Saturday Review* in March, Horace Gregory took a cautionary view of the rising professionalism of poetry in academia, noting that "One reason for a hint of darkness is the lack of an *avant-garde* movement in America . . . ." But even Gregory could see no signs of vigorous opposition. *New Directions* seemed "ancient," its value principally nostalgic: "Its swinging doors have the hospitality, half light, half dark, of McSorley's Saloon. Although little enough happens inside, one would hate to see it

---

[52] It would have been the *New Directions* annuals that exposed young poets like Robert Creeley to the predecessors they would find lifeless. Writing to Olson in 1950 about Cid Corman's literary tastes (which would be in this instance comparable to Laughlin's), Creeley is perplexed by the odd assortment: "If his [Corman's] taste isn't so eclectic that it can condone: Barbara Howes/ Hoskins/ Wilbur/ Eberhart/ you/ Ciardi/ etc., etc. I.e., no NEED to point out, very damn big differences in the roots of each. He seems now, to have a thing on Roethke. Okay. Don't know much of the work, but I respect the straightness. Whereas I loathe Ciardi. Shapiro, et al. Just isn't poetry. And I distrust, equally, Hoskins & Howes. As I do the latter's old man: WJ Smith" (*Correspondence* vol. 3, 16–17).

boarded up and closed" (14). The erosion of vanguardist presence in the decade after the war explains in large part the shock value of the Beats. The poetry world had become so settled, secure, and unadventurous that by 1955 it seemed unthinkable to associate hazard with poetry as Mallarmé once did. Symptomatic of the period was the confident reassertion of views about the avant-garde that had been advanced nearly twenty years before. "This happens *not* to be a time of great innovation in poetic technique: it is rather a period in which the technical gains of past decades, particularly the 'twenties, are being tested and consolidated," Stanley Kunitz stated matter-of-factly in 1959 ("Silver" 178). Two years later, surveying the warring camps emerging in the wake of *The New American Poetry*, Donald Hall explained to the general readership of *Horizon* that " . . . in the 1920 anthologies almost all value would have resided in the more experimental volume. One could try to defend the reverse today and argue that the current experimentalists are the real conservatives, since they are only repeating the actions of their fathers in the twenties." But by this point Hall was already moving toward a meliorist position, and suggested that "the split now is different in type: value resides in both camps" ("Battle" 117).

The splenetic side of the poetry anthology wars will be chronicled later, so my concern at the moment is to emphasize that the poetry establishment of the fifties was built on that sanguinary assumption of the forties—namely, a faith in the obsolescence of the avant-garde. The logic was consistent, from the beginning of World War II until the end of the fifties. Delmore Schwartz's position is emblematic, in that his version of modernism remained unchanged and (in his mind, at any rate) unchallenged from 1941 to 1958, when he confidently proclaimed that

> Once a literary and poetic revolution has established itself, it is no longer revolutionary, but something very different from what it was when it had to struggle for recognition and assert itself against the opposition of established literary authority. Thus the most striking trait of the poetry of the rising generation of poets is the assumption as self-evident and incontestable of that conception of the nature of poetry which was, at its inception and for years after, a rad-

> ical and much disputed transformation of poetic taste and
> sensibility. What was once a battlefield has become a
> peaceful public park on a pleasant summer Sunday after-
> noon, so that if the majority of new poets write in a style
> and idiom which takes as its starting point the poetic
> idiom and literary taste of the generation of Pound and
> Eliot, the motives and attitudes at the heart of the writing
> possess an assurance which sometimes makes their work
> seem tame and sedate. (*Essays* 44)

Schwartz is refering here to the spectre of the Beats, and possibly the
Black Mountain poets. It was a curious assumption, the basis of
which is that poetry has a certain *look*, that the rectilinearity of the
left margin is the norm, and that the stepline characteristic of Pound,
Williams, and others (and with it, the tendency to avoid capitalizing
the initial letters of a line) were deviant and period bound.
Schwartz's confidence appears to derive not from any reading of the
poems, but from a glance at the page.

A few years later George Garrett would make the same point,
adding a useful qualification: "Chiefly . . . the poetry of this advance
guard is conservative. A return to the typography and punctuation of
the 'thirties. With a difference. It is neither social nor economic"
("Grain" 231). The careers of Ginsberg and Snyder have been so conspicuously public and activist, that it takes an effort now to register
the force of Garrett's critique. It was common in the late fifties and
early sixties to characterize the "antisocial" postures of the Beats as
being *asocial*. Garrett's acerbity was not reserved for the Beats alone:
their opponents, the academics, exemplified for him a "General
Motors Aesthetic":

> Persistence of the "romantic" ideal of the poet as unac-
> knowledged priest-prophet-legislator has put a premium
> on novelty, on "originality". Result? The poet is supposed
> to *show* that he is changing, growing, improving, maturing.
> Sometimes a genuine demonstration. More often this
> means merely the grafting of tailfins, chrome and new
> accessories on a basically unchanging model. (225)

This makes the nuances of formal versification sound like opportunistic commercialism, but there is a plausible analogy of tailfins to

the increasingly baroque technical convolutions of fifties' academic formalism. In 1955 Richard Wilbur, responding to similar charges, noted that "As regards technique, a critic has called me one of the 'New Formalists,' and I will accept the label provided it be understood that to try to revive the force of rhyme and other formal devices, by reconciling them with the experimental gains of the past several decades, is itself sufficiently experimental" (quoted in Breslin, *Modern* 25). This statement dramatically reveals how Wilbur, like others of his low-profile generation, countered rhetorical energy and sheer ambition with patient expertise—"artists of the beautiful," as in Hawthorne's tale, resentful of the gross demands of their lusty peers. To point out the "experimental" nature of formalism is useful, but in the context of the period in which Wilbur's statement was made, it's hard not to see a veiled hostility, and an attempt to usurp the name of experiment in the interests of something altogether different. Wilbur's assumption, like that of Schwartz and so many others, was that of a restoration purview following in the wake of a revolution still uncomfortably near in time.

For all the willed amnesia, a case could be made that by 1962 "yesterday's revolution had become today's institution" (Cambon 5). Reacting to the common conservative assertion that the modernist "revolution of taste" had grown stale, Jerome Rothenberg declared in 1966 that "A revolution involves a change in structure; a change in style that is not a revolution" (*Pre-Faces* 65). Feeling himself at the crest of a social revolution, Rothenberg was unwilling to cede the modernist revolution to the chaperons of literary taste.[53] The institutionalizing of modernism inaugurated by the New Criticism had made the very notion of a vanguard coincident with antiquarian and scholarly interests. As James Breslin has remarked, the pervasive assumption that any new vanguard necessarily proceeded from the

---

[53] Rothenberg went on to cite a fascinating passage from Mircea Eliade: "Any form whatever, by the mere fact that it exists as such & endures, necessarily loses vigor & becomes worn; to recover vigor, it must be reabsorbed into the formless if only for an instant." In dispute in the poetry world was the duration of that instant, whether the immersion in the "formless" was confined to high modernism or extended into the postwar years.

old is plainly evident in Donald Allen's anthology, *The New American Poetry*. "Allen perceives no irony in speaking of an avant-garde that is also the continuer of an earlier movement in poetry," Breslin writes, "and he anticipates . . . one of the contradictions of the innovative poets of the third generation: the opposition between their effort to return an authentic spirit of modernity to American poetry and their evocation of literary predecessors as authorities justifying such an effort" (*Modern* 12–13). This is in fact the perennial crisis of the avant-garde, as illuminated by Paul Mann in *The Theory-Death of the Avant-Garde*. Attempts to depose authority in the arts become enshrined as the fetish objects of a new authority. It is certainly the case with regard to modernism, and in postwar poetry we can see opposing views of how best to dispose of that legacy.

The formalist, "academic" position held that modernism was an historically necessary moment, but a moment now past. The non- (and sometimes anti-) academic position was intent on maintaining continuity, searching for ways to expand on the modernist instigation. The most vigorous theoretical advocacy of this latter position—which it would not be inappropriate to call *traditionalist*—is found in David Antin's influential essay of 1972, "Modernism and Postmodernism: Approaching the Present in American Poetry." Antin's antipathy to the Lowell-Schwartz-Jarrell line leads to some hilarious if merciless characterizations, but his position is fundamentally sound as far as it goes. Antin's argument is that the underlying aesthetic principle of modernism is collage, and that this was repudiated by Lowell and other successful poets of the "Metaphysical Modernist" heritage. "The appearance of Olson and the Black Mountain poets was the beginning of the end for the Metaphysical Modernist tradition," Antin insists, "which was by no means a 'modernist' tradition but an anomaly peculiar to American and English poetry" (120). Commenting on the postwar penchant (epitomized in *Lord Weary's Castle*) for combining an historical sensibility with a psychoanalytically inclined introspection, Antin dismisses these as prepackaged notions by which poets and critics attempted to dispel the complexity of the real, while retaining a mild collage principle. "In the main, poets have not resorted to a 'sense of history' or to 'psychoanalysis' because of the success of these viewpoints in reducing human experience to a logical order," he contends, "but because the domains upon which they are normally exercised are filled with arbitrary and colorful bits of human experience, which are nevertheless sufficiently 'framed' to yield a relatively tame sort of disorder" (107). In the case of Eurocentric sensibilities like Jarrell's, "Europe after the end of the second World War offered an unparalleled opportunity. It presented them with a ready-made rubble heap (a collage) that could be rationalized by reference to a well-known set of historical circumstances . . . " (108). The result is what Antin calls "covert collage," and he scornfully dismisses the notion of history subsumed by such practice as "cocktail-party intellectual history. It requires no theory and very few facts, and is a natural collage" (111).

What Antin fails to consider is that there might have been nonaesthetic reasons for these tendencies, such as race. To reflect on the Pound/Williams legacy as it was transmitted through an intermediate generation is to confront the conspicuous fact that the major figures were Jewish: Zukofsky, Reznikoff, Oppen. The same consideration applies to Gertrude Stein, a major figure for Antin, and certainly a pioneer of radical collage. *Partisan Review* was of course the flagship enterprise of New York's Jewish intellectuals (Schwartz among them), but the whole spirit of rapprochement between the *Partisan* and the New Critical quarterlies meant that American poetry would be represented as passing from Eliot (and Yeats) through Ransom and Tate to Lowell: it would be emphatically Christian. Jewish heroes of the *Partisan Review* were Marx, Freud, Kafka, and the fictive Leopold Bloom. Two of the most celebrated poets of Lowell's generation were Jews, Delmore Schwartz and Karl Shapiro. Schwartz epitomized for many the condition of the artist as Jew—a role he embraced, voicing the opinion in 1951 that "the annihilating fury of history" would only be handled by those poets who, like the Jew, were at once "alienated and indestructible" (*Essays* 23). Leslie Fiedler also suggested that "the real Jew and the imaginary Jew [Joyce's Bloom] between them give to the current period its special flavor" (*PR* 872). The emphasis on Dublin's Bloom is revealing, because this is the Jew as isolato, a figure of that silence, exile and cunning for which Joyce was also known. Nothing orthodox, nor anything suggesting solidarity or continuity or community. Being the sanctioned singular Jew, however, proved troublesome to some, like Shapiro, who grew increasingly antagonistic to the literary establishment that had awarded him a Pulitzer at the outset of his career. To name a collection *Poems of a Jew* as he did in 1958 was, if not a transgression, at the very least indiscreet—especially at a time when Allen Ginsberg, ridiculed as a heathen and pervert, was the reigning incarnation of the Jewish poet.

It's not my purpose here to document covert anti-Semitism in American literary politics, but rather to point out the assumptions by which certain poets came to be regarded as the stars of the literary system in the postwar decades. As the anthologies colossally display, the WASP was the figure of choice. Exceptions were very few and far between. There would always be a designated "major" poet who happened to be Jewish, just as there would always be a "significant" woman poet or two. But blacks were invisible. Even Gwendolyn Brooks, who won the Pulitzer for *Annie Allen* in 1950, was rigorously excluded from the anthologies for more than a decade—a situation that provoked Shapiro to complain that the award proved a black poet could win a Pulitzer, but it did not prove that the Pulitzer was worth winning (*Children* 37). The Filipino poet José Garcia Villa had come to the U.S. to college in 1926, established himself in New York, where he was an omnipresent figure in the forties and recipient of numerous prestigious awards and fellowships; but, like Brooks, he was barred from anthologies. Nor was Langston Hughes anthologized, despite his absolute preeminence as dean of the Harlem Renaissance, while his contemporaries Richard Eberhart and Robert Penn Warren became obligatory figures.

These examples are, I think, indisputable evidence of racism. But to leave it at that is insufficient, because of the equally vigorous exclusion of other poets during the fifties (Olson, Duncan, Everson, and others) for reasons that have less to do with racism or sexism. At root is the spirit of conformism that permeated the postwar decade. The tendency was not so much driven by *exclusion* as it was by a specific sense of *inclusion*. The *virile* figure of the youthful poet was a respectable paradigm, and in the age of Auden—or, to be exact, the age of Auden's Anxiety—the virile poet needed to manifest a "rage for order," in Morse Peckham's phrase, a rage that would eventually encroach on madness, but which, in 1950, seemed primarily recuperable to the ministrations of a Christian existentialism, albeit with a sprinkling of the collage host thrown in for ritual effect. It was a comforting diorama while it lasted.

THE AGE OF CONFORMITY

> [J]ust as we had labeled our times the Age of Anxiety, and had managed to point out an ample and redeeming shadow of darkness in just about every writer who had ever lived— just at this point we suddenly found we were midway in a second solid, sensible, wealthy, optimistic, child-bearing era, one not unlike the times of Queen Victoria and Prince Albert. Out of the black earth of our evil authors and evil visions, we have somehow rebuilt our own booming 1970s, '80s, and '90s [sic], complete with their dynasties of Republican Presidents. (Lowell, *Prose* 130)

In 1990 William Harmon, using the resources of the Columbia Granger's index to poetry, put together an anthology, *The Concise Columbia Book of Poetry*, consisting of "The Greatest Hits of Poetry in English." This database anthology reprinted the top hundred poems (i.e. poems appearing most frequently in the anthologies reviewed for the Index), and was followed up by *The Top 500 Poems*. "The Tyger," it turns out, is number one; Keats's "To Autumn" is third; Hopkins's "Pied Beauty" fifth; and the highest ranking American poem is, not surprisingly, "Stopping by Woods on a Snowy Evening." There are only two postwar American poems that rank in the top hundred: "The Death of the Ball Turret Gunner" (#68) and "My Papa's Waltz" (#88). A number of other poems make the top 500, however, including one each by Plath, Ginsberg, Wilbur, Hayden, and Brooks, two by Eberhart, three by Lowell, and four by Roethke. The poems date from the 1940s to the mid 1960s, and it seems reasonable that it would take thirty or forty years for poems to circulate widely enough to make it to the "top 500."[54] However, most of these poems would have made it to the list earlier (if it had existed), because the dominant pattern of American poetry anthologies was established soon after the war, when a select catalogue of poems became in effect the skeletal support on which anthologists strung their wares.

To a surprising extent, "contemporary" American poetry continues even today to be signified by work written thirty to forty—and in some cases more than fifty—years ago. Here, in rough chronology, are the poems that constitute the "top 100" of postwar American anthologies: "The Groundhog," "The Fury of Aerial Bombardment" (Eberhart); "Bearded Oaks," (Warren); "In the Naked Bed, in Plato's Cave," "The Heavy Bear Who Goes With Me" (Schwartz); "90 North," "The Death of the Ball Turret Gunner," "A Camp in the Prussian Forest" (Jarrell); "Open House," "Cuttings," "My Papa's Waltz," "Frau Bauman, Frau Schmidt, and Frau Schwartze," "Root Cellar," "The Waking," "I Knew a Woman," "In a Dark Time," "Dolor," "Elegy for Jane," "The Lost Son," "Meditations of an Old Woman" (Roethke); "Homage to Mistress Bradstreet," "The Ball Poem" (Berryman); "As a Plane Tree by the Water," "After the Surprising Conversions," "The Quaker Graveyard in Nantucket," "Mr. Edwards and the Spider," "Memories of West Street and Lepke," "Skunk Hour" (Lowell); "The Man-Moth," "The Fish," "At the Fishhouses" (Bishop); "The Death of a Toad," "'A World Without Objects is a Sensible Emptiness,'" "Love Calls Us to the Things of This World," "Year's End," "Museum Piece," "A Baroque Wall-Fountain in the Villa Sciarra," "Still, Citizen Sparrow," "Advice to a Prophet" (Wilbur); "Auto Wreck" (Shapiro); "The Kingsfishers," "Maximus, To Himself," "I, Maximus of Gloucester, To You" (Olson); "I Know a Man," "A Wicker Basket," "The Rain" (Creeley); "In Goya's Greatest Scenes" (Ferlinghetti); "Marriage" (Corso); "Howl," "A Supermarket in Califor-

---

54 That Gwendolyn Brooks and Robert Hayden outstrip so many of their peers is a telling indicator of the momentum of the emerging multicultural curriculum over the past twenty-five years. After all, they did not break the color line of anthologies until quite late (1962 for Brooks, 1970 for Hayden); so their appearance in *The Top 500 Poems* can be read as a seismographic register of deep cultural and pedagogic restructuring.

nia," "Sunflower Sutra," "America," "Kaddish," "To Aunt Rose" (Gins-
berg); "Riprap," "Piute Creek," "Myths and Texts" [selections] (Snyder);
"Poem Beginning With a Line by Pindar," "Often I am Permitted to
Return to a Meadow" (Duncan); various poems from the sequence "A
Street in Bronzeville" (Gwendolyn Brooks); "Those Winter Sundays"
(Hayden); "'More Light! More Light!'" (Hecht); "The Drunk in the Fur-
nace" (Merwin); "The Goose Fish" (Nemerov); "Some Trees," "The
Painter," "The Instruction Manual" (Ashbery); "To the Harbormaster,"
"Ave Maria," "Poem ['The eager note on my door']," "Why I Am Not a
Painter," "A Step Away from Them" (O'Hara); "In Memory of Radio"
(Baraka); "The Colossus," "Daddy," "Ariel," "Lady Lazarus," "Fever
103" (Plath); "Aunt Jennifer's Tigers," "Snapshots of a Daughter-in-
Law," "The Trees" (Rich); "Her Kind," "The Truth the Dead Know,"
"All My Pretty Ones" (Sexton); "My Father in the Night Commanding
No," "To the Western World" (Simpson); "April Inventory," "Heart's
Needle," "Mementos," "A Flat One" (Snodgrass); "Love Song: I and
Thou" (Dugan); "The Heaven of Animals" (Dickey); "Travelling
Through the Dark," "At the Bomb Testing Sight" (Stafford); "A Bless-
ing," "Saint Judas," "Lying in a Hammock at William Duffy's Farm,"
"Autumn Begins in Martin's Ferry, Ohio" (Wright); "Poem in Three
Parts" (Bly); "So I Said I Am Ezra" (Ammons).

All of these poems were written, and in most cases anthologized, in the quarter-century after 1940. As the most anthologized
poems of the period, these are the poems by which their authors
have been particularly known to generations of students. While other
poets have advanced in the anthologies to comparable prominence
during the past thirty years, only a few poems have attained an
equivalent canonical rank.[55] So durable has this hegemony proven to

---

[55] Ammons' "Corson's Inlet," some of Berryman's "Dream Songs," a few
late poems by Jarrell, Lowell and Bishop, "The Sheep Child" and "Cherrylog
Road" by Dickey, "Nightmare Begins Responsibility" by Harper, "The Bear"
by Kinnell, "The Jacob's Ladder" by Levertov, "They Feed They Lion" and
"Animals are Passing from Our Lives" by Levine, "The Broken Home" by
Merrill, "For the Anniversary of My Death" and "The Asians Dying" by Merwin, "Diving into the Wreck" and "Planetarium" by Rich, "Keeping Things
Whole" by Strand, and "In Response to a Rumor That the Oldest Whore-
house in Wheeling, West Virgina, Has Been Shut Down" by James Wright.

be that, even as a recent spate of anthologies shows clear signs of moving in a different direction, it will be some time before the *habitual* transmission of these primary units of poetic display cease being shipped out as if by standing order from local jobbers. While it's to be expected that the senior poets of an age will go through a period of being pervasive in the anthologies, what is unusual about the mid-century Americans is that most of them were in effect canonized as younger poets, the result of which was an extremely inflexible canon, since anthologists and critics patiently set space aside to account for every nuance of "growth" and "maturity" in those poets already delegated as significant. F. O. Matthiessen, the dean of American literary scholarship by World War II—author of *American Renaissance* and *The Achievement of T. S. Eliot*—edited the revised edition of *The Oxford Book of American Verse*. Published in 1950, this was one of the few such collections to take the formality of Auden's citizenship seriously and present him as an American poet. Matthiessen's collection culminated with the four poets most consistently designated in the previous decade as the cream of the new poetic crop: Schwartz, Shapiro, Jarrell, and Lowell. Matthiessen's choice proved to be the photographic negative to which subsequent anthologies would invariably be exposed. The charter of postwar verse was established very early in the anthologies, determining rank and file; artificially sustaining the careers of numerous burnouts; and generally setting the protocol for what anthologists up to the present have regarded as an obligatory table of contents.

The most expedient place to begin is with John Ciardi's inventive presentation, *Mid-Century American Poets* (Twayne 1950). Fifteen poets (Wilbur, Viereck, Rukeyser, Roethke, Shapiro, W. T. Scott, Nims, Mayo, Lowell, Jarrell, Holmes, Eberhart, Ciardi, Bishop, Schwartz),[56] each represented by ten to fifteen pages of poems, were

---

[56] Some of these poets will be unfamiliar to contemporary readers. I've already mentioned Viereck in the context of Pound's Bollingen; and about Holmes and Mayo I know little. Nims continues to be a respected translator; but the most interesting of the lesser known of Ciardi's *Mid-Century* poets is Winfield Townley Scott. Scott was one of a circle of Boston area poets organized into an informal club by John Holmes the year Ciardi was assembling

invited by the editor to preface their work by responding to a questionnaire. The adroit blend of text and context assured the seriousness of the undertaking, and also set the conditions for the reception of the poems themselves. As Ciardi was assembling his collection the boom in higher education was in full swing. This pedagogic windfall had dropped into the lap of *Understanding Poetry* by Brooks and Warren (1938, revised in 1950) and comparable anthologies which provided lyric specimens for classroom dissection. Ciardi's strategy thus represents a shrewd bit of market analysis; *Mid-Century American Poets* may be likened to such period marvels as do-it-yourself home kits in woodworking or elementary chemistry, providing the conceptual flasks and beakers with which to conduct experiments on such volatile *materia poetica* as "Still, Citizen Sparrow," "The Quaker Graveyard in Nantucket," and "The Man-Moth."

Ciardi's witty foreword performs a dual function, in which he makes a case for the validity of American verse, then provides a

---

his anthology (others involved were Ciardi himself, Eberhart, Wilbur, and May Sarton) (Donaldson 212). When *Mid-Century American Poets* appeared, William Carlos Williams singled out Scott in a review as the best of the lot (227). Scott was apparently a rousing public reader, and Donald Gallup at Yale informed him, "You now rank by popular acclaim with Eliot as the two poets most successful at reading their own works" (226). He had a wide circle of friends, and his biographer cites, among his visitors in Santa Fe, Malcolm Cowley, Eberhart, Justin Kaplan, M. L. Rosenthal, and William Stafford (288–89). George Elliott, whose textbook *Fifteen Modern American Poets* (1956) included Lowell, Roethke, Wilbur and Jarrell, regarded Scott as the most accomplished of them all (378). Why, then, is he so unknown? I think that, in his case as in so many others, it was a matter of timing—bad timing. Born in 1910, he published six books of poetry before he was forty, including one with New Directions in 1942. But from 1948 to 1958 he published nothing, although he regularly appeared in anthologies during that time. Then, in a brief span, he published voluminously: *The Dark Sister* (a book-length poem, 1958), *Scrimshaw* (1959), *Exiles and Fabrications* (1961), *Collected Poems 1937–1962* (1962) and *Change of Weather* (1964). The problem with all this productivity was timing, as these titles span the years from Lowell's *Life Studies* to *For the Union Dead* and the rise of confessionalism; they also coincide with Donald Allen's *New American Poetry* anthology; and, finally, with the attention-grabbing mid-career stylistic changes of such poets as Merwin, Rich, and James Wright. Scott, a contemporary of Olson's, was in effect putting a cap on a career—and a poetic idiom—forged decades before, and in the turbulent years of the early sixties there was scant interest in what his work amounted to.

series of numbered instructions for reading modern poetry. An historical map justifies the terms of poetic maturity, while the vexing issue of modernity is approached as a technical problem. In a single motion, then, Ciardi corroborates his generation's accomplishments: a canon is subtly but patently formed as a sort of thought-experiment in the milieu of instructional expedience. There is a tacit correlation between the educational prospect of correct reading on the one hand, and a set of exemplary (or at least inevitable) texts on which to perform that reading. Ciardi reviews three factors that he sees enabling the mid-century maturation of American verse, under the following headings: "the barbaric yawp and its exhaustion," "the capture of the American voice-box," and "the ferment of technique." Taken together they form a chronicle of the nation achieving poetic maturity. The "yawp" is a necessary stage now past: "Americas cannot happen without noise. America had to make loud poetry before it could make good poetry" (xi). The second point is cannily worded, as Ciardi distinguishes between the mere reproduction of common speech—vocal mimesis as subordination of higher poetic powers—and the "poetic stylization of that speech" (xii). The vocal chore proposed, then, is one of "capture" and containment. Ciardi's perspective is easily accommodated to the foreign policy preoccupation with "containment" strategies for checking the spread of Communism.

The third factor in Ciardi's account of American verse maturity continues to have the broadest implications. By "ferment of technique" Ciardi means that the unabashed spirit of modernist experimentalism—with Pound as designated "high priest"—is thankfully over. No longer in the clutches of "manifestoes and petty dictatorships," the poets of 1950 can fondly reflect on the "quaintly mad" antics of their predecessors, whose "venturesome excitement" nevertheless "did leave succeeding poets with a stock of techniques . . . " (xiii). There are some contradictory impulses at work in Ciardi's account. He criticizes the modernists for emphasizing technique above subject matter, while at the same time crediting them with enlarging the storehouse of poetic techniques. By now, it's clear that the very poets Ciardi sponsored in his own anthology have claimed the attention of readers, critics, historians, and subsequent anthologists, specifically for their technical skills. Ciardi's conflation of two impulses—antiformalism and "poetic stylization"—has proven characteristic of many of the antagonisms of postwar poetry. Adherents of traditional metrics, from the New Critics of 1945 to the New Formalists of 1985, persistently claim that "technique" is acceptable only when distinguishable from invention or "experimentation." At issue is a misplaced notion of authenticity. Such *tours de force* of traditional prosody as we find embedded in Zukofsky's *"A"* or Duncan's "Seventeenth Century Metaphysical Suite" are irreversibly tainted by their "experimental" contexts, while the bland "purities" of Brad Leithauser are lionized as unimpeachable instances of "strong measures." Ciardi's propositions revealingly implicate the roots of formalism in a fear of the avant-garde. If an "anxiety of influence" may be applied to periods as well as individuals, the current climate of a "return to the basics" of traditional meter is grounded in the anxiety that "technique" may also include the early twentieth century. The 1990s sonnet or villanelle has to work very hard to bypass the technical provocations of the present century. And from Ciardi to the present, the consistent mode of denial has been to associate poetic technique with "tradition," while setting modernist precedent to the side as a technique under erasure, "a bit precious and a bit insane" (xiii).

Having established the credentials of American verse dignity at midcentury, Ciardi enumerates six principles for accurate and pleasurable reading. Ciardi's wit and charm percolate through his ingratiating appeal to the reader. The first point, for instance, "is delight: if you mean to enjoy the poem as a poem, stop cross-examining it, stop trying to force it to 'make sense.' The poem *is* sense. Or if you must cross-examine, remember at least that the third degree is not the poem" (xvii). Point one, then, is that the poem is not to be confused with a paraphrase. This may be grasped by allowing the poem its full physical presence, as suggested in ensuing points. Two: avoid speed reading; discern the natural rhythm of the work. "Look for the notation within the poem. Every poem is in part an effort to reconstruct the poet's speaking voice." Three is a corollary: read it aloud.

Points four through six make fundamental distinctions between modern and traditional poetry. The nineteenth century was susceptible to "one dreadful flaw: it tended to take itself much too seriously" (xviii). Against the gravity of the forefathers, modern readers are to relax with a more inclusive poetry which Ciardi pinpoints in the "tradition [of] the poetry of 'wit.'" This will prove an enormously influential decision in the subsequent mapping of poetic activity, for what Ciardi proposes is that the dank baggage of the previous century be replaced not by the present century but by the *previous* century, the era of wit. The "courtier" poetics of Wilbur—the lead-off poet in Ciardi's collection—are intimated as a solution to a seemingly insoluble dilemma: how to dispose of several centuries while not losing one's footing in the present. To have proposed in 1950, as Ciardi did, that the poetic voice was not to sully itself with pontification, was in effect to withdraw poetry from the increasingly shrill political clamor of the public domain; but it was also to stigmatize political concerns in American poetry for some years to come. In 1956, when the voice of political poetry returned in the person of Allen Ginsberg, the hectoring impieties, the barbaric yawp, and an adolescent irreverence seemed inevitably part of that voice. Some of this may be attributed to the timbre of media discourse, but we might also consider Ciardi's proscription of gravity from the poetic voice. As political poets go, Ginsberg is surely afflicted with a trace of wit, which has made him more congenial to poetic conservatives than, say, the more somber Olson.

Ciardi's fourth point is not actually a proposition about wit (though it does subsume a lengthy excursion recommending wit over zealotry); rather, in keeping with his emphasis on the tactile qualities which preceding points had stressed, Ciardi urges readers to *hear* and heed the poet's intention. Not to be swayed by Wimsatt's warnings about the intentional fallacy, Ciardi affirms: "Judge the poet by his intent" (xix). I detect in this cautionary statement a slight anxiety, perhaps, that the traces of wit may be too delicately woven into the filigree of the text to be noticed. The danger is that these midcentury poets may be mistakenly apprehended as over-serious. Behind this hovers the spectre of that new medium, television, with its appeal to the gutbusting antics and the raucous humor of the music hall and vaudeville (television broadcasting in 1950 was still live). While Ciardi confidently proclaims the curative properties of wit, he is nervously aware that this may be too fey a quality to be apprehended without careful attunement. Accordingly, points five and six are intended to remove all traces of gentility from the prospect of the contemporary poem. This is poetry, he insists, not *poesy*. "Poesy, which is always anti-poetry, wants it pretty" (xxi). Beware the pretty, and the delicate sentiment. These are the feminine features of obsolescent poetry, terminated along with the catalogue rhetoric of the male yawpers chronicling "the sweat-soaked glories of barbaric America" (xi). Finally, Ciardi would cleanse the poem of any taint of potpourri, mop, or crankshaft: "Point six, then: the poem does not exist to confirm moral, political, or religious prejudgments. The poem as a poem is in fact amoral" (xxii). He might as well be describing the atomic bomb: a neutral device, the use of which reflects the moral caliber of the user. He is quick to add that it's the poem, not the poet, that is amoral.

The occupation of a global moral center was of course the primary ideological feature of America's postwar self-definition. Geopolitical strategies were redescribed in terms of geophysics, as the nation moved to the right (no longer occupied by the defeated fascists) in order to "balance" the escalating power of the Soviets. American "good will" was exercised in the form of postwar military occupation, consolidated below the surface with the escalation of intelligence activities. The two components of American identity which the State Department wished to present abroad are curiously adopted by Ciardi to convince his audience to embrace the "midcentury American poets." First and foremost—and unique to this particular generation—is that "these poets *want* to be understood" (xxix). "For preeminently this is a generation not of bohemian extravagance but of self-conscious sanity in an urbane and cultivated poetry that is the antithesis of the bohemian spirit." (Little did he know that they would become the manic-depressive, suicidal tribe, the Confessional Poets.) The second claim, a "fact" that Ciardi professes to find "both impressive and hopeful, is the absence of authority." Now, this is baffling *unless* it is associated, as I've proposed here, with State Department public relations. Ciardi appears to mean that, as these poets are "not imagists, nor vorticists, nor classicists, nor existentialists," they are immune from tyranny. "They will *listen* to the authority of sense and talent," he allows, citing T. S. Eliot as an instance of moderation they have all evidently heeded. The proposition is designed to affirm centrist values, specifically envisioning an ideologically neutral core in which cultural verities align with the individuated mind to afford an *ekstasis* of radiant symmetries. In Ciardi's own description,

> [i]t is never, then, a poetry of movements and manifestoes. It is more nearly a blend of the classical and the metaphysical, a poetry of individual appraisal, tentative, self-questioning, introspective, socially involved, and always reserving for itself the right to meet experience in its humanistic environment—the uncoerced awareness of the individual man, which in art must be subjected always to principles of craftsmanship. (xxx)

It is a poetry that shuns manifestoes, for this would signal the presence of ideology. Politics is only obliquely evident here, as these poets are (somehow) "socially involved" despite their tentative introspection. This "humanistic environment," however, is hardly a *polis*, nor even an *agora*, but simply the uncoerced mind of the individual: an inner sanctum of privacy, secured and guaranteed for the sake of craft; and the principle of craftsmanship aligns the poet with the hegemonic cultural value of technical expertise.

American culture is a spectator culture, the roots of which long precede the advent of the electronic media. The spectatorial impulse may be attributed to a nation of immigrants for whom social realities are in flux, so social positioning requires alert observation. The study of differences with which American culture begins, however, eventually modulates into a self-scrutiny directed at others. Spectator culture is an enigmatic pursuit, as public life becomes a homogeneous field of externalized introspection. Poetry hardly figures in the larger spectatorial venues, of course, so it would be misleading to attribute too much ideological heft to the *public* reception of poetry. But the postwar decade witnessed a drastic transformation of the role of poetry in a specific institutional context: the university. The hegemony of the New Criticism most actively secured the preeminence of poetry among the genres, within that pedagogic setting. Poetry was a uniquely privileged showcase of literary integrity, poems exemplary reflections of humanistic values: hand mirrors for their viewers, in other words. The self-regard privileged in fifties poems was white, male, Ivy League, motivated by domestic liberal consensus and flattered by an international stature unprecedented before the implementation of the Marshall Plan. The American moment such poems inhabited was absolutely secure in its confidence in the first-person plural, and in its assumption of a terminology that reckoned "man's" prerogatives and talents—in poetry and politics alike.

Ciardi's polemical introduction was so attuned to the mood of the day, politically as well as pedagogically, that it can hardly be called tastemaking. Rather, he affirmed the common views in a buoyant and convivial style that proved attractive to the general public. Anthologists of American poetry had often been popularizers, like Louis Untermeyer and Oscar Williams. What distinguished *Mid-Century American Poets* from the other popular anthologies was Ciardi's insistence on letting the poets have their own say, and not subsuming them under his editorial wing. That gesture extended authority to the poets themselves, but it also served to authorize the project as a whole—a most significant consequence of which was the accreditation of Ciardi's choice of poets.

The famous battle of the anthologies that broke out a decade later has overshadowed the trends established earlier, which established patterns that would not be seriously destabilized until Donald Allen's *New American Poetry* in 1960. Because of the schism suggested by Allen versus Hall-Pack-Simpson, there has been an unfortunate tendency to retroactively attribute to Allen's group a revolutionary coherence that it didn't actually possess, as well as to misattribute foundational coherence to the *New Poets of England and America*. Especially instructive in this regard is the list of poets that Kenneth Rexroth, alleged sugar daddy of the Beats, thought to put in an anthology he proposed to James Laughlin for New Directions in 1950:

> You know—I wonder about the USA poets under 50—my god theyre bad most of them—There is [Elizabeth] Bishop, [Richard] Eberhart, [Kenneth] Fearing, Laughlin, [Thomas]

> Merton, [Laura] Riding (under 50?), [Muriel] Rukeyser,
> [Kenneth] Patchen, D[elmore] Schwartz, [Yvor] Winters,
> [John] Wheelwright (under?), [Karl] Shapiro, [Peter]
> Viereck, [Robert] Lowell, [Randall] Jarrell—to make up the
> bulk of the book—but there are some dreary time wasters of
> cooked verse amongst the minors—and Bishop and the last
> four are not to my taste, although I have represented them
> judiciously.[57] (*Letters* 136–37)

Eight of Ciardi's fifteen poets are listed here, and among those remaining only Wilbur and Roethke are surprising omissions on Rexroth's part (the letter is dated March 1950, just before Ciardi's book appeared). And excepting Laughlin, Merton and Riding, the others would all be heavily anthologized in the 1950s and beyond. Those poets with whom Rexroth was to be subsequently associated were not yet known to him at this time. What is significant about his prospect for a midcentury anthology, and what sets him apart from Ciardi and other fifties compilers, is his open disdain for the overall caliber of work to choose from. Where Ciardi was enthusiastic about the present and optimistic for the future, Rexroth's view was tempered by a more diffident assessment of the current crop. The difference between them—which needs to be emphasized because of their mutual respect (Rexroth singled Ciardi out as "singularly independent" of group affiliations, which endows his poetry with "a human, unliterary quality all too rare in his generation" [*American Poetry* 124])—was largely that Rexroth was a bohemian, staunchly antiacademic, while Ciardi loathed everything bohemia stood for and was comfortable in academia.

Ciardi was a typical instance of what he himself called "the G.I. generation."[58] He served in the U.S. Army Air Corps, was decorated

---

[57] Rexroth's anthology was never published. Interestingly, Jarrell and Lowell planned an anthology together in the mid-fifties, at least on the evidence of Jarrell's correspondence (*Letters* 424). It would be interesting to know what they proposed to include. My guess is that it was rendered redundant because all the other anthologies were subservient to the Lowell-Jarrell enterprise already.

[58] "The G.I. generation had its potential rebellion largely blurred by army restrictions and could do little more than grumble or go AWOL on a binge, but that much at least they did manage regularly enough." This is from "Epitaph for the Dead Beats," Ciardi's denunciation of beatnik behavior, followed by a qualified admiration for Ginsberg's "Howl" (*Dialogue* 300).

with the Oak Leaf Cluster Air Medal, married on demobilization in
1946, and proceeded to rear three children. Having taken degrees from
Tufts and the University of Michigan before the war—and having gotten
two years teaching experience before conscription—Ciardi then set to
work at Harvard (1946–53) and Rutgers (1961), with stints abroad in
Salzburg and Rome. He was academically respected enough to become
Director (1955–57) and then President (1958–59) of the National College
English Association. Ciardi served as poetry editor for the *Saturday
Evening Post* from 1956–1973, and was promoted to contributing editor
from 1973–1980. He was also a lecturer at the Bread Loaf Writer's Conference from 1947–1973, and its director from 1956–1972. Ciardi did
well enough from his extracurricular activities to retire from teaching at
age forty-five, becoming host of CBS television's *Accent* program, and
in his later years joining the staff of National Public Radio with his
memorable broadcasts on the English language.

It may be a bit misleading to profile Ciardi's career as typical
of his G.I. generation, given his forays into mass media. My point,
however, is that the role of pundit was available to educated dough-
boys in the postwar years, at least through the Eisenhower era. (The
State Department circuit that sponsored Dizzy Gillespie's globe-hop-
ping as cultural ambassador extended to poets as well.) For poet-veter-
ans, university appointments were plentifully at hand. In his first year
as poetry editor for the *Saturday Review* Ciardi addressed the academic countenance of poetry in an editorial, "Poverty on Parnassus: The
Economics of Poetry." "By now at least 85 per cent of our serious
poets under sixty are working, or have recently worked, at some sort
of university careers" (*Dialogue* 292). He astutely comments on the
increased signs of professionalization, with poet-professors "now fifty-
ish" holding a B.A., the middle generation (Ciardi's own) with an
M.A., and the thirtysomething crowd "tend[ing] to come armed with
the full union-card doctorate."[59] Ciardi's lively retort to accusations of

---

[59] Of the "G.I. generation" (b. 1913–1923) the number of poets with Master's
degrees or the equivalent is fairly astonishing: Berryman, Brinnin, Carruth,
Ciardi, James Dickey, Engle, Ferlinghetti, Hayden, Hecht, Honig, Hugo, Jarrell,
Langland, John Logan, McGrath, Moss, Dudley Randall, William Jay Smith,
Van Duyn, Theodore Weiss, Whittemore, and Wilbur; while the Ph.D was held

ivory tower myopia and middle-class comforts set the stage for his compelling excuse for, and justification of, a generation's detainment in the lecture hall. Ciardi openly concedes that "our faculties are made up of intellectual sheep," and "woe to the poet who marries them in love and for better or worse." It's interesting to read James Dickey's popular poem "The Sheep Child" as a parable of academized poetry, as "Farm boys wild to couple / With anything" are described spooking themselves with tales of a bestial offspring, evidence of which teaches them sexual abstinence from sheep:

> The boys have taken
> Their own true wives in the city,
> The sheep are safe in the west hill
> Pasture but we who were born there
> Still are not sure. Are we,
> Because we remember, remembered
> In the terrible dust of museums?
>
> (*Poems* 252)

Ciardi's advice to budding poet-scholars is: don't mingle; keep it honorably parasitical. "I see no reason for the poets to stay out of the universities," he writes, adding that "[t]oo many of them have joined

---

by Matchett, Nims, Roseliep, Simpson, Stafford, and Viereck. Of the previous generation (b. 1903–1911), Eberhart, Fitzgerald, Francis, Kunitz, Mayo, Olson, Rakosi, Roethke, Robert Penn Warren, and Zukofsky had an M.A., and Cunningham, Lattimore, and Miles had a Ph.D. So Ciardi's estimate that a Bachelor's represented the terminal degree for his predecessors was not really accurate. And while the generation succeeding Ciardi's (born 1924–1932) was conspicuously well educated, some of those who would become well known as poets had doctorates (Bowers, Coulette, Hoffman, Hollander, Koch, James Wright), but most went only as far as the M.A.: Antin, Ashbery, Berry, Bly, Booth, Jane Cooper, Corman, Creeley, William Dickey, Feldman, Finkel, Garrett, Hall, Hanson, Howard, Justice, Kennedy, Kinnell, Kizer, Kumin, Lansing, Levine, Lieberman, O'Hara, Pack, Pastan, Plath, Ray, Rothenberg, Harvey Shapiro, Slavitt, Snodgrass, Spacks, Spicer, Stern, Sward, Van Duyn, Wagoner, and Miller Williams. As educated as these generations were, subsequent generations (born after 1933) continued to advance through a succession of degrees, especially by the late sixties when the MFA became commonplace. The main educational distinction between the earlier and the later generations of American poets (by which I mean pre- and post-1924), is that the later generation is far less likely to include men and women with *only* a Bachelor's degree, and that those like Rexroth and Bukowski of the earlier generation who lacked degrees altogether are unlikely even to have been published later on.

the universities rather than lived off them" (*Dialogue* 298). Ciardi is really addressing the anthropological problem of going native. His solution, as it turns out, is dependent on temperament; one either is or is not prepared to "cheat the poetry in favor of the employment." This fails to address the uniqueness of the occupation. The poet in the insurance company, by contrast, may recognize the either-or as indisputable. But the poet-professor shuffling personal writing with public lecturing can't entertain the same clear separation.

Ciardi's conceptual defense of poets in academe pales in comparison with the stark practical lure he dangles, by way of autobiography, for his *Saturday Review* readers:

> I taught at Harvard for seven years right after the war and when I was working full-time it was a two-afternoon-a-week job. It was no way to get rich, but it kept the family bills paid and it left me large chunks of time in which to write. Moreover, of my last three years at Harvard one was spent on a sabbatical in Europe and one happily doing as I pleased on a Ford Grant. Since then I have taught for three years at Rutgers, and I am now scheduled to spend my fourth year in Rome on an American Academy of Arts and Letters Grant. I call it princely. (*Dialogue* 297–98)[60]

Poets were indeed a new aristocracy, or at least some of them were. The symbolic escalation of poetic stock meant that, for a number of years, the demand for living poets exceeded the supply—bearing in mind, of course, the specific constraints of the role poets were expected to play in an institutional setting. So, as Horace Gregory observed, "The poet as the sentimental professional rebel vanished; in his place

---

[60] Times have changed. Junior professors—those lucky enough to have tenure-track positions—would now be hard pressed to characterize their full-time service as a "two-afternoon-a-week job." Sabbaticals are increasingly a matter of petition, and the promise of time abroad is largely out of financial reach. Ciardi doesn't mention such amenities as affordable housing, of course, which is also increasingly withdrawn as part of the career package for younger academics, as is marriage and/or child-bearing. In the career profile at present—in contrast to Ciardi's glib "earthbound mortgage and the statistical 2.7 children" (295)—one finds a *rentier* class not only of the "thirtyish" but the "fortyish" generation as well, with few professors bearing children till impending menopause forces the issue.

was the young instructor of English in privately endowed colleges wearing a Brooks Brothers uniform" (13). The sartorial aspect was stressed, usually in deprecating terms, and often by the poets themselves. "The world of the younger poets, at present," Jarrell confided to Elizabeth Bishop, "certainly is the world of Richard Wilbur and safer paler mirror-images of Richard Wilbur—who'd have thought that the era of the poet in the Grey Flannel Suit was coming?" (*Letters* 413). A month later, in October 1956, he reported to Shapiro, "I met a really good (and wholly delightful) new young poet named Gregory Corso. He's all that the tea-party or grey-flannel or World-of-Richard-Wilbur poets aren't. Not that I don't like Wilbur, but one is enough" (*Letters* 417).[61] Wilbur was not a private reference, but virtually the public benchmark of the dapper, handsome, collegiate formalist. Horace Gregory, in his 1953 *Saturday Review* survey, felt obliged to mention Wilbur as one of the most accomplished of the younger poets. But he was circumspect in his praise, and noted that Wilbur's work was dangerously close to being "the kind of verse that falls too inoffensively into the blank spaces below an article on 'Where is the World Going?'" (14). Gregory had the insight that the greatest danger facing someone like Wilbur was to "suffer too much unthinking patronage," which is exactly what happened, as Wilbur has become the most widely anthologized of American poets since World War II, and fairly unique among members of his generation in not having undergone any mid-career changes in style or theme.

Delmore Schwartz, who sustained the role of outsider as well as anybody in the inner sanctum of poet celebrities, recognized the spectre of opposition looming in the form of the Beats. In his 1958 lecture at the Library of Congress, Schwartz not only advanced his notorious vision of poetry as "a peaceful public park on a pleasant summer Sunday afternoon," but insisted that there could be no bohemianism in the present, or if there were it was only covert, in

---

[61] Jarrell's infatuation with the young Beat poet was short-lived. Corso visited the Jarrell's and was encouraged to stay for many weeks, during which time the host grew increasingly distressed by Corso's commitment to the principle of spontaneous composition, refusing to revise anything, stubbornly insisting on writing a new poem instead.

the fantasies of suburbanites. "Unlike the Bohemianism of the past," he insisted, "the new non-conformism has no genuine enemy: it is unopposed and permitted to exist in freedom . . . ." Consequently,

> The rebellion is a form of shadow boxing because the Man in the Brooks Brothers suit is himself, in his own home, very often what Russell has called an upper Bohemian. His conformism is limited to the office day and business hours: in private life—and at heart—he is as Bohemian as anyone else. . . . The new rebel is fighting for what he has already won and fighting against a threat which does not exist, since he does not want a grey flannel suit, he is not forced to wear one. . . . (*Essays* 45)

The tranquility Schwartz insists on is bound to seem bizarre because of the latent forces soon to erupt in the sixties. As it was, I'm inclined to hear Schwartz's comments corroborated by media images of the period, from the benign and hapless beatnik Maynard Krebs of the *Dobie Gillis Show*, to the Brooks Brothers figures played with sublime ridicule by Jack Lemmon and Tony Randall in films like *Bell, Book and Candle*, *The Apartment*, *Will Success Spoil Rock Hunter?*, and *Boys' Night Out*. Hollywood was very busy in the wake of the beatnik onslaught assuring its middle class audience that bohemianism was best affirmed in fantasies that everybody, even the most uptight, secretly harbored (and, *ergo*, that the Hollywood dream machine was the best medium in which to entertain those fantasies).

The command of metrics in verse functioned as a corollary to this more general solace, reaching its peak at the end of the decade with *The Drunk in the Furnace* (Merwin), *The Summer Anniversaries* (Justice), *The Country of a Thousand Years of Peace* (Merrill), *Advice to a Prophet* (Wilbur), *Saint Judas* (Wright) and *Heart's Needle* (Snodgrass), when the tensions simmering below the surface threatened to undo the meticulous ornamental crochet. The increasing absorption of poets and poetry into academic life, however, was something that even Schwartz could no longer deny. "This is the change which has affected the condition of poetry more than any other during the past generation," he wrote (*Essays* 36). Shapiro, as usual, sensed what was in the wind, and noted that the real vanguard was not so much aesthetic as institutional. "The revolution here is not in poetry but in education," he observed. "Public education in democracy has burst the confines of the curriculum and taken over the creative element of the community" (*Children* 92). The role poets were often expected to play, as educators, was that of specialist proponents of modern literature. The precedent for such a role had been set by the New Critics in the forties, but the academic industry bent on disseminating modernism was expanding far beyond the sectarian concerns of Ransom, Tate, and their acolytes. Trilling, lamenting "The Teaching of Modern Literature," complained that institutionalized presentation of modernism took all the sting out of it, along with the thrill of discovery. George Garrett noted with alarm that the assimilation of modernism to the university curriculum meant "the exposure of the young student to the *official* history of modern literature within the confines of a formal discipline," the consequences of which were a "simplification of the immediate past" ("Grain" 222–23). Specifically, what was simplified was the lineage by which modernism as avant-garde continued to hold out vanguard potential. What was encouraged by the institutionalization of modernism (a phrase I would like to resonate with a Foucauldean intensity) was the view that the literary radicals of the day were Lowell, Jarrell, and Roethke. It was only within such a monochrome portrait, for instance, that Wilbur's notion of rhyme as "experimental" could come across as anything but ludicrous.

Shapiro satirically noted, "It was clever of you poets, I must say, to switch your affections from the church to the university. Now you are playing second fiddle to sociologists, you are practically respectable" (*Defense* 259). The fifties were indeed dominated by the vision of sociology, the highly respected new science of the democratic masses. Sociologists were popular authors, and titles like Riesman's *The Lonely Crowd*, Whyte's *Organization Man*, and Mills's *White Collar* sparked cocktail conversation as well as symposia. Poetry was not immune from this, and Shapiro offered a formula: "Advertising is the poetry of the American masses; sociology is the poetry of the educated middle class; and academic poetry the poetry of cultural officialdom" (*Defense* 285). Riesman's tabulation of tradition-directed, inner-directed, and other-directed personalities is handily adaptable to poetry;

and as poets resigned themselves to university life they became recognizable variants of the "organization man." Under the pressure of conformity implicit in such institutionalization, the topic of the poet as Brooks Brothers mannequin became a familiar fifties reference. R. P. Blackmur had foreseen the consequences in 1948, noting that "a loss of the real delight in imaginative risk" was what was "ominous about the agglutination of writers in the universities . . . " (*PR* 864). The values that poets celebrated, he feared, would come to be dominated by those sedative reassurances of suburbia, their denizens increasingly obedient to the military-industrial order of the Eisenhower era: "The economic, political, and cultural drifts of our society are toward the institutionalization of all the professions; their special freedoms will lie *only* in their own work." And as Blackmur pointed out, "As a people we are unused to taking our risks in our work."

Risk is a term specifically linked with poetry's fate in the successive wagers that evolve from Mallarmé to the present, finding its most eloquent proponent in Robert Duncan, whose scathing critique of poetry careerism at the height of the Vietnam war explicitly equated the much touted "failure of vision" of the modern world with a flawed poetics. "The modern mind has not only chickened out on God, on angels, on Creation," wrote Duncan in "The Truth and Life of Myth," "but it has chickened out on the common things of our actual world, taking the properties of things as their uses and retracting all sense of fellow creatureliness" (*Fictive* 22). Duncan sees this retraction developing in tandem with a rationalist poetics which, in its contemporary manifestation, would reduce poetry to a branch of psychology.

> In the tribute poets pay, after Dryden, to deliver over their art to the consensus of reasonable men, poetry, like the universe of rationalist science, ceases to be primal Creation and becomes a commodity, a material for human uses and self-development. Poems will be viewed as competing in the great market of values, even as men compete there, and an evaluative criticism grows up. Self-made men and self-made poems take pride in their rise. The operations of allegory and metaphor cease to be magical and become manners of speaking, displays of wit, and historical events themselves cease to be thought of as informed by a creative intent. . . . (*Fictive* 45)

It was feared, as the bland fifties went on, that respectability had been gained at too exacting a price. Poets were prestigious, addressing captive audiences of students across the land. Yet as Randall Jarrell complained in *American Scholar* in 1959, "He"—meaning God—"has given us poets students. But what He gives with one hand He takes away with the other: He has taken away our readers" (277). Readers had been replaced by annotators, not by accident but by design. In the same pages—a special issue on contemporary poetry—A. Alvarez ventured an explanation: "the pressures of academic life sooner or later bring down everything to plain method," he wrote. "For method is impersonal, almost an abstraction. It reduces to clear teachable elements the huge complexity of disciplined response and choice with which the reader otherwise needs to re-create for himself each poem" (367). Clement Greenberg had similarly noted, ten years earlier, the consequences of the New Criticism: "The criticism that concentrates itself on the close analysis of poetry is by and large an American phenomenon and a concomitant . . . of the store we set by techniques and of our concern with the statement of procedures" (*PR* 877). The can-do spirit of the G. I. generation in the universities made poetry recuperable to homespun American pragmatism.[62]

Donald Hall lampooned this gimmick-oriented view of poetry in *New Republic* (April 29, 1957) by proposing as a marketable game a "Make Your Own Poem" kit. But in his contribution to the

---

[62] A somewhat different emphasis is given by George Garrett, recollecting the transition from the immediate postwar influx of veterans to a return to more youthful "norms": "[B]y the early 1950s the last of the World War II veterans were gone from the campuses. . . . It was all *kids* again. There were things that the mature veterans had known, from hard experience, that the kids didn't and couldn't know. Content quickly became less important than form. We taught more about literary aesthetics than essential substance—because we had to. We also tried to teach things relevant to them and their limited experiences. Pretty soon here came *The Catcher and the Rye* and *Lord of the Flies*. We discovered that whatever we *called* the canon *was* the canon. We ate up the forbidden fruit, enjoyed it thoroughly, and our eyes were opened to the possibility of organizing and manipulating the present to be and to mean whatever we said it was. We shared a lot more with the hucksters and tricksters of Madison Avenue than we would ever admit, even to ourselves" ("Future" 50).

American Scholar symposium he defended himself and his peers against the routine jibes at academic compromise. "It is not surprising that reviewers, from the quarterlies to *Time*, should blame the young poets for being married and having children, although fatherhood would seem to be about as conformist as supper." But the fallacy of doing so, in his view, was to mistake the terms of conformity, since "domesticity is not directly connected with conformity, and domesticity is the real enemy. Conformity is social and public and protective; domesticity for the poet has uses that inhibit his extension as an artist" (310). Hall's reasoning here is uncharacteristically strained; but as I understand him, he is advocating the merits of conformity, of peer pressure, defending the right of "the silent generation" to be silent as long as the silence is a unison effect. What is ultimately disabling about private life, Hall implies, is any domestic arrangement that impedes the creative temperament. While this is not a position Hall would later hold to, it suggests why the confessional poets would shortly prevail. Their agonies documented the ill-fit between domesticity and poetry—coinciding, it would seem, with that juncture in the lives of the G.I. generation when mid-career divorce was becoming commonplace, if not habitual. But beyond that, Hall was defending the right of poets to follow the necessities of their art, and even to conform to conformity. After all, it was (as Irving Howe declared in 1954) an "Age of Conformity."

The age of conformity attuned itself to the principles of sociological functionalism, affirming principles of self-regulation in a compensatory consumerism. The standard of the "well-adjusted man" was the result. "Adjustment as the new art for art's sake means far more than merely one more 'age of conformity,'" Peter Viereck wrote in his political manifesto *The Unadjusted Man* (1956). Being "well-adjusted," he warned, easily shades into overadjustment, resulting in "the public-relations personality of public smile, private blank. In effect, an ecstasy of universal voluntary lobotomy" (3). The age of conformity, in his view, was the result of an "abnormal desire for normalcy," and in post-McCarthy America he saw this culminating in "a voluntary cultural thought-control more insidious than the coercive political kind" (4). Its trump was the commercialization of spirituality, not only in huckster revivalism but in the secular marketplace: "when anti-materialism gets publicized like toothpaste . . . then commercial materialism wins its biggest triumph of all: a triumph in the name of anti-commercialism" (9). In addition to being a Pulitzer poet, Viereck was a prominent political conservative. But the term is imprecise, particularly by the reckoning of 1990s conservatism, since he regarded the native strain of American conservatism as "primarily a cultural movement," citing Hawthorne, Melville, Henry James, Henry Adams, and Faulkner as its lineage (40).[63] "Conservatism is spiritual arithmetic. It calculates the price paid for progress" (41). The hero of Viereck's title, *The Unadjusted Man*, is the saboteur, the grit in the machine of instrumentalism and self-adjustment. Citing Clemenceau's remark that "[w]ar is too important a matter to leave to generals," Viereck adds that "atom bombs are too important to leave to scientists; freedom too important to leave to political theorizers; literature too important to leave to English departments" (323).

Viereck was probably alone among political scientists whose theories deliberately took note of poetry (a position more recently inhabited by Bruce Andrews), and portions of *The Unadjusted Man* were published in *Shenandoah* as well as *World Affairs Quarterly*, and delivered as the Whittall Poetry Lectures at the

---

[63] Viereck was explicitly anti-Emersonian and anti-Whitmanian, because they signified in his view an unrealistic drive for autonomy (or self-reliance). His definition of the distinction between liberal and conservative is worth citing as clarification: "The liberal sees outer, removable institutions as the ultimate sources of evil; sees man's social task as creating a world in which evil will disappear. His tools for this task are progress and enlightenment. The conservative sees the inner, unremoveable nature of man as the ultimate source of evil; sees man's social task as coming to terms with a world in which evil is perpetual and in which justice and compassion will both be perpetually necessary. His tools for this task are the maintenance of ethical restraints inside the individual and the maintenance of unbroken, continuous social patterns inside the given culture as a whole" (*Unadjusted Man* 35). The conservative, then, is a paradox—a worldly manichean; and this parallels the liberal antitype, the communist, who is a utopian materialist. The distinction, along with the parallelism, is elaborated: "in temperament liberalism often is the articulate relating of abstraction to abstraction, conservatism the inarticulate relating of the concrete to the concrete" (36).

Library of Congress as well as to the American Historical Association. So it's not surprising to find Viereck devoting an entire chapter in this political treatise to "The Dignity of Lyricism: Form Yes, Formalism No," in which he defines overadjustment in cultural affairs in the phenomenon of "conveyor-belt dons": "The overadjusted style of the critic's poet performs like a chewing-gum slot-machine," he wrote. "It responds to each counterfeit slug of critical jargon by emitting a jaw-breaking wad of allusion; if you listen carefully, you can hear the satisfied metallic click" (280). Lamenting this "art decadent with elegance" (290), he offered as a positive value of unadjustment an "exuberant profligacy," in terms similar to Georges Bataille: "Without wastefulness, no generosity" (282).[64] Affirming form over formalism, Viereck has continued to insist on the formal power of metrics up to the present, although he has judiciously clarified his commitment in terms that grow closer and closer (without mentioning it) to Olson's sense of proprioceptive prosody (see "Anti-Form or Neo: A Curse on Both Houses" from 1993). He has pursued a mediatory position, which is in fact a true conservatism, and the customary ways of narrating the progress of postwar American poetry have yet to find a way to account for such a figure. "[W]hy confine poetry to this false choice between Agit-prop and furniture polish?" he asked in *The Unadjusted Man* (289). The choice continues to pawn its distractions many decades later.

For all his exemplarity as poetic maverick, Viereck's position had its crudities and blind spots. His essay in Ciardi's *Mid-Century American Poets* was openly partisan, polemically titled "My Kind of Poetry." "Right from the start," he began, "I must disappoint many readers by the unexciting conservatism of my poetic techniques" (16). Viereck proclaimed himself a metrical traditionalist in form, and an upstart protester of modernist obscurantism.

---

[64] Viereck's praise of wasteful exuberance has its immediate ancestor in Frost (and Frost gets it from Emerson and Thoreau). In his late talk "On Extravagance" (1962), Frost exclaims "What an *extravagant* universe it is. And the most extravagant thing in it, as far as we know, is man—the most wasteful, spending thing in it—in all his luxuriance" (*Poetry and Prose* 447). And from this thriftless expenditure, Frost exults, comes poetry.

It's not enough to say a poet must belong to none of the arty coteries. It's essential that he actively sin against their rituals. *My own sin is twofold.* 1) I've content—something to say about the profane world they scorn—and not only form; this makes me an "impure" poet. 2) I try to communicate to the qualified layman also, instead of only to fellow poets and critics; this makes me a philistine. (16–17)

Waging the good fight against what he saw as a failure of nerve on the part of critics and readers too cowed by literary authority to do anything but meekly accede to the obscurantist principles of the modernist priests, Viereck lambasted the New Critics with their "cult of [Eliot's] criticism and their accompanying cult of studied obscurity [which] are stifling the growth of poetry today" (29). He recognized it as a dictatorship, "charming and velvet-gloved," uncoercive in its snobbism but all the more appealing for its aloofness.[65]

In the face of a modernism doubly infected by political extremism and formalist mystification, Viereck offered his own avowedly accessible, metrically traditional, and morally stable poems to readers of *Mid-Century American Poets.* Affirming populist virtues, he directed his work to "that audience of intelligent non-experts who are neither professional poets nor professional critics" (29–30). Viereck's claim suffers from a telling misdiagnosis of a cultural and political transfiguration unmentioned in his piece. He appeals to a sentimental image of the literate republic. As the U.S. moved past the midcentury mark, however, there would be increasing signs of alarm as the anticipated "audience of intelligent non-experts" never showed up at the gig. In hindsight it's clear that, however unfashionable modernism seemed for a few literary seasons around 1950, it was preoccupying much more of the intellectual labor of the intelligent audience (casual and expert alike) than poets like Ciardi and Viereck admitted. As concern for the no-show audience increased, on the part

---

[65] He augmented the sartorial image in *The Unadjusted Man*: "Our Mandarins Junior Grade make official uniforms of Eliot's discarded garments but lack the originality with which Eliot so imperially filled those garments. It is not that the emperor has no clothes—he has too many—but that in most cases the clothes have no emperor" (283).

of the poet-professors, audiences began turning up in droves for cultural venues that seemed at the time barbaric or juvenile and thus beneath comment. I refer to popular music, of course, but also to the excoriated "beatnik" writing which took the literary world completely by surprise. Just when the poet-professors thought they'd diagnosed the cause of their dwindling audience, the audience itself appeared like a vast hydra head leering at a competing performance, a performance outside the circus tent altogether.

The anxieties attending the general awareness that academia had swallowed up the American literary community reflect a broader awareness, confirmed indubitably in the wake of the Sputnik launch, that knowledge was power, and that a social readjustment was required in the cold war world in which old-fashioned know-how was insufficient. The spectre of conformity rankled many, but there was a readiness to reinterpret what it meant. As the bland fifties gave way to the turbulence of the sixties, the campus began to seem a lively place after all, and the poets' academic sinecure a subtle prescience. Even the Beats were becoming fixtures of the college circuit. M.L. Rosenthal, an advocate of *both* the Beat and the patrician strains, was able to heave a last reproach (in *The New York Times Book Review* in 1965) to those who had attributed the docility of the previous decade to academia as such. "Behind the more blatant dislike of such work by people whose idea of poetry is purely external—to whom any junkie or hipster looks more 'poetic' than a man quietly writing—lies the subtler contemporary tendency to discredit the whole creative meaning of the humanistic tradition." Humanism was not so easily dismissed by a mere change of venue, however, since every impulse to mount a critique in the first place had its roots in that heritage. "The grove outside Athens where Plato taught has the associations of this tradition, and of the pleasures of sweetly philosophical musings and reverie as well as of learning. It was called Academe" (197).

Rosenthal's reappraisal is indicative of the sixties, however, and was a position altogether unavailable to those in the fifties, especially after the Beats appeared on the scene. Norman Podhoretz, who had been a fellow student of Ginsberg's at Columbia, famously called his Beat peers "the know-nothing Bohemians," but his observations were actually a bit more perspicacious than that phrase would suggest. Linking the image of domestic duties with conformist anxiety, he appraised the sociological appeal of the Beats:

> I think that the unveiling of the Beat Generation was greeted with a certain relief by many people who had been disturbed by the notorious respectability and "maturity" of postwar writing. This was more like it—restless, rebellious, confused youth living it up, instead of thin, balding, buttoned-down instructors of English composing ironic verses with one hand while changing the baby's diapers with the other. Bohemianism is not particularly fashionable nowadays, but the image of Bohemia still exerts a powerful fascination—nowhere more so than in the suburbs, which are filled to overflowing with men and women who uneasily think of themselves as conformists and of Bohemianism as the heroic road. (202)

While he generally opposed and even ridiculed them, Podhoretz perceptively understood the appeal of the Beats as social fantasy. There was nothing unusually insightful in this, since Hollywood had a nearly monopolistic hold on the fantasy of the outsider—*The Wild One*, *Rebel Without a Cause*, with Brando and Dean icons of something as yet unnameable but clearly usurping the role of the bohemian. What was alarming at the time was the fact that these outsiders were not artists or poets, but, like their English counterparts, teddy-boys and toughs, illiterate and antisocial. While the position occupied by poets had varied since the nineteenth century as to its extremity, the fifties confounded everyone because the delegated "major" poets were so implacably centrist, while the mantle of bohemia (in the eyes of the press) had fallen to the dregs of delinquency. However, as Russell Jacoby has written about the 1950s, "The persistent mourning for the passing of rebellious youth has to be set against its opposite, the national mobilization against delinquency" (62). It's only with hindsight we can distinguish the antisocial from the countercultural, and it was clearly the latter to which the Beats belonged.

Much has been asserted, by scholars and historians, about the complacency of the Eisenhower years; and the accommodating careerism of the poets aroused curiosity. But it never lacked for critics. Glauco Cambon wrote in 1962 that "in separating itself from the wild twenties and the committed thirties, the mid-century generation risked forgetting that civilization, especially in literature, is not a matter of suburban comfort" (5). By the end of the decade it was becoming apparent that poets were "committed" in an altogether different sense—Lowell, Roethke, Berryman, Jarrell, Plath, and Ginsberg all having spent time in mental institutions. Ken Kesey's antihero in *One Flew Over the Cuckoo's Nest* (like Bellow's portrait of Schwartz in *Humbolt's Gift*) is the product of a period when the pressures of the center were so great, for the poets and artists who inhabited it, that periodic recuperation in the clinic was inevitable. Poets cracked in the crucible of a central sanity, and their commitment to poetry was unthinkable without some corresponding "commitment" that could restore to them the measure of poetic frenzy.

The central sanity I speak of is inseparable from the sanitizing impulses of dominant values. Politics had become a sort of germ warfare, with the Communist "infestation" seen as something beyond discussion, requiring treatment, pest control. The New Criticism had likewise sanitized literature, acclimating modernism to the pedagogically serviceable streamlining of academic careers. I have not as yet spoken of a poetic "establishment," except obliquely. Poetry in fact hardly needed any official referendum, given the hegemonic representations of mass media, where a corporate structure was the tacit background of any profile. Action painting was as close to being the official art of the day as the Brooks Brothers poets were, except for the obvious fact that the "center" in painting *was* the avant-garde. If an avant-garde is necessarily political, in effect if not by intent, abstract expressionism was different, a "political apoliticism"—"artistic rebellion . . . transformed into aggressive liberal ideology" (Guilbaut 2, 200). Action painting was made to signify a necessary (that is, recuperable) dissidence, and its nonrepresentational character made it amenable to the explanatory liberal reasoning of the voice-over. As "an art of obliteration, an art of erasure," avant-garde art "pretended to tell a story, but no sooner had the telling begun than it began ingeniously to undo itself, to cover its tracks, to cover itself up and disappear" (197).

Guilbaut conveniently summarizes his argument in *How New York Stole the Idea of Modern Art*:

> [F]rom compromise to compromise, refusal to refusal, adjustment to adjustment, the rebellion of the artists, born of frustrations within the left, gradually challenged its significance until ultimately it came to represent the values of the majority, but in a way (continuing the modernist tradition) that only a minority was capable of understanding. (3)

With this, Guilbaut enables us to pinpoint the accommodation of poetry to the "vital center" of liberalism: the understanding minority, in this case, being the academic specialists of Criticism, Inc. The poetic center, with its doctrine of close reading, differed fundamentally in its explanatory impulse from the critical proponents of abstract expressionism. As tortuous, recondite, and bristling with jargon as the analyses of New Criticism could be, there was always a reassuring commitment to the text itself, the words of the poem on the page and, in turn, a presumption of veracity in the relations of words to things. Literary criticism made a commonsense appeal that was perceptually unavailable to the naked eye immersed in the porridge of Pollock's drips. As long as the very notion of "experiment" in poetry was tainted by association with the social milieu of twenties bohemianism, its conceptual pertinence was irrelevant. It had been "historicized" out of existence. Poetry was emphatically and resolutely taken to be an art of reference and representation; an art of depiction and assertion. Furthermore, what was asserted in the poem was the articulated intentionality of "the speaker," a figure of sensibility, perceptual resourcefulness, and determinate contours.

The prospect of a poetic vanguard was disadvantaged precisely by the dominance of the avant-garde in painting. Being a language art, it was assumed the words in a poem couldn't "ingeniously undo" themselves, despite the prodigious demonstrations of Gertrude Stein. Besides, the pedagogic injunction that poems be *about* a demonstrable subject matter foreclosed for a time any chance of reckoning the poem as a record of energies rather than a transcript of viewpoints. (It should also be remembered that Henry James was very much in vogue, glamourizing point of view for literature in general; and however abstracted this can be in his later works, there is always a demonstrable topic or what he called the "donée.") *Life* magazine showcased Pollock ("Jack the Dripper") and Lowell at about the same time, and this is quite instructive about the different criteria accorded to subject matter in the respective arts in the late 1940s. Both Pollock and Lowell were incarnations of what Arthur Schlesinger named for the *New York Times Magazine* of April 4, 1948: "Not Left, not Right, but a Vital Center," although their routes to this center were different. This vital center entailed, in Schlesinger's words, "an acceptance of conflict . . . with a determination to create a social framework where conflict issues, not in excessive anxiety, but in creativity" (Guilbaut 203). The "Age of Anxiety," after all, was the title of a poem before it became a period moniker. In painting, Guilbaut argues, "the avant-garde even became a protégé of the new liberalism, a symbol of the fragility of freedom in the battle waged by the liberals to protect the vital center from the authoritarianism of the left and the right" (202). In the case of painting and poetry alike, the representational preoccupations of the prewar left stigmatized *representation as such* as overly partisan. Pollock's drip paintings abolished the representational residue in a way that couldn't be replicated in poetry, however. So the traumatic function of indexing the present moment without depicting it—the only way around the partisan requirements of McCarthyism on the right and the legacy of an anti-Stalinist left passing through a maze of wickets of successive repudiation and disengagement—put poets in the position of *increasing* the historical surface, rendering it baroque, as thickly present as the strokes of a Kline canvas yet somehow noncomittal.

The solution was ingenious, and it grew out of the New Critics' obsession with tradition and the historical sensibility. "History," as it appeared in postwar poetry, would be the history of premodernity. Especially in the wake of the Bollingen fiasco, in which everyone involved took a public beating over the issue of politics (as "history" in the present moment), there was increased pressure to return, as it were, to the obliquities of the Malatesta Cantos, to represent History as a distant mirror. The results are conspicuous: Berryman's *Homage to Mistress Bradstreet*, Lowell's Puritan divines in *Lord Weary's Cas-*

tle, Hecht's "Gardens of the Villa d'Este," Wilbur's translations from French neoclassicism. So the centrist poetry corresponding in status to abstract expressionism covered its retreat from modernism by accentuating historical materials; but its accent was, for all that, an evasion. The difficulty of diagnosis plagued even attempts by those in privileged positions inside the emerging establishment, like Karl Shapiro, who finally lost patience and snarled at his peers:

> Our generation—the generation of Jarrell, Wilbur, myself, Roethke, Lowell, Schwartz, Bishop, Ciardi, Berryman, Kunitz, Nemerov, Whittemore—one is almost inclined to add Merrill, Lynch, Pearce, Fenner, and Smith—our generation lived through more history than most or maybe any. . . . We were reared as intellectuals and fought the Second World War before it happened and then again when it did happen. We witnessed the god that failed and helped trip him up. We predicted the Alexandrianism of the age and like everybody else we throve on it. We drove our foreign cars to class to teach. And we bit the hand that fed us, but not very hard, not hard enough. The hand went on signing papers. Once upon a time we were all revolutionaries of one stripe or another, but when we got married and settled down, with tenure, we talked technique instead of overthrow. Half of us stopped rebelling and not because of middle age. The age made it so easy to be a poet, or to survive on lobster, the age gave in so sweetly to our imprecations, the age so needed us to help it hate itself, this spineless age ended by softening the backbone of poetry. (*Children* 138)

Shapiro's was the conscience of that generation, even if Lowell's lines in his late poem, "For John Berryman," have been more often and approvingly cited as evidence of his perspicacity: "Yet really we had the same life, / the generic one / our generation offered"—one which for Lowell at the end, surveying his "threadbare art," "seems a snapshot, / lurid, rapid, garish, grouped, / heightened from life, / yet paralyzed by fact" (*Day by Day* 27, 127). Significantly, these celebrated lines themselves derive from a letter to Berryman dated March 18, 1962, in which Lowell exclaims, "What queer lives we've had even for poets! There seems something generic about it, and determined beyond anything we could do" (Hamilton 298).

What provoked Shapiro's self-reflections, it appears, was not the motivated careerism of his own generation but the quiescent enigma of the next. In 1957 Louis Simpson had edited for *New World Writing* a mini-anthology, featuring "Poets of the 'Silent' Generation." "The Silent Generation is as good a name as any," Shapiro thought. "It is a generation of poets who grew up amidst the intellectual wreckage of the century, between two battlefields, a generation deprived by their elders of every standard, every ideal except that of survival. Their sestinas, their Audenese, their footnoting do not promise much of a future for poetry or for anything else. They are the stylistists of the age and even the guardians of style. They are all that is left of the Tradition in a time when the Tradition has become a symbol of bankruptcy" ("Silent" 299).[66] By this point Shapiro was a famous poet, a prominent educator, former editor of *Poetry* and currently of *Prairie Schooner*, notable for its early acknowledgment of the Beats as poets rather than social freaks. He was solicited by *The Nation* in 1957 to contribute to a forum on "The Careful Young Men: Tomorrow's Leaders Analyzed by Today's Teachers," in which he concurred with most of his fellow educators that the current crop appeared to be a "Brain-Washed Generation": "It has been common talk among teachers in universities for a good many years that students have become increasingly bland in every way," he wrote. He had a specific axe to grind, thinking it likely that a lethargic generation was made, not born. The culprit was *Understanding Poetry*, "the book that took poetry off the street and put it in the laboratory," resulting in "the brainless and beautiful poetry of our leading verse magazines . . . " (208).

As Shapiro began hectoring the poetry establishment from within, Kenneth Rexroth continued his flamboyant guerrilla raids from without. The invective is commensurate with Shapiro's, and the message nearly identical:

---

[66] Amusingly, Shapiro had complained in an earlier number of *Prairie Schooner*, "It is time critics stopped generalizing about 'our Age' and started taking a personal interest in books" ("Poetry in 1956" 11). Later in the year this resolve proved no impediment to Shapiro's characterization of the Silent Generation as "stylists of the age."

> From about 1930 on, a conspiracy of bad poetry has been
> as carefully organized as the Communist Party, and today
> controls most channels of publication except the littlest of
> the little magazines. . . . Behind the façade of this literary
> Potemkin village, the main stream of American poetry . . .
> has flowed on unperturbed, though visible only at rare
> intervals between the interstices of the academic hoax.
> Today the class magazines and the quarterlies are filled
> with poets as alike as two bad pennies. It is my opinion
> that these people do not really exist. Most of them are
> androids designed by Ransom, Tate, and Co. . . . This is
> the world in which over every door is written the slogan:
> "The generation of experiment and revolt is over. Bohemia
> died in the twenties." (*Casebook* 188–89).

Not only was bohemia declared obsolete, but evidence of its Whitmanian foreground was expunged. Robert Bly passes on a telling
anecdote from James Wright:

> "I went to a party last night at Allen Tate's with a lot of
> English department people. In the course of it, I made a
> mistake. I said something complimentary about Whitman. I
> should have known better . . . There was silence in the
> room. It was interesting that not one of the men said any-
> thing. Finally one of the department wives burst out and
> said, 'Just name one poem of Whitman's that is good—just
> one!' speaking for the offended husbands." (*American
> Poetry* 72)

The impossibility of answering that question was, for Tate's crowd,
the proof of the pudding (though it should be pointed out that Jarrell
had undertaken to rehabilitate Whitman in *Poetry and the Age*). For
others, like Ginsberg, it was an incentive to abandon the tightlaced
showcase poems of the academy, "the well made mouse trap" as
Shapiro put it ("Auden" 167). Or, in Amiri Baraka's scathing characterization, "a punishingly dry, highly mannered magazine verse
equipped with hot and cold running Latin and Greek phrases mit
footnotes and the emotional significance of a *New York Times* crossword puzzle" ("Cultural Revolution" 150). Much as he admired
Auden, Shapiro freely acknowledged the regressive character of his
example: "Auden has led us back to the art-gallery poem, the poem

suffused with the golden light of the museum and the library." Specifically, the flaw was academic: "[Auden] uses the poem as a blackboard to chalk out his views" (*Defense* 125).

Blackboard verse was the antithesis of the blackboard jungle. The bow-tied egghead leading the science class (lampooned by Jerry Lewis in *The Nutty Professor*), along with the Brooks Brothers poet chalking out metrical patterns to classes of buzz-cut Ivy Leaguers, personified authority and control. The poet was a figure of contradiction, simply because the professional assurance of the poetry career was too much at variance with the romantic image of the vagabond and the bohemian, archaic as those images were. One of the most explicit confessions to come out of that "silent generation" was that of Donald Hall. Hall was one of the first of his generation (the one following Lowell's) to be singled out in the national media, featured (with photograph) in *Time* on the publication of his first book. It didn't take him long to become weary of the comfortable propriety of his own verse, even if it did take him a few decades to state it as bluntly as he did in an interview from the seventies: "I asserted control because the real freedom of poetry, the loosening of the impulse of unconscious things that are primitive and conventionally reprehensible—that loosening frightened me," he explained. "A lot of New England, a lot of Harvard, and a lot of Oxford went along with this fear about poetry" (*Goatfoot* 10). When a renewed primitivism in poetry appeared, in the form of the Beats, Hall felt a double source of anxiety: "I feared the poetry not only because it attacked my stylistic set, but also because it was a danger to my *emotional* set" (18).

Hall's experience was not unique by any means. The emotional tentativeness implicit in the adherence to metrical order was diagnosed by M. L. Rosenthal in 1950, reviewing *Mid-Century American Poets* for *The New Republic*, noting of the poets Ciardi had chosen that "their formal conservatism, their refusal to 'take chances,' is a block of a sort. Perhaps our poets, like their non-readers, fear the very meanings they need to discover" (18). Bly conveys an anecdote—about another party—dating from about the time Wright's work broke with strict metrics and attained that laconic flatness of

diction that made him so popular.[67] But at the time, according to
Bly, a poet of their generation confronted Wright at the party "with
real venom." "Jim laughed as he told the story," Bly reports. "'Listen,
Robert, this is weird: relaxation and gentleness in a poem produces
in some people real fear and rage'" (*American Poetry* 72–73). Bly
was specific in diagnosing the rage: "The generation of 1947 might
very well be called the hysterical generation," he suggested in "A
Wrong Turning in American Poetry." "Its response to the question of
literary style or content is hysterical. In fact, hysteria is often the
subject of these men's poetry . . . " (23–24). Thomas Parkinson would
concur: "In pop art and in *For the Union Dead* (insofar as it participates in the merely confessional mode), the age of anxiety evolves
into an age of panic and ultimate helplessness" (*Poets* 222).

Bly's "Wrong Turning," provocative and accurate as it often
is, overextends its generalizations. His premise is that "two strains—
puritan fear of the unconscious and the business drive toward dealing in outer things—meet in our poetry to push out the unconscious." However, he misdiagnoses modernism altogether, claiming
that the poets of 1917 "tried to adapt poetry to business and science.
They looked for 'formulas.' They tried to deal efficiently with natural
objects. They studied to develop 'technical skill'—like engineers"
(*American Poetry* 21–22). What Bly is doing, actually, is describing
the fifties from the next decade, and generalizing it to include the
whole century. "Our poetry took a wrong turning years ago," he concludes. "Some centuries have a profound spiritual movement: poetry, when vigorous, always is a part of it. We know ours is a century
of technical obsession, of business mentality, of human effort dissipated among objects, of expansion, of a destructive motion outward.
Yet there is also a movement in the opposite direction that is even
more powerful. The best thought in this century moves inward . . . .
The weakness of our poetry is that it does not share in this movement" (34).

---

[67] Apparently partying isn't congenial to Bly. "I can't explain it," he said in
an interview, struggling to express his reservations about Lowell, "but you
get the feeling that he's at parties too often" (*Talking* 197).

Donald Hall's emerging vision of his own puritanical restraints was, as I've indicated, a response to the Beats. Finding his sympathies spanning two supposedly incompatible camps, Hall was able to recognize his own malady pervading the whole field: "There is a puritanism in American thought, among both Palefaces and Redskins, which demands adherence to a code of behavior and judges poems by the actions of the poet" ("Battle" 119). "Actions" is too strong a term: *mood* and *attitude* are more accurate to the sullen brooding of the age of conformity. In 1948 the coming decade was accurately forecast by Blackmur, who realized that the oppositional rhetoric of the vanguard would prove inadequate to the recuperative necessities of postwar-shading-into-cold-war. "There is not even an adequate relation of rebellion. We have instead a vogue for the terms anxiety and euphoria; and we have a growing literary expertness in the techniques of expressing the experience of dismay, and the general techniques for creating the conditions of trouble." It's hard not to surmise *Lord Weary's Castle* as the substantive provocation here (along with, perhaps, Viereck's title *Terror and Decorum*, if not the poems themselves). "It is as if one's private hysteria were the matrix for public disorder. It is as if we believed the only possible unity and enterprise were those of crisis—against any enemy, for survival. We have a secular world stricken with the mood of religious war" (*PR* 861). It was not until Ginsberg published "Howl" that Blackmur's conditional equation could be made explicit, to assert that private hysteria *is* the matrix of public disorder; and that illumination of the decade's subtext seems to have clarified for Lowell the terms of his own work. No longer would he need to encode personal trauma and the sterilities of family history in religious allegory: Lowell's "Howl" would consist of the portraiture of *Life Studies*, still dignified and somewhat regal—*frank*, yet studied.

If Lowell signified determination and sturdiness, the poetry that mushroomed in his shadow was largely frail, withdrawn, anemic. The "battle of the anthologies" that broke out in 1960 pitted Donald Allen's miscellany of Beats and others against the academic formalism of *New Poets of England and America*; but it's essential to realize that *New Poets* was an excellent selection of its kind. The quarterlies periodically drew up mini-anthologies which reveal how fallow the field was. As Richard Stern, prefacing one such portfolio of "American Poetry of the Fifties" in *Western Review*, rather meekly put it, "It is hoped that this collection will help to define this generation of American poets, one which has too frequently been considered . . . quiet technicians, low-tide singers, workers in filigree . . . " (167). Shapiro, brusque as always in his declarations, saw such work as a bedridden terminal case: "Modern Formalistic is in fact Literature, with all the pretensions of that establishment and the life expectancy which surrounds anything that can afford the best doctors and lawyers" (*Children* 70). Finally, with all signs of vigor seemingly drained from the body politic of poetry—approaching more than ever that "dead art" which Pound as Mauberly confessed to being out of step with his time—the Beat declamations arrived like electroshocks galvanizing cadaverous matter in Dr. Frankenstein's laboratory. "After ten years of literary dandies carefully machining their Fulbright poems in a social atmosphere of cold war and general stuffiness, the beats were welcomed" (Parkinson, *Casebook* 277). The "welcome" they received, however, was not immediately from other poets.

THE BEAT PHENOMENON: ANXIETY REGAINED

The impeccable behavior of fifties academic poets is nowhere more evident than in the career profiles of Wilbur, Ciardi, Nemerov, Hecht, Jarrell, Berryman, and similar others. In corporate America, these figures resembled their peers in other vocations, and they obligingly supplied the verse for Criticism, Inc. The brutality of the unexpected appearance of a subterranean poetry as a *popular* phenomenon is only comprehensible against this backdrop—a backdrop reinforced explicitly in Ginsberg's "Howl" when he writes of those "who were burned alive in their innocent flannel suits on Madison Avenue amid blasts of leaden verse & the tanked-up clatter of the iron regiments of fashion & the nitroglycerine shrieks of the fairies of advertising" (*Howl* 14). "[I]n a society where sanitation is an ideal," said Karl Shapiro, "you don't want poetry to get out of hand"

(*Reports* 34). One way of keeping verse in check was to stress the formal means of regulating emotion, as Robert Frost did in *The Atlantic* in 1951. In terms congruent with Allen Tate's preoccupation with "control," Frost wrote: "Emotions must be dammed back and harnessed by discipline to the wit mill, not just turned loose in exclamations. No force will express far that isn't shut in by discipline at all the pores to jet at one outlet only. Emotion has been known to ooze off" (*Poetry and Prose* 413). In the fifties the question of free verse appeared to have been resolved. Not only had it been historically defiled by spurious associations with a moribund bohemianism, but Frost had authorized a cocktail party attitude in the same article with his famous remark, "I had as soon write free verse as play tennis with the net down" (415). In a different climate of opinion this analogy could be heard positively: playing tennis without a net might well require greater skill and quickness. With Frost's authority, Eliot's dictatorship of taste, and the general social atmosphere of button-down constraint, emotions were not only "dammed" but *damned* as well; and the visceral necessities of free verse couldn't be heard as exhortation—to *free* verse, as in Ornette Coleman's album title "Free Jazz"—for another decade.

News of the Beats as a literary force was broached in *The New York Times Book Review* by Richard Eberhart, on September 2, 1956, in which he declared that "the West Coast is the liveliest spot in the country in poetry today" (144). "Poetry here has become a tangible *social force*," he claimed, citing the public frenzy as proof: "The audience participates, shouting and stamping, interrupting and applauding" (145). Kenneth Rexroth, on hand for the famous Six Gallery reading in October 1955—and lampooned by Kerouac in *Dharma Bums* as the weepy Rheinhold Cacoethes, a "bow-tied wild-haired old anarchist fud"—repeated Eberhart's claim that poetry had become a "social force," which he admits to having previously regarded as "a Utopian dream of the William Morris sort" ("Disengagement" 192). By 1955 the lament that poetry was inconsequential and lacking a readership was routine, and poets had become accustomed to the thought that their only social role was in the classroom. But the Beats made Shapiro realize in a flash that "my whole generation was wrong about the Audience and the Poet; 'Howl' gave us the lie. For myself, I was delighted and immediately sent in my resignation to my generation" (*Children* 144).

Rexroth, unaffiliated to any academy or creed, was well positioned to view the emergence of the Beats outside the customary terms of evaluation and characterization:

> The youngest generation is in a state of revolt so absolute
> that its elders cannot even recognize it. The disaffiliation,
> alienation, and rejection of the young has, as far as their
> elders are concerned, moved out of the visible spectrum
> altogether. Critically invisible, modern revolt, like X-rays
> and radioactivity, is perceived only by its effects at more
> materialistic social levels, where it is called delinquency.
> (*Casebook* 179–80)

The delinquency scare of the fifties was based on an image of predatory youth—like Marlon Brando in *The Wild Ones*—but as Rexroth realized, there was a widespread disaffiliation that had nothing to do with criminality. Michael McClure, the youngest of the Beats, captures the sense that it was not he or his friends who were threatening, but rather the militaristic social norm that threatened *them*: "My self-image in those years was of finding myself—young, high, a little crazed, needing a haircut—in an elevator with burly, crew-cutted, square-jawed eminences, staring at me like I was misplaced cannon fodder. We hated the war [Korean] and the inhumanity and the coldness. The country had the feeling of martial law" (12). Hearing Ginsberg read "Howl" at The Six Gallery, says McClure, was to feel "at the deepest level that a barrier had been broken, that a human voice and body had been hurled against the harsh wall of America" (15).

When the Beats were not taken as a threat, they were taken as harmless misfits, goons, "oddballs" and "clowns." "Are you going to let your emotional life be run by Time Magazine?" asked Ginsberg in his poem "America" (*Howl* 32). *Time* responded by profiling Ginsberg as "recognized leader of the pack of oddballs . . . who celebrate booze, dope, sex and despair and who go by the name of Beatniks" ("Fried Shoes," *Time* [Feb. 9, 1959] 16). Thomas Parkinson, who had been Ginsberg's professor when he tried out graduate school in

Berkeley (during which he wrote "Howl"[68]), has testified to the general debasement of the Beats: "the first critical approach to the Beat writers," he says, was "ignore them, don't take them seriously, they are a bunch of clowns" (*Poets* 315). Parkinson was advised by his department chair in 1959 not to cite publications on the Beats in his dossier for promotion, "because there might be somebody on the Budget Committee who lacked a sense of humor. I have always treasured that moment" (314–15).

It took someone as intrepid as Karl Shapiro to register a serious response. Having recently taken over editorship of *Prairie Schooner*, he wrote in 1957 that "[t]hey are, in fact, the first symptom of widespread literary revolt to appear before the walls of modern literary conservatism and the Tradition," adding that "the group has an intrinsic significance: it has drawn talent to its side" ("Romanticism" 182). The talents singled out in the article were Ginsberg, Kerouac, Everson, and Spicer. Shapiro's authority in the matter is not to be undervalued. As I've indicated previously, he was among the leading poets of his generation in terms of public acclaim, honors and prestige; and before taking over *Prairie Schooner* he had been editor of *Poetry* for six years. His recognition of the Beats was important, if not as the *solution* to his generation's peculiarities, at least as an *antidote*: "the invention of 'Classicism' in our time by American poets was possibly a stratagem of delay," he pointed out, "the ostracism of Whitman a military maneuver to re-establish the right esthetic distance between poetry and the world" ("Romanticism" 183). The Beat phenomenon continued to provoke deliberations by Shapiro in the following decades, since he felt it acutely as an overturning of the "bourgeois literary applecart" his generation

---

[68] The specifics of the contact, as reported by Parkinson: "[T]he writers associated with the beat movement became known to me because Allen Ginsberg's little cottage in Berkeley, where I met Kerouac, Snyder, and Whalen, was at 1624 Milvia Street and our old farm house was at 1610 Milvia, so that while Allen was writing 'Howl' he was also taking a special course with me in Whitman's prosody and was in and out of our house as a welcome guest. Kerouac was, as a manic lush, not welcome, and I heard at the time that Rexroth also barred him from his home. For one thing, he bewildered and frightened our young daughters" (*Poets* 258).

had fabricated with the diligence of General Motors engineers.[69] In 1968 he reflected that

> For many years I have been trying to loosen the hold of the academic or "colonial" mind over poetry. It encourages a poetry as well as an entire literature of reference, the kind that refers back in every case to prior commitments, historical, religious, philosophical. In a sense it is a useless battle; attacking the Establishment only tends to strengthen it. It would be better to ignore the existence of the literature of reference and to create whatever we think valid than to go on tilting at windmills. This is what the Beat writers did; they were successful because they refused to take part in the academic dialogue. (*Children* 38)

These comments place Shapiro clearly in the vector of concerns that preoccupied Williams in the wake of *The Waste Land*, which he felt had made poetry hostage to the academy. Shapiro, despite his impulse to resign from his generation, felt constrained about joining the Beats, but resolved to "aid and abet, contribute to and fondle the Revolution and never be a part of it," because he "hated concerted behavior with a passion and would remain an outsider above all" (*Reports* 137).

Closer to the time, facing the emerging factions of the Beats as well as confessional poets, Shapiro declared that "[p]oets don't run in packs. And confessions aren't to be confused with public rants and exhibitions. If we are going to bait academic poets—one of the most wholesome of literary sports—we might as well keep in mind that the Beat poets constitute the most clearly defined and most widely publicized 'academy' in the American world of poetry today" ("Careful" 178). This was a charge many poets made against the Beats, particularly the academic ones who were less disposed

---

[69] In 1990 Shapiro included an anecdote in his autobiography which amounts to a castration scene; whether literally true, it does express the emasculating affront signified by the sexual impact of Beat legends. In this account, Shapiro is having sex with a woman from California (itself a pertinent synecdoche): "He was on the rise," he says—reporting in the third person, as he does throughout his autobiography—"pushing away at her with her legs over his shoulders, when she said to him in a calm voice, 'Allen Ginsberg says you can't write for shit.' His erection immediately shrank and his penis fell out" (*Reports* 136).

than Shapiro to legitimize Ginsberg as a poet; and this is largely because the academic poets refused to recognize themselves and their formalist poetics as constituting an academy as such. "Academe" was an unpalatable term, but they could always disavow it by reducing it to a term for the workplace. Part of what the Beats put on view, with their strictures on spontaneity, bop prosody, and open form composition, was that *all* poetry is method, even the most barbaric. Method on either side could only be confronted by militant response. Guy Daniels in *The Nation* (1958) satirized the arrayed forces in military terms. "The time is the latter part of 1956," he begins, "The Land of Poesy . . . an Occupied Country":

> Wheresoever one looks, one sees the stony, bespectacled faces of the occupation troops (academic critics and poets drilled by Master Sgt. T. S. Eliot). And at one's back one always hears the heavy iambic trâmp, trámp of their boots as they patrol the pages of the literary quarterlies, armed with Seven Types of Ambiguity. . . . Such is the Tale, as told in *The Nation, New World Writing, New Directions, The Evergreen Review, Esquire*, etc. (53)

The competing tale of the conservative quarterlies was different: "According to this version the Land of Poesy was, in the year 1956, a smiling, prosperous realm . . . *almost* a Golden Age." Daniels's intent was to expose the emerging stereotypes, so he insisted that "several of the academic poets are decidedly unprofessorial and freewheeling when they have a mind to be (Roethke, Ciardi), and there is more social consciousness in Robert Lowell than in any ten San Francisco poets" (54). But the stereotype remains in place today, despite Daniels's documentary provocation. Citing a "little mag circuit" overlooked equally by the academics and the Beat enthusiasts, he proposes an extensive underground alternative in James May's *Trace* (L. A.), Leslie Hedley's *Inferno* (S. F.), William Margolis's *Miscellaneous Man* (Berkeley), Lilith Lorraine's *Flame* (Alpine, Texas), all established before Beat notoriety, plus the more recent *Whetstone* (Philadelphia), *Coastlines* (L. A.), and *Mutiny* (N. Y.). "It now becomes apparent that the San Francisco earthquake of 1956–57 was only a late phase of a seismographic phenomenon which had been building up for a long time. Moreover, this late phase was far from being characteristic of the underground movement as a whole" (54). Daniels excepts Rexroth and Ferlinghetti from his general contention that the misnamed "'San Francisco School' . . . played a negligible role in the Underground." If his list of magazines seems unfamiliar, the list of poets he cites as authentic "underground" poets is only slightly less so: Leslie Woolf Hedley, James Boyer May, William Pillin, Thomas McGrath, Curtis Zahn, George Abbe, Henry Birmbaum, and William Stafford (55). Of these, only Stafford rose to the upper echelon of eminence (although his academic reputation is still wanting today); and McGrath has earned some grudging respect in reprints.

The most distracting aspect of the Beats, to members of the poetry world, was the journalistic application of the term to a broader context. So, where "Beat" originally referred to a handful of poets and novelists, the new term Beatnik became a familiar misnomer. "In 1950 these poets gave name to the generation, calling it the Beat Generation," wrote Corso in 1959, but "they did not know when they created that stupid name what the vast extent of the future demand would be" (*Casebook* 88). By 1958 a commentator for *Poetry* could not even mention the Beats without carefully providing a sociological perspective on this originally literary phenomenon:

> As to the poet's situation, "beat" sometimes means pushed into an unsuccessful stratum of society, into a semi-squalid, semi-romantic Bohemianism. . . . But there is a more essential meaning for "beat," keying in with the beat poet's frequent affiliation with jazz. Beat means pulse. The beat poet feels he responds to the pulse of the times, or to an essential reality which beats beneath the forms, the sham, the imperialistic show. This, I take it, is what everyone most properly feels during adolescence, when for a little while he is part of a communal personality made up of his contemporaries. (Rosalie Moore 105)

The jazz connection was foremost in many people's minds, and rightly so. It was by this route that one quasi-Beat affiliate, LeRoi Jones, became the first black poet to be regularly anthologized in a white context, with poems like "In Memory of Radio." For the author of the *Poetry* article on "The Beat and the Unbeat," however, it seemed that "beat poetry is based on a direct use, or misuse, of the poet's own excitement on discovering this identity, this charge"—the charge, that is, of adolescent communion with a peer group.

The Beat ethos was full of contradictions. Jack Kerouac was busy celebrating the asphalt-hugging hijinks of Dean Moriarty in *On the Road*, while the automobile was given a derogatory twist in Corso's definition of a *square* as "some guy who forces himself arbitrarily into a square auto-life mold, because squareness is not a shape that any living creature occurs in" (90). And Robert Duncan, living in San Francisco during the Beat heyday but pointedly keeping his distance (while being idolized by Gary Snyder and Michael McClure), was writing *The Opening of the Field* in part as a deliberate counterpoint to Beat designs: "in the midst of the Beat Movement, by lovely synchronicity," he explained later, "while they're talking about squares, I am dealing with a *square*: my field is square" ("Interview" 533). The hipster ethos permeating the Beat image in the press belied their personal backgrounds. As Snyder testified in 1974, "We weren't high school dropouts. We were graduate school dropouts—all of us" (Knight 9). Without such a background the Beats would not have been able to succeed, for they were called upon to be spokesmen for the inarticulate. Far from writing for the underground magazines, Kerouac went straight to national television and glossy venues like *Esquire*, where he characterized the Beats as "solitary Bartlebies staring out of the dead wall window of our civilization"—which Michael Davidson shrewdly notes was offset by an ad for a mohair suit, with the plug "Dress right. You can't afford not to." "The juxtaposition of Kerouac's antiestablishment Beat bum with what William H. Whyte, in a popular book of the period, called 'Organization Man,' offers a felicitous image of the tensions faced by the Beat writer," Davidson writes, asking "Was he an alternative to mass culture, or a product of it, court jester to the Fair Deal society?" (23).

Davidson has usefully formulated a question that was broadly felt, if latent and unexpressed, in the 1950s. The most chilling aspect afforded by the spectre of the Beats as court jesters was that they disclosed a liability of the poet's role in general. Even the most docile of establishment poets were, in the end, freaks. It soon became impossible to seek salvation for certain poets without vindicating all of them at once, of whatever persuasion. This is the tactic Donald Hall took in 1961 in *Horizon*, in which he described the Beat/square opposition as

> . . . a ritual as old as American literature: East against West, the salon against the frontier, sophistication against ruggedness, learning against experience, the literary life against the life of the bum, Henry James against Mark Twain. Of course these contraries have been valuable to American literature, partly because so many of our writers have commuted from one camp to another. Philip Rahv invented a good phrase for it with his essay "Paleface and Redskin." . . . Sometimes it seems that the West is a place created for Easterners to go wild in. The Beat Generation is a group of New Yorkers who came to light in San Francisco in the late fifties. ("Battle" 116)

This archetypal view sounds celebratory, intent on exonerating all kinds of offenders. It also subtly reasserts a status quo in the image of a tranquil middle ground, not unlike Delmore Schwartz's 1958 image of a peaceful summer park. By stressing deeper continuities over the superficial dissimilarities between Beats and academics, Hall reaffirms the middlebrow need to quell uprising by means of the pervasive functionalist formula of compensation. One reciprocates in wildness for the other's tameness, and those in the middle are relieved of the fear of extremism in their midst. Mood swings assuredly settle down to a central stability in the explanatory lithium of common sense.

This centrist doctrine was adopted only tentatively, of course, since the academic *cordon sanitaire* of 1960 saw itself as thoroughly inhabiting a sage and judicious middle ground. The literary right was represented by modernists like Robinson Jeffers and Ezra Pound, while the left lingered on in the image of antiquated personalities still wringing their hands over Stalinism. The Beats embodied a limit that was neither right nor left in such configurations: they were, instead, underground, beneath attention, with a taint of mass media kitsch and opportunism that verified their Americanness in an age prone to identify deviance as *un*-American. The Beats, however, were *too* public, too intimate with mass culture. So it was that, when Don Allen certified the Beats in the context of a number of other neglected schools in *The New American Poetry*, reviewers generally singled out others and left the Beats behind with a sigh of relief. As Hall put it, "it became quickly obvious that the Beats mattered less, poetically speaking, than the other poets whom their breakthrough uncovered. An orthodoxy was attacked which had become stiff enough to resent anything that did not resemble itself" ("Battle" 119).

That orthodoxy continued to assert itself, in the face of considerable odds, with assurance and complacency. Carolyn Kizer, in a survey of American poetry of the fifties for the first *International Literary Annual* published in London in 1958, had nearly forty pages at her disposal, yet managed to skirt the rupture signified by the Beats, discussing the later work of earlier generations (Williams, H. D., Moore, MacLeish, Ransom, Winters, Humphries, Léonie Adams, R. P. Warren, Lattimore, Fitzgerald, Kunitz, Roethke) and only tentatively inching toward the present with the fortysomething crowd (Berryman, Garrigue, Gardner, Stafford, Lowell, John Holmes, W. T. Scott), the sole "younger" poet being Richard Wilbur (thirty-seven at the time). In June 1962, in *Library Journal*, Louis Untermeyer provided a "Selected List for the Medium Size Library" of modern American poetry. Given Untermeyer's prestige—not to mention his longevity as an anthologist—along with the bibliographic clarity of his list and the authority of *Library Journal*, this was bound to be an influential checklist for librarians across the country (and judging from municipal libraries I've seen, it either set or reinforced purchasing patterns). Given that Untermeyer's focus was "modern," one would expect to find Stevens, Crane, Eliot, and the rest of the modernists; and he accordingly lists twenty-four titles as "absolute 'musts.'" However, he goes on to cite thirty entries by authors largely of the postwar generation and/or somewhat lesser modernist poets (Tate, Van Doren, etc.). These constitute the core of official verse culture of the fifties, with titles by Eberhart, Warren, Kunitz, Roethke, Bishop, Rukeyser, Schwartz, Shapiro, Jarrell, Lowell, Viereck, W. J. Smith, Barbara Howes, Nemerov, Wilbur, and a smattering of new poets (Vassar Miller, Dugan, Snodgrass, and Sexton). Untermeyer concedes the existence of other poets, naming "some forty of a possible hundred who have their admirers and, in some instances, their imitators" (2085). Apart from Muna Lee, David McCord, and Lee Anderson, whom I've never otherwise heard of, the forty consist of those poets anthologized in the mainstream fifties anthologies edited by Ciardi, Humphries, Elliott, and Hall-Pack-Simpson. Rexroth and Olson are the only poets cited from the milieu of Allen's "New American Poets," and Untermeyer pointedly omits the Beats because they allegedly lack "staying power" and belong only "in a library that has a place for poetry as documentaries." The documentary gesture is telling: at the end of a decade in which poetry seemed subordinate to the prestige of sociology, the most sociologically efficacious group of poets is commended not for their poetry but as social document. The gesture meant far more than Untermeyer surely intended.[70]

The latest confirmation of this perspective is by Michael Davidson, in *The San Francisco Renaissance*, albeit in a different vocabulary. His concern is to clarify the nature of the Beats as political poets. The common assumption, and the narrowest for Davidson, is that political poetry is the sort that manifests identifiably political views. But the more intriguing prospect for a political poetry, which the Beats typify, is "their collective role as a kind of oppositional sign" (27).

---

[70] Untermeyer had become quite compliant with the official view of poetry, despite his populist orientation forty years earlier. Surveying the field in *American Poetry Since 1900* in 1923, he celebrated a return "to actuality, to heartiness and lustihood. Latterly the most aristocratic of the arts, appreciated and fostered only by little salôns and erudite groups, poetry has suddenly torn away from its self-imposed strictures and is expressing itself once more in terms of democracy. It is no longer composed chiefly by scholars for scholars. It is democratic in the sense that a great part of it is written of the people, for the people and evidently—judging from the number of magazines devoted exclusively to its practice—by the people" (7–8). His book auspiciously concluded with a survey of "Native Rhythms," covering African American and Native American poetry, cowboy verse, poetry in slang, and poetry by children. His 1962 report to librarians gives no hint of this legacy, confining itself to a kind of social-engineering profile of poetry safely and firmly in the hands of accredited professionals. Frank Lentricchia is right to draw attention to Untermeyer's revolt against the poetic hegemony of voices from "the cosmopolitan finishing schools of genteel America" (82), but by neglecting Untermeyer's subsequent concessions gives a misleadingly romanticized view.

> For our purposes it would be possible to see the San Francis-
> co poets as offering not only a performative poetics . . . but a
> critique of "master narratives." By refusing to propose an
> institutionally "correct" ideology and by celebrating an essen-
> tially plural society, these writers distinguish themselves
> from earlier political poets like Auden and Spender. . . . At
> the same time, their qualities of self-projection, their use of
> popular culture, their exploitation of the mass media allowed
> them a kind of public exposure that turned them, as writers,
> into signs. If they were assimilated by the public imagination,
> they also willfully appropriated it to their own uses. This is
> an oppositional and critical stance that must be mentioned in
> any discussion of the period. (31)

The references to ideological correctness, oppositionality, and the
critique of master narratives here mark the passage as thoroughly saturated with its (and our) moment; but I take this marked moment as
a necessary precondition for speculating on the trauma suffered by
American poetry in the 1950s. The 1980s were themselves preoccupied with various fifties revivals, in music and politics and religion
and styles of personal appearance; and Davidson's book was written
to its cultural moment as much as it was *about* a preceding time. The
New Formalism had arisen from the ashes of fifties formalism, and
part of the task of *The San Francisco Renaissance* was to delineate a
genealogical portrait of a mythopoetic site, by which the revivalism
of the Beats could be transposed not to their direct heirs (second or
third generation Beats) but to the "language" poets of the Bay Area,
who rose to prominence in the eighties by proclaiming a politics of
the sign.

  Davidson's equation is supple and almost works. What
impedes it in the end is the fact that the Beat mystique never faded
away, but has percolated on through the decades in high schools and
on the fringes of college campuses, becoming in the process a semi-
official subaltern anti-intellectualism—the opposite, in other words,
of the theoretically inclined scholasticism of language poetry. The
desultory hipster pose of the 1980s and '90s—often preserved with
the assiduousness of the Civil War buff—is strikingly out of key with
its time. On the other hand, the value of that core of original Beats—

Ginsberg, Snyder, Burroughs—remains undimmed because they recognized, in Snyder's words, that Beat was "a particular state of mind
. . . and I was in that mind for a while." But "[e]ven the state of mind
belongs to that historic window," a window long ago boarded up
(Charters xxxvi). The desire to gaze out that window may never
recede, as long as there are adolescents who read; and in that
respect, there is a certain truth to middlebrow charges in the fifties
that the Beats were immature. But the cost of "maturity," then as
now, is to subscribe to what William Burroughs sagely diagnosed as
"The Algebra of Need," to be addicted to the rat race and its seda-
tions.[71] From that perspective, the Beat or "beatific" impulse may be
adolescent, but as so many have gleaned from that contact, poetry is
enduringly adolescent too.

ANTHOLOGY WARS

The coupling of American with English poetry was endemic
to the Fifties—one might as well say *pandemic*. The auspicious presence of Auden in New York had an impact hard to overestimate,
without which neither the selection of poets by Donald Hall and his
co-editors for *The New Poets of England and America* nor by David
Cecil and Allen Tate in *Modern Verse in English, 1900–1950* would
have seemed so self-evident. In his introduction Tate provides the
genealogy: "The early reception in England of Robert Frost and the
enormous international influence of Pound and Eliot and, later, of
W.H. Auden, have at last produced an Anglo-American poetry that
only by convention can be separated . . . " (40). The inevitability of a
link between British and American traditions was too readily
assumed by Tate, but he was correct in identifying the codependence
of poetry and criticism. "Never have poetry and criticism in English

---

[71] "Junk is the mold of monopoly and possession," Burroughs writes. "Junk is
the ideal product" because "[t]he junk merchant does not sell his product to
the consumer, he sells the consumer to his product" ("Deposition" 137, 138).
Capitalism, addictive behavior, and information are all manifested together in
a simple elegant synthesis in junk, in Burroughs's vital testimonial.

been so close together, so mutually sensitive, the one so knowing about the other. This has been partly but not altogether the result of their appearing so often in the same person," he claimed, singling out as examples of such critics "many of our best poets, Eliot, Ransom, Auden, R.P. Warren, Jarrell . . . " (42). This listing is recognizably an address book of Tate's own associates, of course, and it fastidiously avoids mention of two significant facts: first, that the formalist heirs of this lineage were, by 1958, proving themselves all too clearly abstemious of criticism or theory, and second, that the new wave of articulated poetics was emanating from other quarters, reactivating the significant provocations of Pound, Williams, and Stein, among others, who could not be accommodated to the Eliot line. Tate clearly knew that modern poetry could not speak on its own behalf, no matter how eloquent it was; nor was he among those who imagined that a putative poetic complexity needed to be explained or justified to a general public. The declining modern role for the man of letters might have given rise to poetic speculation, but Tate knew as well as anyone that the practice of verse had become inseparable from the practical elaboration of a poetics. I can only speculate regarding Tate's views on the matter, but it seems reasonable to suppose that *The New American Poetry* was a brutal reminder of the abdication of poetics on the part of those poets who succeeded the generation of poet-critics: it was as if, by being politely circumspect, their muteness had given voice to a raucous and unwarranted opposition. Donald Allen's anthology culminated in a section of "Statements on Poetics," forty pages of concerted poetic theory by fifteen poets, most noticeably Charles Olson and Robert Duncan.

Concluding his introduction to the American wing of *Modern Verse in English*, Tate indicated that "One looks in vain at the work of the brilliant young poets of the fifth decade for the signs of a new poetry such as Pound, Eliot, Stevens, Miss Moore, Ransom, Cummings, and Crane gave us thirty-five years ago" (48). While not recognizing that the dam was about to burst with a *new* poetry, Tate described the imminent change with uncanny precision: "If we suppose that we are at the end of a period, or of a period style (I think we are), we must nevertheless be ready for something entirely new from a poet whose work may seem to be complete, or, from a new poet expect a style altogether new, which persons who have reached middle age would probably dislike." This prescient forecast portends the drastic change in style and idiom that would soon affect Lowell, Merwin, Wright and so many others; and it also gestures toward those in *The New American Poetry* whose new styles were thoroughly disliked by Tate himself. Four years later, at the National Poetry Festival in 1962, Tate had still not come to terms with the immensity of the change at hand, maintaining that "in spite of the brief spasm that we heard about from California a few years ago . . . poets are trying again to write in rhyme and meter" (*NPF* 285).

For a quick vantage on the turbulent transitional years, from the secured hegemony of academic verse in *The New Poets of England and America* in 1957 through the rise of the Beats, the confessional surge, and the consolidation of opposition in Allen's *New American Poetry*, it's useful to review them by way of an observer uniquely positioned astride the Anglo-American interface. Carl Bode, a professor of English, spent three years as Cultural Attaché at the U.S. Embassy in London, where he reported on the fractious American poetry scene for interested British bystanders, subsequently collected in 1965 in his book *The Half-World of American Culture*. Bode's first piece, written for *Time & Tide* in 1959, commented chiefly on "The Poems across the Way" by means of Stevens, Frost, and "a whole school of American experimentalists, all of whom would deny that they belonged to any school whatsoever. Notwithstanding, Roethke, Richard Wilbur, Robert Lowell, and Randall Jarrell have much in common" (191). To an audience presumably basking in the sententious wit and puffery of Betjeman and the crusty naughtiness of Larkin, the American equivalents could seem esoteric: "These men all write a poetry of tension, a poetry which has that intellectuality tightened into obscurity which marks so much of American verse today" (192). While these poets had been prominent for more than a decade, Bode was alert to newer developments, declaring that "[t]he hallmark of current American poetry is its vitality," and adding that "[t]he contrast with current British verse is very sharp. . . . There is no Beat Poet howling in England, or if there is one, he howls alone" (190).

During the next three years Bode would survey the unfolding conflagration for the weekly *John O'London's*. In 1960 he saw "The Changing Face of American Poetry" embodied by W. D. Snodgrass, whose *Heart's Needle* had taken the Pulitzer. It must have been the arch formalism that motivated Bode's odd comment that "[o]ne of the most interesting things about American poetry for the last year or two is that it has begun, in several important ways, to resemble current British poetry" (194). Other prizewinning collections by Eberhart and Kunitz were noted, in part as instances of a new clarity which Bode contrasts with Stevens, "the idol of the obscurantists" (196). Bode disapproved of literary power politics as represented by the New Critics, and was perturbed that "[t]he poets whom the New Critics and editors applauded most were the poets of obscurity" (195). He saw a glimmer of hope in Ransom's retirement, the previous year, as editor of *Kenyon Review*; and approvingly cited Shapiro's assault in *In Defense of Ignorance* on what he called the "culture poets." "The boldest attempt to change the face of American poetry," Bode wrote approvingly, "has been Karl Shapiro's" (195).

The next year, in "The Mixed Romantics," Bode generally confined his remarks to poets he felt deserved wider recognition, William Meredith and Chad Walsh, and puffed Eberhart's new *Collected*. It all added up to a renewal of Romanticism, and Bode added, "I confess that even among the Beats I see Romanticism"—singling out McClure for further comment (203). The ruckus occasioned by *The New American Poetry* could not escape his attention for long, however, and in 1962 Bode disclosed to his London readers "The Hidden War in American Poetry" (retitled "The New Battle of the Books" in 1965). Allen's anthology is not mentioned, except obliquely by way of "the Beats." Bode has the ingenuity to juxtapose the Beats with the Fugitives-cum-New Critics, spending most of the article elaborating on their different attitudes to black culture: "the most vital advantage the Beatnik has over the Fugitive is in the attitude toward the Negro" (207). Bode also perceptively notices that the Beats' success is in part attributable to their disdain of direct confrontation with the academic establishment: "these latest opponents are almost accidental ones, who hardly care that the New Critics exist. They are the Beats. Crude and boisterous . . . [t]hey have simply outdone—and shouted down—the New Critics" (206). Bode was not sympathetic to the New Critics, so he concludes his report by asserting that while "the battle has gone on . . . the real casualties have been the talented writers of the median. Not esoteric enough for the New Critics, not bawdy enough for the Beats, they have often been ignored" (209). Bode's prize example of such neglect turns out to be Daniel Hoffman.

As I discuss in Chapter Three, Hoffman has had a significant role in perpetuating distortions in the history of postwar American poetry. But what did "neglect" signify for Bode as applied to such a poet in 1962? Hoffman at that time was author of two collections, published by Yale and Oxford, as well as three critical studies, including his influential *Form and Fable in American Fiction*. What constituted neglect for Bode, apparently, was the fact that Hoffman was not among the *New Poets of England and America*, and was obviously antithetical to Don Allen's tribes. In fact, the only anthologist who'd taken note of Hoffman was Oscar Williams, which was no help at all. To be a recognized poet in the early sixties was necessarily to be a pawn in some armchair quarterback's version of the Battle of the Anthologies, and the Anthologies in question were specifically Allen's and the Hall-Pack-Simpson one in its two editions. The habitual and often gratuitous mention of this "battle" has permeated the study of American poetry in the past thirty years—so much so, that it would be fair to think of it as a perpetual *rerun* much like a syndicated television program. In the hijinks of the rerun, Beats and Squares face off in 1960 to duke it out for poetry's golden glove award. Because it's such a familiar tale, I propose to review it by readjusting stereotypes rather than narrating it once again.

Surveying "American Poetry's Silver Age" for *Harper's* in 1959, Stanley Kunitz dared his readers to "[o]pen any popular anthology on your shelf and try to find what tribute is paid to Charles Olson or Kenneth Rexroth, who are potentates in their own right" (174). Kunitz revealed himself to be bipartisan before the battle erupted, and was particularly enthused about the New York and Black Mountain poets. "You would have known more about them—such poets as

Robert Creeley and Denise Levertov, for example—if they had created a scandal" (178). While this may have been true, Kunitz's comment indicates how the groupings which Allen documented in his anthology were already tacit in the minds of certain readers. The unfortunate thing about the Beats, for Kunitz and others, was that their notoriety obscured the range of alternative poetries available—a comment that would be frequently repeated in reviews of *The New American Poetry*, although *how* those alternatives would have been noticed without the Beats' notoriety is left unmentioned.

Kunitz was authorized to comment on the poetry scene in the first place by virtue of having won the Pulitzer, "a recognition which many poets felt was long overdue" as the editorial headnote to his article put it (173). It was common practice (and remains so) for authoritative commentary to be justified on the basis of prizes, awards, and professional honors. Kunitz deviated from standard practice at the time in asserting a meliorist vision of the state of poetry. He was approving yet skeptical of the radical and conservative wings alike, and did not overstress the adversarial aspect of that distinction. However, he obliquely questioned the New Critical presumption of custody rights over modernism. Eliot, along with Pound, reports Kunitz, "made a fashion in poetry out of irony, wit, indirection, allusiveness, and objectivity." Glossing over the elaborate institutional consolidation of these practices, he continues: "You can see how the fashion persists by examining *The New Poets of England and America*, the quasi-official anthology of the poets under forty who belong, as of this date, to the literary establishment" (176). Kunitz's point is more clumsily, but plainly, put by Louis Simpson. "The influential ideas about poetry came from the New Critics and in the postwar years there was seen a phenomenon, poetry imitating criticism. Most of the poetry published in the quarterlies was of this kind. And when we put together *The New Poets of England and America* this was the kind of poetry we found" (*Air* 179). Simpson shrewdly selects Nemerov as "the most representative poet in the anthology" of the tendency he describes.

In 1972 Simpson attempted to set the record straight regarding his role in the project. Robert Pack had secured backing as well as publisher, and then asked Hall and Simpson to join him as editors. In Simpson's recollection, the editors were innocent of subsequent charges. "Without intending to, we had created a furor . . . . Now I can see that we were naive. For years there had not been an important collection of contemporary poets, and so the book would be regarded as definitive" (*Air* 176). This is misleading (as well as ambiguous, since it's not clear whether "years" gestures back to Ciardi in 1950, for instance), since George Elliott had consolidated the reputations of *Fifteen Modern American Poets* in a Holt textbook of 1956; and the year before that Wilbur and Shapiro had served as consultants to Untermeyer, who was preparing a shorter revised edition of *Modern American and Modern British Poetry* for Harcourt Brace. These collections virtually assured in advance the success of *The New Poets of England and America*, who were "new" within an established and recognizable idiom. Nor were many of them even very new. Lowell and Wilbur were, by any standard of success, the two most prominent "younger" poets of the fifties, and each had been anthologized annually throughout the decade. And there were others: Merrill, Merwin, Nemerov, Swenson and William Jay Smith had published copiously since the end of the 1940s and had all been anthologized before. This is not to discount the significant number of poets who really were *introduced* by Simpson and his co-editors (among whom many turned out to be very successful: Bly, Hollander, Justice, Meredith, Rich, Snodgrass, and Wright). Simpson was certainly overstating the case to claim *New Poets* as "definitive," and it hardly created a "furor." The furor was altogether consequent on publication of Allen's *New American Poetry* three years later, by which time it was retrospectively clear that Simpson's anthology had consolidated a poetry establishment and successfully launched the careers of the next generation of official formalist heirs. That so many of them underwent drastic stylistic changes in the wake of the anthology wars suggests, among other things, that the collective constraint implicit in *New Poets* was uncomfortable, even suffocating.

Simpson goes on to address the fate of his poets in the wake of the Allen challenge: "It has become, in fact, an accepted part of literary history that *The New Poets* was published according to certain literary prejudices that did not make room for the writing of the Beats, the Black Mountain poets, and other experimental writers"— which was indeed the case at the time of this reflection. "Having tried to set the record straight," he goes on, "I must admit that, though the criticism of our motives was mistaken, much of the criticism of the anthology was justified. It is true that it did not represent experimental verse sufficiently" (*Air* 177). This massive understatement begs the question by adding "sufficiently," since the only justification for associating experiment with *New Poets* is the flimsy claim that the return to metrical formalism was itself an experiment. The best that could be said of Simpson's group was, in Louise Bogan's words, "if few rebellious notes are openly struck, many of these young men and women are capable of satiric poems that indicate the working of a sharp and critical eye" (*Alphabet* 24).

One of the editors, Donald Hall, soon lost confidence in the collection. He was initially circumspect: "The anthology *New Poets of England and America*, which I helped to edit," he wrote in 1959, "confronted many of us with our obvious slightness as a generation of poets; we all knew what was *good* about us, but it took a collective annunciation to show us what was bad" ("Domesticity" 311). The labor of putting a poetic generation on record led to a diagnostic concern: "I feel that I see a pattern among us of provinciality and evasion, which results in a reliance on the domestic at the expense of the historical." James Dickey had argued a similar case in his review of the collection: "most of these poets have every right to admission, being as well as any others representative of a generation that has as yet exhibited very little passion, urgency, or imagination" (*Babel* 9). "Most of these are *occasional* poets," he clarified (12). The problem, in Dickey's view, is a congenial sort of indecision, in which "the Inevitable tends to get blurred, obscured, and finally swallowed up by the imploring crowd of pretty and quite serviceable Possibles" (13). In 1965 George Garrett conceded that "[t]here was, indeed, a kind of uniformity about the poems in the book, though it resulted more from the editorial choices than from the poets themselves . . . " ("Grain" 229). This is a perspective available, perhaps, only from another decade; at the time of publication the domestic quietude and formalist assurance of the work selected was so strictly in the centrist idiom of the day that there was little incentive, on the part of the generally favorable reviewers, to notice what an attenuated range such poetry actually represented. By comparison, the Beats were writing antipoetry, so far removed from the premises of *New Poets of England and America* that nobody reproached the editors for excluding them. As proof of the pall of uniformity which the editorial selection imposed on the contents, it's curious to note that Thomas McGrath was represented by several antiwar poems, yet even his notably leftist views were smoothed over, muted into yet another facet of formalist expertise, in that context. Delmore Schwartz, for one, cast an approving glance at *New Poets* in his Library of Congress lecture of 1958, in an assessment that by stressing the generational aspect ironically effaces the assembled individuals. "The new generation of poets possess a trained and conscious skill, a sophisticated mastery of the craft of versification. And this professional competence may be strengthened by the disciplined knowledge of literary form which the teacher of literature must have" (*Essays* 47). The salient assumptions of the period are firmly in place here: poetry is the craft of sophisticates, a formalist preoccupation which has no real place except in the classroom; poetry is vocational training for professional pedagogues.

Shortly before Don Allen's anthology appeared in 1960, Thomas Parkinson noted of *New Poets of England and America* that "it included none of the beat writers and none of the writers of the San Francisco school and the Black Mountain group." Possibly cued by Allen or some of his poets, Parkinson evoked the precise terrain shortly to be mapped in *The New American Poetry*: "Any anthology of recent poetry now appearing would practically have to include Ginsberg and Snyder, to say nothing of the nonbeat writers who have by accident been associated with them: William Everson (Brother Antoninus), Robert Creeley, Robert Duncan, Denise Levertov, Charles Olson, Kenneth Rexroth, and Jack Spicer, to name only those I take to be most distinguished" ("Casebook" 280). The opposing forces were being arrayed, and the span of security promised by *New Poets* was short-lived. The question remains, however, as to the real visibility of

those excluded from *New Poets*. Might the editors have made a different, more informed, selection? Simpson evidently thought not, though
he was insistent in 1972 that there was no conspiracy of exclusion.[72]
Donald Hall, on the other hand, demurred in a frank response to an
interviewer's question about the omission of Black Mountain poets.

> It's ridiculous, but we did not acknowledge that they exist-
> ed, and we weren't reading them. I speak for myself any-
> way. They were printing; the magazines were there.
>   I know that I avoided looking at the magazines
> because I had decided that the stuff was really no good
> without opening up my mind to it. Obviously, I wanted to
> keep my mind closed. I thought I *knew* how to write poetry;
> I *knew* what to do; I didn't want anybody upsetting me. . . .
> So, I think that the parochialism of the first edition of *New
> Poets of England and America* was a result of a kind of
> *careful* ignorance. (*Goatfoot* 16–17)

In 1961 Hall had perceptively noted that "There is a puritanism in
American thought, among both Palefaces and Redskins, which
demands adherence to a code of behavior and judges poems by the
actions of the poet" ("Battle" 119). He was referring obviously to the
dismissal of the Beats as bohemian misfits, but he was also pointedly
implicating the Beats themselves as fostering a correspondingly misguided assumption about their antagonists. And behind it all was the

---

[72] As in any hegemonic practice, there are meticulous constructions of ignorance that serve to console those delegated to wield influence with what has
become infamously known as "plausible deniability." Simpson and other
junior members of the poetry establishment exercised their authority with
the confidence that other, less knowledgeable agents, would follow their
precepts, but that they themselves could profess innocence. An example is
the handling of agents for powerful granting institutions. Kenneth Rexroth
reports an encounter with the Rockefeller Foundation representative touring
the west coast in 1955. "My treatment consisted of being told first that his . .
. best friend had been Jack Wheelwright and *then* that he thot John Berryman the best 'young' poet . . . . He was utterly unaware of the existence of a
living avant-garde. The people young people talk about—Genet, Beckett, the
late Céline, Artaud, Kerouac, the bonafide little magazines (e.g. *Origin, Gold-
en Goose, Black Mt Review*, etc.) even Olson, Creeley, Denise [Levertov] and
the rest—he actually did not have the slightest inkling suspicion that this
world existed" (*Letters* 208).

spectre of the Pound affair, in which the judgment of poems and poets had been all too messily conflated.

Karl Shapiro, among the first to hail the Beats, kept his distance on the basis of a similar appraisal of the liabilities of group mentality:

> . . . we have official criticism at the helm which determines the standards of work, directs the organs of expression, controls the fellowship foundations, and even reaches into the curricula of schools. The only opposition to this state of affairs comes from a self-styled literary Underground. But this Underground plays directly into the hands of the critical police of letters, being itself only a negative version of culture poetry. It is mostly the form of small life found under stones. But at least it is alive. (*Defense* 27)

The dilemma of the underground was to be helplessly caught up in a deathgrip with its opposite. The "life" of poetic alternatives was animated by its morbid Other, and the ensuing revulsion guaranteed that it would never be possible to consider the poetry world without elaborate defensive postures to neutralize the traumatizing spectre of dissent.

Even before *The New American Poetry* was published, the proscenium on which it would play its part in the poetry world had been constructed, much like a gallows in those frontier towns in westerns, the hammering outside assuring the jurists of the rectitude of their decision. Not surprisingly, it was Lowell who gave the cue in his acceptance speech for the National Book Award:

> Two poetries are now competing, a cooked and a raw. The cooked, marvelously expert, often seems laboriously concocted to be tasted and digested by a graduate seminar. The raw, huge blood-dripping gobbets of unseasoned experience are dished up for midnight listeners. There is a poetry that can only be studied, and a poetry that can only be declaimed, a poetry of pedantry, and a poetry of scandal. (quoted by Kunitz, "Process" 100)

Lowell satisfied pedants and scandalmongers alike with *Life Studies*, and the fact of the award confirmed a pervasive sense that the reigning formalism would have to come to terms with the raw gusto of the Beats. Who better than Lowell to invent the poise of dignified assent, without appearing to give in to anything at all? Stanley Kunitz was mesmerized, as many were, and his description of Lowell's sea-change can be read as symptomatic of a general approval: "These poems . . . boil with energy because they are charged with danger and audacity," he found. "Largely autobiographical in impulse, *Life Studies* reads with the breathless momentum of a novel. One of Lowell's heroic gestures has been to abandon the density of line, the hammer-metrics, the sensational Christian imagery with which he achieved his early reputation" ("Process" 100). Only in the case of Lowell would it seem daring to abandon Christian imagery, but this testifies to the unique sanction given Lowell's career by the end of the fifties: he was the poet who set the tone, as Auden had before him.

His distinction between raw and cooked (which Virginia Woolf had used to distinguish herself from the raw *Ulysses* of Joyce) had the effect of putting words in people's mouths, or at the tip of their pens. Lowell became the ventriloquist of attitudes and opinions. Katherine Garrison Chapin, reviewing *The New American Poetry* for *New Republic*, concluded that "[t]hese are poems which Robert Lowell has rightly called 'raw, huge, blood-dripping gobbets of unseasoned experiences dished up for midnight listeners'" (26). Hers was not an entirely negative review, and she had the sense to recognize, as some did not, that "from the variety of styles one discovers at once that the new poets are not an affiliated group" (25). However, she fell back not only on Lowell's authorizing terminological distinction, but on the habituated response to the Beats, which confused the poetry with the way their (and other) lifestyles were (mis)reported in the media. "Often these poems are like candid-camera shots, presenting feelings and emotions from an unbuttoned angle" (25). Where some saw flippancy, irreverence, and a jocular disposition, Chapin oddly remarks that Allen's poets "are highly self-conscious and articulate, humorless and a little portentous," and that "[w]hat one looks for in vain here is a fresh, creative impulse in poetry" (25). In the end she singled out Duncan, Adam, Levertov, Olson, Creeley, Ferlinghetti, and Corso as poets worth watching.

James Dickey, who had approved of but not raved about *The New Poets of England and America*, savaged *The New American Poetry* as " . . . mindless and jubilant. This is, I think, a fair description of the writers in Mr. Donald Allen's anthology." He did concede that "to an era weary of overrefined, university-pale subtleties, they look interesting; at least they look *different* . . . but put against a really intelligent and *resourceful* poet like Howard Nemerov, even [the best of the New American poets] show up pretty drably," he added (*Babel* 4–5). The term "resourceful" is ambiguous, and regardless of how Dickey meant it, it could be taken to explain the febrile approval which Nemerov's poems garnered, and which I can only understand as an intimation of the eventual triumph of the workshop conceit, as in "The Vacuum" (included in *New Poets*), which begins "The house is so quiet now / The vacuum cleaner sulks in the corner closet . . . " (248).

A more circumspect response was by Louise Bogan, who recognized that this anthology was not a surface flutter but a probing of assumptions which would subsequently have to be taken up even by those disposed to dismiss the new poetry.

> The questions multiply. Does this new poetry arise from sources largely amateur, exhibitionistic, or otherwise out of hand? Is it a revival of an oral tradition? . . . Are these wild talents outcroppings of an underground idealism; does their violence stem from a deliberate attempt to extend consciousness, or are many of them actually out of control? . . . The collection brings up, finally, the perhaps unanswerable query: What degree of anarchy can be projected in poetry? For when its principal tenets and accepted formal procedures are assaulted with utter vigor, this art of language does not merely change, it totally disappears. (*Alphabet* 25–6)

Bogan's tone intimates a private skepticism, but she had the decency to refrain from the spurious dismissals—either of individual poets or subgroups within the anthology—which typified much of the response. Cecil Hemley, for instance, in *The Hudson Review* (in which one might have expected a more gracious response, given its patent enthusiasm for the modernist foreground of the New American

poets, coupled with its resistance to New Criticism), attacked both
the premise of the gathering and Allen's editorial skills. "Anyone
who has had a serious interest in American poetry from 1945 to 1960
must see that this is a very eccentric version of what has been going
on. It represents Mr. Allen's private view, and that is all, and it shows
what happens when a narrow, dictatorial taste attempts to assert itself
as authoritative" (626). If this now sounds comically off-target, it is
nevertheless a vivid reminder of the presumptuousness of the establishment custodianship of the modernist legacy. For *The New American Poetry* to seem "eccentric" was to pit it against a *center* which
seemed so stable that Allen's group could be perceived as quite
beside the point. As Hemley saw it, Allen was shuffling minor players with reputable mavericks in an ungainly attempt to conjure a tradition out of thin air. "This is so obviously *not* the new American
poetry," he blithely asserted (629). Hemley was irritated that, as he
says of O'Hara, these poets were "not interested in writing good poetry in the usual sense." Hemley's fault was in not considering why
anyone, let alone so many, might choose such a course—a point that
drove Bogan to her litany of earnest questions about poetic risk.

Hemley's complaint about eccentricity was of course true, at
one level: Don Allen was decidedly not paying proper attention to the
kind of poetry that had been sanctioned up until that moment. But
while Allen had not given much credence to the official version of
1950s poetry, he *had* managed to produce a prophetic forecast of
what poetry in the 1960s and beyond would look like. What's funny
about Hemley's review is how thoroughly, if unintentionally, it mis-
perceives the scene. Allen's "private view" quickly became common
sense, and the "eccentricity" of his vision was momentary. After all,
Allen was not, in any strict sense, *introducing* these poets. *The New
American Poetry* was in fact the first appearance in an anthology for
most of the poets involved (including Ashbery, Baraka, Blackburn,
Corso, Creeley, Dorn, Everson, Ferlinghetti, Koch, Lamantia, Levertov, McClure, Olson, Schuyler, Snyder, and Spicer, with Ginsberg
being concurrently included in Shapiro's *American Poetry*). But the
Beats had been notoriously prominent for several years, and the beatnik scene was folklore on the *Dobie Gillis* television show (CBS,

1959–1963). Richard Eberhart had applauded the San Francisco scene in the *New York Times*, and when *Howl* was published it included a preface by William Carlos Williams. Furthermore, in his autobiography of 1951 (published by Random House) Williams had given over two full pages to an extended citation from Olson's "Projective Verse." The Black Mountain poets had been publishing vigorously in a broad network of little magazines and presses for most of the fifties. Ashbery had even been one of Auden's choices for the Yale Younger Poets series. Members of the formalist Anglo-American mainstream, then, claiming to have been ambushed by the sudden appearance of such organized opposition, risked exposing themselves as either snobs or ignoramuses. Hemley at least appears to have known enough to admit that "[s]ome of the best writers in the volume have been grossly neglected . . . " (626). His hostility to the editor did not automatically extend to the poets themselves; he proved sympathetic to, and even positively enthused about, Levertov, Duncan, Olson, Dorn, Ginsberg, Ferlinghetti, Barbara Guest, and LeRoi Jones. He justifiably lamented the omission of Rexroth, though his reference seems rhetorically designed as supporting ammunition for his accusation that Lowell and Bishop were unjustly excluded as well. Hemley was also right to quibble about the fact that Allen's compilation was not "truly representative," since it failed to include Roethke or Kunitz (from Olson's generation), nor did it accommodate Wilbur, Swenson, Garrigue, Hoffman, Simpson, or Snodgrass (the list is Hemley's), whose "verse is new in any meaningful sense" (630).

Hemley was rankled most of all by Allen's "confused preface with its outrageous claims" (626). The alarm is hard to account for by consulting the text, which seems in retrospect alarmingly modest. Allen itemizes the late riches of high modernism (citing *Helen in Egypt*, *Thrones*, *Journey to Love*, etc.); accounts for a "second generation, who emerged in the thirties and forties" (naming Bishop, Denby, Lowell, Rexroth, and Zukofsky); and then commits the fatal indiscretion, suggesting "we can now see that a strong third generation, long awaited but only slowly recognized, has at last emerged"— a generation characterized by "one common characteristic: a total rejection of all those qualities typical of academic verse" (xi). Outrageous? Only in a vacuum. Hemley can scarcely have been unaware of the fact that a public debate had been aired in the academic quarterlies themselves for several years prior to the appearance of *The New American Poetry*, questioning the tonal constraints and formal limits of what was widely called "academic verse." In fact, poets in academe consistently repudiated "academic" verse. So the real infraction, on Allen's part, was not to use the epithet but to pack an anthology with 400 pages of work written in clear defiance of—or utter indifference to—academic verse. The terms of the late fifties debate about academic verse had really been determined and monitored by academics, who were therefore in a position to exercise damage control after the embarrassing eruption of *Howl* in 1955. By that point the academy was so saturated with poets that it was possible for the most reactionary metrical technicians to point the accusing finger at someone even more narrow-minded and say "now *there's* the problem: academic verse."

In Hemley's world, the world of academic custody of poetry, the nature of the art is not susceptible of revision; poets are for him—and I take him to be paradigmatic of a widespread view—rather like television scriptwriters, required above all to efface an individuating signature so as better to duplicate the house style. Kunitz was far more tolerant, though even he referred to some of the New American poets as "uncooked or illiterate or both . . . a staggering bore." But he could not dismiss the energy, since that was precisely what he valued in the Lowell of *Life Studies* in his omnibus review "Process and Thing." The title was itself a variation of Lowell's formula of the raw versus the cooked (which is quoted not once but twice in the review) and Kunitz's concern was to strike a balance by nominating Lowell as the one who had synthesized rawness into a culinary treat—*nouvelle cuisine* posing as new poetry. That of course left the "process-oriented" work of the New American poets exposed, implicitly, as *too* processual—even meandering—a point about which Kunitz was explicit: "Most of the poets of this anthology give all to process; the *thing* escapes them." Despite this, he admitted that "a solid core of honest work nevertheless remains, particularly in the Black Mountain and New York sections, with Charles

Olson looming large as the dominant figure of the entire anthology" ("Process" 103). While Kunitz acknowledged Olson's significance as dean of the "process" school, the distinction between process and thing already had efficacy *within* the formalist establishment. In 1959, for example, Berryman contrasted Lowell with Roethke in precisely those terms: "Lowell's work is Latinate, formal, rhetorical, massive, historical, religious, impersonal," in his enumeration, while Roethke's was "Teutonic, irregular, colloquial, delicate, botanical, and psychological, irreligious, personal. It is hardly an exaggeration to say that Lowell is a poet of completed states, Roethke a poet of process" (*Freedom* 310). The availability of such handy contrasts within the establishment went far in justifying neglect of outsiders. If "process" could be associated with the free verse set pieces of Roethke, largely on the basis of thematic peculiarities like his botanical imagery, Olson's pronouncements on such matters as proprioception, dreamtime, and Whitehead's cosmology were bound to place him at the lunatic fringe.

The language of appraisal dominant within establishment circles was emphatically a matter of taste. As late as 1971, Lowell, in an interview, claimed that "I revere Pound and Williams; I think the Black Mountain poets are their journeymen, quite powerful without being inspired or pathfinders. . . . Other younger American poets, Snodgrass, Alan Dugan, and Adrienne Rich, seem more original" (*Prose* 273). Lowell's language reveals much about his own ability to consistently write the award-winning poem the way some actors can deliver the Oscar-nominee performance with monotonous predictability. His claim that certain poets "seem more original" is idle chatter, opinionated bluster delivered in such bland terms that, coming from a poet as eminent as Lowell, had a spellbinding effect. His taciturnity suggested that he was beyond the trifling and messy business of having to *account* for his views, so he simply and irrevocably passed judgment. A phrase like "powerful without being inspired" is literally nonsense—at least without careful definition of the terms. But it doesn't matter, since this is a game, Lowell's favorite sport, which he had routinely bullied old cronies like Jarrell and Berryman into playing and which they called

"Who's On Top."[73] It was the supercilious assumption that only those in on the game counted that kept even Allen Ginsberg from feeling sufficiently *acknowledged* until 1977 when, after a reading with Lowell not long before the latter's unexpected death, he found he was apparently no longer a "barbarian jerk" (Schumacher 618). Lowell was deft and oblique in his put-downs, embodying the tact of his social class. Reading with Frank O'Hara in 1962, after O'Hara read a poem he'd written the same day (and since then frequently anthologized—"Lana Turner has collapsed!"), Lowell "prefaced his poems by apologizing somewhat disingenuously for not having written a poem on the spot" (Gooch 387). Lowell is the sophisticated double in Mailer's *Armies of the Night*, effortlessly winning over an audience that the novelist debases himself to secure the approval of. Mailer watches the poet reading and realizes he is one of those happy few "who give a sense of security to the abdomen." Lowell is tellingly described as the "personification of ivy climbing a column" (58). His patrician manner played very effectively to an audience that thought of poetry as a way of cultivating sensibility and refining an aristocracy of spirit. Lowell's demeanor, unflappably dignified (except in his manic breakdowns, which were politely unmentioned), suggested above all that there was little to say *about* poetry; that its premises were known, were on record, and beyond improvement; and that to engage in poetics was impolite, overbearing, or simply superfluous to the monumental finality of the well-crafted poem itself.

The most considerable distinction between Hall-Pack-Simpson's New Poets and Allen's New Poetry was in the poetics rather than the poetry. *New Poets*, seamlessly bonding English and Ameri-

---

[73] It was also practiced obliquely in the art of blurbs. "Some patient cynic ought to write a definitive study of the art of the bookjacket blurb in our time. Poets, *in character*, each seeing and praising himself in another's work," George Garrett wrote in 1965. He then cites examples from the dustjacket of Kunitz's selected poems: "Kunitz has every technical virtue. What's more he can put his perfected and rather lapidary style at the service of the most fundamental themes and passions" (Wilbur); "I admire Mr. Kunitz's savage, symbolic drive" (Lowell); "Mr. Stanley Kunitz has a bold dramatic imagination that can wrest meanings from bleak and difficult material, turn even the language of science to the lyrical purpose with speed and style" (Roethke) ("Grain" 225).

can authors, offered no statement of method by the poets nor even the editors. Robert Frost's introduction, "Maturity No Object," amounts to a cagy refusal to comment on the work in the anthology. He acknowledges the danger of "rhyming trivia," but tendentiously implies something good will emerge because "all poets I have ever heard of struck their note long before forty, the deadline for contributions to this book" (11). Frost's final appeal is to a hermetic, inscrutable standard of excellence: "There should be some way to tell [good writing] just as there is to tell the excitement of the morning from the autointoxication of midnight." Curiously, he ends on a note that, in retrospect, amounts to a sabotage of the project from within. "If school is going to proclaim a policy of maturing boys and girls," he says, addressing the matter of his title, "it might become necessary for us to stay away from school or at least play hooky a good deal to season slowly out of doors rather than in an oven or in a tanning vat" (11–12). The *New Poets* were schoolroom bound—in mind as well as vocationally—but of course the Beats, at the time of Frost's writing, were exuberantly and insistently out of doors playing hooky.

Much of the vehemence with which the Beats and the Black Mountain poets were greeted is attributable to their insistence on explaining, proselytizing, exhorting: in short, theorizing a poetics. The penchant for writing manifestos tends to draw fire at any time, but most of the pronouncements by Allen's poets were not designed to shock or provoke, nor were they written as manifestos. (O'Hara's "Personism" is a parodic manifesto, although it begs the question of whether such a thing as a non-parodic manifesto exists.) The major distinction here is the patently *individuating* tone, the fact that so many of the "Statements on Poetics" in *The New American Poetry* are journal entries, personal letters, notes from album sleeves—in other words, hardly to be taken as *legislative*. The grandiloquent tone of Olson's "Projective Verse" tended to be misread as typical and paradigmatic of all these poets (mis)conceived as *a* group. The affront was in the open display of poetics as a matter of intense individual concern. The tacit platform of *The New Poets of England and America*, by contrast, was abstemiousness in the matter of poetics: the New Poets appealed, instead, to *taste*. And taste in that context, as in any other, is a surreptitious way of fabricating judgment. "Like the teaching anthology," Ron Silliman suggests, "the poem without theory exists solely as a concealment, the hiding of a primary dimension for the purpose of causing its effects to seem 'natural' or 'self-evident'" ("Canons" 167).

Responding to Cecil Hemley's complaints about *The New American Poetry* by appealing to standards of taste, Robert Duncan offers a chastening clarification: "Since he has no other conceivable route to knowledge of that work, taste must suffice. But I can have no recourse to taste," he says, adding that the work of Olson, Levertov and others "belongs not to my appreciations but to my immediate concerns in living." Duncan's view of form as organic necessitates a resistance to any notion of form as imposed. It is not merely a distinction between internal and external compulsion, but between a view of Romantic individualism versus what la Mettrie called "l'homme machine":

> What form is to the conventional mind is just what can be imposed, the rest is thought of as lacking in form. Taste can be imposed, but love and knowledge are conditions that life imposes upon us if we would come into her melodies. It is taste that holds out against feeling, originality that tries to hold out against origins. For taste is all original, all individual arbitration. (*Fictive* 104)

David Antin, who maintains a position of reverential but adamant distance from Duncan's Romantic hermeticism, nevertheless agrees with the basic premise that the poem is an act of inauguration rather than repetition. So Antin salvages the underlying poetics while conceding that much Beat and open form poetry was flaccid:

> It is part of a great Romantic metaphysic and epistemology that has sustained European poetry since Ossian and Blake and Wordsworth and is still sustaining it now. If the particular representations of reality offered by these poets of the fifties seemed less useful or adequate, this seemed less important and partially inherent in the Romantic metaphysic itself, according to which reality is inexhaustible or, more particularly, cannot be exhausted by its representations because its representations modify its nature. ("Modernism" 133)

Even John Ashbery, who has consistently integrated exercises in formal versification into his books, is pledged to a poetics of process. "Certainly the simultaneity of Cubism is something that has rubbed off on me," he told an interviewer in 1986, "as well as the Abstract Expressionist idea that the work is a sort of record of its own coming-into-existence; it has an 'anti-referential sensuousness' . . . " ("Interview" 202).

Robert Creeley, in his note for Berg and Mezey's *Naked Poetry* anthology, favors "a sense of 'free verse' as that instance of writing in poetry which 'turns' upon an occasion intimate with, in fact, the issue of, its own nature rather than to an abstract decision of 'form' taken from a prior instance" (*Essays* 492). Citing Ginsberg's dictum, "Mind is shapely," he elaborates that, "Mind, thus engaged, permits experience of 'order' far more various and intensive than habituated and programmed limits of its subtleties can recognize" (494). Creeley, in short, values open form precisely for the liberation from habit that motivated Auden, at about the same time, to place a premium on metrics: "Blessed be all metrical rules that forbid automatic responses, / force us to have second thoughts, free from the fetters of Self" (642). At the same time, Creeley's decision commits him, as it does Robert Duncan, to a decisively extraliterary sense of "tradition"—an "intuitive economy of human experience, biological and environmental"—which entails a certain indifference to strictures and "standards" (516).[74] "'Standards' are only interesting in relation to the possibilities they recognize," Creeley insists. "In the forties I

---

[74] Gary Snyder, likewise, stresses form as biological event. "I think of form in terms of biological forms," he told Ekbert Faas in an interview. Citing Adolf Portmann and evoking other biologists, he says, "Those people's work offers to me the most interesting information about what form is and how form changes. Form is always moving and adaptive and always has a function" (Faas, *Poetics* 125). Biological theories of morphogenesis continue to be of significance to a sophisticated open-form poetics. There is now a sizable body of pertinent literature on the concept of "autopoesis," the *locus classicus* of which remains *Autopoiesis and Cognition* by Maturana and Varela. For an ambitious attempt to incorporate this theory into the open-field trajectory of American poetics, see Byrd's *Poetics of the Common Knowledge*. A thoughtful supplement is Paul Ryan's *Video Mind, Earth Mind*.

felt them arbitrarily restrictive and dominated by the practice of criticism apart from the practice of poetry itself" (521). Creeley, like other advocates of open form and process, argues for a poetry of enactment in contrast to a poetry of episodic representation. But the issue of form remains vexed by the sheer scale of the metrical foreground; so, as Warner Berthoff has observed, a principle of order needs to be derived somehow: "Olson, Duncan, and O'Hara all argue directly, and repeatedly, from the great formulations in Keats's letters—'negative capability,' the 'true voice of feeling,' the importance of staying close to the mind's natural confusion ('uncertainties, mysteries, doubts')—which are the nearest thing in Anglo-American writing to a postclassical *ars poetica*"(*Qualities* 84).[75]

Kunitz's "process and thing" and Lowell's "raw versus cooked" were, in the end, altogether misleading. In 1959 they had a *polemical* serviceability as the terms by which the mainstream adjusted to challenges from the fringe. The accessibility of these distinctions ensured their repeated application, which developed into a repetition compulsion. The belief that a certain kind of poetry is chaotic while another is cultivated seems hardly to have tarnished its durability as platitude. In their time, Kunitz's and Lowell's terms of order reinforced the sense that a centrist taste, a discerning sensibility, could (and would) incorporate just the right dose of wildness; and it is this assumption, I believe, that ultimately gave sanction to the workshop phenomenon. Lowell's exalted *center* of refinement gave way to an altogether different center, which has turned out to be demographic: a triumph of the average, and what is more, a democratic vindication of plebeian sanity over the "manic power" of an established poetry elite.

At the moment of confrontation known as the battle of anthologies—which is by no means resolved even now, as we'll see

---

[75] W. S. Di Piero has complained that "Keats's remark about Negative Capability seems to be becoming a literary cult object. The commentators are full of it these days. Some, though, use it as a justification of ignorance," he warned. "We travesty Keats's inquiring, sensuous intelligence, however, if we cite him as an endorsement of the unwillingness to pass judgment, to evaluate, to assert or deny. Negative Capability is no counsel for failed nerve" (73).

in Chapter Five—the raw, process-oriented work was terminological-
ly disadvantaged in that "process" could be processed into "thing,"
and "raw" transformed by a culinary poetics into the "cooked." As
long as the "postmodern" mainstream could gesture toward a tradition and claim filiation, it seemed plausible that modernism might
culminate in precocious formalism. This core began to erode precisely to the extent to which the marginal activists of *The New American
Poetry* took care to explain their poetics with reference to the past.
To make explicit a poetics is not, of course, the same as public relations. But, in the fifties, mainstream formalists mistakenly presumed
that the classroom was a suitable place for elucidating their poetics,
and that in public the decorum of presentational immediacy stipulated performance without comment, poems without context: verbal
icons riveting the gaze by the formal symmetry of their apparition in
a depthless space—or else a space defined in its depths solely by the
blank cipher of "tradition."

When Donald Allen, aided by George Butterick, revised *The
New American Poetry* in the late seventies, the title was changed to
The Postmoderns. The title evokes a shift which, in another context,
is usefully problematized by Thomas Docherty:

> The avant-garde necessarily implies that a merely "conven-
> tional" art cannot offer a moment of cognition, but instead
> indulges in a superficial recognition; and the name for this
> is representation. For the avant-garde, conventional art was
> thus an art built entirely upon *anagnorisis*, upon the struc-
> ture of recognition in which the Subject of consciousness
> finds the comfort of Identity and self-sameness: the world
> as it is represented as it is, *tel quel*. (16)[76]

The perpetual quandary of the avant-garde is its dialectical relation
with the conventional because, through time, the renunciations of the
vanguard become new conventions. The "postmodern," as Docherty
suggests and which Allen and Butterick affirmed, begins by acknowl-

---

[76] A comparable distinction was made in 1941 by Leo Spitzer in *The Southern Review*: "Whereas history of ideas leads toward the *recognition* of general themes, the reading of poetry leads toward the cognition of concrete individual art . . . " (603).

edging this dilemma, which has the status within the postmodern of one of Zeno's paradoxes. The superficial recognitions (the formalist reiterations) celebrated in mainstream poetry were denounced as inadequate by the New American poets. "Open form" has proved a misleading term with which to designate their difference, since what was really at stake was the necessity to desist from *re*-cognition, from reiterating yet again the thoughts, postures, and verbal integrities that the New Critics had prepared readers to recognize as poetry. These poets were spurned by the establishment as "know-nothing bohemians" and comparable epithets that were more clichéd than the vanguard clichés the centrists thought they were censuring.

The mainstream assumed it had tradition on its side, or Tradition as certified by T. S. Eliot; but tradition is not idly to be presumed. Tradition is *acknowledgment.* Without acknowledgment, without credit and homage and the explicit cultivation of lines of force and means of access, there is no tradition. Instead, there is merely public relations and name dropping. "For in and of itself, tradition does not exist. Tradition is a bibliography with implications" (Silliman, "Canons" 152). The intensity of distinctions and discriminations that marked the early criticism of Jarrell, Schwartz, Berryman and others following immediately in the wake of high modernism tapered off, so that for the generation represented by *The New Poets of England and America* the *active* engagement with the past had become passive, tacit. After the smoke of ill repute associated with "Howl" cleared away, it turned out that the "know-nothing" upstarts were a platoon of bibliophiles and wandering scholars, arousing interest not only in themselves but in a radiantly expanding field of poetic lore. Where "tradition" had become narrowly configured by Shakespearean blank verse, a handful of English metaphysicals, and by Dryden, Pope, Wordsworth, Keats, and a cultural Eurocentrism, a much vaster assembly now billowed into sight—borne aloft by renegade autodidacts—ranging from Whitman, Dickinson, Blake, and Smart all the way back to Hesiod, taking into account T'ang China, Mesopotamian dynasties, Sanskrit poetics, Oceanic and native American oral traditions, and a range of modern poetries in other languages that all seemed clamoring to get into English—including Lorca, Vallejo, Neruda, Mandelstam, Breton, Char, Trakl, and scores of others.

The circumambient pressure of a *world* poetry proved too enticing, and almost as soon as the impetus to engage it appeared in the form of a "New American Poetry" it overflowed the boundaries of partisan squabbles, tingeing diverse strands with a more cosmopolitan dye than any of them had hitherto proposed.[77]

~~THE AGE OF~~ LOWELL

The poet who personified the postwar American bard was Robert Lowell. He was the poet whose actions set the pace and dramatized the Puritan backdrop into the bargain. But was he indicative? Was it really, after the Age of Auden, the Age of Lowell? Thomas Parkinson admits "It makes me uneasy to hear the period from c. 1945 to the present referred to as 'The Age of Lowell'—the phrase has a tinny fabricated sound. Lowell was something we reacted to and against, but there was never a sense of coziness about the whole thing . . . " (*Poets* 215). Parkinson's phrasing reveals more than he's willing to concede: his Lowell, it turns out, is not a person but a force, "something we reacted to," or as he subsequently puts it, "an other and representative reality." Lowell was attractive because he personified self-determination and

---

[77] Paul Blackburn, for a brief time poetry editor of *The Nation*, announced in a column of 1962 the advent of "The International Word." "There is an affirmation, a reaffirmation, of values," he wrote, "a searching of the older cultures, both American and foreign, modern and ancient, for values to sustain the individual in a world where all the official values have let us down entirely by being in the main hypocritical . . . " (359). Blackburn, one of Allen's New American poets, sent out signals of rapprochement here, citing the virtues of Merwin and Lowell, while reiterating those of Olson, Creeley, Levertov, O'Hara and others of the Allen anthology; stressing as well the absurdly neglected Zukofsky, and intimating continuities in the young and as yet barely published Robert Kelly, Clayton Eshleman, Ed Dorn, and Jerome Rothenberg, who was to become the foremost synthesizer of "the international word" in his large revisionary ethnopoetic projects (*Technicians of the Sacred, Revolution of the Word, A Symposium of the Whole,* etc.). The impetus was furthered from the late sixties on in a range of magazines devoted to the expanded field of modernism, performance, and an insubordinate dissipation of disciplinary boundaries (*Alcheringa, Io, Caterpillar, Montemora, New Wilderness Letter, Hambone,* and *Sulfur* come particularly to mind).

force of will, at a time when these were the qualities that appeared to have left America intact and endowed with leadership in a broken world. But this was, in the classic Madison Avenue and Hollywood sense, personification as production. Shapiro offers this insight: "Robert Lowell took to poetry instinctively as one of the deepest forms of abuse: he was pliable in the hands of the New Critics, the most powerful literary caucus of the midcentury, and he was not discovered but *created* by them" (*Children* 137). This would be sufficient incentive for a quality that many besides Shapiro noted: "one feels that Lowell writes poetry to *get even*," he said, adding that "competition is the sole inspiration of such a poet" (137).

It's not difficult to see Lowell as the "self-made" poet that Robert Duncan disapproves of, pridefully asserting the marketability of his verse as the public struggle of a *persona*. It was a role Yeats had pioneered, and Lowell made his difference explicit by putting the mask on upside down or backwards from time to time. It's not an accusation Duncan himself levelled, possibly because he saw, as I am inclined to, that Lowell was compelled in part to destroy the terms of valuation that had canonized him in the first place. His career charts a set of hurdles, each of which is a calculated affront to a coterie of admirers. What is alarming about Lowell, in the end, is the amount of *calculation* involved. The will to power is nowhere more brazenly apparent in poetry than in Lowell's trajectory. "Lowell is primarily a figurehead which he himself personally carved out of solid rock," Shapiro observed, contradicting his version of Lowell as New Critical putty (*Children* 136). His success is a classic American perplexity: that of the self-made man who is, for all that, enabled to triumph by powerful backers with their team of handlers and public relations experts. He was *the* poet prepared, golem-like, by the founders of New Criticism, programmed as it were to produce the poems that would confirm for a contemporary audience that their *tastes* (as honed by the curriculum of *Understanding Poetry*) could handle the new poetry as readily as the old.

"'You didn't write, you *rewrote*'," Jarrell's voice says reproachfully in a poem from *History* (135). Lowell's way of explaining his own work was to direct attention to the past, then offer a solution for its liabilities: "Shelley can just rattle off terza rima by the page," he explained. "And I think both Tate and I felt that we wanted our formal patterns to seem a hardship and something that we couldn't rattle off easily" (*Prose* 241). In his final years, when Lowell rattled off volume after volume of blank verse sonnets, it seems that history itself has been grasped as a technical problem, disgorging epiphanies by squeezing equal portions of data and sensibility into a stunted receptacle. Duncan's practice is virtually the opposite of Lowell's. If Lowell aspires to saturate history with his own presence—in the Emersonian sense, reckoning history as biography—Duncan is equally Emersonian in rendering himself porous to historical imperatives. "You've got to be flooded by the world, and yet, more and more, *how* to be flooded by the world becomes the question of the artist" ("Interview" 548). I have in mind not only Duncan's poems, like "A Seventeenth Century Metaphysical Suite" and the "Dante Etudes," but his method as well, for he was as meticulous a formalist as Lowell. Duncan's sense of form, however, involves consent rather than domination.[78] So in his view, "the poem is entirely a protective form": "The realization of form that's in the poem is analogous to the use of a pentragram in magic, where you're going to call up demonic powers" (548).

Lowell certainly called up powers of some kind. His manic-depressive episodes are well documented, and he exemplifies more than anyone the sustaining power of poetry in the face of personal crisis. So, while Parkinson is unwilling to recognize an Age of Lowell, he does validate Lowell as a barometer of public record. "Lowell was a reminder of pain. He dramatized, not knowing it himself any

---

[78] Duncan's sense of organic form stipulated attention to process as compositional medium; and the consequent aura of provisionality is registered in his poems by the suspended phrase, the pendulous unstopped line, and by syntactic ambiguities incumbent on these techniques. Duncan was fond of instructive bivalence, as in his assertion "poetry gives me orders." A position curiously proximate to Duncan's on the matter of order is that of R. P. Blackmur, who held "that an order is not invalidated by disorder; and that if an order is to become imaginative it must be so conceived as to accommodate disorder, and indeed to desire to do so, to stretch itself constantly to the point where it can envisage the disorder which its order merely names" (*Lion* 161).

more than the rest of us, that pain was normal for our generation because of the irreconcilabilities we had chosen as our substance, and then the ultimate numbness that great pain imposes" (*Poets* 215–16). His private pain could signify a public grief, that is, at a time when public space was being remorselessly privatized. In the wake of the McCarthy hearings, which made it clear just how much punishment could be brought to bear on the private lives and beliefs of individuals, a poetry that glamorized laceration offered irresistible attractions. "Pain was what we expected society to impose," Parkinson continues, "and all our cultural conditioning has led us to associate purgation and genuine suffering with that pain." "In the Cage," from *Lord Weary's Castle*, reappears in *History* like a refrain Lowell couldn't stop feverishly handling. "It is night, / and it is vanity, and age / Blackens the heart of Adam" becomes, thirty years later, "I am night, I am vanity." Both versions end "Fear, the yellow chirper, beaks its cage" (*History* 129). But pain with Lowell was a private matter preceding public life (a distinction not so clear in the case of one whose genealogy was notably public): reminiscing about his boyhood pugilism, he admitted in the fifties "I wanted to handle and draw strength from my scar" (Hamilton 17).

Even when he outraged many of his followers with what they saw as the opportunistic and unwarranted exposure of privacies not strictly his own to disclose, in *The Dolphin* and *For Lizzie and Harriet*, Lowell still epitomized control as the approved criterion of "mastery." (If anything, these late poems certify the durability, the determination, of *will* as poetic spark.) The first poem in *The Dolphin*, "Fishnet," comes on with all the swagger of a leadoff hitter in a batting lineup: "the net will hang on the wall when the fish are eaten"—the fish being, in this case, Lowell's subjects, friends and family members, and the net his poems, "nailed like illegible bronze on the futureless future." Yet even this poem offers the characteristic hint of self-deprecation, the controlled glimpse of frailty under the charisma: "Poets die adolescents," he confesses, "their beat embalms them." This could well be what Allen Tate had in mind in 1968, in "Poetry Modern and Unmodern" published in *The Hudson Review*. "Formal versification is the primary structure of poetic order, the assurance to the reader and

to the poet himself that the poet is in control of the disorder both outside him and within his own mind" (256).[79] He could be paraphrasing
Shakespeare's *Troilus and Cressida*: "Take but degree away, untune
that string, / And hark what discord follows" (I.iii.109–10).

Tate's passage was ridiculed by David Antin in his 1972
essay "Modernism and Postmodernism," in which he noted that
Tate's "assurance to the reader" implies consent and obedience:

> Certainly the "assurance to the reader that the poet is in con-
> trol" instructs the reader quite precisely in the way he must
> feel about the objects. He must feel poetical about them, that
> is, he must experience no equivocal impulses that are likely
> to threaten the poetical frame that wraps these objects like a
> "pink ribbon." It is the pathetic hope of a virgin for an expe-
> rienced lover whose competence (detachment) is sufficient
> to lead her to an orgasm, and all to be achieved by mere
> maintenance of a regular rhythm. (117)

This is wickedly funny satire. But Antin's intent is not to besmirch
the purity of Tate's imagination but to point up the clumsiness and
presumption inherited by his student, Robert Lowell:

> The taste for the ironic, moral poem is a taste for a kind of
> pornography which offers neither intellectual nor emotion-
> al experience but a fantasy of controlled intensity, and like
> all pornography it is thoroughly mechanical. But machin-
> ery is quite imperfectly adapted to the human body and
> nervous system, which operates on different principles. As
> a result poetry such as Lowell's seems terribly clumsy as it
> continually seeks to reach some contrived peak of feeling
> while moving in the machine-cut groove of his verse. . . .

---

[79] Tate's apparent insistence on this point is followed by a confession of
uncertainty: "Here is a theoretical difficulty that I cannot deal with any better than I could have dealt with it forty years ago. Yet is not much of the so-
called poetry of the past twenty or more years merely antipoetry, a parasite
on the body of positive poetry, without significance except that it reminds
us that poetry can be written, or has been written?" ("Unmodern" 256). He
attributes his own advocacy of formal metrical control to Yvor Winters's definition of the "fallacy of imitative or expressive form; that is, chaos should
be rendered in chaotic language." In Tate's view, "antipoetry" is the most
rudimentary mimeticism, and the least interesting.

> Lowell attempts to energize a poem at every possible point
> and the result is often pathetic or vulgar. . . . But it is the
> decadence of the metrical-moral tradition that is at fault
> more than the individual poet. . . . (120)

By the time *History* appeared in 1973 there was no longer any moral
to the metric, just the spooked resurrection of the man viewing his
poetic homunculus supine in premature burial, confronting "maturity" as self-internment. "I memorized the tricks to set the river on
fire— / somehow never wrote something to go back to." Yet in "the
wax and honey of a mausoleum"

> this round dome proves its maker is alive;
> the corpse of the insect lives embalmed in honey,
> prays that its perishable work live long
> enough for the sweet-tooth bear to desecrate—
> this open book . . . my open coffin.
>
> (*History* 194)

In the end, Lowell's fantasies of "controlled intensity" constitute a
pornographic exhibit in the medical pathology wing of the Wax
Museum, at least when viewed through Antin's account of its pathos
and vulgarity. Regardless of whether Lowell deserves such invective,
the "metrical-moral" tradition for which he was the standard-bearer
held the field through the 1950s, though most of the "contrived
peaks" achieved by his peers were of much lesser intensity.

What the "age demanded" in Pound's phrase, after the Second
World War, was its "accelerated grimace" in the figure of the poet as
virile youth, a role which fit Lowell to a tee. The poet did not compel
the age (as, in some measure, Yeats, Eliot and Auden had). What had
changed from Pound's time was the way in which literary expectations
were gratified. Lowell was the all but official laureate for an age that
cared little for poetry. Quite apart from his personal traumas, he suffered the indignity of being canonized while alive and installed into
what I hope has been conveyed as the *kitsch* proportions of exhibit in
the Wax Museum. Trapped in a display space nicely prefigured as the
jail cell of "In the Cage," Lowell kept one eye on the idolators, syco-
phants and tourists of literature, and another on the ward bosses, all on
behalf of Poetry with a capital P. "If you look at the poetry of Robert

Lowell," Michael Palmer points out, "a certain amount of it is stultified by having to exist under the sign of Literature. Am I making Great Literature? Is Delmore Schwartz going to be angry with this poem? Is Allen Tate going to scold me?" (*Talking* 131). Lowell may have been The Man, but he was also the front for a committee.[80]

Even his closest admirers could be disconcerted by the way he seemed pliable to the will of others. In his commemorative tribute to Lowell in *The New York Times Book Review*, Kunitz describes how "[h]e made his friends, willy-nilly, partners in his act, by showering them with early drafts of his poems, often so fragmentary and shapeless that it was no great trick to suggest improvements" ("Sense of a Life" 34). Kunitz was both fascinated and disconcerted by the legibility of so many contributing hands in Lowell's finished work. Frank Bidart, Lowell's student amanuensis at Harvard, testifies that "He wanted you to like his poems, obviously, but he didn't want you to be a yes man." Bidart nicely captures the plight of canonization as a kind of premature burial as he describes the process of revision: "I said I didn't think this line was quite right, or something, and he changed it right in front of me, and it was unnerving, it was scary. It was a little like going into a museum and you say, 'I'm not crazy about that arm,' and the statue moves" (Hamilton 392). In his last years Lowell was performing the biopsy of his career, which had been one of perpetual overexposure. Nothing may be quite so haunting as the last lines of "Endings":

> The wandering virus never surmounts the cluster
> it never joined.
>
> My eyes flicker, the immortal
> is scraped unconsenting from the mortal.
>
> (*Day by Day* 50)

The viral poet, never fully dissociated from the pack because he'd been adopted too young to have sensed any personal agency in the

---

[80] Lowell's nickname was Cal, from Shakespeare's Caliban, which he subsequently realigned with Caligula. The brutality of the Roman association is instructive; but even more so is Lowell's concern to obscure a name that would be revealing later on, as he played the brute to Ransom and Tate's Prospero.

matter: helplessly contagious, impassively dominant, a colossus of contradictions. David Perkins writes, "He understood that in poetry 'life' must be an illusion produced by art" (415). The opposite, I think, was the case: Lowell gullibly credited poetry with producing the facticity of a life, the public reputation of which might be illusory but, for all that, needed to be *lived*.

Lowell's evident dismay at his own eminence, in the end, can best be analogized to a prizewinning boxer who knows he had the moxie but whose career was an orchestrated series of fixed fights. Convinced of his own superiority, he's nevertheless haunted by his awareness that the public show was rigged.[81] As indeed it was for Lowell, mascot of the New Criticism during the decades of its imperium. Lowell—along with Jarrell and Schwartz to lesser degrees—represents the establishment's quest for poetry's Right Stuff (to evoke Tom Wolfe's phrase), lofted into canonical orbit; and we see, in the late work especially, the g-force *introjected* into the poetry, the masking function of the personae becoming an apotropaic grimace: the poet, suited up and deposited in the claustrophic body-contour of the space capsule, cultivated like so much raw material for the purpose of Making History. And under it all the suspicion that "The Age of Lowell" is really another movie: *The Set-Up*.[82]

---

[81] Langdom Hammer's study of "Janus-Faced Modernism," *Hart Crane and Allen Tate*, concludes with a symptomatizing reading of "Robert Lowell's Breakdown." Hammer, like Thomas Parkinson, agrees that "at the very least, it is no longer plausible to call the postwar period 'The Age of Lowell.' That it ever *was* possible to do so remains, however, a fact of large interest . . . ." Hammer argues that "Lowell can be instructively discussed as a 'representative,' culturally central poet precisely because he set out to become such a figure, and because he made his way by permitting other persons to make him the poet *they* wanted him to become" (214). Hammer's general thesis regarding Lowell is that he broke from his mentor Tate's reactionary modernism in the late fifties, attempting to recuperate the devalued modernisms of Crane and Williams; but, in doing so, he "recapitulated, rather than resolved" the Janus split, so "his historical importance does not lie in his ability to move 'beyond' modernism, but in his inability to do so" (213).

[82] As I completed this study, Paul Mariani's new biography of Lowell, *Lost Puritan*, appeared, its dust jacket assuring readers that the book captures "not only the man but also his age, the Age of Lowell."

Lowell's epitaph could very well be Mailer's wager, in *Armies of the Night* (subtitled "History as Novel, the Novel as History"): "Once History inhabits a crazy house, egotism may be the last tool left to History" (68). It's not coincidental, I think, that in the wake of global war—under the sign of History as Apocalypse—the poets most notable for energetically engaging history have been figures of complex polymathic egotism, foremost of which are Pound, Lowell, and Olson. Donald Hall, reviewing Olson for *The Nation* in 1961, found his historicizing impulse practically without precedent in recent years: "The peculiarity of Olson's poems in 1961 can almost be called this subject matter. History is *the* subject of modernism: a subject which the other pickers of the fruits of Pound and Williams have avoided" ("Eyes" 485). This might seem a surprising slight of Lowell, but Hall may have discovered by way of Olson that Lowell's variety of history was attenuated. As David Antin complains, Lowell "manages to get as much grade-school history into a poem as he can . . . " ("Modernism" 112). For a friendlier view which I think amounts to the same thing: Elizabeth Bishop enviously exclaimed in a letter to Lowell "In some ways you are the luckiest poet I know!" Most poets could write about their ancestors, "but what would be the significance? Nothing at all. . . . Whereas all you have to do is put down the names!" (Hamilton 233).

Bishop's remark suggests a distinction that cleaves American poetry in two in the anthology wars, and into a myriad of splinters thereafter. Where Lowell could write of "The farm, entitled *Char-de-sa* / in the Social Register, / . . . named for my Grandfather's children: / Charlotte, Devereux, and Sarah" (*Life* 60), a comparable passage in Olson might be "Althan says / Winslow / was at Cape Ann in April, / 1624"—a specification which immediately follows Olson's declaration "I would be an historian as Herodotus was, looking / for oneself for the evidence of / what is said . . . " (*Maximus* 104–05). Lowell tends to monument, Olson to document. The Boston Common statue of Colonel Shaw's troops in "For the Union Dead" ("William James could almost hear the bronze Negroes breathe" [*Union* 71]) is a hieratic view; whereas Olson registers the stark traces of the transatlantic economy that fetched so many millions as raw material in the first place:

On board, San Juan de Lua, 57
Negroes, *optimi generis*, each valued at 160£, or a total of
9,120£ ("Schedule of Property Lost, *State Papers*, Dom.
Elizabeth, liii")

(*Maximus* 67)

The density of Olson's documentation in *The Maximus Poems* is for
most readers distressingly far from anything resembling "grade-
school history." But scholars have been more successful annotating
Maximus than they have *History*, for all the convenience of Lowell's
specimen label titles. The reason is not hard to find: Lowell's work is
accessibly subordinated to the thematic register of the heroic ego. In
his final year, reflecting on his life's work, he concluded that "the
thread that strings it together is my autobiography, it is a small-scale
Prelude, written in many different styles and with digressions, yet a
continuing story . . . " (Hamilton 233). Lowell's work is compulsively fascinating precisely because it takes on the waxwork character of
the freak show, the exhibit of a human life assuming monstrous proportions. What is "monstrous," I should clarify, comes from the root
monstrum and *monere*, portent and warning: Lowell warns us, by
self-exhibition, of the pitfalls of life lived on a pedestal, in the showcase; life as continual self-dramatization; poetry as public monument. His celebrated jawbreaker lines have an integrity that detaches
them from the very poems they inhabit, bringing to mind Albert
Speer's penchant for designing Third Reich buildings for the elegance of the rubble that would eventually be left of them.

To *person* in Lowell it's necessary to contrast *polis* in Olson.
And when he insists "Polis is this" he emphasizes the deictic immediacy of the occasion: the person *is* public for Olson as much as it is
for Lowell, but without the malignant conflation of public with *private*. For Olson, by way of Yeats and Pound, comprehends person as
persona, mask. *Larvatus pro deo*: masked I go forth.[83] Olson's Max-

---

[83] This was Descartes's motto, and it would clearly be misleading to associate Olson with Cartesian rationalism. But I take Paul Rabinow's point to
heart, when he reminds us that "it will be sufficiently tantalizing to remember that Descartes was himself an actor and a dancer and wrote at least three
plays and a ballet, which have been lost to us. Modern interpreters have

imus is specifically figured *as* gigantic, grotesque, in ways that do not impinge on the subjective crisis of self-representation. Maximus is more like the subject construed by Roland Barthes in *The Pleasure of the Text*:

> Then perhaps the subject returns, not as illusion, but as fiction. A certain pleasure is derived from a way of imagining oneself as individual, of inventing a final rarest fiction: the fictive identity. This fiction is no longer the illusion of a unity; on the contrary, it is the theater of society in which we stage our plural: our pleasure is individual—but not personal. (62)

It is as an occupational plurality that Olson can say "I am the Gold Machine and now I have trenched out, smeared, occupied / with my elongated length the ugliest passage of all"—as it is a principle of individuation, not personality, that permits him to give voice to parcels of land: "Gravelly Hill says / leave me be, I am contingent, the end of the world / is the borders / of my being" (*Maximus* 301, 331). It is a principle that reorganizes the very notion of individuation by flooding even the personal with its larger task, its "maximus":

> . . . It is not I,
> even if the life appeared
> biographical. The only interesting thing
> is if one can be
> an image
> of man, "The nobleness, and the arete."
>
> (*Maximus* 473)

Lowell, by contrast, sensing himself prematurely *packaged* as an image (a "poor passing fact" [*Day by Day*, 127])—not of "man" but of "the poet"—could only endure his notoriety as an indignity and incentive for stoic grace.

Lowell's mordant registration of his generic fate is a pathological exaltation, evidence from the center that the center cannot

---

stripped away all of these masks in the name of revealing the true Descartes, the precursor of their modernity, Descartes the scientist. But they want to ignore the blushing, God-ordained actor they find shivering there" (185). Olson was a trained dancer as well.

hold. The critics, meanwhile, were eager to use the conventional terms of appraisal, and were unstinting in applying them. The extreme instance may be Helen Vendler, who as critic and anthologist uses Lowell as a scouring implement for purging the map of competing figures and gutting the diversity of American traditions. A persuasive analysis of why this hero-worship fails is provided by Warner Berthoff in *A Literature Without Qualities*. The title plays on Robert Musil's *Mann ohne Eigenschaften*, and is meant to evoke a literature of dissipations and contingencies, an "adjunct literature" freed from expectations derived from prior models (67). He goes so far as to locate American literary continuity in the very ruptures that seem to violate the principle of literature as such. "What we have had, periodically, are not simply generational progressions, with new incumbencies for fixed literary offices"—assimilated to anthologies and literary histories—"but a fracturing of what currently has been understood as appropriate to literature itself; a rejection of the very notion of orthodox literary making as an acceptable enterprise, with qualities and values peculiar to itself that are worth maintaining and renewing" (25). Oddly, Berthoff doesn't recognize that *renewal* is exactly the wrong notion to apply to a situation that he plainly recognizes as the dissolution of orthodoxy and its replacement by heterodoxy.

The terms of conventional apprenticeship, as Berthoff describes them, have resulted in the postwar period in "a melancholy story for the most part":

> This gifted and superbly taught younger generation of the forties and fifties is surely our American "tragic generation" and not only in the shocking casualties it has taken, its palpable struggle with its own will to self-destruction: Weldon Kees, Theodore Roethke, Delmore Schwartz, Randall Jarrell, Charles Olson, John Berryman, Jean Garrigue, Robert Lowell, down through late joiners, father-haunted, like Anne Sexton and Sylvia Plath. (30)

It is tragic not because of the damaged lives, but because this generation unwittingly stumbled upon the double-bind of a literature agonized by institutional criteria of literariness. Berthoff's is a variant of

Margaret Atwood's thesis of Canadian literature in *Survival*, except that she reads thematically where he understands the American terms of survival as categorical: "The double bind of this intuition—that the condition of being which stings you into counterstatement is the condition you must acquiesce in if you are to complete the work you have undertaken to do—provides the *déformation professionelle* which currently lies in wait for literary ambition in the old sense" (45–46). Literature, in the "old sense," still awaits the gullible and the unwary.

Berthoff's purpose is not to chronicle the devastations of Lowell's damaged generation, but to celebrate serendipitous solutions, moments in which *writing* (rather in the manner of *écriture*) overtakes and disposes of Literature,

> . . . moments when that ruling mode itself, and the conceptions of vocation and performance it presupposes, lose credit and are seemingly abandoned; and the writer begins to write, not to achieve the same kind and degree of mastery he has been schooled to admire, but simply to maintain himself as a functioning being in whatever intentional sphere he can tolerate belonging to. He writes, as it were, to reenfranchise himself; to safeguard whatever fiction of personal agency he can imagine living by from day to day. (32)

Lowell's *Day by Day* is a fitting last title for a career battered by the gradual discrediting of mastery. But it, like all of Lowell's books—and none of Olson's or Duncan's—could still be taken to signify The Poet, The Poem, The Talent, and The Career. And in fact Lowell himself could not give up the urge to monumentalize, to round off blunt edges, to transmute the impediment of ungainliness into a comely package.

It remained—and remains—for a different body of works and authors to disengage poetry from the addiction of literature, the Algebra of its Need. Contemporaneous with *A Literature Without Qualities*, Don Byrd responded to "rumors of a formalist revival" by declaring "We need massive flowing and breaking intensities, not tension; we need universal participation in the pleasures of sight, sound, and intellection, not elegance; we need the analytic, disruptive exercise of the mind, not wit; we need the awkward spectacle of the untried move, not grace" ("Meter" 180). "[I]n the first reaction to this decisive face-about," Berthoff writes, "critical partisans and antagonists alike have felt compelled to raise the question of whether the texts that result really belong to the category *literature* as commonly understood" (27). Berthoff's personal candidates for models (although this impulse itself contradicts the major recognition of his book) are Wallace Stevens and Henry Miller, the sagacity of which is preserved only by seeing them in tandem as Berthoff does. Apart from the question of suitable exemplars, the point is to acknowledge a will to *abandon* the protocols of literature as such, in which case

> . . . it may be that writing that reviewers reasonably characterize as garrulous, monotonous, word-careless and the like, has simply been misunderstood in its primary function—which is to furnish disposable scripts the poet can use in acting out his fiction of personal consequence, in the validating presence of an audience very much like himself and not less hungry for some bluff gesture of self-authentication. (100)

With this Berthoff puts us squarely in the moment of his writing—*A Literature Without Qualities* was published in 1979—when the Associated Writing Programs had recently become the dominant force in American poetry, the first time in any national literature I'm aware of, in fact, that style and function in literature had become a manifestation of demographics—a "generic fate" in a much broader context than Lowell ever conceived—when the "bluff gesture[s] of self-authentification" were institutionally subsidized.

Lowell represents the final flower of a now-lapsed literary power bloc. If he could momentarily signify an "Age," it's because he stood at that delicate but precise juncture between social privilege and professional esteem. His illustrious family background would ensure his reputation in the society columns, whether he wrote poetry or peddled yachting tackle. But he had the wherewithal to resist such easy buoyancy, and migrated to another elite enclave, the New Criticism. The choice was fortuitous—prescient, not opportunistic (since, when he went to Kenyon, it was not at all clear that "Criti-

cism, Inc." would soon become so powerful)—and Lowell was perfectly positioned to represent The Real Thing: a poet-aristocrat for an
aristocracy of poetry. The Jews (Schwartz and Shapiro) were excluded from this final eminence, this singular conjunction of high society, commerce, and academe; and close contenders like Wilbur and
Jarrell were not born to class. Not that Lowell thought much of class.
By pledging allegiance to the New Critics he had forfeited class for
taste, and in the Olympia of taste he was willing to endure even the
bumptious Roethke, albeit warily. What Lowell brought to the poetry
world above all, through his adroit blend of taste, class, and personal
savoir faire, was an inimitable dignity, dignity that could survive
even his manic atrocities.

Despite his core of personal dignity, Lowell was in many
senses a corporate product, the classy chassis of Criticism, Inc. On a
pedestal, he was nevertheless a feature of the showroom and subject
to the marketing strategies of the dealership. It's to Lowell's credit
that when this corporate manifold dissolved, he emerged, if anything, revitalized. The poetry establishment—in which Lowell was
the uncontested prize specimen—was dissolving into the sixties
complex of activism, public appearances, and the ascendancy of the
New American poets. The starting lineup of 1950 no longer held:
Shapiro had broken ranks, yet was of little or no interest to the outsiders; Schwartz had become thoroughly reactionary by the time the
Beats appeared, and even his friends saw nothing but decline in his
poetry; Jarrell drifted on the coattails of his association with Lowell,
his poetry respected because of the ferocity of his critical intellect
and because "Death of the Ball Turrett Gunner" was omnipresent in
the textbooks and anthologies. Only Lowell remained at the top in
the sense that he continued to induce respect from supporters and
foes alike, and his career became a manifestation of the poet's life as
a series of instructive stylistic adventures. Many poets who had
achieved notable success at the onset of the Cold War were all but
invisible (as poets) by the sixties, including Garrigue, Howes, Nims,
Gardner, Brinnin, Ciardi, and Viereck.

That there was still a viable establishment, however, is
abundantly clear in the realm of awards and prizes, which through-

out the sixties affirm strict continuity with the fifties.[84] The bestowal of prizes was a way to arouse public interest, however modestly. A disconcerting example is from *Newsweek*, in which an anonymous reporter, after noting the fragmentation of poetry's audience, pursued an upbeat ending by pointing to the foundational support system, culminating with a brief biography of Maria Bullock, founder of the Academy of American Poets. The article concluded with an itemization of available awards, with Roethke as the system's star player:

> In the last eight months, besides the Ford grant, he has taken the Bollingen Prize ($1,000), the National Book Award ($1,000), a Borestone Mountain Award ($200), and the Edna St. Vincent Millay Award ($200) of the Poetry Society of America. He is thus not only a superb modern master of English [sic!] verse but a fantastic financial performer in the exceedingly limited poetic sweepstakes. ("This Is the Poet Today," [June 15, 1959], 110)

A comparably skewed perspective informed a Gordon Parks photospread for *Life*, in which a soft-focus light-and-leaf-porn, with the

---

[84] The Pulitzer winners of the 1960s were Phyllis McGinley, Alan Dugan, Louis Simpson, John Berryman, Richard Eberhart, Anne Sexton, and Anthony Hecht, with William Carlos Williams winning posthumously in 1963 and, quite against the grain, George Oppen in 1969. Bollingen prizewinners of the sixties were Schwartz, Winters, Eberhart, Warren, Berryman, Shapiro, and seniors Frost, Wheelock, and Horace Gregory. National Book Award recipients were Lowell, Jarrell, Dugan, Stafford, Ransom, Roethke, Dickey, Merrill, Bly, and Berryman. And the Shelley Memorial Award went to Schwartz, Roethke, Stafford, Ignatow, Sexton, Swenson, Ruth Stone, and Ann Stanford. Only in the cluster of *Poetry* magazine's awards (the Oscar Blumenthal Prize, the Levinson Prize, and the Eunice Tietjens Memorial Prize) was there any recognition of non-mainstream poets, including Zukofsky, Olson, Creeley, Duncan, and Snyder, although even these tended to go to recipients of the bigger prizes. The Academy of American Poets was giving fellowships exclusively to senior poets (Ransom, Tate, Pound, Moore, MacLeish, Van Doren) with an occasional "younger" figure like Eberhart, Berryman, Bishop, Kunitz, and Hecht; while the American Academy and Institute of Arts and Letters was disposed to a slightly more eclectic distribution, ranging from Rich, Snodgrass, Garrigue, Nemerov, Cunningham, Hoffman, Hollander, Booth, Brinnin, Moss, and Nims to Dickey, Kinnell, Levertov, Ignatow, Snyder, Ashbery, and Ginsberg.

occasional open view of rolling hills and haystacks, accompanied excerpts from Robinson, Millay, John Peale Bishop, MacLeish, Frost, Jeffers, Williams, Eliot, Crane, and "a standout among the younger poets"—Richard Wilbur ("Kaleidoscope of U.S. Poetry," [February 15, 1960], 73). Lowell's exclusion from this profile, in a magazine that had heralded him as poetry's glamour boy, may well reflect some reservations about the indiscretions of his recent confessionalism.

The last stand of this establishment is linked, by a grotesquely fitting synchrony, to the Cuban Missile Crisis in October 1962, when the Library of Congress, at the initiative of its Consultant in Poetry, Louis Untermeyer, sponsored a fiftieth anniversary festival celebrating *Poetry* magazine. Running from Monday through Wednesday, October 22–24, the Festival program consisted of a full slate of lectures, symposia, and poetry readings. Three former *Poetry* editors were present for the occasion—Morton Dauwen Zabel, Karl Shapiro, and current editor Henry Rago. Rago and Zabel, along with Louise Bogan and Stanley Kunitz, opened the festival with a symposium on "The Role of the Poetry Journal." There was a forum on "The Problem of Form," with a panel consisting of Ransom, Tate, Léonie Adams and J. V. Cunningham. Clearly, in the wake of the Beats and *The New American Poetry*, there were to be no concessions whatsoever to the integrity of the Anglo-American metrical tradition. But the problem of "The Poet and the Public," which had so agonized academic poet-critics in the fifties, was fretted one more time by Wilbur, Nemerov, Shapiro, and Babette Deutsch. Randall Jarrell was given a place of honor as the featured speaker in an evening session, in which he surveyed "Fifty Years of American Poetry." Most of his talk was devoted to the earlier decades of the century, but he pointedly drew up a genealogical heritage in which the bloodlines of the great modernists flowed directly into the veins of Elizabeth Bishop, Robert Penn Warren, Theodore Roethke, Karl Shapiro, Richard Wilbur, and Robert Lowell. Of Lowell, whose work culminated the talk, Jarrell concluded that "You feel before reading any new poem of his the uneasy expectation of perhaps encountering a masterpiece" (*NPF* 138).

The occasion clearly sanctioned the hegemony of the New Critics' choice poets. Lowell himself was not on hand, having suc-

cumbed to another of his manic episodes in September during a trip to
Buenos Aires, where he was frantically sending cables to the Pope and
to Eisenhower (then ex-President) on the subject of "America as the
Roman Empire" (Hamilton 301). Jarrell would persist for a few more
years until he was overtaken by manic depression and suicide.[85]
Schwartz was at the end of his tether as well, and actually broke down
during the festival, trashing (or as Wilbur delicately put it, "hurting")
his hotel room. Berryman and Wilbur had to be called away from a
party hosted by Robert Frost to sign for his release from the police station (Atlas 345). Jeffrey Meyers has an apt phrase for these poets:
"They were competitors in symptoms" (133). Insofar as they were also
competitors in poetry, their poems were their grandest symptoms.
Their poetic competition had always been stabilized by a simple rule:
Lowell as the "major" poet, and as long as this premise went uncontested he would freely dispense the same adjective to his friends (and
work behind the scenes on behalf of their reputations).

　　None of these matters were so much as broached at the
National Poetry Festival, of course. Kenneth Rexroth was on hand to
speak up semi-officially on behalf of alternatives, and he interceded
amidst the chorus of laments about the diminished audience during
the session on "The Poet and the Public": " . . . it's a matter of fact,"
he declared, "the audience for poetry in America is enormous. If we
want vatic poets, why aren't they here?" he went on, referring to the
Festival's invitees. "Kenneth Patchen is not here; Allen Ginsberg is
not here. There are quite a few people like that. Yes, you sneer, but
Ginsberg outsells everyone here put together" (*NPF* 166). Karl
Shapiro, predictably, stood toe to toe with Rexroth in speaking his
mind, insisting that there was no such thing as an American poetry
because "the baby was kidnapped and grew up in captivity." Elaborating by changing metaphors, Shapiro crudely blamed the magazine
being toasted by the Festival: "the great train robbery of American

---

[85] Jarrell's widow contests the suicide verdict in her edition of her hus-
band's correspondence. But regardless of whether on the fatal occasion he
deliberately stepped in front of a car on a highway or not, he *had* attempted
suicide earlier in the year.

poetry coincides curiously with the founding of *Poetry* magazine, for what set out to be the first American poetry journal almost overnight became an Anglo-American review" (164). Despite such interventions, which in that genteel circumstance must have seemed gauche, the National Poetry Festival mustered all the officiousness and self-congratulation befitting such an occasion. The published proceedings constitute one of the more curious, because unwitting, anthologies of American poetry. The poems read are printed in their entirety, along with incidental comments and impromptu preludes by the poets. There were twenty-eight poets delegated to give readings of their work (of whom six were women, two black). The readings (which took place on three consecutive afternoons) featured Léonie Adams, William Meredith, Nemerov, Rukeyser, Schwartz, Shapiro, Van Doren, Untermeyer, Berryman, Bogan, Gwendolyn Brooks, Cunningham, Eberhart, Paul Engle (director of the Iowa Writers' Workshop), Henry Rago, Snodgrass, Tate, Blackmur, Katherine Garrison Chapin, Babette Deutsch, Langston Hughes, Jarrell, Kunitz, Ogden Nash, Rexroth, Wilbur, and Oscar Williams, with Robert Frost headlining an evening of his own.

When Frost died the next year, John Berryman was instantly convulsed with the thought of succession. "Who's number one?" he asked R. P. Blackmur, "Who's number one? Cal is number one, isn't he?" (Beaver 125). Number one indeed; and Irvin Ehrenpreis would shortly broach the big question. Could the new era be called The Age of Lowell? As if in response to such a prospect, Lowell himself began churning out the unrhymed sonnets that in retrospect appear to have dethroned him as soon as he donned his regal attire. Donald Davie cites the increasingly anxious perception "that the Lowell verse-machine was not just overheating but also throwing up ever more sludge and waste" (260). For many the most disturbing denouement of the postwar highbrow sensibility, and a capstone to the senescent career of New Criticism, was Lowell's impetuous recasting of *Notebook* in *Lizzie and Harriet* and *History*. The arrangement struck in *History* exemplifies Lowell's *dutiful* cramming in of all the proper subjects, some of which alarmed because of their seeming impropriety, like the series dedicated to Allen Tate. "Who else would sire twin sons at sixty-eight?" Lowell asks in one poem (122). And in another, he details the death of one of the twins: "Michael Tate / gagging on your plastic telephone, / while the new sitter drew water for your bath, / unable to hear you gasp . . . " (121). This poem strained relations between Tate and his former pupil, but Lowell was faithfully following old precepts, writing the traditional elegy on the loss of an infant heir, violating the occasion not so much by reporting the details as by ticking them off a packing list, an inventory of themes, in a context in which the vaunted *form* was becoming as disposable as a fast food wrapper.

Despite (or maybe because of) such indiscretion and opportunism, the later books are really Lowell's true idiom. He confessed to being dissatisfied with his work overall, noting that the high point was always revision: "revision is inspiration, no reading of the finished work as exciting as writing in the last changes" (*Prose* 289). But with *Notebook* and its prodigious revisions Lowell exulted in the severity and confinement of "rendering appearances": "I was thinking lines even when teaching or playing tennis" (272). It was a cornucopia of text, and best of all for Lowell, the ultimate indulgence: a *perpetuum mobile* of revision. One critic has claimed that Lowell engaged and transcended "a process aesthetic" in these works.[86] But for Lowell—contrary to Ginsberg's "first thought, best thought"—it was "*next* thought, best thought": a constant enchanted indecision, and a momentary suspension of the obligatory closure of form. The arrangement of *History* is ostensibly chronological, but a surprising number of the historical topics have almost no bearing on the poems, as if Lowell had finally had enough and chucked his topic assignments. But there may be another factor, if we recall that the onset of his manic episodes was coincident with Ezra Pound's incarceration in the "bughouse." I suggested that Lowell's own mania was in some degree a form of sympa-

---

[86] Alex Calder makes a persuasive case for *History* as a genealogical epic. He notes that Lowell eschewed orality (as in Olson or Ginsberg) and personality (Berryman): "Instead, the production of a speaking subject in the *Notebook* volumes depended more on formal devices than organic structures of consciousness mapping; the 'kinetics' of Lowell's long poems arose out of writing, out of a process of constant revision rather than a process more committed to speech as a model" (Calder 136).

thetic bonding with the master. Likewise, as the late Pound admitted to bungling the grand vision of *The Cantos*, Lowell produced his own version of the epic (a long poem including history, as Pound famously said) and, like his *miglior fabbro*, duplicated the incoherence as well. "As much with *History* as with any of the *Notebooks* we are really left to do the adding up for ourselves—*if we can*," Donald Davie remarked, "the poet himself having virtually admitted that for his part he can't" (262). At the biographical level Lowell's mania was indubitably all too real; but on the literary plane it attained the uncanny aura of an ephebe's worship, mimetic homage to a damaged patriarch.

For Calvin Bedient, Lowell's madness finally became the infernal method he aspired to; so he overreads *History* as ideological catatonia: "the ideology that reigns in Lowell's late volumes, dully surviving every erotic shudder, is the one Georg Lukács . . . ascribed to literary modernism: despair of history, the reduction of experience to the static and sensational, the solitary and asocial . . . " (142). Bedient's is criticism as diagnosis, predicated on the intentional fallacy, refusing to take into account Lowell's refractory and oblique arrangements—refusing, that is, to credit the compositional process insistently played out in publication as anything more than indulgent self-display. Harold Beaver, on the other hand, recognizes that "[f]or Lowell, increasingly, there could be no secrets. He was (in Hardwick's words) like some 'mythical two-engined machine, one running to doom and the other to salvation.' All his family, his friends, his acquaintances were incorporated into this myth. All history was incorporated into it. His poetry became a place where it was possible for everyone to meet everyone" (129).[87] Lowell's *History* works *because* it is myth.[88] But it brings with it the sobering

---

[87] Donald Davie found himself disadvantaged as a reader of this work: "we feel like people absentmindedly invited to a party where everyone else is in the know and knows everybody else. The least we might expect is to be introduced to at least one other person in the room" (262). Robert Bly, we recall, thought of Lowell as someone who partied too much.

[88] Olson makes it clear why: "It is with EROS that mythology is concerned," he writes in *The Special View of History*. "Which amounts to saying that as a psyche man is only an order comparable to kosmos when he or she is

reminder that myth for Americans is individual, and at its most ferocious may even be private—albeit a private party at which "everyone
meet[s] everyone." It may be solitary, but it's quite sociable, hardly
static, sensational, and asocial as Bedient would have it. It's not "history" at all, of course, but a purely formal exercise of the pretense of
history as it's referred to as being *made*, behind the scenes, under the
table, and in private. A form: a confirmation of conformity regained.

CONFORMITY REGAINED

"'With mankind,'" Herman Melville's Captain Vere is fond of saying,
"'forms, measured forms, are everything,'" and to this credo Vere
abides, sacrificing Billy Budd as proof of its veracity. But Melville
slyly adds that "truth uncompromisingly told will always have its
ragged edges . . . " (*Billy Budd* 1430, 1431). In his contribution to the
poetics section of *The New American Poetry*, Robert Duncan defined
the issue of form as a cosmological and biological event which the
art of poetry develops willy nilly, regardless of whether the poet consciously lays claim to such vast resources. "After Freud," he wrote,
"we are aware that unwittingly we achieve our form." Form is not
entirely a matter of control, of the artful summoning of passionate
forces enticingly subjugated in metrical order. Rather, "It is, whatever our mastery, the inevitable use we make of the speech that betrays
to ourselves and to our hunters (our readers) the spore of what we

---

love—that love is order in the vertical of the self" (54). The *Notebook*-to-*History* years were the period Lowell relocated to England and began a new
marriage, and in light of Olson's thesis it seems particularly intrepid of Lowell to have insisted that "the vertical of the self"—the mythological eros of
this new phase in his life—be called "History." Olson's own traversal of the
path in *Maximus* from history to myth was much criticized, as was Lowell's.
(However, the scope of myth for Lowell is social, not cosmological; so while
he comes to represent an "asocial" despair for Bedient, the very sky—traditional field of cosmic fertility—becomes in *History*'s final line a "carbon
scarred with ciphers" [207].) See Norma Procopiow's summary of the
reviews: *Lowell* 251–52, 267–72. The most pressing version of the critique of
Olson's mythmaking is Robert von Hallberg's study, *Charles Olson, The
Scholar's Art.*

are becoming" (400). The key word is *spore*. The sixties were notably the years when previously formalist poets embraced free verse and process, when urbanity and wit seemed to have evaporated overnight, replaced by the harsh promptings of social conflict, personal crisis, and a growing enthusiasm for wildness. The "spore of what we are becoming" was epitomized at the end of the decade by the concluding lines of Galway Kinnell's famous poem "The Bear":

> . . . the rest of my days I spend
> wandering: wondering
> what, anyway,
> was that sticky infusion, that rank flavor of blood, that
>   poetry, by which I lived?

(Body Rags 63)

For those who underwent dramatic stylistic and procedural changes, the transition was abrupt. W. S. Merwin exemplifies this transit at its least traumatic and most successful. Unlike many others, he did not repudiate his work of the fifties. "In the late fifties, I had the feeling I had simply come to the end of a way of writing," he explains. "I didn't reject it, but it was no longer satisfying" ("Art" 72). Not only did he abandon metrics and the regulatory apparition of the stanza, but punctuation as well. "Punctuation basically has to do with prose and the printed word. I came to feel that punctuation was like nailing the words onto the page" (72–73). In the wake of the Beat phenomenon, public readings dramatically increased in popularity, and in the sixties poets like Merwin could subsist largely off the reading circuit. Lowell attributed the stylistic transfiguration of *Life Studies* to his experience doing readings in the late fifties, and Merwin likewise discovered not only the grammatological restraints of traditional verse, but the appeal of orality in a poetry intent on deep image. "Punctuation as I looked at it . . . seemed to staple the poem to the page. But if I took those staples out, the poem lifted itself right up off the page. A poem then had a sense of integrity and liberation that it did not have before. In a sense that made it a late echo of an oral tradition" (*Observed* 180).

In the sixties there was a resurgence of poetry as public event, supported in part by antiwar activism but more extensively by the fact that colleges and universities were making considerable sums available for readings. For the entrepreneurially diligent, like Diane Wakoski and Gary Snyder, readings could be a primary source of income; and poets were shuffled around the country with the same subordinated constancy as black musicians and dancers had been in the Depression under the auspices of TOBA (Theatre Owners' Booking Association, a.k.a. "Tough On Black Asses"). Rexroth complained that this was "a much bigger thing than the palmiest days of the Orpheum circuit and very much like it. And once you get on it, you feel a little like Singer midgets" (*NPF* 174). This circuit inherently favored poets with effectively *vocal* styles; which is to say, poets working in open forms, attentive to breath units, or otherwise engaged in an accessible colloquialism of vocabulary and speech rhythms. The greatest beneficiaries, of course, were poets of the older generation anthologized by Don Allen, who had effectively *created* the resurgence of interest in poetry readings in the late fifties (an interest fitfully fanned earlier in the decade by Dylan Thomas and John Ciardi), and who by the sixties were not only skilled readers but accomplished public personae and even—there were inklings by the mid-sixties—"major" poets: Ginsberg, Snyder, Olson, Duncan, Levertov, Creeley, and LeRoi Jones (in transition to Amiri Baraka).[89]

As he weathered stylistic transfiguration, Merwin's affiliations extended to both sides of the competing poetic communities. "In the late fifties, all of American poetry was supposed to be divided into two camps," he remarked in 1987. "That never made any sense to me at all. I've always liked disparate kinds of poets—Robert Creeley and Denise Levertov and Gerald Stern and Richard Howard and Anthony Hecht, and so forth—without feeling that there's any

---

[89] It's inconceivable that an operation like John Martin's Black Sparrow Press could have been so successful at any other time. Beginning in the mid-sixties as a small press publishing limited run letterpress editions, Black Sparrow published books which went unreviewed by the mainstream yet the press not only survived but thrived. Why? Not discounting Martin's managerial shrewdness, I attribute it to the magnetism of Black Sparrow poets on the reading circuit. Antin, Rothenberg, Kelly, Wakoski, Eshleman, Dorn and Bukowski were among the earliest Black Sparrow authors, and all were effective stage presences.

disloyalty or impossibility in that" ("Art" 74). Merwin was developing an eclecticism that was even more readily available to younger
poets. Robert Pinsky, as a teenager in the late fifties, abruptly passed
from a kind of adolescent Gongorism to something less mannered:
"From composing allusive rubbish of this kind I felt delivered by
various works, of which I definitely remember three: Allen Ginsberg's *Howl*, Dudley Fitts's *Poems From the Greek Anthology*, and
Alan Dugan's *Poems*" (*World* 153). Just as the jazz world distinction
of hot versus cool eroded by the time Kennedy came to the White
House, the antithetical strands of poetry also began to blur in the
next decade.

In contrast to Merwin, James Wright was among those whose
transition bore traces of high drama. In the *Minnesota Review* in
1961 he vividly denounced not only *The New American Poetry* but
also *The New Poets of England and America* (to which he had contributed). "In spite of certain ostensible differences . . . the two books
are astonishingly similar in their vanity, in the general effect of dull-
ness which they produce, and in their depressing clutter of anxious
poetasters shrieking their immortality into the void" (268). Wright's
review was punningly called "The Few Poets of England and America," and his accent was on the few he approved of and who had been
unforgivably spurned by the editors of both anthologies—James
Dickey, John Logan, and Anne Sexton among them. Wright, along
with Bly, Simpson, Hall, Kinnell, represented the mid-career transition as generationally specific—a point confirmed by Merwin:

> We didn't so much influence each other as feel the same
> things. It was perfectly clear that the things I had felt as a
> kind of straitjacket could be broken out of after all. The
> straitjacket really wasn't there. We didn't have to pay atten-
> tion to it anymore. The other thing about that time—I don't
> know that anyone has described it very thoroughly . . . [is
> that w]e were throwing out all of the apparatus of literary
> careers. . . . ("Art" 73)

The "apparatus" Merwin apparently means is linked to the formalist
protocol. But this is not to say that literary *careerism* didn't persist;
if anything, it thrived as never before. Instead of a small center of

core authors, there was a dispersed network of unlikely alliances formed around other issues with which poetry intersected, such as feminism, the antiwar movement, ecology, and civil rights. As Louis Simpson recalled in 1974, "the Vietnam War readings cut across a lot of lines, a lot of poets who ordinarily wouldn't have been on the same platform were" (*Company* 262).[90]

The rules of poetic comportment having changed, there was a reactionary assumption that the new freedom was contingent on prior achievement in traditional prosody. Galway Kinnell dissented, insisting that "I think that those of my age who say you have to 'learn the rules in order to break them' are wrong to generalize from their own experience. That experience was a historical quirk"(*Walking* 19).[91] Kinnell's remark, made in 1971, has since been repeatedly confirmed. His generation—which includes Ginsberg, Creeley, O'Hara, Ashbery, Bly, Merrill, Snodgrass, Merwin, Rich, and Wright, among many others—stands out for the uniformity with which it straddled divergent formalist imperatives. Ammons and Eigner are among the few exceptions, poets whose commitment to open form has been unwavering from the beginning. The pressures on that generation can also be felt in strictly demographic terms. The acquiescence of a fifties' "quiet

---

[90] Comparable situations recur from time to time, like the 1982 Town Hall (New York) benefit for the nuclear freeze movement, "Poetry Against the End of the World," featuring Amiri Baraka, Robert Bly, Jane Cooper, David Ignatow, June Jordan, Galway Kinnell, Etheridge Knight, Stanley Kunitz, Denise Levertov, Philip Levine, W.S. Merwin, Josephine Miles, and Simon Ortiz. Baraka thought it "rather remarkable . . . because of the *reach* and breadth of the group" which was successful, despite its "disparity of ideology and aesthetic." "I know that certainly there were a few poets there that I myself had castigated from time to time with the *nom de guerre* 'academic' and likewise other poets I have felt closer to aesthetically who have been jumped on, as I myself have been, by some of the first mentioned as perhaps 'lacking discipline.'" But no matter, it turned out, since they achieved solidarity in focusing together on a good cause: "To focus on the real world in one's work or one's life is to violate the basic dictates of bourgeois aesthetics and philosophy" ("Poets Against the End of the World" 302, 304).

[91] Kinnell's conversion was unapologetic and uncompromising. Alan Shapiro, recalling his writing classes, says that Kinnell "refused to let his students write anything but free verse on the grounds that rhyme and meter repress emotion and free verse liberates it" (93).

generation" marked individuals *as* members of a generation, which had its own "generic fate" (if not quite in Lowell's sense). So, when many of them had switched from strict measures to looser forms, there were bound to be signs of resistance to the collective implications. This drove James Wright to observe in 1979,

> For a while during the fifties most writers were tending to write in too facile, too glib a way in regular meters and rhyme. Some of us turned away to free verse. Since then I think that whenever one opens a magazine nearly all the poems one sees will be in free verse. More and more they strike me as being just as facile and automatic in their way as the earlier poems had been in other ways. (207)

Yet, either oddly or fittingly, Wright himself became a hero of the workshop free verse he was criticizing.

Richard Wilbur, who has never made any concessions to change, provided some insight in a 1974 interview. He, like Allen Tate, was still preoccupied with control, but held that habits of mental association might amount to control of a negative kind.

> I have no case whatever against controlled free verse. Yet I think it is absurd to feel that free verse—which has only been with us in America for a little over a hundred years— has definitely "replaced" measure and rhyme and other traditional instruments . . . [Traditional techniques] are not simply a strait jacket, they can also liberate you from whatever narrow track your own mind is running on, and prompt it to be loose and inventive, to entertain possibilities it hadn't foreseen. (*Craft* 183–84)

Wilbur's position clearly reflects the predominance of free verse, particularly its routinization in the workshops, along with the largely unexamined equation of free verse with social liberation that gathered momentum in the sixties.[92] (As early as 1961 Allen Ginsberg was not-

---

[92] William Harmon, surveying the 1980s New Formalism (with considerable skepticism), is far more precise than Wilbur on the commonplace objection to metrics and rhyme as tyranny and bondage: "There are three things to say in response. One: If you decide to use language as your medium, you've already submitted your art to a system of rules, laws, conventions,

ing, "I do get into ruts that lead to Habits that thin my consciousness," and that poetry as such could be "a block to further awareness" ["Prose Contribution" 338, 340].) What is astonishing about Wilbur's position is his failure to consider metrics, in the same light, as habit-forming; although from the beginning of his career critics had warned of habituation as his primary risk. Randall Jarrell, known for the sharpness of his wit and respected for his refusal to pander to friends in reviewing their work, singled out Wilbur in a resounding condemnation in public (and in Wilbur's presence) at the National Poetry Festival in 1962. The passage deserves full citation, because it is as close to being a castigation of poetry establishment practice from an insider's point of view as anything I've found from its time.

> There is . . . [a] group of poets who, so to speak, come out of Richard Wilbur's overcoat. The work of these academic, tea-party, creative-writing-class poets rather tamely satisfies the rules or standards of technique implicit in what they consider the "best modern practice," so that they are very close to one another, very craftsman-like, never take chances, and produce (extraordinarily) a pretty or correctly beautiful poem and (ordinarily) magazine verse. Their poems are without personal force—come out of poems, not out of life; are, at bottom, social behavior calculated to satisfy a small social group of academic readers, editors, and foundation executives. (*NPF* 135)

Jarrell's comments are leveled against poetry in the Age of Sociology, an age mesmerized by the latest gadgets and the "best modern practice[s]." It was this that compelled Bly to dismiss Olson's poet-

---

and regulations so enormous and despotic that you might as well surrender a few more freedoms for the powerful benefits that the new constrictions can bring. Two: The feeble alphabet makes it impossible for you to write *at all* in the same way as you think or talk. Forget about writing the way you talk: Write the way you write. Three: When you centrifuge yourself to the Eden of free verse, you probably give up one set of repetitions (rhyme, say) only to embrace another (anaphora . . .)" (102). With such strictures in hand, Harmon (unlike most of those professing enthusiasm for metrics) is prepared to credit language poetry with a sagacious commitment to the new set of formal constraints that invariably emerge when traditional forms are abandoned.

ics as a "formalist obsession . . . the middle-class worship of technique which he represents and which he feeds" (Perkins 358). Bly was wildly off target, I think, yet it's worth recalling that Olson spoke of form in the fifties—when formalism was uppermost in discussions about poetry—and in the sixties went on to myth (as did Bly himself).

Bly's remark was a defensive strategy, a way of resisting anything resembling an academy. Not only did he repudiate the Brooks Brothers academics and the Black Mountain bardic mystique, but he distanced himself from other young poets working on "deep image" in New York in the late fifties (when Bly had lived in the city and known them). The result was that Jerome Rothenberg and Robert Kelly became known as "deep imagists," while Bly took on the role of midwestern maverick using the same terminology as if by coincidence. This is characteristic, in that it has been a familiar syndrome in American poetry to deny the poetic efficacy of collective action; to insist on the integrity of the heroic ego; and to mistrust anything that smacks of the committee room. These have been disabling denials because they set impossible demands on the individual, as well as discounting the facticity of social reality. Postwar American poetry is an archipelago of sites (academic, Beat, Black Mountain, New York school, "deep image," "confessional," "workshop," New Formalist, language poetry) which the occupants repudiate, one by one, yet the cumulative effect is collective; and so *all* poets seem characteristically wary of diagnosis, and by their protests become unwitting examples of what Harold Rosenberg called "The Herd of Independent Minds" (in *Commentary*, September 1948).

When the Beats appeared they exposed, by contrast with their own solidarity, the incipient group mentality of conformism in the established poets who had serenely supposed themselves individuated merely by being poets. The Beats disclosed the class and race profile of those who had been elected to personify "postwar American poetry." Clayton Eshleman has anatomized the field of social pressures facing younger poets in the 1960s, along with the options for affirming solidarity without succumbing to institutionalization:

As a young poet in the early 1960s, I felt that an experimental front had established itself, not as a new "academy," but as a flexible, communal proposal: American poetry had to be informationally acute, historically and prehistorically curious and psychically bold—or accept the fate of being the minor, decorative art used as "filler" in the pages of *The New Yorker* and *Atlantic Monthly*.

The conventional poetry of the time had split in two directions: As exemplified by the poetry of Richard Wilbur, it was formally anecdotal, dressed up in rhymed verse; as represented by the "Confessional" poets, it was autobiographical gossip shocking to polite society, rendered as "free verse." While the poetry of Wilbur and Sylvia Plath, say, looked different on the page, the poetic assumptions were quite similar: Development was predictable, as in a joke or story, implying that life itself was made up of self-contained, explainable units.

In contrast, the poetry that was exciting me argued that experience was discontinuous, the mind unstable and sexuality of all sorts a power to be confronted in the poem itself. This was the point at which many of the previously outcast minorities—women, blacks, Indians, gays and lesbians—began to invade the essentially WASP stronghold of American poetry. (*Antiphonal* 246)

Eshleman's essay, "The Stevens-Artaud Rainbow," was written in 1986 (the title echoes Jesse Jackson's "rainbow coalition") and reflects a quarter-century *rapprochement* between the raw-versus-cooked factionalism of the anthology wars. That situation stabilized into a truce or stalemate during the sixties (one measure of which is Donald Hall's remark in 1972 that "You can tell the dominance of a school by the prevalence of bad versions of it"—citing "bad Wilbur" in the late fifties, "bad *Life Studies*" in the early sixties, and "bad Creeley" by the end of the decade [*Contemporary* 36]). Eshleman concludes with a recognition that "Writing significant poetry today is more complexly adversarial than in the past. It is no longer a matter of the Dionysian *vs.* the Apollonian, the experimental *vs.* the traditional, the legendary oppositions which have for the most part divided poets against themselves" (251).

Eshleman's own work has maintained its allegiances to those integrities of attention he has found equally manifest in Stevens and Olson, enabling him to posit a poetry "seen both as a synthesis *and* a melee" (251).

Eshleman's terms seek to reconcile what he sees as an artificially prolonged dispute between control and release, order and energy. In retrospect, it's remarkable how long the confrontation was stalled at the level of form. What was really at stake in the end was the formal apparition of community as a field of heterogeneous claims and calls to order, *social* order. The poetry establishment that seemed so secure after World War II was a refined but precarious meritocracy, able to sustain the pretense, for a time, that the narrow circle of its initiates were producing the canon of "American poetry." The commitment to orderly form was hardly specific to that moment, but what has proven so mesmerizing about it is the clarity with which metrical order was homologous with social decorum: so that the irruption of the Beats connoted the bellicose disturbance of a melee, something as rude as speaking "out of order" in a civic assembly. American poetry, under its official cover, was a security vessel, a sanctuary for the ceremonial nourishment of sensibility, pluralizing its lyric ego in a tight circle of privileged initiates. Eshleman's reference to a "WASP stronghold of American poetry" is precise; and in the American milieu, democratic idealism being what it is, the antidemocratic injustice of such a situation was bound to become controversial.

The presence of Gwendolyn Brooks and Langston Hughes at the 1962 National Poetry Festival signified a dramatic turnaround in the thorough, if silent, segregation that is in retrospect so conspicuous a feature of the fifties poetry establishment. Brooks won the Pulitzer in 1950 but was shunned from the anthologies until Paul Engle and Joseph Langland included her in *Poet's Choice* in 1962.[93]

---

[93] That was obviously not among the canon-making collections, nor was her next appearance, in Lucien Stryk's regional *Heartland: Poets of the Midwest* in 1967. It was not until 1970, twenty years after her Pulitzer, that Gwendolyn Brooks was chosen to appear in a general and ambitious anthology, Hayden Carruth's *The Voice That Is Great Within Us*.

Hughes had a different sort of reputation, having been the premier poet of the Harlem Renaissance between the world wars. It would be several years yet—and even then only in the wake of race riots— before mainstream white poets would note the fact of such long-standing exclusion. "I do not think there has been a conspiracy to 'keep the Negro out of poetry' in America," Louis Simpson wrote in *Harper's* in 1968 (tentatively backing off from his own flagrant racism of a few years earlier[94]), "but there has been indifference to the poetry of the Negro, which is just as bad." He named Robert Hayden as the author of poetry "new to me though in quality and ambition it is superior to the work of white poets who have been much anthologized" (*Company* 113). The obvious thing to do, then, was for anthologists to select someone like Hayden to *replace* an inferior white poet (much as Donald Hall "discovered" Etheridge Knight for the 1972 revision of his Penguin anthology, *Contemporary American Poetry*). Tokenism is the inevitable result—even when expanded to majority proportions as in recent revisions of teaching anthologies of American literature.[95] The presence of the "exceptional" individual is invariably configured as the exception that proves the rule; and as many have lately noted, commenting on canon revision, the increased visibility of minorities does not necessarily call into question the *form* of the canon, the social rule canon-

---

[94] Reviewing Gwendolyn Brooks for the *New York Herald Tribune Book Week* in 1963, Simpson declared: "I am not sure it is possible for a Negro to write well without making us aware he is a Negro; on the other hand, if being a Negro is the only subject, the writing is not important" (quoted in Kalaidjian 172).

[95] Despite this revisionary industry, the map of postwar American poetry as constructed in trade anthologies and critical studies is predominantly white, the attention oscillating back and forth between raw and cooked, radical and conservative. I know of only one thoroughgoing effort to integrate an account of Native, African American and Hispanic American poetry into the more familiar context of confessionals, Beats, Black Mountain and other factions; and that, typically, is by a foreigner: Ingrid Kerkhoff's *Poetiken und lyrischer Diskurs im Kontext gesellschaftlicher Dynamik: USA: "The Sixties."* Kerkhoff rightly points out that only in the wake of the anthology wars was it possible for the "Anthologiegeneration" to reflect on what had been systematically excluded (*Sixties* 337).

icity enforces.[96] "So we must face the essential chauvinism of what is taught as American literature," Amiri Baraka noted in 1978.

> It should be obvious that it, like all other aspects of American life, represents the choice of a white elite, and what's more, even deemphasizes some aspects and confuses American literature, the white part of it, so that in many instances the anthologies and survey courses that we learn literature from are the choices of or have been influenced to a great extent by some of the most reactionary elements in this society. (*Prose* 242–43)

It is a *perpetuation* of the reactionary perspective, in Baraka's view, that certain blacks are selected for "walk-on roles" (243). The theatrical analogy itself indicates who's scripted the event, and what its outcome is likely to be.

The covert pretense of tokenism is that race (or gender, or sexual orientation, or any other disconcerting "difference") is accident, a contingency of existence, not essence. This naturally plays into the hands of the discourse of "anti-essentialism," with the present conundrum of a revised canon in which it is *essential* that minorities be included, yet their minoritarian features must not be essentialized in any way. In the newly configured revolving-door multicultural canon a procedure that always was arbitrary is now more openly disclosed as such. Which is to say, we now see the shameless opportunism of a curriculum designed to reflect political correctness; whereas, formerly, the connivance of a sanitary cordon of

---

[96] In fact, as Richard Brodhead suggests, one of the things that canon revision appears to unwittingly reinforce is consumerist mentality: "The inclusionistic American literature means to celebrate cultural difference, but it is possible that the smorgasbord or bit-of-each practice of inclusion neutralizes the difference it is meant to celebrate, first by abstracting and miniaturizing cultural worlds that are themselves historically complex and variable into the texts that 'represent' them . . . then by rendering these 'different' worlds interchangeable in the domain of consumption. As the current generation can see how the previous one used its literary values to support hierarchies of social privilege, so a later world may decide that the current order used a promised literary egalitarianism to underwrite the operative assumptions of consumer culture: the assumptions that everything exists *for us* and that everything can be accessed through consumption" (66).

white men fielding a canon of taste could masquerade as Literature, or Poetry, "the voice that is great within us" where the deictic term (*us*) was conveniently ambiguous and thus seemingly open to all.

Shortly before he became Baraka, LeRoi Jones clarified some pertinent features of the terrain in "Hunting is Not Those Heads on the Wall." He had been associated primarily with the Beat/Black Mountain axis, having been introduced in *The New American Poetry* (Allen's sole black poet), but was soon to be a commanding force in the Black Arts Movement. "Hunting" is poised midway between the New American orientation of his anthology *The Moderns* (1964) and his far more influential collection *Black Fire: An Anthology of Afro-American Writing* (1968). At the center of Baraka's evolving affiliations was an attention to process. "The artist is cursed with his artifact, which exists without and despite him," he complains. "And even though the process, in good art, is everywhere perceptible, the risk of perfection corrupts the lazy public into accepting the material *in place of* what it is only the remains of" (*Home* 173). His purpose was, in part, to vanquish the mystique of fifties formalism by subordinating the artwork to the primacy of the *quest*, the social struggle. "The most valuable quality in life is the will to existence, the unconnected zoom, which finally becomes in anyone's hands whatever part of it he could collect. Like dipping cups of water from the falls. Which is what the artist does. Fools want to dictate what kind of dipper he uses" (175). Fools, that is, like academic formalists: metrical thought police. For Baraka, as for the New American poetics generally, dippers are legion; what's to be prized is the style of the scoop. Baraka, then as now, was guided above all by musical precedent, and jazz history as he conceived it in *Blues People* (1963) was inevitably social history. Conversely, as "Hunting" makes clear, social history is itself a phenomenon in the history of forms. "A saxophonist who continues to 'play like' Charlie Parker cannot understand that Charlie Parker wasn't certain that what had happened had to sound like that," but "to understand *why* Parker sounded like he did" is to apprehend something of value (176). Social forms are residues of struggle and desire—such, at least, was evident to Baraka and other blacks in the forefront of civil rights issues in the sixties—

and social form is therefore malleable: the trace of a process. The social risk is commensurate with artistic risk, which is congealed form, the lazy acceptance of a particular set of arrangements "in place of" aspiration.

Baraka was soon to proclaim that the sole calling of the black artist was to upend an oppressive social order—a strategy specific to its moment, perhaps, but true to the commitment of a process-oriented art in general, which is to recognize the provisionality of forms, and eventually behold a continuum of forms within forms, a cascade of implication and explication, in which the "limits" of individual attention and social admonition alike are but momentary stops in an Emersonian "circuit" of things through forms. "No one should fool around with art who is only trying to 'make sense,'" Baraka proclaimed. "We are all full of meaning and content, but to make that wild grab for more! To make words surprise themselves" (175). From this promontory, of course, it's quite plausible to claim that the most stringent rules procure the most exhilarating surprises: that is, the principle of constant striving does not disavow order, but recognizes the contingency of its appearance and the chimera of its stability. This was not a conclusion to which Baraka was inclined, but it is available within the dialectic of his negotiations with contrastive communities and styles of self-making.

Nathaniel Mackey elucidates Baraka's apparent contradictions in "The Changing Same," and offers a particularly germane reading of his paradoxical (if only occasional) anti-intellectualism: "In its best aspects, this anti-intellectualism is not so much a repudiation of thought as an effort to rethink, to as it were *unthink* the perversions of thought endemic to an unjust social order . . . " (*Discrepant Engagement* 42). The adjectival form "unthinking" is strictly negative, but Mackey recognizes an affirmative possibility by making it a verb, *to unthink*. The intransigence of one usage animates a renewal, and satisfies Baraka's insistence that words surprise themselves. Such innovations are a vital aspect of the American poetic tradition of self-renewal, and form an even deeper continuum in African American culture, both of which Mackey is positioned to chronicle. The apparent anomaly of his book *Discrepant Engagement* is its selection of authors for sustained appreciative readings—Baraka, Clarence Major, Duncan, Creeley, Olson, Wilson Harris, and Edward Kamau Brathwaite—but this dissolves once we recognize that Mackey is not concerned with canonical adjudication and its tendering of theoretical penalties, but is intent instead on affirming that "[c]reative kinship and the lines of affinity it effects are much more complex, jagged, and indissociable than the totalizing pretensions of canon formation tend to acknowledge" (3).[97]

Mackey's advocacy of creative kinship is a canny alliance with open form and process. The conventional means of presenting the case for process is to cite Olson's "Projective Verse"—a bad habit I've deliberately shunned by turning instead to Baraka and Mackey.[98]

---

[97] Mackey is very nearly alone in his pursuit of "creative kinship," particularly in the current scholarly climate in which the admissible terms of affiliation are legislative, not creative. (One need only look at the terminology imported with the discourse of French critical theory to see why this is the case: to read Derrida, Foucault, Lacan, Barthes, Kristeva, and Irigaray is to be constantly subjected to a vocabulary of legislation [law, regulation, constitution, gaze, code, discipline, etc.].) I don't mean to single him out as symptomatic of some recuperative insurgency, a maverick disaffiliation from the undertow of institutional habits; but it is worth noting that Mackey's criticism (impeccable as conventional scholarship) is deeply informed by the resources of kinship he advocates, inasmuch as the essays in *Discrepant Engagement* tacitly reflect (and are at times cunningly intricated with) his own poetic and fictive writing, *Bedouin Hornbook*, *Djbot Bhagostus's Run*, *Eroding Witness*, and *School of Udhra*, as well as his innovative editing of *Hambone*. I mention this with trepidation lest I be construed as saying that poets take care of their own, or that the tribal sympathies of the creative imagination bar access to the uninitiated academic. It was in fact a common complaint of the New Critics that philologically inclined scholars were devoid of productive sympathy for the works they anatomized. What is valuable in Mackey's critical work is a quality of sympathy which need make no appeal to partisanship because it is resoundingly commensurate in its passions with the energy of the "original" texts. It is, in short, a process-oriented criticism quite willing to make specific claims of judgment because it never seeks to hypostatize such claims or to adumbrate its judgments into a binding cardinal order.

[98] By way of example, see Kuberski's essay "Charles Olson and the American Thing," by far the most searching inquiry to date into Olson's idiomatic macho posturing. Kuberski discloses the very traditional duplicitousness of Olson's search for origins—aligning him with Puritan Jeremiads, Emerson, Whitman, Melville and Pound—yet perplexingly succumbs to a parallel foundationalism himself. Kuberski provides a compellingly clever reading of Olson's "Mayan Letters" and "Projective Verse," but in order to deconstruct projectivism as a (psychoanalytic) "projection of a metaphysical sense

Not that Olson isn't still redolent with instruction, but it's in keeping with his provocation for me to withdraw support from the stereotypic iteration of the sort that has made his own (provisional, if stentorian) pronouncements on open form so easily available to prospective enthusiasts and susceptible to ridicule from others. Olson appeared to embody dogmatism because of his partisan mannerism; whereas formalist dogma went unnoticed because it was impersonal and couched in the studied neutrality of polite criticism. As many process-oriented poets of the 1960s attest, the poem is the record of its occasion—more a manifestation than a representation. Olson looms large in this, as poet and even more influentially as theorist. As the poetry world became politicized in the sixties, *process* could be taken as a political gesture. Significantly, however, it was in African American poetry that this pursuit was most pronounced. The separatist insurgency of the Black Arts Movement provided a forum for poets to develop a community-based audience and to divest from themselves those hankerings, so common among their white peers, to generalize poetry into abstract indicators of "major" and "minor." Since this study is specifically concerned with the vicissitudes of that abstraction—concretized in the image of the Wax Museum—I'll refrain from going into a detailed account of proliferating alternative communities.[99]

---

of loss" (192) he is forced to read Olson's double (and repressed) meanings by taking Derrida and Freud at their (literal) word. Kuberski cites Derrida's texts as foundational gestures in a critique of Olson's hankering after origins, manifestly ignoring the Derridean sense of *écriture* as desiring-production and thus inaugurating, with each citation, a veritable rebirth of metaphysics.

[99] My hope is that, having documented the context of exclusiveness here, others better informed than I may provide a complementary record of struggles on the margin. It would be useful to have a postwar supplement to Cary Nelson's *Repression and Recovery*, in part as a corrective to some of its (probably unintended) implications. Nelson notes, for instance, that in the postwar years "A number of highly interested interpretive moves . . . need[ed] to be installed as facts of nature," citing as example the way that "political challenges of black poets need[ed] to be subsumed under race and race made a matter of black self-interest rather than national concern" (166). It was the separatist drive of black "self-interest" that gave the Black Arts movement such buoyancy in the sixties, however; and here, as with such other arts scenes as the Teatro Campesino in California's Latino community, we need to recognize that the politics of exclusion was not unilateral, and that certain acts of cultural *secession* are vital forms of noncompliance.

As I have chronicled, an American poetry establishment reigned with absolute security from the forties through the fifties, and was destabilized in the sixties only by internal schisms (formalist poets abandoning metrics), by the theoretical challenge of the various contingents anthologized by Donald Allen, and by the ongoing popularity of the Beats. Where poets had been somewhat mystified on the question of audience before 1956—a mystification intensified by the capricious notion of a "general public"—the Beats rediscovered audience in a subculture, demonstrating that a local and decidedly *un*general community might well provide poetry's most viable audience. This was a nightmare for the many suburbanized academic poets, who tended to be defensive enough about where they lived without having to engage with their neighbors as prospective readers of poetry. But for people disposed to affiliate themselves with others on the basis of race, class, oppositional politics, etc., the prospect was enticing. Adrienne Rich cites a refractory continuum of poetry's alternatives:

> The San Francisco Renaissance of the 1940s and 1950s . . . the poetic voices of the Black and antiwar movements of the 1960s had created a strong mix of antiestablishment poetics in the United States. But the poetry of women's liberation in the 1970s was *women's* antiestablishment poetry, challenging not just conventional puritanical mores, but the hip "counterculture" and the male poetry culture itself. (*What Is Found There* 167–68).

Rich reiterates again that the prospect of a communal poetics was the specific legacy of the San Francisco scene and the Black Arts Movement (175), even as she goes on to document a hive of feminist poetics, citing scores of presses, magazines, anthologies, and bookstores. Rich importantly remembers that the consolations of a given community, no matter how intense or gratifying, do not constitute the whole picture; and in a series of declarations in response to the question "What does a poet need to know?" she sustains a principle of nonconformist aggregation: "—That the poetries of men and women unlike you are a great polyglot city of resources, in whose streets you need to wander, whose sounds you need to listen to, without feeling that you must live there" (216). The irony here is that the proliferation of special interest or community based poetry venues tends to reinforce consensus building and homogeneity of poetic practices. I say "tends" because within feminist circles, say, consensus meant recognition of and negotiation between competing claims—lesbian and heterosexual, white and colored, middle class and working class—but we need nonetheless to recognize that Rich's "polyglot city of resources" is, in practice, often an encampment attenuated by its uniformity of purpose. To retain what's most useful in Rich's appeal is to consider above all that "encounters with poems that do not speak to 'us' may well provide 'us' with one of poetry's most crucial acts of education" (Lazer, "Politics of Form" 522).

Apart from the haphazard but useful contributions to *The Poetry Reading* edited by Vincent and Zweig (1981), no one has attempted to document the complex proliferation of poetry subcommunities in the past quarter-century, with the result that nearly all discourse about poetry still proceeds on the premise of a "tradition" that, in the postwar period, begins with Lowell and Roethke and Wilbur and (inexplicably) swerves to include Ginsberg and Snyder and Olson, after which the lineage sprawls in a tangle of untraceable detours, with spasmodic attempts at getting back on track by means of Dickey, Bly, Wright, Rich, Merwin, Merrill, Ammons, and others. But this is literary history for the convenience of anthologies. The confusion is latent in the prospect of a democratic poetry in the first place, as prompted by Whitman. The U.S. is continually disoriented by the spectre of an orderly succession of literary masters who, like presidents, would be popularly elected yet still possess some regal charisma. It has proven very awkward to have a tradition dominated by exiles and expatriates, cranks and fascists, alcoholics, manic depressives and suicides, to say nothing of all the mavericks who are not pathologically afflicted but (even more troublesome, perhaps) see the culture itself as a vast sociopathic complex. This legacy has given many an incentive to seek out and affirm the virtues of normalcy, valuing "craft" and "workmanship." Little wonder, then, that blacks and Chicanos and Asian Americans, along with gay and lesbian and other secessionist groups, have pointedly resisted having anything to do with the *humanist* claims and rhetoric of the poetry mainstream.

That Olson's theories are *not* neohumanist is not readily apparent from titles like *Human Universe* and his insistence, cited above, on composing "an image of man."[100] The frequency with which Olson is mentioned in D.H. Melhem's *Heroism in the New Black Poetry*—which consists of essays on and interviews with Gwendolyn Brooks, Dudley Randall, Haki Madhubuti, Sonia Sanchez, Jayne Cortez, and Amiri Baraka—is a vivid indicator of his difference from, say, Lowell (about whom these poets have nothing to say). Likewise, Olson appears prominently as an exception to the general rule of poetic xenophobia documented by Aldon Nielsen in *Reading Race: White American Poets and the Racial Discourse in the Twentieth Century*. In other words, Olson is resonant with black culture despite his obvious lack of involvement with any black community, not only because of his insistence on documenting the slave trade in Gloucester's history in *The Maximus Poems*, but also because he is a reliable guide to a poetic practice outside the vo-tech mentality of the mainstream. For those who find themselves peripheralized by social injustice, such thought is not option but necessity. (It's not merely of idle interest, but evidence of a forcible and insightful connection, that Olson's private supporter, Harvey Brown, was also deeply involved in the black jazz community: his patron-

---

[100] Olson's influence has been so obsessively figured in terms of Black Mountain that it's difficult to get a sense that he was anything but a cult figure, absorbed in (and only relevant to) a special enclave. That he became a figure of referential force in the sixties is evident in a surprising but instructive way in a comment by William Stafford. "I had been hearing about [Olson's poetics] all my life and sort of giving a general assent, not being negative," he told an interviewer in 1972, admitting that by the time Olson's *Selected Poems* appeared in 1967 he thought a closer look was overdue. Stafford found that "many of the positions taken about writing, about poetry, lines, and so on, seemed quite congenial to me," so much so that "it didn't seem like news . . . it seemed like, yeah, that's what I thought everyone thought" (*Crawl* 98). In the combat zone of poetic factionalism in the anthology wars, I think it likely that many other poets responded to Olson as Stafford did, with the sense that his advice on breath units as the basis of the measured line was sensible and indeed obvious—an assumption, however, that mistakenly takes Olson's concerns to be narrowly aesthetic.

age, in other words, spanned alternate, but complementary, worlds.[101]) Much of the attention brought to bear on poetry stresses its purity and autonomy, claiming for it as privilege a univocality which Bakhtin insisted was its impediment, the mark of poetry's inferiority to the heteroglossic novel. This emphasis has persisted despite the trouble that Whitman and Dickinson brought to monologism: a tensional wager at the threshold of self and other, same and different, which modern American poetry has repeatedly explored. At stake is what Ingrid Monson, discussing black jazz practice, calls "divergent cultural knowledges that *coexist* in particular individuals" (311). William Matthews has succinctly said that "much of the nonsense spoken in the debate over traditional vs. free verse could be avoided, I like to think, by inciting the combatants to learn a little jazz history" (167). Certainly the polyphonic ambition to "do the police in different voices" (as Eliot's *Waste Land* was originally titled) needs to be retained not only as validating a national poetry

---

[101] Fittingly, Brown's one published book of poetry was *Jazz Playing*. The intersection of Black Mountain and Beat aesthetics with black music is itself a topic of notable proportions. Creeley has repeatedly testified to the fact that his rhythmic orientation, his sense of the dynamic interplay of motion and rest, sound and silence, was indebted to Charlie Parker and Miles Davis. The jazz ethos that permeates Kerouac's work is well known. But the indebtedness of poets to jazz in the past fifty years is so pervasive as to cut across conventional lines of confrontation like open versus closed form. This is immediately apparent on looking into *The Jazz Poetry Anthology*, edited by Sascha Feinstein and Yusef Komunyakaa, and *Moment's Notice: Jazz in Poetry and Prose*, edited by Art Lange and Nathaniel Mackey (and Mackey's literary essays in *Discrepant Engagement* are saturated with his attentions to music). Recently David Meltzer (the youngest poet in Allen's *New American Poetry*) has edited a superb documentary collection called *Reading Jazz*, the first such book to successfully integrate perspectives from poets into the more conventional potpourri of comments by critics, historians, and the musicians themselves. "It was the poet's community responsibility to make accurate perceptions, not false metaphor," Stephen Vincent reflects on the Bay Area public reading scene of the sixties: "The music emergent would be part of the cure, the liberation. Jazz was part of the medium: Charlie Parker, Miles Davis, Eric Dolphy, John Coltrane, Thelonious Monk were essential guides to how the language could break, lift, and move" (*The Poetry Reading* 25). And finally, if belatedly, a book by Charles O. Hartman (*Jazz Text*) appeared in 1991, juxtaposing discussions of Creeley, Antin, and Mac Low with musicological studies of Lee Konitz, Ornette Coleman, and Joni Mitchell.

composed of different social groups, but also as the agent of complexity within individual voices—a co-inherence of "divergent cultural knowledges," and an "ethics of antiphony" which Paul Gilroy
commends as the hybridized legacy of "the Black Atlantic" with its
"bifocal cultural forms" (200, 3).

    Insofar as black history has had any standing as a licit sub-
ject in anthologies and studies of American poetry, it is largely history as scenic cue-card. While the transmission of the same poems
from one anthology to the next impinges on the presentation of most
poets, the handful of blacks included in the general anthology context seems particularly driven by tokenism. Brooks, Hayden,
Michael S. Harper, and most recently Rita Dove (who became the
youngest Poet Laureate at forty) are each known by a handful of
poems, all of which are short, accessible, and give little intimation
of the depredations of black history as *collective* and complex.
LeRoi Jones/Amiri Baraka was, from the sixties into the mid-seven-
ties, the favorite black poet for white anthologists—largely, I suspect, because he had been introduced in *The New American Poetry*,
whereas other blacks had appeared, if at all, in less forceful contexts, or in contexts less visible to the white world. But while Baraka has always retained a specific sense of black locution and the
oral occasion, he became overtly political in a way that anthologists
tend to resist ("The 'Race Line' is a Product of Capitalism"), and the
impact of history he proposed to chronicle began to seem as recondite, in its own way, as Olson's:

> Say did you know, brothers, sisters, did you hear
> about the parade the long long line, of nigger servants
> of evil. Did you know that Belgian Congo had changed to
> Zaire, and Mantan Moreland Mobutu starves our people still
> Or intellectual Eric Wms, after fighting against the rule
> of the white man, the british colon, had took up oppression
> on his own, linked his hot thing to the same imperialism
> and trinidad moaned under his bullshit
> there are fools tell you the bullets black reactionaries
> kill with
> dont hurt

(Poetry 302)

The historical complexities evoked here require nothing less than a personal commitment to reeducate oneself.[102] Antin's point about Lowell and "grade school history" comes to mind: mainstream American verse has often blithely taken history to amount to little more than an evocation of images retained from childhood initiation in the platitudes of nationalist rhetoric; and the "sophisticated" poets appear to be those, like Lowell, who extend their references to Renaissance Florence, Periclean Athens, or Hannibal crossing the Alps—in short, set pieces suitable to 19th century kitsch genre painting.[103] By way of

---

[102] Confronted with the discomforting fact of Baraka's development, from Black Mountain to Black Nationalism and then to revolutionary Communism—all of which was inexorably front and center in his poetry—white anthologists tended to reprint poems from his earliest phase (via Allen's selection in *The New American Poetry*) or, more often, trade him in for milder alternates. Don L. Lee (Haki Mabhuti) and other poets exemplifying the verbal aggressions of the Black Arts Movement were also phased out during the 1970s; though I mean nothing disparaging by noting the tempered accessibility of their replacements—Gwendolyn Brooks, Robert Hayden, Etheridge Knight, Dudley Randall, Michael S. Harper, and, most recently, Rita Dove.

[103] Europe was idealized by the devotional attitude to its culture adopted by many of the modernists (Pound, H. D., Stevens, Eliot). A case might well be made that poets displaying too much disrespect or even indifference toward Europe (Williams and Zukofsky, for instance) have appeared a bit suspect to official literary sensibility. Even Bishop's Brazilian settings probably seemed a bit risqué to her Manhattan admirers. The New Critics, of course, were originally motivated by the romance of the old South, which in Ransom's view had facilitated the aesthetic life ("I subordinate always Art to the aesthetic life . . . " [Fekete 69]); but during the Depression and the New Deal, with their increasing concern about the predatory industrialism and corporate mentality of the Northeast, the New Critics began to shift allegiance to Europe, particularly in that Eliot's formal affiliations were with European institutions of civil, religious, and cultural authority. For the generation of their students, Europe became a continent-wide Disneyland of art tourism. "Europe is wonderful," gushed Jarrell to Lowell after a 1948 junket to Salzburg, "you ought to see if you can't get a passport and go next summer on your Guggenheim; I guarantee, *guarantee*, that you'll be glad, glad, glad as Pollyanna" (*Letters* 203). (He did: Lowell happily immersed himself in Europe for a couple years in the early fifties.) In contrast to Salzburg, Jarrell thought American cities were infernal: "This *is* Hell. Hell must be exactly like this," he said of New York (229). The European sojourn was not only becoming a cultural obligation for intellectuals of the G.I. generation, but an advantageous monetary venture as well. This is, for obvious historical reasons, a postwar romance. But I'm suggesting that the New Critical ethos of

contrast—to cite Louis Simpson's infamous formula—"if being a Negro is the only subject, the writing is not important" (Kalaidjian 172). In the face of such inanities, it is certainly worth asking, with John Beverley, "Are there experiences in the world today that would be betrayed or misrepresented by literature as we know it?" (69).

The problem of poetry by poets of color is a complex issue for critical discourse, bringing to the surface, once again, the vexed terms that have polarized the scene for decades: open versus closed form; form versus content. Poetry that engages the specificity of ethnic communities is easy for the white establishment to ignore, because its "content" doesn't compute. (The tastemakers and canonizers are naturally as fussy about content as about form.[104]) The centrist demand

---

the poem as a radiant episode of controlled intensity merged with, and became inseparable from, a notion of aesthetic cultivation which could be assimilated to a *specific* site (Europe), acceding to *its* terms of order—terms explicitly resisted by Olson in his poem addressing Rainer Gerhardt (a German admirer). But for the New Critics and their epigones, the symbolic order of Europe was as scintillating in its paradoxes and ironies as the internal dynamic of any metaphysical poem. The Eurocentrism of the official pantheon of American poetry still exerts a powerful lure. Geoff Ward notes that in Ashbery's "Self-Portrait in a Convex Mirror" "the attention to a Renaissance portrait gives the poem a 'European' air . . . and who can doubt the cultural reassurance that would have given the judges of the Pulitzer Prize and other awards won by the book *Self-Portrait* in 1976 . . . " (161–62).

[104] A case in point is Melvin B. Tolson, a black poet with notably formalist affiliations to the New Critical trajectory of high modernism, whose works were prefaced by Allen Tate and Karl Shapiro, yet who remains a nonentity in the anthologies and a footnote in the chronicles. As I've already indicated, there was little hope for black poets to cross the color line into white (a.k.a. "American") anthologies until the late 1960s; but by that time Tolson had died (in 1966), and his major work, *Harlem Gallery* had only recently been published (1965). Michael Bérubé has produced a thorough reading of "Tolson's Neglect" in *Marginal Forces/Cultural Centers*, but he focuses largely on the (mis)handling of Tolson's reputation in anthologies of Afro-American literature and by black critics, in part to consolidate his overall thesis that "authorization" and canonization diverge racially "precisely because American writers of different races have historically been assigned radically different author functions" (61). To Bérubé's diagnosis that Tolson's modernism was misconstrued by black custodians of their own literary heritage, I would add that, for the white world of poetry's national canon, Tolson's timing was all wrong: the late sixties was the worst possible time for a major poem of closely ordered multivalent symbolism in a tensional structure, particularly by a black poet visibly associated with Allen Tate, who by then seemed hope-

for referential clarity is often a veiled repudiation of any experience not already indexed in and legitimated by canonical precedent.[105] Formally, some ethnic poetry is situated in a pragmatic oral context, and that too renders it inadmissible. Poems that appear on the page like transcripts of songs belong to a generically suspect medium (though Louise Bogan, for one, welcomed the prospect of a polyphonic anthology blending oral with written traditions). Also, the *implications* of form in ethnic contexts takes on manifestly different connotations, as in the resistance to free verse in the Harlem Renaissance (free verse representing the quintessence of white Eurocentrism). The complexity of the situation is compounded by insufficient consideration of the matter of form and formalism, or most concisely, form *as* formalism. Form is not to be idly dismissed as platonism, escapism, or dilletantism; after all, we speak of "life forms." Life is form, as lives are informed by contacts and connections with others (who are likewise *formed*). The legacy of New Criticism has exacerbated the issue of form, to the extent that a resourceful critic like Aijaz Ahmad

---

lessly retrograde. Tolson's invisibility is in part attributable to another factor, which is that his generational peers were the poets of the Harlem Renaissance of the 1920s, and his very belated publications thirty years later seemed bibliographically consigned to a period aura by virtue of his birthdate.

[105] The sometimes reactionary tone of canonical restructuring may be partly attributable to the simplemindedness of the status quo that needed deposing. But there are clearly revisionary excesses of simplification, not least of which is Adrienne Rich's preemptive discovery that traces of a "deliberately racial language" in Wallace Stevens constitute "*a key to the whole*" of his work (*What Is Found There* 205). Alan Shapiro, probably thinking of more rigorous academic instances, counsels that "When applied to literature, a 'hermeneutics of suspicion' in and of itself, despite its intellectual sophistication, is as crudely incomplete as a sympathetic imagination divorced from the disciplines of intellectual and historical inquiry" (179). Nathaniel Mackey's warning that "there has been far too much emphasis on accessibility when it comes to writers from socially marginalized groups" is also relevant: "This has resulted in shallow, simplistic readings that belabor the most obvious aspects of the writer's work and situation, readings that go something like this: 'So-and-so is a black writer. Black people are victims of racism. So-and-so's writing speaks out against racism.' It has yet to be shown that such simplifications have had any positive political effect, if, indeed, they have had any political effect at all." And what's worse: "the confinement of the work to racial readings that tell us only what we already know, is a symptom of the social othering that such readings presumably oppose" (17–18).

can comment on its "practice of reified reading" as "altogether hegemonic in American literary studies," a convenient "pedagogic tool in the American classroom precisely because it required of the student little knowledge of anything not strictly 'literary'—no history which was not predominantly literary history, no science of the social, no philosophy . . . " (52). Ahmad goes on to acknowledge that New Critical formalism could stress objective rigor "thanks to its prior commitment to squeezing a particular ideological meaning out of each literary text" (52–53). He apparently fails to see that "literary history" for the New Critics *was* precisely a "science of the social," and that this "prior commitment" was nothing short of *the content of the form* (in Hayden White's phrase). In light of this, *formalism* can best be described as acceding priority to the contents inured to certain forms. The derelict omission of ethnic writing from the postwar poetry canon was a matter of form in this sense. Form and content are agents of reciprocal assimilation. The canonical authors clearly had to *look* the part of the delegated role, a role for which it was essential that the custodians and tastemakers could use the first-person plural as the proper term for a felicitous relation. "Our poets" is deceptively democratic; in fact, such a phrase has never implied a radius bigger than an exclusive country club, and we can't discount the snobbism of "good form" that attends canonical choices in such an environment.

While objections to elitism and the taint of racism are pertinent, it is problematic to dismiss New Criticism on formalist grounds, as virtually everyone now appears overeager to do, forgetting the temperamental and procedural advantage of a critical approach which stresses the quiddity of the object and regards literature as a sort of gnosis. New Criticism advanced the view of literature as a practice of knowledge, a practical manifestation of imagination, rather than a derivative and transitory representation. The New Critics were predominantly poets themselves, so their pronouncements have a decidedly polemical bite. Not significantly different from the rhetoric of the New Critics is Charles Olson's declaration at the 1965 Berkeley conference to the effect that "that which exists through itself is called meaning" (reported in Creeley, *Contexts* 93); nor, for that matter, is Olson's view that far from Emerson's "Experience": "the definition of *spiritual* should be, *that which is its own evidence."* (*Essays* 475). The New Critical insurrection, then, needs to be seen as an aspect of that (otherwise New England) continuum from Emerson to Olson, which reclaims the universe as an event of the poem.[106] "The value of the universe contrives to throw itself into every point," Emerson wrote in "Compensation" (289). The complexities of response to the prospect of the art object as a concentration of regenerative impulses are germane to a broader context. Linked in the 1950s with the action-ethic of Kerouac's r.p.m. prose and the kinetic insistence of bebop, Jackson Pollock was celebrated by Clement Greenberg (in 1943) as an advocate of painting as "something valid solely on its own terms, in the way nature itself is valid, in the way a landscape—not its picture—is aesthetically valid . . . " (Brookeman 196). Forecasting the Creeley-Olson formulation, worked out in their correspondence in the early fifties, to the effect that form is nothing more than an extension of content, Greenberg appraised the avant-garde aesthetic as one in which "content is to be dissolved so completely into form that the work of art or literature cannot be reduced in whole or in part to anything not itself" (197). The failing of the poetry sponsored by the New Critics is that it was, in the end, *less* than rigorous about the unity of form and content. Completely incapable of recognizing the Black Mountain poets' commitment to form—open though it may be—these poets were just as inept at calculating the consequences of their own covert criteria for a *formalist content.*

The symbiosis between form and content sought by New Criticism was predicated in part on a critique of the modernist tendency to transpose social chaos onto form: collage method as sympathetic magic, homeopathic mimesis. The postmodernism pioneered by the New Critics reasserted the same principle in reverse: metrical stability and formal unity as bulwark of sanity in an uncertain world. Modernist collage may have redistributed the order of the parts, but the relation of part to whole was preserved by appealing to organic form (only transparently different from that of Romanticism); so the

---

[106] For an elaboration, see Rasula, "The Compost Library" and "Exfoliating Cosmos."

reallocation of sensibility from part to whole in high modernist practice was not unprecedented. In fact, as far as the New Criticism was concerned, the trajectory (and its unity) was plainly evident in Eliot's progress from *The Waste Land* to *Four Quartets*. A formalist content (to infer from Eliot's example) would thus involve a psychological pledge of allegiance to images of formal unity (the "crowned knot" resolving the fire and the rose at the end of "Little Gidding") as defining features of a sustaining sanity. The formal complex constituted by the conjunction of organic unity, cultural redemption, and a sanitary preoccupation with modes of thought is commonly known as *fascism*. This is not to suggest (as it's all too easy to do) that either high modernism or its New Critical recuperation are inherently fascist. Rather, I regard them as autotelic hierarchies *analogous* to, but not necessarily in concert with, the totalitarian impulse. If Walter Benjamin's essay on "The Work of Art in the Age of Mechanical Reproduction" has attained canonical status as the definitive summary of the conjunction of fascism and aesthetics, it's because he clarifies as no one else has the fact that an aesthetic principle is *the* vital precondition for the rise of fascist collectivity. The lure of fascism is precisely the lure of organic unity and thrives on identification compulsion. It's hard to imagine anything more auspicious and prescient than Benjamin's concluding remark that human "self-alienation has reached such a degree that it can experience its own destruction as an aesthetic pleasure of the first order" (*Illuminations* 242).[107] Unity is achieved by maximizing disunity and aestheticizing it as spectacle (for the masses) or fetishizing it as art (for the elite). Thoughts of racial purity in fascism correspond to aesthetic anxieties about the integrity of formal means. This homology needn't be taken as evidence of a motivated link (after all, one might also note the proliferation of organic symmetry in nature and conclude that the

---

[107] Hollywood sensibility has unwittingly followed Benjamin's lead; and it has now become axiomatic to associate high art with lethal weapons, as in *True Lies* (directed by James Cameron and starring Arnold Schwarzenegger, 1994), in which ancient Assyrian monuments imported for the art market turn out to harbor nuclear warheads. The point of the film, of course, is to display the weapons and their firepower, not the art.

natural order displays fascist tendencies). But what I would retain, to clarify what I mean by *formalist content*, is a recognition that the content of any "formalism" is contingent on the notions of purity or integrity identified with "form" in the first place.[108]

The collectivizing impulse in the postwar American poetry establishment invariably appealed to images of plurality drawn from the image bank of identity rather than difference, familiarity not alterity, recognition not estrangement. It didn't need to be actively racist or sexist (nor did these need to be "intended") because *form* passively transmitted principles of conformity in which racism and sexism were mere byproducts, delayed structural effects. Private moments, for such a poetry, needed to be absorbed into the organic project of collective unity; indeed, this could be read as the defining rationale for Lowell's entire body of work. Lowell's career exemplifies a series of formal wagers of the incubating sensibility. Lowell himself was ready to admit that *Life Studies* was his idiomatic response to Beat orality, his own release from the metrical constraints of *Lord Weary's Castle*. His work exemplifies as well a continual readjustment of content to each new formal solution; and if *Life Studies* seemed a daring disclosure, as well as heralding confessional verse, the later sequence cobbled out of *Notebook* clearly exceeded the acceptable bounds of formalist content. For some, this late work is of value precisely because it publicly violated the tacit

---

[108] For Donald Wesling, the compulsion to achieve purity in modern poetry is historically contingent. "Self as voice as style, or what I should call technique as sincerity, is the literary response to a historical moment; the more the public world becomes a mass world, the more the private world is by compensation interiorized: the more a personal voice must seem tangled in the words of the poem," he contends. "In this setting the hope to de-emphasize anterior forms grows from a sense that poetry must become more transparent to the world of reference and ordinary language" (10). Yet even this compulsion takes the form of technical and procedural dogma: "So modernity must both despise and require the device" because "under historical conditions of modernity, poetry and commentators alike are enmeshed in a contradictory structure of thought where the highest twin values are the corporeality and the transparency of the medium of language" (3, 133). These "twin values," I would suggest, are the form/content pair that lends clandestine energy to either one presumed to be scrutinized alone (either ~~the content of the~~ form or ~~the form immanent in the~~ content).

recipe of the reigning literary trust; for others, it belatedly confirmed its bankruptcy. In either case, the Lowell scandal extended beyond him, implicating his set, his circle, and his backers.

Lowell, strapped into his assigned seat in the rocket of reputation, had found himself in a position which under the aura of the Right Stuff revealed that the controls were elsewhere, and that the previous occupant had been a chimpanzee (maybe the very same, in the anecdote of information theory, who could produce Shakespeare's works at a typewriter in a paroxysm of statistical improbability). He may have been "number one" as Berryman feared, but that meant being buckled into a suffocating set of expectations. On the strength of his "Dream Songs," Berryman's own stock soared during the sixties, prompting Win Scott to ask Horace Gregory "Do you suppose any besides you and me have this feeling that the whole Berryman boom is a managed, phony thing?" (Donaldson 330). Surely the insecurities that plagued so many of those in Lowell's orbit—where human carnage had endowed the inner sanctum with an aura like a duelling scar—were attributable in part to suspicions like Scott's, that their success was not deserved but part of a cynical entrepreneurial design. The paraphernalia of the literary life, in these terms, proved uninhabitable to many; and it coincided historically with a growing sense of the futility of literary politics (not to mention politics as such). W.S. Merwin, for instance, reflected that "When I wrote *The Lice* I thought that things were so black, that what we as a species had done was so terrible that there was very little hope, and certainly not much point in writing. The arts really were over—the culture, the salutary role of the arts in our lives—that was finished. There was nothing left but decoration" ("Art" 75). The issue was Olson's as well, on January 15, 1962, when he specified as the work of poetry "that we act somewhere / at least by seizure"—bringing to mind Whitman's thought a century earlier of a national crisis driven by "convulsiveness"—a consequence of which was Olson's recognition that "In English the poetics became meubles — furniture / . . . after 1630 / & Descartes was the value" (*Maximus* 249). It is a distinction between lives lived and fates fronted, or else name-cards on placemats and rooms full of immaculate furniture under plastic dustwrap.

The distinction was decisive in the mid-sixties and remains a point of contention. Michael Palmer was sufficiently vexed by the prevailing terms of literary careerism in 1989 to exclaim, "I don't really care if something is literature when, in fact, that particular category bothers me in terms of what goes along with it, in terms of decorum, political decorum and decorum in relation to taste: the clothes you wear in the poem and the table manners of the poem" ("Interview" 3). By contrast, James Merrill felt motivated in 1967 to make the opposite claim:

> Manners for me are the touch of nature, an artifice in the very bloodstream. Someone who does not take them seriously is making a serious mistake. They are as vital as all appearances, and if they deceive us they do so by mutual consent. It's hard to imagine a work of literature that doesn't depend on manners, at least negatively. One of the points of a poem like Ginsberg's "Howl" is that it uses an impatience with manners very brilliantly . . . ("Interview" 148–49)

There's a certain irony in my juxtaposition of these passages, inasmuch as Merrill and Palmer epitomize elegance in literary manners for their respective generations, and personify that quality of "taste" which the New Critics silently applied as innate to poetic judgment.[109] Defining manners as part of nature, Merrill tacitly opposes them to culture—a significant reversal of customary associations—and this explains his resistance to the concept of history. "I'm an enemy of history," he declared in the same interview, quoting A. D.

---

[109] One of the most ludicrous episodes in the wake of the Mapplethorpe scandal that led to scrutiny of National Endowment for the Arts funding guidelines was the brandishing in Congress of a passage of Palmer's poem "Theory of the Flower." The poem begins inauspiciously: "I will read a few of these to see if they exist / (We will translate logos as logos)" but shortly proffers in inverted quotes the lines "'Now kiss her cunt' / 'Now take his cock in your hand'" (*First Figure* 22). For all I know, the big game pornography hunters in Congress may have taken "logos" to be scandalous as well! It's hard not to be amused by the thought of Palmer identified as a panderer of filth, given the austere aestheticism of his poetry, as well as the Harvard elegance of his personal demeanor. Notably, during the time he held his NEA grant, Palmer shrewdly probed the genuinely obscene: "Write this. We have burned all their villages / Write this. We have burned all the villages and the people in them" (*Sun* 83).

Hope's distinction (itself cribbed from Aristotle) between the poet as "the 'eater of time'" and "that 'anus of mind, the historian'" (141).

There is poignant desperation in Merrill's handling of the historical prospect in the poem "Domino" in *Late Settings* (1985). It begins with a precise conceit of the poet as a sociocultural sweetener, an historical additive:

> Delicious, white, refined
> Is all that I was raised to be,
> Whom feeling for the word
> Plus crystal rudiments of mind
> Still keep—however stirred—
> From wholly melting in the tea.

He then contrasts himself with the downtrodden, the implicitly dark men who "cut / The sea-wide, sea-green fields of cane," whose historical destiny is on the (multicultural) rise, threatening Merrill and other members of the old leisure class.

> The better to appraise his mess,
> History's health freak begs
> That such as we be given up.
> Outpouring bitterness
> Rewards the drainer of the cup . . .
> He'll miss those sparkling dregs.
> (*Late Settings* 17, ellipsis orig.)

The poem concedes the gratuity of the aesthetic sugar (the "sparkling dregs") while at the same time condemning the subliminal ambition of revolutionary progressivism, the utopian dream of scouring away noxious historical residue in order to begin the wager of civility anew. Perhaps only Merrill would have the temerity to rebuke multiculturalism with the insouciance of courtly wit; yet his apparent anachronism hangs fire in the end, firmly implying that cultural progress is invariably reckoned by damaged sensibility.

For poets of the "G. I. generation," broaching history in poetry required tact. In a weak version, as in Wilbur's "Looking into History," we get platitudes ("Reflect how history's / Changes are like the sea's") and paeans to an informing organic grace that survives the changes, "Resembling at the last / The self-established tree / That draws all waters toward / Its live formality" (*Poems* 85). In a slightly stronger version, as in Anthony Hecht's "Still Life," the familiar genre piece concludes with a twist:

> As in a water-surface I behold
>   The first, soft, peach decree
> Of light, its pale, inaudible commands.
> I stand beneath a pine-tree in the cold,
> Just before dawn, somewhere in Germany,
> A cold, wet, Garand rifle in my hands.
>
>   (*Poems* 211)

For most of these poets "history" was thoroughly integrated into a vision of conjugal opposites, largely derived from Yeats (his "terrible beauty"), often epigrammatically modulated by Auden. History, in short, was a set-piece, part and parcel of the standard literary furnishings. The disturbance of Hecht's Garand rifle is confined to the pastoralism of his poem, as if it had no application otherwise. The tangible combat experiences of Hecht and other soldier poets are not to be denied; but they faltered in not recognizing that the scope of the formalist poetry they embraced made no concessions to their experience; or else allocated the nightmare of history to the baroque trim of irony and indirection, the battlefield become an oblique thematic counterpoint to the suburban lawn. This formal balance of contrasts would admit no asymmetrical detours into the ghetto, the kitchen, or any other setting not congruent with poetic tasks equivalent to what Nina Baym calls "melodramas of beset manhood."

A curious travesty in recent attempts to "represent" historical experience in poetry is Carolyn Forché's anthology *Against Forgetting: Twentieth-Century Poetry of Witness* (1993). A broad array of international poetry is summoned to chronicle historical catastrophes from (I cite section headings) The Armenian Genocide, Revolution and Repression in the Soviet Union, The Holocaust, War in the Middle East, and the Struggle Against Apartheid in South Africa, among others. Forché is well aware of the limited exposure of North Americans to depredations on such a scale (at least since the Civil War), but she offers a section on Civil Rights and another on Vietnam as a way of showcasing American poets in this heterogeneous political context, and includes thirteen Americans in the section on World War II. "Extremity," she writes in the introduction, "demands new forms or alters older modes of poetic thought. It also breaks forms and creates forms from these breaks." She allows that fragmentation is not contingent on specific historic experience, but suggests that the fragment "might well be the feature that binds this anthology together" (42). This cogent formulation, it turns out, is abandoned when it comes to the selection of American poetry. On the one hand, Forché's choice of poets seems crassly commercial; Lowell, Nemerov, Simpson, Hugo, Hecht, Levertov, Dugan, Simic, Rukeyser, Kinnell, and Baraka are among the most heavily anthologized postwar poets. On the other hand, most of the poems she has selected by these and other Americans are (or could have been) textbook samples for *Understanding Poetry*. Only George Oppen's "Route" intimates what fragmentary form might look like in an American idiom.[110] Forché has too literally construed eligibility by biographical accident, favoring poets who served in the armed forces or, in the case of civil rights and Vietnam, were jailed for protesting (hence the inclusion of Kinnell, but not Merwin, Bly, or Antin). But her choices reveal another agenda at work, one long familiar in its presumptuous affirmation of Americanism certified by prizes and publishers. So we find no reflection on the Holocaust by Reznikoff, Olson, or Rothenberg; no psychogenetic critiques of American imperialism by Duncan, Ginsberg, Dorn, or Eshleman. In the American context, Forché's editing implies, formal innovation is irrelevant to historical experience; so instead of the explosive prospects of Silliman, Andrews, Taggart, or Scalapino—to mention recent poets who have significantly contributed to the emergence of an historically inflected grammar of fragments—Forché favors the centrist workshop mode with its investment in ego-building and pithy

---

[110] "The first person, free-verse, lyric-narrative poems of my earlier years has given way to a work which has desired its own bodying forth: polyphonic, broken, haunted, and in ruins, with no possibility of restoration," Forché writes of her own poems in *The Angel of History* (81). This book does in fact substantially jettison the trappings of her former work, and is a more persuasively fragmented engagement than most of the poetry by Americans that she selected for *Against Forgetting*.

vignettes of "authenticity." To read her selection of Vietnam war poetry is to be astonished at the prospect that she (and maybe even her
selected poets) are unaware of the extraordinary verbal ballistics of
Michael Herr's famous *Dispatches*—a book of "prose" that deftly
exposes most poetry about Vietnam as conceptually and semantically
retrograde. For a book entitled *Against Forgetting*, it's disheartening to
discover (once again) that much of what passes for American poetry is
a product of forgetting. "The truly historical imagination involves the
co-presence of the alien," Donald Hall wrote in 1959, "not the domestication of the strange into the familiar" ("Domesticity" 316).

The Freudian challenge posits forgetting as a productive
source of psychic momentum. To the trauma of repressive transcendence there is also a fatality of remembrance; and the dialectical
vortex opened up between them seems the special province of confessional verse. Stephen Spender has a useful qualification: "The
term 'confessional' attached to the work of certain modern American poets, is a bit misleading," he wrote. "These poets don't confess
in order to reveal the truth about themselves . . . . Instead they cut
open a vein of their lives onto the psychotic, the abnormal, some
energy below the sociability of consciousness" (227). For all the
posturing, we should remember, the psychotic *ambiance* could be
fatal. Confessional poetry as a "generic fate" makes no sense without the explicit proddings of Ginsberg's "Howl," and the fact that
Ginsberg's challenge was, at the time, unassimilable to the conventions of mainstream poetry. If it *had* been readily assimilable it
would have been converted into a stylistic option, given the prevalent formalism. But the suicides and manic episodes of Plath, Sexton, Berryman, Lowell and Snodgrass are not to be resolved into the
stylistic continuities each of them resolutely certified in their verse,
as if mania were a simple authenticating feature like a dairy seal on
homogenized milk. "Wanting to Die," in Sexton's plaintive poem,
involves "drooling at the mouth-hole" with "the phone off the hook
/ and the love, whatever it was, an infection." Suicide, the revelation goes, is "a special language" (142). Confessional poetry was the
Rx inscription on a bottle of metrical sleeping pills. The spellbinding irridescence of Plath and Sexton in particular is the metallic

sublunar glow of unwholesome metals, throbbing in fissures, just out of reach.

When Robert Langbaum speculated on a "New Nature Poetry" for *American Scholar* in 1959 he surely didn't realize how clairvoyant his evocation was, or how soon its poetry would flourish:

> Our nature philosophy has been made not only by Darwin but by Freud and Frazer. It connects not only man's body but his mind and culture to the primeval ooze; and you cannot convey that sense of nature in poems about the cultivated countryside of England or New England. . . . [T]he new nature poetry is really about that concept by which living unconsciousness has come to be understood as a form of consciousness and, paradoxically, the most vital form of it. (331, 332)

Langbaum's evocation seems to fit the stance adopted by Wright, Bly, Kinnell and others in the 1960s. Bly, tracing a "wrong turning" in American poetry, held that

> Poetry is forgotten, if by poetry we mean exploration into the unknown, and not entertainment; an intellectual adventure of the greatest importance, not an attempt to teach manners, an attempt to face the deep inwardness of the twentieth century, not attempts to preserve the virtues of moderation. (*American Poetry* 19)

To his claim that poets shirked the great adventure of "deep inwardness," Bly specifically charged that "The forties generation succeeds in forgetting both the revolution in language and any revolutionary feeling toward society." The sixties generation would recall those revolutionary feelings; but it would recall too many of them *as* feelings in its inability to detect any difference between feeling and revelation, sensibility and vision. For a poet like Bly, with (to use the Jungian vocabulary he has favored) a strong intuitive side and dormant intellect, "A poem is something that penetrates for an instant into the unconscious" (*American Poetry* 33). Bly generally conflates reason with consciousness, and attacks both *as if* they were the incarnation of ideology, or Sartrean *mauvaise foi* ("ideology" not being an active term in Bly's vocabulary). But he's been betrayed by the purity of his faith in *image*, in the integrity of the flashpoint of subconscious insight, insofar as he has failed to credit the extent to which North American culture is saturated with images; that images are utterly debased yet endlessly recouped through the manipulations of data banks and audience sampling procedures.[111] Images are the basic form of currency in mass media. It is a sublime kind of naïvete to pledge allegiance to image as the gold standard of emotional currency, when emotions are so ruthlessly manipulated. The recourse to the corrosive sublime of image eventually led Bly to the self-help forum of the men's movement, and the ecological concerns of *News of the Universe* were reconfigured and clarified in *Rag and Bone Shop of the Heart*, not so much an anthology as a relief agency primer for middle class white males traumatized by multiculturalism. The surrealistic impulse of *Kayak* and similar sixties magazines became thoroughly congenial to the poetry workshops, where, under pressure of cordial exchange and the evaluative criteria of the classroom, images moved back to the surface, while the inept intimations of depth went uncontested in a context that was a combination of therapy and vocational training. The workshops captured poetry for the universities on a scale unprecedented by the "academicizing" of poetry during the 1950s. There was now an institutional base sanctioning free verse and and metrics, process and thing, all at once. It is in the nature of such accommodation that the "creatively maladjusted" (as Parkinson called Gary Snyder [*Poets* 184]) would now be marginalized more than ever, since the superficial indicators of creativity implied that everything a young poet might aspire to was to be found in one workshop or another.

There is a sobering synchrony in the fact that the American involvement in Vietnam came to an end precisely during the years when the national network of poetry workshops was being consolidated. It's a symmetry that, in a most oblique way, haunts Robert Duncan's insistent silence for fifteen years after *Bending the Bow*, published in 1968. When *Ground Work: Before the War* finally appeared the landscape of poetry had become so banal and unresponsive to the

---

[111] See Rasula, "*Selected Poems* by Robert Bly."

imaginative demands of Duncan's work that his book passed with scarcely a ripple. (In 1984 *American Primitive* by Mary Oliver won the Pulitzer; The National Book Critics Circle Award went to Sharon Olds for *The Dead and the Living*; and Fred Chappell got a Bollingen.) Duncan was far too secure in his faith in a sustaining community of fellow poets to be disconcerted by such a slight. But his book had, in its own way, already taken it all into account. The subtitle could be read as prewar, before Vietnam; or in a longer view, prior to Korea or World War II, both of which Duncan had engaged in earlier poems.[112] Given the conspicuous placement of "Achilles' Song" at the head of the book, it could even evoke a time before the Trojan war. Duncan's theme, in Achilles' voice, was of larger scope even than that—it was a "deeper unsatisfied war beneath / and behind the declared war . . . " (4). And as he enumerates all that is registered by that *before*, "the rubble of the beautiful" comes to suggest another conflict, a war of anthologies; a war before which Duncan was a novice, then an unknown master, but following which he was a veteran of poetic combat, impassioned and ardent and devoted to registering every temblor of national crisis into the Whitmanian sweep of his verse. Whitman was a preoccupation for him, as much for *his* own war as for his homosexuality. And as the pervasiveness of war emanated from Vietnam into a grand hermetic cosmology in Duncan's late work, culminating in "The Regulators" in *Ground Work: In the Dark*, war was not of a temporal order at all. Duncan affirms Williams's vision of "The Birth of Venus," that there is no getting back to a time prior to conflict,

---

112 Muriel Rukeyser had been an early supporter of Duncan's during the period of his first war/postwar poems. She was living in the San Francisco Bay area in 1949 when her book *The Life of Poetry* was published, in which she reflected on the continuity of war as a "basic premise" of American poetry: "American poetry has been part of a culture in conflict. . . . We are a people tending toward democracy at the level of hope; on another level, the economy of the nation, the empire of business within the republic, both include in their basic premise the concept of perpetual warfare" (61). These two principles are dramatized for Rukeyser by Melville ("the poet of outrage") and Whitman ("the poet of hope") (86). Presaging Duncan's later position in *The Truth and Life of Myth*, she suggests that "these conflicts are the same old war—I believe so—and truth or reality, process or movement, gods or half-gods, are the terms for immortal necessities" (68).

because to be situated in the world was to be just that, *in situ*, so placed as to be before or *in front of* a continual ripple of undeclared war. A lucid declaration of all that he was moving into in his "ground work" was published in *Caterpillar* 8/9 in 1969 as "Man's Fulfillment in Order and Strife" which begins with Heraclitus's dictum, "'War is both King of all and Father of all.'" "Among poets throughout the world or within any nation, men are at war, even deadly war, with each other concerning the nature and responsibility of poetry," Duncan began, making quite clear the terms with which he was personally confronted: "Conventional poets and avant-garde poets are at war. . . ." He went on to specify subdivisions of strife, until the only thing left to say was that "Every order of poetry finds itself, defines itself, in strife with other orders. A new order is a contention in the heart of existing orders" (*Fictive* 111). Duncan's principle of fulfillment amidst contending orders is far-ranging and subtle ("Poetry . . . gives me orders" he writes at one point [124]); but what I want to do is give Duncan the last word on the matter of the war of anthologies, which is assuredly among his many subtexts, because of the catholicity of his recommendation, which includes the recognition that there is no consistency in an open universe, and that the consequent waywardness ("vagrancy" in the term preferred by Thoreau; "extravagance" for Frost) means, in effect, learning to fight on behalf of every side while at the same time fighting against *sides*:

> Not only do we have different languages, we have different worlds and different orders; and within our American "world" and the particular language that the art of poetry creates there are communities of all kinds; each idea of poetry in so far as it is vitally concerned is charged with the conviction that it has a mission to change, to recreate, the heart of poetry itself. Each of us must be at strife with our own conviction on behalf of the multiplicity of convictions at work in poetry in order to give ourselves over to the art, to come into the idea of what the world of worlds or the order of orders might be. We must go beyond the sincere into the fiction whose authors, Blake tells us, are in Eternity. We must set up in the midst of the truth of What Is, the truth of what we imagine. (*Fictive* 111–12)

CHAPTER THREE

Consolations of the Novocain

Officially Covering Contemporary American Poetry

At an MLA panel on "The Institutions of Criticism" in December 1993, I watched a fascinating pantomime unfold involving two poets: Charles Bernstein (speaking on "Provisional Institutions: Alternative Presses and Poetic Innovation") and Richard Tillinghast (defending "The Contemporary Reviewing Establishment"). Bernstein pressed the point that literature is not indifferent to its institutions, and that the official monitors of the poetry world are out of touch with what really goes on. Tillinghast, on the other hand, defending the honor of high profile metropolitan reviews, pointed out that as a regular reviewer of poetry for *The New York Times* and the *Washington Post* he was constrained by editorial decisions beyond his control. He felt that, despite such constraints, poetry benefits from the exposure; and he was particularly solicitous of the "general reader," the rare person somewhere out there for whom the slight seismic shift in sensibility occasioned by a poetry review makes the institutional control of review outlets tolerable. Tillinghast's credulous faith in the general reader was familiar to me, of course, and I was not surprised when he characterized "voice" and "image" as beyond dispute, simple operative features of what he called "poetry as such." In the question and answer session following the presentations, Brian McHale intervened, calling the panel a "dialogue of the deaf." He proposed that the terms of the discussion would be clarified if the word "poetry" were abandoned—or, he added, maybe Tillinghast would be content to keep it. Bernstein's response was immediate and firm: "I'm not willing to give it to him." The panel, and the exchange, seemed emblematic. Bernstein and Tillinghast epitomize contrasting, even irreconcilable, approaches to poetry; but they also represent distinct critical attitudes—one historicizing, the other ahistoric; heteroglossia versus monoglossia; the politics of partisanship and the politics of a neutrality predicated on nostalgia.

The discussion of American poetry since World War II has tended to be schizophrenically cast in the contrasting but related modes of cynicism and boosterism. The New Formalists and the language poets sneer at one another across a vast populace of antiformalists (practitioners of what Jonathan Holden calls the "centrist" mode) dedicated to poetry as the tenuous practice of selfhood.[1] Outwardly convivial as always, the scholars meanwhile extend their salutations across the ramparts, then hunker down to resume shelling. M.L. Rosenthal, Helen Vendler, Marjorie Perloff, Charles Altieri, and Robert von Hallberg occupy nearly irreconcilable positions which cannot be boiled down to Robert Lowell's cliché, raw versus cooked. The refinement and gentility of much of the commentary belies the culinary implications of this binarism, concealing what Ed Dorn exposed in 1978—namely, that criticism is in reality a form of inspection:

---

[1] Smith and Bottoms, introducing their Morrow anthology poets, frankly typify their young poets as "haunted by a life that seems inconsequential or less than fully lived." Hence the notion that "[i]n his poems the younger poet tends to be himself, an invented version of himself" (*Morrow* 19). Larry Levis more precisely calls this a "new homelessness," in which recent poets are paradoxically bound together by "an intimate, *shared* isolation." This results in a generic fate more extensive than that of Lowell's circle of fellow poets—a generic generation. "Instead of the private loneliness of the first person point of view, there appears to be, even when unstated, a narrator who behaves as a 'we' rather than an 'I'" (473).

Inspection

Poetry is now mostly government product
therefore we can dispense with the critical apparatus
the grades assigned to beef will do nicely:

Prime
Choice
Good
Commercial
Canners
Utility

(*Hello* 80)

Why not adopt the criteria of the Food and Drug Administration? After all, there is little concern to historicize poetry's genres and practices, especially when critical vocabulary—disposed to Tillinghast's decontextualized common sense—habitually seeks to locate poetic value in generalized (or "universal") timeless (or "eternal") modalities. And anyway, "the lifeless, automaton-like nagging and head-patting that characterises most current reviewing practice reflects a real difficulty in finding an honorable 'commentary mode' where poetry is concerned" (Easthope and Thompson 210). Critics are all too often content to utilize little more than the code of flag signals derived from anthologies, which in practice rarely extends beyond simple binaries that constitute a cover, or decoy, seeming to provide clarity without actually *informing*.

Repression and Recovery, Cary Nelson's energetic and spirited survey of "forgotten" American poetry from 1910–1945, is a calculated challenge to anyone writing about the postwar period as well. Nelson warns of the anaesthetic function implicit in our prevailing lust for the autonomy (or purity) of poetic discourse. Political verse of the Depression era has been left behind as if it had been issued with an expiration date, like cottage cheese. "The insistence that the political past is *not usable* assists a resistance to politicizing the study of literature in the present and helps mask the knowledge that everything in the present is already politicized" (133). Likewise, it's futile to pretend some aspect of the present is unusable. To purify poetry of its tangible political traces is to sever its potential alliances with credible discourse.[2] Poetry then has little use but as puppetry for animating academic pantomimes.

I've suggested that these pantomimes have staked out competing and irreconcilable positions, as if it were a martial affair; and, while the agonistic spirit of scholarly exchange is readily acknowledged, the *politesse* that prevails in academic writing about contemporary poetry seems to prohibit open confrontation. This exaggerated reserve and cordiality among opposing factions, I would suggest, ultimately derives from the ideological trauma of the Cold War years, when poetry was (briefly) a subject of national notoriety, as hot and cool, Beat and tweed were caricatured for journalistic edification of the middlebrow public. Neither the ivory tower purists nor their hipster nemeses occasioned more than dismay or ridicule. In an ideological climate in which the concept of collectivity was being subordinated to the privatizing tasks of consumption, regulated by criteria of taste, poetry appeared as a paradigm of the indigestible. The poem remained an icon of taste, but the infamous acrimony of actual poets tainted poetry as cultural enterprise with an opportunism and partisanship altogether suspect during the Cold War. Liberal administration finally caught up with poetic subcommunities in the 1970s, when NEA subsidies contaminated the entire ethos of an underground or a countercurrent. Critical custodianship escalated dramatically, aligning the voice of "authenticity" with an ideological ventriloquism of the attenuated first-person lyric; and American poetry has continued to be traumatized by insinuations that "the voice that is great within us" has gotten *into* us by forces outside our control.

"American poetry in our time has been a brilliant form of introspective photography. But the famous photograph album of the modern anthology is only to leaf through in some unborn dentist's office, a momentary and mindless distraction before the consolation

---

[2] Nelson adds: "In fact, because political poetry typically reads specific historical crises in the light of other more general discourses—morality, ethics, religion, aesthetics, social justice, human identity, epistemology, national destiny—it provides dialogic discursive models that are often capable of being adapted to, revitalized by, and reinterpreted in different historical conditions" (133).

of the novocaine," Karl Shapiro wrote in the fifties (*Children* 58). In short, poetry is prelude to anaesthesia. But the anaesthesia is different now, as the powers of introspection have increased, and the mindless distractions have grown more prolific and cunning. Ron Silliman has also been concerned with the "literary forgetfulness" of public discourse about poetry, suggesting that "poetry, particularly in the United States, is a profoundly amnesiac discourse" ("Canons" 150). Unfortunately, forgetfulness implies something that was known in the first place, whereas the periodic factionalist hysterias punctuating the world of American poetry suggest that such knowledge has been resisted by all parties. What we have really had is an institutional negligence, and the serene confidence in the success story of certain careers has been administered *as* the Novocain itself, numbing us to the loss of major portions of a usable poetic legacy.

CRITICAL AUTHORITY BY DEFAULT

Scholarship on contemporary American poetry has been slow to arrive, yet even to say so understates the case. (See Appendix 9 for a chronology of critical studies.) For the fact is that from 1950 to 1980 the management of reputations was almost exclusively a function of anthologies, awards, and reviews. Richard Howard's compendium of essays on forty poets, *Alone With America*, published in 1971, assumed a singular prominence not so much because of the celerity of his wit and insight, but because it was a large and agreeable entry in a miniscule field. Previously, a handful of poets had been discussed in Hungerford's collection *Poets in Progress* in 1962 (with a few more added for the 1967 edition); while Stepanchev's *American Poetry Since 1945* (1965), Mills's *Contemporary American Poetry* (1965), Rosenthal's *The New Poets* (1967) and Carroll's *The Poem in its Skin* (1968) were virtually the first book length studies of postwar poetry. The sixties also saw the publication of two general histories—by Babette Deutsch and Hyatt Waggoner—which dealt briefly with living figures. To search out books on contemporary poetry around 1970, one was as likely to encounter titles by poets as by critics: *A Quick Graph* by Creeley, *Babel to Byzantium* by Dickey, or *Poetry and Fiction* by Nemerov. Furthermore, only a few studies devoted to specific poets had appeared by 1970 (on Berryman, Bishop, Eberhart, Ginsberg, Levertov, Lowell, Nemerov, Plath, Roethke, and Warren).[3]

In the following decade, studies of postwar poetry favored thematic criticism and close readings of a handful of poets—typified by Donoghue's *Seven American Poets from MacLeish to Nemerov* (1975), Lensing and Moran's *Four Poets of the Emotive Imagination* (1976), Kalstone's *Five Temperaments* (1977), Oberg's *Modern American Lyric* (1978, featuring four poets), and Mazzaro's *Postmodern American Poetry* (1980, six plus Auden). Other studies included chapters on topics permitting a more wide-ranging discussion, but were neverthe-

---

[3] Considering the privileged role played by poetry in the New Critical canon, along with the New Critics' establishment of a hegemony of leading poets—not to mention the decisive criticism by Schwartz, Jarrell, and Berryman—it's baffling to find scholarly scrutiny so late in arriving. An obvious factor is the precariousness of contemporary poetry as a topic for a scholarly monograph for several decades after the war. Of the titles listed above, only Rosenthal's was published by a university press. There is another compelling consideration, having to do with the *discursive* momentum created by the trenchant poetics of Donald Allen's *New American Poets* and carried on in such journals as *Kulchur*, *City Lights Journal*, and *Evergreen Review*. Allen's anthology offered a conspicuous impetus, by way of example, to consider poets occupying a more aggressive and engaged stance than the "silent generation" had. Incited and empowered to speak before, after, and between poems, poets became known (if not notorious) for being proselytizers, theorists, and reviewers. It is not simply by temporal coincidence, then, that the studies of the sixties earnestly attend to Black Mountain poets. Rosenthal's *New Poets* are Olson, Creeley, Duncan, Levertov, Blackburn, Ginsberg and Baraka, juxtaposed with Lowell, Plath, Berryman, Sexton, and Roethke. This equilibrium of raw and cooked is preserved in Stepanchev's history and in Waggoner's.

What happens in the seventies represents a curious readjustment. Various poets from Donald Allen's anthology continue to figure prominently for a few years, until roughly the end of the war in Vietnam. Then, in the second half of the decade, there is a notable increase in scholarly studies and a corresponding decrease in the visibility of Black Mountain and Beat poetics. *Alone With America* had as much to do with this shift as any other single factor. Published by Atheneum, Howard's book was in essence a reader's guide to Atheneum poets (Finkel, Hecht, Hine, Hollander, Justice, Merrill, Merwin, Moss, Strand), a medley of others in the lineage stemming from *The New Poets of England and America* who had been somewhat overlooked in

less dominated by the chapter-per-poet approach: Mills's *Cry of the Human* (1975), Molesworth's *The Fierce Embrace* (1979), Miller's *The American Quest for a Supreme Fiction* (1979), and Nelson's *Our Last First Poets* (1981).[4] Despite their good intentions, the precedent set by

the sixties (Bowers, Dugan, Feldman, Hoffman, Hugo, Kizer, Logan, Meredith, Swenson, Wagoner, Weiss), and a sampling of better-known figures at the time of publication (Bly, Corso, Creeley, Dickey, Ginsberg, Kinnell, Levertov, O'Hara, Plath, Rich, Sexton, Snodgrass, Snyder, and Wright). Ammons and Ashbery were also featured, although neither had yet achieved the prominence they would shortly when Harold Bloom singled them out in his books on poetic influence. Howard's mass of poets, along with the sheer size of the volume (nearly 500 pages), tended to obscure what was missing: Berryman, Jarrell, Lowell, Shapiro, Bishop, Roethke, Wilbur, and Nemerov, among those whose reputations were secure; as well as Olson and Duncan. All these poets are dealt with two years later in Karl Malkoff's *Crowell's Handbook of Contemporary American Poetry*, which features short essays on seventy-three poets, the selection of which offers a telling counterpoint to Howard's. Malkoff covers thirty of Howard's forty poets. His other additions are in three key areas: race, gender, and New American poets. Malkoff breaks the color line which is so conspicuous in *Alone With America*, including profiles of Baraka, Brooks, Cruz, Mari Evans, Giovanni, Hayden, Lee, Sanchez, and Margaret Walker. Only five of Howard's poets are women, whereas Malkoff discusses (in addition to the five black women) Bishop, Gardner, Glück, Jong, Kizer, Levertov, Plath, Rich, Sexton, Swenson, and Wakoski. Finally, Malkoff fills in the New American roster by including nine poets from *The New American Poetry* in addition to the nine Howard discussed, and extends the map by adding Kelly and Rothenberg. With Howard and Malkoff, it would seem that two ample informative sources were available by 1973 that offered a thorough guide. However, neither of them included Zukofsky, Reznikoff, Oppen, Kunitz, Rexroth, or Warren from Roethke's generation, nor the slightly younger Everson and Rukeyser. Apart from these oversights, however, they actually *do* manage to encompass between them a nearly complete roster of poets born before 1930 who continue to generate critical interest and occupy space in anthologies.

[4] The thematized close reading of individual poets persists in numerous subsequent studies, such as Libby's *Mythologies of Nothing* (1984), Breslin's *From Modern to Contemporary* (1984), Stitt's *The World's Hieroglyphic Beauty* (1985), Jackson's *The Dismantling of Time in Contemporary Poetry* (1988), Spiegelman's *The Didactic Muse* (1989), Gardner's *Discovering Ourselves in Whitman* (1989), Gilbert's *Walks in the World* (1991), Scott's *Visions of Presence in Modern American Poetry* (1993), and Shetley's *After the Death of Poetry* (1993). The close reading protocol "often remains the dominant methodology," writes Hank Lazer, "for most historicized, cultural, political, and theoretical approaches to contemporary American poetry. So too does thematization come in as a ghostly essentialism which reins in more adventurous varieties of individual critics as they are indicative of a generic difficulty in writing criticism of contemporary poetry" ("Politics of Form" 507).

these studies has tended to inhibit the development of investigative scholarship. While scholars of modernist, Victorian, or Romantic poetry and poetics have felt it incumbent to know something about context, the study of contemporary American poetry has been dissipated by a metaphysics of the intimate encounter, the interpersonal reckoning between the sensibility of the reader and the tuning fork of the poet's confidential imagination. This is the tacit model that has enabled university presses and critics to offer collections of book reviews as "scholarly" responses to American poetry.[5] Laurence Lieberman's *Unassigned Frequences* (1977) was honestly subtitled "American Poetry in Review," but this concession was dropped in the case of Helen Vendler's two omnibus compilations, *Part of Nature, Part of Us* (1980) and *The Music of What Happens* (1988). The mix of essays and reviews in the form of historical chronicle endows Sherman Paul's *Hewing to Experience* (1989) and M. L. Rosenthal's aptly

---

[5] A liability of this sanctioning of casual commentary as scholarship has resulted in consistent errors of fact which would be intolerable in other fields. Vernon Shetley, for instance, makes the absurd claim that "Ashbery did not appear in the leading antiformalist anthology, Donald Allen's *The New American Poetry*" (107). If only he had bothered to consult the table of contents! Andrew Ross also errs on the subject of Ashbery, speculating on the difference between the more easily consumable publications by "major presses" and "the John Ashbery of, say, the Ecco Press, from the seventies" ("New Sentence" 370). The Ecco Press titles were actually reprints of volumes issued previously by Holt and by Dutton. Christopher Beach is apparently unaware that $L=A=N=G=U=A=G=E$ magazine was co-edited by Charles Bernstein with Bruce Andrews, since he notes that "[p]oets such as Bruce Andrews, Lyn Hejinian, and Steve Benson also appear to be strongly committed to language-oriented work . . . " (239). In his contribution on poetry to *The Columbia Literary History of the United States* James Breslin assigns Peter Viereck to a generation born "between 1920 and 1940"—but he was born in 1916 (1081). He also mistakenly places Robert Kelly as a student at Black Mountain College (1091). Daniel Hoffman, whose problematic accounts of contemporary poetry I'll be discussing shortly, is particularly prone to errors of fact. In his contribution to Spiller's *Literary History of the United States* (1974), he dates Olson's *Maximus Poems* 1953–1961, apparently unaware that the work was ongoing until Olson's death in 1970 (1430). Elizabeth Bishop's "Roosters" is one of her *least*, not "most frequently anthologized" poems (1436). Merwin spent two years, not one, tutoring Robert Graves's children on Mallorca (1440). (Hoffman gets it right the second time around, in his own *Harvard Guide* [538].) It is probably a typo, however, rather than an error, when Hoffman dates "deep image" to work of Rothenberg and Kelly in 1950 (read: 1960) (1441).

named *Our Life in Poetry* (1991) with a useful character, suggesting a format that would have made Vendler's books seem less imperial. Mariani's *A Usable Past* (1984), Dave Smith's *Local Assays* (1985), Ehrenpreis's *Poetries of America* (1989), McClatchy's *White Paper* (1989), and Henry Taylor's *Compulsory Figures* (1992) are other instances of miscellanies of reviews being rearticulated into pseudoscholarly publications.[6] A default mode has been implemented, in which "purely qualitative judgments of dominance simply use dominance as a synonym for excellence," as Charles Altieri puts it. Critics in this default mode "return us to the ideal of paying close attention to individual poets without worrying about shared contexts and problems" (*Self* 9). There are some exceptions. In the 1970s, two studies by English critics—perhaps under pressure of cultural difference—represented the sole attempts to flesh out a sociohistorical context: Raban's *The Society of the Poem*, and Thurley's *The American Moment*. Not until *American Poetry and Culture, 1945–1980* by Robert von Hallberg appeared in 1985 did an American attempt to cover comparable ground. Since then there have been encouraging signs of interest in what Walter Kalaidjian calls the "social text" of American poetry, including Kalaidjian's own *Languages of Liberation* (1989), Davidson's *San Francisco Renaissance* (1989), Perloff's *Radical Artifice* (1991), and Damon's *The Dark End of the Street* (1993); although, again characteristically, the most thorough documentary approach comes from elsewhere: Ingrid Kerkhoff's *Poetiken und lyrischer Discurs im Kontext gesellschaftlicher Dynamik* (1989).

There are a considerable number of other studies of American poetry I haven't mentioned, since my purpose is not to provide a superficial taxonomy of approaches. Rather, this quick review is meant to serve as an indication of certain operative norms, norms which have made silence about the historical legacies of American

---

6 The *documentary* value of reviews is obvious, of course, and constitutes the rationale behind Donald Hall's series for the University of Michigan Press. Beginning as a way to bring together interviews and prose ephemera from prominent poets like Kinnell, James Wright, Bly, Stafford and others, it has also accommodated portfolios of reviews (by Tom Clark, David Lehman, Peter Davison, and Daniel Hoffman in recent years).

poetic heterodoxy acceptable. In the face of meticulous evidence of various subaltern and renegade traditions, critics and scholars have apparently felt more comfortable focusing on final soliloquies of the interior paramour. For all its apparent studiousness, the scholarship offers nothing to rival the work of the poets themselves, in their coupling of intellectual adventure with meticulous awareness of history and tradition. It is commonplace to assume the pertinence and acumen of essays by Pound, Williams, Eliot, Stevens, H. D., and other modernists. But, to a dismaying extent, academic scrutiny of postwar poetry has settled on poets who have largely refrained from theoretical excursions; one consequence of which is a critical indifference to poets' self-professed contexts of assumptions, discoveries, and research. Rukeyser's *The Life of Poetry*, Olson's *Human Universe* and Duncan's *Fictive Certainties* will readily seem examples of what I mean here; but I have in mind an even more expanded field, which in the case of the latter two poets is signified by Duncan's dispersed and still uncollected *H. D. Book*, and Olson's *Additional Prose, The Special View of History*, and the "Chiasma" lectures. Gary Snyder's *Earth House Hold* is obviously concordant, along with *The Real Work, The Old Ways*, and *The Practice of the Wild*. Olson and Snyder expand the implications of "poetry" far beyond a literary purview, toward a larger perspective that regards poetry as contemporaneous with the Paleolithic (in Clayton Eshleman's view), the Blakean/Jungian *aion* (in John Clarke's magisterial *From Feathers to Iron*), the antinomian (in Susan Howe's *The Birth-mark*), the ethnopoetic bandwidth of Rothenberg's *Technicians of the Sacred* and *Symposium of the Whole*, and the hybrid tectonics of overlapping cultures in Mackey's *Discrepant Engagement*. Don Byrd's *The Poetics of the Common Knowledge* offers an invaluably extensive perturbation of poetry's complicity with the (logocentric) project of "*Language*, that peculiar abstraction which . . . has confused its own systematic requirements with the world's . . . " (25–26).

By contrast, the critical temperament appears to have confused proficiency with English department reading lists for specialist area exams—which are themselves derived from the Norton and other teaching anthologies. Poets may be justified in thinking of scholarly critics as educated halfwits, unable or unwilling to fill in even the most rudimentary connections between text and context, or between reputation and institutional hegemony. It's only in such an impoverished medium that Harold Bloom's scenarios of revisionism could have canonical impact despite their obvious inapplicability to much (or even most) poetic activity; and it was not until 1992 that another critic (Christopher Beach) took care to explain in historical terms the inadequacy of Bloom's model. I should be explicit about my own gratitude to Bloom, whose magisterial intertextual reading of Emerson, Nietzsche, Stevens, Freud, and the Romantic sublime is a genuinely pioneering work in a new idiom—hermeneutic angelology, which in Bloom's case is given a weird and wonderful aura as an applied hybrid, gnostic pragmatism.[7] But everything that Bloom attempts is achieved at the cost of history. "Criticism and poetry are not primarily political, social, economic or philosophical processes," he declares, yet insists that "the history of poetry and criticism" is only to be understood as "a poetic and critical view of history" (*Agon* 41). This is not far, as it happens, from Olson's "special view" of history; but Bloom is creating a tautological chiasmus with which he can evade materialist history altogether. His assertion that poetry is not "primarily" social liberates him

---

[7] "As performative knowledge, Gnosis is pragmatic and particular," Bloom writes in *Agon* (13). Bloom is so able an interpreter of Emerson precisely because he takes the full measure of Emerson's neoplatonism to heart, recognizing that his pragmatism derives in large measure from a cosmic fatalism that sees, or is willing to imagine, the earth utterly dissolved in the larger scheme of things. Yet, for all the intricacy of his speculations on the gnostics and kabbalists of late antiquity—or maybe because of it—Bloom fails to recognize the extent to which Emerson and Whitman alike found final confirmation of their views in Eastern religions. Bloom, adhering to gnosticism, acquiesces finally in the view that the dissolution of the earth is the path of wisdom, and that a combatant's mentality represents the pinnacle of poetic sapience. However, for Emerson and Whitman, informed by Hinduism and Buddhism, the dissolution is to be achieved not by destruction but release, by desisting from grappling—in fact, by means of a Keatsian negative capability. Bloom presumes, with the gnostics, cosmic alienation; whereas, for Emerson, alienation is beside the point when one is addressing *difference* as the constitutive force of that "great and crescive self" he writes of in "Experience," for which the proper perspective is to acknowledge "I am a fragment, and this is a fragment of me" (*Essays* 491).

from the consideration that it may nevertheless be *partially* so. But to consider that partiality is to discover, as does Christopher Beach, that a work like the *Cantos* "constitutes not a poetry of 'veiled imitation,' not a 'swerve' from or a 'revision' of past models, but a nexus, a 'vortex,' of formal and expressive possibility derived from a plenitude of openly declared sources" (*ABC* 65).[8] Pound's "paideuma" is a concept that leads to historical particularity and to paradisal vision, without implying irreconcilability between them. For a poem purporting to "include" history, paideuma is a utopian tradition, one which favors community over conflict, recognizing at the same time that community is only achieved by means of patterned conflict—that "plenitude of openly declared sources" which can, will, and must be contested to be tested.

I take Bloom to be the most forceful practitioner of what I've called the default mode. He makes overt many of the assumptions that are covert in other critics: contextual isolationism, ahistoricism, and readings that are so "close" that the critic's own claustrophobia permeates the text, which then seems available as an exercise in colossal autobiography (in Emerson's sense of "history"). Bloom's is a bravura performance, which is to be valued in the context of studies in contemporary poetry (not, admittedly, Bloom's own preferred field of intervention) inasmuch as it reveals how little energy and insight is to be found in other monographs. As a recent example of critical anemia I want to look at Wyatt Prunty's *"Fallen from the Symboled World": Precedents for the New Formalism*, published by Oxford University Press in 1990. The title is derived from a poem by Howard Nemerov, who is undergoing a revival of attention at the moment. Mary Kinzie, for instance, gives Nemerov a pivotal place in a huge essay at the center of *The Cure of Poetry in an Age of Prose: Moral*

---

[8] Beach avoids dealing with the complex revisionism of Canto I, which is the obvious place to engage Bloom's criteria—*in the text*, which in Pound's case involves as foundational gesture for his epic a conjunction ("And then . . . ") leading to a textual palimpsest (Andreas Divus's Latin version of Homer's Greek, transposed by Pound into a deciduous English bearing morphological and semantic traces of its medieval origins). *Palimpsest* is a concept which literally throws Bloom's revisionary ratios into disarray.

Essays on the Poet's Calling (1993). Nemerov may well be the perfect poet for such an age, if "prose" is taken to signify diminished expectations for poetry (which it obviously didn't for Pound, thinking of James; nor Olson, thinking of Melville; nor should it for anyone now, thinking, for instance, of Pynchon). Kinzie, describing Nemerov's "best mood, the one that brings out the tenderest and most credible language, is that mood of pitying praise in the presence of natural law and intellectual construct." These are terms of *approval*, mind you. Kinzie goes on to concede Nemerov's ways of being out of key with his time: "In another age, Nemerov would have been bard to the Royal Society or an enclave of Thomists. He was framed to celebrate the edifice of mind from a gargoyle's niche; he depends, that is, on a tradition of shared intellectual achievement to which he can pay orthogonal homage in the form of tears" (196). Read as an entry in a dictionary, I might assume this to be the definition of "poetaster."

To turn to Nemerov's other champion: Wyatt Prunty labors to restore dignity to metrical forms that nevertheless retain what Pinsky in *The Situation of Poetry* calls "prose virtues." Nemerov's vindication must come at the expense of a prevailing countertrend, which is here identified with certain open form poets. To make his case against what he obtusely calls "organism" (meaning organicism), Prunty acknowledges without explanation that "I restrict my examples to anthologized poems by Robert Creeley, A. R. Ammons, and James Wright" (17). Prunty's concern is "to demonstrate the arbitrariness of what have become certain free-verse conventions" (303, *n*2). He does not bother with the sociological problem of how these conventions came to prominence, nor with the vital role of anthologies. He simply opts for Creeley and Ammons as "interesting and useful examples" of what he dubs "emaciated poetry" (58). Prunty's interest in formalism leads him to restrict his discussion of Creeley to the matter of lineation, since he can intuit no other formal features in the work. The characteristic brevity of Creeley's lines, "a shrinkage in margins," Prunty derogates as "a stylish, highly marketable thinness" (58). What does this mean other than that Creeley has been one of the most influential poets in recent decades? Prunty wants to cast doubt on Creeley, as he avows; but at the same time he wants to use Creeley as a stick to beat unnamed but supposedly teeming hordes of others. There are more odious elisions, however. In castigating as "stylish" the shorter line, Prunty ignores its lineage. Creeley is made to seem opportunistic and, by analogy, journalistic as well. But there is no mention of the precedent set by Zukofsky, whom Creeley has repeatedly credited for many things, not least of which is his narrow lineation. This egregious omission is compounded by that of Olson, at whose urging Creeley developed a rationale of "breath units" to justify breaking lines into shorter elements to reflect his staccato style of oral delivery. Nor does Prunty make mention of orality as a determinant in line length. He appears, in fact, to be perfectly ignorant of the cluster of related issues which have been frequently and hotly debated for nearly forty years.

Lest this be taken *ad hominem*, it remains important to acknowledge that Prunty proceeds with an articulate context. The larger claim of his book is that allegory and symbolism have lapsed in the face of postwar skepticism, and Prunty comes forward in favor of tropology as the poet's remaining means of perpetuating the art while engaging the mind's claim on the real. This argument is restated in miniature in the midst of his critique of Creeley, and is worth quoting in full:

> Because of the theistic assumptions embedded in their traditional uses, symbol and allegory had become problematical in the face of a postwar skepticism, and on the surface the classroom virtues of irony, paradox, and ambiguity taught by Cleanth Brooks and other influential critics half a generation earlier also appeared to have been set aside. Beneath that surface, however, the temporal problems that the Brooksian categories addressed did not disappear; poetry continued to respond to them. Whether one was concerned with religious experience (as Eliot was), with "preternatural" experience (as Winters at times said he was), or with the unconscious mind, poetry's task continued to be that of ferreting order out of the doubt and disorder of modern existence. What actually happened was that a poor man's version of irony, paradox, and ambiguity sprouted as part of an excessive reliance upon enjambment. (59–60)

"Poor man" is especially apposite, as Prunty goes on to quote Creeley's famous "I Know a Man," written when the poet was living in
Mallorca because it was the cheapest place he could find. Despite
his frequent denunciations of any trace of platonism (of which he
takes allegory and symbol to be the material culprits), Prunty rein-
states idealism in the form of "the reader," to whom he appeals in
protest of the poet's sophistry. Prunty's tactic is simple: with a poet
he disapproves of, like Creeley, formal devices are "tricks" (61),
while with those he favors, like Nemerov, they are "tropes" in
which "[t]hought and thing engage in a dynamic play, and word is
where they play" (191).

Prunty offers as a "watershed" instance (apparently without
intending the pun) Nemerov's "The Loon's Cry," a two-page poem
(thirteen seven-line stanzas) quoted complete. "This poem," he
claims, "is a complex example of synaposematic mimicry" (179). It
certainly sounds more dignified than Creeley's mere "tricks." A definition is required: "Synaposematism is a defenseless species' mimicry of another species that possesses some means of protection"
(19–20). Nemerov's poem is central to Prunty's enterprise, and it also
provides him with his title (177):

> But I could think only, Red sun, white moon,
> This is a natural beauty, it is not
> Theology. For I had fallen from
> The symboled world, where I in earlier days
> Found mysteries of meaning, form, and fate . . .

Nemerov's is a poem of pedestrian observation and plain statement. Prunty is charmed by the parallelism employed throughout,
culminating in the train whistle which, in the final line (in case
the reader hasn't already made the connection) is shown to be
"like a loon." Are we to imagine for a moment that the loon is a
defenseless creature synaposematically imitating the trainwhistle
of that incorrigible blight, man? Or is it humans who are imperiled, and have shrewdly launched the iron horse in a mutant inter-
species competition with this bird? "The Loon's Cry" is celebrated
by Prunty for its mirroring tropes, a mimicry revealing that "what

balance is possible comes from similitude . . . " (179). Northrop Frye, for one, would have been surprised to find this offered as antidote to allegory.

But there remains the troubling allure of Prunty's "synaposematic mimicry." Disposed as he is to read poems as systems of tropes—and thus to rewrap them in the tinfoil of allegorical correspondences which he declares moribund—Prunty is as oblivious to sound values as he is to the implications of lineation. Nemerov's moderate speech mannerisms place the poem midway between verbal utterance and academic prose, without inhabiting either. The archaism of "The world a stage, its people maskers all / In actions largely framed to imitate / God and His Lucifer's long debate" is juxtaposed with the plain statement, as in

> . . . I simplified still more, and thought that now
> We'd traded all those mysteries in for things,
> For essences in things, not understood—
> Reality in things! and now we saw
> Reality exhausted all their truth.

Nowhere in the poem is there even a hint of the loon's cry as a synaesthetic component in a world of sound shared with humans. The loon remains Nemerov's *idea*, and he can't even register the "savage cry" in its alterity without feeling himself transformed into allegory: " . . . and Adam I became, / Hearing the first loon cry in paradise." Reading Nemerov's poem, I wonder whether he or Prunty have any recollection of Thoreau's loon, which sports with Edenic insouciance in a way that mocks any pretension Thoreau might have had to paint himself into paradise on Walden Pond.

Applied to Creeley, Prunty's notion of synaposematic mimicry is actually serviceable. Dispensing with the traditional set-piece antithesis of man and beast, or creature of earth and creature of air, Creeley manages to introduce a savage intimidation by disclosing (with enjambment, spelling, and the mimicry of oral diction) the spectre of the advantaged and the disadvantaged, the defenseless and the protected, with a power the German romantics spoke of as "unheimlich," uncanny:

> As I sd to my
> friend, because I am
> always talking,—John, I
>
> sd, which was not his
> name, the darkness sur-
> rounds us, what
>
> can we do against
> it, or else, shall we &
> why not, buy a goddamn big car,
>
> drive, he sd, for
> christ's sake, look
> out where yr going.

(Collected Poems 132)

"I Know a Man" requires no trick of parallelism of the sort Prunty admires in "The Loon's Cry." The oscillation here of self and other—frighteningly complicated by the nominative power of the speaker ("John, I // sd, which was not his / name")— strikes me as an exemplary instance of "articulating the jeopardies of a decentralized metaphysics," which is precisely what Prunty claims for Nemerov (20). Prunty shrewdly observes of Creeley's poems that "[t]he reader's pace is slowed to such an extent that what would be recognized as a commonplace when confronted at ordinary mental speed sounds oracular at this halting pace" (61). Of course, if one is disposed to oracular pronouncements, this may be the case. What is really at stake, however, is that for Prunty, Nemerov is oracular because his poems can be rewritten as prose summaries with their arguments intact; whereas, in Creeley, "there is not enough here to sustain wit or argument." It appears never to have occurred to Prunty that Creeley's poem is performative in its intent, hieroglyphic in its means, and neither wit nor argument are of any relevance. There has indeed been an oracular residue (if you want to call it that) from Creeley's poem: the phrase "drive, he sd" has attained a life of its own, circulating not only as the title of a film (directed by Jack Nicholson, 1972) but even as a rhetorical commonplace of the language.

At issue is not the (il)legitimacy of Prunty's critique of Creeley, but his paucity of means, which in turn impoverishes the very
issues he wants to raise. Creeley suffers from "excessive reliance upon
enjambment," in Prunty's view; but he has not bothered to consider
Creeley's own poetics. There is an abundance of material by Creeley,
Olson, Levertov, and numerous commentators, on "breath units" in
poetry; and it requires little ingenuity to see that Creeley's lines register a contest of faculties, a struggle between the integrity of the breath
unit—which solicits a certain autonomy for the line as such—and the
semantic value of unfolding grammatical requirements which
inevitably result in enjambment. Enjambment is, apart from a brief
neoclassical resistance, a dominant feature of English poetry; hardly
something for which postwar Americans can be held accountable. If
Creeley's enjambment seems "excessive" to Prunty it's because he's
incapable of recognizing that excess may signify not an inattention,
but a solution to enjambment as a "problem." Olson and Creeley were
both keenly attentive to the prosodic ambiguities of enjambment, and
instead of seeking to "solve" the problem opted to dramatize it.

Because Prunty is not unique, I'll refrain from itemizing further instances of his contextual myopia. There have been very few
discussions of American poetry *as discourse*[9]: Pinsky's *The Situa-*

---

[9] I do not intend by this phrase the sense proposed by Antony Easthope in
Poetry as Discourse. His purpose there is "to describe English poetry as discourse defined in the way it foregrounds and promotes a position for the reader
as subject of the enounced while aiming to disavow the reader's position as
subject of enunciation" (162). Easthope is an advocate of the reader as (co)pro-
ducer of the text, a position he sees consistently denied by a tradition which
valorizes textual transparency as affording privileged access to the transcendental ego of the *specified* ("enounced") subject position stipulated by the poet—
or, in the long view he would have us consider, by the tradition itself. While
Poetry as Discourse is a useful challenge to the integrity of the English poetic
tradition, it elides the American difference. There is a chapter on Pound and
Eliot, but intended only to show that "Modernist poetry can be seen as denying
a position for the transcendental ego. By insisting on itself as production it
asserts the subject as made, constituted, relative rather than absolute" (135).
What I am calling "poetry *as discourse*" here, then, has to do with the ongoing
American struggle to initiate and inaugurate that poetic *difference* which, since
Whitman, American poets have consistently felt to be a native prerogative. The
difficulty of doing so can be seen as the mark of Americanness, just as the relative *ease* of perpetuating the tradition may be characteristically English.

tion of Poetry in 1976 and Altieri's *Self and Sensibility in Contemporary American Poetry* in 1984 have been the only studies conspicuously setting for themselves the task of addressing what poetry *means* as a scene of operations impinged upon by the rhetoric of social forms. Or, to put it another way, Pinsky and Altieri examine the poetic longing to purify a monoglossic genre amidst rival versions of discursive heteroglossia. The burden of anachronism weighs heavily on poetry, which is in part why there has been such pressure to claim vernacular authenticity. Most critics at their best either produce solid readings of poems or precise articulations of underlying poetics (or a combination of both functions, as in the work of Marjorie Perloff), but few produce work that actually challenges the premises of poets themselves; and this is exactly what Altieri does in *Self and Sensibility.* Since this book is in some measure a response to Pinsky's diagnostic approach in *The Situation of Poetry*, it will be useful to begin there in order to see what additional concerns Altieri brings to the discussion.

Pinsky advocates an embrace of discourse ("prose virtues"), yet avoids any mention of poets who have aroused suspicion *because* of their discursivity (Olson, Duncan, Spicer, Dorn, Whalen, Oppen, Rich, Kelly, Eshleman, Antin), and who may have been more pertinent figures with which to discuss the "situation" of 1975 than many of those Pinsky chooses instead. On the other hand, Pinsky makes no mention of Merrill, Hecht, Hollander, or Dickey either. So what is going on here—is *The Situation of Poetry* mistitled? The first words of Pinsky's preface are a disclaimer: "This is not a survey, nor a selection of the best or most promising work being done. Rather, I try to explore principles: some of the problems and opportunities of this current moment in poetry" (vii). The emphasis should clearly be on *some.* The reason is simpler than it appears. Pinsky is neither a sloppy researcher nor a careless chronicler. He simply represents the predominant critical stance, which is to conflate poetry with *lyric.*

The preoccupation with voice—the subject of Pinsky's second chapter—is symptomatic of this conflation. It would be worthwhile to pursue the emergence of the concept of poetic voice in terms of the history of the telephone, with its detachment of voice from personal presence, and the reattachment of the floating voice to the grounded material transmitter as "speaker." This is another instance in which the mass media have predicated a situation internalized in poetic discourse as prediscursively natural or original. But the prosthesis here precedes the bodily thesis. The aversion to these technological considerations has a poetic foreground, which is also discussed by Pinsky in his third chapter, "The Romantic Persistence," along with its legacy, "Descriptions of Wonder" (Chapter Four). The concerns of Romantic wonder are notably lyrical (or so it's too readily supposed—forgetting Byron's satires, Shelley's dramas, and Blake's prophecies), so it's not surprising that Pinsky concludes (in "The Discursive Aspect of Poetry") by anticipating discursive transfiguration on the narrow proscenium of the lyric. His example of discursive archetype is Stevens's "Sunday Morning," which predisposes him to think of discourse without reference to serialism and the long poems that constitute the primary legacy of modernism. It also precludes serious consideration of collage methods. So, while Pinsky is ostensibly concerned with the attrition represented by what, in 1975, was fast becoming the going currency of workshop free verse ("the horrible ease with which a stylish rhetoric can lead poetry unconsciously to abandon life itself" [163]), he ends up confining the terms for renewal to the very ground which his argument has revealed to be fallow. This expectation of miraculous resurrection from barren soil was also, one recalls, a central thematic preoccupation of Anglo-Agrarian modernism.

Pinsky's hopes for poetry offer a variety of mind-cure theology with its faith in the power of positive thinking. Altieri comes prepared to deal with the anomalous credence given to poetry as secular miracle, but recognizes that this, like any miracle, is a matter of setting the stage, framing the scene. Dramatic and theatrical analogies permeate *Self and Sensibility in Contemporary American Poetry*. For instance, the Enlightenment demystification of religion was itself modelled on the "dramatic flair" of conversion narratives; yet, as Altieri notes, "[t]he ideals of Baconian empiricism do not engage enough emotional life to establish this theatre on its own; nor do they afford the dramatic principles required for appreciating what takes the stage" (12). In other words, lyric empiricism is an inhospitable medium in which to glimpse the sublime. Late in the book, Altieri returns to the theatrical metaphor when he insists that "the most severe pressure of reality in our time is a compulsion to irony that undermines ideals of sincerity and makes our only interpretive orientation one that suspects the moral theater rather than applauding the moral performer" (196). It appears that Altieri has followed Marshall McLuhan's adage that the form of one medium is always the content of another; in this case, the constrictions of lyric cut a certain figure of deficiency in the moral theatre.

The brunt of Altieri's critique is levelled against what he takes to be the dominant poetic idiom of the 1970s, the "scenic mode,"[10] in which the central aim "is not to interpret experience but to extend language to its limits in order to establish poignant awareness of what lies beyond words" (11). The problem is the ontological weight that must be borne by evoking silence, absence, emptiness and other ratios of inversion as the ciphers of an imponderable burden. Altieri is doubly suspicious because the expressive norms of sincerity are so patently artificial: "the sincere self has no theater on which to stage itself except the theater it constructs. But such construction is pure rhetoric, the traditional opposite of sincerity, because the individual acts of self-staging shape what is made to appear as natural" (22–23). As an operative paradigm of the poetic power to evoke greater mysteries, silence acquires special status; Altieri calls it "perhaps the last metaphysic left to Western culture" (51). However, "[t]oo large a claim for silence returns us to *symbolisme* and the romantic image," while "too comprehensive or serious

---

[10] Altieri's "scenic mode" is an accurate term for what was "dominant" in the seventies only from a demographic perspective. Now, two decades later, the picture that is emerging is one in which the language poets loom into prominence, bringing with them a long foreground. Regardless of any final sorting out of reputations, the impact of issues raised by the spectre of language poetry means that, in terms of literary history, the seventies are more likely to be regarded as the decade of radical break with the logocentric legacy of fifties formalism and sixties vocalism (to use Whitman's term). Meanwhile, the proliferation of workshop writing in the scenic mode will subside in retrospective accounts, assuming less prominence than Altieri gives it, until it will finally be safe to characterize it as being for the seventies what genteel verse was when Pound and Eliot fled to Europe.

a use of discursive metaphor entraps us in an anachronistic bardic role of imposing vague profundities on the narrow basis of scenically grounded lyric emotion" (25). Altieri here reveals his own prioritization of lyric as the model of poetry as such, since he too succumbs to the easy generalization of "contemporary poetry" as little more than the comportment of lyric sensibility in salient moments of self-doubt or self-assurance. He is thus positioned to commit a singular error, approvingly citing Olson's warning about the interference of the lyrical ego, yet accusing Olson of betraying his insight by making "an ineluctably parodic lyrical ego the basic instrument for resisting the deadening impersonality of a consumer society" (24). Maximus, however, is *not* a parodic ego; rather, *The Maximus Poems* are an expanded field in which ego is revealed *as* limit, not to be sustained by means of parody or any other artificial stimulant. "Contrary to what most critics of the modernist long poem have said," Peter Baker writes in *Obdurate Brilliance*, "poets writing long poems in the twentieth century *are not interested in* extending the dramatic or narrative lyric into the modern long poem" (2). Robin Blaser, noting Spicer's initiative in moving poetry into seriality and open form, says "I call this openness worldly because it measures the I of the poetry and includes the poet in a world" (289). It may even be debatable whether writers of *short* poems are invariably drawn to the lyric; or, that those who favor the lyric also aspire to inhabit the old brittle shell of its ego. Marjorie Perloff, likewise, suggests that complaints about the "belatedness" of a given poet often fail "to consider that it may be the genre itself, not the particular poet, that is 'belated'" (*Dance* 176).

Altieri's paradigm for literary capability is, as I've indicated, theatrical. He occasionally cites Kenneth Burke on other matters, but not on the concept of "dramatism." Nevertheless, he adheres to Burke's principle of dramatism as involving figure/ground ratios: "scene is to act as implicit is to explicit," Burke writes (7). The concept of "voice" in the lyric focuses attention on the grammatical scope of the speaker, which is the poetic corollary to the dramatic *scene*. But to enlarge the perspective from scene to act also has its corollary, which entails a shift in poetry from lyric to discourse. Theatre is Altieri's trope of discourse; but in fact it covertly shifts attention from Pinsky's nomenclature while occupying the same ground. In the process, however, Altieri makes the misleading claim that modernism is "radically nondiscursive." "Modernist works had to be self-contextualizing, essentially dramatic, constructions, because they had to maintain an adversarial relation to discursive canons" (89). If the adversarial is nondiscursive, it is because "discursive canons" declare discourse off-limits to countercurrents. Altieri is obviously sensitive to the political depredations of hegemonic discourse, so what is surprising is that he chooses as his positive term ("dramatic") something which, by his own definition, lacks efficacy. Commenting on Bloom, he allows that it makes sense "to insist that strong poets create and elicit interpretive conflicts. But the cause is less their psychological relation to their predecessors than their creative relations to the cultural theater where values are dramatized and discussed" (200). Here we have Altieri suggesting that Bloom's revisionary psychodramas are, like the "scenic mode," too narrow a platform on which to sustain the full drama of values in contention. But at the same time, he has depicted the adversarial theatre of modernism as radically nondiscursive, which is to say, producing a dramatization that has no discursive credibility. Altieri has thus created all over again, but with more cunning and metaphysical ingenuity, the terms by which the lyrical ego condemns itself to a prison of its own making, stymied by the spectre of hegemonic forces patrolling the stage on which a coerced utopia of free speech is produced—which, in poetry, consists of those "orthogonal" tears Mary Kinzie evokes in the case of Nemerov. With his precedessors of the 1950s, Altieri falls back on an intuited model of functionalist adjustment (poetry as consolation for the ideologically confounded), with lyric's duty the emotional maintenance of a self beset by inopportune neediness. One might, by the same logic, consider the importance of poetry as juvenile innoculation to cultural contradictions by exciting false magnitudes of autonomy and transcendence. In those terms, poetry has not "failed" the culture: rather, it has *answered* it in precise ways, analogous to the social requirements met by heavy metal or televangelism.

Altieri argues that poetry is disempowered because it has ceded discursive complexity to other genres; and that the dominant discourse is now critical theory. The "dramatic principles" of the moral theater oscillate between the "ideals of lucidity and ideals of lyricism," and "[t]he tension between these ideals makes for the longest-running play in our cultural history" (12). The paradoxical goal of "demystifying ideals and idealizing a mode for a sense of values that resists all demystification" leaves poetry in an exposed position. The ideal of lucidity is jettisoned in the performative wager of modernism, since lucidity itself is seen to be a value constructed by an official and officious culture. But "once all claims to lucidity are dropped, lyricism is too isolated to have much cultural force." An age of criticism arises, then, because "[s]peculative criticism . . . feeds on forms of discourse that apply to several disciplines, so it brings emotional pressure and imaginative life to topics by dramatizing how much depends on a given stance or how much is buried within our traditional allegiances" (205).[11] It is worth pausing to ask: from what perspective does lyricism qualify as an ideal? The claim of lucidity is obvious enough as a dominant category of Enlightenment thought; but when did lyricism ever become a correspondingly pervasive cultural aspiration? Here the precariousness of Altieri's insistence on lyric comes into play. For in fact the ideals of lyricism are incommensurate with the ideals of lucidity, unless we expand the term beyond the generic bounds of poetry to encompass lyric moments in theater, fiction, public rhetoric, and so on. From that perspective, of course, lyricism is far from being too isolated to have cultural force: quite the contrary, it would seem to be pervasive. The lyri-

---

[11] By 1991, from the perspective of England at least, the rage for theory had subsided somewhat, and it became plausible to address poetry and theory on equal footing, as in *Contemporary Poetry Meets Modern Theory* edited by Easthope and Thompson. The editors propose that critical theory succeeded in part because of the theoretically unsophisticated literary texts it dealt with. "This is not so easy to do," as in the case of language poetry which dominates this collection, "when the text that theory is to handle threatens to be stranger, more baffling, more political, more personal than theory itself" ("Afterword" 210).

cism of the mass media (in the sense in which Baudelaire said that
screwing is the lyricism of the masses) turns out to wield an influence undreamed of by speculative criticism.

Altieri creates an elegant series of aporias, which represent
an exceptional challenge to contemporary poetry; but he has, if anything, lent too sympathetic an ear to poets' own claims to significance. That is, Altieri is willing to accede to the compulsion, developed as the credo of the scenic mode, to make absolute claims for
lyricism. But he also recognizes (largely by an unflinching assessment of generic practices in the scenic mode) the constraints of this
lyricism. He has failed, however, to examine the premise that lyricism deserves to be the signature trait of poetry as such. His conclusion comes breathtakingly close to acknowledging all this, without
quite doing so, particularly when he notes that "The dominant style
[the scenic mode] vacillates between minute attention to a subdued
elegance of technique and the most general leaps into the metaphoric
infinite, without allowing the style itself to evoke powers of mind
capable of making the infinite seem, in fact, within our grasp" (211).
One solution, it seems clear enough, would be to relinquish lyricism
as an ideal. The abiding American preoccupation with serial form,
from Whitman (and, it's now clear, Dickinson) to the present has to
be recognized as a *kenosis of lyricism*, a loosening—at times even a
purging—of the lyric ideal. Lyricism persists, then, not as an ideal,
but as a contingent feature (as Robert Duncan might say) of moments
in which there happen to be lyric impulses. Lyricism as *intermittent*
has a much greater chance of infiltrating the fabric of cultural life
than does the resurrection into some putative dominance of a specific literary genre. What Altieri shares with poets he otherwise has little patience with, then, is a subliminal faith in poetic triumphalism,
a faith that an entire cultural order may be rectified by the right kind
of poetry.

I have taken as symptomatic Altieri's deft critique of contemporary poetry in somewhat the same spirit in which he takes
Vendler as a symptom. "It is precisely Vendler's capacity for sympathy that makes criticism like this so disturbing a symptom," he
writes. "She reflects the intellectual stance the age's poetry

demands, and she becomes an index of the quality of the questions or discourses the scenic mode can generate"(203).[12] Altieri takes Vendler as symptomatic of an artificial swelling of sympathies produced in the endless seriality of one-on-one encounters with "the mind of the poet," the "poet's voice," and so forth. A basic premise of Altieri's book is that "criticism of contemporary poetry ignores some of its basic responsibilities if it rests content with describing the work of individual poets," which is exactly what Vendler does (191). To do so is to presume a context, and to persist in vaporous appeals to a "general public" and the "common reader" without any investigation into the continuing existence of these fabled species (or whether they ever did exist: "The so called 'general culture' that the critics of creative writing claim our poetry no longer speaks to is an antiquated fiction," writes Alan Shapiro [177]). Such contexts do not exist autonomously, like rooms awaiting their human conversationalists. They are rather in a process of constant dissolution and reformation, and thrive by an open contest of what Altieri calls "contrastive languages." His strength is that he recog-

---

[12] A comic intertext here: in Dorn's *Gunslinger* the lyric ego, "I," is deceased, but retained as "the perceptual index / of Everythings batch"— this batch being LSD in Dorn's narrative. The poet goes on to speculate: "What then, if we make I / a receptacle of what / Everything has, / our gain will be twofold, / we will have the thing / we wish to keep / as the container of the solution / we wish to hold / a gauge in other words / in the form of man. / It is a derangement of considerable antiquity" (60–61). Do I overread Altieri's text by suggesting his attribution of indexicality to Vendler is commensurate with the "perceptual index" of Dorn's antique "derangement"? It's hard to say in the case of a book, like Altieri's, which openly avows its *allegorical* relation to the material it covers. "I shall be content with an essentially phenomenological treatment of a limited set of psychological problems informing characteristic attitudes and anxieties of the cultural groups poets primarily write for," Altieri professes. "Then readers can fill out for themselves the possible application of my claims while they reflect on the poetry" (*Self* 20). What is this but to claim critical method as allegory, in which the reader's role is to reapply interpretive dicta to whichever texts are most familiar? Altieri later goes on to produce his own "allegory" of the dialectic of discourse and the nondiscursive, based on Ashbery's *Three Poems* (26–27). The result is deft and imaginative, and convinces me at any rate that *Self and Sensibility* is indeed a broader allegory, and thus susceptible of more expanded application than Altieri himself can accommodate within the text.

nizes the mutual responsibility of poets and critics for the creation—or in this case the failure to create—contrastive languages.[13]
Just as in the scenic mode the poet relies on the constraining
assumption of the ideal of lyricism, so too the critic must adhere to
a correspondingly narrow set of assumptions, which are aesthetic.
Vendler is symptomatic for Altieri of a tenuous aestheticism. Ron
Silliman sees her as more than a symptom: she is the disease itself,
which he christens "canonic amnesia or Vendler's Syndrome"
("Canons" 169).

Vendler's collection of essays and reviews, *Part of Nature,
Part of Us*, was launched by Harvard University Press with a major
publicity campaign. Reviewers were encouraged to regard her as
the leading authority on the contemporary scene, and her publisher took out auspicious ads in *The New York Times Book Review*
substantiating that view with the usual array of supporting quotes.
In short order, Vendler was heralded as expert commentator with
infallible taste, and her book ironically received more reviews
than the work of all but the most famous poets she had originally
reviewed. This inaugural episode in the saga of "Vendler's Syndrome" was followed by *The Harvard Book of Contemporary
American Poetry* in 1985 (about which one reviewer noted that
"even before we crack the cover, we sense an uneasy alliance
between taste and institutional weight" [Doreski 85]), another collection of essays and reviews, *The Music of What Happens* (1988),
and the PBS television documentaries (also a college credit course)
Voices and Visions. During the 1980s, then, Vendler emerged as
the premier authority on contemporary poetry: but the verb is too
docile, acquiescent. Vendler was institutionally *produced* as an
authority in terms that parallel the institutional backing of her

---

[13] Of critics, Altieri claims that "We fail our culture and we fail the poets if
we do not seek some contrastive basis on which to establish the significant
tasks poets must perform" (*Self* 191). On the other hand, "When we turn
from theory to practice, we immediately see that we have paid an enormous
price for our poets' commitments to the expressive norm of sincerity and the
thematic ideal of articulating a silence beyond cultural frameworks. In seeking absolutes, they cease to address one another or to take responsibility for
making and testing contrastive languages" (200–01).

coterie of preferred poets.[14] There is, at least, a symmetrical just-
ness in this. If Harold Bloom is something of an avenging angel in
the matter of assessing contemporaries, Helen Vendler is just the
opposite. She is generally positive about the poets she reviews,
and her critical approach is generously sympathetic. Yet she is
imperial in her method, which is denunciation by indifference,
silence, and subtle strategies of omission. She is, in short, a late
blooming New Critic who, rather than engage in the polemics of a
frankly heteroglossic domain, imperiously presumes unanimity (of
taste) where none exists, and so imposes herself as foremost among
tastemakers.

Two texts expose Vendler's presumptions with tremendous
clarity, neither of them collected in her books: a review of *America a
Prophecy* in *The New York Times Book Review* in 1973; and her
Presidential Address to the Modern Language Association in 1980.
The Presidential Address is deceptively titled: it could be more accurately called "Presidential Sermon on *The Prelude*." Like a sermon,
it discusses a general condition by means of examples drawn from a
specific text, in this case Wordsworth's. The lines she cites to anchor
her theme are: "What we have loved, / Others will love, and we will
teach them how." What she proposes to teach as a general precept is
the superior integrity of innocence. Before being exposed to vario-
rum editions or critical terminology, Vendler begins, we form an

---

[14] The force of that institutional backing palpably impressed itself on me in
the wake of *Part of Nature, Part of Us*. I was active as a book reviewer from
1977 into the early 1980s, and for several years hosted a program on books
for the Pacifica network radio station KPFK in Los Angeles. I reviewed
Vendler's book on air, elucidating the way in which Harvard University
Press had launched its publicity campaign to secure for Vendler the status of
supreme authority on the basis of what was (I pointed out) a collection of
book reviews. I used that occasion to lament, as I have done here, the relative dearth of investigative scholarship in the field of contemporary poetry.
My review was hardly vicious, simply informative and contextualizing. Yet,
after transcripts were sent to the publisher, there was apparently considerable displeasure at some level, and I was deleted from the Harvard reviewers
list. I have reviewed hundreds of books published by scores of trade and
university presses, and this was the only occasion in which a negative
review resulted in a punitive response.

"innocent . . . attachment to literature." This is not phenomenological description, but the ground for critical practice: "In every true reading of literature in adult life we revert to that early attitude of entire receptivity and plasticity and innocence before the text . . . " ("Address" 344). The figure of youth's virginal encounter with the text is rich with connotation, as Vendler intends it to be. But I detect other, unsolicited connotations. Her image of innocence corroborates a damaging naivete: for the child the text (the "text itself" of New Criticism) simply appears. The child is not concerned with text production, of course, nor with any system of distribution, circulation, and censorious authorities. A choice among poets may seem to Vendler like discriminating apples from oranges and pears; but, as in Vegas, there is always a *house* that determines what comes up—and what goes down. Texts do *not* swim innocently into view. This point has been exacerbated considerably in canon debates in recent years; and even in 1980 Vendler might have considered the implications, but this was a strategic omission. Her serene confidence in the intimacy of textual exposure reveals a breathtaking indifference to worldly institutions, one which is perhaps available only to those positioned, like Vendler herself, at the pinnacle of such institutions; those for whom authority is so casually congruent with their personal views that they see the exercise of power as indistinguishable from matters of taste and sensibility.

Vendler's tranquility masks the sheer brutality of her review of *America a Prophecy*, edited by Jerome Rothenberg and George Quasha.[15] Subtitled "A New Reading of American Poetry from Pre-Columbian Times to the Present," *America a Prophecy* admits no ambiguity as to its intent. A *reading* is proposed, not the erection of a monument; and the temporal scope involved not only exceeds the parameters of any other anthology of American poetry, but openly indicates how provisional the contents will be. While Vendler is

---

[15] As a lead review in *The New York Times Book Review*, Vendler's hatchet job was bound to have detectable impact. Jerome Rothenberg in fact believes that Vendler's review fatally stalled chances for the anthology's success (personal correspondence, October 1993).

normally meticulous in her reading, she appears not to have bothered with the subtitle of the book, nor even with the editors' introductory disclaimers regarding comprehensiveness. Her undeviating purpose in a long review is to chastise Rothenberg and Quasha for, in effect, refusing to play by the rules, by violating the decorum of more conventional collections which offer unproblematic rosters of "major" poets without bringing up the tactless issue of inclusions and exclusions. The editors frankly indicate that they've excluded Eliot, Auden, Frost, Ransom, Lowell, and Jarrell, for instance, as "securely established poets about whom we had little new to say in the present context." "Needless to say," they add, "exclusion does not in itself imply judgment" (xxxvi). Their "context" consists of a sequence of "Maps" on set topics: Origins, Losses, Visions, and Renewals; these are in turn punctuated by a sequence of "Books," on Rites and Namings, Histories, Music, and Changes. There is little effort to arrange the selections chronologically within these groupings, or to conform to the generic prescriptions of literary taxonomy. This is clearly a book of poems *as* rituals, and poems selected to *inform* the ritual choreography of an unabashedly idiosyncratic vision. The arrangement is interrupted throughout by editorial interpellations, sometimes anecdotal, sometimes annotative, sometimes contextual; and the sections, like the volume as a whole, are painstakingly introduced and prefaced. In other words, there's no mistaking the intent, which is in fact bluntly spelled out: "Our general intention has been to show modes of poetry rather than individual poets, and any reader who takes what follows as an attempt to draw up definitive lists of poets or to chart chronologies of careers will have missed one of the most fundamental premises of this anthology" (xxxvi).

Where violation of canonical decorum is a concern, however, Vendler is clearly immune to such clarification. "[T]he major poets [are] excluded or very skimpily represented," she complains; and what is worse, the editorial agenda forgoes "the best work of our best poets" for "poems of H. D., Zukofsky, Rexroth, Oppen, Fearing, Patchen, Olson, Duncan, etc." ("Alas" 7). These are names of vilification for Vendler; but the very nature of the list discloses her contemptuous unwillingness to be involved enough even to discriminate among them. Who else but Vendler would juxtapose Zukofsky and H. D. with Fearing or Patchen in a litany of *et ceteras*? She belittles the editors' intentions by the supercilious assertion that "[a] revolt against high culture is a stage in the life of many authors"— the implication being that this anthology is arrested at a stage of juvenile dissent. Yet here too, as in her MLA Presidential Address, the figure of the child is prominent. "American children no longer read any poetry to speak of in the schools," she observes. But "with Chaucer, Shakespeare, Milton, Wordsworth, Keats and Whitman not yet given to them, are they to read Pawnee Bear Songs and Dadaist experiments, aleatory 'art' and Hoodoo chants?" (7). This is the canonical version of the domino theory with a vengeance. Confronted with trickster Coyote, African American "dozens," selections from the Book of Mormon, and Mayan codices, Vendler lets out a long wail of disapproval: "the hungry sheep look up and are not fed; the worthy bidden mouths of our greatest poets appear not at the feast . . . " (8). The Miltonic conceit recurs in her MLA address: "Can we not, in foreign languages, include, even at the earliest levels, some simple genuine literature, myths, or parables, so that the hungry sheep are not fed only pattern drills?" (345). By this point it's clear that, for all her solicitous concern about the integrity of childhood and the rights of budding students, they're really little more than a variety of domesticated livestock for Vendler. The nobility of higher education—which Vendler links to a core curriculum emphasizing "the indispensable background of the general literary culture," a "literary inheritance, from the Bible to Robert Lowell" ("Address" 349)—turns out to be highbrow fodder with which to force-feed those "hungry sheep."[16]

---

[16] Vendler, like so many American cultural supervisors, readily adopts such platitudinous phrases as "every adult needs," "the general public," and "we owe it to ourselves." The most informative context for considering Vendler is in a lineage including Frederic Wertham, author of *Seduction of the Innocent*, a 1954 harangue on the depredations of comic books, television, and other forms of mass culture as perversions of youthful purity (see Rasula, "Nietzsche in the Nursery").

> We owe it to ourselves to show our students, when they
> first meet us, what we are; we owe their dormant appetites,
> thwarted for so long in their previous schooling, that deep
> sustenance that will make them realize that they too, hav-
> ing been taught, love what we love. (350)

The chauvinistic plurality of these, her concluding words, is taken
up in the title (from Stevens) *Part of Nature, Part of Us.* This is the
punitive "we" of British public schooling that raps the lads' knuck-
les or canes their posteriors for any sign that they've not adapted to
the way we do things here.

The two sides of Vendler's disposition, then, are the cheery,
upbeat profession of "love" for literature, and that stern, rebuking
curatorial gaze intolerant of attempts to redefine what literature consists of. "We owe it to ourselves to teach what we love on our first,
decisive encounter with our students and to insist that the freedom
to write is based on a freedom of reading" (350). This sounds all very
well until placed against her denunciation of such freedoms as practiced by Rothenberg and Quasha (which she consigns to "the freak-
ish eddies of human culture" [7]). The ideal of "a freedom of reading" is, for Vendler, an ideal predicated on the banishment of texts
like *America a Prophecy.* The solace of good reading subsists on a
censorious subtext; and the landscape of American poetry has been
rendered subservient to a patronizing philistinism masquerading as
love of literature and commiseration for underprivileged innocents.
I'm well aware that some of her critical opponents, like Altieri and
Perloff, never fail when mentioning her to acknowledge their respect
for her interpretive skills. What I'm objecting to is in fact hardly
unique to Helen Vendler, which is why I cited Silliman's proclamation of "canonic amnesia" as "Vendler's Syndrome." What she has,
others have contracted too, and some even *aspire* to catch it—to
reclaim, that is, the wonder of first glimpses into literary vistas, the
allure of virginal induction into a transfiguring order. There is a crucial difference, however, between *respect* for the integrity of such
liminal passages and the hankering to legislate them. To credit
Vendler with the status among critics of "foremost," "keenest,"
"most astute," "penetrating," and other such superlatives, is to

demean poetry; or at least to demean poetry by those whose work is not an exercise in nostalgia.

When Hugh Kenner's work of epic scholarship, *The Pound Era*, was published in 1971, it set a precedent for writing literary history as colossal biography in the Emersonian vein. Kenner's book is openly partisan, a work of homage. Vendler's work is comparable in that she is equally obsequious of Lowell. Maybe she will yet present us with an "Age of Lowell." As it is, she has devoted her energies to chronicling a considerable portion of postwar activity in American poetry, as critic, reviewer, and anthologist; but in doing so she has grotesquely rearranged the entire field in order to amplify Lowell's preeminence. She, like most critics, shirks the task of engaging poetry as discourse, as social text; and, also like so many others, refuses to read significant counter-figures.[17] The cost of this approach is to confuse the critical function with canon formation. The furtive passion behind Vendler's lavish "readings" of poets is to assign ranking, and in this she has been an able heir of Lowell's own trivial game "Who's On Top." Despite its triviality, it could even be a disarmingly enjoyable game, if only it were played by someone willing to consider that the gaming pieces need not have been shrinkwrapped in advance by the toy company that's taken out a patent on what is, after all, part of the public domain. But it's still a game either way. "What poetry belabors is more important than what poetry says, for 'saying is not a game' . . . " (Bernstein, *Poetics* 8).

---

[17] Sectarian evasions should not be exclusively associated with an establishmentarian perspective; disinformation and hostility are as likely to emanate from the vanguard as well, a point Keith Tuma made on the Buffalo poetics listserv on the Internet (a group notably oriented to experimental poetics): "There are also talented writers among the so-called 'mainstream,' many of whom are completely ignored by the alternative scene, which prefers to create bogeymen. . . . There is considerably more sophistication out there than we're sometimes led to believe. And the old binaries—'mainstream' and 'alternative,' you name them—no longer obtain, or, rather, they are transparently falsifying rhetoric without careful delineation and definition." Tuma's advice, in conclusion: "If the so-called 'mainstream' ignores you, don't ignore it, and don't be predictable in your responses to its products." (UB Poetics discussion group <poetics@ubvm.cc.buffalo.edu>, August 7, 1994). The present study, it should be clear by now, is dedicated to reckoning the social costs of predictable responses.

The cost of those left out of the game is hard to assess. Generations of American poets (virtually since Whitman and Dickinson) have labored in obscurity, arousing little more than indifference and occasional scorn. The margins they've occupied have been seething with life for much of this century; and in many ways it has benefited the overlooked poets not to be burdened by "Who's On Top." On the whole, American literary history is a sorry tale of talent aborted on contact with fame. But it's important to remember that the "game" of reputations and tastemaking is, for all its triviality, demonstrably a medium of social oppressions. The appeal to taste and sensibility pretends to operate outside the fractious spaces of history and politics, yet this very pretense is one of the most ancient and brutal forms of political dominance. Robert Duncan, a perennial outsider—indeed, *exemplary* of the outsider in several senses, as homosexual, as nonacademic autodidact, and as a poet not only outside the establishment but even wary of the counter-establishment that would claim him—did not mince words responding to the critical presumptions of the tastemaking institutions. "Professors of literature do not always have minds of the same inspiration as the minds of writers whose work they interpret and evaluate for consumption," Duncan wrote in an understatement, "and an age of criticism has grown up to keep great spirits cut down to size so as to be of use in the self-esteem of sophisticated pusillanimous men in a continual self-improvement course" ("Homosexual" 61).

Linda Wagner-Martin justifiably claims that "[t]he pall of the snobbery of the intellectual elite has doomed new writing since the 1950s. There was a break in that snobbery in the 1960s and early 1970s, with the genuine interest in minority and women's voices, but the 1980s seem shadowed with the same fear and disapproval of innovation" (36). Bruce Andrews, responding to the same symposium on the state of American poetry in 1987, offers a lucid summary of poetry as a productively contested field:

> Poetry . . . works within a fretwork of contests and fadeouts and differences (stifled and otherwise) which always displays a series of social—political—edges. (The political *edge* results in part from the political *opportunity* given to

writing—the opportunity to radically reconstruct the contexts which give it value.) So an implied notion of "American poetry" as an active contemporary praxis—instead of a
corpse readily assimilable to the established canon—would
be one which *takes on* such a dominant (literary, and
social) paradigm. In writing, in art, this national context of
sense offers praxis an *outside*, a contestable horizon, the
basis for a national social reflexivity and self-reflexivity. (4)

Stephen Rodefer, speaking on behalf of an honorable "practice of the
outside" (originally Robin Blaser's phrase for Jack Spicer), has an
anecdote about his childhood that I offer here as a parable of the
poetry world.

Fourth grade was my best year. I invented a way to subtract
fractions without all that refiguring and shorthand notation
rigamarole they taught you and insisted you "show." The
teacher was a good one or she wouldn't have tolerated it.
Miss Biehl. It was a contest at the board between me and
the smartest kid in the class, as to who could do it faster,
he with the book's way and me with my new short-cut
method. And I won, much to everyone's astonishment but
mine. And Miss Biehl had to admit that it was an interesting alternative, but she still made everyone else do it the
long way. I didn't understand. It was a victory but my way
didn't win. (188)

LITERARY HISTORY AS DEMONOLOGY

One approach to the trauma of poetic authenticity would be to examine poets' own hypotheses about predecessors, about source materials, about "inspiration." Harold Bloom's stimulating theory of revisionism is so intractably situated in the gnostic palace of the psy-
chodrama that it would seem to permit no consideration of documentary material. However, Bloom's thesis bears reconsideration in
light of the political economy of American letters, for it is apparent
that the material world, in the American mind, is thoroughly (if anxiously) integrated with fantasy. To study the facts is necessarily to

engage the fantasies. Various versions of infection and purgation could be anatomized, ranging from the antistylistic posturing of poets like Levine and Bukowski, through the middle zone of quasi-traditionalists who imagine that the sheer durability of the sonnet guarantees its immunity from ideological pressures, to the avowedly "derivative" poetics of Robert Duncan. Another approach, which I'll pursue here, is to look at the ostensibly less opinionated medium of the scholarly reference work, the authoritative history. Daniel Hoffman's *Harvard Guide to Contemporary American Writing*, the work I have in mind, strikes me as embodying what Andrew Ross calls "the Cold War intellectuals' liberal pluralist model of checks and balances and veto power . . . " (*No Respect* 56). The Gramscian spectre of hegemonic "blocs," or coalitions of overlapping interests, is pertinent. A dominant ideology is achieved not through coercion or subjugation but by means of legitimation. The work I'll examine here is congruent with a liberal pluralist Cold War hegemony, in which the distribution of "talent" across a spectrum of "individual styles" is presumed to add up to that coherent spectacle, "history"; and it's also a work in which the "veto power" looms large.

John Guillory has made the point that the truly canon-making works of criticism do not consist of prophetic certifications; quite the contrary, the canon waxes by means of the sedate, meticulous labors of evident sobriety, in "essays whose serene judgments upon poetic careers or complex close readings seem far removed from the realm of interest, indeed whose very claim upon our attention is their detachment, their disinterestedness" ("Ideology" 338). The ideologically *effective* argument, then, is the argument cleansed of its explicit affiliations. Such argument positions itself as centrist and levelheaded, with its lucid claim on the indubitability of formal comeliness as a measure of its motto, *mens sana in corpore sano*. The body enshrined by the canon-making argument is a *corporate* body, a body sanitized of its quotidian associations, a body that labors to effect the ideological transfiguration of *work* into The Work (and flesh into wax).

The Harvard Guide to Contemporary American Writing, edited by Daniel Hoffman (1979), contains three chapters authored by

Hoffman himself on postwar poetry. These interlocked essays—"Poetry: After Modernism," "Poetry: Schools of Dissidents," and "Poetry: Dissidents from Schools"—constitute what is in effect a book inside a book (439–606). This copious report on poetry is not only invested with authority but occupies the culminating position as the final three of the volume's twelve chapters. As we'll see, Hoffman's chronicle elaborates a bizarre thesis camouflaged by wit, erudition, and the necessary measure of *apparent* objectivity.[18] What he attempts is an obfuscation of lineage and heritage in which the direct heirs of modernism would appear to be the very poet-professor-formalists with whom Hoffman identifies.

Lowell naturally plays a central role, with Hoffman regarding *Life Studies* as "the fulcrum of American poetry after the war" (485). In Lowell's collection the formalist sensibility absorbs a new post-Beat formalism, a "breakthrough from received to provisional rhythms and forms." *Life Studies* is paradigmatic for Hoffman because it affirms his primary thesis that stylistic renovation is characteristic of the major postwar poets. "There has perhaps never been a generation of greatly talented poets who, whatever their individual proclivities, have so widely shared in a stylistic revolution" (460). The burden of proof here lies, of course, with poets whose careers

---

[18] Hoffman's work has not gone uncontested. Donald Hall attacked *The Harvard Guide* on publication as "an unrivalled map to slovenly academic America," reserving his most virulent criticism for Hoffman's own contributions: "Daniel Hoffman achieves an appearance of eclecticism and wide reading by the quantity of poets mentioned, but he gets his facts wrong, he makes absurd groupings, he is as conservative as Genghis Khan, and he omits mention of many remarkable poets." Also: "He seems unaware of the prominence of women in recent American poetry" (*Times Literary Supplement*, Sept. 5, 1980, p.989). Hall enumerates a half-dozen factual errors (and there are others as well), blasts Hoffman's prose style, and comments on a few of the many misleading sociological assumptions. Unfortunately Hall was the sole dissenter, as is often the case with an authoritatively titled compendium like *The Harvard Guide*. The anonymous *Choice* reviewer singled out Hoffman's essays as three of the four "superb" chapters in the volume (17 [March 1980]: 72). Denis Donoghue was sceptical of the unifying theme of crisis, but approving of Hoffman's handling of the poetry scene (*New York Times Book Review*, Oct. 28, 1979, p.9). Earl Rovit in *The Nation* acclaimed the effort as "thoroughly responsible, judicious" (230 [Jan. 26, 1980]: 85).

demonstrate "continuity" with traditional versification while at the same time allowing for some loosening of metrical rigor, increased attention to the vernacular, or in extreme cases conversion to free verse. Warren and Kunitz are viewed as "elder statesmen" exemplifying this trend, along with Eberhart who is pointedly characterized as having "gone his own way, scarcely touched by the seismographic shifts in the work of others" (461). Observations to this effect are repeated in the case of such poets as Merrill, Hecht, Wilbur, Nemerov, Weiss, and Wagoner, among whom Hoffman finds an exemplary integrity in their refusal to make concessions to the idiom of the day. Hoffman's cardinal (if undeclared) task is not to map the field as such but to certify the achievements of certain poets as native sons of a revolutionary legacy. Hoffman favors a particular set of poets presumed to have "shared" in a stylistic revolution, while those who saw themselves extending such a revolution are accorded no share at all. The thesis is made plausible by a subtle shift of emphasis, from revolution to style. It is common but grossly inaccurate to refer to modernism as a "stylistic revolution." To be fair, this is hardly attributable to Hoffman, who shares with many in his generation a need to disavow the patently ideological energy of modernism while preserving its stylistic *gifts*. But, as Jack Gilbert complained in 1964, "My quarrel is with the poetry that presents itself as a successor [to modernism]. It is exactly because the previous poetry was so great that I refuse to be tolerant of poetry that expects to prevail by default" (106).

It's essential to Hoffman's scheme that the mid-career turn to a more colloquial free verse on the part of Lowell and others be attributable to poetic volition rather than peer pressure. By making Lowell's career exemplary for postwar poets in general, Hoffman is in essence describing the establishment of an official verse culture. Yet, curiously, the conservative "elders" are cited (Warren, Roethke, Eberhart and others), along with a younger generation, as evidence that there never was an "establishment" in the first place: "younger poets as individual in accomplishment as James Merrill, Anthony Hecht, John Hollander, Richard Howard, David Wagoner, Theodore Weiss," Hoffman implies, can hardly be said to constitute "The Enemy" as the

Beats construed it (497). As further proof of the nonexistence of "alleged academicism" he cites Kinnell, Simpson, Dickey, Ammons, and Stafford. After a few other key figures come under review—notably Merwin, Rich, Plath, Lowell, Berryman, Wright—the case appears closed. Hoffman takes the stylistic alterations in these poets' work as evidence of their innate gifts, proof of integrity, and, above all, as indications that they are compounding the blessings of modernism. There is a world of difference, I submit, between the panic alterations undertaken by the postwar generation, and the lifelong interest in expanding the parameters of poetry characteristic of the modernists. Robert Bly's biting denunciation of the "war generation" is worth citing: "Their convictions about poetry are so impersonal and changeable that it would be truer to say they have no convictions at all," Bly wrote in 1963. "The generation of 1947 might well be called the hysterical generation. Its response to the question of literary style or content is hysterical. In fact, hysteria itself is often a subject matter of these men's [sic] poetry . . . " (*American Poetry* 23–24).

Hoffman is intrepid if nothing else in his rewriting of the entire thrust of modern American poetry: "When I speak of a conservative or academic poetry, I refer to tendencies within the context of the modernist movement" (461). This is counterinsurgency with a vengeance. Hoffman, like other cold war pundits, wants to retain an anaesthetized version of the modernist revolution. A succinct assessment of this historical Novocain is offered in James E. B. Breslin's survey of postwar poetry for the *Columbia Literary History of the United States*: "Called the 'New Formalists,' they imagined themselves completing the modernist revolution when their return to tradition actually undermined modernism" (1082). Even as early as 1953 one outside observer—Geoffrey Moore, the English editor of a Penguin anthology of American verse—noted that "I do not think that the young poets and their students are quite the custodians of revolution that some . . . critics have tended to think" (30). It's been observed of Hoffman's generation that they were poets reticent about committing themselves to theorizing, and extremely reluctant to engage in polemic or overt partisanship. What emerged, instead, was the clandestine factionalism of committee work, fellowship and grant support, prize nominations, and so forth. It is in this spirit that Hoffman publicizes his fraternity here, albeit as a kinship of taste. As he meticulously assembles a moiety of backroom allies and associates, Hoffman introduces them as independent spirits, marching to different drummers, and finally—subsumed into a chapter heading— "dissidents from schools." In this light Simpson, Hecht, Davison, Weiss, Wagoner, Hollander, Justice, Booth, Howard and others are deftly interspersed with such apparent mavericks as Finkel, Swenson, Berry, Kinnell, Stafford, Ammons, and Dickey to make Hoffman's aversion to other poets appear a sensible repudiation of cliquishness and opportunism. In Hoffman's view, it is always the others—not himself or his fellow "dissidents from schools"—who rumple the level playing field:

> This balkanization of contemporary poetry has produced an acrimonious spirit of discussion in which partisans of each splinter group make exclusionary claims for their own aesthetic against what they presume to be the literary establishment and, sometimes, against each other. (497)

The implication is that there is no literary establishment except in the hysterical accusations of paranoiacs. The only acrimony Hoffman acknowledges is identified with the partisanship of the balkanized tribes, characterized by "incivility," "shrill attention-seeking," and "bloated propaganda" (498). These are the groups gathered under the clever title "Schools of Dissidents" (Beats, Black Mountain, confessionalism, deep image, and pork barrel surrealism), incisively discharged in the chapter's epigraph (from Yeats): "What are all those fish that lie gasping on the strand?" (496). The spectre of opposing gangs of poetic thugs infects Hoffman's previous reference work entry for Robert Spiller's *Literary History of the United States*.[19]

---

[19] Hoffman's wariness of poetic contenders was more openly acrimonious in 1960, when he prefaced a survey of the year in poetry for *Sewanee Review*: "Fortunately there are no entries here from either the tranquillized or hopped-up schools of dreariness which were the fifties' contributions to poetic history. None of these books is mere graduate-workshop scrabble nor deadbeat bongo from the drummers of disaffiliated Zensibilities" ("Arrivals" 118).

There he sees them not only quixotically sparring with an illusory "establishment" but, "as is the custom among members of a movement," busily "praising each other as though no other poets had claims to legitimacy" and "mutually reinforcing . . . one another as influences or dedicatees of one another's poems" (1430, 1431). It's ludicrous to suppose that dedications somehow militate against other poets. But in Hoffman's conspiracy theory, affiliation is seditious, the work of polemical rather than properly poetic temperaments.

The matter of temperament, or sensibility, is germane to the kind of poetry Hoffman favors. It must be mounted from the deepest reservoir of "stoicism and grace" (1445, on Hecht), individuated in "spare, precise, and brooding" metrical realizations (1434, on Kunitz), in verses "glistening with the patina of a highly worked finish" (507, on Merrill), or if the poet is female, sustaining "close and loving attention to the particulars of experience" (602, on Swenson). This poetic self "must reconstitute the very terms of its being from its own experience, which is, as it were, without precedent" (542, on Merwin). Omit the names of the poets and one might suppose these extracts to be about Baudelaire or Mallarmé and the tight, opalescent hermeticism of the French symbolists. Some of Hoffman's highest praise is reserved for Richard Wilbur: "With meticulous craft he responded to the madness of the modern world by shutting it out from his verse" (1433). Hoffman is an enthusiast of lyric sensibility, which it's not my intention to disparage. My concern is with the contortions required to represent postwar American poetry as solicitous of, and achieving its true vocation in, the isolate and manicured—indeed, the obsessive compulsive—individual talent. Hoffman's case is exemplary because, despite his intentions, he makes it clear how far-fetched this thesis is. To make such a case requires belittling or maligning a longstanding tradition of alternative poetry and poetics, not to mention erasing all historical evidence of its cultural viability and influence. This is achieved by redescribing a tradition as a series of internecine "movements," cynically and opportunistically refusing to play by the rules. While Hoffman is probably correct to recognize that, in the long run, individuals rather than groups survive in the cultural memory, it is spurious to foreshorten the canonizing pressure of centuries and to conclude, as he did in 1974, that "[a] number of poets whose work may prove among the most lasting of the period have joined no movements, issued no corporate manifestoes, but rather have written in the honorable American tradition of individualism" (1445). Ignoring the fact (of which he was well aware) that neither the Beats, the Black Mountain poets, nor the confessional poets ever claimed such labels—and never issued group manifestos—Hoffman nevertheless fires all his rounds into this straw dog to make poets of his pantheon appear more robust in their honorable individualism: "By not being self-categorized in any movement," he concludes, "they are not limited to any particular prescriptive aesthetic." Hoffman seems impervious to the prospect that "honorable individualism" is itself a prescriptive aesthetic. The legacy of an untainted temperament freely disposing its poetic talents is so pervasive in Hoffman's account that it is uninspectable. But, I would argue, it is a primary and not an incidental concern of critics to review the occluded (or even the all too transparent) ideological dimension that supports the "free" enterprise of the lyric occasion.

The politics of community organization are very much at issue in Hoffman's evasions. Hoffman, like so many critics, has trouble recognizing signs of solidarity as anything but incivility. Such anxieties are symptomatic of an enduring postwar tension between competing ideologies of the poet's role. The legacy of transcendentalism, augmented by the peculiar isolation of Whitman and Dickinson, has been received in the postwar era as sanctioning a spirit of individualism. Even the great modernists, who are relentlessly stuffed into tight spaces together to make modernism coherent, emerge as powerfully individuated figures. Individualism has thus come to appear inseparable from the quest mentality of the lyric sensibility. The great trauma which attends this explanatory idealization is the obvious fact that not all individuated temperaments are treated as equal. A criterion of excellence that is based primarily on a principle of non-congregation—individualism without community—is nonsensical.[20] The collective value implicit in the canonical procedure is useless if there is no collective impulse in the poets themselves. In short, the organization of poets into Hoffman's map of postwar poetry is plagued by the Daniel Boone syndrome: social values and rugged individualism are awkwardly merged in a single figure, and society (or the canon) is presumed to be the merely additive function of pooling individual talents together as avatars of national motive.

Recent scholarship obviates the link between canon maintenance and nation-building. The specific tenor of Hoffman's efforts can, I think, be accurately subsumed under what Michael Paul Rogin calls "political demonology," a particularly virulent and characteristically American rhetoric. What's most pertinent is that this demonology tolerates individuation only as a function of the inside, against which the faceless aggregation of an outside looms dangerously. But—and this is where Hoffman is perhaps most clearly what Michael Rogin calls a "demonologist"[21]—the collectivity implied by the clustered hordes outside is explicitly denied recognition as community. If the role of the inside is order, its collective will is legislative; the will of the infectious outside, on the other hand, is seen as conspiratorial.

The roots of Hoffman's splenetic comments on poets in groups—the pervasive Other in both of his reviews of the period—can

---

[20] It may of course be rendered sensible in terms of mysticism, which has been a predominant obsession in critical studies devoted to contemporary American poetry, in which the poets are so many peas in the pod of ecstasy, as critics squeeze each one in turn to see which is plumpest: Molesworth's "fierce embrace," Mills's "cry of the human," and Donoghue's "Connoisseurs of Chaos" are indicative.

[21] "The demonologist splits the world in two, attributing magical, pervasive power to a conspiratorial center of evil. Fearing chaos and secret penetration, the countersubversive interprets local initiatives as signs of alien power. Discrete individuals and groups become, in the countersubversive imagination, members of a single political body directed by its head. The countersubversive needs monsters to give shape to his anxieties and to permit him to indulge his forbidden desires. Demonization allows the countersubversive, in the name of battling the subversive, to imitate his enemy" (Rogin xiii). Hoffman's preferred poets, I remind you again, are valorized precisely for their ability to imitate the enemy—that is, to write free verse better than the supposed ideologues of free verse.

now be addressed directly, since his own standing as a poet needs to be taken into account as a contributing feature of his "scholarship."[22] Condescending remarks about "campus poets" have dogged Hoffman's generation, and he is obviously vexed by them. "[T]he poets of the forties, who before V-J Day had been called the War Poets, soon became known in literary journalism as the University Wits. This was a label most of them would eventually repudiate" (471). Or, as he put it in 1974: "'University Wits' [is] a designation which smudges their readily identifiable talents" (1427). As I indicated in Chapter Two, quarterlies of the fifties routinely reviewed poets under such collective headings as "Four Campus Poets." Soon after his collaboration with Simpson and Pack on *The New Poets of England and America*, Donald Hall came to see that "We are a provincial generation, largely unaware of the past, of our own tradition, or of the nature of our limitations. Most of us have sheltered in the protection of the intimate" ("Domesticity" 318). This is sufficient reminder that the "paleface" poets were not simply idling in the mode of career gratification until rudely chafed by bohemian upstarts. Doubts about the university as a supportive environment for poets were widespread, and the undeniable success of anti-academics in the late-1950s only exacerbated residual anxieties about the use of poetry. Had poetic sensibility become a mere training in complacency? At what point did poets in academe devolve into professors? Richard Ohmann, summarizing his book *English in America*, points out that

> . . . English teachers have helped train the kind of work force capitalists need in a productive system that relies less and less on purely manual labor. More, we have helped inculcate the discipline—punctuality, good verbal manners, submission to authority, attention to problem-solving assignments set by someone else, long hours spent in one place—necessary to perform the alienated labor that will be the lot of most. (*Politics* 8)

---

[22] I don't mean to impugn his genuine scholarship elsewhere, which is varied and distinguished, including *Form and Fable in American Fiction* (1961), *Barbarous Knowledge* (1967) and *Poe Poe Poe Poe Poe Poe Poe* (1973).

The broader implications of this functionalist compliance are spelled out by James E. B. Breslin in terms that help relocate Hoffman's *Harvard Guide* from 1979 back to its primal scene in the fifties:

> Intimidating literary grandfathers, disappointing fathers, prosperity, and social and political conservatism combined to create the bland literary hegemony of the fifties. In literature, as in practically all spheres of American life, the basic procedures had already been invented. Theories, alternative ways of understanding present practices and imagining new future ones, were not just unnecessary but positively harmful. What was needed were skillful but deferential practitioners—new formalists, new critics, literary bureaucrats who could be relied upon to keep providing new answers to old questions. ("Poetry" 1082)

Breslin's "literary bureaucrats" are functionaries, agents of functionalism, creatures of the culture factories that regulate the emergent canons. The uncanny double function of the poet-professor was at once to write the poems and "receive" them, placing them in time, historically, and hierarchically assessing them for the fantasyland of "the timeless."

It is characteristic of the doctrine of neutrality to which verse culture initiates adhere that discussions of poetry abstain from engaging the sociological dimension, the careerism behind the poems. What we get, typically, is an adventure of sensibility roughed up on the shoals of life (madness, alcoholism, and suicide thus become eminently narratable events, unseemly excrescences, perhaps, but worth mentioning anyway, like the anthropologist's off-color asides). Walter Kalaidjian claims that "Like other academic practices, contemporary poetry's staging of the private self—along with the critical industry that recruited a readership for it—proved a bourgeois aesthetic: one that was blind to the social foundations of its own anxious malaise" (23). In Kalaidjian's allegation, "most of our enduring verse writers are academics whose poetry typically seeks to repress and transcend their institutional lives" (27). Many critics, of course, are not poets themselves, so their aversion to social text may involve other factors like the contingencies of academic training; but in Hoffman's case the pertinence of Kalaidjian's diagnosis is obvious: his essays on the postwar poetry scene exemplify the tactic of repressive transcendence.

Hoffman was among the select group handpicked by Auden for the Yale Younger Poets series, and one of the few young poets chosen by Oscar Williams for his popular omnibus collections of American verse in the fifties. His poetry has been published by Oxford and Random House. He has served as Consultant in Poetry to the Library of Congress, won a considerable number of awards, and in 1972 became Chancellor of the influential Academy of American Poets—a post he held until being succeeded by John Ashbery in 1991. Hoffman is, as much as anyone, a fully credentialed delegate of official verse culture. It seems to me the most obdurate pretense to seize the occasion of public authority for vindication of private allegiances; but this is precisely what Hoffman did in assigning to himself the authorship of three long chapters in his *Harvard Guide.* Given the inordinate space Hoffman as general editor was willing to allocate to the topic, here, if anywhere, there was room for instructive disagreement.[23] Nor does he refrain from coyly setting his own name amidst the roster of poetic dignitaries: "Since the persona through whom I have spoken in these chapters is neither confessional nor autobiographical, to speak of my own work here would scarcely be appropriate," he says, adding that "I can, however, mention Richard Howard's chapter, 'Daniel Hoffman,' in *Alone with America,* and 'A Major Poet' by Monroe K. Spears . . . " (603).

Taking his cue from Lionel Trilling to the effect that culture is a form of debate or dialectic, Hoffman (as general editor) suggests that the dialectic is the unifying theme of the volume at hand. The commissioned essays, he claims, do not "substitute a critical analy-

---

[23] "What has proved disabling is not the failure of humanists to *agree* on objectives," Gerald Graff claims, "but their failure to *disagree* on them in ways that might become recognizable and intelligible to outsiders" ("Teaching" 263). Graff is discussing the institutional tessellation of "disciplines" and, within these quarantines, the additional disengagement perpetuated by specialization. Theory, he hopes, may become "the generalized language for staging conflicts in ways that increase rather than lessen institutional visibility."

sis for the work itself, recasting the reading of a novel or a poem 'into a problem instead of an experience.'" Fair enough; but then he adds: "The criticism of intermediation thus resists becoming 'an instrument of power' at the expense of the literature it serves" (viii). What more fitting description of Hoffman's practice could we ask for? His own elaborate "intermediation" *taxes* the subject mercilessly, even as it masquerades in the innocuous trappings of scholarship, wielding its sanctioned powers with the kind of assurance that would preclude any thought of resistance. It is only those tiny pricks that alert our conscience (those small but significant rhetorical lapses) that remind us of the needle that administered the Novocain.

IN A FOG

Even if it's not taken as egregious, the case of Hoffman raises the suspicion that there may be a certain futility in writing literary history, especially one that involves the recent past. After composing his two-volume *History of Modern Poetry*, David Perkins wondered, in another book, *Is Literary History Possible?* As long as publishers (and reference desks) are receptive, however, the histories will be written, even if prematurely, carelessly, or malevolently. The Columbia Literary Histories were inaugurated with two distinguished volumes, *The Columbia Literary History of the United States* and *The Columbia History of the American Novel*, both under the general editorship of Emory Elliott. Deviating from precedents, these volumes favored a topical format within a broadly chronological arrangement. The risks were obvious, as certain authors fell through the general thematic net (in the volume on the novel, for instance, Henry Miller is never mentioned). The gain was in a prodigious annotation of authors and texts, in contexts that rendered them pragmatically visible. For the recent *Columbia History of American Poetry* (heir apparent to the *Harvard Guide*) editor Jay Parini adheres to the chronological format with only modest concessions to topical innovation. Apart from entries on "Nature's Refrain" and a fascinating consideration of "Longfellow in the Aftermath of Modernism" by Dana Gioia, the topics are utterly commonplace: "What Was Confessional Poetry?" and "The Postconfessional Lyric." There are also the increasingly familiar curatorial ghettos on native, black, and women poets. Eleven poets are featured in essays devoted exclusively to their work (Longfellow, Dickinson, Whitman, Poe, Frost, Pound, Eliot, Stevens, Williams, Crane, Auden); and this, coupled with the eight other articles on pairs or trios of poets, means that the bulk of the volume is explicitly dedicated to the protracted exposition of two dozen figures.[24] If one were assembling a collection of explications, of course, there would be nothing untoward about this allocation of space; but in a compendium purporting to be a *history*, it turns out to be a colossal evasion.

It might be objected that my criteria for literary history simply differ from Parini's. It would be more accurate to say that Parini has no criteria. Some of the things that might be expected from a literary history—even one, like this, which is the work of many contributors—are examinations of discursive formations; community networks and collective action; the material dimension of publication, distribution, reviewing; the original contexts of poets' own debates and rivalries; and, not least, a text that can be *consulted* (as one should expect to do in the case of a "reference" work) for information about poets who have not received much, or any, critical commentary. This Columbia project is almost exclusively dedicated to a well-worn itinerary of "major" poets and salient themes (transcendentalism, confessionalism, nature, the long poem). Parini, in short, has vacated all claim to literary history and filled the gap instead with normative theme and career profile essays in literary criticism. What's more, the most resounding reproach comes from the inaugural volume in the series. The entries on poetry in *The*

---

[24] Several essays topically coordinate a pair of poets. The elegy provides an occasion for Lea Baechler's essay on Berryman and Roethke; the visionary theme allows Edward Hirsch to mumble on about Philip Levine and Charles Wright; and Elizabeth Bishop is paired (inevitably) with Marianne Moore. John Shoptaw brings Merrill and Ashbery together on the premise that they are godparents, respectively, of the New Formalists and the language poets, and then proceeds to show how much they have in common. The most successful pairing is in W. S. Di Piero's "Public Music," an original meditation on the dream of a common language in Pound and Oppen.

Columbia Literary History of the United States are uniformly superior to those in *The Columbia History of American Poetry*, the defining difference generally being that contributors to the former are conscientious about providing historical information, while those in the latter volume are comparatively negligent. Coming nearly fifteen years after the forceful advent of New Historicism—which articulates the approaches in the previous Columbia literary histories—the retro–New Critical ahistoricist tendency of this volume is an embarrassment.

Because so much of the space is taken up with profiles of individual poets, the informing strategy appears to be to "historicize" by documenting the vicissitudes of careers. But there does not even appear to be any strong Emersonian pragmatist compulsion to render history as biography—except Gioia's Longfellow, who convincingly emerges as "representative man." Christopher MacGowan, an editor of the superb *Collected Poems* of William Carlos Williams, largely cleaves to a mix of the poet's biography and publishing history. Claude Summers, writing on "American Auden," squanders what could have been a fascinating discussion of Auden's *influence*; so we get an indulgent summary of biographical minutiae. But what end is served—in a history of American poetry—by five pages devoted to the domestic arrangements and versification of Auden's later years in Italy and Austria? Lynn Keller contributes a usefully eclectic catalogue of long poems, despite which she manages to omit Kelly's *The Loom* (or any of his other longer poems), Reznikoff's *Testimony*, Oppen's "Of Being Numerous," Ronald Johnson's *RADI OS* and *Ark*, Schwerner's *Tablets*, McClure's *Rare Angel*, Rothenberg's *Poland/1931*, Blackburn's *Journals*, Viereck's *Archer in the Marrow*, McGrath's *Movie at the End of the World*, or any of the longer works by Rexroth, Mac Low, Enslin, Winfield Townley Scott, and many others. At the very least, one might expect a reference work entry on the long poem to provide a *list* (or an appendix) of relevant titles.

Overall, this is literary history as calculated (or—maybe worse—casual) obscurantism. This is a volume in which Lowell appears as inevitably as Madonna does in the mass media, in which

Life Studies is enshrined virtually without reference to the fifties context in which it appeared to exacerbate yet resolve conflicting traditions. If the 1960 "battle of the anthologies" has been overstressed in the editorial apparatus of subsequent anthologies, to judge by *The Columbia History of American Poetry* it has no status as "history" whatsoever—not even in Ann Charters's survey of the Beat scene. For this history, in fact, the emphasis is so exclusively on the poem and the poet that one might never glean that anthologies had been significant, let alone volatile; nor even that the issue of literary prizes has affected the public demeanor of the poets involved. Not only are significant contexts missing from *The Columbia History*, but a great many poets have disappeared as well. The specific fatalities are numerous.[25] *The Columbia History* continues to marginalize Zukofsky, Olson, and Duncan—those traditional "signifiers of eccentricity" as Ron Silliman calls them ("Canons" 156), and Creeley is limited to the role of follower of Williams and mentor of Baraka. Despite Parini's adulatory reference to her as "one of our most essential contemporary poets" (xxx), Adrienne Rich is mystifyingly given short notice. W. S. Merwin scarcely rates a mention. But the list is too copious to annotate. How do we regard a project purporting to be a history of American poetry that makes *no* mention of the following poets: Reznikoff, Niedecker, Stafford, Ignatow, Hall, Antin, Rothenberg, Eshleman, Robert Kelly, Ronald Johnson, Blackburn, Mac Low, Berrigan, Wakoski, Simic, Meltzer, Bromige, Berry, Bronk, Hugo, Simpson, Viereck, Justice, Kumin, Dugan, Woods, Clampitt?—a

---

[25] Despite 800 pages of text, only 200 are devoted to poetry before the twentieth century (of which nearly 150 are exclusively concerned with six dominant figures). The recent appearance of John Hollander's selection of nineteenth century verse for the Library of America constitutes a veritable slap in the face to this anemic survey, in which we find scant reference to the Fireside poets or to Melville (although John McWilliams, scanning the prose of *Moby-Dick*, makes a persuasive case for Melville and Cooper as constitutive of any view of epic in the nineteenth century); nothing at all on Lanier, Timrod, Tuckerman, Stickney, Boker, Emma Lazarus, or the Cary sisters (Alice and Phoebe). What about Bayard Taylor, author of "The Echo Club" ("When upon my gaiters / Drops the morning dew, / Somewhat of Life's riddle / Soaks my spirit through")?—to say nothing of more considerable poets like Stephen Crane and E. A. Robinson, mentioned fleetingly without discussion.

study that makes only incidental reference to Karl Shapiro, Riding, Rukeyser, Hayden, Miles, McGrath, Everson, Kees, Ciardi, Swenson, Lamantia, Spicer, Blaser, Bly, Merwin, O'Hara, Hecht, Hoffman, Logan, Schuyler, Kizer, Stern?[26]

The Columbia History is a disconcerting record of indulgence and patronage. What else could account for the fact that J. T. Barbarese authors two essays (on Pound and Crane) occupying seventy pages? Surely the most egregious editorial transgression is for Parini to have gathered as contributors what appears to be a *cordon sanitaire* of friends and associates. Two of them are colleagues of Parini's at Middlebury; a full half of the contributors teach in New England, and two-thirds are situated in the northeast. This parochial bias may account for peculiarities in credential: half of the contributors have not published a book on the subject of their entries. Profiles of the contributors suggest, in fact, that eight of the thirty authors are qualified primarily by having published poetry. This raises an interesting and potentially revolutionary strategy, to solicit versions of poetic history from poets themselves—particularly for a reference work. But here it largely backfires: some of the poets appear disinterested, their contributions perfunctory; others seem barely competent; none have apparently given any thought to (nor received editorial guidance regarding) what literary history might encompass. (There *are* numerous historically informed poets who have published exacting critical commentaries, and who would clearly have produced more satisfying contributions: Charles Bernstein, Nathaniel Mackey, Rachel Blau DuPlessis, Michael Davidson, Bob Perelman, Ron Silliman, Joan Retallack, Susan Howe, Don Byrd, William Harmon, David Antin, Jerome Rothenberg, among others.) It's only fair to ask what might have been done to make a better col-

---

[26] These are necessarily approximations, since the index is quite unreliable. Blackburn, Hugo, and Kumin, for instance, are not found in the index, yet are named on pages 635–36. Since many poets are mentioned in that passage in associational clusters, it's possible the editors thought it useless to index them all. However, Wendell Berry isn't indexed either, despite being discussed on page 720; whereas Jorie Graham and Mark Strand are indexed at 391, where Vendler lists them without further comment as examples of poets influenced by Stevens.

lective literary history. Even a cursory glance at published scholarship suggests preferable alternatives: Cary Nelson on populism, Walter Kalaidjian on social text, Alan Golding on anthologies; Stephen Fredman on the prose poem; Robert K. Martin on the homosexual tradition; Charles Altieri on lyric idioms; Robert von Hallberg on poetry's modes of socialization; Motlu Blasing on the rhetoric of forms; Charles O. Hartman on musicality; Johanna Drucker on the materiality of production; Maria Damon on marginality; Marjorie Perloff on experimentalism; not to mention historical networks like Objectivism (Michael Heller or Guy Davenport) and Black Mountain (Sherman Paul or Christopher Beach).

There are of course no unequivocably satisfying solutions to the task of producing an historical record of a national poetry; but there are minimum requirements of documentation and usefulness which *The Columbia History of American Poetry* evades. By an uncannily suitable oversight, the final word should be given back to the publisher: in the press release, after a boldface "STRIKE UP THE BAND: COLUMBIA DOES IT AGAIN," a typo has crept in (symbolic retribution?) to Frost's claim that "Poetrty [sic] is a way of taking life by the throat." Unfortunately, as this sorry production proves, it also works the other way around. It is further evidence (as if any more were needed!) that institutionally authorized treatments of American poetry proceed without license, and with minimal standards of scholarship. The periodic diagnoses of an ailing poetry are misplaced. The real disease is amnesia, and it's not the result of "natural" causes but has often been craftily administered, like Novocain. *The Columbia History of American Poetry* is merely the latest injection. Given that the two most prominent official guides to American literature published in the 1970s were those edited by Spiller and Hoffman, and that Hoffman composed the entries on poetry for both, he may be accurately said to have *covered* the field. Hoffman exercised his veto power with considerable skill, and *The Harvard Guide* is an exemplary consolation for those who desire the contestatory relevance of modern poetic history to vanish; and now the Columbia tome has arrived as reinforcement. The nosological analogy is instructive when dealing with the uses or abuses of power that seem to emanate from

power "centers." Jonathan Holden, University Distinguished Professor
and Poet-in-Residence at Kansas State, proclaims virtues of centrism,
but is a bit testy as anybody would be speaking from a geographical
center so sparsely populated. Daniel Hoffman, on the other hand,
inhabiting multiple positions of authority under the shadow of the
Liberty Bell, can confidently claim that there is not and never has
been a poetry "establishment" (as would, I suspect, Parini, ensconced
in the Bread Loaf at Middlebury). Finally, there's the position of
Charles Bernstein, David Gray Professor of Poetry and Letters at SUNY
Buffalo, who suggests that "the center is a projection from the periphery. Or rather, there is no center, only peripheries that agglomerate in
various ways—like blood clots at the sites of trauma" (*Poetics* 188).[27]
He, like Ron Silliman, retains the vocabulary of pathology, which here
disturbs what would otherwise sound all too close to Hoffman's view
that the center is merely the collective hallucination of provincials.

The traumas that concern us at this particular literary moment
are canonical. The most obvious trauma is the fact of selectivity; but
this is superficial. Canonical figures succeed one another like members of Congress, but the change of names doesn't seem to alter the
institutional way of doing business, either on Capitol Hill or on Mount
Helicon. The lives are lived and the poems are circulated elsewhere,
despite massive and even oppressive interference from the only centers that count because they *are* institutional. Literary history, I would
argue—even when written under the auspices of an institutional setting—should be resistant to the Marvel Comic Superhero syndrome,
which is the historian's version of a canonical roll-call. But the celebration of a Lowell or a Rich need not be partner to cultural genocide.

Politics is always about the use of the first-person plural.
Discourse about poetry has been recalcitrant in addressing this fact,

---

[27] Bernstein speaks from a position of exemplary complexity: Manhattan
native, Harvard educated, he is famous (or infamous) as co-conspirator of
the language poetry movement that has been vilified and embraced with
roughly equal measures of righteousness. Except for this Harvard publication, all of his other books (prose and poetry) have been by small presses,
often quite ephemeral (even in production values, which have included
mimeo and staples). Nevertheless he was appointed to succeed Robert
Creeley to the distinguished David Gray chair at Buffalo in 1990.

despite a certain critical eagerness to embrace a selection of poets as quintessentially "ours." The *we* of the convivial scholarly address easily obscures a predatory claim. History is a matter of public record, but literary history inevitably reproduces private life as public event without accounting for its *social* (and sociable) dimension. As I've suggested, Daniel Hoffman's version derives finally from a particularly tremulous ideological moment which Cary Nelson has usefully sketched:

> The collapsing of modern poetry's wild diversity into a hypostatized combat between literary titans mirrors the most simplistic of 1950s North American political world views. It resembles the ideological strategy of those who promoted a vision of a world contest between freedom and communism, the United States and the Soviet Union, with most of the world's diverse cultures simply invisible to us. (*Repression* 37)

Difference, in other words, is politically simplified into the binary system Rogin calls "political demonology." We have yet to reckon the cost of our refusal—in this most heterogeneous of nations—to acknowledge conflict as a function of diversity rather than polarity. Charles Bernstein's *A Poetics* opens with an auspicious recognition that

> There is of course no state of American poetry, but states, moods, agitations, dissipations, renunciations, depressions, acquiescences, elations, angers, ecstasies. . . . The state of American poetry can be characterized by the sharp ideological disagreements that lacerate our communal field of action, making it volatile, dynamic, engaging. (1)

There are hopeful signs that there are others interested in preserving this dynamic volatility.[28] Despite such signs, the "canonic amnesia"

---

[28] See for instance *Conversant Essays: Contemporary Poets on Poetry* (1990), edited by James McCorkle, which houses Bernstein and other language poets alongside Gioia and the New Formalists, workshop veterans along with the permanently disaffiliated. Significantly, such diversity was accommodated not in an anthology of poetry but of poets' prose.

perpetuated by Vendler's Syndrome, *The Harvard Guide* and *The Columbia History* are not unique to them but are endemic to American anxieties about cultural capital, representational obligations, permissible association, and the status of authority when the canonical gatekeeping roles are ambiguously delegated. The trauma of literary politics in the U.S. is that there is no center without coalition. The pundits who fear the center cannot hold invariably yearn for the virile politician and the strong poet to occupy that fantasy space in the center, a zone that on closer inspection is really a vacuum. So: the solution? As long as we keep thinking of solutions as happening only once we perpetuate the trauma of our native insecurities. In our quest for poetic supreme fictions, we have yet to have a chronicler as intrepid as Stevens's lines:

> It feels good as it is without the giant,
> A thinker of the first idea. Perhaps
> The truth depends on a walk around a lake . . .
> . . .
> Perhaps there are moments of awakening,
> Extreme, fortuitous, personal, in which
>
> We more than awaken, sit on the edge of sleep,
> As on an elevation, and behold
> The academies like structures in a mist.
>
> (*Palm* 212–13)

CHAPTER FOUR

Politics In, Politics Of

NORMAL CHANNELS

In 1950 Wallace Stevens wrote "As at a Theatre," which can be viewed as a contribution to the genre of New World verse—which would include Keats's "On First Looking into Chapman's Homer," Whitman's "Starting from Paumanok," Crane's "O Carib Isle!" and Adrienne Rich's "Diving into the Wreck." While it may seem improper to connect the austerities of Stevens's style of old age with the buffoonery of *I Love Lucy*, Stevens's new world emporium is not, after all, a theatre, but *as at* a theatre, and is furthermore "the artifice of a new reality, / Like the chromatic calendar of time to come" (*Palm* 361). Still in its black and white infancy, television had not yet achieved its chromatic calendar; but Stevens's poem ends with the question that must be put to any new medium that engages imagination and skepticism in equal portions: "What difference would it make, / So long as the mind, for once, fulfilled itself?"

In 1950 only 9 percent of American homes had television sets, but when Stevens's *Collected Poems* appeared in 1955 the figure had risen to 65 percent (Spigal 32). By the end of Eisenhower's tenure in the White House, the saturation of household habits by

363

television schedules was nearly complete. Throughout the copious selection of "American Poetry Since 1945" in the fourth edition (1994) of *The Norton Anthology of American Literature*, however, the poems give almost no indication that the authors had ever bothered attending to radio, film, television, or the pervasive billboard environment (not even the ingenious serially versified Burma Shave roadside jingles).[1] How is it, then, that a common poet's lament of the period has been: "If only poetry didn't have to compete with tv. . . ." What is it that makes this fantasy so durable? Surely, with a little reflection, those tempted to compare poetry with television would be hard put to contend that a permanent electrical outage would send droves of people to poetry as an alternate form of entertainment. What is misleading about aspirations by poets to compete with television programming is the corollary that poetry is an entertainment medium. "It would be better to speak not of the *disappearance* of poetry and the other arts in their bourgeois manifestations but of their transformation by media which are more efficient and democratic" (Byrd, "Learned Ignorance" 175).[2] There *was* a time when poetry was read as bite-sized moral edification; but the moral was gone long before television packaged the edification into the half-hour sitcom, the hour-long

---

[1] Among the few exceptions are Olson ("where shall you listen / when all is become billboards, when, all, even silence, is spray-gunned?" [*Norton* 2423]) and Lowell ("When I crouch to my television set, / the drained faces of Negro school-children rise like balloons" [2501]).

[2] Don Byrd is responding here to Christopher Clausens's *The Place of Poetry*, an exercise in nostalgia for the reign of Palgrave and Queen Victoria. Clausens hankers after the humanizing qualities of a moderate and moderating verse culture. But as Byrd usefully reminds us, "We have persistent testimony that the pleasures of poetry are extreme" ("Learned Ignorance" 175). The virtues of moderation readily become acquiescent to prevailing norms. Michael Palmer accordingly vilifies certain venues as *most* damaging to poetry: "I think the ultimate marginalization of poetry comes from people who trivialize it, poets who turn poems into commodities. The truly marginalized poetry is the poetry next to the cartoons in the *New Yorker* or the kind of rote composition and commentary that occupies most pages of the *American Poetry Review*. That is self-marginalizing verse because it is commodified and can be discarded" ("Interview" 6). As an aside, it's worth noting that Clausens appears to have been the source of the widely touted

drama, and the soap-opera serial. Nineteenth-century pulpit homiletics were an equivalent menace, except for those who, like the American "fireside" poets Whitman rebelled against, saw their work as an extension of the devotional impulse in another medium. Likewise, as Byrd points out, the *uses* of poetry are not distinct from those of television and popular music; poetry is simply "entertainment for the most demanding audience, those who require greater complexity, which is to say, those who have more surplus attention to absorb" (175).

A cogent point of comparison would rephrase Pound's dictum about poetry being as well written as prose: poetry should be at least as well written as a network television episode. The work of Richard Wilbur or James Merrill patently avoids the comparison by its baroque elegance and wit. The same could be said of the bardic orations of Ginsberg. But the garrulous medium of the free verse lyric positively invites comparison to television. The old sense of poets as wordsmiths of a high order is challenged every night by network television fare. Partisans of poetry would no doubt be able to demonstrate the superior verbal prowess of their favored medium. But I am speaking of the sort of *instantaneous* demonstration television thrives on; and in that sense any prospective comparison favors the tube's amplified media resources over poetry's penury. Poets complaining about television are apt to forget that almost as soon as the films became talkies Hollywood producers started raiding the precincts of stage and fiction for fresh talent. Ben Hecht and Preston Sturges were perhaps the most successful converts to Tinseltown formulae, but Faulkner, Fitzgerald, West, Chandler, Huxley, and many others underwent a notable apprenticeship in scriptwriting. The classist spurning of television began with the film studios which, unlike poets, really were in competition with the new medium. The storytelling bias of Hollywood media perhaps accounts for the persistent

mass media "factoid" (CNN's apt term) that Alice Walker and Toni Morrison have driven Shakespeare and Milton nearly out of the curriculum—a charge Stanley Fish usefully demythologizes in *There's No Such Thing as Free Speech* (1994).

exclusion of poets from the ranks of recruited writers.[3] But the more accurate formulation of the issue at hand is that poetry is in competition with *writing* as such, in any other medium.

Where poetry is unwittingly drawn into comparison with television is in the lyric integrity that informs the grace notes or other poignant exchanges that television writing thrives on. The witty nonsequitur of the sitcom has, to some extent, influenced the composition of dramatic series. Furthermore, the periodic disruption of commercials mitigates against any sustained exchange of the sort ancestrally prepared for in drama or fiction. So, as television has refined its allotted space of exposition, it has inevitably encroached on the sort of verbal felicity that characterizes the lyric. Recently, offbeat series like *Twin Peaks* and *Northern Exposure* have narrowed the gap, providing extended monologues that, if transcribed in free verse lines, could imperceptibly slip into the domain of published poetry without any trace of their genealogy. Insofar as poetry has become synonymous with the free verse lyric, "poetry" is in dangerous competition with television, because the inscrutable rhetorical foundation of free verse abandons all the immunizing paraphernalia of prosody, putting poetic language on a free and equal footing with felt intensities in any medium that also happens to use words.

What is surprising, then, is not that poetry should be in competition with television but that it could ever be imagined as occupying a noncomparative autonomy in the first place. Poetry is not a linguistic oasis, and is not immune from the discursive norms of society at large. To assert this is to go against the grain of critical practice, however. It is alarming that the inaugural study of contemporary poetry in a mass media context (Marjorie Perloff's

---

[3] Interestingly, poets have had some success in Hollywood, including Peter Coyote, Michael Lally, Lewis MacAdams, and Harry Northup. In the late 1980s the star-studded poetry reading became a Tinseltown vogue, as more and more actors started 'coming out' with their closet productions. The thespianized flamboyance—or at times the underplayed drama of celebrity—of this scene may be responsible in part for the rise of "poetry slams" in metropolitan centers around the country, an indigenous if belated populist revolt against the complacencies and etiquette of poetry's public venues.

Radical Artifice) was published as late as 1991. The modernist verification of art latent in the quotidian has been chronicled (by
Perloff herself in *The Futurist Moment*, among others), but the
myth of poetic autonomy has proven intractable in the face of the
modernist legacy, consistently favoring the high road of tradition
over the low of mass media culture. But the modernists had to confront the crystallization of appearances in commodity forms; and
Walter Benjamin was mesmerized by Baudelaire as the first (and
thus *ur*-modernist) poet to recognize this: "It was Baudelaire's
endeavour to make the aura which is peculiar to the commodity
appear," he noted. "Baudelaire had the mass-produced article
before his eyes as a model. His 'Americanism' had therein its most
solid foundation" ("Central Park" 42, 52). Ironically, American
poets either lack or aspire to shed this Americanism. The modernist ambience of the mobile sign as well as the monumental
hieroglyph is responsive at once to daily and to esoteric provocations. So Benjamin, disposed to detect gnostic wisdom in the mundane, observed: "Now the letter and the word which have rested
for centuries in the flat bed of the book's horizontal pages have
been wrenched from their position and have been erected on vertical scaffolds in the streets as advertisement" (quoted in *Radical
Artifice* 93). Words and letters have gotten up and wandered
around, settling into the quotidian in postures of assertive independence. The "liberation of the word" announced by Marinetti
has become a dominant feature of the environment, thanks to corporate advertising rather than artists and poets. Not surprisingly,
there is a reserve, even outright hostility, on the part of poets
regarding these strategies that materialize the sign. The typescript
norm that dominates the presentational strategy of the book of
verse obdurately resists such sensationalism, affirming in its
machine-tooled template and its steady rectilinear movement a
humanizing stability.

If there is a "death of the author," poetry says, it's out there in
the world of billboards—not here in the sanctuary of subjectivity. The
irony is that individuation is so sedately associated with the uniformity of the medium. Someone like Bob Brown, then, who liberated

his words by orthographic means, is shunned as a crank.[4] The typographic variety of the compositor gave way to the standardized parameters of the typewriter. The typewriter put a mode of production directly into the hands of the poetic worker. However, the *conveniences* prevailed: kerning between letters, spacing between lines, and left-margin axis determined the look of the typescript. Typewriter deviants like cummings, Williams, Olson, and Duncan proposed variations of these default characteristics as a necessary exercise in poetic composition, only to have the exactitude of their typewriter specifications mistaken as approximations of typography. The standardization of the typescript/print continuum adapted the mechanical reproducibility endemic to modern media, and poetry is not immune to the pervasive features of print culture. The typographic variables implicit in much twentieth-century work and often explicit in eighteenth-century writing are uniformly denied. The teaching anthology, the poetry anthology, and even the individual poet's published book, participate in a design habit that subordinates authorial impulse to generic production specifications. The glamour of a uniquely individualized voice emerging from the bland consistency of typographic norms is what we've accustomed ourselves to—so much, in fact, that the poetic issue of articulated spacing as trace of vocal impulse, as well as the grammatological deferral of the metaphysical presumptions of such notation, are marginalized as arcane theoretical matters extraneous to poetry. But of course "poetry itself," from the bastions of such a defense, is a purely Platonic *form*, most suitable to that corresponding form, the Republic, from which Plato would banish poets.

Typography is not at issue here, however. My concern is rather to stress the normalizing propensity of the medium that happens to impinge on poetry's appearance in the world. All media

---

[4] Jerome McGann has recently drawn attention to Brown in *Black Riders*, a book ranging throughout nineteenth and twentieth century poetry, intent on recovering a hidden dimension of modernism as materialist poetics. In terms that are useful in this context, McGann says that Johnson's edition of Dickinson "goes astray . . . because it has approached her work as if it aspired to a typographical existence." But, in McGann's view, "Dickinson's poetry was not written *for* a print medium, even though it was written *in* an age of print" (38).

impose norms. These technical norms are in turn ascribed to the contents, the substantive texts transmitted through the medium's particular channels. Debate about television has long been divided on this point, between those who regard the programming as a deficient use of a proficient medium, and those who insist that the medium itself forecloses other options. This split is sustained demographically: viewers, like addicts, plug into the tube for their fix, so "watching tv" seems a generic response to the medium. On the other hand, target groups can be researched and pinpointed with moderate success by programmers. It's obvious that television accommodates both dispositions equally, the indiscriminate as well as the discriminating viewer. Regardless of the distinction, vernacular usage refers "television" to whatever is watched, not to the electronic instrument as such. Likewise, "poetry" specifies the content or substance of a (usually printed) speech act, along with its production values (prosody), but not the actual typographic medium.[5] The poem in Caslon is presumed to be the same poem in Times Roman. A corollary to this effacement of the material dimension of the sign is the generic assumption perpetuated by the dominant media of poetry— book, anthology, commentary—that what counts as a poem must typographically reflect the design standards of the collection itself.

Conventionally, typeface and other design features have come to seem incidentals and accidentals, not essentials. The *channels* through which a medium is felt to operate are generic, ideal rather than material. They are ideal in the sense that they are hosts or transmitters of ideology, a subliminal shaping of experience. Ideology is the hidden hand that focuses a medium, a seemingly technical effect like the self-focusing feature in cameras. When Americans refer to television, as in

---

[5] Thomas Vogler points out the generic debilities associated with the means of production: "By the middle of the nineteenth century, printed text had become the exemplar of mass production and nondifferentiation, hence the opprobrious terms 'stereotype' and 'cliché,' both derived from the advanced stages of automated print technology. The sound produced by the new typesetting machines led to the onomatopoeic verb *clicher*, for the copying process, and the noun *cliché* for the metal plate (the same device is called a 'stereotype' in English) from which identical reproductions of print or design could be made indefinitely" (*Books as Objects* [7]).

"watching tv," the device appears secondary to the program. But after a childhood's acculturation, in fact, most Americans become accustomed to conflating a few primary programming formats with the medium itself; commercials appear inevitable, dramatic sequence seems indisputably naturalized into eight-minute segments, comic incidents bonded to a laugh track, and so forth. For the television viewer the norm assumes the parameters of the dominant model. So "normal" channels have been the major networks, with other programming venues appearing (either positively or negatively) eccentric.

"Normal channels," then, are the dominant channels. Dominant channels mean channels that dominate the attention of a large, diffuse, and generally unknown audience. In the Victorian era, Wilkie Collins (*The Moonstone* and *The Woman in White*) concerned himself with the new mass hydra that devoured his novels, speculating that the "unknown public" was "now waiting to be taught the difference between a good book and a bad. It is probably a question of time only." Collins optimistically imagined that this unknown mass "must obey the universal law of progress and must, sooner or later, learn to discriminate" (191). It's now later than he ever would have thought possible, inasmuch as discrimination is exercised between media, not within a medium. People prefer to watch television rather than read poetry, it seems. But that's as specific as it gets. The viewer of a television movie dramatizing victimized women is not likely to have opted for that instead of Sharon Olds's *Satan Says*. If television dominates the mass audience it's because television producers stand to gain from that domination in ways that clearly exceed the gains of poets and critics. But it's misleading to imply an opposition between electronic and print media. In the late 1970s Richard Snyder, president of the publishing firm Simon & Schuster, admitted that "[i]n a certain sense, we are the software of the television and movie media" (Whiteside 65). It's not evident that poetry has any place as "software" in the brokerage between publishing firms, television networks, and movie studios. Poetry is a cultural oddity—like the Amish, the smithy, the ballroom quadrille; but that doesn't exempt readers from being under the (toxic) influence of the dominant media, regardless of whether they find poetry exalting or simply irrelevent. Those intoxicated by it tend to see their addiction as a culturally generic condition of consciousness; but television marshalls superior forces in producing the genres of awareness that fibrillate public mood. Television, after all, is nothing less than "an architectural aperture . . . a metronome of the quotidian" (Crary 285).

In the aftermath of World War I, when the present communications oligarchies were established, the notion of the audience was strategized in terms of domination, even when it assumed a benevolent demeanor—what Anthony Smith in *The Shadow and the Cave* calls "enforced enlightenment of the mass audience" (32). Dominant channels are now operated by media entrepreneurs who deploy a product in a medium in order to get the attention of an audience. This is the hook inside the bait of entertainment. This marketing angle estimates the unknown audience as accessible only in captivity. The audience is transported invisibly and electronically as statistical integers in the contractual bargaining agreement between network and advertiser.[6] The implicit injunction to the captive audience

---

[6] Advertising rates are calculated by consulting Nielsen's ratings, which is a monopoly business. This business projects statistical aggregates by sampling a small number of "Nielsen families." These families are, in effect, unelected congressional delegates in a national literacy forum, determining what goods and services we all have access to by means of normal channels. In recent years the networks have threatened legal retaliation against the Nielsen agency because its method of eliciting viewing-information from the statistical sample showed a massive overall decline in the size of the audience for network television. The statistics on home viewing indicate a dwindling share of the audience for the networks, and it has become evident that this is due to home video and cable. People have adapted themselves to a modulation of the norm, and the networks have had to adjust, painfully, to the awareness that the means by which they had retained a captive audience changed when the medium developed. So the latest and most successful compensatory tactic has been target marketing. The updated Nielsen system—introduced to placate the sponsors' demand to reach specific audiences—required each individual in the family to enter a personal code when watching a program, to facilitate demographic identification. As long as an audience can be targeted demographically (product X for baby boomers) then the statistical sampling methods are acceptable; but when the sampling procedure allows (or requires) too much intervention or interference on the part of individual audience members, then something must be wrong. (The strategist's horror: perhaps the ten-year-old girl switching on the tv and not punching in her code name is refusing to produce herself as a subject for that object.)

(name, rank and serial number) is to concede volition to the broadcast medium, in exchange for the privilege of "participating" in the statistical process—just another episode in the lifelong mini-series of political abstinence: " . . . the renunciation of the question of political right through the private pursuit of well-being" (O'Neill 89).

This is the participation mystique of an industrial-communications society. It is also a residual sort of mind-cure theology. Donald Meyer, writing on the "positive thinking" cults of the nineteenth and early twentieth centuries, notes that "[m]ind-cure theology was purely expressive. That is, it was the immediate projection of uninspected wish" (81)—an impeccable description, as well, of commercial advertising, in which a product is projected into the virtual psychological space where wishes congregate. Products in this zone of captivities—of predator and prey, producer and consumer—offer themselves as charismatic magnetizers, objects which can't be resisted. They are "strange attractors,"[7] inducing catastrophic transitions, which in a capitalist environment assume the paradigm of rags to riches. Products engage the psyche with such allures. Instantaneity becomes a value; and the quotidian becomes invested with a latent potency, as the mediated projection of uninspected wishes.

When the public realm has been outfitted as a spectacle, a theatrical assemblage, the whole world is revived as evidence of the bizarre and the miraculous—the very categories institutionalized by Robert L. Ripley. Whether we Believe It Or Not is a diversionary tactic, for belief is no longer at issue when the continuum is choreographed as *display*. We may be mesmerized, or annoyed, but volition is held in abeyance by the illusory spectacle of a cornucopia of choices. Meyer provides an illuminating vantage here, for as he observes, "The wish for plenty was not the wish to have one's wishes fulfilled; it was the wish not to have to wish wishes of one's own

---

[7] "Strange attractors," also known as "chaotic attractors," are "singularities" in phase space in topological mathematics. Strange attractors have been cited frequently enough elsewhere by now so as to constitute a cultural reference, which is the usage intended here. For a cogent synopsis from the cultural perspective, see Manuel De Landa, *War in the Age of Intelligent Machines*, 234–37, n9.

at all" (207). The attraction of mind-cure theology is to keep alive the fanciful apparition of volition, but in a state of suspended animation, so that no real effort is involved. Television, for forty years, has succeeded by gratifying wishes its audience never even knew they had until they found them gratified. This is not secular entertainment so much as huckster miracle—and it is apt that one of the more perspicacious industries is televangelism: the medium has found its own exemplary display. Televangelists thrive on their recognition that viewers *believe in television.* "We may not be conscious of it," says Martin Esslin, "but television culture is the religion by which most of us actually live . . . " (quoted in Twitchell 259).[8] Watching television is keeping the faith; so combining *that* faith (which is a subliminal duty) with the avowed terms of Protestantism, is a characteristically American deal: two for one. At the same time it reverses the traditional subordination of the human to the divine, as this spectatorial role positions the observer in a dispassionate deific posture: "Man, the consumer, is used so as to replace the absolute God as the indifferent spectator with a God who is carnally represented in real life. There must be TV for the *divina comedia* to have real existence in the flesh" (Avens 45).

Poetry, unlike television, is not contingent on belief. David Jones, the Welsh poet, succinctly diagnosed the prospect: "It must be understood that art *as such* is 'heaven'—it has outflanked 'the fall'—it is analogous not to faith but to charity" (164). Jones, writing during World War II on "Art in Relation to War," addressed the situation

---

[8] Wolfgang Giegerich has also described the devotional milieu of mass media, noting that "Advertising is the *constant proclamation of salvation and the constant confirmation of the belief in salvation*" (quoted in Avens 46). Twitchell observes of mass media culture: "In many respects popular culture resembles a secular religion promising release, not in the next world, but in this one. Wishes are fulfilled, not later, but NOW. Gratification is instant because for the first time it can be" (38). Twitchell's documentary approach is invaluable for the information presented and summarized, but his perspective is problematically—if self-consciously—naive. His thesis is that modern mass media are the most genuinely democratic media yet invented, and that we've gotten precisely what we asked for. While he is careful to document corporate control of media formats, he places far too much faith in marketing analysis as an accurate referendum on audience desires.

which continues to predominate today, for he recognized that the arts "compete" (if that's the term) with forces of an altogether different magnitude—now, he noted, "the art most practised is that of war . . . " (132). As we seek the "efficacious sign," the mystery of transubstantiation (136), the arts of war import such signs into our lives with astonishing industry and effectiveness; and Jones enjoins his readers to respect such efficacious art for its gifts, its bestowal of creative energies. "Man must first of all be considered as a creative beast, and a creative beast he will be, one way or another" (150). One way is the path of hostilities, the other is the path of charities: both, Jones insists, are arts. When he concludes that art is analogous to charity, not faith, he sees the arts arising from a blessed superfluity, like the temperamental gift of charity in the individual. Charity, that is, is not the means to an end; not a strategy. Charity is the end, or what Jones says lies outside time (as "heaven"). Art is to society what charity is to the individual, a space secured outside the teleological insistence of the system. This is not to say that great artworks are "eternal," unless by such a term one would indicate an available and contingent attribute, analogous to charity. Jones's concern was with how the arts were to survive in wartime, in a time in which the technical resources of the *art* of war clearly exceeded the resources of the "arts" as such. He recognized that both sorts of art could deposit an uncanny eternity at our doorstep, and his diagnosis has been proven prescient.

Since 1942, the time of his writing, we have inhabited an "eternity" of war—what Paul Virilio calls "pure war."[9] Living in

---

[9] "All of us are already civilian soldiers, without knowing it. . . . People don't recognize the militarized part of their identity, of their consciousness" (*Pure War* 18). Pure war, for Virilio, is a form of state terrorism, in which military logistics ("communications, vectorization" [20]) permeate everything because there's no *declaration* of war and thus no collectively directed—and therefore containable—effort. Pure war, ideologically transparent to everyday life, becomes a pervasive feature of consciousness. Jean-François Lyotard has indicated the direction taken by our unwholesome embrace of pure war in *The Inhuman*, a study of what persists (culturally) as *human* long after the "human" has failed to keep up with its inventions. Culture becomes a predatory force, using and disposing of raw human material, there being no goal, but simply a drive, a drive for *acceleration*. Lyotard's

England during the Blitz, David Jones was in a position to recognize and hail an emerging state that would remain invisible to many of his American counterparts involved in the war effort. In the United States the war meant productivity and economic resurgence for an overseas engagement. The war effort impinged on domestic life in the form of shortages, whereas in civilian combat zones such as England individuals were forced to confront the mentality of war as it became integrated with lifestyle and was thus purified in Virilio's sense. "The War has been reconfiguring time and space into its own image," Slothrop intuits in Pynchon's *Gravity's Rainbow* (257). "[T]he real business of the War is buying and selling," and the show of combat merely "serves as spectacle, as diversion from the real movements of the War" (105). In the U.S. we began to inhabit pure war only when it became available as the myth of "postwar." The communications technologies engineered by the hyperindustrious laboratories of the war became the predominant features of civil existence, so our way of inhabiting war has been thoroughly cozy. Television has given us the living room armageddon. It is fatally disorienting to imagine that television has anything to do with art, if art is analogous to charity. For the fact is that the television in the home converts the home into a virtual environment, a tactical linkup with technical weapons systems. This paramilitary reality emerged clearly for the first time during the Cuban missile crisis, and then with the assassination of President Kennedy. Every television monitor was annexed to the scope of a rifle, trained on a head of state, in a perpetual "rerun"

---

question then is "what if what is 'proper' to humankind were to be inhabited by the inhuman?" (2). What would our collective habitat, our culture, become, if we fell prey to the simple compulsion of an idea heedlessly realizing itself? Lyotard calls this force "development": "Development is not attached to an Idea, like that of the emancipation of reason and of human freedoms. It is reproduced by accelerating and extending itself according to its internal dynamic alone" (7). But Lyotard is cautioning us to beware the way in which we're in the grip of an ideology—not simply a system of ideas but "a power of realization" (6)—that has no identity, but has a power of industry to persist, parasitically, on its surrogate extensions, the prosthetic elaboration of its "tele-graphic" impulses. These impulses favor acceleration and abbreviation (3) and are anchored in microchip launching sites.

that became, in effect, a forecast of telecommunications' compliance with the state of pure war. The *focus* of that scope extends in an unbroken line from the Bay of Pigs to Bagdad. And it may be said with reasonable accuracy that the only possible resistance to the Gulf War was to *not watch tv.* It has been widely bemoaned that television trivializes serious issues and events; but, in light of research by Virilio and such books as *War in the Age of Intelligent Machines* by Manuel De Landa, it is evident that the reverse is the case. War and other forms of hostility have been domesticated, in a complex leasing arrangement whereby the civilian population *signs on* to technical systems developed militarily. And now, as more and more people in the humanities go online in the Internet, their precarious status increasingly becomes a matter of political concern, since, after all, this is a military communications network.

When poets rue the "competition" of television, they are ultimately registering their dismay that poetry will seem inept and unappealing in comparison with the technical lure of telecommunications, video games, or personal computers. Printed words—and even words sonorously declaimed—are subordinate to the glamour of weapons systems. This is not due to some deficiency in the use of words (though this is a claim made by traditionalists, that free verse laxities sink poetry because the technical basis of verse is eroded), but in the relation of words to the dominant systems. Instead of words that buzz with prosodic energy, and have a palpable heft, we have "buzz words." "In the sphere of art," Jones writes, "conditions can arise where the men of a whole culture are made eunuchs, owing to the particular demands that utility and materiality, profit and power make within that culture" (150). Language is a technology, a fact we forget amidst our proficiency with microchip technologies. Linguistic deficiency is a deprivation, "analogous to a sterilization or a castration" as Jones suggests. We are presently sustaining the loss of a "technology" with which—in the vocabulary of more recent technologies—we appear to be hardwired. The lapse of poetry is more serious than any supposed competition with television suggests, for what is at stake is

not simply cultural displacement but the erosion of a species'
trait.[10]

"Television culture is no oxymoron," James B. Twitchell
has recently written in *Carnival Culture*. "It is rapidly becoming the
species culture, the nervous system of the animal, just as print had
been for generations before" (261). Twitchell's "just as" is wrong:
print had prestige, but prestige does not occupy the nervous system
of a culture—furthermore, "generations" is misleading, since the
literate population was highly select until recently, with the advent
of compulsory mass education. The hours we log viewing television and movies, listening to the radio and to recordings, are a pervasive socio-physiological activity. It is a form of addictive behavior which the concept of prestige cannot begin to account for. We
are repeatedly exposed to incidents from around the world which
are reported under the rubric of the "hostage crisis." It is one of the
failsafe attention-grabbing news genres. What we fail to notice,
meanwhile, is the hostage *norm* that prevails in the fabric of everyday life. Herbert I. Schiller has analyzed this as a "corporate
takeover" or (more ominously) a "capture of the sites of public
expression" and Neil Postman characterizes it as the "surrender of
culture to technology" (to cite the subtitles of their books). Schiller

---

[10] The New Formalism has been seen as a vindication of prosody as a natural feature of the central nervous system, with iambic pentameter starring as
Consciousness Itself. The most vigorous champion of a return to metrical
rules as a bioenergetic adaptive mechanism of the species is Frederick Turner, whose *Natural Classicism* collects several influential essays, including
"The Neural Lyre: Poetic Meter, the Brain, and Time." Turner proposes "an
archaic genetic armature" as the basis for artistic value (11); but the useful
interdisciplinary research he has undertaken is unfortunately plagued by a
reactionary repudiation of "modernists" and "deconstructionists," the sim-
pleminded bogeys in his account who lack standards, refuse to play by the
rules, and are somehow accountable for a collapse of story, an abandonment
of prosody, a defiant assault on representation in the visual arts and on
melody in music. There are obvious parallels between Turner's critique of
modernism and Adolf Hitler's, in that both are disposed to see a biomedical
disorder at the root of nontraditional activities in the arts. While I respect
Turner's insistence on a biogenetic patrimony for the creative impulse, I
find it absurd to insist, as he does, that "rules must be followed" (222). For a
more detailed critique, see Rasula, "The Catastrophe of Charm" (1987).

chronicles the procedures by which the corporate "host" inverts its parasitic nature by media control, or to be precise, by ownership. "The American audience remains encapsulated in a corporate-message cocoon" (168). The airwaves, for instance, are public access in principle, but are deeded to private interests (like television networks) that are in fact monopolies. (It is impossible to imagine NBC having its license revoked.) The "corporate-message cocoon" Schiller refers to is constituted not only by the conspicuous "sponsor" whose logo appears in commercial breaks, but by the program itself as well. If the program is seen as bait, it's clear that the real activity of television is the network herding of its audience into contractual enclosures for the benefit of the sponsors. The networks are press gangs, hijacking and conscripting demographically desirable populations for the private uses of sponsoring corporations. We inhabit a hostage situation that is not recognized as a crisis simply because it's so pervasive, durable, normative.

It is regarded as a crisis only by those who feel themselves impinged upon as cultural producers, like poets. Culture is an ideologically intensive labor, not at all the leisure activity which corporate sponsorship makes it out to be. We work hard to stay relaxed: such is the tacit message of the media, the First Commandment of which is "Stay Tuned." Poets have keenly felt the ways public space has been privatized.[11] The often hectoring rhetoric of ambitious poets is in fact a profoundly agonized howl of alarm: Ginsberg's "Howl" is the most shrewdly named poem of the period. It is a cry of dismay at the species' auto-dismemberment. Poetry, as a minor public servant in the cultural disciplines, finds itself with little to do but to perpetuate the legend of its own dignity. The humanities as a whole are socially conscripted in a service arrangement—wherein the corporate raider becomes an arts benefactor, and the arts cozy up accordingly—and if television is denounced as

---

[11] Anthologists have absorbed poetry into a public display of privacy which compromises the prodigious poetic labor of resistance. To make an analogy: one might assume, from the contents of anthologies—not to mention the prevailing idiom of free verse—that *history* is sufficiently represented by "Kodak moments."

a kind of mental whoring, it must be admitted that poetry is little different, even if it would aspire to a more dignified directory listing like "escort service." To admit this is to concede that any "crisis" of poetry is at present a public relations fiasco. Few people actually *care* whether poetry is written, so whether it is written well or poorly is a moot point, and what is written *about* it is of even less consequence.

I am speaking of poetry as public event, which is to say as commodity, for that's the only kind of event recognized as public in the U.S.—a commodity manifesting itself politically as the "photo opportunity." A replay in a baseball game may receive corporate sponsorship—a "Norelco Highlight"—but poetry is obviously not interested in securing this kind of attention. It would be impressive if it could!—imagine opening the latest volume by Marge Piercy, and finding corporate logos gracing the white space at the bottom of the pages. This kind of presence is a *detailing* of the environment, but while the individual logo may be perishable, or in place for a limited duration, the conversion of public space to the insignia of corporate sponsorship ultimately revokes the public dimension altogether, as the *logos* gives way to the logo. Corporate sponsors' logos are appearing with greater frequency and ingenuity—on tennis players' T-shirt sleeves, between yard-line markers on football fields—and it is easy to imagine that the entire public realm may eventually give way to the billboard syndrome. The "reality effect" anatomized by Barthes has been adopted by the major corporations as a cost-effective form of advertising. The casual baseball cap or T-shirt that reads "Nike" migrates effectively through the pedestrian milieu, its bearer unpaid for what is, after all, manual—or, to be precise, pedal—labor. By these and other means the environment is being tattooed, the public realm stenciled with fine-print instructions for care and maintenance of the corporate sponsors and their servomechanisms, those agents of subjectivity that are, even now, nostalgically referred to as "citizens." Politics, as Murray Bookchin attests, "has acquired a sneeringly pejorative meaning" which attends "the transformation of citizens from publicly active human beings into atomized, trivialized 'constituencies' who are preoccupied with their individual survival in a world over which they exercise no control. This wound is still hemorrhaging in the 'body politic' and threatens to bleed people of all their humanity" (28).

Charles Olson may have been the last poet to address himself to fellow inhabitants of this threatened polis as "citizens." It is difficult for us, in the 1990s, to transport ourselves back forty years to Olson's early *Maximus Poems* without suspecting him of either some campy usage or political naiveté. But the bite of his plaint still holds, in his objection to

> . . . words, words, words
> all over everything.
> > No eyes or ears left
> to do their own doing (all
>
> invaded, appropriated, outraged . . .
> > > (*Maximus* 17)

It is only recently that the outrage, so evident as an affliction of the domestic economy in *Maximus*, has been restored to Olson's *oeuvre* as the global afterbirth of pure war. As had been known before, Olson abandoned a budding political career for poetry in the aftermath of the atomic bomb and the disclosure of the Holocaust. But the appearance of the *Collected Poems*, edited by George Butterick (1987), made it clear that Olson turned to poetry as the most imaginatively expedient means of reckoning the cost, to the species, of such historical traumatization.[12] The documentation of postwar American poetry, unfortunately, continues to mark the threshold of the new world order in terms of the formalist privacies of Lowell and Roethke; and critical reckoning has favored Stevens's rhetoric of a "violence within" as its preferred response to the "violence

---

[12] The most pertinent early poem remains "La Préface," previously published. *The Collected Poems* contextualizes it amidst several years' obsessions with the Holocaust's industrial absorption of human flesh as fuel for the ovens (as in "The Town," "A Lustrum for You, E. P." and "Canto One Hundred and One").

without"—one consequence of which is the formal segregation of the testimonial impulse in Carolyn Forché's Norton anthology *Against Forgetting: Twentieth-Century Poetry of Witness*, a project which is trivialized by its genre; so Forché's documentary of political violence is topically coded, one among a series of options ranging from Bly's anthology of men's poetry to inanities like *The Poetry of Chess.*

William Carlos Williams's portrait of a quite different sort of *violence within* is instructive of how frail the fulcrum of political awareness is amidst the minutiae that constitute a poetic terrain:

> What is there to say? save that
> beauty is unheeded   . tho' for sale and
> bought glibly enough
>
>   But it is true, they fear
> it more than death, beauty is feared
> more than death, more than they fear death
>
>   Beautiful thing
>
> —and marry only to destroy, in private, in
> their privacy only to destroy, to hide
>   (in marriage)
> that they may destroy and not be perceived
> in it—the destroying
>
>   (*Paterson* 106)

Williams, like Olson, was stricken by "So much talk of the language—when there are no/ ears." Milton's "paradise within," so forcefully inhabited by Stevens, refuses to admit such corporeal erosion. But in the matter of poetics the issue may be simply put: is poetry—that paradise—sullied by speaking the offending names? Is it all the same, for instance, to say Satan where Hitler is meant, as implied by Wallace Stevens's line "The deer and the dachsund are one" (*Palm* 153). Stevens skirted the issue by populating his poems with baroque figures with names like Phosphor, Ercole, Nanzia Nunzio, Professor Eucalyptus and Mrs. Alfred Uruguay, and the barest smattering of "real" people like Nietzsche and Santayana (and only then somewhat anonymously, as the "old philosopher in Rome").[13] It may be said on his behalf that Stevens was composing in that sublime space of the "interior paramour" a poetic equivalent to the Unknown Soldier—an Unknown Auditor. But this is in a time "when there are no / ears." So what is to be addressed, the persisting echolalia of the mind, or the "violence without" that has clipped the ears in the first place?

THE REAL WAR AND THE BOOKS

One of the more conspicuous political gestures made by a poet in the 1960s was Robert Bly's use of the 1968 National Book Award ceremony to denounce his publisher's tacit support of the war in Vietnam. Bly handed over his prize money (for *The Light Around the Body*, published by Harper & Row) to the draft resisters' league. But this was a rare forum, a fortuitous coupling of public occasion and the will to assert political values. Another, more private, protest was registered by Robert Lowell when he declined an invitation by Lyndon Johnson to the White House, reportedly infuriating the President. The milieu of protest surrounding the war provided a handy forum for poets to make effective political declarations, but that platform was short-lived—and was also readily viewed as opportunistic, even in the case of a committed activist like Denise Levertov. In Bly's topically and autobiographically arranged *Selected Poems* in 1986 he prefaced the section of war poems with these reflections:

---

[13] As with the belated attention to the actual media environment as impinging on poetry, it is only in the last few years that Stevens scholars have discovered the novelty of situating Stevens in the "real world." See the challenging articles collected in Albert Gelpi, ed., *Wallace Stevens: The Poetics of Modernism* (1985); and Alan Filreis, *Wallace Stevens and the Actual World* (1991), Thomas C. Grey, *The Wallace Stevens Case: Law and the Practice of Poetry* (1991), and Mark Halliday, *Stevens and the Interpersonal* (1991).

> The war brought a new corruption of language. The practice
> of doing ugly things, then describing them in bland words
> . . . became national policy. Since the leaders admitted to
> no shadow, the opposition called them all shadow, and the
> exaggerations on both sides damaged the language of public
> debate in the United States. By the end of the war, I felt
> some affinity gone in me, and I wanted to return to privacy
> rather than to go on judging, useful as judgment is. (63)

Bly's long antiwar poem "The Teeth Mother Naked at Last" had
already expressed the weariness vividly in 1970: "We all feel like
tires being run down roads under heavy cars" (*Selected* 83). Bly recognized, as so many of the politically engaged poets did, that too
deep a submersion in demagoguery—even in a good cause—would
begin to infect the language of poetry.[14] Some, like W. S. Merwin,
had foreseen this prior to the protests, and his war poems in *The
Lice* and *The Carrier of Ladders* seem now inscrutably resolved back
into the tone of intimate anonymity he had been nurturing since the
late fifties. Only the title of "The Asians Dying" provides any clue to
the identity of the victims: "Rain falls into the open eyes of the dead /
Again again with its pointless sound" (*Lice* 63). Robert Lowell, who
led the most *public* career among officially prominent postwar
poets, refrained from writing antiwar poetry, while he did participate in many antiwar acts. His much belabored and scintillating
book-length sequence *History*, read in the wrong frame of mind, can
seem like a perplexing and interminable mumble, somehow curt
and wordy at the same time. Like Bly, Lowell emerged from the Viet
Nam years wearied to the core: "Sometimes I sink a thousand centuries / bone tired then stone-asleep" he begins "Memorial Day" at
the end of *History*, " . . . But nothing will be put back right in time /
done over, thought through straight for once . . . " (206).

---

[14] Bly's account of the cessation of antiwar sentiment highlights those issues
which would emerge as his characteristic concerns from 1975 to the present—male bonding (*Iron John*) and ecology (*News of the Universe*): "After its
years of storm, the war ended in 1975. The war had eroded the confidence of
men in each other, especially the confidence of younger men in older men,
and it emphasized how estranged from nature the entire nation was. It was as
if the hostile mountain spirit had defeated the entire nation."

The weariness, as it happens, may have had less to do with war than with decades of *postwar*. "War, in all its senses, is the condition not the crisis of our lives; this at least we know in the late forties," wrote Leslie Fiedler in his *Partisan Review* statement for its symposium on American literature in 1948 (875). Shapiro later lamented that "the tragedy of our generation . . . was that our army never melted away. It remained, it grew bigger, it was more and more all over the world. It became a way of life, the state . . . " (*Children* 153).[15] Robert Bly, too, remarked that "[t]he continuity of our wars stretches through each of us" (*American Poetry* 135). Of the antiwar poets, only Robert Duncan persisted in the exploration of war as an outbreak of hostilities latent not only socially and psychologically but also cosmologically. Volume One of his final two-volume *summa, Ground Work*, subtitled *Before the War*, is a quest for a time before chaos and strife, a topological orientation as well as a spatial discovery, since "before" also means "in front of." The poet, exploring the war as his mirror—and therefore imaging himself (as on a video screen) as a *monitor* of the war, discovers warlike intimations of another self:

> I know but part of it and that   but distantly,
> a catastrophe in another place, another time,
>   the mind addresses
> and would erect within itself   itself
>   as Viet Nam
>
> . . .
>
>   For a moment,
> ephemeral,   we keep
> alive in the deepening shame of Man,
>   this room where we are,   this house,
>   this garden,   this home
>   our art would make
>   in what is threatend from within.
>
> (*Ground Work: Before the War* 80, 81)

---

[15] Shapiro, sensitive not only to the militarization of domestic life in the fifties, but himself a veteran of World War II, had an unorthodox but accurate way of assessing what was at stake regarding "form": "An overnight collapse of the stanza might be as dangerous as the abolition of the army," he mocked. "Poets still need close-order drill and the barracks mentality," adding that "poets are still the hostages of convention" (*Children* 58).

In *Ground Work* Duncan served notice that he, at least, felt the Blakean force of Stevens's distinction between a violence within and a violence without as the given terms of an empowering poetic dialectic, neither of which would be realized without the other. Duncan's preoccupation culminated in the exceedingly powerful sequence "Regulators" in *Ground Work II: In the Dark*, in which he followed out wartime malignancies on a Manichean scale, through the bloodstream into the molecular rage of infection, and out to an ominous "peace" that did not surpass his understanding:

> The other face of the Angel, not now   of War but of Peace-
>   time uses—
>   from the promised power stations   radioactive
>   waste   death-leakings
>
>   come into the hour glass.
>
>   (*Ground Work II* 70)

Even in Duncan's last published poem, "After an Illness," the spectre of war is a paradigm for life as such:

>   ... In the World, death after death.
> In this realm,   no last thrall of Life stirs.
>   The imagination alone knows this condition.
> As if this were before the War,   before
>   What Is,   in the dark this state
> that knows nor sleep nor waking, nor dream
>   —an eternal arrest.
>
>   (*Ground Work II* 90)

With this, Duncan is where he'd want to be; concluding with Dante the task of resolving public crisis in spiritual autobiography. It is an old and venerable journey which few poets have undertaken, and even fewer managed with success.

As in so many other things, Whitman and Dickinson, in their response to the Civil War, set the definitive American precedent for hearing war as a turbulence of the soul. The elaborate arrangement of poems Whitman devised in 1860, to absorb into *Leaves of Grass* the prodigious outpouring following the first two editions in 1855–56, was smashed in the next few years by the hostilities of long campaigns, Washington ballrooms and offices alike filled with the wounded he nursed. Later, in *Specimen Days* when Whitman collected his wartime notes and observations, he included a few pages on the subject of how "The Real War Will Never Get in the Books"—implying, uneasily, that what got into *his* book was not the real war either. In the final arrangement the war poems are, as it were, under quarantine in "Drum Taps." There, the booster rhetoric is not quite Whitman's familiar swag, a shade too porous to prevailing sentiment. The elegies for Lincoln are paradigmatic: there is "Lilacs . . . " which is suffused with Whitman's personal vulnerability, in contrast to which is "O Captain! My Captain!" which he later came to despise for its enduring popularity. Whitman left two legacies for politics in poetry with these two laments, a private record and a public record; he also left a precedent for American poets' frequent repudiation of the public record, the poem tainted by its complicity with the public mood.

Since Whitman, the vexing issue of politics in poetry has continued to be aggravated by the ambiguity of American political discourse in the first place, as well as by the shifting planes of attention which various literary strategies put forward, obscuring the view of their ideological parameters. The nature of American politics precludes poetry as a significant social discourse; so the choice of poetry as a medium instantly sidelines the poet. The poetic voice is devoid of political consequence. We lack, for instance, a tradition of political song, which in Latin American countries provides the material base for a genuinely political poetry for a mass audience. Furthermore, the adaptability of the novel to mass-market circulation has proven especially preemptive of any social status for poetry. The espionage thriller, escapist though it may be, requires considerable complicity on the part of the reader to make the historic/political data cohere; whereas comparably information-intensive poetry appears esoteric and remote, inviting pedantic response at best. We have nothing quite like the epic ambition of Pablo Neruda (excepting perhaps Pound, who is hardly a populist), documenting the political destiny of Latin America in *Canto General* and interweaving the politically topical with the psychotropic phantasmagoria of surrealism in *Residencia en la Tierra.* Apart from Neruda's poetic gift, however, his work persists in part because Latin America continues to inhabit the same historical dimension, its people struggling with the same conditions and issues. In the U.S., by contrast, the political verse of the Depression compassionately resurrected by Cary Nelson in *Repression and Recovery* often reads like bulletins from another planet. It's not that the poetry has expired, but that we suffer from such severe cultural amnesia that the parameters of political reality faced by our parents and grandparents have prematurely become a *terra incognita.*

Reflecting on his decision to abandon poetry during the Depression, George Oppen remarked that a poem is simply not a politically efficacious form: "If you decide to do something politically, you do something that has political efficacy. And if you decide to write poetry, then you write poetry, not something that you hope, or deceive yourself into believing, can save people who are suffering" ("Interview" 187). Oppen unwittingly discloses the real problem here, which is determining what can possibly be politically efficacious in a world in which "politics" is itself a form of show business. We might even fancifully refer to national politics as a "poetry" of public gesture—albeit maudlin and embarrassing. (Surely, though, George Bush's "thousand points of light" has to be reckoned America's most successful haiku.) For Oppen, in the 1930s, it was clear how to proceed if one made the choice to abandon poetry for politics. This is no longer the case. Following a trip to the (old) Soviet Bloc—where censorship politicized all literary activity—Clayton Eshleman lamented that in the United States "You cannot speak versus / you can say anything and it does not matter" (*Hades* 58). Increasingly, Americans have come to feel that you can *do* anything and that that, too, fails to make a difference. If political efficacy is hard to find even in the domain of politics, it's still more difficult to imagine the political business a poet might propose to take up.

In the postwar decades there have been few, if any, prominent poets possessed of anything like Kenneth Rexroth's polymathic political savvy; instead, we have had enthusiasts, partisans, and the occasional "village explainer" (to use Gertrude Stein's disparaging tag for Pound). Some of the more durable political roles occupied by American poets have included the public-personality activism of Allen Ginsberg, Adrienne Rich, and Amiri Baraka, and the ecological regionalism of Gary Snyder and Wendell Berry. There is also the deeply considered determination to write a poetry responsive to human rights violations, exemplified in the work of Clayton Eshleman. Jerome Rothenberg's ceaseless quest for an ethnopoetics—an ongoing consultation with non-Eurocentric traditions, coupled with a strong affiliation to the European avant-garde—precedes the current enthusiasm for post-colonial and minority literatures; and "Khurbn" (1989), his poem confronting ancestral losses in the Holocaust, is one of the most moving sustained threnodies of the postwar era. But Rothenberg's poem, with its debt to surrealism, is not likely to be counted as "political," even in so enervated a sense of that word as applies in the U.S. The great cultural traumas—ecological disaster, refugee populations, genocide, starvation—which might otherwise be cited as political have little political status here, because they're not public policy categories. Politics "as usual" is simply the administration of resources, and the allocation of funds and funding opportunities. So the continuing plight of refugees (which Hannah Arendt identified as the single dominant feature of the modern world order [266–302]) is reduced to a regional nuisance.

It is perhaps a sign of the continuing decline of the cultural prominence of poets that only Carolyn Forché, among a younger generation, has achieved recognition as an American "political poet"—an anomolous tag, considering that the "politics" of The Country Between Us is exclusively focused on El Salvador. Forché, in other words, is what I would call an *issue-oriented* poet, a practice that has emerged as the most dominant gathering ground for readers motivated by non-aesthetic considerations. The issue-oriented, socially expository poetry of women, gays, and ethnic minorities has generated a more motivated readership than the work of those whose appeal is simply that they may be "good" poets. This is a salutary sign that poetry may yet be taken as news that stays news. Ron Silliman has speculated that the yearly total of reported rapes in the U. S. exceeds the total number of volumes of poetry sold ("Political Economy" 59). An appalling statistic, it nonetheless suggests one reason for the predominance of topical, experience-oriented women's poetry: whether it addresses the experience of rape, or simply conveys feelings of vulnerability, such work clearly leads to dialogue, solidarity, and political conviction. The risk run by topical poetry, however, is it may prove to be expendable after its suit is resolved. But it's an interesting symptom of our situation that this is seen as a liability, for it testifies to our compulsive need for *monumentality*, for works that "endure" in part because they appear to have no local applicability. In fact, poems stripped of defining context—epitomized by those of Mark Strand—occupy a locale *so* local it's virtually private; and even in less extreme cases the verse masquerades as an *Architectural Digest* photospread of fabulously appointed mental and emotional interiors.

Politics depicted in or by means of poems may reflect poetic value; but then, poetic value (as in Blake or Pound) is likely to generate its own matrix of political reference. Poetic value is a kind of capital invested in the genre itself, the genre as institution. "Genres are essentially literary *institutions*," Fredric Jameson contends, "or social contracts between a writer and a specific public, whose function is to specify the proper use of a particular cultural artifact" (*Unconscious* 106). While Jameson has done much to illuminate the "political unconscious" of the modern novel, it would be expedient to consider the lingering contractual arrangements between readers and writers of lyric poetry—particularly in light of the ways in which the poem (as Jameson says of narrative in the novel) is an "ideologeme whose outer form, secreted like a shell or exoskeleton, continues to emit its ideological message long after the extinction of its host" (151). We have grown accustomed to hearing repeated declarations of the "continuity" of a tradition. Such claims may be recognized as precisely the sort of ideological emission Jameson cites, particularly in this century of a permanent avant-garde and the revoking of genre as social contract. Tradition (and its "individual talent") is an ideologeme that insists that the pleasures of poetry as genre continue unabated, and that the exchange value of a certain experience is holding steady. The official coverage of postwar American poetry—on the part of editors, reviewers, and scholars—has tended to operate like the FDIC, ensuring coverage of emotional currency invested in the Bank of the First Person Singular. But, as I argue in the previous chapter, this has amounted to a *cover story* at best.

POLITICS OF THE REFERENT

In a forum on *Politics and Poetic Value* in 1987, Charles Altieri was invited by the editor, Robert von Hallberg, to respond to Jerome McGann's "Contemporary Poetry, Alternate Routes." Altieri appears to believe in the social contract that stipulates for poetry a role in public life commensurate with its concessions to public discourse. He insists that poetry is devoid of political consequence unless it submits itself to "those accommodations to a collective that are the precondition of effective social action" ("Consequence" 307). But as Altieri must realize, politics in the United States has itself constantly made concessions to the ascendant public rhetoric of self-promotion and product endorsement. (If we look for accommodations of this order in contemporary poetry, a caterwauling legion of candidates presses forward, including the Care Bears soft-touch of Hugh Prather, the carnival geek antics of Charles Bukowski, and the soft-core pop surrealism of Mark Strand.) McGann, for his part, draws on von Hallberg's distinction (in *American Poetry and Culture, 1945–1980*) between a poetry of accommodation and a poetry of opposition ("Alternate" 255). This distinction is highly misleading as a political measure. As Altieri readily observes, formally conservative poets can be just as oppositional in their politics as any of the language poets celebrated by McGann.[16]

---

[16] I delete the equal signs from between the letters of "language," and shift back and forth between references to language writing and language poetry in order to make the generic specification productively fuzzy. McGann says "I think the institutional character of this movement should be emphasized" (255, *n*4), speaking of "L=A=N=G=U=A=G=E Writing" in order to preserve the graphic trace of the spelling of the flagship magazine of a generation of affiliated "language poets." By iterating institution, McGann contaminates his reading of language writing by alleging a consistency antithetical to what even he admits is a "loose collective enterprise." For more on the imposed coherence of a "collective author" for language poetry, see Michael Greer (1989).

The problem with this distinction is that it posits politics as a realm separate from poetry, which poetry can only report on or represent, by means of "analogies drawn from specific effects" (305). In this account, poetry is inevitably secondary, stripped of whatever political issues might be found intrinsic to its own arena of action. But there is, in fact, more than politics *in* the poem; there is also a politics *of* poetry, and this is what language poets have largely chosen to address from the outset. "All writing," insists Charles Bernstein, "is a demonstration of method; it can assume a method or investigate it" (*Tree* 590).[17]

The politics of poetry is not predicated on the façade of "opposition" versus "accommodation": this is, rather, a distinction to be made about the politics of poets as citizens. Bernstein discerns two methodologies that provide a more generative polarity:

> Compare / these two views / of what / poetry / is.
> In the one, an instance (a recording perhaps) of reality / fantasy / experience / event is presented to us through the writing.
> In the other, the writing itself is seen as an instance of reality / fantasy / experience / event. (*LB* 41)

In the first view, the issue of oppositional practice is mitigated right away, because there is *already an accommodation* to an unexamined medium. Language writing, by embracing the second view, approaches the poem in a clinical way to discover what sort of reality or event was constituted by the medium of language—both as a "given," and as deconstructed, interrupted, estranged in transmission.

The investigations undertaken by language poets go back twenty years, and it's now possible to see a third view of poetry emerging in practice: poetry as presenting a reality/fantasy/experience/event through writing which at the same time examines its own

---

17 For the reader's convenience—and also to illustrate the diversity of views collected in the two primary anthologies of Language-centered writing— most of the citations in this section are drawn from *In the American Tree* edited by Ron Silliman (1986, cited as *Tree*), and *The L=A=N=G=U=A=G=E Book* edited by Bruce Andrews and Charles Bernstein (1984, cited as *LB*).

material exigence, its own self-exposition discovered to be an event charged with partisanship *beyond* the neutrality which any (re)presentational transparency would suggest. Surely the initial investigations of language writing have been disseminated broadly if Jorie Graham—a MacArthur recipient and faculty member at the Iowa Writers Workshop, and thus as "mainstream" a figure as anyone in her generation—can submit her work in *The End of Beauty* and *Region of Unlikeness* to strategies of forwarding the device; strategies that, a decade earlier, would hardly have endeared her to a critic like Helen Vendler. A skeptic might simply call the diversification of individual talent among the core language writers "poetic maturity." If language poetry is undergoing a comparable seasoning, it is not attributable to the determination of an isolated coterie, but to a thoroughly prepared foreground of provocations and instructive irresolutions. This century's project in American poetics has been a continual examination of assumptions and first principles, from Pound, Williams, Stein, Stevens, Moore, Riding and cummings through Zukofsky, Olson, Duncan, Creeley, and such immediate progenitors of language poetry as Jack Spicer, Jackson Mac Low, David Antin, and Jerome Rothenberg.

Given this tradition of a radical, investigative poetics, what is confounding in retrospect is the continuing prevalence of formally conservative (not necessarily "accommodational"), self-expressive, family-snapshot verse. This tendency is obviously buttressed by the proliferation of workshops, at both professional and recreational levels, in which poetry acquires the accessory functionalism of arts and crafts. A Marxist analysis might recognize in this a good example of the continued existence of an obsolete mode of production. The work of Amy Clampitt or J. D. McClatchy, then, might prove interesting by comparison with bestselling fiction, where its filigree artistry could be more instructively compared with that of Anne Rice or John Cheever than with the poetry of Lyn Hejinian or W. S. Merwin. Considering such work from the point of view of dialectical materialism, Raymond Williams describes this as "writing of a residual kind," and adds that "most writing, in any period, including our own, is a form of contribution to the effective dominant culture" (44). Jonathan Raban has char-

acterized the predominant verse practice as "low mimetic realism,"
stating that it "deliberately compromises itself by submitting to the
only common, available language that we have, [that of] the submerged and mortgaged middle class, that is promoted by property
developers, television advertisements, feature writers for popular
newspapers, and politicians with the common touch" (137, 72). Such
writing has as its main social consequence the maintenance of recreational literacy; Auden's passion for crossword puzzles is symptomatic. It appeals at its highest level (Merrill, Hecht, Bishop) to a commitment to the civilizing pleasures of style, taste, and sensibility; and
at its lowest to a faith in literary masquerade as a way of life.

The great liability of the mode of low mimetic realism is its
unexamined urge to find the soft emotional center of its issues. But
as Canadian poet Brian Fawcett noted in *L=A=N=G=U=A=G=E*, "the
emotional is the least reliable source of information we now have,
because it's the most thoroughly manipulated" (*LB* 154). Poetry that
is often credited as "political" actually consists more of *mood* than
of any developed political consciousness. Furthermore, it is formally
cautious in direct proportion to the anticipated size of the audience.
One of the agonies of reading such work is witnessing the awkward
obligation of political reference while the poet struggles to sustain a
swollen poetic intensity. Adrienne Rich bluntly admits in "Contradictions: Tracking Poems," that there may be "no art to this but
anger" (*Native Land* 98). She also concedes there the risk of a writing
"in danger of mistaking / our personal trouble for the pain on the
streets" (101). But what does it mean that we so readily succumb to
politics in poetry if it's grounded in methods of emotional manipulation? The ultimate "accommodational" argument would be that this
is absolutely consistent with the dominant culture of movies,
records, and television; as such, it has its proper historical role to
play as an unwitting chronicle of its time. By the same token, however, the most accurate chronicle would be the most vitiated poetry.
The claim for representational viability conflicts with the urge to
acclaim excellence.

The resentment caused by language writing in some circles in
recent years is a sign that the unexamined emotional center of low

mimetic realism (that Ford Mustang of the American lyric) has been impinged upon.[18] It's doubtful that this can be attributed to a conscientious reading of the numerous theoretical publications by language poets; it appears, rather, to be a rudimentary alarm at the spectre of group solidarity. The very notion of the group is worth examining since, as Bernstein observed in "The Conspiracy of 'Us'," as soon as there was external opposition to a perceived group identity of "language-centered" poets, " . . . what's in common within and different from without both [got] exaggerated" (*LB* 186). Group identity among language poets was initially a matter of internal cohesion of the sort needed to sustain local dialogue and facilitate debate, set up a structural network of publication and distribution, and mount readings and talk series—in other words, to make public the conceptual underpinnings of issues that had originated in private exchange. The term "language poetry" should be taken strictly as an historical marker for the willingness of a few dozen American poets to go public, in the late 1970s, in a mutually supportive way. It was not, as Bernstein cautioned in 1979, "the latest fashion splash of the 'up & coming'" (*LB* 187). There was no party doctrine, in the manner of surrealism; language poets were not signatories to any manifestos or circulars. Yet now, with articles by Lee Bartlett, Albert Gelpi, Marjorie Perloff, and Jerome McGann—and books or chapters in books by a younger generation of scholars—"language poetry" has acquired a portable new façade, reconstituted from the outside.[19] Language poetry has been made to speak in a unified or typical voice, in which the internal disputes and diversity are, in effect, erased. The tactical issues that formed rallying points for a fairly diverse group of writers have become ripe for interpretive codification. A unified group identity is so unproblematically given that the moniker "L=A=N=G=U=A=G=E Writing" reappears in Altieri's critique of

---

[18] Throughout the 1980s pages of the Bay Area's *Poetry Flash* sustained an emotional polemic from both sides. Some of this spilled over in the doctored objectivity of Tom Clark's "'Stalin as Linguist,'" *Partisan Review* 2 (1987).

[19] Gelpi's essay on "The Genealogy of Postmodernism" is indicative of the inclination to speak disparagingly of the group in order to single out exemptions—in his words, "to sort out the mandarins from the poets" (537).

McGann without a flicker of hesitation. That Altieri should not even have raised the issue of group solidarity is the clearest indication of McGann's persuasiveness on this point.

McGann reads Bernadette Mayer's "Experiments" (reprinted in *The L=A=N=G=U=A=G=E Book*) as a "mini-manual" of orthodox language writing procedures. But Mayer is in fact singled out by Barrett Watten in *Total Syntax* as evidence of a structural liability of the avant-garde:

> While the advantage of Mayer's techniques is their adherence to the quotidian, there is no further integration. The "permanent avant-garde" vaporizes, leading to more conventional roles. As actually happened—in the course of Mayer's later editing of *United Artists*, the stylistic opening-up returns all these techniques to "the self." (56–57)

The impediment of McGann's approach is further signalled by his repeated formulation that Language writing "typically" argues a case univocally, or by such prescriptive phrases as "in the view of L=A=N=G=U=A=G=E Writing . . . " ("Alternate" 266).[20] Language poetry, it would appear, offers an exemplary opportunity for exploring Raymond Williams's recommendation of Lucien Goldmann's concept of the "collective subject": "For it is no longer the reduction of individuals to a group, by some process of averaging; it is a way of seeing a group in and through individual differences: that specificity of individuals, and of their individual creations, which does not deny but is the necessary way of affirming their real social identities . . . " (28–29). This project is impeded by the compulsion to typify collective effort—even when practiced, as by McGann, in the most benign and supportive spirit.

What distinguishes language poetry from similar group efforts is that it was contested as actively from within as from without, during its formative years. Barrett Watten, editor of *This* and

---

[20] Language Poets "*typically* foreground their oppositional politics . . . " (256), McGann writes, acknowledging that his goal is "to indicate the kind of intervention L=A=N=G=U=A=G=E work *typically* seeks to make . . . " (258). He subsequently argues that this work "*typically* deploys a consciously antithetical political content" (263, emphasis mine).

subsequently co-editor with Lyn Hejinian of *Poetics Journal*, observed that "attempts at a program seem to divide the stylistic congruence into dissimilar intents" (*Tree* 485). Bruce Andrews, co-editor of *L=A=N=G=U=A=G=E* with Charles Bernstein, cautioned that such formalist explorations as those pursued by language poets "may risk a more homogenized meaninglessness," bound as they were to be perpetually outstripped by the maniacal inventiveness of the capitalist pitch (*LB* 135). "Indeed, all forms," wrote Bernstein, "all modes, all methods are coercive in that they have a relation to power" (*Tree* 597). Steve McCaffery noted, "[t]he danger in *L=A=N=G=U=A=G=E* would be a certain ossification around the area of consensus and the rigidifying of its heteroglossia into a monologic canon" (119). Catchwords like "nonreferentiality" and "language-centered" were attacked in the early pages of *L=A=N=G=U=A=G=E* by Jackson Mac Low, a dean of chance-generated and other procedural compositional techniques, who pointedly asked "What could be more of a fetish or more alienated than slices of language stripped of reference?" (*Tree* 492).[21] Ron Silliman astringently branded language poetry as "the grouping together of several, not always compatible, tendencies within 'high bourgeois' literature" (*LB* 168). Such withering assessments usually come from outside a group, not from its supposed members.

While a common agenda was clearly a motive in the formation of disparate writers into a network (predominately New York, Washington D.C., and the San Francisco Bay), it must be stressed that diversity of opinion proved the most significant bonding agent.

---

[21] Mac Low's point was later more famously elaborated by Fredric Jameson in his essay on postmodernism as the cultural logic of late capitalism, in which he took Bob Perelman's poem "China" as symptomatic of the latest trends. Elsewhere, Jameson succinctly summarizes the problem which continues to vex language poetry and poetics: "For when modernism and its accompanying techniques of 'estrangement' have become the dominant style whereby the consumer is reconciled with capitalism, the habit of fragmentation itself needs to be 'estranged' and corrected by a more totalizing way of viewing phenomena" ("Reflections" 211). Of course, this is to accede to the directive force of capitalism as the tail to the horse: whatever "corrections" are devised in opposition to dominant styles are still subservient, in that they require a dominant style in the first place to substantiate their critiques.

> The abrasive assertiveness and lack of agreement among
> persons of warmly shared interests encourages them to
> reconsideration of individual custom. The truism that the
> only people who now read poetry are themselves poets is
> thus understood rather as potential than as limitation: the
> reader is presumed not as a consumer of the experience
> sustained by the poem but as a fellow writer who shares
> contentiously in the work and can willingly answer the
> uses of the medium which the writer feels impelled to
> undertake. . . . (Benson, *Tree* 486)

Steve Benson here situates language writing within a contested site.
He makes evident the most notable stance common to language
poets: membership in a community of *readers.* It is a socially singular phenomenon that poets should come together as active readers of
one another's work rather than, as is the custom, mutual celebrants
of poetry as initiatory cult.

Reading through the mass of theoretical statements and position papers in *The L=A=N=G=U=A=G=E Book, In the American
Tree*, and the book-length issue of *L=A=N=G=U=A=G=E/Open Letter*
(Volume 4), it's evident that the only issues about which a consensus
may be said to have been reached were the restoration of the reader
as coproducer of the text, and an emphasis on the materiality of the
signifier. Yet even these—commonplaces of poststructuralism in
other venues—are subject to reconsideration. Steve McCaffery, for
instance, discovered that

> In light of the Baudrillardian "proof" that use value is but a
> concealed species of exchange value, I would say now that
> the gestural "offer" to a reader of an invitation to "semanti-
> cally produce" hints at an ideological contamination. (124)

This is the same contamination, I would suggest, that Charles Altieri
notices when he says that "many of McGann's images of class struggle
and projections of audience freedom and responsibility can easily be
recast to reflect basic capitalist practices . . . " ("Consequence" 305).
He then poses a pertinent question: " . . . is not such freedom to recast
inherited materials a perfect exemplar of the right to treat language as

a commodity to be manipulated?" It was the overdetermined commod-
ification of language as such that provided the initial incentive for the
founding of the journal *L=A=N=G=U=A=G=E*. The resolve shared by
the editors and the contributing authors was to explore the politics of
a literary bill of rights that would *not* admit of "the right to treat language as a commodity to be manipulated"—not, at any rate, without
protest (and a large dose of theoretical analysis). The notion of a *right*
to manipulate language as a commodity presupposes a diminished
language, fit only for consumption, not communication. Emphasizing
the materiality of the signifier is one way of indicating the excess, the
surplus, residual to language above and beyond any call of duty in a
system; but it risks reifying distraction in a new complacency—as
Adrienne Rich warns, remarking that "[avant-garde] attempts to shat-
ter structures of meaning may very well be complicit with a system
that depends on our viewing our lives as random and meaningless or,
at best, unserious" (*What Is Found There* 226–27).

But language is larger than any of us—and "language itself
can be experienced as other" (Blaser, "Poetry and Positivisms" 23).
As Barrett Watten eloquently contends:

> If at some point language walked in the open door, we
> would show it some respect. Our response would be more
> immediate than to use it as a sign. So we respect language
> by not being content to operate in any one part of it. It's
> greater than we are. That has implication for the form. The
> sense is larger than one can say. (*LB* 18)

The sense is larger than *one* can say: the prospect of group effort, then,
is not unanimity, but *community*, particularly one that preserves and
values its conflicts. As Gerald Graff has argued, intellectual freedom
in the university is occluded without "staging conflicts in ways that
increase rather than lessen institutional visibility" ("Teaching" 263).
Graff is an advocate of "theory" as the ground for staging such disputes. John Koethe, discussing the "tension between poetry and theory," has noted the ideological presuppositions of the workshop evasion of theory. "In the absence of explicitly articulated theoretical
principles regarding the nature and purpose of poetry, [writing pro-

grams] inculcate, by default, a poetics of the 'individual voice' that valorizes authenticity and fidelity to its origins in prepoetic experience or emotion" (70). Language is a Trojan horse, and an untheorized language invariably reinforces prevailing hegemonic values.

If one concedes a right to manipulate language, a concession has already been made to the manipulation of human beings. It is here that the fulcrum of the reader/writer alliance so central to language poetry is found. The question of language is above all a question of value:

> The question is always: what is the meaning of this language practice; what values does it propagate; to what degree does it encourage an understanding, a visibility, of its own values or to what degree does it repress that awareness? To what degree is it in dialogue with the reader and to what degree does it command or hypnotize the reader? (Bernstein, *Tree* 589)

On one hand Charles Bernstein is cautioning here against the hypnotic lure of language-as-commodity (a cereal called Kix, a car called Cougar); but he is also addressing a venerated principle germane to the poetic tradition of the high sublime: the hypnotic reverie, the stupefied assent of the reader, drugged with bewitching words. Little wonder, then, that Watten proposes to read Kit Robinson's poem "In the American Tree" as a demonstration of the Brechtian "alienation effect": "The transformation in Robinson's poem is not the coming into being of the image but of something even deeper—the perception of mind in control of its language. Distance, rather than absorption, is the intended effect" (*Syntax* 64). As Brecht himself insisted, "There's no A-effect when the actor adopts another facial expression at the cost of erasing his own. What he should do is to show the two faces overlapping" ("Binocular" 368); in short, "that the showman Laughton does not disappear in the Galileo whom he is showing . . . " (*Theatre* 194). A self-critical method of poetic delivery need not entail a less impassioned spectacle; it simply serves as a means of maintaining a functional perspective that visibly operates alongside the passion it conveys. "Before familiarity can turn into awareness the familiar must be stripped of its inconspicuousness; we must give up assuming that the object in question needs no explanation" (*Theatre* 144). American poetry of the past twenty-five years, by contrast, seems compulsively to seek a familiar inconspicuousness as the guarantor of its authenticity; and, as Charles Altieri persuasively contends, "we have paid an enormous price for our poets' commitments to the expressive norm of sincerity and the thematic ideal of articulating a silence beyond cultural frameworks. In seeking absolutes, they cease to address one another or to take responsibility for making and testing contrastive languages" (*Self* 200–01).[22]

The enchantment of the Romantic sublime—in which the individual was still perceived against an encompassing world of social consequence—deteriorated in its Symbolist twilight to intoxication and fantasia as social absenteeism. The stirring of modernism took such truancy as a given (think of the deeply layered antiquarianism of early Pound or Rilke), but the urgency of political issues rapidly made their impact felt. Historical pressures translated in modernist practice, as often as not, into a megalomania no less bewitching than etherial reverie. Hugo Ball was one of the exceptions, and Watten approvingly cites Ball's dictum that "the distancing device is the staff of life" in order to emphasize his own interest in a method that can restore the text to its status as public fact, shaking off in the process the lethargy of the authored (supervised) text. Whether it's called a "distancing" or an "alienation" effect, such a method insists on the political necessity of returning to the reader/auditor a measure of social aptitude. Given the predominance in the U.S. of expository, emotive, first-person verse, Watten's emphasis on distance can easily be miscon-

---

[22] As Altieri elaborates earlier in his book: "The 'sincere' self, then, is one poets are tempted to posit as always beyond language. Heightened sensitivity is a path to secular transcendence. But secular transcendence has no ritual, no public confirmation of the patterns that warrant the pursuit. And for most contemporary poets, claims about form cannot replace ritual, since they only return one to the inflation of modernist metaphysics. So, like the child spoiled by his parents' indulgences but unable to attract their attention, the sincere self has no theater on which to stage itself except the theater it constructs. But such construction is pure rhetoric, the traditional opposite of sincerity, because the individual acts of self-staging shape what is made to appear as natural" (*Self* 22–23).

strued.[23] The point is to resist the demagoguery that saturates the emotive deluge of all first-person fixations, singular *and* plural. The reliance on means of distancing that splinter the textual surface has the beneficial effect of destabilizing the central authority of the writer: " . . . the differentiation of meanings produced calls into question the person at the center. The mediator ultimately is directed to a larger scale" (*Syntax* 64).

In Watten's critique of "The Politics of Poetry" the weak point in the chain of signification that passes through text to reader is the reification of the writer as dominant figure. In much contemporary verse the reader is expected to accommodate herself to the poet's vision as conveyed through the (conveniently transparent, unfractured) medium of referential language. Such an act of patent submissiveness is comparable to the adulation of fans in the music world. When Ornette Coleman, for example, first broke into the jazz scene in the late 1950s, public response ranged from disdain and dismay to allegations that he couldn't play. And while he could, in fact, play superbly in the conventional sense, he chose not to. He opted instead to pursue a different musical economy, commenting that "it was when I found out I could make mistakes that I knew I was onto something" (quoted in M. Williams 240). "Free jazz" in Coleman's music was a setting demanding increased responsibility among all the musicians in order for the performance to cohere; and this in turn meant that a listener had to be equally attuned to the continually changing parameters of the music. No longer could a hip fan deride a musician for playing a "wrong" note. To *make* a mistake is to bring the mistake into the realm of creation.

---

[23] John Koethe, for instance, advances a critique of language poetry's strategy of emphasizing artifice to dispel the illusion of referential transparency. Summoning aid from Stanley Cavell, Koethe points out that "locating the source of our notions of language, thought, and the mind in contingent human practices does not automatically render them illusory" (71). His point is somewhat belated: publications by language writers for a number of years now have obviously absorbed that realization in practice—to the extent, perhaps, that affirmative exploration of representational *possibilities* (rather than, strictly, limits) may have emerged as their dominant preoccupation.

"How will I know when I make a mistake," Ron Silliman writes in *Ketjak*, confronting the same fertile liberation as Ornette Coleman (5). It's not a gratuitous question. Both Coleman and Silliman are intent on performative conditions in which listener and reader are as fully implicated *and* as firmly invested with responsibility as are the musician or writer. They are alert to the dense obligations of a consequential materiality. In both cases—and they are indicative of many others—a change in the *form* of the medium is mistakenly identified as a violation of *content*. (Commonly, formal innovators in both poetry and jazz are accused of abandoning the emotional base of the art, it being assumed that "feelings" are transparent to some putatively more "natural" exercise of the medium.) But Coleman didn't seek to succeed in the jazz world by running changes on "Green Dolphin Street," and Silliman is manifestly not wrestling "An Ordinary Evening in New Haven" into the stubbornly unaccommodating molds of *Ketjak* or *Tjanting*. Like Coleman's music, Silliman's poetry fashions a temporally sustained and materially consistent space inviting cooperative involvement by virtue of the integrity of its means.

"Lonely Woman" and *Tjanting* are both "user friendly": but that does not mean there is any master code one can bring from outside the listening or reading occasion. Every accommodation is made within the text, for the purpose of self-orientation; there is innate support for the reader's writerly proficiency. Silliman's poetics—his ongoing principles of composition—are enfolded into the *perpetuum mobile* of his large prose recitatives, *Ketjak* and *Tjanting*. The recursive structure of both works provides a frame for the proto-Odyssean return of the reader to first principles, to reflection on writing and reading as labor: from "Reading rewrites this" to "Rewriting reads this" (*Tjanting* 40, 91). Silliman's urbanity is utopian; it is the nowhere of readers and writers congregating invisibly on the page, that enigmatic public space where everyone can be alone together, yet where *all* can be there at once, one by paradoxical one. While the procedural and compositional statements of *poiesis* are diffused throughout the utopic fabric of *Ketjak* and *Tjanting* (and in the subsequent volumes *Lit*, *What*, *Paradise*, and

Demo to Ink), in *The Age of Huts* they are concentrated in one piece, "The Chinese Notebook." This mathematically Wittgensteinian series of propositional investigations poses variations on the question "What if I told you I did not really believe this to be a poem? What if I told you I did?" (*Age* 59). Answering the question is the reader's prerogative—that is, deciding whether to respond to its interrogative or to its rhetorical facticity. Even the moments of self-interrogation summon a readerly response: "If this were theory, not practice, would I know it?" (44).

While the distinction between theory and practice is problematized in Silliman's books of poetry—typographically prose—this was not generally true of other language poets during their first public decade. The robust critical and theoretical energies of these poets were applied, by and large, outside the context of the poetry itself. Poetry and politics, like church and state in the Constitution, remained formally distinct. Given the rigor of some of the theoretical work and its relevance as direct stimulus to the poetry, it's surprising that this should have been the case. But the schism was maintained throughout the tenure of *L=A=N=G=U=A=G=E* (as theory depository), with the poetry segregated in the concurrent journals *This, Roof,* and *Hills.* It persists in essay collections by Bernstein (*Content's Dream*), Watten (*Total Syntax*), Silliman (*The New Sentence*), Davies (*Signage*), McCaffery (*North of Intention*), and in the generically marked poetry collections by the same authors. And, despite Silliman's recursive and self-probing structures in his own books, his anthology *In the American Tree* continued the rift by relegating the theoretical pieces (otherwise brilliantly chosen) to the back of the collection, contained under the unflattering heading "Second Front." There have been exceptions, of course. Bruce Andrews's first chapbook, *Edge* (1973), contains a full page exposition of theoretical issues pertinent to a reading of the poems. (It is also the earliest statement I'm aware of, by any of the language poets, that clearly articulates the ideological principles of non-referentiality and non-representational text production.) Barrett Watten interspersed similar reading cues in *Conduit* (1988), and Alan Davies's *Candor* (1990) adroitly mixes poems, reviews, and theoretical statements; so there have been some reconsiderations of the cost of the split.[24]

The significance of this generic bifurcation—however it may have been redressed by some of the poets—has unfortunately marked the critical response. Albert Gelpi, for instance, usefully synopsizes a theoretical platform (525–26), only to then produce readings of the poems that fall back on a stubbornly humanist skepticism: "stunt" and "gimmick" are the terms of reference with which Gelpi summarizes works by Christopher Dewdney and Jackson Mac Low (528, 529). Marjorie Perloff and Jerome McGann also tend to read the theoretical pronouncements as a supplementary aid to reading the "real" work; and George Hartley in *Textual Politics and the Language Poets* (1989) separates theory from practice with almost doctrinal consistency. Curiously, Charles Altieri prescribes as a political responsibility something like the very split I've been documenting. He suggests that " . . . the actual arguments, the relation between what art discloses and politics can be made to pursue, will depend first on a responsible criticism, then on a willingness to submit its descriptions to the analytic and narrative modes of discursive judgment required for serious political thought" ("Consequence" 306). Altieri is of course reproaching language poetry not directly, but as accounted for by McGann, who argues that language writing is non- or anti-narrative, antagonistic to representation and description. He frequently cites the "oppositional politics" of language writing, but does not make clear that this political assertiveness is largely carried out through what Altieri calls "responsible criticism" in which analytic and narrative modes are indeed applied in the service of "discursive judgment."

Criticism written by poets has often been misread as a deviant method of self-justification, which it then becomes the crit-

---

[24] To the above list should be added Leslie Scalapino's *How Phenomena Appear To Unfold* (1989), which gathers talks interspersed with verse plays; Charles Bernstein's *Artifice of Absorption* (1987), a verse essay in the manner of Karl Shapiro's *Essay on Rime* (1945); and James Sherry's *Our Nuclear Heritage* (1991), a collection of short prose pieces (prose poems?) that are generically ambiguous.

ic's job to decode and realign with the poetry. With the language poets the case is complicated by the patently *dialogic* character of the theoretical adventure. Consequently, developed critical works are appearing which take care to retain the traces of their concrete situations and provocations. Charles Bernstein's *A Poetics* is such a work, documenting the poet's group affiliations during a period in which the sense of solidarity was actually loosening, and individuals like Bernstein were finding themselves moving rapidly along career paths that awkwardly emphasized their singularity. As holder of an endowed chair in poetry at SUNY Buffalo, his essays published by Harvard, Bernstein had to confront the burden implicit in his situation—that of being spokesman for his compatriots, explaining their works and means.

> Here's my theory of surplus explanation:
> Multiple incompatible hypotheses are needed to provide an adequate account of any phenomenon—aesthetic, material, or psychological.
> Which of course means no explanation at all.
>
> (*Poetics* 168)

This is not to say that Bernstein has refused to address the strategies of his peers—which is done at length in *Artifice of Absorption*, reprinted in *A Poetics*—but that he has "explained" the legacy of language writing by eroding the claims of truth verification in the theory/criticism side of the ledger.

It is apparent from the existing body of language writing that poetic praxis and theoretical examination have rarely been so intimately bound together in American poetry. It is here, in the structural integrity of this symbiosis, that we find an internalized political struggle in language poetry. The writers themselves, by adhering to a separation of theory and practice, have unwittingly fulfilled Altieri's requirements for a politically responsible criticism. The cost has been a practice, in the poetry, of isolation and apparent autonomy. Language poets have thereby courted the spectre of preciousness, art for art's sake, and esotericism—despite repeated denunciations of these qualities throughout their theoretical pronouncements. The critical accusation that language poetry treats language as a manipulable commodity has been frequently made—usually by critics ignorant of Jackson Mac Low's initial charge to that effect, and thus equally ignorant of the significance of *debate* as a communal workshop of theory.[25]

Language writing's most conspicuous contribution to a discussion of politics and poetic value has been an examination of the sublimated political asymmetries of the reader/writer relationship. The argument for a politics *in* poetry has been mounted at the level of the poem seen as a social integer of applied labor, with reader and writer both recognized as workers. Various discourses—including psychoanalysis, linguistics, and philosophy—have provided language poets with an abundance of methods for analyzing the material event of the text as such, and have led to an exposure of the submerged power relations of conventional verse practice. Language poets have insisted that we know the *prescription* that our linguistic lenses have been made to fill. Foremost among these, in the predominance of the *soft lyric* (by which I mean free verse, first person singular, sedated epiphany), is the complicity required of the reader as voyeur.[26] In the end, the poem serves a subpoena to the reader, who becomes a sedentary witness to the security system of another's privacy.

---

[25] I don't mean to impute such ignorance to McGann, Perloff, or Gelpi, who exercise the necessary scholarly research preparatory to writing. But even they have been gullible perpetuators of the praxis/theory split generated in the first decade of language poetry publications. Another misconception perpetuated by academic attention to the language writers is a reverence for their theoretical references. Bernstein summarizes the dilemma nicely, reporting that "a scholarly poet friend was telling me that he thought he would have to undertake two years of background reading in philosophy and literary theory and linguistics to find out what $L=A=N=G=U=A=G=E$ was all about. In which case he would have read far more comprehensively in this area than most of the poets published in $L=A=N=G=U=A=G=E$" (*Poetics* 175). Bernstein himself provides a handsome case in point. In the initial publication of *Artifice of Absorption* Brecht's "Verfremdungseffekt" is mangled as "verfrundunseffect" (*Artifice* 48). Reprinted in *A Poetics* the error is not corrected as such, but the poet inserts evidence of his struggle with this foreign term: "*verfrem*dumdum*den* effect" (66).

[26] Even the best works in this mode succeed only marginally as performance monologues, but without the attendant risk of the thespian. Spalding Gray's *Swimming to Cambodia*, for instance, whether in live performance or documented on film, preempts the space of a considerable portion of the

ELECTING THE MARGIN

It is against the background of a docile readership that exhortations for politics *in* poetry should be heard. For it is here, when the reader is revealed as a surrogate viewer, that we see that the most egregious response is switching channels, or reading another poet. If choice is constrained by taste, the exercise of political will is in trouble; and to this extent poetry is, as I've already indicated, an unwitting documentary of American political abstinence.[27] The despair of the poet at effecting charged response is understandable, given the lack of a viable tradition of political poetry and song, along with the prevailing public inertia. However, this malaise is contingent upon a view that associates poetic language with an Orwellian plain style. Rarely are the size, shape, or internal distorting mechanisms of that style examined. Brian Fawcett, considering strategies for dealing with the atrocities of the Khmer Rouge in *Cambodia*, says: "Dramatizing individual episodes will not capture the essentials of Cambodia. Such an approach will inevitably distort the issues by introducing lyric elements of pathos and character that are precisely what is absent in mass reality" (46). The social scale of what Fawcett calls mass reality is simply beyond our previously established methods, genres, and habits of representational accountability.

---

soft lyric terrain. Gray achieves this in part because of a quasinarrative structure, but protonarrative often hovers in the background of lyric poetry as well. Where Gray's audience is openly being courted—as interlocutors, almost as co-conspirators in the performer's own undoing—the reader of contemporary lyric is noted mainly for docility.

[27] "Abstinence" is misleading; the proper term might be bulimia. As spectators we are caught up in a binge-and-purge cycle. We submerge ourselves in politics, but none of it sticks. Our exemplary political medium is the public opinion poll, a form of instant politics—poll-taking has increased in frequency, because it's clear that a constitutional indecisiveness is the character of the American voter. A ratio (for and against) of 60/40 one day might actually be 35/65 within 24 hours. The message (for television reporting, at least) is clear: political inclination is like body temperature, to be taken every hour during a fever. We are invalids of our own political destiny, in that we have to follow the doctor's orders, stay in bed (or on the couch), avoid activity, and take plenty of fluids.

The representational limits of the plain style were admirably charted by Charles Reznikoff in his epic serial volumes *Testimony* and *Holocaust*, which chronicle political atrocity, industrial mismanagement, and human rights violations in the muted eloquence of the legal affidavit. It's difficult to read much of *Testimony* in a single sitting, for the incidents portrayed are so brutal and the details so unsparingly enumerated.

> . . . When her sister came home,
> she left the outer door shut
> but not locked
> and the rooms full of smoke from gunpowder.
> His wife lay dead on the floor,
> the body still warm and bleeding from bullet wounds;
> at her side, the broken frame
> in which she had kept her marriage certificate hanging on
>   the wall
> but the certificate itself was gone.

> > (*Testimony* I 190)

Testimony is also taxing because the poet provides no framing device, no commentary, no overview, nor any impassioned interjections. The work serves as a haunting reminder that, confronted with unmistakable evidence of inhumanity, we rely on the emotional crutch of outrage as a purgative. Indignation is our catharsis. Reznikoff's work, much of it dating from fifty years ago, still stands as a reproach to the conventional emotive strategies of "political poetry." "It's easy enough to feel victimized by the daily news," writes Barrett Watten, "and that may be what is intended. Lyrical horror is our 'participation in democracy' at the level of violence of compulsory voting in El Salvador" ("XYZ" 6).

Reznikoff's representational method would on the surface appear to be antithetical to language poetry. However, I think it likely that the somber particularity of his style may have served as a stimulus for probing the layers of manipulation in more recent (and better known) political poetry. Furthermore, his text is so massive and unflinching in its details, and the authorial presence so adamantly remote and uncoercive, that the reader is in no way beckoned in,

lured, assuaged, or mesmerized. To read *Testimony* is to bear witness
to a record of human malice, on a scale that continually reflects the
reader's commitment to persevere, to keep cool, but care (as in Pynchon's famous motto in *V*). As such, Reznikoff's procedure is theoretically insistent in much the way language poetry can be: both require
a collaborative reader, and both are unstinting in rewarding applied
labor. Several books by Bob Perelman (*To the Reader*, *The First
World*, *Face Value*, *Captive Audience*) are commendable instances of
a political poetry which deliberately sullies the inevitable instrusion
of lyric pathos. Perelman often deploys the rhetoric of expert testimony, study cribs, consoling voice-over, and other varieties of mediaspeak in order to display history and politics as kitsch. He is also
intent on incorporating the vexatious theory/praxis rift into the
work—as anxiety, if not solution. In "Speeches to a City No Larger
Than the Reach of a Single Voice" Perelman squarely juxtaposes self-
reflexive language poetry principles against an "other" claiming to be
free from the constraints of "method":

> The other says: I have no method.
> I merely undress in powerful moonlight
> delighting the wretched few
> and plunge in and drown each time.
>
> I say: I turn to Dallas, to baseball, to Prince, sushi, fractals
> —note the intrusive plane of explanation
> tied up finally in some diplomatic pouch of noncombatant
>   pro-life pro-choice pre-ontology movie-like stasis—I mean
> a person, in quotes, on earth, quotes
> sited in the aporia of toilet paper in Nicaragua
> of jobs in Youngstown, if you don't already own the shop-
>   ping center then go shopping, which is why in the late
>   afternoon on weekdays, after the heat of the searing sex-
>   ual repression and age war of midday has abated, and
>   the talk shows have grown cool and delightfully empty
>   with discussions of kitchens and embarrassing moments
> which allows the viewer to go out and turn
> theory into practice, in short
> to rule the world
> until the news at six enacts the State . . .
>
> And now I see that some enchanter has spoken my words.

(*First World* 13–14, ellipsis orig.)

Perelman's "enchanter" is nothing less than the *voice-over*, the confidential insinuation of a controlling point of view by the dominant cultural media. The difficulty that arises in language poetry is that, once the soft lyric voice has been deconstructed or deposed, the remaining linguistic material is susceptible of further unforeseen subordinations. This is what Fredric Jameson noted in his critique of an early Perelman poem, "China," analyzing it as an example of postmodern "schizophrenic disjunction or *écriture*, when it becomes generalized as a cultural style . . . " (*Postmodernism* 29).

> The former work of art, in other words, has now turned out to be a text, whose reading proceeds by differentiation rather than by unification. Theories of difference, however, have tended to stress disjunction to the point at which the materials of the text, including its words and sentences, tend to fall apart into random and inert passivity, into a set of elements which entertain separations from one another. (31)

This nebulous realm has been engaged by David Antin quite literally as cloudscape (German *Nebel* is mist, fog), in a skywriting poem over Santa Monica Beach on May 23, 1987. The text Antin prepared for his hired fleet of Skytypers was necessarily limited in duration, which he compounded by introducing large spaces within the lines; and through ground-to-air radio communication he deferred the appearance of each line until the previous one had vanished. So the complete text that Memorial Day sunbathers in Los Angeles *could have* seen, if they happened to look up at the beginning, and happened to sustain the sense through the gaps and delays, was:

IF WE   GET IT   **TOGETHER**
CAN THEY   **TAKE IT**   **APART**
OR   **ONLY IF WE LET THEM**

("Furs" 154–55)

Antin's poem engages as *materially consequent* Jameson's observation that textual disjunction leads us to entertain separations. Appearing without warning in the sky, Antin's piece is first of all entertaining. The text, on the other hand, is ominous, pointedly

delivering a political warning, but in the jargon of commercial advertising (let's get together). And finally, as poem, it advances by familiar tropological means, as the idiom "getting together" comes undone
(as it materially evaporates) and is reformed into its semantic inversion, "taking apart."

To say that Antin's poem is a resounding success—as art, as
performance, as politics, as entertainment—is not to say there aren't
problems inherent in his medium. Contextualizing the piece in an
article in *Critical Inquiry*, he argues against monumentality and on
behalf of the transitory. The best thing about his own skypoem, Antin
implies, is that it wasn't there for very long. That made it arresting
and valuable while it was there, and its planned obsolescence liberated it from the burden of monumentality. He contrasts this evanes-
cence with the oppressive monumentality of Richard Serra's "Tilted
Arc," coming out on the side of the court that ordered the removal of
Serra's vast steel curtain from its New York plaza: "There was no reason for Serra to iterate his single utterance forever. Perhaps the right
to repeat yourself endlessly in a given space is not freedom of speech.
It may become a form of tyranny" ("Furs" 162). Obviously, Antin's
criticism may just as accurately have been directed at the prevailing
use of public airwaves, where the "enchanter" of the voice-over
reigns supreme, iterating itself endlessly in a speech "free" to coerce
continuing public compliance with consumerism.

The success of Antin's skypoem, in my view, has as much to
do with what is usually called "form" as it does with his content. Politics is engaged not so much in the poem as in the *delivery system*. In
Antin's case, in this particular instance it's a refusal of monumentality—albeit in a momentarily monumental apparition. There are other
practices of comparable negation having to do with the medium of
publication. The social history of the publishing of American poetry
is—or should be—of paramount interest to any reader concerned not
only with politics *in* but the politics *of* poetry. Antin went out of his
way to mount his skypoem, a conspicuously flamboyant medium; but
this is consistent with his other venues, which have included "talk
poems" in galleries, fairs, libraries, and elsewhere. What Antin has
never done is publish his poetry with a trade publisher or a university

press, and this is instructive, for he is far from alone in disowning the conventional network of publication. Among his allies in insurrection are the language poets, whose assiduous cultivation of their own means of production—including talks, reading series, performances, magazines, reviews, and books—is exemplary. Jerome McGann's characterization of this alternative network as "painstakingly constructed" is accurate; for there is in fact a long tradition of alternative publishing, coupled with occasional wary contacts with the mainstream, that has constituted the lifeblood of what can be regarded as an American tradition not unlike *zamizdat*.

The cornerstones of this tradition are Whitman's self-publication of *Leaves of Grass* and Emily Dickinson's personalized preparation of her poem packets. Simply to point out this much is to indicate the dignity of the ongoing American *salon de refusées*. The American poetic tradition as such, then, begins with a repudiation of, and by, the dominant media. But it's essential to realize, as well, that Whitman and Dickinson are in this respect *not anomalous*. The second and modern phase may be pinpointed in New York in 1934, when William Carlos Williams could find no publisher willing to bring out his *Collected Poems*. A group of younger admirers—including Reznikoff, Oppen, and Zukofsky—consented to produce the book themselves, under the imprint of The Objectivist Press. This private initiative was followed a few years later when James Laughlin founded New Directions, to bring (and keep) Pound, Williams, and others into print. The politics *of* poetry in the United States has been waged as a social struggle of this tradition. The scale may be small, relative to other cultural activities, but it's no mean thing to develop and sustain an alternative system of production and distribution within a capitalist society. This has been managed with considerable difficulty, but the unique result has been a more viable link between poet and reader than afforded by the mainstream publishers and their relatively aleatory and anonymous mode of poetry distribution.

A politics in and a politics of American poetry can never achieve a full collaborative interaction between writer and reader without the deliberate cultivation of a specific audience. The poetry printed by mainstream publishers (generally, New York trade houses and university presses) is, in practice, abandoned to the marketplace like a note in a bottle cast out on the waves. It washes up in libraries like so much flotsam, haplessly deposited. Any functional correlation between poet and potential reader is randomized, becoming a different sort of alienation effect in the reification of commodity relations. And since poetry has so attenuated and marginal a status in the mainstream publishing world anyway, its appearance in print seems accidental, unpremeditated, until finally poetry itself appears quaint, and dispensable. For fifty years now, the most vital American poetry has operated *on* those margins that it has conscientiously allied itself with, rather than haphazardly submitted itself to. "The margin is not a habitat but an event, a state of becoming and devolving in constant flux" (Damon 2).[28] Considering the suffocating monotones that official (statistically dominant) media culture has spawned, it's a good thing—and a politically expedient tactic—that some members of the culture have *elected* to inhabit the margins and learned to cultivate their modes of production and communication at the edge, practising their social ecology in a strategically declassed American zone which, after all, is Whitman's "liquid rims and wet sands," where "the spirit that trails in the lines underfoot" is endlessly rocking.

---

[28] Marginality has been so opportunistically pursued in the discourses of post-colonialism, multiculturalism, and cultural studies that it is threatened with illegitimacy before it's had much chance to develop. However, Maria Damon's *The Dark End of the Street: Margins in American Vanguard Poetry* is a superb application, as is Michael Bérubé's *Marginal Forces/Cultural Centers: Tolson, Pynchon, and the Politics of the Canon.* Bob Perelman's self-consciously precious poem/essay "The Marginalization of Poetry," is also commendable in its tracking of multiple applications—and sites of application—of marginality. Antony Easthope and John Thompson propose a new task for critical theory, which is to construct an interface between two distinct yet equally valid margins, "a poetry of the marginalized voice [and] a poetry which, by injecting the principles of the margin *into* the voice, torques or fractures the 'sayable' irremediably" (*Contemporary Poetry Meets Modern Theory* 210).

CHAPTER FIVE

The Empire's New Clothes

A "WEIRD ETHER OF FORGOTTEN DISMEMBERMENTS"

In the redaction of anthologists, in editorial voice-over, American poetry has been framed in idiomatic personal tones, fabricated as a "first person" for whom any thought of "we the people" is unsupportable. Yet this version must sustain—like the pretense of Hoffman's *Harvard Guide* or Parini's *Columbia History of American Poetry*—the illusory display of critical objectivity. The scholar's job, then, has often been to sketch in the missing collective, as is evident even in such titles as *Our Last First Poets*, *Part of Nature, Part of Us*, *Discovering Ourselves in Whitman* and *Our Life in Poetry*. While the most tantalizing title remains Richard Howard's *Alone With America*, his methodological precedent unfortunately remains ascendent. The paradigm of the individual talent is obsequiously ministered to, and the dominant critical approach is still the chapter-per-poet New Critical model of close reading. It has been extremely difficult to sustain serious commentary on the *situation* of poetry in an atmosphere claustrophobically encased in *the* mind of *the* poet. The solitary white male has, naturally, been the beneficiary of this approach, because the ideological superstructure saturates the environment with his inevitability. There is now a discernible slippage in the self-evident status of this solitary stalwart. Because multiculturalism is not the vanguard of change, but accommodation to changes already at hand, the mystique of "individual talent" has taken on a peculiar aspect, like the "weird ether of forgotten dismemberments" in Ashbery's line (*Houseboat Days* 6). The predominance of the Associated Writing Programs has fostered these conflicting currents simultaneously: having trained and accredited diverse constituencies in large numbers, the workshops have in fact contributed to some "opening up" of the canon. At the same time, the attenuated lyric personalism that is the dominant workshop mode has constricted the range of expression and blotted out the diversity of ethnopoetic traditions. John Koethe's analysis is astute: "Writing programs are not usually 'schools,'" he points out. But, "[i]n the absence of explicitly articulated theoretical principles regarding the nature and purpose of poetry, they inculcate, by default, a poetics of the 'individual voice' that valorizes authenticity and fidelity to its origins in prepoetic experience or emotion" (70). In other words, ethnic diversity at the applicant and trainee level does not automatically translate into poetic diversity. So the writing programs have become a safe haven, a refuge from the sociocultural perplexities signified by "theory" and "postmodernism" (not to mention "late capitalism"), promoting a return to the now paradoxically reassuring anxieties of self-doubt.

In 1991 Jonathan Holden confidently estimated that "[b]y the mid-1980s, probably more good poetry was being written and published in America than in any country at any time in human history" (29). Deferring for the moment my incredulity at this claim, I would add that the astonishing proliferation of poetry in the United States since the 1960s cannot be innocently acclaimed as a surge of creativity without bearing in mind the institutional imperatives for the production of poetry. The situation resembles that diagnosed by Jack Gilbert, who complained in 1964 that "most poets in America today are concerned with their careers as poets far more than with their poetry" (106). The masthead of poetry careerism, the AWP Newsletter, has a circulation of some 12,000, and should really be regarded as an inhouse corporate publication (the "corporation" being the amalgam of some three hundred affiliates of the Associated Writing Programs).[1] The "creative" outlet of the AWP has generally been *The American Poetry Review*, the tabloid founded by Stephen Berg in 1972. While there has been no *official* anthology, the hefty *Morrow Anthology of Younger American Poets* (1985) has, in its fidelity to the workshop mode, preempted the need for one. Edited by Dave Smith and David Bottoms, the Morrow volume is in Holden's view the Pierian spring of contemporary abundance, "display[ing] the depth and strength of the mainstream, 'centrist,' realist mode" (48). Holden's claims for centrism are wily. But this "center" is, I think, merely demographic. Fifty years ago there were probably as many people writing mediocre poems (the adjective prematurely disclosing my own bias here); the difference now is that there is a national clearing house, so we know more than before about this peculiarly industrious solipsism.

Holden's defense of current poetry is not mounted without provocation. In recent years there has arisen a cottage industry of laments, diagnoses, and even funeral orations for an art purportedly suffocated by mediocrity, typical of which is an expansive feature in *The Atlantic* by Dana Gioia, who observed that

---

[1] The "institution" in this case is the consortium of hundreds of MFA programs, coordinated under the professional umbrella of the Associated Writing Programs. The AWP was founded by R. V. Cassill, who stunned members at an annual convention in the 1980s (in George Garrett's account) by "making a strong case for the deinstitutionalization of creative writing. The writing programs were a good idea whose time had come and gone. He argued that the results of the association of writers and artists with the Academy were now more negative than positive, for everyone concerned. He urged that the AWP disband. Some people thought it was some kind of a joke" ("Future" 59). As to Holden's sense of poetic productivity, I think his globalism is presumptuous, considering that in China poetry has long been a commonplace practice of literate people; and this domestic or nonspecialist competency was surely a contributing feature in the extraordinary efflorescence of poetry in the T'ang Dynasty. (While other cultures have also practiced poetic composition on a broad social scale, I cite China simply to offset Holden's hyperbolic estimation of America.)

> by opening the poet's trade to all applicants and by employ-
> ing writers to do something other than write, institutions
> have changed the social and economic identity of the poet
> from artist to educator. In social terms the identification of
> poet with teacher is now complete. . . . The campus is not a
> bad place for a poet to work. It's just a bad place for all
> poets to work. (102)

It's hyperbolic to situate all poets in the university, but possibly all the ones he has in mind *do* teach. (Gioia fails to distinguish *what* poets teach: there is a telling difference between the MFA careerist who is compelled to breathe, eat, sleep and talk poetry all the time, and the poet-scholar.) Gioia's is symptomatic of the prevailing perception, fixated on a sociological trend (the proliferation of workshop programs) as a lamentational synecdoche for poetry in general.[2] It's routine to cite university workshops and blame the legions of graduates who have nowhere to go with their MFA degrees but back into the classroom, compelled to drag poetry into the publish-or-perish cycle of academia, but this is only a partial analysis. What also needs to be considered are the material consequences for poetry

---

[2] Walter Kalaidjian offers the more perceptive assessment that "[f]or better or worse, most of our enduring verse writers are academics whose poetry typically seeks to repress and transcend their institutional lives" (*Liberation* 27). Gioia, like Christopher Clausen, yearns for the good old days (before the anxiety of influence) when poets crooned directly into the gratified ear of the body politic. That fantasy depends on the assumption that the enlightened, independent readers of the past were synonymous with "the general reader." But *that* reader, in all likelihood, never cast a glance past *Palgrave's Treasury*. The substantive cultural environment is now so remote from these fantasies of cultural empowerment that it strikes me as perverse to imagine reclaiming the past by moral rectitude, which is finally what Gioia suggests in a six point plan for resuscitating the art. His solutions (106) appeal to that buccaneering streak of American mercantilism, which presumes that "community" is safest in the hands of a stalwart individual. Oddly, Gioia's cure consists exclusively of interventions on the part of administrators, teachers, editors, media programmers, critics, and anthologists: that is, despite his warning about the institution, he can't envisage anything but a different kind of behavior in the same institutional setting. The hidden dimension, for Gioia, as for so many other partisans of a golden age, is the actual complex specificity of the present, which is not confined to the classroom, nor are all classrooms identical.

caught up in the ratios of "career productivity" and corporate "performance." The truly astonishing fact is that, of all things, *poetry* has successfully been quantified and integrated into the marketplace—and the vast domain of the writing programs indubitably constitutes a market. If it's difficult now to distinguish the contributor's notes from curriculum vitae, it's just as hard to focus on the lyric as anything other than a credit voucher, a sign that the place is being held in the event that anything more important comes along. This is not to suggest that lyric is an exhausted medium, but to reassert Olson's warning from "Projective Verse" (1950) about "the lyrical interference of the individual as ego" (*Selected* 24). "I believe, I know!: these are sentimental idealisms against which the current sociological practices of American poets (the entrepreneurial management of positioning being a more subtle body of knowledge than previously admitted) are perhaps our 'real' commonality," Michael Heller wrote in response to *American Poetry*'s questionnaire of 1987, "Is There, Currently, an American Poetry?" (23).

The splenetic invective directed at creative writing programs is hardly limited to Gioia, of course; but Heller provides a clue as to why this should be the case. Few poets and critics are so righteous as to accuse the AWP of degrading poetry as such. More germane is the "entrepreneurial management of positioning" which has enabled a particular consortium of self-accredited poets to occupy a secure institutional niche. Furthermore, this institutional security functions as a safe haven, insulating its inhabitants against cognitive and cultural challenges from outside. If this sounds like academe it's because it is; but unlike the English departments that generally house them, creative writing programs have doggedly claimed diplomatic immunity from disciplinary reconfiguration. The cost, however, is an inbred trepidation and intellectual xenophobia.[3]

---

[3] David Dooley's account of "The Contemporary Workshop Aesthetic" is remorseless: "The workshop aesthetic is dominated by three terrors," he writes, "terror of emotion, terror of thought, and terror of language. Emotion is replaced by blandness; thought by self-presentation; and attention is deflected from the poem's language to the poet's 'voice,' that is to say, the poet's shtick or self-imitation." "Caution, complacency, self-regard, technical

Increasingly, poets don't give evidence of reading out of their field any more than other academics do, nor do they appear to have read with much catholicity within it. As Eve Shelnutt elaborates, "That teachers in M.F.A. programs need no longer aspire to be men and women of letters is a phenomenon coinciding, roughly, with the growth of M.F.A. programs" (7). Shelnutt recognizes that the workshop poet is structurally isolated from "the broader intellectual life of the university," and is consequently burdened with an intellectual insecurity (9). The culprits in her account are MFA faculty, who have succeeded too well in winning territorial concessions from the host institutions. In order to protect their municipal autonomy, then, AWP faculty members end up protecting their students from the bogey of intellectualism, that virus of the scholarly environment they're hemmed in by. "M.F.A. students and their faculty knit themselves into tight cocoons of unexamined curricula, of defensive postures to literature and composition programs, and of provincial views of success in the field of writing" (19). "Whether intended to or not," notes Alan Shapiro, "the effect of this [MFA] curriculum is to isolate the beginning poet from the literary past." Consequently, "creative writing programs are unable to provide a firm grounding in the literary past [and] our poets are left with no one to imitate but their own contemporaries or their teachers" (168, 172). William Gass draws up just short of declaring the whole enterprise fraudulent: "No one is asked to write against the little grain they've got. Relations grow personal before they grow professional," he charges. "Here many hide from academic requirements and from intellectual challenge" (quoted in Moxley xv).

As long ago as 1959 Reed Whittemore remarked that creative writing was, "to apply an old remark of Robert Frost's, education with the net down" (345). He was skeptically assessing a workshop

---

inadequacy: these terms characterize most American poetry of the last quarter century. Fear of imagination" (261, 278). R. S. Gwynn is equally withering: "Greg Kuzma recently quipped that soon there will be a creative writing program within safe driving distance of everyone in America . . . . About all that is lacking here is a program offering *remedial* creative writing for the functionally illiterate" (317).

ethos that was evident long before it had mushroomed into the pervasive institutional phenomenon it is now. But is Whittemore's netless instruction a harbinger of the "aggressive anti-intellectualism" Shelnutt sees today (7)? As I've elaborated throughout this study, the development of a postwar poetry pantheon secured a credible basis for associating poetry with self-development. Fifties prototypes ranged from Lowell to Ginsberg, in the conventional accounting; but in any case the celebrated models were intellectually cultured. So the workshop demeanor can hardly be said to derive unmodified from earlier poetic models of selfhood. The pressure is more broadly social, less generically specific, in fact. David Dooley's identification of "the workshop lyric's connection with what Christopher Lasch has called the culture of narcissism" is apt (278). The boom years of the Associated Writing Programs as a growth industry were the 1970s, a decade notable for the rise of the self-help publishing market.[4]

The most recent estimates are that some fifteen million Americans are members of between 500,000 and 750,000 self-help groups—although in 1983 the U.S. Department of Health and Human Services projected that there would be a million groups by 1990, so the strong growth phase may be levelling off (Katz 1). As a social movement phenomenon, self-help has a broad historical pedigree ranging from guilds, brotherhoods, and trade unions to philanthropies, "Friendly Societies," and mutual aid groups (Katz 3–8). American varieties of self-help have been typically evangelical, with a tendency to conflate religion and business in the "positive thinking" tradition that runs from Mary Baker Eddy to Norman Vincent Peale and up to the present televangelists. The American vision of social bonding readily settles into cultism. "The self-help tradition has always been covertly authoritarian and conformist, relying as it does on a mystique of expertise," warns Wendy Kaminer. "But the authoritarianism of this tradition is cloaked most effectively in the

---

[4] Some of the leading "nonfiction" bestsellers of the 1970s: *I'm Ok, You're Ok, How To Be Your Own Best Friend, TM: Discovering Energy and Overcoming Stress, Passages: The Predictable Crises of Adult Life, Your Erogenous Zones, Pulling Your Own Strings, Looking Out for #1,* and *My Mother/My Self.*

power of the marketplace to make it seem freely chosen" (6). In Kaminer's account the self-development movement is predominately conformist, and she sees that this has political overtones. "Self-help literature tends to ensure that the selves readers find or make are standardized and socially congenial. The potentially disruptive quest for individual identity is collectivized" (164). While the effectiveness of support groups may be considerable (most of them are modelled on Alcoholics Anonymous), the proliferation of self-help primers in various media is another matter. Kaminer notes the predominant talk-show mode of the testimonial, and observes that "Testifying, as a substitute for thinking, is contagious. You even find it in the halls of academe" (41).[5] And the most eligible sphere within academe for this dubious activity is that of the writing workshops, whose motto, Alan Shapiro suggests, may as well be "My poem's OK, your poem's OK" (175).[6]

Because the workshops took self-development as a seemingly unschooled or "natural" incentive for writing, virtually anything per-

---

[5] A singular instance of the power of testifying in academe is Maxine Hong Kingston's 1976 bestseller *Woman Warrior*, which practices "talk story" in order to testify to the dignity of Chinese women. That this book *also* vindicates in its testimonial the immigrant experience situates it at an institutionally powerful confluence: identity politics, self-help agency, multiculturalism, and feminism. This is not to deny the intrinsic qualities of Kingston's text, but to note the extraordinary nexus of extrinsic issues facilitating its instantaneous canonization. I would also note, in passing, the troubling ambiguity of generic status: as Frank Chin has frequently charged, *The Woman Warrior* is patently fictional, yet it's classified by the Library of Congress as history. Kingston herself does not deny its fictive nature, acknowledging that a formative model was Williams's *In the American Grain*, which (unlike *The Woman Warrior*) chronicles conventionally denominated "historical" episodes yet which has the status of literature, or fiction. In view of the public protocols of *testifying*, however, this ambiguity can be alleviated, since from a semiotic perspective the important thing is not truth or falsity but the consistency of indexical transport between them. To "make up" stories about one's past, one's relatives, or one's heritage is precisely to *validate* them; and increasingly, truth is not what is proven but what is validated— that is, certified to signify the true.

[6] For a stimulating review of the fate of orality and "natural speech," see Marjorie Perloff, "The Changing Face of Common Intercourse: Talk Poetry, Talk Show, and the Scene of Writing" (Chapter Two of *Radical Artifice*).

sonally asserted was admissible without qualification.[7] This, I believe, is at the root of the anti-intellectualism Shelnutt speaks of; and it also links the poetry compulsion with testifying as a socially validated palliative for thinking. "Poetry in an age of psychology," W. S. DiPiero realizes, means "the equivalent importance of all impressions. Poems as interchangeable parts in the 'descriptive insight' machine. The result, however, is the diminution or thinning out of mental qualities" (*Memories* 73). In the workshop, the anxiety occasioned by the conspicuous shadows of critical theory, literary history, and everything else convened in the university could be dispelled by waving the poem as the wand of selfhood—and appealing to the supreme validation of personal experience. Experience, of course, is indisputable, beyond scrutiny: a charmed circle into which criticism dare not trespass. Self-validation by reference to the inscrutable endowment of "experience" has been given enhanced credibility in the wake of identity politics, in which those disenfranchised on the basis of race, gender, or class have been able to counter their deficits in cultural capital by appealing to the authority of personal experience. This has in turn led to criticism of the *ease* of the conversion from marginality to authority; so Gayatri Spivak speaks of a need "not merely to enlarge the canon with a countercanon but to dethrone canonical *method*: not only in literary criticism but in social production; the axiom that something called concrete experience is the last instance" (276). The erosion of a public sphere and the increased privatization of American life have been frequently noted in recent decades; but we should not overlook the escalated infiltration of the private by the public sphere in the form of media: mediated environment, mediated sensibility; nor its important historical corollary, which is the strident reassertion of privacy in the self-help movements. If the appeal to personal experience is attenuated by the

---

[7] I take it as axiomatic that those who pursued creative writing rather than membership in self-help groups were not consciously sizing up these parallel routes as alternate options. The aspiration to be a poet in America generically reflects a highbrow inclination of some sort—enough so, at any rate, to distinguish it from the decidedly low and middlebrow connotations of mass media generally, and the self-help publishing market in particular.

pervasiveness of target marketing—soliciting emotion as a stabilizing resource is misguided in light of marketing strategies that enlist loyalty precisely by appealing to emotion as "the last instance" of concrete reference—the icon of the person is nonetheless worshipped with religious intensity in the self-help venues and the creative writing workshops alike. "We have museums of passions, waxworks, taxidermy," Adrienne Rich says surveying the scene, "emotional cram notes, emotional theme parks, emotional tourism" (*What Is Found There* 16).

We need to rethink the social role of creative writing, especially when we recognize that *writing* is the least significant part of it. The workshop values of self-development, interpersonal bonding through plain speech as the certificate of confidentiality, and appeal to the primacy of experience and emotion are a function of professionalization (yet constituted to appear "natural," innate). The certification of MFA graduates as writers is merely incidental. What's really at stake is a more pervasive process of social inscription and subjectification. Fred Pfeil speaks of "the virtual dissolution of the university as an autonomous public sphere," and emphasizes "its reconstitution as meritocratically legitimated sorting mechanism for the market in labor power" (103). The "labor" in question is not merely induction into the consumer mentality, but the attainment of self-possession *as* the very demeanor that enables an educated populace to comply with market demands. The writing programs have nurtured the rise of the new Professional Managerial Class, identified by Barbara and John Ehrenreich in 1979, consisting of "salaried mental workers . . . whose main function in the social division of labor may be described broadly as the reproduction of capitalist culture," "a class specializing in the reproduction of capitalist class relationships" (12, 14). However, we should be wary of any cleanly delimitable posture of consumerism as such in the actual writing generated in these programs; for what's involved here is not the recruitment of consumers (which is accomplished in childhood anyway), but the conversion of simple consumers into complex entities of self-management—the development of "self-expression" being a paramount feature of market autoregulation.[8] Public opinion polls, audience sampling calls, demographic profile cards provided with purchases exhorting the consumer to respond with information the company needs in order to "keep the customer happy"; the discursive function distributed throughout this network requires a steady focus on the purported "needs" of selfhood.

Lest this sound improbable—and to dispel any lingering sense that the real purpose of poetry workshops is the innocuous one of teaching people how to write—I would reiterate again the *professional* motivations integrated into the Associated Writing Programs. Galway Kinnell complained in 1975 that the workshops "seem to be breeding grounds of the careerism one sees in the poetry world today" (77). As a national organization with hundreds of affiliates, the AWP engineered professional autonomy, becoming successful enough that its members could be permanently disaffiliated from the Modern Language Association, so the AWP hosts its own convention. Albert Goldbarth, roaming the aisles, summons the atmosphere:

> But just a bourbon ago it was easy to feel a load less chummy. I *know* these people, and know of these people: their days are devoted to teaching poetry, reading poetry, editing poetry journals, mailing out poems of their own to poetry journals, keeping track of poetry grants and contests like inveterate race buffs scanning their sheets for track tips,

---

[8] This account follows from, and extends, Herbert Marcuse's 1937 essay on "The Affirmative Character of Culture." Marcuse sees personality as "the bearer of the cultural ideal" (122), and thus thinks of "affirmative culture" in terms of a functionalist compensation. His essay concludes with a tentative consideration of the lapse of affirmative culture and the complete integration of personality into social solidarity. What he envisions (correctly, in light of the workshop phenomenon I'm focusing on here) is that this will entail not the abolition but the *realization* of personality (133). If we now inhabit such a space, it's clear that we no longer need to address "the lonely crowd" or "the authoritarian personality," but the principle of personality extended without interruption across the whole social fabric. What does it mean for the prospect of heterogeneity and polymorphic social alliances when the entire culture is saturated with personality as its sole concern— when the social is unthinkable except as a material support, a launching pad for that paradoxical monster, the individuated mass?

> gossiping poetry, networking poetry, carrying poetry and
> self-promotional flyers in their attaché cases, playing poetry
> tennis, organizing poetry lobbying and poetry-for-social-
> change and a range of poetry therapies, reviewing poetry,
> scoring poetry points for reviewing poetry . . . . (*Sympathy*
> 166)

This may be satire, but it's immanent in the concrete social situation. Goldbarth lets the issue drop without analysis, but analysis is indispensible; so it's necessary to turn to another poet, Hans Magnus Enzensberger, whose 1970 essay "Constituents of a Theory of the Media" offers a passage of increasing relevance to the phenomena I've been discussing.

> The sentence "The medium is the message" transmits yet
> another message . . . and a much more important one. It
> tells us that the bourgeoisie does indeed have all possible
> means at its disposal to communicate something to us, but
> that it has nothing more to say. It is ideologically sterile. Its
> intention to hold on to the control of the means of produc-
> tion at any price, while being incapable of making the
> socially necessary use of them, is here expressed with com-
> plete frankness in the superstructure. It wants the media *as
> such* and *to no purpose.* (119)

The role of the workshops has been nothing less than an extension of this principle of bourgeois control of the means of production; and the vacuity of much workshop product is stunning confirmation of Enzensberger's point that "it wants the media *as such*" even without anything to say. The purpose of the workshops, all along, has not been to produce poetry but to produce poets. And, in light of the homology between the workshops and the self-help movement, poets are *made* by unimpeachable testimony.

The production of poets imposes a mutation on the public role of the poet: under the auspices of the New Criticism poets were taken to be spokesmen for "the age," but in the workshop regime poets speak only for themselves. Indeed, the very *posture* of public declamation on behalf of others is often seen as an anachronism, a relic of the old stump-speech and lyceum circuit. One reason why scholars have had such difficulty addressing the tidal swell of workshop verse is that the available critical vocabulary is designed to nominate representative figures, charismatic public dignitaries to whom the nation-building vocabulary of "we" and "ours" could be applied. When critics bemoan a supposed "decline" in poetic standards (which is merely the flipside of Holden's euphoric proclamation of poetic ascendancy), what is actually being registered is a dismay at the obsolescence of a critical vocabulary. That such a vocabulary necessitates a shift from the aesthetic to the sociological and the political is in fact much of the point of the present study.

In 1981, writing from a different milieu in England, J. P. Ward addressed the relation of poetry to society in *Poetry and the Sociological Idea*. Ward's commendable study pursues a fairly simple claim; namely, that even so much as to ask the familiar question of the poet's relation to society is to succumb to "the sociological idea," and thereby subordinate poetry to the normative criteria of language use derived from that idea in the first place.[9] "The general,

---

[9] Ward explains that "the very term, 'society' . . . is now saturated sociologically" and so renders suspect the seemingly innocuous concern for the poet in "the society of his time" (26, 27). Ward contends that criticism has long since acceded to the priority of the sociological idea, and that disciplinary configuration as such, along with the challenges of critical theory, "are themselves a product of the evolution of the sociological idea . . . " (16). "My general argument then is that we are subject, in this era, to the sociological idea perhaps above all other modes of cognition . . . and that criticism has moved massively across into accepting that dominance. The broad critical mode, allowing for its undenied differences in Marxism, structuralism, linguistics and so on, is to see the sociological dimension as the context of meaning within which literary works are structured" (21). To adhere firmly to the conviction that "poetry" is a concept and a practice that precedes the sociological era is to risk reducing it to a vestigial primitivism, or to elevate it to an idealism. While I share Ward's anxiety about the preponderance of concessions to a "sociological" concept of society, I think it futile to pretend that *poets* (if not poetry as such) are less deeply immersed in that concept than the rest of us. To have noted the postwar compulsion to think of an "Age of Auden" or an "Age of Lowell" is to recognize at once the extent to which the thought of poetry has come under the sway of the sociological idea. To apply the idea as a device for interpreting the poetry, however, is to seek a more intimate compliance with socio-logic, and that is what I believe Ward is really objecting to. What I've attempted (in considering the case of Lowell, most

familiar point to be made is that the sociological mode of thought comes into the world as a result of the materializing or secularizing of the descriptions of all other phenomena" (9). It's a fairly straightforward task, then, for Ward to demonstrate the ineffectuality of "Donne and Symbolic Interactionism" or "Pope and Social Functionalism." When he turns to poets contemporaneous with the rise of sociological discourse (nineteenth century and later) the issue is obviously more complicated; so Ward attempts to show, for instance, how Eliot and Pound turn to *Kulturgeschichte* to nullify competing versions of cultural history in sociological thought. What Ward leaves undone—unattempted, in fact—is to address the phenomena I've been considering in this book, which means asking: What becomes of poetry when it is *initiated* by "the sociological idea," when its ground of appeal is *to* that idea, and (as in the case of the workshops) when it is openly *legislated* by it?

With the dramatically expanded role for poets in educational institutions, the slim volume has ceased to be a matter of poetic etiquette and become instead professional exigence. The subject matter in turn has understandably been affected. The European atmosphere that suffuses the stately verses of Wilbur, Hecht, and other beneficiaries of the postwar boom has been replaced by the suburban epiphany.

---

notably) is to trace a rift between the poet and the poem; or the person afflicted by the sociological attitude on the one hand, and the poem which resists it (or is indifferent to it) on the other. The most familiar submission of poetry to the sociological idea is its deployment as a means of courting approval, acceptance, financial success, sexual adventure, social status, and—on a seemingly more elevated sphere of considerations—canonicity, that mystifyingly agentless "judgment of time" (Berryman being, for Ward, the paramount example). It seems indisputable that, insofar as poets are interpellated as citizen-subjects, their poetry is not immune from conscription either. The error is in conceiving poetry entirely from within the dispensation of the *specific* social formation which happens most recently to have comandeered the sociological "right" to name the social and anatomize its codes and purposes. Poetry *should* be regarded as in some crucial sense archaic, which is to say, out of our time, and beyond the reach of our concepts. To practice poetry *may* be (but rarely is) a commitment to a temporal othering. This can be merely anachronistic, but that is its risk, and (allowing that the very notion of risk may be subordinate to the vanguard temper of the age of sociology) "poetry" appears to be an honorific term for that risk.

Robert von Hallberg's affirmation of poetry's suburbias, in *American Poetry and Culture, 1945–1980*, lays claim to the necessity of understanding rather than condemning suburban experience, inasmuch as that experience has set the terms of national thought and character (242). But von Hallberg has not taken his analysis as far as politicians recently have, forced to take a second look at the supposed affluence of the suburbs. The point is, after all, not affluence but stability. The epiphany sought by the poetics of suburbia centers on the spectral enticement of "family values" as such, in an age when the family rarely occupies any of its traditional functions. With family members increasingly exposed as child molesters, perpetrators and victims of incest, drug abuse, divorce, fiscal impropriety or financially catastrophic investments, and as the cost of higher education forces suburbanites to increase their loan obligations on the only resource they have, the home mortgage, the very paradigm of the Oedipal nest-egg— "Mommy-Daddy-me"—seems as remote as the manger in Bethlehem. A suitable fantasy for lyric epiphanies, in other words. What von Hallberg fails to notice is that the poetics of suburbia relies on a strong dose of fantasy, compensating for the professional obligations and social maladjustments endemic to late capitalism. Furthermore, poets have been disadvantaged by novelists when it comes to contending with the suburban milieu. While the G.I. generation was adapting to suburbia by keeping a Eurocentric distance from it, their counterparts in fiction, like Updike and Cheever, were investigating it with a naturalist fastidiousness. The belated poet of the 1980s had the even stiffer task of competing with the poetically wizened fictional lens of Don DeLillo, whose *White Noise* threatens to render the whole genre of suburban poetry gratuitous, so insightful is its investigation into the apocalyptic imagination of the mundane. DeLillo, like Pynchon, is a novelist whose work reproaches poetry all over again with Pound's dictum that poetry should be at least as well written as prose. All that is left for the suburban poet is the epiphany, begrudgingly elaborated to accommodate principles of workshop display, like so many numbered parts in an engine block.

    An exemplary instance is "Under the Boathouse" by David Bottoms, in his anthology, co-edited with Dave Smith (and introduced by Anthony Hecht), *The Morrow Anthology of Younger American Poets* (1985). I don't propose a reading of the poem as such—which I assure you can be anatomized to put on display all of the most desirable features of the workshop poem—but I want to suspend here, like a dangling mobile, the epiphany, which is, after all, the rationale of such verse. The scene: nude poet, not heeding the calls of his wife for help with the groceries, jumps into the lake. "Halfway between the bottom of the lake / and the bottom of the sky," Bottoms (or his poet surrogate, the ever-ready workshop "I") hangs suspended in a cocoon of pain, something stinging his hand, imagining himself

> . . . hanging there forever,
> a curiosity among fishes, a bait hanging up
> instead of down. In the lung-ache,
> in the loud pulsing of the temples, what gave first
> was something in my head, a burst
> of colors like the blind see, and I saw
> against the surface a shadow like an angel
> quivering in a dead-man's float,
> then a shower of plastic knives and forks
> spilling past me in the lightened water, a can
> of barbequed beans, a bottle of A.1., napkins
> drifting down like white leaves,
> heavenly litter from the world I struggled toward.
> What gave then was something on the other end,
> and my hand rose on its own and touched my face.
> Into the splintered light under the boathouse,
> the loved, suffocating air hovering over the lake,
> the cry of my wife leaning dangerously
> over the dock, empty grocery bags at her feet,
> I bobbed with a hook through the palm of my hand.

(Morrow 99)

The epiphany centers obscurely on the matrimonial relation. The wife, "calling for help" in the fifth line of the poem, reappears as angel, in what Harold Bloom might call a metaleptic reversal of Whitman's head in "Crossing Brooklyn Ferry," spokes of light radiating Christ-like from its aquatic reflection. The poet has been transumptively "caught" in the underwater paraphernalia of marriage, its mundane debris a "heavenly litter" floating past like nominalized bubbles (A-1 sauce and beans). The life-giving air over the lake—where the wife is "dangerously" perched—is, significantly, both loved and suffocating. The matrimonial attachment is figured as both *introjection* (the poet is pierced by a hook) and *projection* (the wife appears in the upper air like an angel)—the "psychic defenses" Bloom specifies for the rhetorical trope of metalepsis (which operates under his revisionary ratio of apophrades, when threatening spirits drive inhabitants from their homes). Metalepsis, the attribution of a present effect to a remote cause, is precisely the relation between the hook and the wife in Bottoms's poem. It also alludes to the anxieties that ensure the continuing predominance of suburban poetry—which, as I've indicated, can hardly be seen as a complacent celebration of bourgeois life.

While there are complacencies which afflict the actual practice of poetic suburbia, its symptomatic and compelling resources are beyond poetic intention, even as aroused and then tamed by workshop procedures. I doubt, for instance, whether the poetic virtues Bottoms might admit to in his poem include the metaleptic proposition that his wife is a thorn in his flesh, and he the bait to her designs. But this rapacious relation is fully figured in "Under the Boathouse." The laconic need for a surface naturalism, which in workshop poetry is mystified as "voice,"[10] generally works as an impediment to such inadvertent epiphanies as Bottoms's. In Maura Stanton's "Childhood," from the same anthology, the spectre of voice has thoroughly domesticated the poetic impulse: "How do I ever get back to the real house / Where my sisters spill milk, my father calls, / And I am at the table, eating cereal?" (664–65). This is what we

---

[10] W. S. DiPiero usefully summarizes the poetics of workshop conventions (circa 1978): "'voice' is the new form of poetry; tone is the new prosody; the lyric is essentially a blend of tone and personality; poetry generally is a verbal configuration of personality, a talisman carved in the image of the personality of the poet; the poem therefore is a charm, should charm, be charming" (63). By the time of the *Morrow Anthology* the prescriptive energy had been toned down, and in 1984 DiPiero more casually evokes a "personhood, the 'natural' quality or character of the person in the poem, which usually amounts to a likable, presentable sort of benign self-absorption" (83).

might call the social welfare version of the epiphany, the tacit message of which is simply "make me happy." And of course the fabulous resource, the object of maximum desire for workshop poets of the past two decades, has been the suburbia of their childhoods.

One reads through a collection like *The Morrow Anthology of Younger American Poets* with the stupefying sense that each poem is a registered letter to that *annis mirabilis* 1955, saying "Open Me First." Everything that has happened in the intervening decades appears to have no social or political implication at all, as if history were incommodiously nonpersonal, and the attraction/repulsion of childhood were strictly a matter of the family romance. In short, the suburban poetry of the 1980s merits scrutiny as a symptom of our broader cultural nostalgia for the recent past. This is tantamount to saying that such work is only justified sociologically; but for postwar generations, trained to review their position in generational niches as an obligatory index of consciousness, individuality has become indistinguishable from the sociological imperitive. The *Morrow* younger poets never dare name themselves or lay claim to a fully individual identity in the poems; rather, the poems are monologues for "the speaker," in an appeal made on the basis of generic abstractions, which swell collectively into an "I" registering muted disappointment, while the reader as social worker attends patiently and sympathetically to each voice.

Nevertheless, the Morrow anthology performs a valuable service, because in its tight juxtaposition of 104 poets it renders the poetic voice anonymous and collective as perhaps no previous anthology has done. It's not the intention of the editors to do this, but it is indisputably an effect of the anthology and of the choice of poets. Anthony Hecht professes relief in his introduction that these poets do not "fancy the use of archaic diction, in the manner of Ezra Pound or Robert Duncan" (38); but the lack of such, or of any corresponding identifying trait, is what reduces the Morrow workshop poets to anonymity. That anonymity, I've been suggesting, is their strength, insofar as it might be viewed instead in terms of a *collectivity*. But that will not soon occur, since the very *ethos* of workshop poetry is individuality. Collective values are edited out, along with the will to collaborative responsibility. The poetry, as a result, bemoans the small parcelled fate of suburban lifestyles, and each poem echoes in its isolate chamber the terrors of a voice that is more truly unnameable for being studied, learned, developed, and professionalized. The white-collar subject of Whyte's *Organization Man* in the 1950s has, in the 1990s, become the Organization Poet, studiously and obediently working up *curriculum vitae* itemizing the published "McPoems" (as Bly, along with Donald Hall calls them) by which such careers are profiled (*American Poetry* 140).

A full assessment of workshop verse remains to be done (and it awaits a critical vocabulary). But it would have to account for a mass collective refusal to address the "manifold otherness" Robin Blaser sees driving "the fundamental push of twentieth-century poetry [which] has been to break out of the 'confines of the lyric voice and sensibility'" ("Poetry and Positivisms" 22). The canon of postwar poetry often strives, meekly, to creep back into the abandoned lyric sanctuary. When Warner Berthoff surveyed reviews of poetry during the first couple seasons of *Parnassus* (the mid-1970s) he was intrigued to find that "[w]hat is described and scrupulously illustrated on all sides is a shrinkage of the imaginative field of poetic statement to the contemplative and merely reactive, or abreactive, self" (90). Because Berthoff was not attempting an exhaustive chronicle of postwar poetry, he didn't go back far enough to realize that this imaginative shrinkage was not recent, but fastidiously cultivated in the postwar years. "To maintain itself in at least a semblance of its remembered functions, poetic utterance withdraws into exercises of self-preservation," he goes on. "No more the egotistical sublime of high Romanticism, early or late, but egotism terrorized and turned spectral, or . . . turned self-parodic and self-consuming." In the realm of the workshops, the parodic and the self-consuming poem might provide some relief from the monotonous moonscapes of the lyric ego, shrinkwrapping its experiences in cellophane epiphanies of a poetic voice long since displaced by an institutional voice-over.

The voice-over is dimly perceived by Larry Levis in a 1980 lecture on "Eden and My Generation." Citing an "orphaning by and in America," Levis contends that what many younger poets have in common is a "new homelessness," and that "what they tend to hold in common is, at heart, a contradiction: an intimate, *shared* isolation." What's especially compelling about Levis's remarks is that he identifies a commanding sociological factor, yet is content to see it as a predication of the poems, which (again) achieve commonality in a transfiguration of the first person into "a narrator who behaves as a 'we,' rather than an 'I'" (473). "Part of what got lost is the possibility of wholly believing in the grand fiction of Romantic alienation and individuation" (477). Levis and his expelled generation are thus dismayed by the intuition that the individuation they seek may be nothing other than the remorselessly socializing process of technocratic subjectification, and that even the specular enchantment of alienation has long since been recuperated for the mainstream as a prepackaged endorsement of deviance.

In their academic affiliation the workshops were structurally positioned to cater to the young.[11] Not surprisingly, the adolescent quest for selfhood would become the *de facto* theme of workshop verse. It's to the credit of some of the more venturesome of the MFA poets that they've either shed this technical/adolescent baggage as they've entered middle age, or else learned (albeit tentatively) to develop poetic techniques for moderating it. So we see a shift away from the lyric croon and the confidential talkshow patter (dominant features of the poems selected for the *Morrow Anthology*) in the development of tracking-shot sensibility in Levis's *The Widening Spell of the Leaves* (1991) or Jorie Graham's *Region of Unlikeness* (1991) and *Materialism* (1993), the Jamesian loquacity of syntax in C. K. Williams's *Flesh and Blood* (1987) and *A Dream of Mind* (1992), the aura of gratuity and palimpsest in Alice Fulton's *Powers of Congress* (1990), the pop science kitsch wizardry garnishing Albert Goldbarth's *Arts & Sciences* (1986), *Popular Culture* (1990) and *Heaven and Earth, A Cosmology* (1991), or the historically oriented parataxis of much of Norman Dubie's work since the seventies. For Levis, in

---

[11] "Much as in the old days," writes Galway Kinnell in a telling analogy, "the eunuchs were put into the service of ladies, so in our day the poets are hired to serve and pamper the young" (74).

his impressively ambitious sequence "The Perfection of Solitude," the obsessions of personal memory that stocked his earlier poetry like ornamental carp still recur, but as an almost remorseful admission of failure: "You are thinking of Berkeley & Telegraph Avenue in 1970" (he writes after detailing an unsettling encounter with a "Teenage girl on display in a glass cage in Denver's porno district"), "Because you cling to a belief in the Self, which memorizes, which is nothing, / Which grows over everything like the wild, cracked glaze of frost outside / As, once again, she puts her left nipple into the little hole in the glass" (*Spell* 32–33). The danger here, as always with the workshop sensibility, is that *petit récits* can seamlessly revert to the petty receipts of transacted guilt and awkward yearnings. There's nothing regressive as such about the compulsion to chronicle the trials of individuation—Whitman, after all, claimed as much for himself; but Whitman's unsettling ambition to put a person "freely, fully and truly on record" is shirked by the lyric idiom with its intermittent flashes of cognition and sensation, coy maneuvers of disclosure, and (strangest of all, for poetry) its nervous evasion of linguistic prodigality.

The poetry workshops have been around long enough, and been successful enough, to stimulate historical scrutiny. That this has not been attempted is attributable to the fact that workshop initiates are not encouraged to develop the research skills required for such investigation, along with the fact that poets in other traditions tend to be so scornful of the workshops that they pretend they didn't exist or didn't matter. But there are considerations germane to poetry in America, *as such*, which the workshops illuminate. It's worth recalling Lionel Trilling's fears about the organizational initiatives of liberal humanism, and the tendency "to select the emotions and qualities that are most susceptible of organization." Federal paternalism was extended to poetry by way of NEA funding beginning in the mid-sixties, creating much of the financial infrastructure conducive to a federation of workshops in a national executive apparatus. This government bankrolling of poetry also supported dissident projects unaffiliated with the workshops, with the result that nearly *all* poetic activity in the United States for the past thirty years has been subjected to the pressures of centralization and bureacratic cost-accounting. "Support" for poetry, under these auspices, readily translated into actuarial considerations injurious to poetry: the calibration of success in terms of grants, publishing records, geographic and demographic quotas. Poetry came under an administrative umbrella that derived in the first place from social welfare; and so it is that *funded* American poetry has consistently reflected concerns congruent with the self-help industry, where the bonding agent of commonality is damage, breakdown, deficiency, deprivation, loss—factors that appear susceptible of alleviation. To the extent that *traditional* poetic themes of what the Germans call *Sehnsucht* (a near cosmic craving) are admitted, they render the poem ineligible for support. On a very practical and rudimentary level, American poets have been institutionally constrained to conceive of poetry as "deserving" or requiring *support*. Support as funding, housing, marketing; or publishing, teaching, honoring. But not often discussing, criticizing, or contextualizing.

The contexts of poetry are diverse, but the spectre of workshop verse as I've set it forth demands that we acknowledge a vital difference in the *undertaking* of poetry (a term I mean to retain its ominous double). As Walter Benjamin deftly put it, speaking of modern cultural affairs generally, "The greatly increased mass of participants has produced a change in the mode of participation" (*Illuminations* 239). Jonathan Holden's confidence in contemporary poetic productivity, whatever one makes of his claim of excellence, reflects this. There *are* an inconceivable number of poets writing and publishing in the U. S. Demographic splintering into special interest groupings is at some level a prudence of sanity. To think of "American poetry" as an open market is possible only for the naïve or the deceitful, for that is to think it plausible to somehow adjudicate the work of thousands. Even to confine the sphere of investigation to those poets listed in Appendix 2 (those most anthologized in the postwar period) is to confront an implausibility. Quite apart from matters of preference and inclination, who is prepared to step forward and claim critical authority over the work (to cite by alphabetic metonymy a mere half dozen) of William Meredith, James Merrill,

Thomas Merton, W. S. Merwin, Robert Mezey, and Josephine Miles? Who's prepared to invest the time to read 4,000 pages to advance from Me- to Mi- in the alphabet of "prominent" American poets? The change in mode which Benjamin refers to compels evasion, dishonesty, or hyperbole. Does this mean, then, that a national literature is baseless pretense? Obviously, yes; but a more informed historical perspective can instruct us in the fallacy of demanding such a thing in the first place, because it would provide us with an indelible image of "nation" and its purported cultural realizations as a mode of production, as specifically oppressive in its means and as exhorbitant in its claims as Liberty Paints in Ralph Ellison's *Invisible Man*, which produces the brand of "Optic White" used on national monuments.

Determinations of national representativity are haplessly insular. In the canonical ranking of poets, race and class clearly play a major role, as does educational privilege; but so do such "accidents" as timing and acquaintances. In the previous chapter I identified some varieties of critical parochialism, particularly those that make an effort to denounce sectarian association as such, thinking it unseemly or even seditious that poets might group together. "Black Mountain" has often been used as a pejorative term, but only by discounting its value as specificity. By contrast, Lowell and his associates could not be correspondingly stigmatized (unless one referred vaguely to "Lowell's circle"). One might conclude that the poets most likely to succeed as delegates of the national type are those who have shed traces of formal affiliation, or who are privileged to occupy those institutional sites which are not marked by debilitating sectarian connotations. Harvard, Black Mountain, and Iowa are the names of educational institutions, yet only one of them is exempt from denominational taint (which is to say, a Harvard background is still neutral when it comes to naming formative influences on poets). There has been, in fact, a reigning consortium of poets and critics, as I've documented in Chapter Two. On the surface it would appear that the New Critical regime was destabilized by the New American Poetry, and that the workshops arose as the anthology wars subsided. (This version is legible in Donald Hall's itinerary from the 1957 *New Poets* to his own conciliatory map in the Penguin *Contemporary American*

Poetry anthology of 1962, and its revised version in 1972.) Until recently this seemed plausible, but there is now significant evidence linking the New Criticism to the rise of the creative writing idea more than fifty years ago.

D. G. Myers's important account of "The Rise of Creative Writing" overturns the familiar tale of Iowa as the prototype of subsequent workshops. What Iowa contributed was a mutation of an original concept that had proven enormously influential as long ago as the 1890s. Writing as a technical component of college teaching gained currency at Harvard, where Barrett Wendell developed courses in composition which he popularized in a textbook that went through thirty editions (284). Wendell's rationale was not remedial, but intended as an enrichment of the study of literature. Under Wendell's incentive, creative writing was proposed as the effort "to restore the idea of literature as an integrated discipline of thought and activity, of textual study and practical technique" (279). In its institutional setting, composition was a pragmatic immersion in the activity out of which literature grew. In the 1920s composition was given a new slant by Hughes Mearns, who popularized Dewey's concept of education as personal growth. *Creative Youth* and *Creative Power* (1925 and 1929)—appraised and approved by Robert Frost— cemented the emphasis on *creative* writing which the Iowa workshop was soon to capitalize on. Mearns was explicit: the goal of creative writing was "to develop personality" (289). This key proviso marks a shift of focus, as it portends an emancipation of creative writing from subordination to the study of literature.

The effort to liberate writing was not meant as a repudiation of literary study. But it was indeed linked to a dissatisfaction with the philological norms of scholarship, norms that also gave incentive to Ransom and Tate to pioneer a "new criticism." The final *persona* in the development of creative writing is Norman Foerster, the first director of Iowa's School of Letters from 1930 to 1944. During the very years that the Southern Agrarians refashioned themselves into proponents of Criticism, Inc., Foerster was waging a comparable fight against philological and historical scholarship: he too proposed to restore a critical sensibility to the study of literature, to which creative writing would contribute. "[C]reative writing," Myers summarizes, "was an effort of critical understanding conducted from within the conditions of literary practice" (293). In contrast to the New Critics, Foerster was keen on synthesizing writing, historical scholarship, and criticism (the School of Letters, it should be noted, only later evolved in a separatist direction as the Writer's Workshop).[12] And while he took issue with their tendency to aestheticism, Foerster paid the New Critics the compliment of having inspired his efforts at Iowa to put writing on an equal footing with scholarship, lending credence to poetry writing as being "as pertinent and honorable in the training of a literary doctor as an academic study in language or literary history or literary criticism" ("Esthetic" 71). Foerster favored a more overtly humanistic (in Babbitt's sense) orientation than the New Critics, but shared with them the ambition "to restore the full meaning of literary scholarship so that it shall imply not only accuracy, thoroughness, and the sense of time, but also aesthetic suggestiveness, the ability to write firmly, a concern for general ideas, and an insight into the permanent human values embodied in literature" (*Scholarship* 20). By 1941, when these statements were made, Foerster was working in concert with the New Critics not only thematically but collaboratively. These extracts are from two volumes published that year: *Literary Scholarship* which included essays by René Wellek and Austin Warren, and *The Intent of the Critic*, with contributions by Ransom, Auden, and Edmund Wilson. 1941 was also the year Tate's *Reason in Madness* and Ransom's *The New Criticism* appeared. The point of this excursion is to augment the previous discussion of the patronage system that New Criticism represented for poetry, and to indicate that the New Critics were by no means inimical to the establishment of creative writing in the university curriculum.

---

[12] Gerald Graff attributes to Foerster the "impulse toward synthesis and integration [that] more than anything gave the new field an iconoclastic and populist aura that continued to be part of its image for decades to come" (*Professing* 214). The "new field" in question is American Studies, in which Foerster was *also* a key instigator. (Foerster was an editor of Houghton Mifflin's *American Poetry and Prose*, a textbook that went through many editions during the postwar decades.)

In 1988 Ron Silliman claimed that "Academic colonization is contemporary poetry's fundamental social problem" ("Negative Solidarity" 175). True, but the colonization he evokes omits the foreground I've just sketched, which is important to include because it makes visible the broadly coordinated network constituted within academe by poetry, specifically modern poetry. To take the point further: the academy as we know it does *not* predate the current situation, to which it would stand as imperial power colonizing recent poetry. Quite the contrary: modern poetry (in a certain canonical version as the institutional site for the ongoing production of more poetry) can be said to be *foundational* with respect to the modern university. So who colonized whom? Like any chicken and egg question, the answer is, as they say, "academic." The result is the same in either case: a thorough imbrication of poetry and pedagogy, in which the two can be distinguished only by the most peremptory *fiat*. It's now possible, before going on to visit the final curiosity cabinet in the Wax Museum, to summarize the genealogical contours of contemporary American poetry.

The poetry world is now configured by four zones. Utterly disproportionate in terms of size, material resources, and internal stability, they are nonetheless broadly discernable: (1) the Associated Writing Programs, consisting of some three hundred institutionalized venues of creative writing instruction; (2) the New Formalism, with a small but visible number of adherents, whose goals are supported by a combination of small presses, large trade publishers, and a few highbrow quarterlies; (3) language poetry, with a well established alternative press network, and a considerable critical reputation; and (4) various coalitions of interest-oriented or community-based poets (which obviously renders this fourth zone more heterogeneous and fluid than the others).

Tracing the lineage of these groups or zones is tricky, although going back thirty years the four easily resolve into two: formalism, and open-form poetry. These two, in turn, are resolved into a split or fractious One inasmuch as they represent a dispute over the legacy of early twentieth-century modernism. The formalist-academic school can be depicted as a triumph of New Critical appropriation of the modernist tradition for a so-called postmodernist neoformalism.

The underground (in Donald Allen's 1960 gathering) arose partly with indifference to, and partly in dispute of, academic custodial claims to modernism. A key distinction is that the school of civility sought closure in relation to the modernist provocation, whereas the "New American" antitypes claimed modernism as an ongoing unfinished project. Hence the emergence of a vocabulary distinguishing open from closed poetics. There is another contrast as well: where the old New Critical formalism emphasized craft, the New American Poetry preferred to speak of poetics (consisting of a complex amalgam of method, polemic, religious dicta, and social critique).

The Associated Writing Programs arose in the wake of a tentative rapprochement between these two factions. Which is to say: the rapid growth phase of institutionalized creative writing signifies a momentary and unsatisfactory resolution of the problem of modernism (or modernism *as* problem). AWP preserved the formalist emphasis on craft, but dispensed with the specific metrical tradition associated with it. The formal disposition was toward free verse, the mystique of open form having gained ascendancy steadily through the 1960s in the wake of the battle of anthologies. A further characteristic of the writing programs derives from their setting: institutionally housed, the workshops were designed to promote careers and, as a byproduct, careerism, specifically on the model of the host institution. In addition, the writing programs embraced the open-form aesthetic, but only by detaching it from the nimbus of associations specific to the New American Poetry. Issues of religion, cultural critique, and social justice faded away in the workshop emphasis on craft and self-expression. Both the New Formalism and language poetry arose in part as responses to the ascendancy of AWP.

The New Formalism was a revolt against the laxity of workshop free verse which, combined with the professional takeover of nearly all venues of publication and public readings, had led to an institutionalization of metrical ignorance—such, at least, was the gist of New Formalist diagnoses of the situation. But New Formalism represents a more complex challenge, because its critique of the dominant workshop mode was not merely technical, but sociological as well; and some practitioners advanced anthropological and neurological perspectives substantiating the case for traditional metrics. So, much as one might be inclined to see New Formalism as an uncomplicated assertion of continuity with the older claims of craft and versification, it also participates to some degree in the contrasting discourse of poetics. This compulsion amounts to an interesting tension within New Formalist proselytizing, because the elaboration of poetics (as culture critique) is a specific legacy of modernism, and the New Formalists have consistently vilified modernism as the root cause of the harm.

Like New Formalism, language poetry spurns the bland serenities of the workshop mentality (to which a number of language poets were exposed in MFA programs early in their careers). But clearly the more significant orientation of language poetry was not reactive but proactive. The main anthologists (Silliman and Messerli) assert a New American Poetry genealogy. What distinguished language poetry from the outset was its emphasis on articulating a poetics: that is, preserving and extending the sense of poetics as social engagement as well as methodological provocation. Language poetry specifically laid claim to the vanguard impulse within modernism that had been effaced by New Critical recuperations, and consistently ignored by the AWP; and it was aided in this quest by the concurrent rise of critical theory in academia. (Language poetry can be thought of as the specific attempt to rethink New American poetics in light of continental critical theory—structuralism, semiotics, Frankfurt school ideology critique, and discourse theory.) This syncretizing impulse eventually drummed up renewed academic interest in contemporary poetry, with the language poets emerging as most eligible for study.[13]

---

[13] Academic attention to contemporary poetry has been fairly dormant until recently, for understandable institutional reasons. Coincident with the rise of AWP, English departments split into rival factions. Old style liberal humanists looked on aghast as young turks declared the bankruptcy of humanism in the wake of theory. Meanwhile the in-house creative writers kept their distance, busy consolidating their own institutional turf. The writing programs became safe havens from the theory wars, and creative writing was stigmatized for many scholars as an academically sanctioned anti-intellectualism. So, when the flagrantly intellectualized, theoretically inflected poetics of the language movement began to surface in academia, it drew the attention not of the house poets but of scholars, critics, and theorists.

A fourth sector remains to be considered, consisting of various coalitions of subcommunities, linked by identity politics. The women's movement and the Black Arts movement, both emerging in the 1960s, are the groups with the deepest taproots, with securely established modes of production and circulation. Both can be seen as having either arisen from, or gained momentum in the wake of, sixties counterculture; and that culture was clearly indebted to the Beats and other dissident provocations of the fifties. Identity politics is thus hypothetically linked to a New American poetics. However, there is a persistent antimodernism attributable to the academic crescendo that has become (too easily) identified as multiculturalism. Academic multiculturalism has generally rallied around the common desire to open up the canon; and insofar as the canon had thoroughly integrated the New Critics' version of modernism during the 1950s, opening up the canon meant (among other things) deposing modernism. In addition, much of the more broadly based discourse of cultural studies has developed institutionally as a way of either refuting or correcting the provocations of critical theory. The populist disposition of identity-politics poetry tends to be antitheoretical; yet in academe the same issues are configured on and as the theoretical platform of canon revision. Many of the writers who are beneficiaries of a multicultural emphasis are proteges of the workshops; so, while their identities have complex and nuanced theoretical significance, their writing has been nurtured in a nontheoretical and even anti-intellectual environment.[14]

---

[14] The situation is a setup for egregious claims and particularly insidious forms of institutional power politics, as theoretically sophisticated academic critics position themselves as custodians of "disenfranchised" writers. However, some of them are going to be disenfranchised in another sense, since the theoretical naïvete evident in their workshop orientation leaves them permanently disadvantaged with regard to the theoretical maneuvers that have positioned them as relevant in the first place. In this new Darwinian environment, only those *trained* to be the fittest will thrive—like Toni Morrison, who as a trade book editor learned everything she'd ever need to know about institutional power plays and the tactical escapades of intellectual fashion.

With these four sectors or zones in place, it's possible to see what a thoroughly contradictory space is convened. Every group has unwitting alliance with another, which can be dismaying for those who yearn for some clarity of lineage and purity of purpose. The fractured and discrepant apparitions of these groups indicate something about the perils of grouping, the fragility of alliance, and, in the background, that consistent bogey of American literature: poets in school, schools of poetry, poetry in the schools, and school mentality in poets. In light of so many decades of celebrating, and accounting for, the appearance of poets (exciting or disturbing as the case may be), and the orchestration of appearance as a group phenomenon, maybe we should leave some conceptual space open for considering the disappearances, not so a new group might be convened (the officially registered neglected poets[15]) but in order to alleviate going orders from the monotony of their success, and to disabuse the past of its all-too-available retrospective glamour of solid fronts rolling their canons into place in the Wax Museum's Waterloo panorama—the "museyroom" of *Finnegans Wake.*

ANTHOLOGISTS' ONTOLOGIES

In a valedictory contribution to the final issue of *Caterpillar* in 1973, Robert Bertholf acknowledged Clayton Eshleman's editorial finesse while at the same time claiming that the magazine had had little effect on the poetry scene. This is rather startling, considering that the paid circulation of *Caterpillar* in 1971 was 2,700 copies.[16] Bertholf goes on to contextualize his assessment, citing the hegemo-

---

[15] What needs to be remembered, in addition to the liability of the group-effect, is the sheer number of the uncounted and the unaccountable outside of such groups. What to make, for instance, of a border-hopping (Berkeley/Vancouver), gay, New American free-verse poet and theoretical sophisticate like Robin Blaser?

[16] This is according to the "Statement of Ownership, Management and Circulation" statement printed inside the back cover of *Caterpillar* 17 (October 1971).

ny of New Criticism and the rise of the MFA programs.[17] In high-brow circles and the cornbelt world of the workshops, Bertholf insists, *Caterpillar* never made a ripple. His thesis, bold at the time, was that the schools had swallowed poetry almost whole, and that *Caterpillar* represented that vital but ineffectual puddle left outside. Diane Wakoski (a friend of Eshleman's, but with much practical experience in the academic world which Bertholf claims was unpenetrated by *Caterpillar*) responded in the new *American Poetry Review* in her regular column. In her view, *Caterpillar* had not been shut out so much as it had shut itself out by cultivating its own special poetry enclave. "[I]f Iowa has had a bad influence, it is not really Iowa's fault, but all of our faults for only embracing our own and fearing to like anything outside our own camps" (*New Poetry* 53). She concluded with a heartfelt but naïve appeal: "Surely it is not necessary any longer to have a cold war in the poetry world?" (56). This poetry variant of the concurrent Lennon-Ono line, "Give peace a chance," was out of step with the *Realpolitik* of institutional factionalism. Poets in the academy, no less than poets outside it, will fight for their kind of poetry, despite the pervasive (and perverse) mystique of "poetry" as an incentive to amicability.

Bertholf was inclined to see a conspiracy, which makes sense given the looming fiasco of Watergate; and Wakoski was perhaps

---

[17] Bertholf reproduces two salient documents, worth reprinting here. The first is the "Letter to the Teacher" accompanying desk copies of Brooks and Warren's *Understanding Poetry* in 1938: "The editors of the present book hold that a satisfactory method of teaching poetry should embody the following principles: 1. Emphasis should be kept on the poem as poem. 2. The treatment should be concrete and inductive. 3. A poem should always be treated as an organic system of relationships, and the poetic quality should never be understood as inhering in one or more factors taken in isolation" (125). The second document is a comparable appeal by the editors of *American Poetry Review* (then in its inaugural season): "Dear Professor," it begins, "*The American Poetry Review*, published six times a year, is the only continuous text for classes studying poetry in all its forms (original translations, critical essays, reviews, columns, worksheets). Unlike other texts (anthologies, for example), it isn't a one shot thing; it's ongoing. You receive your issues in class—a new text every two months. It helps you to organize your classes openly, as the class is developing. It is also a perfect supplementary reading text to other texts you may be using," and it goes on to recommend itself as "Ideal for poetry writing classes" (132–33).

under the sway of sixties dreams of peace and accord. Another sixties platitude comes to mind here: "If you're not part of the solution, you're part of the problem," a magnetic slogan that *contributes* to another problem, which is the vexing legacy of binarism. And as we've seen, the poetry world was riven by the raw/cooked binary for several decades. As I'll discuss shortly, there is a pretense that this whole show of opposition was a sham, or else insignificant. There is also the contrasting tendency to view the conflict as definitive and ongoing. What's at issue here, however, is not a degenerate present and a distinguished past, but multiple versions of what actually constitutes the present (not that the past is beyond dispute, either). The present will naturally seem impoverished if we focus only on the senseless proliferation of an attenuated form, amply displayed in the bulging anthologies of workshop poetry of the past decade. The segregation of poets into anthologies emphasizing their formal affiliations ("younger" [i.e. workshop] poets, New Formalists, language poets, university press poets, Bread Loaf poets, St. Mark's poets) makes every presentation seem a shrill reiteration of the same stance, intention, and goal, despite the obvious documentary benefits of these approaches. Maybe it's futile to expect any kind of general map, given the almost grotesque editorial deformities inhibiting recent attempts like *The Harvard Book of Contemporary American Poetry* edited by Helen Vendler (1985) and the popular textbooks *Contemporary American Poetry* edited by Poulin (5th edition, 1991) and *The Longman Anthology of Contemporary American Poetry* edited by Friebert and Young (2nd edition, 1989). However, the difficulty runs deeper than this: not only is an accurate global view unattainable, to judge from recent anthologies, but we lack even those heterogeneous collections that forego rank and status for variety and provocation, exemplified by *America a Prophecy* edited by Rothenberg and Quasha (1974). At this point we're a long way from that instructive experiment of 1965, *A Controversy of Poets* edited by Robert Kelly and Paris Leary, which (alphabetically) juxtaposed John Wieners with Richard Wilbur, and Robert Lowell with Jackson MacLow. It's even been a quarter century since anyone attempted a catchall everybody-who's-anybody omnibus like Hayden Carruth's *The Voice That is Great Within Us*.

What are the impediments to the appearance of an anthology that is at once eclectic and representative?[18] There are any number of anthologies that adequately depict the claims of particular constituencies; at the same time, it's in the nature of such projects to take on a monologic cast. "Just think what a fine anthology some 'we' could make if we stood together in differences, in the pluralism of constructive experiment," Rachel Blau DuPlessis muses (adding, "[t]hat would be the anthology to counter incessantly 'prize winning' poets") (193). However, the presentational matrix of anthologies involves a show of ideological immunity from such awkward considerations, substituting aesthetic quality as the only viable determinant. The neutralizing effect of this nonpartisan pretense is devastating, as trends and countertrends are aired in a vacuum, with each anthology promoting its poets in a context that mimics, at the collective level, the solipsism notable in so much of the poetry.[19] The implications of

---

[18] Robert von Hallberg complains about the incoherence of anthologies with his accusatory observation that anthologists "hedge their bets by taking on all comers, as though we might be living in the Age of Ashbery, or of Ginsberg, Creeley, Wakoski, Howard, Hollander, or Hecht—who knows? The dimmest prospect is that this may turn out to be the Age of the Anthology, when only errant sampling can reflect the worth of poetry, even though in such uncertainty anthologies lack their use as reflections of the cultural coherence of the age" (*American Poetry* 26).

[19] By way of instructive contrast, Silliman offers his "language poetry" collection, *In the American Tree*, as an exercise in community development. "While the old dichotomy of 'academic' (i.e., the follower of received European forms) and 'nonacademic' (everybody else) has not disappeared, it now sits within a very different context," he writes, without specifying what that context is or how it got that way. "This makes it possible to see that each audience is a distinct social grouping, a community whether latent or manifest. It is now plain that any debate over who is, or is not, a better writer, or what is, or is not, a more legitimate writing is, for the most part, a surrogate social struggle. The more pertinent questions are what is the community being addressed in the writing, how does the writing participate in the constitution of this audience, and is it effective in doing so" (xxi). Silliman's anthology is helpfully organized to accentuate this focus, and he is explicit about his indebtedness for such organizational principles to Donald Allen. Many anthologies are of course gatherings of associates, but few are *articulated* that way, so any clarification about community remains latent. This is as true of regional and special-topic anthologies as it is of the canon-making general surveys.

fractiousness are so traumatic to Americans, apparently, that a deliberate confederacy of variables is unthinkable. Yet as Alan Golding points out, even when pluralism is identified as a positive value, as in the revisionary Norton anthology, it is "systematized" for the benefit of the academic community, which is busily securing its own autonomy by making a show of diversity (301).

If it now seems unlikely that any anthology could be cohabited by Jorie Graham, Bob Perelman, Albert Goldbarth, Leslie Scalapino, Mei-Mei Berssenbrugge, and Nathaniel Mackey (all of the generation born just after World War II), it's worth recalling that in 1960 it seemed unthinkable that Lowell and Plath and Snyder and Ginsberg could be found in a single volume. That particular alignment has often been made since the end of the 1960s, becoming to some extent everybody's favorite example of anathema overcome, unity triumphant over diversity, excellence prevailing over mediocrity, or mountaineers from different expeditions amicably clasping hands at the summit. A clear image, a simple story: too simple. But the simplicity of the solution was prepared for, long ago, by that binary convenience of Lowell's Raw versus Cooked. He seemed to be elegantly summing up, in neutral terms, the arrayed forces. Yet his culinary metaphor had its own implications: *all* food is raw at some point, yet only some of it is cooked. Language as such can be regarded as intrinsically raw, something which we elevate into discourse and, if adequately prepared ("cooked"), endowed with style. "Raw" poetry, then, would be that initial inchoate state through which *all* poetry passes—the implication being that poetry lingering in its raw condition is undeveloped, unaccomplished.

The point may have lost its associative edge now, when a diet of fresh fruits and vegetables is a pervasive and positive image. Lowell's remark needs to be heard against its Eisenhower era barbecue backdrop for its imputation of raw unpalatability. The face-off has been evoked to the point of fatigue, so the near symmetry of anthology titles will serve to evoke what was at stake: the conceptual and pragmatic urgency of *new poetry* versus a generational succession of *new poets*. In anthologies, the two camps merged by the 1970s, with the "cooked" patricians regularly appearing alongside their "raw" adversaries. By 1993 Vernon Shetley could confidently assert the demise of Lowell's binary, a "polarization [which] no longer prevails. The battle of the anthologies ended long ago, with the result not so much a victory by one side or the other as a blurring of the divisions, as many of the erstwhile formalists—Merwin, Hall, Wright, and Rich, among others—switched sides to adopt 'open' forms" (17). Shetley asserts what is in fact a commonplace assumption. But the appearance of two recent anthologies suggests either that the battle is far from over, or that the editors are seriously deluded. The aspect of J. D. McClatchy's *Vintage Book of Contemporary American Poetry* and Eliot Weinberger's *American Poetry Since 1950* that invites comparison is the fact that they include, between them, most of the poets from the anthology wars of the 1960s (there are only eight poets in both books: Olson, Duncan, Creeley, Levertov, Ginsberg, Snyder, O'Hara, Ashbery—all eight, notably, "raw"). Despite their claims to contemporaneity, then, Weinberger and McClatchy are waging a massively retrospective combat. The confrontational impulse is held in check, largely confined to nostalgic evocations of the 1960 anthology wars, with the editors cavorting about in period dress like history buffs reenacting the battle of Gettysburg.

McClatchy's rhetoric of collective identification has a proprietary demeanor, manifest destiny as manifest synecdoche. Much of his introduction is devoted to detailing the "pluralistic" strands, the "competitive energies" that flourish in American poetry "because we have no single literary capital—no London or Paris—but a patchwork of regional centers . . . " (xxvii, xxiv).[20] "There is no need for

---

[20] It's disingenuous to omit New York, but it seems initially plausible in light of McClatchy's decision to claim two New Englanders, Lowell and Bishop, as his figurehead poets, whom he situates (contrary to his chronological scheme) at the beginning, devoting twenty pages to each of them (twice as much as to any other poets in the volume). Nor does he refrain from claiming as regionalists Snyder, Hass, Wagoner, Kizer, Levine, Hugo, Charles Wright, Dave Smith, Glück, and Wilbur (xxvii). What *is* emphatically omitted is any mention of the dynamics of publishing and the affiliations implied thereby. The acknowledgment credits tell a story McClatchy is unwilling to address: Norton, Atheneum, Knopf, Harper & Row, Houghton Mifflin, etc. Apart from Copper Canyon and City Lights, there's nothing in the credits to suggest that poetry actually gets published outside of the New York trade vortex and the

any anthology to choose sides," says McClatchy, with odious sub-
terfuge (pulling the wool over the eyes of at least one reviewer, who
asserts "the editor has successfully avoided making selections based
on political criteria"[21]). "No critic has to deploy our poets into
opposing battle lines with names like Paleface and Redskin, or Academic and Avant-Garde" (xxi). Indeed not. Why should an editor
bother with such distinctions when they can simply be ignored and
dropped? For that is precisely what McClatchy has done in assembling "our poets" into an array he claims, at the end of his introduction, to be quite simply "the best," with no qualification whatsoever
("sixty-five men and women, the best poets of our time, alone with
their art, with their passions, with the truth they would hold us
steady to until we can make it our own" [xxx]). Who are these poets?
They are overwhelmingly paleface and academic, to use the terms
McClatchy professes himself eager to discard. Five of the sixty-five
poets in *The Vintage Book of Contemporary American Poetry* are
African American; nobody of Asian or Latin background, and no
"redskins." Didn't anybody on the editorial staff at Vintage recognize
the profound rebuke implicit in McClatchy's opening remarks (or at
least have the sense to tuck in a reference to Philip Rahv's 1939
Kenyon Review article "Paleface and Redskin")? Are "redskins" so
beneath consideration as poets that they can be summoned for the
menial task of playing editorial straw dogs? Apparently the Vintage
editors were taken in, as readers are clearly intended to be, by the
editor's confident assertion that there's no need for an anthology to
take sides. By declaring his disdain for choosing sides, McClatchy
implies there are no viable alternatives to be considered; and this
position in turn lends credibility to his proclamation that the poets
he's chosen are simply "the best." McClatchy dispels the spectre of

---

occasional university press reprint. Furthermore, his selection of poets
betrays a certain attraction to (and in 1990 what amounts to a *nostalgia* for)
an urbane wit—as embodied in the work of Moss, Hecht, Nemerov, Schuyler,
Justice, Feldman, Howard, and Hollander—a style that typifies New York
trade poetry publishing in the genteel fifties.

[21] Uncredited review, *Virginia Quarterly Review* 67 (Spring 1991), 66.

ideological confrontation, and with it the need to acknowledge "sides," in two ways. First, he discredits as immature anything that would appear oppositional. Then, by admitting contrariety might exist, he evaporates the issue by citing an exemplary antinomy from the Eisenhower era.[22] To cite a contemporary example of contrariety would unavoidably engage in the partisanship McClatchy pretends to disdain.

McClatchy's non- or antipartisan position is of course the dominant style of advocacy today. It replicates liberal ideology by declaring the romantic efficacy of the person, the centered subject whose artistic proclivity bestows (on "us") that indubitable icon of value, the work of art. The "hazards of the self," McClatchy declares, are "the primary focus of contemporary poetry" (xxvi). McClatchy doesn't mention what a shrivelled and attenuated self this has become, but some of the poetry speaks adequately if inadvertently on his behalf. Mona Van Duyn's "Into Mexico," for one, stakes its hazards of self on a visit to the privy: "I am brave / out back in a court-yard, by a shack that might be the toilet . . . " (McClatchy 144). If we're really going to gesture towards some primal territory that implicates selfhood in hazardous developments, shouldn't there be more at stake? McClatchy, aware of the charge of imaginative shrink-age, takes pains to emphasize the liability of the grand Symbolist quest for the perfect object or exemplary lesson: "Many poets have been—or been made—wary of the Privileged Moment" (xxvii). But in the end he reverts to the verbal icon, conceding that his, like "any anthology, is finally a gathering of poems rather than of poets . . . "

---

[22] *If* alternatives are admitted—particularly in so ideologically tense an opposition as Academic vs. Avant-Garde—then one should openly declare an allegiance, or take the trouble to deconstruct the operative binary. McClatchy in fact goes on to chronicle legendary antipathies (Williams's Eliot, Whitman's Poe), only to dismiss them as "merely sibling rivalries and territorial imperatives" (xxi). True poets, he insists, grow up, and in their maturity learn to partake of "underground streams of sympathy and influ-ence" (xxii). He illustrates adult civility by citing Lowell and Ginsberg tran-scending their adversarial roles to acknowledge one another's gifts and stature. This sounds gentlemanly enough, proof that choosing sides is use-less; but whose sides are on view here? Reciprocal courtesy on the part of "the Beat and the patrician" (xxi) was hardly news in 1990.

(xxviii). Summarizing the traits of his privileged poetic objects, McClatchy resorts to platitudes one might have thought long ago eroded by torrents of continental philosophy: "[T]he lyric poem—the song of the self—best captures the mind in collaboration with the heart, the psyche with the rhythms of verse; best isolates aspects of the individual in history, best joins the human with intimations of the divine" (xxviii). There is no irony in any of this, nor any aware-ness that the lyric poem as such was the first thing jettisoned by Whitman in his aspiration to compose a song of the self. "Song" and "lyric" for Whitman were, like "aria" and "dirge," metaphors and analogues of a new poetic practice, more copious, impromptu, and hectic than the discrete lyric occasions on display in the shopwin-dow format from Samuel Kettell's *Specimens of American Poetry* in 1829 right up to the present in *The Vintage Book of Contemporary American Poetry*.

Since McClatchy's notion of poetry is confined to issues of craft, there is no sense of poetic *investigation* involved, no probing or testing; rather, each poem appears in a blank proscenium, comporting within the limits of sensibility to the muffled delight of some interior paramour. The setting is conceptually attenuating, and many poems seem to struggle audibly for ventilation in this context, like Ashbery's "Pyrography," Hass's "Meditation at Lagunitas," or Merrill's "Lost in Translation": all too much is lost because there is no articulation of context—instead, there is McClatchy's serene declaration that the energies of contention and conflict have either subsided or are trivial and do not merit notice. Since the contestatory features of a poetics are not on view, how does McClatchy provide any means of elucidat-ing resources and strategies? He's not so anachronistic as to appeal to the spectre of *sensibility*, that internal register of acute perception and poetically heightened intuition; so what differentiating principle is operative in the *Vintage*? The answer is brutally simple, and very tidy: reputation, public notice. McClatchy carefully prefaces his selection from each poet with biographical information, and is preoc-cupied with awards ("His poetry has been honored with a National Book Critics Circle Award and the Rome Prize from the American Academy and Institute of Arts and Letters"). At least McClatchy plays the cards of reputation straight up—well, almost: his title should have been *The Vintage Book of Contemporary Prizewinning American Poetry*. McClatchy's reliance on prizes as a standard of excellence provides the ulterior rationale for his denial that "opposing battle lines" exist. It's nothing less than a Trojan horse; awards and prizes (the spoils system of the metropolitan literary enclave) provide the mobility with which he smuggles in those poets who do in fact constitute the core of official verse culture. At that level of accreditation, the canon of American poets is easy to ascertain: McClatchy includes nearly all the Pulitzer and National Book Award prizewinners since the mid-fifties.[23] By contrast, Weinberger (who points out that William Carlos Williams won a Pulitzer only after he died) has only Williams, Ashbery, Ginsberg and Snyder from that prizewinning elite. McClatchy's *Vintage* is an affadavit that unwittingly testifies to the bankruptcy of poetry-establishment discourse in the United States: its rhetoric denies context and effaces the historical record even as it perpetuates the received canon.

It would hardly be worth bothering with the twin issues of history and canon if McClatchy weren't so ambitious, proposing to offer "the best" and brandishing the collectivizing jargon of nationalism. Canonical precedent during the past two centuries has been forcibly articulated by the print media of national self-regard. The nations that came into existence in the era of democratic revolutions set themselves up as culturally cohesive entities by means of vernacular documents such as poetry anthologies. In the anthologies at hand, however, a curious reversal is evident. The nationalist rhetoric employed by McClatchy prefaces a collection of generally unambitious lyrics—or, to be precise, his selection inadvertently equates lyric with a parochial frugality and modesty. On the other hand, Weinberger's

---

[23] Most of the exceptions are those like Auden, Sandburg, Stevens and others too old for inclusion in *The Vintage Book*. The remaining poets McClatchy foregoes are Pulitzer winners Kunitz (1959), McGinley (the humorist, 1961), Oppen (1969), Mary Oliver (1984), and Henry Taylor (1986); and from recipients of the National Book Award (which was discontinued after 1979), McClatchy omits only Stafford (1963) and Bly (1968), among those eligible.

avowedly unofficial gathering of "outsiders" swells with prideful enterprise. McClatchy's volume bears in its title the imprint of its publisher, part of the vast S. I. Newhouse media congolomerate. Weinberger's anthology is published by an Italian firm (expanding into the North American market), while the text is itself an English version of a compilation originally issued in Mexico, where it was a bestseller. This is pluralism of an order quite unlike anything conceived of in the Vintage anthology. The eclecticism Weinberger claims for his version of the field is attributable to its internationalism, "as though Pound's dream of the vortex had been realized: the whole world was rushing into American poetry" (403).[24]

What's most valuable about *American Poetry Since 1950* is its rigorous documentation of alternatives, its demonstration that there is a tradition of dissidence in the domestic legacy of modernism. The documentary impulse can be redundant, however: while it's accurate to place Ginsberg or Snyder in this lineage, for instance, their work is widely available, so the larger purpose of the anthology could have been served by stressing their role in the introduction and using the space for poets less well known but surely as pertinent, like Irby or Dorn. This collection is unwittingly documentary in another sense, for

---

[24] In his account, the international affiliations and travels of American poets make their work distinctly American, as they forge alliances with an ethnopoetic cornucopia perceptible along two axes—diachronically, as in the palimpsests of modernist textuality, and synchronically, in the itinerant contacts of travelers like Eshleman, Tarn, Snyder, Ginsberg, and others. Weinberger is so committed to the romance of elsewhere that even the criteria for his selection of poems is determined by it. William Carlos Williams's Mexico poem "The Desert Music" sets the tone, followed by a number of comparable global intertexts—Oppen's "Route," Olson's "Kingfishers," Creeley's "Mazatlán," Ginsberg's "Kyoto-Tokyo Express" and "Wales Visitation," Ashbery's riverine catalogue "Into the Dusk-Charged Air," along with the Paleolithic Dordogne of Eshleman's "Hades in Manganese," Gustaf Sobin's Provence, and the Egypt and Peru of Clark Coolidge. Weinberger has reinforced the cosmopolitanism of these selections by including translations (by Pound, Rexroth, Zukofsky, Rothenberg, and Blackburn), an unusual tactic which helps convey the porousness of the American idiom. "Thanks to the vastness and precision of the English language, with by far the largest vocabulary in the world," Weinberger writes with booster confidence, "American poetry has been much less abstract and rhetorical than the poetries written in the European languages" (408).

it chronicles a colossal enterprise of cultural imperialism which was poetically inaugurated with Whitman's euphoric claim of Kanada (his spelling) as one of "these States," and extending through his figure of the transcontinental railroad running westward to the Pacific rim with its resurrection of Columbus's dream of Asian markets ("A Thought of Columbus" was, according to Horace Traubel, Whitman's last poem). For Pound, of course, China was an event in his passage through Europe. The result is the same in any event: the confident assertion that the oldest poetic traditions are germane, even native, to America: India (Whitman, Ginsberg, Snyder), China (Pound, Rexroth), Mesopotamia (Zukofsky, Olson), pre-Homeric and Homeric Greece (Pound, H. D., Olson, Duncan), and pre-Columbian America (Snyder, Rothenberg). The common name for these manifold relations is ethnopoetics, which Weinberger declares the "most vital movement or tendency" of the 1960s, and it is clearly a momentous inspiration for his anthology (402). But Weinberger doesn't address the issue of cultural imperialism—he fails even to intimate that such a problem exists. Inasmuch as these poets have generally been outsiders within their own culture (or worse: "most of the poets here are, or have been, outside the outside," Weinberger contends [xii]), they have inhabited only a tenuous position of imperialist empowerment in relation to the cultures they survey—unprivileged but thereby opportunely situated "poachers" in Michel de Certeau's sense. However, *any* collection of American attitudes and responses to its cultural others requires a clarification of intent, arising from a sensitization to oppressions that are predictable to all but those who undertake them. In fact, apart from Oppen's brief exile during the McCarthy years and Baraka's police harrasment, Weinberger's poets have generally been "privileged" by most American standards of success. They represent, in particular, those generations born into the postwar cradle of American prosperity, for whom a high standard of living on the homefront readily translated into ease of access to exotic and impoverished peripheries. These are poets who have (often, not always) been "outside" the coteries of New York trade publishing and literary prizes; but few of them ever made any effort to "join" in the first place. In other words, their outsider status does not really signify affliction or debasement, so

much as a privileged ability to abstain from the messy squabble over
domestic cultural spoils.

In the current scholastic climate, with its often self-congratulatory insistence on multiculturalism, the compliance with ethnic
quotas so conspicuous in the latest *Norton* (where Sylvia Plath is
the sole white among the nine poets born after 1930) and other
teaching anthologies is less evident in either of these commercial
publications. Langston Hughes and Amiri Baraka are the only nonwhites chosen by Weinberger, who offers aesthetic justification:
"And though the academy and its publications and reading series
now pride themselves on 'diversity,' it is one based on ethnicity,
not poetry: it is sometimes astonishing how such varied backgrounds can lead to the same poems" (405–06). While conceding
some justice to this remark, I can't refrain from noting its intemper-
ance and obtuseness. Weinberger was surely aware that his selection would be brusquely scrutinized for its political correctness,
and found wanting.[25] Weinberger specifies his editorial criteria in a

---

[25] As it promptly was, by John Yau, in *The American Poetry Review*. Yau
charges Weinberger with an assimilationist and imperialist vision of cultural
others, claiming that this derives from an injudicious heroicizing of the
Pound tradition. Yau mercilessly prolongs his charges of racism, sexism,
and colonialism, transforming a plausible critique into a case of rhetorical
dementia—as was noted by all the respondents in the next issue of *APR*.
Weinberger himself responded to what he characterized as a "nervous breakdown in print," and accused Yau of lying, practicing "intellectual
apartheid," flaunting a "sneering ignorance," succumbing to "demagoguery"
and "scumbag race-baiting" ("To the Editors" 43). These outbursts distract
from what is otherwise a sage, even cordial, response. He specifically asks
that his anthology be read "for what it is," which is "not a census, a top ten
list, a literary canon, a hiring committee, a clubhouse or a newspaper."
Yau's response to this judiciously sticks to recapitulating the basic charge
levelled in his review. Noting that Weinberger "fails to address the primary
and simple issue I raised in my essay" (44)—which is true—Yau insists that
the anthology "reduces the provocative wildness of the past fifty years of
radical poetry" to what his review characterized as a "tidy patrilinear tradition" (49). The pertinence of Yau's critique was initially derailed by the
injustice of his rhetoric—inadvisably *ad hominem*—and one wonders why it
took publication and rebuttal for him to trim his position to a clear argument.
At any rate, Yau originally held that the "job" of the anthology was to reform
and deform the received map of modernism (54). And in his later commentary
he accuses Weinberger not only of having failed at this task, but of introducing

prefatory "Note on the Selection": "The demographic complexity of the United States is reflected in the work itself, rather than in the police-blotter profiles of the individual poets. The book opens on the Mexican-American border, and is concerned throughout, as the poetry has been, with the migration of cultural stuff from every part of the world" (xiii). In other words, the claim of adequate representation is to be met substantively in the texts, not by demographic tokenism. At the same time, Weinberger is making an appeal based on quality, not quantity; rather than meet a quota with work he considers inferior, he would opt for a more fulsome selection from those privileged to occupy multiple positions. The way I've phrased it, of course, discloses the fragility of his decision.[26] It is

---

"a willful distortion" in the process. Yau's accusation is misplaced, I think, for what Weinberger provides is demonstrably a documentary clarification of a specific poetic lineage. At one level, Yau would simply prefer that Weinberger edit another anthology with different aims. At another level, Yau recognizes that Weinberger is the least likely candidate for this (unattempted) job, and that he is "strangely out of sync with the times" (46). This, I take it, is his most devastating criticism; it pinpoints the peculiar sense one has, reading Weinberger's anthology, that it was published exactly twenty years too late. Steve Evans, in a discussion of this debate on the SUNY Buffalo Poetics list-server in July 1994, observed that, apart from any consideration of who was "right," "Weinberger and Yau are playing two sides in a single game, a game in which 'marginality' has been converted into the stake and highest honor even by intellectuals who feel few of its withering social effects." Finally, an ironic note on literary gamesmanship: in 1988 Yau was awarded the General Electric Foundation Award for Younger Writers for his poetry by a panel consisting of none other than Eliot Weinberger and two of his former teachers (John Ashbery, Robert Kelly).

[26] The most damning thing to be said about Weinberger's anthology in the present climate of cultural politics is that twenty-eight of the thirty-five poets are white men. But, as he preemptively retorts in his Introduction, "[t]hose who count heads according to gender and race should first consider how many poets genuinely qualify within these chronological limits [i.e. born by the end of World War II]." Weinberger concedes that "a subsequent selection of the innovators from the post-World War II generations would probably contain a majority of women, with a greater number of nonwhite poets, male and female" (xiii). Yet, having considered the alternatives, as he advises, I find his decisions wanting. Among black poets, for instance, he understandably overlooks Robert Hayden—probably too mainstream for his taste—but he also ignores Gwendolyn Brooks who, despite her acclaim, has sustained an exemplary resistance to official verse culture. Most dismaying is Weinberger's ignorance (or omission) of Melvin B. Tolson, the most

important to note, though, that the editorial apparatus of *American Poetry Since 1950* invites such considerations, whereas McClatchy (like most other anthologists) obfuscates the issue altogether.

Both of these anthologists are eager to champion poetry as a stalwart holdout against the institutionalizing pressures of modern life—Weinberger by adumbrating a lineage of "outsiders," McClatchy by the imperturbably Olympian atmosphere of aesthetic "excellence." What's to be made, then, of the omission of language poetry from these collections? An arresting discrepancy, for language poetry has occasioned the most conspicuous scholarly attention during the past decade, but remains largely unacknowledged by official registers of the poetic community. Academic scrutiny of language poetry is impressive, particularly for a small press movement of poets, now mostly in their forties, who have yet to win any literary awards. In the domain of poetry anthologies, however, they are all *persona non grata*: there are *no* language poets to be found in over five thousand pages comprised by the following anthologies: *New American Poets of the 80s* edited by Myers and Weingarten (1984), *Singular Voices* edited by Berg (1985), *The Morrow Anthology of Younger American Poets* edited by Smith and Bottoms (1985), *The Harvard Book of Contemporary American Poetry* edited by Vendler (1985), *The Direction of Poetry* edited by Richman (1988), *The Longman Anthology of Contemporary American Poetry* edited by Friebert and Young (1983; 2nd edition, 1989), *Contemporary American Poetry* edited by Poulin (4th edition, 1985; 5th edition, 1991), *New American Poets of the 90s* edited by Myers and Weingarten (1991), nor in McClatchy or

---

indebted of all postwar black American poets to modernist precedent. And what about Bob Kaufman, the street hipster published by New Directions, a press whose backlist includes works by seventeen of Weinberger's thirty-five poets (not to mention two books of essays by Weinberger himself)? Among women who "qualify," to use Weinberger's injudicious term, what about Barbara Guest, Joanne Kyger, Diane DiPrima, Beverly Dahlen, Diane Wakoski, Sharon Olds, Rosmarie Waldrop (another New Directions poet), Rachel Blau DuPlessis, Anne Waldman, Alice Notley, Bernadette Mayer, Joan Retallack, or Lyn Hejinian (not to mention numerous others cited by John Yau)?

Weinberger.[27] Needless to add, they're not to be found in any of the omnibus textbook anthologies of American literature (where their contemporaries and ethnically appropriate juniors are favored).[28] Yet this group of *outré* poets has been repeatedly and favorably singled out in prestigious scholarly journals (including *Critical Inquiry, New Literary History, South Atlantic Quarterly, Boundary 2, American Literary History* and even *The Southern Review*), and they are routinely discussed in monographs.[29] So

---

[27] Weinberger has had a contestatory relation to language poetry, complicated by the fact that he is on the editorial board of *Sulfur* along with Charles Bernstein. He anthologizes Michael Palmer, Clark Coolidge—both on the *Sulfur* masthead as well—and Susan Howe, all of whom were absorbed into the language poetry context in the Silliman and Messerli anthologies (1986 and 1987). But otherwise Weinberger obtusely persists in regarding language poetry as "a kind of moving-wallpaper literature for the current generation of grad students who were raised in front of the tube—a harmless entertainment not unlike the '7 types of ambiguity' poetry produced for students in the 1950s" ("On Language Poetry" 184). The kernel of a substantial research article might be extracted from such a claim, but neither Weinberger nor anyone else has attempted it. As it is, his inclusion of Coolidge, Palmer, and Howe should be recognized as a strategic preemption of the need to consider the position of language poetry in relation to the lineage it claims for itself, which (awkwardly for him) happens to be Weinberger's tradition as well.

[28] Jeffrey Nealon surveys this exclusion, exposing the multiculturalism of teaching anthologies as extending "a kind of epiphanic white experience to many other groups." In Nealon's view, the registration of otherness here is thoroughly integrated into representational frameworks already saturated with (one might as well say, but he doesn't) *white* criteria of self-making. He shrewdly cites the *Heath Anthology*'s editorial claim that, for the writers selected, "[r]eadability is their primary consideration"—commenting: "If a consumable 'readability' and emphasis on 'expressi[on]' is the ante to get into the game, it's not surprising that language poetry isn't asked to play . . . " (*Double Reading* 156).

[29] Even Daniel Hoffman includes a chapter on language poetry in his 1993 collection of essays, *Words to Create a World*. Language poetry has occasioned two books: George Hartley's *Textual Politics and the Language Poets* (1989) and Linda Reinfeld's *Language Poetry* (1992). Apart from the now common sprinkling of references to language poetry in books and articles not otherwise concerned with the phenomenon, recent years have seen a growing tide of chapter length discussions: *The Sun Is But a Morning Star* by Lee Bartlett (1989), *The San Francisco Renaissance* by Michael Davidson (1989), *The Poetry Beat* by Tom Clark (1990), *Obdurate Brilliance* by Peter Baker (1991), *Unending Design* by Joseph Conte (1991), *Disjunctive Poetics* by Peter Quartermain (1992), *The ABC of Influence* by Christopher Beach (1992),

what's going on—is this an academic delusion? Is there a conspiracy on the part of anthologists and publishers to deny the existence of language poetry? Or is this simply another instance of what Billy Collins calls "antireputation," in which certain poets "become somewhat well known for *not* being well known" (297)?

At the moment it becomes possible to ask these questions, as it happens, they're rendered more or less obsolete by the appearance of the two largest and most ambitious poetry anthologies in many years: Paul Hoover's *Postmodern American Poetry: A Norton Anthology* (701 pages) and Douglas Messerli's *From the Other Side of the Century: A New American Poetry 1960–1990* (1135 pages), both of which enshrine language poetry front and center, and (like Weinberger) capitalize on what is by now a very secure and familiar "outsider" lineage. Unlike McClatchy and Weinberger, the editors of these anthologies are relatively abstemious in their presentational rhetoric. Each resists making grand claims and restricts comment to a sketchy evocation of traditions that are clearly part of the public record. Hoover and Messerli have in common a concern to place language writing in the context of the New American Poetry, but they otherwise diverge, with Hoover favoring a more extensive mapping of the New York scene, while Messerli goes north of the border to include Canadians whose work is manifestly interactive with the American scenes he documents. Hoover, operating under the profession-sensitive directives of Norton, makes space for a more prodigious ethnic variety than Messerli, and he carefully indicates what's "multicultural" about his selections in the introduction. Hoover's success at integrating multicultural requirements into a collection of avowedly "experimental" poetry is itself an important challenge to Weinberger's confidence in their incompatability. In homage to Allen's precedent in *The New American Poetry*, Messerli lists

---

Statutes of Liberty by Geoff Ward (1993), *After the Death of Poetry* by Vernon Shetley (1993), *Black Riders* by Jerome McGann (1993), and *American Culture Between the Wars* by Walter Kalaidjian (1993—unlikely, given the title, but the subtitle is "Revisionary Modernism and Postmodern Critique"). Language poetry is also a running theme in Marjorie Perloff's *Dance of the Intellect* (1985), *Poetic License* (1990), and *Radical Artifice* (1991).

addresses of "Publishers of American innovative poetry" (1134–35), while Hoover includes a section of statements on poetics. Given the enormity of Messerli's collection, it's regrettable that he didn't do the same, since the space was clearly there. However, Messerli's selection of poems offers considerably more variety in terms of actual *praxis*, and this is clearly attributable to his editorial procedure, which was to solicit from the poets themselves suggestions for work to include in this context.

Weinberger, Messerli, and Hoover, in pledging allegiance to *The New American Poetry*, seem obliged to perpetuate the sectarianism that was manifest there. In 1960, of course, there was a certifiably establishmentarian poetry canon which did not so much exclude Allen's poets as it was indifferent to them; and Allen responded to that indifference with *difference*. There is a disabling nostalgia, however, symptomatic of all four of these recent ambitious anthologies. McClatchy is nostalgic for a time when an editor could in good conscience rely on prizes and public acclaim as a preliminary sorting process—not that that was *ever* possible except as an exercise in bad faith, as it is here. Weinberger, Hoover, and Messerli are all transported by the reverie of the outside, the experimental, the dissident; yet all three pursue an explicitly conservative function in purporting to trace a genealogy of the vanguard. The romance of the outsider, moreover, patently haunts the interstices of all our public institutions, including the mass media, the educational system, and political rhetoric. In the case of these anthologists, it's a nostalgia predicated on a "recuperation" of New American poetic dissidents, but the logic is flawed because they've come too late to get in on the fruits of first acclaim.[30] All aspire to huddle with Donald Allen on that peak in Darien, beholding a new vista for poetry. As

---

[30] By "recuperation" I mean the conspicuous inclusion of underanthologized poets who might have been (but weren't) in Allen's anthology: Rexroth, Oppen, Bronk, MacLow, and others. Published in the 1990s, of course, these anthologies extend the recuperative impulse to figures from the post-Allen generation, now senior poets who have been overshadowed by the continuing prominence of Allen's canon: Antin, Rothenberg, Kelly, Johnson, Bromige, Tarn, Irby, Sobin, Berrigan, and many more.

latecomer anthologists (for which Harold Bloom's map of anxieties has no name), they compensate for their belatedness by monumentalizing what, in 1960, was a tactical assault, turning it into a ponderous genealogical system of certifications.

A problem of the "outside" all too legible from the inside is that even indigence can appear heroic. As critics of Allen's anthology recognized at the time it was published, only a few of his poets proposed and enacted serious challenges to the prevailing conditions of American poetry. The rest were (it was claimed) hangers-on, friends or toadies. A comparable charge could be made again today. These anthologies in each instance justify a selection of the present by appealing to a former occasion of exclusion, and so avoid addressing *present* exclusions and contestations either conceptually or pragmatically. It literally goes without saying for Weinberger, Hoover, and Messerli that poets appearing in a context like the *Morrow* anthology are excluded from consideration. Consequently, they all end up including work by the "correct" poets that, written by others, wouldn't even be considered. Likewise, they deny in advance the possibility that somebody from the workshop milieu might be experimentally challenging. They refuse to consider the obvious but awkward fact that the factionalism of 1960 has long since eroded, and that regardless of institutional affiliation many different poets may have found stimulus in and guidance from rebels of a previous generation. These new anthologies thus unwittingly perpetuate the same cycle they ostensibly combat as they, like McClatchy's *Vintage*, would like to avoid present contentions by appealing to a sanitary (because familiar) image of past disputes. What happened in the 1950s was a bifurcation of poetic communities on the issue of modernism, specifically its reception and transfiguration; the result being (to summarily allegorize it) Lowell versus Olson and their respective camps. The same thing is happening all over again, as the custodians of the New American Poetry tradition are evidently blind to the prospect that their own equivalent of high modernism—the New American poetry—has been broadly disseminated and has consequently inspired a range of poets outside those enclaves (language poetry, New York school, etc.) which they designate as the official transmitting mechanism of the original spark.

The messianic temptation of oppositionality has proven too tempting, apparently. But we should be motivated to wonder about this latest pride in heresy. If real countermeasures are intended, what purpose is served by making an orthodoxy of the unorthodox? These anthologists unwittingly reinvest in the Hegelian premise of the master-slave dialectic. The fallacy of revolutionary thinking in the literary milieu, suggests Wolfgang Iser, is the temptation "to believe that by negating something, you have already grasped its otherness. . . . With pure negation, the revolution remains dependent upon that which it negates, and the more radical the destruction, the more inevitably it must lead to self-destruction" (200). The spectre of autonomous opposition summoned by these anthologies ends up servicing the reactionary forces they oppose—partly because they set up clear targets, but more so because they reaffirm the power of the binary. Ron Silliman entertains the idea that "the challenge facing any oppositional poetics is how to remain marked, literally stigmatized . . . " ("Negative Solidarity" 175). I doubt whether he had in mind the sort of marking practiced by Weinberger, Hoover and Messerli, for whom the stigma has given way to the team logo. Jeffrey Nealon defends language poetry as "a discourse that recognizes a certain postmodern necessity in mediating institutions. It recognizes, in short, that there is no 'outside'" (155). He recognizes that language poetry staked its success on an institutional gambit comparable to that of other marginal groups for whom "the great institutional lesson [of] the past twenty-five years has been the necessity of mediating institutions—the recognition that, despite the potential problem of cooptation, the presence of traditionally oppressed or excluded groups within society's institutions is absolutely necessary, as is a simultaneous and ongoing engagement with problems of institutionalism" (154). As has often been noted, however, cooptation turned out not to be the danger; institutional absorption has successfully redistributed the provocations of women's studies and African American studies into special concentration areas that are a form of quarantine in which the fever of opposition burns fiercely in containment. Nealon is, I think, too optimistic when he imagines that language poetry "calls into question the entire balkanizing logic of consensus pluralism . . . " (158). Rather, it *confirms* it by providing such a lucid model of group identity; and the identity politics most institutions are poised to recognize now settle precisely on *groups*: how to recognize them, solicit their cooperation, sequester them, and contain them.[31] It is salutary to be explicit about the strategies of consensus building—which, in the best light, is what the Weinberger, Hoover, and Messerli collections do—particularly as the "opposition" (in this case the establishment world of McClatchy, and the MFA programs) practices its consensus without acknowledging that there's a need for anything so patently ideological. It seems to me that the more effective strategy requires a certain cunning and guile: the truly seditious anthologist now should go poaching, retain the genealogical profile as a courtesy, but not rely on it for the crutch of indignation or heroic pride. When the world of Associated Writing Programs has to contend with an anthology that puts Jorie Graham and C. K. Williams next to a swarm of language poets, then and only then will it be forced to confront its own ideological dispensation beginning to erode as if from within.

Even the most homogeneous anthologies will *appear* to initiates and insiders to capture some variety. The problem facing us now is the uniform demeanor of the "outside" delegated by these

---

[31] Charles Stein offers a concise recapitulation of the limits of the struggle: "Organized political minorities demand of those who bear the mark of membership that they behave accordingly. The need for this assembling of humans under the kinds that their oppressors have discriminated in order to oppose that oppression is perhaps unarguable. But surely this banding together, this demand for solidarity, this enforcement of an identity that has, in fact, been forced upon one, is at best a necessary and hopefully temporary evil to be put aside as successful struggle brings brighter times. That 'identity' and 'pride' of membership in any group should be elevated to ontological status, however tactically useful, is a species of the very evil all such struggle is most justified when it opposes" (25). It's worth adding that Charles Stein is omitted from all of the anthologies I've been discussing here, although he is an exemplary instance of a nondenominational poet whose work would be instructively interactive in a language context, an open form post-Olsonian context, a New York school context, or a postmodernist context, to cite the areas most insistently claimed by Weinberger, Hoover, and Messerli. Other poets shamefully overlooked by all three anthologists include Gerrit Lansing, John Clarke, Duncan McNaughton, and Ted Pearson.

recent anthologies, for none of them attempt to conceive heterogeneity from outside their own partisan coordinates. All are fueled by a certain energy of indignation at the complacency of the poetics they oppose, but this indignation becomes a mirroring denial. In this context, it seems likely that language poetry has been canonized as the official opposition, a status that should bring chills to anybody unfortunate enough to be tagged a language poet, because they'll be henceforth set up as predictable, reliable, containable under the terms of that stiff pose of oppositional detente which Hoover and Messerli have negotiated on their behalf. It will at this point appear that I've taken a particularly skeptical line on the matter; but at this late stage in my study—and hopefully for those who have followed the argument and documentation this far—this shouldn't be surprising. I've consistently evoked the Wax Museum as the site of canonical debasement, a paradox of ambiguous elevation, and in these recent anthologies I see all too clearly a canonizing or waxmaking impulse likely to do for this generation's poets exactly what Ciardi, Hall, Pack, Simpson, Allen, Strand, and Halpern did for previous generations. Institutionalization is not necessarily an abasement, but the rhetoric of antiprofessionalism in the romance of the vanguard suggests—for these anthologists and despite their own contributions *to* the canonical sorting process—that it is.

The indisputable value foregrounded in these anthologies is their determination to elucidate a cartography. The traditional ambiguity with which poems in anthologies stand in for poetics—or more accurately are *posed* as the fruition of a poetics which it would be redundant to include or even make editorially explicit—is attributable to an editorial fetishization of the unique aesthetic object. With this reluctance to amplify the social and cognitive context within which poems appear, it's not surprising that anthologists have failed to conceive their own work in terms other than that of allocating compartmentalized space to a discrete series. The prevailing practice of bureaucratic allotment has proven a purely logistical affair, as though editors were dealing with troop transport rather than poetry. Rare is the anthology—and these (excepting the *Vintage*) are among the few—driven by a determination to do more than take a random (if

aesthetically filtered) groundsample. Weinberger is the most successful in owning up to his organizational protocol, elucidating in his
editorial matter the polemical dispositions of the poets he includes;
yet he, like Hoover and Messerli, succumbs to the temptation to
showcase isolate poems, concurring with McClatchy that letting them
"speak for themselves" is the editor's primary obligation. That poems
"speak for themselves" is an editorial pretension, deflecting attention
from the ventriloquial ambience.

However diverse their originating contexts, poems on display
in anthologies begin to look alike: this is an effect of the showcase
environment. Poems, like women on view in a Miss Universe
pageant, look more like one another than like anybody around them.
Any breach in this façade—this means of advertising coherence, unanimity of purpose, and "universal" relevance[32]—amounts to a disabling infraction. Weinberger, Hoover, and Messerli openly advertise
formal affiliations, those wagers of creative indebtedness and compensation, which amount to something more than colorful biographical detail. Avoiding such partisan genealogies, appealing instead to
that abstract third-person plural of a conflated readership/citizenship,
McClatchy's pitfall is to impute an immaculate neo-Kantian disinterestedness to the reader, who becomes a neutral arbitrator of the pure
event of the (The) Poem. To the diachronic axis of the "anxiety of
influence" we need to recognize a synchronic counterpart, which I
would define as an anxiety of contact, a neurosis that fears collaboration as much as confrontation; and this fear is equally germane to editorial strategies of evasion or nostalgia. The emphasis on poetry as a
medium of pure individualism has played havoc with the social functions of literary community. Perhaps the surest proof of the institutional dereliction of poetry is that anthologies have consistently
failed to "teach the conflicts," which in Gerald Graff's view dogs
academia as a whole. What we now have in the U. S. is an official

---

[32] "We have to get over, as in getting over a disease, the idea that we can
'all' speak to one another in the universal voice of poetry," Charles Bernstein succinctly states (*Poetics* 5). Alan Golding argues that anthologists, in
particular, set the standards which "each literary generation is so easily
seduced into thinking 'universal' . . . " (284).

verse culture with its workshops, laboratories, grants and awards, credentialing boards, and licensed practitioners and overseers. McClatchy, in Official Verse Culture, is simply a corporate manager supervising a sales and services division. On the other side of the coin, there has been a serious attrition of what one might call oppositional poetry, as the Allen *New American* poets have *also* been institutionalized insofar as they have successfully represented The Outsider for thirty years—a role they're nominated for, yet again, in the rosters assembled by Weinberger, Hoover, and Messerli. The custodial labors on view here are preoccupied with anterior accreditation, and thus recapitulate the familiar image of the anthology as genealogical certificate of good manners, the dutiful transfer of poetic property and cultural capital from one generation to another.

The kind of community represented by the taste-making postwar anthologists masquerades as the spontaneous flower of market forces, frothing the cream to the top. In the canonic-heroic mode—ultimately fashioned on *The Aeneid*—this "cream" of transcendent individuality is the bonding agent of social will. As a canonical model, the image is that of an anticollective ascent to Olympian summits, on which a cordiality among peers predominates above and beyond the miasmic mists of the lower slopes, where the heathen bardic clans are astir. Our views of the imaginal resources of poetry are still under the sway of what Jerome McGann calls the "Romantic ideology," which privileges a poetry that obscures traces of *interest*, and thus accommodates the view that poets want nothing more than election to a hall of fame. The kind of poetry favored in such an account is that which can be glossed without reference to ideology as such, because the ideological disposition of the canonizing institutions would stand revealed. To concede the existence of the canonical ideology is at the same time to admit that it may not, after all, be *natural* for everybody to crave fifteen minutes of fame. The institution—even one so dominant as the canon—subsists in the aura of what seems natural. The moment the spell is broken, the culture that steps forth from the husk of nature is starkly ideological; and that ideology stipulates for poets the role of linguistic subalterns in the production of subjectivity.

Insofar as the cultural capital of literacy is minted in academia, poetry as writing and as written will be inextricable from that institutional matrix. This is, of course, to concede that other poetic practices, less dependent on literacy skills, may not suffer such dependency. I would concur with John Guillory's thesis in *Cultural Capital* that "the center of the system of social reproduction has moved elsewhere, into the domain of mass culture" (80). So what *is* reproduced in poetry is a specific strain of verbal attention to words on a page that engage, in complex ways, the mystique of logocentrism—the originary psyche, the animated breath, the founding utterance. We need to recognize that logocentrism is a metaphysical term specific to literacy as a social formation. Poetry in all of its modern modes is acutely dependent on literacy (even sound poetry is scored), and is therefore increasingly hampered by its association with the kind of cultural privilege perpetuated by literacy as a vernacular standard, sustained by "the transmission of tensed delight before the word," as George Steiner puts it, and which traditionally derived "from power-relations, from pretenses, from silences by the majority which our present world is no longer prepared to put up with" (17, 16). Meanwhile, the culture is clearly prepared to put up with "tensed delight" before the visual and the acoustic image. Even this abridged account should suggest the futility of any appeal to "tradition and the individual talent," inasmuch as our mediascapes warp tradition out of any linear reckoning and at the same time displace the burden of talent onto those viewers and auditors who are accustomed to considering performative "talent" as a pure simulation of promotional agencies.

Postwar traumatization about the diminishing efficacy of poetry has invariably clouded mainstream anthologists' and reviewers' sense of their present, so for forty years the representation of American poetry has been predicated on a fallacious supposition: that only that poetry may be officially sanctioned that *would be* efficacious if the *proper* cultural patrimony were still dominant. Consequently, the claims for poetry made by anthologists and reinforced in such review organs as *The New York Times*, *Atlantic*, and *The New Yorker* relegate poetry to a strictly symbolic role, as an icon of high cultural legacy which "we" cannot do without, even if we don't know what to do *with* it. In the display windows of poetry anthologies we continue to see an outward conviviality, an intimation of solidarity, with the amicable nod and wink between imperial functionaries that says, more succinctly than words, "we know who we are." The result is a spectacle of confusion and dismay, naive confidence as well as incredulity, as different communities (of poets, belles lettrists, and scholars) contest in pantomime the uses of poetry in a republic in which there is no use for poetry but theirs, much as they struggle mightily, like the emperor calisthenically donning his new clothes, to pretend otherwise.

WHITMAN'S BIBLE: "BOLD, MODERN, AND ALL-SURROUNDING AND COSMICAL"

> The canon changes—books and authors entering and exiting through revolving doors—by mysterious processes, but a real canon nonetheless exists. Like the Church, the Poetry Establishment honors some of its dead by conferring a kind of sainthood. Lacking England's Poet's Corner in Westminster Abbey where the Greats are interred, this country maintains a Poetry Hall of Fame, invisible but as tightly controlled as the one in Cooperstown. Robert Frost is American poetry's Babe Ruth.
>
> Neglect by the Poetry Establishment becomes its own kind of reputation, the reputation of a poetry-singer for being himself unsung. Poets may become somewhat well known for *not* being well known. This kind of antireputation is bred and maintained within the hyperactive world of Small-Press-Little-Magazine publication . . . . (Collins 297)

While I would not want to overestimate the benefits of "antireputation," Billy Collins is certainly correct in his insistence that there *is* a canonical establishment and that it *is* to some degree successfully opposed by a countercanon. This has lately been accorded a certain lustre in the romance of marginality: "paradoxically," John Guillory notes,

> the most surprising aspect of the current legitimation crisis
> is the fact that the "noncanonical" is not what fails to
> appear in the classroom, but what, in the context of liberal
> pedagogy, *signifies exclusion*. The noncanonical is a newly
> constituted category of text production and reception, per-
> mitting certain authors and texts to be *taught* as noncanon-
> ical, to have the status of noncanonical works in the class-
> room. (*Capital* 9)

For over thirty years, for instance, the Beats have been signifiers of
exclusion, and the familiarity of the role has clearly attenuated
what is signified by the renegade posture. Guillory also provides a
clue to phenomena like the *Norton Anthology*'s inclusion of poets
of color whose work unproblematically conforms to standards of
representational translucency, documenting the experience of a
putative marginality. "The typical valorization of the noncanonical
author's experience as a marginalized social identity necessarily
reasserts the transparency of the text to the experience it represents" (10). To Wimsatt and Beardsley's *intentional* fallacy and
affective fallacy, and Mary Kinzie's *rhapsodic* fallacy, we might
add a *liminal fallacy*, or the assumption that race, class, and gender
automatically privilege certain people as reliable witnesses for the
prosecution of the canon. In fact, oppositionality is not so easily
assumed. Michael Davidson, for instance, chronicles how the
Beats—forced to recognize themselves as icons of mass media—
struggled to convert their own iconicity to the status of oppositional sign. Maria Damon's thesis in *The Dark End of the Street: Margins in American Vanguard Poetry* is that the vanguard is contingent on an actual experience of marginality, and that its "often
neglected work becomes canon-fodder in the construction of a
respectable façade of American letters that would erase the indigence and illegitimacy of its vital sources" (xi). She, like Davidson,
recognizes that "'[r]esistance' implies organization and some degree
of intentionality, unity, and unanimity" (xi). To inhabit the margins, then, is not to be bereft of companionship: quite the contrary,
the margins can more readily facilitate congregation and mutual
recognition.

As margins have come under greater scrutiny, and acquired a certain discursive advantage, marginality as such has drawn fire. Peripheral spaces, after all, are privileged sites of tourism, and "[m]odern mass tourism," writes Dean MacCannell, "is based on two seemingly contradictory tendencies: the international homogenization of the culture of the tourists and the artificial preservation of local ethnic groups and attractions so that they can be consumed as tourist experiences" (176). The degrading spirit of tourist consumerism in the academic celebration of margins has prompted Henry Louis Gates's parodic discontent with his forced conscription to the ranks of "official marginality," hearing the siren call, "Be oppositional, please—you look so cute when you're angry" (185). The condition of marginality most worth talking about is not the calculation of qualifications and merits in the honor-roll of oppressions suffered, nor is it the disappointment of being left out or unrecognized; rather, *marginality* most tellingly names the disadvantage of having to bear the brunt of material and ideological labor that replenishes the center.

The canon of postwar American poetry compounds the problem because of the afflictions suffered by core personae like Lowell, Jarrell, Berryman, Plath, and Sexton. If the canon is maintained by pathological crisis at the center, then suffering at the perimeter is not so much tolerated as *expected*. It is, however, an old dilemma, for which I propose a neologism: *canontology*, signifying the *mode of being* germane to canonicity. *Canontology* finds the word "canon" overlappingly appended to the word "ontology" to signify the criteria for existence—the modes of being and of appearance—that are stipulated by canonical issues. Insofar as a canon is more than a roster of names, it is a collocation of attributes, a showcase for modalities of the exemplary. Canontology has to do with sanctioned prescriptions for being, which translates in a given generic setting to *styles of belonging*. Canontology regulates *membership*. Sacred canons patently render canontology apparent, since the goal of the text is to facilitate rectitude in its readers. Secular canons don't promise as much, except by implication; so it is in the subtext—that ideological residuum of a submerged but tacit group identity—that we must look for evidence of the favored agencies of canonical existence.

Marginality is relative, estimated strictly by the standards of whatever seems central. In First World centers, poetry doesn't figure prominently, but this is only by comparison with the things that do engage centers (which are largely administrative, anyway—including, of course, the administration of "entertainment"). So it makes sense to think of poetry marginalized in another domain, the cultural-pedagogic matrix which manufactures coherence (of a sort) but isn't synonymous with political centrism. Far from marginalizing poetry, this matrix couldn't do without it—though what it does *with* it may be odious. Poetry is at the center of a pedagogic matrix, where it is administratively put to work for *canontology*. For several centuries, anthologists have labored in the canonical mine at the center of national cultures, separating the purported ore from a murky amalgam of subterranean deposits. I want to suggest by this fanciful analogy that anthologists devoted to the Enlightenment task of sorting the grains of wisdom and beauty have really been working in the dark. To summarize quickly (and stress the obvious), this is because poets don't write for anthologies, by and large, and as a result only certain sorts of poems can be identified as harboring canonical aspirations. That such poems dominate in the anthology game should alert us to the syndrome of the teacher's pet: the mischievously solicitous abandon of Beats and Confessional Poets alike in the 1960s, for instance, served only to cloud the fact that both parties courted the canon, but from different directions.

The case of Walt Whitman is curiously appropriate to the topic of anthologies. Whitman devoted his life to one book. Instead of producing a series of books culminating in a *Collected Poems*, Whitman reprinted the same book over and over again, with textual emendations, deletions and additions, rearrangements. In other words, Whitman treated his book the way anthologists tinker with their collections for a revised edition. Whitman thought of *Leaves of Grass* as "the new Bible" (Kaplan 228). This is interesting, because the Bible is not a book but an anthology, a collection of writings. It is the prototype of all anthologies that aspire to transmit a canonical imperative, and in doing so establish a binding relation between Being and Text, life and book. The Bible is at once the most encompassing ontology in the West, and the definitive anthology.

As a book that is a collection of books, the Bible is a canon; that is, the selection of its contents is said to be canonical, and Western canonicity, in turn, is modeled on Biblical precedent. The Bible, like any canon, is identified with a particular people and a nation— Israel. Whitman repeatedly and unabashedly claims a people and a nation for his book too: it is the first word of the preface of the first edition of *Leaves of Grass*: "America . . . ." In the late essay "Poetry To-day In America—Shakspere—the Future," the odd corporation of the title suggests a "fusion" in the sense of that "adhesiveness" Whitman celebrated in his quest for "a new world of democratic sociology and imaginative literature" (538). The political destiny of democracy (synonymous for Whitman with America) is "the grand experiment [of] the forming of a full-grown man or woman . . . "—"standing apart from all else . . . sole and untouchable by any canons of authority . . . " ("Vistas" 484, 479). Here is a peculiarity: a canonical book beyond the reach of canonical authority. For Whitman, canonical credibility inheres in the person.

By "canons of authority" Whitman has in mind something like a council of the elders, a patriarchal editorial board who might censure his poetic disposition. Hence his emphasis on what he called "Personalism": "The problem, as it seems to me, presented to the New World, is, under permanent law and order, and after preserving cohesion, (ensemble-Individuality,) at all hazards, to vitalize man's free play of special Personalism . . . " (497). "This idea of perfect individualism it is indeed that deepest tinges and gives character to the idea of the aggregate" (479). So Whitman does this in the most effective way he knows, in his "attempt, from first to last, to put *a Person*, a human being (myself, in the latter half of the Nineteenth Century, in America,) freely, fully and truly on record" (444). But the written self-portrait was only half the puzzle, to be completed by the living, embodied reader: "Not the book needs so much to be the complete thing, but the reader of the book does" (523). In the 1876 Preface he simply claims "'Leaves of Grass,' as publish'd, to be the Poem of average Identity (of *yours*, whoever you are, now reading these lines)" (534).[33]

Whitman's call for complete readers is a compensation for the poet's own impediments. Whitman's poems are sometimes bardic, oracular; but they are often bashfully self-aware, equivocal, tentative—"baffled, balk'd, bent to the very earth, / Oppress'd with myself that I have dared to open my mouth . . . " ("As I Ebb'd" #2). Now, what does this tell us about the proclamation of cultural authority? How can the bard of the new Bible admit perplexity and impediment? Whitman characteristically secures the linguistic act to the sociopolitical prospect, when he submits that "Behind all else that can be said, I consider 'Leaves of Grass' and its theory experimental—as, in the deepest sense, I consider our American republic itself to be, with its theory" (432). This position cuts against the grain of canonical priorities; you simply can't have experimental righteousness. To alter the form of government requires collective will; but in positing the American political revolt as the tacit backdrop for his revolution of the word, Whitman has to claim collectivity in singularity, the poetic containment of multitudes. Confident that the time had come for "a readjustment of the whole theory and nature of Poetry" Whitman was adamant in "Backward Glance"—over thirty years after the first *Leaves of Grass*—that "It is certainly time for America, above all, to begin this readjustment in the scope and basic point of view of verse; for everything else has changed"

---

[33]Whitman may not have been cognizant of a contemporaneous labor, in the perfection of actuarial tables, involving the wholesale conversion of a populace to its statistical base, which is the modern form of the electorate. It is a strictly mathematical and probabalistic computation of what constitutes a "majority"—probabalistic because the majority of registered voters no longer vote, so the contentious minorities that do vote need to be reconfigured mathematically as a viable majority. Whitman's appeal to the "average Identity" does not even envisage a statistical norm, though he goes on to suggest a sampling procedure ("whoever you are, now reading these lines"). Whitman's sample is hardly random, relying as it does on readerly motivation; but what the poet requires of his constituency here, in this apparent randomness, is precisely the contingency that someone *does* take the trouble to read the poem: that "someone" is then among the elect, personally addressed as such, in a kerygmatic embrace, by the distant bard.

(436, 433). Despite the glamour of a national verse enterprise that so absorbed Whitman's fancy, the kind of change he was calling for could only be individually undertaken. What Whitman discloses here is a tension between cultural authority and personal authenticity. It is intended to be a productive tension, but it cannot be regulated by canons of authority. In his noteworthy phrase from the 1855 Preface, the poet "does not stop for any regulation . . . he is the president of regulation" (453).

A "perfect individualism" may well end up sanctioning or even centralizing the bizarre, the grotesque, the perverse. Emerson's "representative men" were all heroes, in his friend Carlyle's sense. But as Borges pointed out, "the mere happy vagabond proposed by the verses of *Leaves of Grass* would have been incapable of writing them" (72). In fact, even the scrupulous author proved incapable of augmenting his book significantly after the Civil War, and became instead its editor, custodian, and memorialist. By 1876 Whitman conceded that the radiant physiology of 1855 had yielded to "the pathology which was pretty sure to come in time from the other" (533). The *song* of the self became the *diagnosis*; melody replaced by malady.[34] The "electric self" haughtily declaiming poems, "seiz'd by the spirit that trails in the lines underfoot" turned out to be "but a trail of drift and debris . . . " ("As I Ebb'd" #1, 3).

Leaves of Grass is both attractive and exemplary because it encompasses such extremes (as do, later, Pound's *Cantos*). Whitman proposes in it a book inseparable from the nation, yet indistinguishable from its author; and what is more, coextensive with its reader's privacy, a reader whose personal compact with author and nation is rendered in terms of Whitman's uncompromising list at the end of *Specimen Days* " . . . the costless, average, divine, original concrete."

---

[34]Reflecting on Poe in *Specimen Days*, Whitman persists in identifying ailment as necessary to the complete poetic achievement: "Comprehending artists in a mass, musicians, painters, actors, and so on, and considering each and all of them as radiations or flanges of that furious whirling wheel, poetry, the centre and axis of the whole, where else indeed may we so well investigate the causes, growths, tally-marks of the time—the age's matter and malady?" (708).

(754).[35] The case of Whitman clarifies for us what it means to think of anthology as ontology. In his succinct oxymoron, the issue is "ensemble-Individuality." Whitman's project engages public and private, self and other, typical and marginal, central and peripheral, average and exceptional. These polarities vivify the options available to the anthologist.

The *American Heritage Dictionary* defines anthology as "a collection of literary pieces, such as poems, short stories, or plays, usually suggesting a theme." ("Here the theme is creative and has vista," Whitman says ambiguously of his book and the nation [452].) Throughout *Leaves of Grass*, Whitman tells us how to live and work and love as individuals and in the aggregate. "This is what you shall do: Love the earth and sun and the animals, despise riches, give alms to every one that asks, stand up for the stupid and crazy" he exhorts in the 1855 Preface (454). His theme, in other words, is ontological, prescribing a theory of being. An anthologist likewise asserts a theory of being by designating a theme, and by asking of the congregation of pieces: How do these many things taken together achieve congress? What binds them? Can a positive identity be distilled from such a constellation?

The crucial point at which anthologists diverge from Whitman has to do with aesthetic value. Whitman makes no claim for the excellence of his poems, only for their pertinence, relevance, fit. Representation is less important than presentation—not in the sense of "presentable," but as implying intrusion, ungainly sprawl, protrusion. If his book includes the prophetic with the maudlin, the visionary with the trite, so much the better. Whitman's precedent enables Ezra Pound, surveying his own rag-bag, to see that "it coheres all right." Can we think of an anthology of poetry that makes comparable claims, and that bears itself with Whitmanesque nonchalance, or an anthologist proudly declaring a blend of the shabby with the

---

[35] *Democratic Vistas* concludes with a nearly identical summation: " . . . the main thing being the average, the bodily, the concrete, the democratic, the popular, on which all the superstructures of the future are to permanently rest" (524).

superior? At most, anthologists concede that the standards of excellence are not uniformly high throughout.

There are a handful of rudimentary priorities assumed by virtually all anthologists whose labors are explicitly canonical. The poems chosen for a collection of national literature will be said to be typical with respect to literary practice, and the authors will be representative of some purported "range" of thematic affiliations and concerns. These options seem reasonable. But these alone do not satisfy editors (or publishers), for the chosen poets and poems *also* have to demonstrate excellence, or accomplishment ("of the highest order"). The burden turns out to be double, and insoluble: the typical, the representative, must somehow exemplify the exceptional. The normal must be abnormally fine. How did we come to this impasse, this impossible dream?

I should point out the obvious fact that not all anthologies aspire to canonical service. A collection of literary pieces may be bound together by a peripheral and incidental, rather than central and official, theme. Before the printing press, manuscripts were bound together, more as a convenience to a binder than as a thematic assembly. The practice continued after printing, and in 1790 the British Museum had a category for such books: Polygraphy, or the collection of separate works bound together, classed with Poetry, Novels, and Letters. In other words, disparate works could be casually brought together; immediate juxtaposition of texts did not signify totalization. At the same time, we can see the epistemological trouble that lurks ahead for polygraphy after its recognition by British Museum bibliographers. These items, with their capriciously affiliated component parts, tend to make the ephemeral look permanent, simply because the medium is print.

But print is also inert. Library stacks harbor novelties like *Stag Lines: An Anthology of Virile Verse*, arranged by the lunar cycle in such sections as "The Stag and Eve," "The Stag Murmurs to His Mate," and "The Stag and the Scarlet Stain." Despite what you may think, this is far from pornographic; it is simply an adventurous way to package a bland batch of pedestrian poems. Still, idiosyncratic and renegade projects can end up servicing nationalism inadvertently, as does *The Beauties of Poetry Display'd*, published in 1757. This anthology in two volumes has an indexical relationship to English verse, which is "display'd" here entirely in excerpts, arranged alphabetically by such topics as Stars, Ridicule, Fishing, Luxury, Basilisk, Abandoned, and Petitions. The cumulative impact of such arrangement is the implication that English poets have penned captions sufficient for any and all occasions. Not all nationalist anthologies are canonical. An early ambitious collection of American poetry, *The Poets and Poetry of America*, edited by Rufus Griswold, flatly declares the mediocrity of its contents, but claims to be performing the service of accurately representing the state of the art as of 1842.[36] This is rare, however. Anthologies like *Stag Lines* can forgo excellence in pursuit of novelty; but a national affiliation invariably burdens editors with an Olympic quest for the gold.

What is it about nationality that makes the anthology so ponderously ambitious, so clumsily responsible? Nation-states are comparatively recent institutions, having developed simultaneously with the vernacular languages and the printing press. These communications media are intimately fused in the nation-building

---

[36] Anthologists of the early nineteenth century, despite their invariable modesty with respect to the calibre of American verse, justified their selections on documentary, moral, and anthropological grounds. In 1834, for instance, the anonymous editor of *Selections from the American Poets* issued in Dublin noted that "The character of the poetry of a country has always been justly regarded as indicative of its general moral and intellectual progress" (vii). John Keese apologetically presented his *Poets of America* (New York, 1840) with a reminder that in undertaking the "mighty work of preparing a spacious home for the thronging multitudes of our population, and building up for their protection, a great polity . . . . American poetry has hitherto been little more than a happy accident, and seems to have arisen in spite of the practical tendencies of our country, and the prosaic character of our time" (9). "We have left our pearls unstrung," Keese sadly concludes (10). George B. Cheever (*The Poets of America*, Hartford, 1847) consolingly points out that "[a]ll the pieces in this volume are of the purest moral character, and, considering its limits, and the comparative scantiness of American poetry, a good number of them contain, in an uncommon degree, the religious and poetic spirit united" (5). For a useful account of the eventual growth of nationalist rhetoric in anthologies of the late nineteenth and early twentieth century, see Alan Golding, "A History of American Poetry Anthologies," and *From Outlaw to Classic: Canons in American Poetry* (University of Wisconsin Press, 1995).

enterprise. The stabilization of the vernacular was aided by print-fixity: printed writing literally regulated speech. Nation-states exist largely as what Benedict Anderson calls "imagined communities"— and the collapse of the Soviet Union is sufficient reminder of the perils of community negligently imagined. The determination of social congress is as much a cultural as a political activity. The cultural imagination nominates types of affiliation; cultural institutions evaluate and thereby stratify people and objects; and the protocol of the whole sociopolitical ensemble is to regulate passage from inside to outside and vice versa. One of the key regulative tools that has grown to prominence during the age of Gutenberg nationalism is the museum. Museums are not only collections of things but indices of practices. In this respect a museum is a strategic model for the anthology.

The modernized version of the curiosity cabinet, the museum, is a device for taming and ordering diversity. It is also through the museum that the cultural project of centralizing and enshrining the typical as the exceptional comes into focus. The Wunderkammer unpretentiously collects and displays the grotesque, the unique, the atypical, accentuating marginalia and stressing exceptionality as difference. The Wunderkammer determines value quantitatively, as an assertion of rarity or irregularity, while the museum registers value as qualitative. The pivotal distinction between Wunderkammer and museum is that the latter moves typicality and representation into the center of concern. We go to museums not to marvel at the bizarre or grotesque wonders on display, but to reflect on the typicality of exemplary items spread out before us.

Malraux's concept of the museum without walls alerts us to the violent resocialization involved whenever artifacts are detached from one environment and rendered emphatically significant in another. Detached from original contexts, artworks become synecdoches of everything so sundered: "How indeed could this mutilated possible fail to evoke the whole gamut of the possible?" (Malraux 15). Donna Haraway, in "Teddy Bear Patriarchy," helps us recognize art as a species of wildlife, bagged and tagged. To which I would add: gagged. If artworks are in some sense mutilated by their forced resocialization in museum culture, it is their muteness that is on display. (Isn't it uncanny how quiet museums are? Maybe this is why audio-headset tours are so popular, to quell the silent clamor of dismemberment. These places are holding tanks, penitentiaries of eyes.) The important thing to take into consideration here is that anthologies are public relations agents for "poetry" the way museums are for "art"—and both are sites all too susceptible to "the various executive commodifications of the administrative attitude" (Said, "Blackmur" 48). As with any intermediary agency, there are behavioral prescriptions involved. Foremost among these for the anthology is that the peculiarities of the contents must be subdued. Each poem has to "represent" the exceptional without actually being excessive. It has to be *typically different.*

Art, mediated by the cultural apparatus of the museum, is the category in which most of us first come into contact with the exceptional (which captions and catalogs won't let us forget). It is, however, also the means by which we experience an explicit staging of the uncommon and the original, the marginal and the aberrant. To actually comprehend the scale of displacement that makes a museum's collection or an anthology possible is to encounter there an extradited population—the stateless, the deportee, the refugee. When you see Kandinsky in a museum, I'm suggesting, you don't see Kandinsky; you are witness to the ruin of Kandinsky, the dispersal of a coherent body of work into a thousand places. In the same manner, four or five "characteristic" poems by H. D., Snyder, or Rich in an anthology put displacement on display. The objects in museums and anthologies are prized and enshrined, but they are also ostracized by virtue of their forced resocialization. But isn't it useful, the argument goes, to have these works circulated anyway, even if the circumstances are not ideal? To answer that, I would point out that it is precisely the museum, the canon, the anthology that advertise themselves as agents and custodians of the ideal. Museums and anthologies borrow their authority from objects which they certify as authentic. But what is authenticated by the resocialization of objects into icons? The objects themselves become ideal forms; so "The Waste Land" loses its character as shaggy residue of pathological catastrophe, the disordered script of an aborted project, and it circulates instead as one of a series of ideal forms rendered conceptually homologous (Modernism : Waste Land : Postwar : Mythopoiesis : Collage : Culture Crisis).

The international character of early twentieth-century art now tends to be redistributed into national canons, not because of the failure of modernism, but because of the vigor of nationalism. For several centuries the anthology has been an optical tool for focusing the idiom of the tribe; the lyric was grooved to run on iron rails of prideful enterprise; the culture was abbreviated into a book, a synecdoche of the nation. Anthologies in the language-world of nation-states are the steroids of canon-building. The anthology poem in this environment, to be truly competitive, must be synthetically manipulated to bear up under great pressure. Anthologies teach canonical poems how to eject their contexts as so much material detritus hindering the trajectory of the ideal. Recontextualized in canon-building anthologies, poems become monumental configurations of cultural centrism. The central status of canonical poems converts them, in effect, to inscriptions on monuments—and who bothers to read plaques? So the canonization of poems has, paradoxically, worked to marginalize poetry.

Literature and language merged in the seventeenth century as a field in which the central problem was figural stability. Rhetoric had been until then the prevailing system of linguistic deviation. But the lapse of rhetoric exposed language as intrinsically deviant. Since then, literature—and within it, poetry especially—has borne a double burden. As it assumes a canontology (or maintenance of the being of a canonical core), poetry is made responsible for stabilizing identity, both psychologically and sociologically. On the other hand, poetry is expected to exemplify the gratuitous, the ludic, the untethered. It must speak the truth in the midst of play; it needs to make a killing while on holiday. You may recognize here the Kantian moment in which a nonutilitarian pleasure is dignified by its cognitive endowment. The Romantic prospect follows from this: poetics is no longer a theory of writing but a theory of knowing. Poetry is not literature but consciousness.[37] Having now absorbed the ancient discipline of rhetoric, with all its *topoi*, tropes, figures, commonplaces—and having been elevated to the status of one of the branches of learning by Bacon, and one of the means of knowing by Kant—poetry in the post-Romantic phase is expected to accommodate radically conflicting claims and demands. Poetry begins to seem poetic to the degree that it engages complexity; this is the kind of center that cannot hold. Poetry occupies that junction where the information maximized in it slides over to entropy, starting to sound like noise. It's like the waveband in the inner city, with an oversaturation of broadcasts bleeding into each other: you have to go out past the city limits, out to the margin, to pick up a clear signal. In the entropic densities of our cultural centers, it makes perfect sense to think of poetry marginalized. Poetry can—and *should*—be our term for a language in crisis, driven to the outskirts to hear itself speak.

Museums and anthologies have long been the sites of a gladiatorial display; far from being things on holiday, their contents are contestants seething with desperation. When Walter Benjamin warned that the aestheticizing of politics results in war, I think he had something like this in mind. The canonical anthology smells bad, like the cattle-pens up Interstate 5 (the "Golden State Freeway") between L. A. and Sacramento. The aesthetic equivalent of genetic engineering has yielded a glut of identical perfect specimens, which demonstrate only too well the grotesque obligation to be typically distinctive. What seems in danger of being lost is the audacity of Whitman's attempt to make up a canon all by himself, sensing in the center cause for bereavement, because the sterilizing altitude of the "universal" is in the end just a moribund stereotype—all that sur-

---

[37] The rise of modern free verse—and here Whitman again looms large—is thus susceptible to notions of a "natural" utterance, a voice unsullied by technical or stylistic decoration. In acceding to this fantasy, of course, poets begin to prioritize selfhood as a phantom accomplice. What's lacking in the Anglo-American tradition is anything like Rimbaud's "*dérèglement*" or the surrealist commitment to discerning self in nonnormative utterance. So the hectic scramble of voices in language poet Bruce Andrews's work, for instance, is likely to appear as a perverse abandonment of "self" and "voice," and thus ineligible for serious consideration as Poetry.

vives the eradication of the particular. William Carlos Williams's particularism, like Whitman's, values things as "universal" in and of themselves, not because they conform to some greater type. "One has to learn what the meaning of the local is," Williams wrote, "for universal purposes. The local is the only thing that is universal" (*Imaginations* 358). "[A]ll we can be sure of is that at our most subjective we are universal," Muriel Rukeyser affirmed in *The Life of Poetry*. "For this is the world of light and change: the real world; and the reality of the artist is the reality of the witnesses" (202). As Sidney Mintz says, "It is not our human nature that is universal, but our capacity to create cultural realities, and then to act in terms of them" (quoted in Wallerstein 158). The universal is everywhere instantaneously congealed in the sprawl of singularities, dispersed and recollected, abandoned and sustained.

> The universality of things
> draws me toward the candy
> with melon flowers that open
>
> about the edge of refuse
> proclaiming without accent
> the quality of the farmer's
>
> shoulders and his daughter's
> accidental skin, so sweet
> with clover and the small
>
> yellow cinquefoil in the
> parched places.
>
> (Williams, *Imaginations* 117–18)

The privilege of poetry is this drift, this insouciant disregard for the exemplary pose—and the tyrannous attitudes—of those figures in wax.

APPENDIX 1: AMERICAN POETRY ANTHOLOGIES, 1950-1994

Anthologies consulted are listed below chronologically. When several anthologies share the same year, they are arranged within that year in alphabetical order by the editor's name. For example: P85 (*Contemporary American Poetry* edited by Poulin) precedes V85 (Vendler's *Harvard Book of Contemporary American Poetry*). Textbooks are indicated by an asterisk (*) before the editor's name. Of the 143 titles listed below, 13 were published in the 1950s, 25 in the 1960s, 52 in the 1970s, 40 in the 1980s, and 13 in the 1990s.The distribution of selected anthologies across the decades reflects each decade's reliance on the anthology as a medium of expressive intervention in the marketplace. The number of textbooks increases as the market for instructional anthologies expands with increasing enrollments. There are 48 textbooks cited—including, however, multiple editions of several of them; different editions are represented only when there is substantial revision of selections.

The criterion for selecting the anthologies in this list was above all to include the most ambitious, the ones attempting either to be definitive (generally, or within an ambitiously claimed domain). A secondary consideration was documentary; thus the leading magazines of postwar poetry, when compiled into anthologies, are all represented. I avoided anthologies on specific topics (whether Vietnam or Chess); and I also avoided anthologies that by definition exclude particular types of people—i.e. none of the numerous collections devoted to poetry by blacks, gays, women, or men were consulted. I did include those regional anthologies that offer some scope. As to the publishers, there is a considerable range here. There are hardcover collections as well as mass market paperbacks, trade and university as well as a few small press anthologies. I've included anthologies published in Canada and England, to incorporate a view from abroad but still within the purview of English. I've sampled an array of anthologies that don't limit themselves to contemporary poetry, so there are some titles that begin with Chaucer and conclude with Lowell, others that are American from the nineteenth century to the present, and others that are Anglo-American from modern to contemporary. The textbooks cited are of two kinds: anthologies indistinguishable from trade anthologies except that they're marketed by textbook divisions, like Poulin's; and those modelled on the prototype of the famous Brooks-Warren *Understanding Poetry.* In every instance I included only those that made a substantial commitment to including contemporary American poetry, which generally means using the work of some dozen postwar poets. Finally, a supplementary list of foreign language anthologies of postwar American poetry follows the list of "Most Anthologized Poets," itemizing the poets selected.

In Appendix 2, "Most Anthologized Poets," the anthology citations are listed chronologically. (The poets are listed alphabetically.) Listings from anthologies issued in consecutive revised editions are cited as follows: P71–91 would mean the poet appears in all editions of Poulin, inclusive from the first edition in 1971 through the fifth edition in 1991. Certain anthologies by the same editors are not treated this way because, though the poets may be repeated, the selections of poems were entirely revised by the editors; for instance, the second edition of *Naked Poetry* (BM76) includes none of the poems from the first edition (BM69); so BM69 and BM76 are separated in the list by all the intervening anthologies published between 1970–76. Annual volumes edited by John Hall Wheelock, each featuring three poets, were published by Scribner's as *Poets of Today* with the designated roman numeral for the series entry, beginning with I in 1954. These are indicated in the text by **PT** followed by roman numeral and year, for instance, **PTVI.59** is *Poets of Today VI* published in 1959. The Wheelock volumes are accounted for in the "Most Anthologized Poets" list, but are *not* listed below.

C50   Ciardi, *Mid-Century American Poets,* Twayne

MO50 Matthiessen, *The Oxford Book of American Verse,* Oxford U. P.

H53   Humphries, *New Poems by American Poets,* Ballantine

M54   Moore, *The Penguin Book of Modern American Verse,* Penguin

W54   Williams, *A Pocket Book of Modern Verse,* Washington Square

U55   *Untermeyer, Shapiro, Wilbur, *Modern American and Modern British Poetry,* revised shorter ed., Harcourt Brace

RS55   *Rosenthal, Smith, *Exploring Poetry,* Macmillan

A56   Auden, *The Criterion Book of Modern American Verse,* Criterion ["Faber" in U.K. edition and title]

E56   *Elliott, *Fifteen Modern American Poets,* Holt, Rinehart

H57   Humphries, *New Poems by American Poets #2,* Ballantine

HPS57   Hall, Pack, Simpson, *The New Poets of England and America,* Meridian

T58   Cecil, Tate, *Modern Verse in English 1900–1950,* Eyre & Spottiswoode

W58   Williams, *A Pocket Book of Modern Verse,* revised ed., Washington Square

A60   Allen, *The New American Poetry,* Grove

BW60   *Brooks, Warren, *Understanding Poetry,* 3rd edition, Holt

S60   *Shapiro, *American Poetry,* Crowell

EL62   Engle, Langland, *Poet's Choice,* Dial

H62   Hall, *Contemporary American Poetry,* Penguin

HP62   Hall, Pack, *New Poets of England and America,* 2nd edition, Meridian

U62   *Untermeyer, *Modern American Poetry,* 8th edition, Harcourt

BR63   *Brinnin, Read, *The Modern Poets: An American-British Anthology,* McGraw-Hill

K64   Kessler, *American Poems,* Southern Illinois U. P.

W64   *Walsh, *Today's Poets,* Scribner's

ARR65   *Allen, Rideout, Robinson, *American Poetry,* Harper & Row

D65   DeLoach, *The East Side Scene,* Anchor

KL65   Kelly, Leary, *A Controversy of Poets,* Anchor

M66   *Martz, *The Distinctive Voice,* Scott, Foresman

OW66   Williams, *An Anthology of American Verse from Colonial Days to the Present,* World

BBL67   *Bradley, Beatty, Long, *The American Tradition in Literature,* 3rd edition, Norton

R67   Rosenthal, *The New Modern Poetry,* Macmillan

S67   Stryk, *Heartland: Poets of the Midwest* Northern Illinois U. P.

A68   *Adams, *Poetry: An Introductory Anthology,* Little, Brown

C68   Carroll, *The Young American Poets,* Follett

H68   Hollander, *Poems of Our Moment,* Pegasus

BM69   Berg, Mezey, *Naked Poetry,* Bobbs-Merrill

G69   *Gleeson, *A First Reader of Contemporary American Poetry,* Charles E. Merrill Pub. Co.

NY69   *The* New Yorker *Book of Poems,* Viking

S69   Strand, *The Contemporary American Poets,* NAL Mentor

BR70   *Brinnin, Read, *The Modern Poets,* McGraw-Hill [trade edition: *Twentieth Century Poetry*]

C70   Carruth, *The Voice That Is Great Within Us,* Bantam

E70   *Eastman et al., *The Norton Anthology of Poetry,* Norton

F70   *Foerster, Falk et al., *American Poetry and Prose,* 5th edition, Houghton Mifflin

K70   Kostelanetz, *Possibilities of Poetry,* Dell

SM70   *Mark Schorer, *The Literature of America: Twentieth Century,* McGraw-Hill

PS70   Padgett, Shapiro, *The New York Poets,* Grove

SNR70 *Sanders, Nelson, Rosenthal, *Chief Modern Poets of Britain and America,* 5th edition, Houghton Mifflin

E71   Eshleman, *A Caterpillar Anthology,* Anchor

G71   Gillam, *Eight Modern American Poets,* Harrap

L71   Lee, *The Major Young Poets,* Meridian

MS71   McMichael, Saleh, *Just What the Country Needs, Another Poetry Anthology,* Wadsworth

P71   *Poulin, *Contemporary American Poetry,* Houghon Mifflin

WD71   Witt-Diamant, Fukuda, *53 American Poets of Today,* Folcroft

C72   Clark, *All Stars,* Grossman/Goliard

H72   Hall, *Contemporary American Poetry,* 2nd edition, Penguin

W72   *Walsh, *Today's Poets,* 2nd edition, Scribner's

WS72   Williams, Sobiloff, *The New Pocket Anthology of American Verse from Colonial Days to the Present,* Washington Square

C73	*Chace, *Making it New*, Canfield
E73	*Evans, *New Voices in American Poetry*, Winthrop
EN73	*Ellmann, *The Norton Anthology of Modern Poetry*, Norton
F73	Fox, *The Living Underground*, Whitson
G73	*Geddes, *20th Century Poetry and Poetics*, 2nd edition, Oxford U. P. (Canada)
K73	Kherdian, *Visions of America by the Poets*, Macmillan
MK73	Klonsky, *Shake the Kaleidoscope*, Pocket Books
RS73	*Rosenthal, Smith, *Exploring Poetry*, 2nd edition, Macmillan
W73	*Williams, *Contemporary Poetry in America*, Random House
U73	*Untermeyer, *50 Modern American and British Poets*, McKay
BBL74	*Bradley, Beatty, Long, Perkins, *The American Tradition in Literature*, 4th edition, Grosset & Dunlop
GQ74	Gross, Quasha, *Open Poetry*, Grossman
H74	Howard, *Preferences: 51 American Poets Choose Poems from Their Own Work and from the Past*, Viking
HB74	*Brady, Price, *Poetry Past and Present*, Harcourt, Brace
K74	*Kennedy, *An Introduction to Poetry*, 3rd edition, Little, Brown
Q74	Quasha, *Active Anthology*, Sumac
RQ74	Rothenberg, Quasha, *America a Prophecy*, Random House
W74	Weiss, *Contemporary Poetry: A Retrospective from the Quarterly Review of Literature*, Princeton U. P.
CO75	Corman, *The Gist of Origin 1951–1971*, Grossman
CW75	*Ciardi, Williams, *How Does a Poem Mean?*, 2nd edition, Houghton Mifflin
D75	*De Roche, *The Heath Introduction to Poetry*, Heath
E75	*Eastman et al., *The Norton Anthology of Poetry*, 2nd edition, Norton
H75	Halpern, *The American Poetry Anthology*, Avon
P75	*Poulin, *Contemporary American Poetry*, 2nd edition, Houghton Mifflin
S75	Stryk, *Heartland II: Poets of the Midwest*, Northern Illinois U. P.
BM76	Berg, Mezey, *The New Naked Poetry*, Bobbs-Merrill

EO76   Ellmann, *The New Oxford Book of American Verse*, Oxford U. P.

H76   Heyen, *American Poets in 1976*, Bobbs-Merrill

L76   Lally, *None of the Above*, Crossing Press

M77   Moore, *The Penguin Book of American Verse*, 2nd edition, Penguin

HP78   Hine, Parisi, *The* Poetry *Anthology 1912–1977*, Houghton Mifflin

K78   *Kennedy, *An Introduction to Poetry*, 4th edition, Little, Brown

F79   Field, *A Geography of Poets*, Bantam

KN79   *Kalstone et al., *The Norton Anthology of American Literature*, Norton

B80   Bly, *News of the Universe: Poems of Twofold Consciousness*, Sierra Club

E80   Enright, *The Oxford Book of Contemporary Verse 1945–1980*, Oxford U. P.

M80   Moss, *New York: Poems*, Avon

P80   *Poulin, *Contemporary American Poetry*, 3rd edition, Houghton Mifflin

N81   *Nims, *The Harper Anthology of Poetry*, Harper & Row

R81   Ray, *From A to Z: 200 Contemporary American Poets*, Swallow/ Ohio U. P.

AB82   Allen, Butterick, *The Postmoderns* [*New American Poetry*, revised edition], Grove

K82   *Kennedy, *An Introduction to Poetry*, 5th edition, Little, Brown

E83   *Eastman et al., *The Norton Anthology of Poetry*, 3rd edition, Norton

F83   *Frye, Baker, Perkins, *The Practical Imagination: An Introduction to Poetry*, Harper & Row

FY83   *Friebert, Young, *The Longman Anthology of Contemporary American Poetry*, Longman

D84   Dow, *19 New American Poets of the Golden Gate*, Harcourt Brace

H84   Heyen, *The Generation of 2000*, Ontario Review

MW84   Myers, Weingarten, *New American Poets of the 80s*, Wampeter

W84   Warren [intro], *Fifty Years of American Poetry*, Abrams

B85   Berg, *Singular Voices*, Avon

BL85   Pack, Lea, Parini, *The Bread Loaf Anthology of Contemporary American Poetry*, U. P. of New England

G85   *Geddes, *20th Century Poetry and Poetics,* 3rd edition, Oxford U. P. (Canada)

KN85   *Kalstone et al., *The Norton Anthology of American Literature,* 2nd edition, Norton

MM85   *McMichael, *Anthology of American Literature,* 3rd edition, Macmillan

P85   *Poulin, *Contemporary American Poetry,* 4th edition, Houghton Mifflin

SB85   Smith, Bottoms, *The Morrow Anthology of Younger American Poets,* Morrow

V85   Vendler, *The Harvard Book of Contemporary American Poetry,* Harvard U. P.

DJ86   Dacey, Jauss, *Strong Measures,* Harper & Row

H86   Halpern, *The Antaeus Anthology,* Bantam

K86   *Kennedy, *An Introduction to Poetry,* 6th edition, Little, Brown

S86   Silliman, *In the American Tree,* American Poetry Foundation

C87   Codrescu, *Up Late: American Poetry Since 1970,* Four Walls Eight Windows

GR87   Lindberg, Corey, *Keener Sounds: Selected Poems from* The Georgia Review, U. of Georgia P.

L87   Lehman, *Ecstatic Occasions, Obedient Forms,* Macmillan

M87   Messerli, *"Language" Poetries,* New Directions

R87   *Rosenthal, *Poetry in English,* Oxford U. P.

S87   Stokesbury, *The Made Thing: An Anthology of Contemporary Southern Poetry,* U. of Arkansas P.

EN88   *Ellmann, O'Clair, *The Norton Anthology of Modern Poetry,* 2nd edition, Norton

R88   Richman, *The Direction of Poetry,* Houghton Mifflin

C89   Christopher, *Under 35: The New Generation of American Poets,* Anchor

FY89   *Friebert, Young, *The Longman Anthology of Contemporary American Poetry,* 2nd edition, Longman

HA89   Harris, Aguerro, *An Ear to the Ground,* U. of Georgia P.

KN89   *Kalstone, Wallace et al., *The Norton Anthology of American Literature,* 3rd edition, Norton

W89 Wallace, *Vital Signs: Contemporary American Poetry from the University Presses,* U. of Wisconsin P.

K90 *Kennedy, *An Introduction to Poetry,* 7th edition, Little, Brown

L90 *Lauter, *The Heath Anthology of American Literature,* Heath

M90 McClatchy, *The Vintage Book of Contemporary American Poetry,* Random House/Vintage

PR90 Plimpton, *The* Paris Review *Anthology,* Norton

HB91 *Miller, *Heritage of American Literature,* Harcourt Brace Jovanovich

JP91 Johnson, Paulenich, *Beneath a Single Moon: Buddhism in Contemporary American Poetry,* Shambhala

MW91 Myers, Weingarten, *New American Poets of the '90s,* Godine

P91 *Poulin, *Contemporary American Poetry,* 5th edition, Houghton Mifflin

W91 Waldman, *Out of This World: An Anthology of the St. Mark's Poetry Project,* Crown

PH91 *Elliot et al., *American Literature: A Prentice Hall Anthology,* Prentice Hall

BC92 Phillips, Reed, Strads, Wong, *The Before Columbus Foundation Poetry Anthology,* Norton

F92 Field, Locklin, Stetler, *A New Geography of Poets,* U. of Arkansas P.

W93 Weinberger, *American Poetry Since 1950: Innovators and Outsiders,* Marsilio

H94 *Hoover, *Postmodern American Poetry,* Norton

M94 Messerli, *From the Other Side of the Century: A New American Poetry 1960–1990,* Sun & Moon

APPENDIX 2: MOST ANTHOLOGIZED POETS, 1950–1994

Ai. MS71. H75. F79. H84. W84. SB85. H86. EN88. BC92.

A. R. Ammons. H68. S69. BR70. C70. K70. H72. EN73-88. K73. MK73. W73. H74. HB74. K74-90. W74. E75-83. EO76. M77. HP78. F79. KN79-89. P80-85. N81. F83. BL85. MM85. V85. H86. R87. M90. HB91. P91.

Jon Anderson. C68. NY69. H75. S75. HP78. MW84. SB85. DJ86. H86.

Bruce Andrews. L76. S86. M87. W91. H94. M94.

David Antin. NY69. E71. GQ74. Q74. RQ74. C87. W91. W93. H94. M94.

John Ashbery. A60. H62-72. KL65. H68. S69. BR70. C70. K70. P71-91. PS70. WS72. C73. EN73-88. MK73. U73. H74. HB74. W74. E75-83. EO76. M77. HP78. K78-90. F79. KN79-89. M80. N81. AB82. FY83-89. W84. BL85. V85. DJ86. H86. GR87. R87. W89. L90. M90. PR90. HB91. W91. W93. H94. M94.

Jimmy Santiago Baca. HA89. K90. MW91. BC92. H94.

Amiri Baraka (Leroi Jones). A60. KL65. BBL67-74. R67. G69. S69. C70. E70-83. FF70. P71-80. WD71. WS72. EN73-88. K73. MK73. RS73. U73. HB74. K74. D75. EO76. M77. HP78. F79. KN79-89. AB82. K82. MM85. R87. L90. PR90. PH91. HB91. BC92. F92. W93. H94. M94.

Marvin Bell. C68. NY69. S69. L71. E73. H74. CW75. H75. S75. HP78. F79. R81. FY83. P85-91. W84. B85. BL85. DJ86. H86. M90.

Michael Benedikt. C68. S69. BR70. MS71. L71. H72. MK73. W74. H75. HP78. W89. PR90.

Stephen Berg. BM69. NY69. HP78. JP91. MW91.

Bill Berkson. C68. PS70. C87. W91. H94.

Charles Bernstein. S86. C87. M87. W91. H94. M94.

Ted Berrigan. D65. C68. G69. K70. PS70. C72. RQ74. C87. PR90. W91. H94. M94.

Wendell Berry. ARR65. C70. U73. D75. HP78. F79. B80. H84. BL85. H86. S87.

John Berryman. M54. A56. T58. S60. EL62. U62. BR63. ARR65. OW66. R67. BM69. NY69. S69. BR70. C70. K70. SM70. P71-91. WD71. WS72. EN73-88. MK73. RS73. U73. W73. BBL74. HB74. K74. D75. E75-83. EO76. M77. HP78. KN79-89. E80. M80. N81. F83. FY83-89. W84. G85. MM85. V85. DJ86. H86. R87. L90. M90. PH91. HB91.

Frank Bidart. H75. V85. KN85. L87. EN88. M90.

Elizabeth Bishop. C50. M54. W54-58. RS55. U55. A56. E56. H57. T58. BW60. S60. EL62. U62. BR63. M66. OW66. R67. A68. NY69. S69. BR70. C70. SM70. WD71. W72. WS72. MK73. U73. W73. BBL74. H74. HB74. K74-90. W74. D75. EO76. M77. HP78. F79. KN79-89. B80. E80. M80. P80-91. N81. E83. EN83-89. FY83-89. W84. G85. MM85. V85. DJ86. R87. R88. L90. PH91. HB91. M90.

Paul Blackburn. A60. D65. KL65. R67. NY69. C70. E71. EN73. K73. Q74. RQ74. CO75. M77. M80. AB82. W91. W93. H94.

Robin Blaser. A60. KL65. E71. WD71. AB82. M94.

Michael Blumenthal. BL85. SB85. V85. EN88. R88.

Robert Bly. HPS57. H62-72. R67. S67. BM69. G69. S69. C70. MS71. P71-91. WS72. C73. EN73-88. F73. MK73. W73. BBL74. HB74. K74-90. W74. E75-83. BM76. EO76. H76. M77. HP78. F79. B80. M80. FY83-89. B85. GR87. W89. PR90. HB91.

Philip Booth. H53. H57. HPS57. HP62. BR63-70. M66. NY69. S69. C70. HP78. F79. R81. W84. BL85. DJ86. GR87. PR90.

David Bottoms. HP78. F79. K82-86. W84. BL85. SB85. S87. F92.

Edgar Bowers. HPS57. EL62. H62-72. S69. WD71. HP78. S87. M90.

Richard Brautigan. G69. MS71. K73. MK73. K74-90. PR90. W91.

John Malcolm Brinnin. M54. U55. EL62. BR63-70. NY69. U73. H74. W74. H76. HP78. F79. M80. K86.

William Bronk. NY69. C70. CO75. F79. W93.

Gwendolyn Brooks. EL62. S67. C70. E70-83. SM70. P71-91. C73. EN73-88. RS73. U73. W73. K74-90. D75. EO76. M77. HP78. F79. KN79-89. N81. F83. MM85. DJ86. R87. FY89. HA89. L90. HB91. PH91.

James Broughton. A56. A60. WD71. F79. F92.

Michael Brownstein. C68. C87. PS70. W91. M94.

Charles Bukowski. K73. MK73. W73. GQ74. RQ74. M77. F79. E83. F92. H94.

John Cage. K70. GQ74. Q74. RQ74. L87. JP91. W93. H94. M94.

Hayden Carruth. R67. NY69. C70. W74. BM76. HP78. F79. R81. B85. BL85. DJ86. H86.

Lorna Dee Cervantes. EN88. HA89. KN89. L90. MW91. BC92.

Fred Chappell. GR87. S87. W89. PR90. F92.

John Ciardi. C50. M54. S60. EL62. BR63-70. W64-72. M66. R67. NY69. WD71. W73. K74. HP78. K82. BL85. DJ86. W89. K90.

Amy Clampitt. V85. DJ86. H86. L87. EN88. M90. F92.

Tom Clark. C68. S69. PS70. C72. H72. HP78. C87. PR90. W91. H94.

Lucille Clifton. BR70. C73. K74. H75. F79. H84. P85-91. K86-90. W89.

Peter Cooley. E73. H75. S75. MW84. SB85. DJ86. GR87. W89. MW91.

Clark Coolidge. C68. PS70. C72. S86. C87. M87. PR90. W91. W93. H94. M94.

Cid Corman. C70. E71. K74. CO75. F79.

Alfred Corn. HP78. M80. BL85. KN85. SB85. DJ86. L87. M90. PR90.

Gregory Corso. A60. KL65. A68. H68. S69. C70. WD71. C73. EN73. K73.
MK73. W73. HB74. E75-83. M77. F79. M80. BA82. F83. DJ86. W91.
H94.

Henri Coulette. HPS57. EL62. HP62. K64. NY69. S69. W84. R88. PR90.

Robert Creeley. A60. H62-72. K64. W64-72. ARR65. KL65. R67. BM69. G69.
S69. C70. SM70. P71-91. WD71. C72. WS72. C73. EN73-88. K73.
MK73. RS73. W73. H74. HB74. K74-90. CO75. E75-83. EO76. H76.
M77. HP78. F79. KN79. N81. AB82. FY83-89. G85. DJ86. R87. W89.
L90. M90. PR90. HB91. W91. W93. H94. M94.

Victor Hernandez Cruz. C73. M80. L90. W91. H94.

J. V. Cunningham. H53. W54-58. T58. EL62. U62. R67. A68. S69. C70. K70.
WS72. MK73. W73. H74. K74-90. HP78. N81. F83. W84. DJ86. M90.

Philip Dacey. MS71. E73. H75. S75. F79. R81. MW84. DJ86. W89. F92.

Alan Davies. S86. M87. JP91. W91. M94.

Peter Davison. KL65. NY69. BR70. K74-90. W84. DJ86. R88. W89.

James Dickey. PTVII.60. H62-72. HP62. W64-72. ARR65. KL65. M66. R67.
A68. H68. G69. NY69. S69. BR70. C70. E70-83. K70. SM70. P71-91.
WD71. WS72. C73. EN73-88. K73. MK73. RS73. U73. W73. BBL74.
H74. HB74. K74-78. W74. D75. EO76. HP78. F79. KN79-89. M80.
N81. F83. FY83-89. B85. MM85. V85. DJ86. S87. W89. L90. M90.
PR90. HB91. F92.

William Dickey. EL62. NY69. S69. W73. HP78. F79. R81. BL85. GR87. W89.

Ray Di Palma. L76. S86. M87. H94. M94.

Diane Di Prima. D65. K73. Q74. F79. AB82. JP91. W91. H94.

Stephen Dobyns. HP78. MW84. W84. B85. BL85. SB85. H86. MW91.

Edward Dorn. A60. KL65. C70. E71. C72. H72. K73. EO76. M77. BA82.
PR90. W91. BC92. H94.

Rita Dove. H75. MW84. BL85. SB85. V85. GR87. EN88. FY89. KN89. W89.
K90. M90. HB91. MW91. P91.

Norman Dubie. H75. FY83-89. H84. MW84. SB85. H86. EN88. MW91.

Alan Dugan. BR63. ARR65. M66. R67. NY69. S69. BR70. K70. P71-91.
WS72. EN73-88. MK73. W73. H74. HB74. K74-86. M77. HP78. F79.
M80. N81. DJ86. H86. W89.

Robert Duncan. A56. A60. R67. G69. C70. E70. SNR70. E71. WD71. H72. WS72. C73. EN73-88. MK73. HB74. W74. CO75. P75-91. BM76. EO76. M77. HP78. F79. B80. AB82. R87. KN89. M90. PR90. BC92. W93. H94. M94.

Stephen Dunn. E73. H75. S75. F79. R81. BL85. DJ86. H86. GR87. W89. MW91. F92.

Richard Eberhart. C50. H53. M54. W54-58. RS55-73. U55. A56. E56. H57. T58. BW60. S60. EL62. U62. BR63. W64. M66. OW66. BBL67-74. R67. NY69. BR70. C70. E70-83. SM70. SNR70. WD71. WS72. U73. W73. K74-90. W74. D75. M77. HP78. F79. B80. N81. F83. W84. BL85.

Russell Edson. MS71. MK73. GQ74. RQ74. H75. F79. FY83-89. MW84. H86. W89. H94.

Larry Eigner. A60. KL65. C70. MK73. GQ74. RQ74. CO75. R81. AB82. W91. H94. M94.

Kenward Elmslie. C68. PS70. W91. H94. M94.

Lynn Emanuel. SB85. GR87. HA89. W89. MW91.

John Engels. W74. BL85. DJ86. H86. GR87. W89.

Paul Engle. A56. EL62. S67. NY69. HP78.

Theodore Enslin. D65. KL65. E71. Q74. RQ74. W74. CO75.

Clayton Eshleman. C70. E71. GQ74. Q74. RQ74. W93. H94.

William Everson (Brother Antoninus). A60. W64-72. R67. C70. K70. WD71. EN73-88. W73. F79. B80. AB82. E83. F83. W93.

Irving Feldman. BR63-70. K64. NY69. H74. F79. M80. M90.

Lawrence Ferlinghetti. A60. EL62. W64-72. KL65. R67. BBL67-74. G69. C70. E70. P71-91. WD71. C73. EN73-88. K73. W73. HB74. D75. M77. F79. AB82. G85. MM85. L90. F92. H94.

Edward Field. A60. KL65. G69. NY69. S69. WD71. WS72. C73. MK73. H74. D75. F79. M80. R81. W84. HA89. F92.

Donald Finkel. HPS57. PTVI.59. HP62. KL65. A68. NY69. S69. W73. H74. K74-90. W74. HP78. F79. BL85.

Robert Fitzgerald. M54. A56. T58. BR63-70. NY69. C70. HP78. M80. N81. W84.

Carolyn Forché. H75. MW84. W84. B85. SB85. H86. EN88. W89. L90.

Robert Francis. H53. H57. EL62. NY69. C70. K74-90. HP78. F79. B80. FY83-89. W84.

Kathleen Fraser. C68. NY69. H75. D84. W91. H94.

Alice Fulton. MW84. GR87. L87. W89. MW91.

Tess Gallagher. H75. F79. H84. MW84. B85. SB85. H86. MW91. F92.

Isabella Gardner. OW66. S67. NY69. S69. WS72. F79. R81. P85-91.

George Garrett. H57. PTIV.57. W73. DJ86. S87. W89. F92.

Jean Garrigue. W54-58. T58. BR63-70. NY69. C70. WD71. W74. EO76. M80. H86. M90.

Margaret Gibson. W84. SB85. S87. W89. JP91.

Gary Gildner. H75. S75. F79. R81. DJ86. GR87. W89. PR90. F92.

Allen Ginsberg. A60. S60. EL62. K64. D65. KL65. M66. R67. A68. H68. BM69. G69. NY69. S69. BR70. C70. E70-83. FF70. K70. P71-91. WD71. H72. W72. WS72. C73. EN73-88. K73. MK73. RS73. U73. W73. BBL74-82. H74. HB74. K74-82. D75. BM76. EO76. M77. F79. KN79-89. M80. N81. BA82. F83. G85. MM85. V85. DJ86. R87. FY89. K90. L90. M90. PR90. PH91. HB91. W91. BC92. F92. W93. H94. M94.

John Giorno. K70. PS70. GQ74. Q74. RQ74. C87. W91. H94.

Nikki Giovanni. EN73. MK73. GQ74. K74. E75. F79. M80. HB91.

Louise Glück. C68. NY69. S69. E73. H75. HP78. F79. B80. H84. B85. KN85. SB85. V85. DJ86. H86. EN88. M90. HB91. MW91. PH91.

Albert Goldbarth. E73. S75. H84. MW84. SB85. V85. DJ86. MW91.

Paul Goodman. S69. C70. RS73. W74. HP78. M80. R81.

Jorie Graham. D84. MW84. B85. BL85. SB85. V85. H86. GR87. W89. M90. MW91.

Linda Gregg. H75. D84. MW84. SB85. H86. K90. PR90.

Arthur Gregor. NY69. C70. W74. F79. R81. F92.

Robert Grenier. S86. C87. W91. H94. M94.

Barbara Guest. A60. K64. WD71. M80. AB82. W91. H94. M94.

Marilyn Hacker. H75. HP78. F79. M80. W84. BL85. SB85. DJ86. L87. EN88. R88. M90. W91. F92.

John Haines. S69. MS71. H72. MK73. K74. D75. H76. F79. B80. FY83. BL85. H86. W89. K90.

Donald Hall. H57. HPS57. BW60. EL62. HP62. BR63. OW66. R67. NY69. S69. BR70. H72. W73. K74-90. HP78. P80-91. N81. FY83-89. W84. B85. BL85. DJ86. R88. PR90. W91.

Daniel Halpern. H75. M80. R81. MW84. SB85.

Michael S. Harper. MS71. E73. W74. H75. FY83-89. H84. P85-91. V85. H86. EN88. KN89. W89. L90. M90. HB91.

Jim Harrison. C70. EN73. MK73. U73. W73. GQ74. RQ74. H75. S75. JP91.

Carla Harryman. S86. M87. W91. H94. M94.

Robert Hass. C68. H75. E83. D84. H84. MW84. B85. SB85. H86. W89. M90. MW91. P91. F92.

William Hathaway. R81. MW84. DJ86. C87. L87. W89. MW91.

Robert Hayden. BR70. C70. E70-83. FF70. W72. C73. EN73-88.W73. HB74. K78. F79. B80. P80-91. N81. FY83-89. W84. V85. DJ86. K86-90. KN89. L90. M90. HB91.

Anthony Hecht. A56. HPS57. W58. EL62. H62-72. HP62. BR63. KL65. OW66. R67. H68. NY69. S69. BR70. C70. WS72. MK73. U73. W73. H74. HB74. K74-90. W74. EO76. M77. HP78. E80. M80. N81. E83. W84. BL85. DJ86. H86. GR87. EN88. R88. M90.

Michael Heffernan. S75. HP78. DJ86. W89. F92.

Lyn Hejinian. S86. C87. M87. W91. H94. M94.

William Heyen. H75. H76. HP78. F79. H84. SB85. DJ86. GR87. JP91.

Daryl Hine. H68. NY69. S69. BR70. H74. HP78. F79. L87.

Edward Hirsch. MW84. W84. SB85. DJ86. L87. R88. M90. MW91.

Daniel Hoffman. W54-58. EL62. BR63-70. KL65. OW66. H68. NY69. S69. C70. K70. WS72. H74. F79. W84. DJ86.

Jonathan Holden. R81. SB85. GR87. W89. MW91.

John Hollander. HPS57. EL62. HP62. BR63-70. K64. H68. NY69. S69. K70. W73. H74. HB74. K74-90. HP78. F79. M80. E83. W84. DJ86. H86. GR87. EN88. R88. M90.

Anselm Hollo. MK73. GQ74. Q74. RQ74. R81. AB82. C87. W91. F92. H94.

John Holmes. C50. H53. A56. H57. EL62. NY69. W74.

Garrett Hongo. SB85. K86-90. W89. L90. MW91.

Richard Howard. H68. NY69. S69. BR70. H74. W74. HP78. F79. M80. DJ86. H86. GR87. EN88. R88. M90. PR90.

Susan Howe. S86. M87. BC92. W93. H94. M94.

Barbara Howes. H57. T58. EL62. U62. BR63-70. NY69. S69. WD71. U73. W73. F79. M80. DJ86. H86. W89.

Robert Huff. S67. S69. W73. F79. DJ86.

Richard Hugo. S69. H74. W74. H76. HP78. F79. M80. P80-91. K82-86. E83. FY83-89. W84. KN85-89. DJ86. H86. GR87. EN88. M90.

Terry Hummer. MW84. SB85. DJ86. GR87. S87. W89. MW91.

David Ignatow. D65. NY69. S69. BR70. C70. K70. H72. K73. K74-86. W74. P75-91. BM76. H76. HP78. F79. B80. M80. F83. W89.

Randall Jarrell. C50. MO50. M54. RS55-73. U55. A56. E56. T58. BW60. S60. EL62. U62. BR63. ARR65. M66. R67. NY69. S69. BR70. C70. E70-83. K70. SM70. SNR70. WD71. WS72. C73. EN73-88. MK73. U73. W73. BBL74. HB74. K74-90. W74. EO76. M77. HP78. KN79-89. B80. E80. M80. P80-91. N81. F83. FY83-89. W84. MM85. V85. DJ86. R87. S87. M90. HB91. PH91.

Ronald Johnson. C68. C70. MK73. W93. M94.

Erica Jong. E73. MK73. U73. H75. F79. M80. SB85. BL85. PR90.

Donald Justice. HPS57. BW60. EL62. H62-72. HP62. A68. NY69. S69. BR70. C70. W73. H74. HB74. K74. D75. HP78. F79. FY83-89. W84. B85. BL85. P85-91. DJ86. H86. K86-90. S87. EN88. R88. W89. M90. PR90. F92.

Bob Kaufman. BR70. C70. C73. K73. GQ74.

Weldon Kees. BM69. NY69. S69. C70. C73. MK73. HB74. M77. HP78. M80. F83. DJ86.

Robert Kelly. D65. KL65. C68. C70. E71. MK73. GQ74. Q74. RQ74. CO75. AB82. JP91. W91. BC92. W93. H94. M94.

X. J. Kennedy. EL62. H62-72. KL65. A68. NY69. S69. BR70. RS73. W73. HB74. D75. HP78. W84. BL85. DJ86. R88. W89. PR90. F92.

Jack Kerouac. A60. K73. MK73. RQ74. AB82. H94.

Galway Kinnell. H53. W54-58. H57. EL62. H62-72. HP62. BR63. KL65. R67. BM69. NY69. S69. BR70. C70. K70. MS71. MK73. RS73. U73. W73. H74. K74. W74. D75. E75-83. P75-91. BM76. EO76. HP78. F79. B80. M80. K82-86. F83. FY83-89. W84. B85. BL85. DJ86. H86. R87. EN88. KN89. M90. PR90. F92.

Carolyn Kizer. H57. HP62. R67. A68. G69. S69. C70. H74. W74. HP78. F79. F83. P85-91. H86. M90. F92.

Etheridge Knight. H72. EN73. GQ74. BM76. M77. F79. R81. K82-86. B85. DJ86. S87. HA89. W89. L90. BC92.

Bill Knott. WS72. MK73. K74. GQ74. K90. PR90.

Kenneth Koch. A60. K64. H68. G69. S69. C70. E70-83. K70. PS70. P71-80. WS72. C73. EN73-88. K73. MK73. HB74. K74-90. W74. M77. HP78. F79. AB82. F83. PR90. W91. H94.

John Koethe. W74. HP78. L87. W89. PR90.

Ted Kooser. S75. F79. DJ86. GR87. W89. F92.

Maxine Kumin. NY69. E73. W73. HP78. K78-82. F79. R81. B85. BL85. P85-91. DJ86. GR87. EN88. F92.

Stanley Kunitz. A56. EL62. U62. BR63. M66. R67. NY69. BR70. C70. K70. SM70. WD71. WS72. U73. H74. HP78. F79. M80. P80-91. N81. W84. B85. BL85. DJ86. H86. R88.

Greg Kuzma. NY69. E73. F73. K74. W74. H75. S75. HP78. F79. GR87. F92.

Joanne Kyger. GQ74. L76. AB82. C87. W91.

Philip Lamantia. A60. C70. K70. MK73. RQ74. C87.

Joseph Langland. PTIII.56. HPS57. EL62. BR63. S67. NY69. DJ86.

Richmond Lattimore. H57. EL62. NY69. C70. HP78. W84.

Sydney Lea. M80. MW84. BL85. SB85. DJ86. GR87. W89. MW91.

Don L. Lee. W72. C73. EN73. GQ74. E75. M77. F79.

Brad Leithauser. W84. SB85. DJ86. K86-90. L87. R88. F92.

Denise Levertov. A60. EL62. H62-72. HP62. W64-72. ARR65. KL65. BBL67-74. R67. A68. BM69. G69. S69. BR70. C70. E70-83. FF70. G71. P71-91. WD71. WS72. C73. EN73-88. K73. MK73. RS73. W73. H74. HB74. K74-90. W74. CO75. D75. BM76. EO76. HP78. F79. KN79-89. B80. M80. AB82. FY83-89. B85. MM85. DJ86. R87. L90. M90. HB91. PH91. W93. H94.

Philip Levine. EL62. HP62. K64. BM69. NY69. S69. C70. MS71. EN73-88. H74. K74-86. BM76. EO76. HP78. F79. M80. P80-91. FY83-89. W84. BL85. DJ86. H86. GR87. KN89. W89. M90. PR90.

Larry Levis. MS71. E73. H75. R81. FY83-89. MW84. W84. SB85. H86. W89. MW91.

Laurence Lieberman. KL65. NY69. S69. W73. W74. S75.

John Logan. H62-72. HP62. K64. R67. NY69. S67. G69. S69. K70. P71-91. WS72. W73. H74. W74. BM76. H76. HP78. B80. FY83. DJ86. PR90.

William Logan. SB85. DJ86. H86. L87. R88.

Audre Lorde. F79. M80. E83. KN85-89. EN88. L90. M90.

Robert Lowell. C50. MO50. M54. W54-58. U55. A56. E56. HPS57. T58. BW60. S60. EL62. H62-72. U62. BR63. W64-72. KL65. ARR65. M66. OW66. BBL67-74. R67. A68. BM69. G69. S69. BR70. C70. E70-83. FF70. K70. SM70. SNR70. G71. P71-91. WD71. WS72. C73. EN73-88. MK73. RS73. U73. W73. H74. HB74. K74-90. W74. D75. EO76. M77. HP78. KN79-89. E80. M80. N81. F83. FY83-89. W84. G85. MM85. V85. DJ86. R87. L90. M90. HB91. PH91.

Susan Ludvigson. SB85. GR87. S87. W89. F92.

Thomas Lux. E73. H75. MW84. DJ86. FY83-89. H86. PR90.

Jackson Mac Low. KL65. E71. GQ74. Q74. RQ74. AB82. M87. JP91. W91. W93. H94. M94.

Gerard Malanga. D65. C68. NY69. R81. W91.

William Matchett. W54-58. HPS57. EL62. NY69. S69.

William Matthews. E73. H75. MK73. W74. H76. H84. BL85. SB85. H86. GR87. L87. P91.

Bernadette Mayer. PS70. RQ74. L76. S86. C87. W91. H94. M94.

E. L. Mayo. C50. EL62. S69. HP78. R81. BC92.

Mekeel McBride. MW84. SB85. DJ86. GR87. W89.

J. D. McClatchy. HP78. W74. L87. R88. HA89.

Michael McClure. A60. KL65. G69. C72. K73. MK73. RQ74. F79. B80. AB82. W91. H94.

Phyllis McGinley. A56. H57. EL62. U62. NY69.

Thomas McGrath. HPS57. S67. C70. RQ74. BM76. F79. B80. R81. DJ86. BC92.

Heather McHugh. H75. H84. MW84. SB85. H86. PR90. MW91.

Sandra McPherson. H75. HP78. F79. FY83-89. H84. MW84. SB85. DJ86. H86. W89. M90.

David Meltzer. A60. E71. K73. Q74. F79. AB82.

William Meredith. HPS57. T58. BW60. EL62. NY69. S69. WS72. W73. H74. CW75. H76. HP78. M80. N81. E83. W84. DJ86. EN88. M90. F92.

James Merrill. H53. M54. U55. HPS57. EL62. H62-72. HP62. BR63. H68. NY69. S69. BR70. C70. SM70. WD71. WS72. EN73-88. MK73. W73. H74. HB74. K74-90. W74. E75-83. EO76. M77. HP78. F79. KN79-89. M80. P80-91. N81. W84. BL85. V85. DJ86. H86. GR87. R87. R88. FY89. M90. PR90. HB91. PH91.

Thomas Merton. A56. KL65. NY69. C70. GQ74. RQ74. W74. HP78.

W. S. Merwin. M54. W54-58. HPS57. EL62. H62-72. BR63. ARR65. KL65. M66. OW66. BBL67-74. R67. H68. BM69. G69. NY69. S69. BR70. C70. E70-83. G71. MS71. P71-91. WD71. WS72. C73. EN73-88. MK73. U73. W73. H74. HB74. K74-90. W74. D75. BM76. EO76. M77. HP78. F79. KN79-89. M80. N81. F83. FY83-89. W84. MM85. V85. DJ86. H86. GR87. R87. W89. M90. PR90. HB91. PH91.

Robert Mezey. HPS57. H62. K64. W64. A68. BM69. NY69. MS71. H75. M77. HP78. B80. R81. W84. DJ86. PR90.

Josephine Miles. A56. E56. EL62. NY69. C70. SM70. WD71. C73. EN73-88. W73. K74-90. W74. HP78. F79. E83. W84. R88. BC92.

Vassar Miller. HPS57. EL62. HP62. U62. W64-72. KL65. A68. W73. F79. R81. DJ86. S87. PR90.

Robert Morgan. F79. H84. SB85. DJ86. L87. S87.

Howard Moss. H53. U55. HPS57. EL62. HP62. BR63. OW66. NY69. S69. BR70. WS72. MK73. H74. W74. HP78. K78-90. F79. M80. BL85. DJ86. H86. R88. M90.

Stanley Moss. S69. C70. M80. DJ86. F92.

Lisel Mueller. H57. S67. NY69. S69. HP78. F79. W84. GR87. W89.

Howard Nemerov. M54. E56. HPS57. T58. W58. EL62. H62-72. BR63. W64-72. OW66. BBL67-74. R67. NY69. S69. BR70. E70-83. WD71. WS72. EN73-88. MK73. RS73. W73. H74. K74. W74. D75. M77. HP78. F79. E80. M80. N81. K82-90. W84. MM85. V85. DJ86. GR87. R87. R88. W89. M90. HB91. F92.

Lorine Niedecker. C70. GQ74. RQ74. CO75. K90. PR90. W93. M94.

John Fredrick Nims. C50. M54. T58. EL62. S67. W73. K74-90. HP78. W84. BL85. DJ86. GR87. R88.

Alice Notley. C72. C87. L76. W91. H94. M94.

Naomi Shihab Nye. F79. MW84. SB85. S87. MW91. F92.

Joyce Carol Oates. W73. H76. H84. GR87. L87. W89.

Frank O'Hara. W58. A60. KL65. H68. G69. S69. C70. PS70. P71-91. WD71. H72. WS72. C73. EN73-88. K73. MK73. W73. HB74. BM76. EO76. M77. HP78. KN79-89. M80. AB82. V85. DJ86. R87. FY89. M90. PR90. HB91. W91. W93. H94. M94.

Sharon Olds. W84. BL85. SB85. K86-90. W89. PR90. MW91. F92.

Mary Oliver. S67. B80. P85-91. K86-90. GR87.

Charles Olson. A60. KL65. R67. G69. S69. C70. K70. SNR70. E71. WS72. C73. EN73-88. MK73. RS73. W73. K74-90. Q74. CO75. E75-83. EO76. M77. KN79-89. P80-91. AB82. G85. R87. W89. M90. PR90. HB91. BC92. W93. H94. M94.

George Oppen. NY69. MK73. GQ74. RQ74. BM76. HP78. F79. W93. M94.

Joel Oppenheimer. A60. D65. KL65. C70. Q74. RQ74. AB82. W91.

Gregory Orr. H75. H84. BL85. SB85. H86.

Simon Ortiz. RQ74. F79. SB85. HA89. KN89. L90. PH91. HB91. F92.

Rochelle Owens. D65. KL65. GQ74. Q74. RQ74.

Robert Pack. PTII.55. HPS57. HP62. KL65. OW66. NY69. S69. WS72. W73. HB74. F79. R81. BL85. DJ86. GR87. PR90.

Ron Padgett. C68. PS70. C72. H72. Q74. C87. PR90. W91. F92. H94. M94.

Michael Palmer. D84. S86. C87. M87. W91. W93. H94. M94.

Linda Pastan. W74. H76. M80. R81. BL85. K86-90. H86. GR87.

Kenneth Patchen. M54. A56. EL62. U62. W64-72. BM69. C70. WD71. K73. MK73. W73. RQ74. W74. HP78. N81.

Molly Peacock. SB85. DJ86. L87. W89. PR90. MW91. F92.

John Peck. W74. H75. H76. DJ86. H86.

Marge Piercy. BR70. K74. F79. H84. P85-91. EN88. W89. L90.

Robert Pinsky. D84. KN75. HP78. MW84. BL85. SB85. V85. DJ86. H86. EN88. R88. W89. M90. HB91. MW91.

Sylvia Plath. HP62. BR63-70. BBL67-74. R67. A68. H68. BM69. NY69. S69. C70. E70-83. K70. SM70. SNR70. P71-91. H72. W72. WS72. C73. EN73-88. RS73. U73. W73. HB74. K74-90. MK73. W74. D75. EO76. M77. HP78. KN79-89. N81. F83. FY83-89. W84. G85. MM85. V85. DJ86. H86. R87. L90. M90. HB91. PH91.

Stanley Plumly. W74. H75. S75. H76. FY83-89. H84. MW84. B85. BL85. DJ86. H86. GR87. W89. MW91.

Ralph Pomeroy. KL65. NY69. F79. M80. F92.

Carl Rakosi. RQ74. W74. S75. HP78. F79. PR90. M94.

Bin Ramke. MW84. SB85. GR87. S87. W89.

Dudley Randall. H72. F73. EN73-88. K74. N81. DJ86.

David Ray. HP62. C70. S75. R81. DJ86. W89.

Ishmael Reed. C73. K74-78. RQ74. H76. E83. F83. C87. L90.

James Reiss. H75. S75. M80. H86. W89.

Kenneth Rexroth. A56. T58. R67. BM69. C70. K70. G71. WD71. K73. MK73. RS73. RQ74. W74. BM76. M77. K78-86. F79. B80. F83. W84. W93.

Charles Reznikoff. C70. WS72. K73. MK73. K74. RQ74. HP78. M80. F83. W93. M94.

Adrienne Rich. HPS57. H62-72. HP62. KL65. BBL67-74. H68. NY69. S69. C70. E70-83. P71-91. C73. EN73-88. U73. W73. H74. HB74. K74-90. W74. D75. BM76. EO76. H76. F79. KN79-89. M80. FY83-89. G85. MM85. V85. DJ86. H86. R87. W89. L90. M90. PR90. HB91. PH91.

Alberto Ríos. F79. MW84. SB85. DJ86. C87. EN88. KN89. MW91. F92.

Theodore Roethke. C50. H53. M54. W54-58. U55. A56. E56. H57. T58. BW60. S60. EL62. U62. BR63. W64-72. ARR65. M66. OW66. BBL67-74. R67. A68. BM69. NY69. S69. BR70. C70. E70-83. FF70. K70. SM70. SNR70. G71. WD71. WS72. C73. EN73-88. MK73. RS73. U73. W73. HB74. K74-90. D75. P75-91. EO76. M77. HP78. KN79-89. B80. N81. F83. FY83-89. G85. MM85. V85. DJ86. R87. W89. L90. M90. HB91. PH91.

Pattiann Rogers. MW84. SB85. GR87. S87. W89. MW91.

William Pitt Root. NY69. E73. H84. SB85. DJ86. W89.

Jerome Rothenberg. D65. KL65. R67. E71. K73. GQ74. H74. Q74. RQ74. BM76. AB82. W91. W93. H94. M94.

Gibbons Ruark. K82-90. SB85. DJ86. S87. R88. W89.

Muriel Rukeyser. C50. M54. W54-58. RS55. U55. E56. U62. BR63. OW66. BBL67-74. R67. NY69. BR70. C70. WD71. WS72. U73. H74. K74. BM76. HP78. F79. M80. FY83-89. W84. DJ86. H86. EN88. W93.

Vern Rutsala. F79. R81. HA89. W89. F92.

Michael Ryan. H75. S75. MW84. B85. SB85. DJ86. MW91.

David St. John. H75. FY83-89. MW84. SB85. DJ86. H86. W89. MW91.

Sonia Sanchez. C73. RQ74. M77. F79. L90. W91. BC92.

Ed Sanders. D65. PS70. C72. GQ74. Q74. RQ74. AB82. C87. PR90. W91. BC92. H94.

Sherod Santos. MW84. SB85. DJ86. H86. MW91.

Aram Saroyan. C68. PS70. C72. MK73. PR90. W91.

May Sarton. H53. H57. NY69. HP78. F79. DJ86.

Leslie Scalapino. D84. C87. JP91. BC92. H94. M94.

James Schevill. E56. EL62. R67. G69. WD71. R81.

Dennis Schmitz. S67. C68. E73. H75. R81. FY83-89. D84. H86.

Gjertrud Schnackenberg. HP78. W84. DJ86. H86. K86-90. R88. EN88. M90.

James Schuyler. A60. S69. PS70. C72. WS72. C73. MK73. HP78. M80. AB82. E83. W84. M90. PR90. W91. F92. H94. M94.

Delmore Schwartz. C50. MO50. M54. W54-58. RS55-73. U55. A56. E56. T58. BW60. S60. EL62. U62. BR63-70. OW66. R67. A68. NY69. C70. K70. WD71. WS72. EN73-88. MK73. BBL74. EO76. M77. HP78. M80. F83.

Armand Schwerner. D65. K70. E71. GQ74. Q74. RQ74. JP91.

Winfield Townley Scott. C50. H53. M54. A56. E56. BR63. R67. NY69. S69. C70. WD71. RS73. HP78. K86.

Anne Sexton. EL62. HP62. U62. BR63. W64-72. KL65. M66. R67. NY69. S69. BR70. C70. SM70. P71-91. WD71. H72. WS72. C73. EN73-88. RS73. U73. W73. H74. HB74. K74-90. W74. D75. H76. M77. HP78. KN79-89. M80. MM85. V85. DJ86. H86. GR87. R87. FY89. L90. M90. PR90. HB91. PH91.

David Shapiro. H68. K70. PS70. HP78. C87. W91. H94.

Harvey Shapiro. NY69. C70. K70. W74. HP78. F79. M80. R81. W89. K90.

Karl Shapiro. C50. MO50. M54. W54-58. U55. A56. E56. T58. BW60. S60. EL62. U62. BR63. W64-72. ARR65. M66. OW66. R67. S67. NY69. S69. BR70. C70. SM70. SNR70. WD71. WS72. EN73-88. W73. BBL74. K74-90. M77. HP78. F79. N81. DJ86. HB91.

James Sherry. S86. C87. M87. W91. M94.

Charles Simic. C68. S69. L71. MS71. C73. E73. MK73. GQ74. Q74. H75. BM76. K78-90. F79. B80. M80. E83. FY83-89. H84. W84. BL85. V85. H86. GR87. M90. PR90. P91.

Louis Simpson. H53. PTII.55. H57. HPS57. EL62. H62-72. HP62. BR63-70. M66. R67. A68. H68. NY69. S69. C70. E70. WS72. EN73-88. MK73. U73. W73. H74. HB74. W74. D75. P75-91. EO76. H76. F79. E80. M80. F83. FY83. B85. DJ86. K86. W89. PR90.

L. E. Sissman. NY69. S69. BR70. H74. M80. DJ86. R88.

David Slavitt. PTVIII.61. W73. M80. DJ86. W89. K90.

Dave Smith. E73. S75. H76. HP78. M80. H84. BL85. SB85. V85. DJ86. H86. GR87. S87. EN88. W89. M90. MW91. F92.

William Jay Smith. H53. H57. HPS57. T58. EL62. U62. BR63-70. NY69. S69. WD71. WS72. U73. W73. K74-90. HP78. R88.

W. D. Snodgrass. HPS57. W58. BW60. EL62. H62-72. HP62. U62. BR63. K64. W64-72. ARR65. KL65. M66. BBL67-74. R67. A68. H68. NY69. S69. BR70. E70. K70. SM70. P71-91. WD71. WS72. EN73-88. MK73. U73. W73. K74-90. W74. D75. M77. F79. N81. E83. W84. B85. MM85. DJ86. R88. M90. PR90.

Gary Snyder. A60. H62-72. KL65. R67. H68. BM69. G69. S69. C70. E70-83. K70. E71. G71. MS71. P71-85. WD71. W72. C73. EN73-88. K73. MK73. RS73. W73. BBL74. H74. HB74. K74-90. CO75. D75. BM76. EO76. M77. HP78. F79. KN79-89. B80. N81. AB82. G85. FY83-89. V85. DJ86. L90. M90. PR90. HB91. W91. BC92. W93. H94.

Cathy Song. SB85. EN88. KN89. W89. L90.

Gary Soto. F79. D84. MW84. SB85. EN88. L90. HB91. F92.

Barry Spacks. NY69. W73. K74. HP78. F79. K82. DJ86. W89.

Jack Spicer. A60. KL65. C70. E71. WD71. RQ74. AB82. W91. W93. H94. M94.

Elizabeth Spires. SB85. GR87. R88. W89. MW91.

William Stafford. H57. EL62. H62-72. M66. OW66. R67. A68. S67. BM69. NY69. S69. C70. E70-83. MS71. WD71. WS72. C73. K73. W73. BBL74. K74-90. W74. D75. P75-91. BM76. H76. HP78. F79. B80. N81. FY83-89. B85. BL85. DJ86. H86. GR87. EN88. PR90. HB91. PH91. F92.

Maura Stanton. H75. MW84. SB85. DJ86. W89. MW91. F92.

George Starbuck. HP62. BR63-70. NY69. C70. K82-90. W84. BL85. DJ86.

Timothy Steele. K74-90. HP78. DJ86. R88. F92.

Charles Stein. E71. GQ74. Q74. RQ74. JP91.

Gerald Stern. B80. M80. K82. W84. B85. BL85. P85-91. H86. GR87. FY89. PR90. MW91.

Leon Stokesbury. E73. F79. SB85. DJ86. S87. F92.

Ruth Stone. U62. OW66. NY69. HP78. F79. MW91.

Mark Strand. C68. H68. NY69. S69. BR70. L71. MS71. E73. EN73-88. MK73. W73. H74. HB74. W74. D75. HP78. K78-82. F79. M80. H84. W84. BL85. P85-91. V85. DJ86. H86. GR87. FY89. M90.

Lucien Stryk. H76. F79. R81. B85. P85-91. GR87. JP91. F92.

Dabney Stuart. NY69. E73. W73. F79. DJ86. S87. F92.

May Swenson. PTI.54. H57. HPS57. BR63-70. R67. H68. NY69. S69. C70. WS72. MK73. U73. H74. K74-86. HP78. F79. M80. N81. F83. W84. DJ86. H86. R88. M90.

Robert Sward. KL65. S67. NY69. S69. C70. F83.

Nathaniel Tarn. GQ74. Q74. RQ74. JP91. W93.

James Tate. S67. A68. C68. NY69. S69. E70-83. BR70. L71. MS71. K74-78. MK73. W74. H75. M77. F79. R81. MW84. SB85. DJ86. H86. EN88. FY89. W89.

Lorenzo Thomas. L76. C87. W91. H94. M94.

Richard Tillinghast. MW84. BL85. SB85. DJ86. S87. W89. MW91.

David Trinidad. C87. C89. HA89. W91. F92. H94.

Lewis Turco. NY69. W73. H76. DJ86. L87.

John Updike. NY69. K74-90. W84. DJ86. L87. PR90.

Mona Van Duyn. OW66. U73. H74. W74. HP78. F79. N81. W84. DJ86. L87. W89. M90. F92.

Peter Viereck. C50. M54. A56. S60. EL62. U62. NY69. S69. WD71. W73. HP78.

Paul Violi. C87. L76. L87. W91. H94.

Ellen Bryant Voigt. E83. BL85. SB85. DJ86. H86. GR87. S87. EN88.

David Wagoner. H57. EL62. HP62. S69. C70. K70. SM70. W73. HP78. K78-86. F79. N81. W84. BL85. DJ86. H86. GR87. EN88. R88. W89. M90. PR90. F92.

Diane Wakoski. D65. KL65. C68. NY69. S69. C70. E71. W72. C73. EN73-88. K73. MK73. W73. GQ74. H74. E75. H75. M77. HP78. F79. R81. F83. DJ86. W91. F92. H94.

Anne Waldman. C68. Q74. AB82. C87. PR90. JP91. W91. H94.

Rosmary Waldrop. K78-90. C87. L87. H94. M94.

Robert Penn Warren. MO50. M54. W54-58. A56. E56. T58. S60. EL62. U62. BR63. OW66. NY69. BR70. C70. E70-83. SM70. WD71. WS72. W73. BBL74. H74. HB74. EO76. M77. HP78. F79. KN79-89. M80. N81. K82. W84. B85. BL85. DJ86. H86. GR87. S87. R88. FY89. L90. M90. HB91.

Barrett Watten. S86. M87. W91. H94. M94.

Hannah Weiner. GQ74. S86. M87. W91. H94. M94.

Theodore Weiss. H57. KL65. R67. A68. NY69. S69. BR70. C70. H74. W74. M77. HP78. F79. B85. H86. R88. EN88.

Marjorie Welish. C87. L87. W91. H94. M94.

Philip Whalen. A60. G69. C70. WD71. C72. K73. CO75. AB82. JP91. W91. H94.

John Hall Wheelock. H53. H57. T58. EL62. OW66. NY69. WS72. MK73. H74. HP78. M80. W84.

James Whitehead. W73. F79. BL85. DJ86. S87. W89. F92.

Reed Whittemore. HPS57. T58. EL62. H62-72. R67. NY69. S69. E70. K74-78. M77. F79. M80. F92.

John Wieners. A60. D65. KL65. G69. C70. AB82. PR90. W91. BC92. H94. M94.

Richard Wilbur. C50. H53. M54. W54-58. U55. A56. E56. H57. HPS57. T58. BW60. S60. EL62. H62-72. U62. BR63. W64-72. ARR65. KL65. M66. OW66. R67. A68. NY69. S69. BR70. C70. E70-83. FF70. SM70. SNR70. G71. P71-91. WD71. WS72. EN73-88. MK73. RS73. U73. W73. BBL74. H74. HB74. K74-90. W74. D75. EO76. M77. HP78. F79. KN79-89. B80. E80. N81. FY83-89. W84. B85. BL85. G85. MM85. V85. DJ86. R87. R88. L90. M90. PR90. HB91. PH91. F92.

C. K. Williams. NY69. L71. K74. H84. MW84. B85. P85-91. H86. M90. PR90.

Jonathan Williams. A60. KL65. C70. C73. MK73. RQ74. F79. R81. AB82. HA89.

Miller Williams. W73. K74-86. F79. M80. BL85. DJ86. S87. W89. F92.

Yvor Winters. W54-58. RS55-73. T58. U62. C70. WS72. MK73. K74-78. EO76. HP78. K86-90.

David Wojahn. MW84. SB85. DJ86. W89. MW91. F92.

John Woods. KL65. S67. MS71. H72. F79. W89.

Charles Wright. A68. NY69. S69. MS71. W73. H75. HP78. FY83-89. W84. BL85. KN85. P85-91. V85. DJ86. W89. M90. PR90. HB91. F92.

James Wright. HPS57. BW60. H62-72. K64. M66. BBL67-74. R67. S67. A68. H68. BM69. G69. NY69. S69. BR70. C70. K70. P71-91. WD71. W72. WS72. C73. EN73-88. K73. MK73. U73. W73. H74. K74-90. W74. E75-83. BM76. EO76. H76. M77. F79. KN79-89. B80. M80. N81. F83. FY83-89. W84. MM85. V85. DJ86. H86. GR87. W89. M90. PR90. HB91.

Al Young. E73. W73. D75. F79. D84. DJ86. W89. F92.

Paul Zimmer. H76. F79. R81. BL85. DJ86. GR87. W89. F92.

Louis Zukofsky. D65. KL65. C70. K70. WS72. GQ74. MK73. RQ74. W74. CO75. M77. HP78. R87. W93. M94.

APPENDIX 3: NUMBER OF ANTHOLOGY APPEARANCES

70	Wilbur
67	Lowell
62	Ginsberg, Roethke
59	Bishop
57	Merwin
55	Jarrell
53	J. Dickey
52	Levertov, J. Wright
50	Berryman, Snyder
48	Creeley
46	Plath
45	Ashbery, Kinnell, Merrill
44	Sexton, Snodgrass
43	Nemerov
42	R. P. Warren
41	Stafford, Eberhart
39	Rich
38	Hecht, Simpson
37	Baraka, K. Shapiro
36	O'Hara
35	Bly
34	Olson
33	Duncan
31	Ammons, Justice
30	Schwartz
29	Rukeyser, Strand
28	Brooks

27   Levine

26   Koch, Kunitz, Simic, Wakoski

25   Ferlinghetti, Hall

24   Dugan, Hollander, Swenson

23   Moss, Tate, Wagoner

22   Corso, Hayden

21   J. Logan, Cunningham, Rexroth

20   Bell, Glück, Meredith

19   Ignatow, Kennedy, C. Wright

18   Blackburn, Hugo, Miles, Schuyler, D. Smith

17   Booth, Field, Kelly, Weiss

16   Ciardi, Howard, Kizer, Mezey, Pack, W. J. Smith

15   Dove, Harper, Hoffman, Howes, Knight, Patchen, Pinsky, Plumly, Rothenberg, Zukofsky

14   Dorn, Everson, Finkel, Hacker, Hass, Kumin, Scott

13   Brinnin, Haines, Miller, Nims, Van Duyn, Whittemore

12   Benedikt, Berrigan, Carruth, Dunn, Eigner, Kees, Mac Low, Matthews, McClure, Sanders, Stern

11   Berry, Coolidge, Edson, Garrigue, Graham, Kuzma, Levis, McPherson, Padgett, Reznikoff, Spicer, Viereck, Whalen, Wieners

10   Antin, Bukowski, Clark, Dacey, W. Dickey, Fitzgerald, Harrison, Hollo, McGrath, H. Shapiro, C. K. Williams, J. Williams

9   Ai, Anderson, Cage, Cooley, Corn, Coulette, Forché, Gallagher, Gildner, Heyen, Jong, Mueller, Oppen, Ortiz, Ríos, M. Williams

8   Bottoms, Bowers, Clifton, Davison, Di Prima, Dobyns, Dubie, Gardner, Giorno, Giovanni, Goldbarth, Guest, Hine, Hirsch, Lea, Mayer, Merton, Niedecker, Olds, Oppenheimer, Palmer, Pastan, Piercy, St. John, Schmitz, Schnackenberg, Soto, Spacks, Starbuck, Stryk, Voigt, Waldman, Young, Zimmer

7   Brautigan, Clampitt, Enslin, Eshleman, Feldman, Garrett, Goodman, Gregg, Hathaway, Holmes, Hummer, Langland, Lee, Leithauser, Lorde, Lux, McHugh, Peacock, Rakosi, Ryan, Sanchez, Schwerner, D. Shapiro, Sissman, Stanton, Stuart, Tillinghast, Whitehead

6   Andrews, Bernstein, Bidart, Blaser, Cervantes, Engels, Fraser, Gregor, Hejinian, Howe, Kerouac, Knott, Kooser, Lamantia, Lattimore, Lieberman, Mayo, Meltzer, Morgan, Notley, Nye, Oates, Orr, Randall, Ray, Reed, Rogers, Root, Ruark, Saroyan, Sarton, Scalapino, Schevill, Slavitt, Stokesbury, Stone, Sward, Trinidad, Updike, Weiner, Wojahn, Woods

5   Berg, Berkson, Blumenthal, Bronk, Broughton, Brownstein, Chappell, Corman, Cruz, Davies, Di Palma, Elmslie, Emanuel, Engle, Fraser, Fulton, Gibson, Grenier, Halpern, Harryman, Heffernan, Holden, Hongo, Huff, Johnson, Kaufman, Koethe, Kyger, W. Logan, Ludvigson, Malanga, Matchett, McBride, McClatchy, McGinley, S. Moss, Oliver, Owens, Peck, Pomeroy, Ramke, Reiss, Rutsala, Santos, Sherry, Song, Spires, Steele, Stein, Tarn, L. Thomas, Turco, Violi, Waldrop, Watten, Welish

Supplementary List of Poets

The threshold appears to be between four and five appearances, since the number of poets in four anthologies is nearly double that in five. The following are each in four anthologies. They are not included in Appendix 2, but are listed here for convenience.

4   Helen Adam, James Agee, James Applewhite, Rae Armantrout, Gerald Barrax, Mei-Mei Berssenbrugge, David Bromige, Michael Dennis Browne, Paul Carroll, Turner Cassity, Siv Cedering (Fox), Maxine Chernoff, Dennis Cooper, Jane Cooper, Harold Dicker, George Economou, Elaine Equi, Alvin Feinman, Dick Gallup, Dan Gerber, John Godfrey, Patricia Goedicke, Ted Greenwald, Debora Greger, Jessica Hagedorn, Kenneth O. Hanson, David Henderson, Robert Horan, Colette Inez, P. Inman, Thomas James, Mark Jarman, June Jordan, Yusef Komunyakaa, Melvin Walker LaFollette, Gerrit Lansing, Ann Lauterbach, Al Lee, David Lehman, Rika Lesser, Lou Lipsitz, Ron Loewinsohn, Lewis MacAdams, Clarence Major, Morton Marcus, Harry Mathews, James McMichael, Peter Meinke, Frederick Morgan, Leonard Nathan, Ed Ochester, Steven Orlen, Maureen Owen, Greg Pape, Bob Perelman, John Perrault, Robert Peters, Kenneth Pitchford, George Quasha, Kit Robinson, Raymond Roseliep, Ira Sadoff, Frank Samperi, Reg Saner, Peter Schjeldahl, Philip Schultz, Herbert Scott, Frederick Seidel, Hugh Seidman, Judith Johnson Sherwin, Ron Silliman, Gilbert Sorrentino, David Steingass, Adrien Stoutenberg, Henry Taylor, Tony Towle, Leslie Ullman, Constance Urdang, Jean Valentine, Michael Van Walleghen, Mark Vinz, Alice Walker, Marilyn Waniek, Diane Ward, Rosanna Warren, Lewis Warsh, Michael Waters, Lew Welch, Terence Winch, John Yau

APPENDIX 4: POETS BY BIRTHDATE

1894 Reznikoff

1903 Niedecker, Rakosi

1904 Eberhart, Mayo, Zukofsky

1905 Kunitz, Rexroth, R. P. Warren

1906 Lattimore

1908 Oppen, Roethke

1910 Fitzgerald, Olson, Scott

1911 Bishop, Cunningham, Goodman, Miles, Patchen

1912 Cage, Everson, Sarton

1913 Broughton, Hayden, Nims, Rukeyser, Schwartz, K.Shapiro

1914 Berryman, Garrigue, Howes, Ignatow, Jarrell, Kees, Randall, Stafford

1915 Gardner, Merton

1916 Brinnin, Ciardi, McGrath, Viereck, Weiss

1917 Brooks, Langland, Lowell

1918 Bronk, W. J. Smith

1919 Duncan, Ferlinghetti, Meredith, Swenson, Whittemore

1920 Bukowski, Clampitt, Guest, Nemerov, Schevill

1921 Van Duyn, Wilbur

1922 Kerouac, Mac Low, Moss

1923 J. Dickey, Dugan, Gregor, Hecht, Hoffman, Hugo, Levertov, J. Logan, Schuyler, Simpson, Whalen

1924 Bowers, Corman, Field, Haines, Huff, V. Miller, Mueller, H. Shapiro, Stryk

1925 Blaser, Booth, Enslin, Justice, Kaufman, Kizer, Koch, Kumin, Spicer, Stern

1926 Ammons, Blackburn, Bly, Creeley, Ginsberg, Merrill, O'Hara, Pomeroy, Snodgrass, Wagoner, Woods

1927 Ashbery, Coulette, Eigner, Kinnell, Lamantia, Merwin, Schwerner, J. Wright

1928 Davison, W. Dickey, Feldman, Hall, Levine, Sexton, Tarn, Sissman, Weiner

1929 Dorn, Elmslie, Finkel, Garrett, Hollander, Howard, Kennedy, Pack, Rich, J. Williams

1930 Corso, Oppenheimer, M. Williams

1931 Engels, Knight, Rothenberg, Spacks, Starbuck

1932 Antin, Gallagher, McClure, Pastan, Plath, Ray, Updike

1933 Brautigan, Sward

1934 Baraka, Berg, Berrigan, Berry, Di Prima, Hollo, Kyger, Lorde, Rutsala, Sanchez, Strand, Turco, Wieners, Zimmer

1935 Benedikt, Edson, Eshleman, Giorno, Kelly, Lieberman, Mezey, S. Moss, Oliver, Slavitt, Waldrop, C. Wright

1936 Chappell, Clifton, Hine, Owens, Piercy, Whitehead, C. K. Williams

1937 Bell, Fraser, Harrison, Howe, R. Johnson, Meltzer, Schmitz, Stuart, Wakowski

1938 Gildner, Harper, Oates, Reed, Simic

1939 Berkson, Bidart, Coolidge, Dacey, Dunn, Kooser, Plumly, Sanders, Young

1940 Anderson, Cooley, Heyen, Pinsky, Rogers, Tillinghast

1941 Clark, Dobyns, Grenier, Hass, Hejinian, Holden, Ortiz, Peck, Reiss, Root, Ruark

1942 Gregg, Hacker, Heffernan, Jong, Lea, Lee, Ludvigson, Matthews, Olds, Padgett, D. Smith

1943 Brownstein, Corn, Di Palma, Giovanni, Glück, Malanga, McPherson, Palmer, Saroyan, Tate, Voigt

1944 Gibson, Hathaway, Kuzma, Morgan, Stein, L. Thomas, Violi, Welish

1945 Dubie, Halpern, Koethe, Mayer, McClatchy, Notley, Stokesbury, Waldman

1946 Levis, Lux, Ryan, Sherry, Stanton

1947 Ai, Orr, Peacock, Ramke, D. Shapiro

1948 Andrews, Goldbarth, McHugh, Scalapino, Steele, Watten

1949 Blumenthal, Bottoms, Cruz, Emanuel, St. John, Santos

1950 Bernstein, Forché, Hirsch, Hummer, W. Logan, McBride

1951 Graham, Hongo

1952 Baca, Dove, Fulton, Harryman, Nye, Ríos, Soto, Spires

1953 Leithauser, Schnackenberg, Trinidad, Wojahn

1954 Cervantes

1955 Song

APPENDIX 5: FIRST ANTHOLOGY APPEARANCES

This list is designed to show at a glance which anthologies exerted a formative influence on the subsequent careers of poets introduced in them. In that
sense, the anthologies most successful at launching careers have been *Mid-
Century American Poets* (Ciardi, 1950), *The New Poets of England and
America* (Hall, Pack, Simpson, 1957), *The New American Poetry* (Allen,
1960), *The Young American Poets* (Carroll, 1968), and *The American Poetry
Anthology* (Halpern, 1975).

[*= poets whose first appearance was in the *Poets of Today* series edited by John Hall
Wheelock. Brackets are used to indicate poets introduced concurrently by more than
one anthology in the same year.]

Matthiessen 1950 R. P. Warren [Jarrell, Lowell, Schwartz, Shapiro in C50]

Ciardi 1950 Bishop, Ciardi, Eberhart, Mayo, Nims, Roethke, Rukeyser,
Scott, Viereck, Wilbur [Jarrell, Lowell, Schwartz, Shapiro in MO50]

Humphries 1953 Booth, Cunningham, Kinnell, Merrill, Moss, Sarton,
Simpson, W. J. Smith

Moore 1954 Berryman, Brinnin, Fitzgerald, Nemerov, Patchen [Merwin in
W54]

Williams 1954 Garrigue, Hoffman [Merwin in M54]

Auden 1956 Broughton, Duncan, Hecht, Kunitz, Merton, Rexroth [Miles in
E56]

Elliott 1956 Schevill [Miles in A56]

Humphries 1957 *Garrett, Howes, Kizer, Lattimore, Mueller, Stafford,
*Swenson, Wagoner, Weiss [Hall in HPS57]

Hall, Pack, Simpson 1957 Bly, Bowers, Coulette, Finkel, Hollander, Justice, *Langland, McGrath, Meredith, Mezey, V. Miller, *Pack, Rich, Snodgrass, Whittemore, J. Wright [Hall in H57]

Williams 1958 O'Hara

Allen 1960 Ashbery, Baraka, Blackburn, Blaser, Corso, Creeley, Dorn, Eigner, Everson, Ferlinghetti, Field, Kerouac, Koch, Lamantia, Levertov, McClure, Meltzer, Olson, Oppenheimer, Schuyler, Snyder, Spicer, Whalen, Wieners [Ginsberg in S60]

Shapiro 1960 [Ginsberg in A60]

Engle, Langland 1962 Brooks, W. Dickey [Kennedy in H62; Levine, Sexton in HP62]

Hall 1962 [Kennedy in EL62; *J. Dickey, J. Logan in HP62]

Hall, Pack 1962 Plath, Ray, Starbuck [Levine, Sexton in EL62; *J. Dickey, J. Logan in H62]

Untermeyer 1962 Stone

Brinnin, Read 1963 Dugan, Feldman

DeLoach 1965 Berrigan, Di Prima, Ignatow, Malanga, Schwerner, Sanders [Enslin, Kelly, Owens, Rothenberg, Wakoski, Zukofsky in KL65]

Kelly, Leary 1965 Davison, Lieberman, Mac Low, Pomeroy, Sward, Woods [Enslin, Kelly, Owens, Rothenberg, Wakoski, Zukofsky in D65]

Williams 1966 Gardner, Van Duyn

Rosenthal 1967 Carruth

Stryk 1967 Huff, Oliver, Schmitz, Tate

Adams 1968 C. Wright

Carroll 1968 Anderson, Bell, Benedikt, Clark, Coolidge, Fraser, Glück, Hass, Padgett, Simic, Waldman [Strand in H68]

Hollander 1968 Ammons, Hine, Howard, D. Shapiro [Strand in C68]

Berg, Mezey 1969 [Berg in NY69; Kees in NY69 and S69]

Gleeson 1969 Brautigan

New Yorker 1969 Antin, Bronk, Gregor, Kumin, Kuzma, Oppen, Root, H. Shapiro, Spacks, Stuart, Turco, Updike, C. K. Williams [Berg in BM69; Kees in BM69 and S69; Sissman in S69]

Strand 1969 Goodman, Haines, Hugo, S. Moss [Kees in NY69 and BM69; Sissman in NY69]

Brinnin, Read 1970   Clifton, Piercy [Hayden, Kaufman in C70]

Carruth 1970   Corman, Eshleman, Harrison, Niedecker, Reznikoff [Hayden, Kaufman in BR70]

Kostelanetz 1970   Cage [Giorno in PS70]

Padgett, Shapiro 1970   Mayer [Giorno in K70]

Eshleman 1971   Stein

McMichael, Saleh 1971   Ai, Dacey, Edson, Harper, Levis

Hall 1972   Knight, Randall

Walsh 1972   Lee

Chace 1973   Reed, Sanchez

Evans 1973   Cooley, Dunn, Goldbarth, Lux, D. Smith, Stokesbury [Jong in MK73 and U73; Matthews in MK73; Young in W73]

Ellmann 1973   [Giovanni in MK73]

Kherdian 1973   [Bukowski in MK73 and W73]

Klonsky 1973   Hollo [Bukowski in E73 and K73; Giovanni in EN73; Jong in E73 and U73; Matthews in E73]

Untermeyer 1973   [Jong in E73 and MK73]

Williams 1973   Oates, *Slavitt, Whitehead, M. Williams [Stuart, Young in E73; Bukowski in K73 and MK73]

Kennedy 1974   Steele

Gross, Quasha 1974   Kyger

Rothenberg, Quasha 1974   Ortiz [Rakosi in W74]

Gross, Quasha 1974 and **Rothenberg, Quasha 1974** and **Quasha 1974**   Tarn

Weiss 1974   Engels, Koethe, Pastan, Peck, Plumly [Rakosi in RQ74]

Halpern 1975   Bidart, Dove, Dubie, Forché, Gallagher, Gregg, Hacker, Heyen, McHugh, McPherson, Orr, St. John, Stanton [Gildner, Reiss, Ryan in S75]

Stryk 1975   Heffernan, Kooser [Gildner, Reiss, Ryan in H75]

Heyen 1976   Stryk, Zimmer

Hine, Parisi 1978   Bottoms, Corn, Dobyns, McClatchy, Schnackenberg

Field 1979   Lorde, Morgan, Nye, Ríos, Rutsala, Soto

Bly 1980   [Stern in M80]

Moss 1980 Lea [Stern in B80]

Ray 1981 Hathaway, Holden

Kennedy 1982 Ruark

Eastman 1983 Voigt

Dow 1984 Palmer, Pinsky, Scalapino [Graham in MW84]

Myers, Weingarten 1984 Fulton, Hummer, McBride, Ramke, Rogers, Santos, Tillinghast, Wojahn [Graham in D84; Hirsch in W84]

Warren 1984 Gibson, Leithauser, Olds [Hirsch in MW84]

Pack, Lea, Parini 1985 [Blumenthal in SB85 and V85]

Smith, Bottoms 1985 Emanuel, Hongo, W. Logan, Ludvigson, Peacock, Song, Spires [Blumenthal in BL85 and V85]

Vendler 1985 Clampitt [Blumenthal in BL85 and SB85]

Codrescu 1987 Trinidad

Georgia Review 1987 Chappell

Ellmann, O'Clair 1988 Cervantes

Harris, Aguerro 1989 Baca

APPENDIX 6: ANTHOLOGIES OF AMERICAN POETRY IN TRANSLATION

Bosquet, Alain, ed., *Anthologie de la poésie américaine: des origines à nos jours* (Paris: Librairie Stock, 1956) [19th-20th c.]—R. P. Warren—Roethke—Patchen—K. Shapiro—Jarrell—Viereck—O. Williams—Eberhart—Kunitz—Rexroth—C. H. Ford—Roditi—Bishop—Goodman—Rukeyser—Schwartz—Laughlin—Merton—Lowell—Wilbur—Hoffman

Rizzardi, Alfredo, ed., *Poesia americana del dopoguerra* (Milano: Schwarz editore, 1958) Ammons—Ashbery—J. Bennett—Burford—Gregor—Hall—Hecht—Hoffman—Horan—Howes—J. Logan—McAllister—Merrill—Merwin—H. Moss—Nemerov—O'Connell—J. Randall—Rich—Simpson—Swenson—Tamkus—Wagoner—Wilbur—J. Wright

Corso, Gregory, and Walter Höllerer, eds., *Junge Amerikanische Lyrik* (München: Carl Hanser Verlag, 1961) Olson—Corso—Ginsberg—Creeley—O'Hara—Koch—Wieners—[Turnbull]—Persky—Kerouac—S. Thomas—J. Stern—Oppenheimer—Blaser—McClure—Snyder—Whalen—Ansen—

Blackburn—Heliczer—Jones [Baraka]—Guest—Loewinsohn—Orlovsky—G. Douglas—Duerden—A. Weinstein—Laughlin—Eigner—Ferlinghetti—Ashbery—L. Brown—Bremser—E. Marshall—DiPrima—Meltzer—Lamantia—K. Johnson

Steinbrinker, Guenther and Rudolf Hartung, eds., *Panorama Moderner Lyrik: Gedichte des 20. Jahrhunderts in Uebersetzungen* (n.p.: Sigbert Mohn Verlag, 1962) [global modernism]—L .Adams—Cunningham—Eberhart—Ginsberg—Hecht—Hoffman—L. Joseph—D. Laing—Laughlin—Lowell—Mayo—Merrill—Merton—Merwin—H. Moss—Patchen—Pitney—Rexroth—Roethke—Rukeyser—Schwartz—W .T. Scott—K. Shapiro—W. J. Smith—Sobiloff—Solomon—Swenson—Wheelock—Wilbur—Winters

Pivano, Fernando, ed., *Poesia degli ultimi americani* (Milano: Feltrinelli, 1964) Bremser—Corso—Creeley—DiPrima—Dorn—Duncan—Ferlinghetti—Ginsberg—Jones [Baraka]—Kaufman—Kelly—Kerouac—Koch—Lamantia—Levertov—Loewinsohn—McClure—Mailer—O'Hara—Olson—Oppenheimer—Orlovsky—Sanders—Snyder—Sorrells—Welch—Wieners—J. Williams

Girri, Alberto, ed., *Quince Poetas Norteamericanos* (Buenos Aires: Bibliografica Omeba, 1966) Kunitz—Eberhart—Roethke—Patchen—Bishop—Berryman—Jarrell—Lowell—Ferlinghetti—Nemerov—Wilbur—Levertov—Ginsberg—Creeley—Merwin

Wenseleer, Luc, ed., *Adam & Eve & de stad: amerikaanse poëzie van de 20c eeuw* (Den Haag: Bert Bakker, 1966) [moderns]—Rexroth—Roethke—Patchen—K. Shapiro—Rukeyser—Jarrell—Nims—Lowell—Ferlinghetti—Nemerov—Wilbur—Levertov—Merrill—Bly—Ashbery—Hall—Kennedy—LaFollette—Corso—Layzer—Jones [Baraka]—Mezey

Fauchereau, Serge, ed., *41 poètes américaines d'aujourd'hui* (Paris: Les Lettres Nouvelles, 1970) [described by Perloff (*Poetic License* 316 n14): "has a section on Objectivists, on Black Mountain poets and the New York school, as well as one entitled 'La Nouvelle subjectivité,' which does include poetry by James Wright, Galway Kinnell, Louis Simpson, W. S. Merwin, and Robert Bly, and another section called 'Nouvelles tendances,' with poems by James Merrill, Robert Creeley, and Tom Clark, among others."]

Izzo, Carlo, ed., *Poesia Americana 1850–1950,* vol. 3 (Parma: Garzanti, 1971) Eberhart—R. P. Warren—Rexroth—Roethke—L. Hughes—C. H. Ford—Patchen—Schwartz—Rukeyser—K. Shapiro—Hayden—Berryman—Jarrell—Laughlin—Merton—Ciardi—Viereck—Lowell

Roubaud, Jacques, and Michel Deguy, eds., *Vìngt poètes américaines* (Paris: Gallimard-NRF, 1980) [G. Stein]—Zukofsky—Oppen—Duncan—Levertov—Schuyler—Corman—Spicer—Blackburn—Olson—Ashbery—Eigner—Merwin—Mathews—Koch—Rothenberg—Antin—R. Waldrop—Eshleman—Tarn

Hocquard, Emmanuel and Claude Royet-Journoud, eds., *21 + 1: Poètes américaines d'aujourd'hui* (Montpellier: Delta, 1986) [Raworth]—Armantrout—Auster—Bernstein—Berssenbrugge—Coolidge—Davidson—Gizzi—Grenier—S. Howe—R. Johnson—Mayer—Palmer—Perelman—Samperi—Scalapino—Silliman—Sobin—Taggart—K. Waldrop—Ward—Yau

APPENDIX 7: PRIZES AND AWARDS

I. FELLOWSHIPS

Academy of American Poets Fellowship

1946   Edgar Lee Masters

1947   Ridgely Torrence

1948   Percy MacKaye

1949   [no award]

1950   e. e. cummings

1951   [no award]

1952   Padraic Colum

1953   Robert Frost

1954   Oliver St. John Gogarty and Louise Townsend Nicholl

1955   Rolfe Humphries

1956   William Carlos Williams

1957   Conrad Aiken

1958   Robinson Jeffers

1959   Léonie Adams and Louise Bogan

1960   Jesse Stuart

1961   Horace Gregory

1962   John Crowe Ransom

1963   Ezra Pound and Allen Tate

1964   Elizabeth Bishop

1965   Marianne Moore

1966	John Berryman and Archibald MacLeish
1967	Mark Van Doren
1968	Stanley Kunitz
1969	Richard Eberhart and Anthony Hecht
1970	Howard Nemerov
1971	James Wright
1972	W. D. Snodgrass
1973	W. S. Merwin
1974	Léonie Adams
1975	Robert Hayden
1976	J. V. Cunningham
1977	Louis Coxe
1978	Josephine Miles
1979	Mark Strand and May Swenson
1980	Mona Van Duyn
1981	Richard Hugo
1982	John Ashbery and John Frederick Nims
1983	James Schuyler and Philip Booth
1984	Richmond Lattimore and Robert Francis
1985	Maxine Kumin and Amy Clampitt
1986	Irving Feldman and Howard Moss
1987	Alfred Corn and Josephine Jacobsen
1988	Donald Justice
1989	Richard Howard
1990	William Meredith
1991	J. D. McClatchy
1992	Adrienne Rich
1993	Gerald Stern
1994	David Ferry

Rome Fellowship in Literature (poetry only) *[American Academy of Arts and Letters]*

1951	Anthony Hecht
1954	Richard Wilbur
1956	John Ciardi
1957	Robert Francis, Louis Simpson
1961	George Starbuck
1962	Alan Dugan, George Starbuck
1963	Anne Sexton (Travelling Fellow)
1967	A. R. Ammons (Travelling Fellow)
1976	Miller Williams
1978	John Peck
1981	Edward Field
1983	Gjertrud Schnackenberg
1984	David St. John
1988	Edward Hirsch

MacArthur Fellowships *[MacArthur Foundation]*

1981	A. R. Ammons, Joseph Brodsky, Derek Walcott, Robert Penn Warren
1983	Brad Leithauser, A. K. Ramanujan
1984	Robert Hass, Galway Kinnell, Charles Simic
1985	John Ashbery
1986	Daryl Hine, Jay Wright
1987	Douglas Crase, Richard Kenney, Mark Strand, May Swenson
1989	Allen Grossman
1990	Jorie Graham, Patricia Hampl, John Hollander
1991	Alice Fulton, John Hollander, Eleanor Wilner
1992	Amy Clampitt, Irving Feldman
1993	Thom Gunn, Ann Lauterbach, Jim Powell
1994	Adrienne Rich

II. PRIZES AND AWARDS: ACADEMY OF AMERICAN POETS

Lamont Poetry Selection

1954   Constance Carrier, *The Middle Voice*, Swallow

1955   Donald Hall, *Exiles and Marriages*, Viking

1956   Philip Booth, *Letter from a Distant Land*, Viking

1957   Daniel Berrigan, *Time Without Number*, Macmillan

1958   Ned O'Gorman, *The Night of the Hammer*, Harcourt

1959   Donald Justice, *The Summer Anniversaries*, Wesleyan U. P.

1960   Robert Mezey, *The Lovemaker*, Cummington

1961   X.J. Kennedy, *Nude Descending a Staircase*, Doubleday

1962   Edward Field, *Stand Up, Friend, With Me*, Grove

1963   [no award]

1964   Adrien Stoutenburg, *Heroes Advise Us*, Scribner

1965   Henri Coulette, *The War of the Secret Agent*, Scribner

1966   Kenneth O. Hanson, *The Distance Anywhere*, U. of Washington P.

1967   James Scully, *The Marches*, Holt

1968   Jane Cooper, *The Weather of Six Mornings*, Macmillan

1969   Marvin Bell, *A Probable Volume of Dreams*, Atheneum

1970   William Harmon, *Treasury Holiday*, Wesleyan U. P.

1971   Stephen Dobyns, *Concurring Beasts*, Atheneum

1972   Peter Everwine, *Collecting the Animals*, Atheneum

1973   Marilyn Hacker, *Presentation Piece*, Viking

1974   John Balaban, *After Our War*, Pittsburgh U. P.

1975   Lisel Mueller, *The Private Life*, LSU

1976   Larry Levis, *The Afterlife*, Windhover

1977   Gerald Stern, *Lucky Life*, Houghton Mifflin

1978   Ai, *Killing Floor*, Houghton Mifflin

1979   Frederick Seidel, *Sunrise*, Viking

1980   Michael Van Walleghen, *More Trouble With the Obvious*, U. of Illinois P.

1981   Carolyn Forché, *The Country Between Us*, Harper

1982   Margaret Gibson, *Long Walks in the Afternoon*, LSU

1983   Sharon Olds, *The Dead and the Living*, Knopf

1984   Philip Schultz, *Deep Within the Ravine*, Viking

1985   Cornelius Eady, *Victims of the Latest Dance Craze*, Ommation

1986   Jane Shore, *The Minute Hand*, U. of Mass. P.

1987   Garrett Hongo, *The River of Heaven*, Knopf

1988   Mary Jo Salter, *Unfinished Painting*, Knopf

1989   Minnie Bruce Pratt, *Crime Against Nature*, Firebrand

1990   Li-Young Lee, *The City in Which I Love You*, Boa

1991   Susan Wood, *Campo Santo*, LSU

1992   Kathryn Byer, *Wildwood Flower*, LSU

1993   Rosanne Warren, *Stained Glass*, Norton

1994   Brigit Pegeen Kelly, *Song*, Boa

Walt Whitman Award

1975   Reg Saner, *Climbing into the Roots*, Harper

1976   Laura Gilpin, *Hocus-Pocus of the Universe*, Doubleday

1977   Lauren Shakely, *Guilty Bystander*, Random

1978   Karen Snow, *Wonders*, Viking

1979   David Bottoms, *Shooting Rats at the Bibb County Dump*, Morrow

1980   Jared Carter, *Work, For the Night is Coming*, Macmillan

1981   Alberto Ríos, *One Night in a Familiar Room*, Sheepmeadow

1982   Anthony Petrosky, *Jurgis Petrakis*, LSU

1983   Christopher Gilbert, *Access the Mutual Landscape*, Graywolf

1984   Eric Panky, *For the New Year*, Atheneum

1985   Christian Balk, *Bindweed*, Macmillan

1986   Chris Llewellyn, *Fragments from the Fire*, Penguin

1987   Judith Baumel, *The Weight of Numbers,* Wesleyan U. P.

1988   April Bernard, *Bye, Bye Blackbird,* Random

1989   Martha Hollander, *The Game of Statues,* Atlantic

1990   Elaine Terranova, *Cult of the Right Hand,* Doubleday

1991   Greg Glazer, *From The Iron Chair,* Norton

1992   Stephen Yenser, *The Fire in All Things,* LSU

1993   Alison Hawthorne Deming, *Science and Other Poems,* LSU

1994   Jan Richman, *Because the Brain Can Be Talked Into Anything,* LSU

III. PRIZES AND AWARDS: AMERICAN ACADEMY OF ARTS AND LETTERS AWARDS

American Academy of Arts and Letters Awards

1945   Kenneth Fearing

1946   Gwendolyn Brooks, Langston Hughes, Marianne Moore

1947   Lloyd Frankenberg, Robert Lowell

1948   Dudley Fitts, Genevieve Taggard, Allen Tate

1949   Léonie Adams

1950   John Berryman, Hyam Plutzik

1951   Elizabeth Bishop, Louise Bogan, Randall Jarrell

1952   Theodore Roethke, Yvor Winters

1953   Paul Goodman, Delmore Schwartz

1954   Richmond Lattimore

1955   Richard Eberhart, Robert Horan, Chester Kallman

1956   Josephine Miles

1957   Robert Fitzgerald, W. S. Merwin, Robert Pack

1958   William Meredith

1959   Stanley Kunitz, James Wright

1960   Adrienne Rich, W. D. Snodgrass, May Swenson

1961   Jean Garrigue, Daniel McCord, Howard Nemerov

1962   Galway Kinnell

1963   John Hollander

1964   Thom Gunn, David Ignatow, Kenneth Rexroth

1965   Ben Belitt, Robert Bly, J. V. Cunningham, Denise Levertov

1966   James Dickey, Edwin Honig, Gary Snyder, Melvin B. Tolson

1967   Philip Booth, Daniel Hoffman, David Wagoner

1968   John Malcolm Brinnin, Fred Chappell, Reuel Denney, Howard Moss, John Frederick Nims, Julia Randall

1969   John Ashbery, George P. Elliott, Allen Ginsberg, L. E. Sissman

1970   Brewster Ghiselin, Richard Howard, N. Scott Momaday

1971   Wendell Berry, Barbara Howes

1972   Peter Davison, Michael S. Harper

1973   Irving Feldman, Philip Levine

1974   Donald Justice, James Tate, Henry Van Dyke

1975   John Peck, Mark Strand

1976   Kenneth Koch, Charles Simic, Louis Simpson, Louis Zukofsky

1977   A.R. Ammons, Cynthia Macdonald, James Schuyler, Charles Wright

1979   Dave Smith

1980   William Dickey, Maxine Kumin, George Oppen, Robert Pinsky

1981   Louise Glück, William Stafford, Jay Wright

1982   Daryl Hine

1983   Alfred Corn, Robert Mezey, Mary Oliver, George Starbuck

1984   Amy Clampitt, Robert Hass

1985   Alan Dugan, Carolyn Kizer, Gilbert Sorrentino

1986   Robert Kelly

1987   Sandra McPherson

1988   David Bottoms

1989   David R. Slavitt

1990   Debora Greger, Rachel Hadas, David Lehman

1991   Edgar Bowers, J. D. McClatchy

1994   Marvin Bell

Award of Merit Medal (poetry only)

1945	Wystan Hugh Auden
1960	Hilda Doolittle
1970	Reed Whittemore
1975	Galway Kinnell
1980	Richard Howard
1986	Kenneth Koch
1992	Charles Wright

The Gold Medal Awards (poetry only)

1953	Marianne Moore
1958	Conrad Aiken
1963	William Carlos Williams
1968	Wystan Hugh Austen
1973	John Crowe Ransom
1978	Archibald MacLeish
1985	Robert Penn Warren
1991	Richard Wilbur

Jean Stein Award

1986	Gregory Corso
1989	Rodney Jones
1992	James Applewhite

Loines Award for Poetry (discontinued)

1948	William Carlos Williams
1951	John Crowe Ransom
1954	David Jones

1956   John Betjeman

1957   Edwin Muir

1958   Robert Graves

1960   Abbie Huston Evans

1962   Ivor Armstrong Richards

1964   John Berryman

1966   William Meredith

1968   Anthony Hecht

1970   Robert Hayden

1972   William Jay Smith

1974   Philip Larkin

1976   Mona Van Duyn

1981   Ben Belitt

1983   Geoffrey Hill

Morton Dauwen Zabel Award (poetry only)

1971   Charles Reznikoff

1974   John Logan

1977   David Shapiro

1980   Donald Finkel

1986   Philip Whalen

1989   C. K. Williams

1992   Jorie Graham

Witter Bynner Prize for Poetry

1980   Pamela White Hadas

1981   Allen Grossman

1982   William Heyen

1983   Douglas Crase

1984   Henry Taylor

1985   J. D. McClatchy

1986   C. D. Wright

1987   Antler

1988   Andrew Hudgins

1989   Mary Jo Salter

1990   Jacqueline Osherow

1991   Thylias Moss

1992   George Bradley

1993   Patricia Storace

1994   Rosanna Warren

IV. PRIZES AND AWARDS: COLUMBIA UNIVERSITY

Pulitzer Prize

1945   Karl Shapiro, *V-Letter and Other Poems*, Reynal

1947   Robert Lowell, *Lord Weary's Castle*, Harcourt

1948   W.H. Auden, *The Age of Anxiety*, Random

1949   Peter Viereck, *Terror and Decorum*, Scribner

1950   Gwendolyn Brooks, *Annie Allen*, Harper

1951   Carl Sandburg, *Complete Poems*, Harcourt

1952   Marianne Moore, *Collected Poems*, Macmillan

1953   Archibald MacLeish, *Collected Poems, 1917–1952*, Houghton

1954   Theodore Roethke, *The Waking*, Doubleday

1955   Wallace Stevens, *Collected Poems*, Knopf

1956   Elizabeth Bishop, *Poems—North and South*, Farrar Straus

1957   Richard Wilbur, *Things of This World*, Harcourt

1958   Robert Penn Warren, *Promises*, Random

1959   Stanley Kunitz, *Selected Poems, 1928–1958*, Little Brown

1960   W. D. Snodgrass, *Heart's Needle*, Knopf

1961   Phyllis McGinley, *Times Three*, Viking

1962   Alan Dugan, *Poems*, Yale U. P.

1963   William Carlos Williams, *Pictures from Breughel*, New Directions

1964   Louis Simpson, *At the End of the Open Road*, Wesleyan U. P.

1965   John Berryman, *77 Dream Songs*, Farrar Straus

1966   Richard Eberhart, *Selected Poems*, New Directions

1967   Anne Sexton, *Live or Die*, Houghton

1968   Anthony Hecht, *The Hard Hours*, Atheneum

1969   George Oppen, *Of Being Numerous*, New Directions

1970   Richard Howard, *Untitled Subjects*, Atheneum

1971   W. S. Merwin, *The Carrier of Ladders*, Atheneum

1972   James Wright, *Collected Poems*, Wesleyan U. P.

1973   Maxine Kumin, *Up Country*, Harper

1974   Robert Lowell, *The Dolphin*, Farrar Straus

1975   Gary Snyder, *Turtle Island*, New Directions

1976   John Ashbery, *Self-Portrait in a Convex Mirror*, Viking

1977   James Merrill, *Divine Comedies*, Atheneum

1978   Howard Nemerov, *Collected Poems*, U. of Chicago P.

1979   Robert Penn Warren, *Now and Then*, Random

1980   Donald Justice, *Selected Poems*, Atheneum

1981   James Schuyler, *The Morning of the Poem*, Farrar Straus

1982   Sylvia Plath, *Collected Poems*, Harper

1983   Galway Kinnell, *Selected Poems*, Houghton

1984   Mary Oliver, *American Primitive*, Little Brown

1985   Carolyn Kizer, *Yin*, Boa

1986   Henry Taylor, *The Flying Change*, LSU

1987   Rita Dove, *Thomas and Beulah*, Carnegie-Mellon U. P.

1988   William Meredith, *Partial Accounts: New and Selected Poems*, Knopf

1989   Richard Wilbur, *New and Collected Poems*, Harcourt

1990   Charles Simic, *The World Doesn't End*, Harcourt

1991   Mona Van Duyn, *Near Changes,* Knopf

1992   James Tate, *Selected Poems,* Wesleyan U. P.

1993   Louise Glück, *The Wild Iris,* Ecco

1994   Yusef Komunyakaa, *Neon Vernacular,* Wesleyan U. P.

V. PRIZES AND AWARDS: JOHN S. GUGGENHEIM FOUNDATION

John Simon Guggenheim Memorial Fellowships

1945   Ben Bellitt, Stanley Kunitz, Marianne Moore, Theodore Roethke

1946   Gwendolyn Brooks, Randall Jarrell

1947   Elizabeth Bishop, Gwendolyn Brooks, Robert Lowell

1948   Agustí Bartra Lleonart, Douglas LePan, Kenneth Rexroth, Peter Viereck

1949   William Everson, Agustí Bartra Lleonart, Kenneth Rexroth

1950   Rosalie Moore Brown, Theodore Roethke

1951   Rosalie Moore Brown

1952   Adrienne Rich, Richard Wilbur

1953   Edgar Bogardus, Paul Engle

1954   Jorge Guillen, May Sarton, Peter Viereck

1955   Barbara Golffing, Barbara Howes

1956   Margaret Avison, Barbara Golffing, Ned O'Gorman, David Wagoner

1957   Paul Engle, Marcia Nardi, Alastair Reid, Jonathan Williams

1958   Philip Booth, Edgar Bowers, Katherine Hoskins, Alastair Reid

1959   J. V. Cunningham, Paul Engle, Jorge Guillen, Edward Hughes, Adrienne Rich, May Swenson

1960   Agustí Bartra Lleonart, Jane Cooper, Jean Garrigue

1961   Wendell Berry, James Dickey, Kenneth Koch, Agusti Bartra Lleonart, George Starbuck

1962   Galway Kinnell, Denise Levertov, Ned O'Gorman, Louis Simpson

1963   Alan Dugan, Robert Duncan, Edward Field, Alberto Girri, Donald Hall, Richard Wilbur

1964   Robert Bly, Philip Booth, Robert Creeley, Jack Gilbert, Jerome Maz-
        zaro, Robert Sward, James Wright

1965   Hayden Carruth, Allen Ginsberg, John Haines, David Ignatow

1966   A. R. Ammons, Homero Aridjis, J. V. Cunningham, Donald Finkel,
        Richard Howard, William Stafford

1967   John Ashbery, Paul Blackburn, Thomas McGrath, Marco Montes de
        Oca, Tomás Segovia

1968   Thomas Kinsella, Howard Nemerov, Alejandra Pizarnik, L. E. Siss-
        man, Gary Snyder

1969   Carlos Belli de la Torre, Jose Becerra Ramos, Michael Benedikt,
        Edgar Bowers, Alberto Girri, Jim Harrison, Anne Sexton

1970   James Reed, William Pitt Root, Raphael Rudnik, Louis Simpson

1971   Edward Braithwaite, Tom Clark, Robert Creeley, Thom Gunn,
        Thomas Kinsella, Marco Montes de Oca, Ruth Stone

1972   Robert Bly, Donald Davie, Alan Dugan, Donald Hall, Nicanor Parra,
        Charles Simic, W. D. Snodgrass, Mona Van Duyn, Diane Wakoski

1973   John Ashbery, Irving Feldman, Isabel Fraire Benson, David Ignatow,
        X. J. Kennedy, Philip Levine, Michael McClure, W. S. Merwin, Stan-
        ley Plumly, James Scully

1974   Stephen Berg, Russell Edson, Jill Hoffman, Galway Kinnell,
        Etheridge Knight, Christopher Middleton, Jerome Rothenberg,
        Javier Sologuren, Mark Strand, C. K. Williams, Jay Wright, Al
        Young

1975   Ai, Marvin Bell, Peter Everwine, Louise Glück, William Meredith,
        Tomás Segovia, Ruth Stone, Charles Wright

1976   Jon Anderson, James Applewhite, Henri Coulette, Michael S. Harp-
        er, Donald Justice, Sandra McPherson, Czeslaw Milosz, Leonard
        Nathan, James Tate, Jean Valentine, Enrique Verástegui Peláez

1977   Joseph Brodsky, Francisco Brodsky, Norman Dubie, William Heyen,
        Richard Hugo, James McMichael, Robert Mezey, Gregory Orr, David
        St. John

1978   Elizabeth Bishop, Antonio Cisneros Campoy, Clayton Eshleman,
        Carolyn Forché, Tess Gallagher, David Huerta Bravo, John N. Mor-
        ris, Dennis Schmitz, Ellen Voigt, James Wright, David Young

1979   Homero Aridjis, Frank Bidart, Hayden Carruth, John Engels, Freder-
        ick Feirstein, Robert Hass, John Logan, John Montague, Gonzalo
        Rojas, Gary Soto

1980   Olga Broumas, Donald Davie, Kathleen Fraser, Marilyn Hacker, Daryl Hine, Philip Levine, William Matthews, Mary Oliver, Robert Pinsky, Abelardo Sánchez León, Gerald Stern

1981   Mary Madeline DeFrees, Daniel Leyva, Carol Muske, Sharon Olds, John Peck, Michael Ryan, Wendy Salinger, James Schuyler, Dave Smith, David Wevill

1982   David Budill, Jared Carter, Amy Clampitt, Jorie Graham, Linda Gregg, Allen Grossman, Brad Leithauser, Larry Levis, Heberto Padilla, Vern Rutsala, Pamela Stewart

1983   Christopher Bursk, Stephen Dobyns, Rita Dove, Daniel Epstein, Reginald Gibbons, Albert Goldbarth, Sam Hamill, Omar Lara, Susan Ludvigson, Cynthia Macdonald, W. S. Merwin, Hilda Morley Wolpe, Ed Sanders, Sherod Santos

1984   Rubén Bonifaz Nuño, Wanda Coleman, Douglas Crase, Carl Dennis, Stephen Dunn, John Haines, Lawrence Kearney, Richard Kenny, Eduardo Lizalde, Michael Ondaatje, Alicia Ostriker, Pattiann Rogers, Roberta Spear, Timothy Steele, Raúl Zurita

1985   Charles Bernstein, William Di Piero, Edward Hirsch, Jane Hirshfield, Colette Inez, Rodney Jones, Mary Kinzie, Jackson Mac Low, Jay Meek, Liam Rector, Alan Shapiro, John Wieners

1986   Rafael Cadenas, Alfred Corn, Alice Fulton, Denis Johnson, Ann Lauterbach, Wesley McNair, John Nims, Ron Padgett, Gjertrud Schnackenberg, Vikram Seth, Tom Sleigh, Theodore Weiss

1987   Carlos Belli de la Torre, Robert Bringhurst, T. Carmi, Louise Glück, Debora Greger, John Koethe, Sydney Lea, J. D. McClatchy, Katha Pollitt, W. Dabney Stuart, Carolyn Wright

1988   Michael Blumenthal, Deborah Digges, Brendan Galvin, James Galvin, Emily Grosholz, Rachel Hadas, Daniel Halpern, Tamara Kamenszain, Thomas Lux, James Miller, Robert Morgan, Alberto Ríos, Jordan Smith

1989   Jonathan Galassi, Laura Jensen, August Kleinzahler, Li-Young Lee, David Lehman, Heather McHugh, Michael Palmer, Franz Wright

1990   John Ash, Garrett Hongo, Albert Moritz, Paul Muldoon, Marlene Philip, Leonard Roberts, P. Chase Twichell

1991   Mark Jarman, Laurie Sheck, Jane Shore, Dara Wier, Alan Williamson

1992   T. R. Humner, Jane Kenyon, Susan Mitchell, Néstor Perlongher, Donald Revell, Elizabeth Spires, Adam Zagajewski

1993   Diana Bellessi, Nicholas Christopher, Billy Collins, Cornelius Eady, Lars Gustafsson, Mary Jo Salter, Frederick Seidel

1994   Mark Doty, Eamon Grennan, Brenda Hillman, Karl Kirchwey, Elizabeth Macklin, James McManus, María Negroni

VI. PRIZES AND AWARDS: LOS ANGELES TIMES

L.A. Times Book Award

1980   Robert Kelly, *Kill the Messenger,* Black Sparrow

1981   Ntozake Shange, *Three Pieces,* St. Martin's

1982   Allen Ginsberg, *Plutonium Ode,* City Lights

1983   James Merrill, *The Changing Light at Sandover,* Atheneum

1984   Charles Olson, *The Maximus Poems,* U. of California P.

1985   X. J. Kennedy, *Cross Ties,* U. of Georgia P.

1986   Derek Walcott, *Collected Poems 1948–1984,* Farrar Straus

1987   William Meredith, *Partial Accounts: New and Selected Poems,* Knopf

1988   Richard Wilbur, *New and Collected Poems,* Harcourt

1989   Donald Hall, *The One Day,* Ticknor

1990   John Caddy, *The Color of Mesabi Bones,* Milkweed

1991   Philip Levine, *What Work Is,* Knopf

1992   Adrienne Rich, *An Atlas of the Difficult World,* Norton

1993   Mark Doty, *My Alexandria,* U. of Illinois P.

1994   Carolyn Forché, *The Angel of History,* Harper Collins

VII. PRIZES AND AWARDS: NATIONAL BOOK FOUNDATION

National Book Award [for a period in the early 1980s the National Book Award was renamed the American Book Award, but all of the Awards are now referred to as National Book Awards]

1950   William Carlos Williams, *Paterson: Book III* & *Selected Poems,* New Directions

1951   Wallace Stevens, *The Auroras of Autumn*, Knopf

1952   Marianne Moore, *Collected Poems*, Macmillan

1953   Archibald MacLeish, *Collected Poems 1917–1952*, Houghton

1954   Conrad Aiken, *Collected Poems*, Oxford U. P.

1955   e. e. cummings, *Poems 1923–1954*, Harcourt
        Wallace Stevens, *Collected Poems*, Knopf

1956   W. H. Auden, *The Shield of Achilles*, Random

1957   Richard Wilbur, *Things of This World*, Harcourt

1958   Robert Penn Warren, *Promises*, Random

1959   Theodore Roethke, *Words for the Wind*, Doubleday

1960   Robert Lowell, *Life Studies*, Farrar Straus

1961   Randall Jarrell, *The Woman at the Washington Zoo*, Atheneum

1962   Alan Dugan, *Poems*, Yale U. P.

1963   William Stafford, *Traveling Through the Dark*, Harper

1964   John Crowe Ransom, *Selected Poems*, Knopf

1965   Theodore Roethke, *The Far Field*, Doubleday

1966   James Dickey, *Buckdancer's Choice*, Wesleyan U. P.

1967   James Merrill, *Nights and Days*, Atheneum

1968   Robert Bly, *The Light Around the Body*, Harper

1969   John Berryman, *His Toy, His Dream, His Rest*, Farrar Straus

1970   Elizabeth Bishop, *The Complete Poems*, Farrar Straus

1971   Mona Van Duyn, *To See, To Take*, Atheneum

1972   Howard Moss, *Selected Poems*, Atheneum
        Frank O'Hara, *The Collected Poems*, Knopf

1973   A. R. Ammons, *Collected Poems, 1951–1971*, Norton

1974   Allen Ginsberg, *The Fall of America*, City Lights
        Adrienne Rich, *Diving into the Wreck*, Norton

1975   Marilyn Hacker, *Presentation Piece*, Viking

1976   John Ashbery, *Self-Portrait in a Convex Mirror*, Viking

1977   Richard Eberhart, *Collected Poems, 1930–1976*, Oxford U. P.

1978   Howard Nemerov, *The Collected Poems*, U. of Chicago P.

1979   James Merrill, *Mirabell: Book of Numbers*, Atheneum

1980   Philip Levine, *Ashes*, Atheneum

1981   Lisel Mueller, *The Need to Hold Still*, LSU

1982   William Bronk, *Life Supports: New and Collected Poems*, North Point

1983   Galway Kinell, *Selected Poems*, Houghton Mifflin
        Charles Wright, *Country Music*, Wesleyan U. P.

1991   Philip Levine, *What Work Is*, Knopf

1992   Mary Oliver, *New and Selected Poems*, Beacon

1993   A. R. Ammons, *Garbage*, Norton

1994   James Tate, *A Worshipful Company of Fletchers*, Ecco

VIII. PRIZES AND AWARDS: PARNASSUS

National Book Critics Circle Award

1975   John Ashbery, *Self-Portrait in a Convex Mirror*, Viking

1976   Elizabeth Bishop, *Geography III*, Farrar Straus

1977   Robert Lowell, *Day by Day*, Farrar Straus

1978   E. L. Sissman, *Hello Darkness*, Little Brown

1979   Philip Levine, *Ashes and Seven Years from Somewhere*, Atheneum

1980   Frederick Seidel, *Sunrise*, Viking

1981   A. R. Ammons, *A Coast of Trees*, Norton

1982   Katha Pollitt, *Antarctic Traveller*, Knopf

1983   James Merrill, *The Changing Light at Sandover*, Atheneum

1984   Sharon Olds, *The Dead and the Living*, Knopf

1985   Louise Glück, *The Triumph of Achilles*, Ecco

1986   Edward Hirsch, *Wild Gratitude*, Knopf

1987   C. K. Williams, *Flesh and Blood*, Farrar Straus

1988   Donald Hall, *The One Day*, Ticknor

1989   Rodney Jones, *Transparent Gestures*, Houghton

1990   Amy Gerstler, *Bitter Angel*, North Point

1991   Albert Goldbarth, *Heaven and Earth,* U. of Georgia P.

1992   Hayden Carruth, *Shorter Collected Poems,* Copper Canyon

1993   Mark Doty, *My Alexandria,* U. of Illinois P.

IX. PRIZES AND AWARDS: POETRY MAGAZINE

Bess Hokin Prize

1948 William Abrahams	1972 Sandra McPherson
1949 Barbara Howes	1973 Jane Shore
1950 Lloyd Frankenberg	1974 Margaret Atwood
1951 M. B. Tolson	1975 Charles O. Hartman
1952 L. E. Hudgins	1976 Norman Dubie
1953 Ruth Stone	1977 Gary Soto
1954 Hayden Carruth	1978 Richard Kenney
1955 Philip Booth	1979 Robert Beverly Ray
1956 Charles Tomlinson	1980 Gerald Stern
1957 Sylvia Plath	1981 Caroline Knox
1958 Alan Neame	1982 Pattiann Rogers
1959 Jean Clower	1983 Lawrence Raab
1960 Denise Levertov	1984 Grag Glazner
1961 X. J. Kennedy	1985 Linda Pastan
1962 W. S. Merwin	1986 Stephen Dobyns
1963 Adrienne Rich	1987 Ralph Angel
1964 Gary Snyder	1988 George Starbuck
1965 Galway Kinnell	1989 Alice Fulton
1966 Thomas Clark	1990 Billy Collins
1967 Wendell Berry	1991 Gary Fincke
1968 Michael Benedikt	1992 Richard Foerster
1969 Marvin Bell	1993 Julie Suk
1970 Charles Martin	1994 J. D. McClatchy
1971 Erica Jong	

Eunice Tietjens Memorial Prize

1945	Marie Boroff	1975	James McMichael
1946	Alfred Hayes	1976	Richard Kenney
1947	Theodore Roethke	1977	David Wagoner
1948	Peter Viereck	1978	William Heyen
1949	Gwendolyn Brooks	1979	Robert Morgan
1950	Andrew Glaze	1980	Sandra Gilbert
1951	Robinson Jeffers	1981	Pattiann Rogers
1952	e. e. cummings	1982	Stephen Dobyns
1953	Elder Olson	1983	Robert Pinsky
1954	Reuel Denney	1984	Wesley McNair
1955	James Wright	1985	J. D. McClatchy
1956	Mona Van Duyn	1986	Reynolds Price
1957	Kenneth Rexroth	1987	Gregory Djanikian
1958	James Merrill	1988	Lisel Mueller
1959	Barbara Howes	1989	William Matthews
1960	Marie Ponsot	1990	Mary Karr
1961	Karl Shapiro	1991	Sandra McPherson
1962	Muriel Rukeyser	1992	Enid Shower
1963	Helen Singer	1993	Joe-Anne McLaughlin-Carruth
1964	Hayden Carruth	1994	Molly Bendall
1965	Pauline Hanson		
1966	Galway Kinnell		
1967	Robert Duncan		
1968	Adrienne Rich		
1969	Charles Wright		
1970	Jean Malley		
1971	Louise Glück		
1972	Maxine Kumin		
1973	Judith Moffett		
1974	Judith Minty		

Frederick Bock Prize

1981	John Morris		1988	Robert Wrigley
1982	Baron Wormser		1989	J. Allyn Rosser
1983	Richard Kenney		1990	George White
1984	Rodney Jones		1991	Neal Bowers
1985	Dana Gioia		1992	Billy Collins
1986	Cathy Song		1993	Jane Kenyon
1987	Kevin Sain		1994	Tom Disch

Harriet Monroe Lyric Prize (discontinued)

1945	William Gibson		1958	H. D.
1946	Patrick Anderson		1959	Howard Nemerov
1947	Nicholas Moore		1960	Robert Duncan
1948	Richard Wilbur		1961	Robert Lowell
1949	Paul Goodman and Thomas Merton		1962	Ezra Pound
			1963	John Ashbery
1950	Richard Eberhart		1964	Denise Levertov
1951	James Merrill		1965	Donald Justice
1952	Kathleen Raine		1966	Winfield Townley Scott
1953	Ruth Herschberger		1967	W. S. Merwin
1954	Reed Whittemore		1968	Mona Van Duyn
1955	John Ciardi		1969	Richard Howard
1956	David Jones			
1957	Dorothy Donnelly			

Levinson Prize

1945	Dylan Thomas		1949	James Merrill
1946	John Ciardi		1950	John Berryman
1947	Muriel Rukeyser		1951	Theodore Roethke
1948	Randall Jarrell		1952	Saint-John Perse

1953	Vernon Watkins	1975	Howard Nemerov
1954	William Carlos Williams	1976	Judith Moffett
1955	Thom Gunn	1977	John Ashbery
1956	Stanley Kunitz	1978	Brewster Ghiselin
1957	Jay Macpherson	1979	Philip Levine
1958	Hayden Carruth	1980	Marilyn Hacker
1959	Delmore Schwartz	1981	James Dickey
1960	Robert Creeley	1982	Alfred Corn
1961	David Jones	1983	Frederick Turner and Ernest Popperl
1962	Anne Sexton		
1963	Robert Lowell	1984	Gary Soto
1964	Robert Duncan	1985	David Bottoms and Raymond Carver
1965	George Barker	1986	Maxine Kumin
1966	Basil Bunting	1987	Stephen Dunn
1967	Alan Dugan	1988	Reynolds Price
1968	Gary Snyder	1989	Brendan Galvin
1969	A. D. Hope	1990	J. D. McClatchy
1970	A. R. Ammons	1991	Linda Gregerson
1971	Turner Cassity	1992	W. S. Merwin
1972	Michael Hamburger	1993	May Sarton
1973	Richard Howard	1994	David Wagoner
1974	John Hollander		

Oscar Blumenthal Prize

1945	Yvor Winters	1951	Randall Jarrell
1946	George Moor	1952	Roy Marz
1947	James Merrill	1953	William Meredith
1948	Weldon Kees	1954	Anne Ridler
1949	Barbara Gibbs	1955	William Carlos Williams
1950	Richard Wilbur	1956	Sydney Goodsir Smith

1957	Ben Belitt	1976	David Bromwich
1958	Howard Nemerov	1977	Alfred Corn
1959	Josephine Miles	1978	Robert Pinsky
1960	Charles Tomlinson	1979	Lynne Lawner
1961	Kathleen Raine	1980	Robert Beverly Ray
1962	e. e. cummings	1981	Sherod Santos
1963	Karl Shapiro	1982	Pamela White Hadas
1964	Robert Creeley	1983	William Matthews
1965	Charles Olson	1984	Reynolds Price
1966	Louis Zukofsky	1985	Jennifer Atkinson
1967	Guy Davenport	1986	Albert Goldbarth
1968	James Wright	1987	Tess Gallagher
1969	Turner Cassity	1988	J. D. McClatchy
1970	Jon Anderson	1989	Carl Dennis
1971	Geoffrey Grigson	1990	Stephen Dunn
1972	Doulas Le Pan	1991	Charles Wright
1973	Brewster Ghiselin	1992	Richard Kenney
1974	David Wagoner	1993	Billy Collins
1975	Sandra McPherson	1994	Gerald Stern

Ruth Lilly Poetry Prize

1986	Adrienne Rich	1991	David Wagoner
1987	Philip Levine	1992	John Ashbery
1988	Anthony Hecht	1993	Charles Wright
1989	Mona Van Duyn	1994	Donald Hall
1990	Hayden Carruth		

Union League Civic and Arts Poetry Prize

1951	Horace Gregory	1964	Louis Zukofsky
1952	Robinson Jeffers	1965	Gael Turnbull
1953	Robert Penn Warren	1966	John Ashbery
1954	Dorothy Donnelly	1967	Robert Creeley
1955	Anne Ridler	1968	Clayton Eshelman
1956	Jean Garrigue	1969	Margaret Atwood
1957	Robert Duncan	1970	Dick Allen
1958	James Dickey	1971	Philip Murray
1959	William Stafford	1972	Tom Disch
1960	Ben Bellitt		*Discontinued 1973–1992*
1961	Charles Tomlinson	1993	William Matthews
1962	William Dickey	1994	Debora Greger
1963	William Jay Smith		

X. PRIZES AND AWARDS: POETRY SOCIETY OF AMERICA

Melville Cane Award

1962   Richard Wilbur, *Advice to a Prophet*, Harcourt

1963   Emery Clark, (unavailable)

1964   Joseph Langland, *The Wheel of Summer*, Dial

1965   Jean Hagstrum, *William Blake, Poet and Painter*, U. of Chicago P.

1966   James Dickey, *Buckdancer's Choice*, Wesleyan U. P.

1967   Lawrence Thompson, *Robert Frost: The Early Years*, Holt

1968   Jean Garrigue, *New and Selected Poems*, Macmillan

1969   Ruth Miller, *The Poetry of Emily Dickinson*, Wesleyan U. P.

1970   Rolfe Humphries, *Coat on a Stick: Late Poems*, Indiana U. P.

1971   Harold Bloom, *Yeats*, Oxford U. P.

1972   James Wright, *Collected Poems*, Wesleyan U. P.

1973   Jerome J. McGann, *Swinburne: An Experiment in Criticism*, U. of Chicago P.

1974   William Stafford, *Someday, Maybe*, Harper

1975   Richard Sewall, *The Life of Emily Dickinson*, Farrar Straus

1976   Charles Wright, *Bloodlines*, Wesleyan U. P.

1977   Donald Howard, *The Idea of the Canterbury Tales*, U. of California P.

1978   Michael S. Harper, *Images of Kin*, Harcourt

1979   Andrew Welsh, *Roots of Lyric*, Princeton U. P.

1980   Richard Hugo, *Selected Poems*, Norton

1981   Paul Fry, *The Poet's Calling in the English Ode*, Yale U. P.

1982   Gerald Stern, *The Red Coal*, Houghton

1983   Ian Hamilton, *Robert Lowell*, Random

1984   Alan Dugan, *New and Collected Poems*, Ecco

1985   Raymond Nelson, *Kenneth Patchen and American Mysticism*, U. of North Carolina P.

1986   Louise Glück, *The Triumph of Achilles*, Ecco

1987   Lewis Turco, *Visions and Revision of American Poetry*, U. of Arkansas P.

1988   Stephen Dobyns, *Cemetary Nights*, Viking
        Margaret Gibson, *Memories of the Future*, LSU

1989   Edward Butscher, *Conrad Aiken: Poet of the White Horse Vale*, U. of Georgia P.

1990   John Hollander, *Harp Lake*, Knopf

1991   J. D. McClatchy, *White Paper*, Columbia U. P.

1992   John Frederick Nims, *The Six Cornered Snowflake*, New Directions

1993   Jacques Barzan, *An Essay on French Verse for Readers of English Poetry*, New Directions

1994   Nicholas Christopher, *In the Year of the Comet*, Viking

Shelley Memorial Award

1945   Karl Shapiro

1946   Rolfe Humphries

1947   Janet Lewis

1948   John Berryman

1949   Louis Kent

1950   Jeremy Ingalls

1951   Richard Eberhart

1952   Elizabeth Bishop

1953   Kenneth Patchen

1954   Léonie Adams

1955   Robert Fitzgerald

1956   George Abbe

1957   Kenneth Rexroth

1958   José Garcia Villa

1959   Delmore Schwartz

1960   Robinson Jeffers

1961   Theodore Roethke

1962   Eric Barker

1963   William Stafford

1964   Ruth Stone

1965   David Ignatow

1966   Anne Sexton

1967   May Swenson

1968   Ann Stanford

1969   X. J. Kennedy and Mary Oliver

1970   Louise Townsend Nicholl and Adrienne Rich

1971   Galway Kinnell

1972   John Ashbery and Richard Wilbur

1973   W. S. Merwin

1974   Edward Field

1975   Gwendolyn Brooks

1976   Muriel Rukeyser

1977   Jane Cooper and William Everson

1978   Hayden Carruth

1979   Robert Creeley

1980   Alan Dugan

1981   Jon Anderson and Leo Connellan

1982   Robert Duncan and Denise Levertov

1983   Denise Levertov and Robert Duncan

1984   Etheridge Knight

1986   Gary Snyder

1987   Mona Van Duyn

1988   Dennis Schmitz

1990   Thomas McGrath and Theodore Weiss

1991   Shirley Kaufman

1992   Lucille Clifton

1993   Josephine Jacobsen

1994   Kenneth Koch and Cathy Song

William Carlos Williams Award

1979   David Fischer, *Teachings,* Back Roads

1980   David Ray, *The Tramp's Cup,* Chriton

1981   Robert Hass, *Praise,* Ecco

1982   Brewster Ghiselin, *Windrose,* U. of Utah P.

1983   John Logan, *Only the Dreamer Can Change the Dream,* Ecco

1984   David Wojahn, *Icehouse Lights,* Yale U. P.

1985   Robert Pinsky, *History of My Heart,* Ecco

1986   William Harmon, *Mutatis Mutandis,* Wesleyan U. P.

1987   Alicia Ostriker, *Imaginary Lover,* U. of Pittsburgh P.

1988   Alan Shapiro, *Happy Hour,* U. of Chicago P.

1989   Diane Wakoski, *Emerald Ice: Selected Poems,* Black Sparrow

1990   Ivan Arguelles, *Looking for Mary Lou,* Rock Steady

1991   Joy Harjo, *In Mad Love and War,* Wesleyan U. P.
       Safiya Henderson-Holmes, *Madness and a Bot of Hope,* Harlem
       River

1992   James Tate, *Selected Poems,* Wesleyan U. P.

1993   Louise Glück, *The Wild Iris,* Ecco

XI. PRIZES AND AWARDS: UNIVERSITY OF CHICAGO

Harriet Monroe Poetry Award

1946	Wallace Stevens	1980	Charles Simic
1948	Louise Bogan	1981	W. S. Merwin
1950	e. e. cummings	1984	Donald Justice
1952	Robert Lowell	1985	James Merrill
1954	Léonie Adams	1986	W. S. Merwin
1955	Richard Eberhart	1987	Anthony Hecht
1957	John Berryman	1988	William Meredith
1958	Stanley Kunitz	1989	Edgar Bowers
1961	Hayden Carruth and Yvor Winters	1990	Galway Kinnell
		1991	Allen Ginsberg
1974	Elizabeth Bishop	1992	Louise Glück
1975	John Ashbery	1993	C. K. Williams
1976	Philip Levine	1994	Adrienne Rich
1977	Robert Penn Warren		
1978	Richard Wilbur		

XII. PRIZES AND AWARDS: YALE UNIVERSITY, BEINECKE RARE BOOK AND MANUSCRIPT LIBRARY

Bollingen Prize

1949 Wallace Stevens

1950 John Crowe Ransom

1951 Marianne Moore

1952 Archibald MacLeish and William Carlos Williams

1953 W. H. Auden

1954 Léonie Adams and Louise Bogan

1955 Conrad Aiken

1956 Allen Tate

1957 e. e. cummings

1958 Theodore Roethke

1959 Delmore Schwartz

1960 Yvor Winters

1961 John Hall Wheelock and Richard Eberhart

1962 Robert Frost

1965 Horace Gregory

1967 Robert Penn Warren

1969 John Berryman and Karl Shapiro

1971 Richard Wilbur and Mona Van Duyn

1973 James Merrill

1975 A. R. Ammons

1977 David Ignatow

1979 W. S. Merwin

1981 Howard Nemerov and May Swenson

1983 Anthony Hecht and John Hollander

1985 John Ashbery and Fred Chappell

1987   Stanley Kunitz

1989   Edgar Bowers

1991   Laura Riding Jackson and Donald Justice

1993   Mark Strand

APPENDIX 8: "CRITICAL INDUSTRIES" [MLA CD-ROM SEARCH]

This list is derived from the MLA Bibliography on CD-ROM, in the Silver Platter Mode, inclusive from January 1981 through May 1994. The results are indicative, not absolute, as the nature of the Bibliography permits multiple listings of certain items under different reference categories, and so forth. To key in a poet's name one gets a numerical reading like "40 entries," but on closer examination it may turn out that for whatever reason this will result in only 34 articles or chapters in books that are about that poet's work. The situation is compounded in the case of common names, where entries may refer not to the poet as subject of scholarship but rather to scholars who happen to have the same name and are listed in the Bibliography as authors. A final difficulty in assigning absolute significance to such a tabulation is that some poets are the subject of multiple approaches: most of the citations for Robert Penn Warren, for instance, may be studies of his fiction. In order to increase the utility of this exercise in the face of such variables, the unusually high number of CD-ROM entries, which typically reflect the familiarity of poets' names or their extensive work as either translators (Robert Fitzgerald, Robert Francis, and Richard Howard) or critics (Daniel Hoffman and Yvor Winters), are given in parentheses and preceded by a tally which represents only those items relevant to this study. A double tally is also provided for authors whose principal works include both prose and poetry, as a means of isolating criticism specifically on poetry. In instances where the large number of entries prevents an exact tally, keyword searches, with the marker "poetry," have been used to isolate core materials. The results of these searches are indicated by an asterisk. In spite of these adaptations the significance of this key-word name search remains of limited use. Its most interesting result is the revelation of substantial discrepancies between a poet's prominence in anthologies and a clear lack of scholarly interest, or vice versa. W. D. Snodgrass, among the top twenty most anthologized postwar poets, yields only thirteen listings; while George Oppen, one of the lesser anthologized figures, gets an astonishing 111. It is contrasts of this magnitude that make this numerical exercise of more than trivial interest.

Authors	Items	
Ai	1	(280)
A. R. Ammons	65	
Jon Anderson	7	
Bruce Andrews	4	
David Antin	8	
John Ashbery	148	
Jimmy Santiago Baca	4	
Amiri Baraka (Leroi Jones)	15*	(56)
Marvin Bell	27	
Michael Benedikt	2	
Stephen Berg	16	
Bill Berkson	0	
Charles Bernstein	28	
Ted Berrigan	3	
Wendell Berry	53	
John Berryman	81	
Frank Bidart	10	
Elizabeth Bishop	179	
Paul Blackburn	10	
Robin Blaser	7	
Michael Blumenthal	1	
Robert Bly	152	
Philip Booth	9	
David Bottoms	3	
Edgar Bowers	0	
Richard Brautigan	0*	(34)
John Malcolm Brinnin	1	
William Bronk	24	

Gwendolyn Brooks	77	
James Broughton	4	
Michael Brownstein	1	
Charles Bukowski	50	
John Cage	14*	(47)
Hayden Carruth	22	
Lorna Dee Cervantes	11	
Fred Chappell	22	(39)
John Ciardi	45	
Amy Clampitt	13	
Tom Clark	7	
Lucille Clifton	12	
Peter Cooley	4	
Clark Coolidge	13	
Cid Corman	18	
Alfred Corn	11	
Gregory Corso	7	
Henri Coulette	3	
Robert Creeley	85	
Victor Hernandez Cruz	1	
J. V. Cunningham	1	
Philip Dacey	4	
Alan Davies	43	
Peter Davison	2	(41)
James Dickey	157	
William Dickey	5	
Ray Di Palma	0	
Diane Di Prima	3	
Stephen Dobyns	2	
Edward Dorn	33	

Rita Dove	20	
Norman Dubie	10	
Alan Dugan	3	
Robert Duncan	106	
Stephen Dunn	9	
Richard Eberhart	28	
Russell Edson	3	
Larry Eigner	0	
Kenward Elmslie	1	
Lynn Emanuel	2	
John Engels	1	
Paul Engle	4	
Theodore Enslin	11	
Clayton Eshleman	15	
William Everson (Brother Antoninus)	30	
Irving Feldman	10	
Lawrence Ferlinghetti	15	
Edward Field	2	
Donald Finkel	0	
Robert Fitzgerald	1	(16)
Carolyn Forché	24	
Robert Francis	8	(40)
Kathleen Fraser	11	
Alice Fulton	7	
Tess Gallagher	15	
Isabella Gardner	0	
George Garrett	45	
Jean Garrigue	5	
Margaret Gibson	2	(28)
Gary Gildner	3	

Allen Ginsberg	82	
John Giorno	3	
Nikki Giovanni	12	
Louise Glück	20	
Albert Goldbarth	2	
Paul Goodman	25	
Jorie Graham	7	
Linda Gregg	1	
Arthur Gregor	4	
Robert Grenier	4	
Barbara Guest	9	
Marilyn Hacker	8	
John Haines	6	
Donald Hall	51	
Daniel Halpern	2	
Michael S. Harper	24	
Jim Harrison	3	(6)
Carla Harryman	1	
Robert Hass	15	
William Hathaway	2	
Robert Hayden	17	
Anthony Hecht	21	
Michael Heffernan	2	
Lynn Hejinian	0	
William Heyen	10	
Daryl Hine	2	
Edward Hirsch	20	
Daniel Hoffman	9	(35)
Jonathan Holden	18	
John Hollander	39	

Anselm Hollo	4	
John Holmes	30	
Garrett Hongo	3	
Richard Howard	10	(52)
Susan Howe	23	
Barbara Howes	0	
Robert Huff	0	
Richard Hugo	57	
Terry Hummer	1	
David Ignatow	16	
Randall Jarrell	81	
Ronald Johnson	13	
Erica Jong	0*	(18)
Donald Justice	15	
Bob Kaufman	4	
Weldon Kees	14	
Robert Kelly	9	(19)
X. J. Kennedy	13	
Jack Kerouac	14*	(204)
Galway Kinnell	39	
Carolyn Kizer	4	
Etheridge Knight	9	
Bill Knott	1	
Kenneth Koch	15	
John Koethe	3	
Ted Kooser	14	
Maxine Kumin	26	
Stanley Kunitz	22	
Greg Kuzma	7	
Joanne Kyger	1	

Philip Lamantia	1	
Joseph Langland	2	
Richmond Lattimore	3	
Sydney Lea	12	
Don L. Lee (Haki Madhubuti)	7	
Brad Leithauser	13	
Denise Levertov	84	
Philip Levine	34	
Larry Levis	10	
Laurence Lieberman	9	
John Logan	9	(22)
Audre Lorde	37	
Robert Lowell	173	
Susan Ludvigson	1	
Thomas Lux	3	
Jackson Mac Low	3	
Gerard Malanga	0	
William Matchett	1	
William Matthews	11	(19)
Bernadette Mayer	1	
E. L. Mayo	3	
Mekeel McBride	0	
J. D. McClatchy	14	
Michael McClure	9	
Phyllis McGinley	0	
Thomas McGrath	39	
Heather McHugh	5	
Sandra McPherson	9	
David Meltzer	3	
William Meredith	15	

James Merrill	60	
Thomas Merton	34*	(120)
W. S. Merwin	82	
Robert Mezey	2	
Josephine Miles	9	
Vassar Miller	18	
Robert Morgan	6	(16)
Howard Moss	17	
Stanley Moss	1	
Lisel Mueller	6	
Howard Nemerov	35	
Lorine Niedecker	25	
John Fredrick Nims	0	
Alice Notley	1	
Naomi Shihab Nye	5	
Joyce Carol Oates	1*	(137)
Frank O'Hara	24	
Sharon Olds	5	
Mary Oliver	10	
Charles Olson	111	
George Oppen	111	
Joel Oppenheimer	11	
Gregory Orr	7	
Simon Ortiz	17	
Rochelle Owens	4	
Robert Pack	19	
Ron Padgett	22	
Michael Palmer	12	(35)
Linda Pastan	6	
Kenneth Patchen	5	

Molly Peacock	2	
John Peck	14	
Marge Piercy	10	(63)
Robert Pinsky	31	
Sylvia Plath	177*	(235)
Stanley Plumly	16	
Ralph Pomeroy	3	
Carl Rakosi	10	
Bin Ramke	10	
Dudley Randall	3	
David Ray	13	
Ishmael Reed	5	(66)
James Reiss	2	
Kenneth Rexroth	76	
Charles Reznikoff	51	
Adrienne Rich	98*	(116)
Alberto Ríos	8	
Theodore Roethke	86	
Pattiann Rogers	3	
William Pitt Root	0	
Jerome Rothenberg	19	
Gibbons Ruark	0	
Muriel Rukeyser	13	
Vern Rutsala	0	
Michael Ryan	24	
David St. John	11	
Sonia Sanchez	13	
Ed Sanders	11	(52)
Sherod Santos	6	
Aram Saroyan	3	

May Sarton	22	(46)
Leslie Scalapino	8	
James Schevill	4	
Dennis Schmitz	2	
Gjertrud Schnackenberg	2	
James Schuyler	25	
Delmore Schwartz	22	
Armand Schwerner	5	
Winfield Townley Scott	0	
Anne Sexton	115	
David Shapiro	13	
Harvey Shapiro	2	
Karl Shapiro	11	
James Sherry	2	
Charles Simic	20	
Louis Simpson	33	
L. E. Sissman	1	
David Slavitt	5	
Dave Smith	19	
William Jay Smith	17	
W. D. Snodgrass	13	
Gary Snyder	80	
Cathy Song	3	
Gary Soto	10	
Barry Spacks	0	
Jack Spicer	34	
Elizabeth Spires	5	
William Stafford	53	
Maura Stanton	0	
George Starbuck	1	

Timothy Steele	10	
Charles Stein	7	
Gerald Stern	23	
Leon Stokesbury	1	
Ruth Stone	15	
Mark Strand	18	
Lucien Stryk	16	
Dabney Stuart	1	
Robert Sward	1	
May Swenson	26	
Nathaniel Tarn	10	
James Tate	5	
Lorenzo Thomas	3	
Richard Tillinghast	9	
David Trinidad	0	
Lewis Turco	12	
John Updike	18*	(192)
Mona Van Duyn	2	
Peter Viereck	3	
Paul Violi	0	
Ellen Bryant Voigt	6	
David Wagoner	8	
Diane Wakoski	32	
Anne Waldman	6	
Rosmary Waldrop	0	
Robert Penn Warren	94*	(232)
Barrett Watten	6	
Hannah Weiner	1	
Theodore Weiss	14	
Marjorie Welish	0	

Philip Whalen	1	
John Hall Wheelock	2	
James Whitehead	3	
Reed Whittemore	1	
John Wieners	0	
Richard Wilbur	56	
C. K. Williams	10	
Jonathan Williams	6	
Miller Williams	37	
Yvor Winters	26	(36)
David Wojahn	19	
John Woods	10	
Charles Wright	24*	(43)
James Wright	83	
Al Young	4	
Paul Zimmer	11	
Louis Zukofsky	97	

APPENDIX 9: CRITICAL DISCUSSIONS

Key: poets enclosed within an m-dash (—) are the focus of a chapter; a parenthetical numeral following a poet's name indicates the number of essays or chapters devoted to that poet; several poets listed together with slashes (/) are collectively the focus of a chapter; names in square brackets ([]) are either non-Americans *or* Americans of a pre-WWII generation; poets in ornamental brackets ({}) figure substantially in the work, but are not ostensible subjects (i.e., the frequency of references to their work enables the reader to recognize them as a serious subtext). Authors marked with an asterisk (*) are significant poets. Since the purpose of this list is to indicate the state of scholarship, only those works by poets are listed which have scholarly standing apart from the author's poetic achievement, or which have had an authoritative impact commensurate with scholarly work. The following list is chronological.

Rosenthal, M. L., *The Modern Poets: A Critical Introduction* (NY: Oxford U. P., 1960) Lowell—{Roethke—Nemerov}

Luytens, David B., *The Creative Encounter* (London: Secker & Warburg, 1960) [Jeffers-MacLeish-Crane] Lowell

Cambon, Glauco, *Recent American Poetry* (Minneapolis: U. of Minnesota P., 1962) Wilbur—Merwin—Snodgrass—Kinnell—Logan—{Kunitz—Hecht—Wright}

Hungerford, Edward, ed., *Poets in Progress: Critical Prefaces to Thirteen Modern American Poets* (Evanston, Ill.: Northwestern U. P., 1962) Roethke—Lowell—Kunitz—Wilbur—Eberhart—{1967 ed. add: Levertov—Simpson—Sexton}

Deutsch, Babette, *Poetry in Our Time: A Critical Survey of Poetry in the English-Speaking World 1900–1960* (NY: Doubleday, 1963) {Bishop—Eberhart—Garrigue—Kunitz—Lowell—Rexroth—Roethke—Shapiro—Warren—Wilbur—Winters}

*Nemerov, Howard, *Poetry and Fiction: Essays* (New Brunswick, NJ: Rutgers U. P., 1963) [MacLeish]/Viereck—Shapiro/Roethke/ Winters—Whittemore—Kees—{[Auden]/Jarrell—Brinnin/Eberhart/Jarrell/Merrill/Schevill—Garrigue/D. Hughes et al.—Booth/V. Miller/ Wright}

Ostroff, Anthony, ed., *The Contemporary Poet as Artist and Critic* (Boston: Little, Brown, 1964) Wilbur—Roethke—Kunitz—Lowell—[Ransom—Auden]—Eberhart—Shapiro

Stepanchev, Stephen, *American Poetry Since 1945* (NY: Harper & Row, 1965) Lowell—Jarrell—Shapiro—Bishop—Garrigue—Wilbur—Merwin—{subchapters:} Olson—Duncan—Creeley—Levertov—Wright—Bly—Ashbery—Dickey—Dugan—Jones[Baraka]—Simpson—Stafford—Swenson

Ehrenpreis, Irvin, ed., *American Poetry* (London: Edward Arnold 1965) {Warren}—Lowell—{Lowell/Olson/Levertov}

Mills, Ralph J. Jr., *Contemporary American Poetry* (NY: Random House, 1965) Eberhart—Kunitz—Roethke—Bishop—Everson—Shapiro—Gardner—Lowell—Wilbur—Levertov—Wright—Sexton—{Foreword emphasizes bibliography}

Rosenthal, M. L., *The New Poets: American and British Poetry Since World War II* (NY: Oxford U. P., 1967) Lowell—Plath—Ginsberg—Roethke—Berryman—Sexton—Creeley—Olson—Duncan—Levertov—Blackburn—Baraka

Frankenberg, Lloyd, *Pleasure Dome: On Reading Modern Poetry* (NY: Gordian, 1968) [Eliot-Moore-cummings-Stevens-Pound-Williams-Nash-Auden-Thomas] Lowell—Bishop

*Dickey, James, *Babel to Byzantium: Poets and Poetry Now* (NY: Farrar, Straus & Giroux, 1968) {all brief reviews} Jarrell—Ignatow—Nemerov—Whittemore—Ginsberg—Ashbery—Booth—Patchen—Sarton—W. Smith—Warren—Eberhart—Merrill—Scott—Everson—Carruth—Sexton—Kinnell—Olson—Stafford—Merwin—Weiss—Miles—Roethke—Logan—Nims—Wilbur—Duncan—Winters—Cunningham—Simpson—Meredith—Berryman

Waggoner, Hyatt, *American Poets From the Puritans to the Present* (Boston: Houghton Mifflin, 1968) {Modernism ends with Ransom—Tate—Warren} Roethke/Lowell/Shapiro/Wilbur/Dickey/Nemerov/Duncan/Levertov/Creeley/Kelly

Carroll, Paul, *The Poem in its Skin* (Chicago: Follett, 1968) Ashbery—Creeley—Dickey—Gardner—Ginsberg—Logan—Merwin—O'Hara—Snodgrass—Wright

Mazzaro, Jerome, ed., *Modern American Poetry: Essays in Criticism* (NY: David McKay, 1970) [Whitman-Dickinson-Robinson-Frost-Stevens-Williams-Pound-Jeffers-Moore-Eliot-cummings-Crane] Roethke—Lowell—Snodgrass

*Howard, Richard, *Alone With America: Essays on the Art of Poetry in the United States Since 1945* (NY: Atheneum, 1971) Ammons—Ashbery—Bly—Bowers—Corso—Creeley—Dickey—Dugan—Feldman—Field—Finkel—Ginsberg—Goodman—Hecht—Hoffman—Hine—Hollander—Hugo—Justice—Kinnell—Kizer—Koch—Levertov—Logan—Meredith—Merrill—Merwin—Moss—O'Hara—Plath—Rich—Sexton—Snodgrass—Snyder—Stafford—Strand—Swenson—Wagoner—Weiss—Wright—{2nd ed.:} Simpson

Charters, Samuel, *Some Poems/Poets: Studies in American Underground Poetry Since 1945* (SF: Oyez, 1971) Olson—Spicer—Duncan—Snyder—Welch—Ginsberg—Ferlinghetti—Creeley—Everson—Eigner

Bloom, Harold, *Ringers in the Tower* (U. of Chicago P., 1971) {Romantics, 19th c.} [Auden-Borges]/Ginsberg—Ammons—{Feinman}

Raban, Jonathan, *The Society of the Poem* (London: Harrap, 1971) {topics + British} {Olson—Snyder—Dorn—Lowell}

*Nemerov, Howard, *Reflexions on Poetry and Poetics* (New Brunswick, NJ: Rutgers U. P., 1972) Dickey—Belitt—Jarrell—{Naked Poetry}

Shaw, Robert B., ed., *American Poetry Since 1960* (Carcanet, 1973) Lowell—Berryman—Merwin—Ashbery—O'Hara—Rich—Dickey—Plath—Tate—Strand

Malkoff, Karl, *Crowell's Handbook of Contemporary American Poetry* (NY: Crowell, 1973) Ammons—Ashbery—Baraka—Bell—Benedikt—

Berryman—Bishop—Blackburn—Bly—Brooks—Carroll—Corso—
Creeley—Cruz—Dickey—Dorn—Dugan—Duncan—J. Emanuel—
M.Evans—Ferlinghetti—Field—I. Gardner—Ginsberg—Giovanni—
Glück—Hayden—Hecht—Howard—Ignatow—Jarrell—Jong—
Kees—Kelly—Kinnell—Kizer—Knott—Koch—Lee—Levertov—
Levine—Logan—Lowell—McClure—Merrill—Merwin—Mezey—
Moss—Nemerov—O'Hara—Olson—Oppenheimer—Plath—Rich—
Roethke—Rothenberg—Sanchez—Schuyler—Sexton—Shapiro—
Simpson—Snodgrass—Snyder—Stafford—Strand—Swenson—
Wagoner—Wakoski—M.Walker—Weiss—Whittemore—Wilbur—
Wright

Mersman, James, *Out of the Vietnam Vortex: A Study of Poets and Poetry Against the War* (U. of Kansas P., 1974)   Ginsberg—Levertov—Bly—Duncan

Stauffer, Donald B., *A Short History of American Poetry* (NY: Dutton, 1974)
Warren/[et al.]—Lowell/Roethke/Bishop/Kunitz/Jarrell/Shapiro/
Berryman/Nemerov/Wilbur/Eberhart/Cunningham—I.Gardner
/Weiss/Simpson/Garrigue/Snodgrass/Sexton/Koch/Hollander/
Dugan /Corso/Plath/Merwin/Wright/Dickey/Hecht/Ashbery/Gins-
berg/ Snyder/Olson/ Creeley/Duncan/Levertov/Baraka

Boyers, Robert, ed., *Contemporary Poetry in America: Essays and Interviews*
(NY: Schocken, 1974)   Lowell—Jarrell—Berryman—Roethke—Ash-
bery—Plath—Rich—Olson—Belitt—Merwin—Wright—Nemerov—
Dickey—Ammons—Dugan—Bishop—Wagoner—{interviews:
Kunitz—Snodgrass—Kinnell}

Donoghue, Denis, ed., *Seven American Poets from MacLeish to Nemerov*
(Minneapolis: U. of Minnesota P., 1975)   [MacLeish]—Eberhart—
Roethke—Jarrell—Berryman—Lowell—Nemerov

Mills, Ralph J. Jr., *Cry of the Human: Essays on Contemporary American
Poetry* (Urbana: U. of Illinois P., 1975)   Roethke—Ignatow—Kinnell—Hall—Levine—{Berryman—Bly—Dickey—Levertov—Lowell—Merwin—O'Hara—Olson—Plath—Simpson—Wright}

*Pinsky, Robert, *The Situation of Poetry* (Princeton U. P., 1976)   Lowell—
Berryman—[Hardy/Ransom]/Berryman—[Bogan]/O'Hara—Cunning-
ham/Bidart/Ammons—{Ashbery—Merwin—Plath—Roethke—C.
Wright}

Bloom, Harold, *Figures of Capable Imagination* (NY: Seabury, 1976)   Mer-
win/Ashbery/Ammons—Strand/Ammons—Ashbery—Ammons—
Hollander

Lensing, George S., & Ronald Moran, *Four Poets of the Emotive Imagination*
(Baton Rouge: LSU P., 1976)   Bly—Wright—Simpson—Stafford

*Lieberman, Laurence, *Unassigned Frequencies: American Poetry in Review,
1964–1977* (Urbana: U. of Illinois P., 1977)　Ashbery—Ammons—
Dickey(2)—Garrigue—Howard—Merwin—Moss—Strand—Wag-
oner—Wright—Ammons/Dickey—Merwin/Hecht—Berryman/
Stafford/Dickey—Stafford/Morgan—[Walcott]/Harper—{short
notices: Benedikt—Duncan—Hugo—Kinnell—Kunitz—Miles—V.
Miller—Nemerov—Roethke—Rukeyser—Shapiro—Snodgrass—
Viereck—Weiss—Whittemore—M. Williams}

Homberger, Eric, *The Art of the Real: Poetry in England and America Since
1939* (London: Dent, 1977) {topics} {Berryman—Braun—Creeley—
Ginsberg—Hall—Jarrell—Kinnell—Lowell—Olson—Oppen—
Plath—Reznikoff—[Rich]—Roethke—Snodgrass—Snyder—
Wilbur—[Zukofsky]}

Kalstone, David, *Five Temperaments* (NY: Oxford U. P., 1977) Bishop—Lowell—Merrill—Rich—Ashbery

Malkoff, Karl, *Escape from the Self: A Study in Contemporary American
Poetry and Poetics* (NY: Columbia U. P., 1977) {topics} {Berryman—
Duncan—Ginsberg—Lowell—Olson—Plath—Roethke—Schwartz}

Thurley, Geoffrey, *The American Moment: American Poetry in the Mid-Century* (London: Edward Arnold, 1977)　Wilbur—Berryman—Low-
ell/Sexton/Roethke—[H. D./Moore]/Levertov—Olson—Duncan—
Rexroth/Patchen—Ginsberg—Wieners/Baraka/McClure/Whalen/
Corso—Kinnell/Bly/Simic

*Simpson, Louis, *A Revolution in Taste* (NY: Random House, 1978)
[Thomas] Ginsberg—Plath—Lowell

Faas, Ekbert, *Towards a New American Poetics: Essays and Interviews*
(Santa Barbara: Black Sparrow, 1978)　Olson—Duncan—Snyder—
Creeley—Bly—Ginsberg

Oberg, Arthur, *Modern American Lyric* (New Brunswick, NJ: Rutgers U. P.,
1978)　Lowell—Berryman—Creeley—Plath

Molesworth, Charles, *The Fierce Embrace: A Study of Contemporary Ameri-
can Poetry* (Columbia: U. P. of Missouri, 1979)　Roethke—
Lowell/Ginsberg—O'Hara—Kinnell—Bly—Levine—Ashbery—
{Berryman—Bishop—[Creeley]—[Merwin]—Olson—Plath—
Roethke—Sexton—Snodgrass}

Altieri, Charles, *Enlarging the Temple: New Directions in American Poetry
During the 1960's* (Lewisburg, Pa.: Bucknell U. P., 1979)　Lowell—
Bly/Olson/O'Hara—Snyder/Duncan—Creeley/Merwin—Levertov

Altieri, Charles, *Modern Poetry* (Arlington Heights, Ill.: AHM, 1979)　[bibli-
ographies, including British and American modernists]　Ammons—
Ashbery—Baraka—Berryman—Bishop—Bly—Creeley—Dickey—

Duncan—Jarrell—Levertov—J. Logan—Lowell—Merwin—O'Hara—
Olson—Plath—Rich—Roethke—Sexton—Simpson—Snyder—
Stafford—R. P. Warren—Wilbur—J. Wright—Zukofsky

Gilbert, Sandra M., & Susan Gubar, eds., *Shakespeare's Sisters: Feminist Essays on Women Poets* (Bloomington: Indiana U. P., 1979) {Part IV, Contemporaries}: Swenson—Brooks—Plath—Sexton—Levertov/Rich/Rukeyser

*Hoffman, Daniel, ed., *Harvard Guide to Contemporary American Writing* (Cambridge: Harvard U. P., 1979) {topics} {Ammons—Ashbery—Baraka—Berryman—Bishop—Bly—Brooks—Creeley—Dickey—Duncan—Ginsberg—Hayden—Hecht—Hollander—Howard—Jarrell—Kinnell—Koch—Levertov—Lowell—Merrill—Merwin—Nemerov—O'Hara—Olson—Plath—[Rexroth]—Rich—Roethke—Schwartz—Sexton—[Simic]—Simpson—Snyder—Stafford—Wagoner—Warren—Wilbur—[C. Wright]—Wright}

Martin, Robert K., *The Homosexual Tradition in American Poetry* (Austin: U. of Texas P., 1979) [Whitman-Crane] Ginsberg—Duncan—Gunn—Field—Howard—Merrill—Corn

Miller, James E., Jr., *The American Quest for a Supreme Fiction: Whitman's Legacy in the Personal Epic* (U. of Chicago P., 1979) [Whitman-Stevens-Pound-Eliot-Williams-Crane] Lowell/Berryman—Olson—Berryman—Ginsberg

Greiner, Donald J., ed., *American Poets Since World War II* [Dictionary of Literary Biography, Vols. 5–6], (Detroit: Gale, 1980) [*="master entries"] *Ammons—*Ashbery—Baraka—Barks—Belitt—Bell—Benedikt—Berg—D. Berrigan—T. Berrigan—Berry—*Bishop—Bly—Boer—Bowers—P. Bowles—Brautigan—*Brooks—Broughton—Bukowski—Carruth—Casey—Ciardi—Clifton—Corman—Corso—Coxe—Creeley—Cunningham—Davison—*Dickey—Dillard—DiPrima—Dorn—Dugan—*Duncan—Eigner—Eshleman—Everson—Ferlinghetti—Forché—Galvin—Garrett—*Ginsberg—Giovanni—Glück—Guest—Haines—Hall—Hayden—Hecht—Heyen—Hochman—Hoffman—Hollander—Honig—Howard—Hoyem—Hugo—Ignatow—Jong—Kelly—Kennedy—Kinnell—Kizer—Klappert—Koch—Kumin—Levertov—Levine—J. Logan—*Lowell—Madhubuti [Lee]—Matthews—Meinke—Meredith—*Merrill—Merwin—H. Moss—*Nemerov—Nims—Oates—O'Hara—Oliver—*Olson—Oppen—Oppenheimer—Orlovitz—G. Owen—Pack—Padgett—Pastan—Plath—Plumly—Ray—Reed—*Rich—*Roethke—Rosenthal—Rothenberg—Schuyler—Sexton—Simpson—Sissman—Slavitt—D. Smith—W. J. Smith—Snodgrass—Snyder—Sorrentino—Spicer—Stafford—Stanford—Strand—Swenson—Tate—H. Taylor—Updike—Van Duyn—Viereck—Wagoner—Wakoski—Weiss—Whittemore—*Wilbur—Wild—Willard—C. K. Williams—J. Williams—J. Wright—Zimmer—*Zukofsky

Bernstein, Michael André, *The Tale of the Tribe: Ezra Pound and the Modern Verse Epic* (Princeton U. P., 1980) [Pound-Williams]—Olson

Bové, Paul, *Destructive Poetics: Heidegger and Modern American Poetry* (NY: Columbia U. P., 1980) Olson

Vendler, Helen, *Part of Nature, Part of Us* (Cambridge: Harvard U. P., 1980) [Stevens-Moore-Eliot] Warren—Bishop—Jarrell(2)—Berryman— Lowell(5)—Nemerov—O'Hara—Ginsberg(2)—Merrill(3)—Merwin— Rich(2)—Wright—Smith—Glück—Ammons/Berryman/[cummings]

Mazzaro, Jerome, *Postmodern American Poetry* (Urbana: U. of Illinois P., 1980) [Auden] Jarrell—Roethke—Ignatow—Berryman—Plath— Bishop

Davenport, Guy, *The Geography of the Imagination* (SF: North Point, 1980) [Pound-Cummings-Moore] Olson—Zukofsky—J.Williams—R. Johnson

*Holden, Jonathan, *The Rhetoric of the Contemporary Lyric* (Bloomington: Indiana U. P., 1980) {topics} Dunn—Ashbery

Jones, P., *A Reader's Guide to Fifty American Poets* (London: Heinemann, 1980) {18th–20th c.} Zukofsky—Warren—Roethke—Olson—Bishop—Schwartz—Jarrell—Berryman—Lowell—Duncan—Wilbur—Dickey—Ginsberg—Ammons—Merwin—Ashbery—Rich—Snyder—Plath

Kostelanetz, Richard, *The Old Poetries and the New* (Ann Arbor: U. of Michigan P., 1981) {topics & reviews; *=article} {*Ashbery— *Cage—*Coolidge—Dickey—*Field—*Ginsberg—Giorno—Higgins—Hollander—Ignatow—Koch—Kunitz—Lowell—MacLow— O'Hara—Olson—Roethke—*Rothenberg—Schwartz—Schwerner— *H.Shapiro—*Solt}

Paul, Sherman, *The Lost America of Love* (Baton Rouge: LSU P., 1981) Creeley—Duncan—Dorn

Nelson, Cary, *Our Last First Poets: Vision and History in Contemporary American Poetry* (Urbana: U. of Illinois P., 1981) Roethke—Kinnell—Duncan—Rich—Merwin—{Ginsberg—Levertov}

Berke, Roberta, *Bounds Out of Bounds: A Compass for Recent American and British Poetry* (NY: Oxford U. P., 1981) {topics} {Ashbery—Bly— Dickey—Ginsberg—Lowell—O'Hara—Olson—Plath—Wilbur}

Géfin, Laszlo, *Ideogram: History of a Poetic Method* (Austin: U. of Texas P., 1982) [Pound-Williams] Olson—Duncan/Creeley—Ginsberg/Snyder

Castro, Michael, *Interpreting the Indian: Twentieth-Century Poets and the Native American* (Albuquerque: U. of New Mexico P., 1983) Olson—Rothenberg—Snyder(2)

Piggory, Terence, *Yeats and American Poetry: The Tradition of the Self* (Princeton U. P., 1983) [Emerson/Poe/Thoreau/Whitman-Pound-Frost-Williams-Stevens-Eliot-Jeffers-MacLeish]—[Tate-Ransom]/ Warren—Roethke—Berryman—Lowell

Rosenthal, M. L., & Sally Gall, *The Modern Poetic Sequence: The Genius of Modern Poetry* (NY: Oxford U. P., 1983) [Whitman-Dickinson-[British]-Masters/Eliot-Pound(2)-Williams-Stevens/Auden] [Crane]/Olson—Lowell/Snodgrass/Berryman/Ginsberg/Plath/ Sexton

Rotella, Guy, *Three Contemporary Poets of New England* (Boston: Twayne, 1983) Meredith—Booth—Davison

Altieri, Charles, *Self and Sensibility in Contemporary American Poetry* (NY: Cambridge U. P., 1984) Creeley—Ashbery—Rich—{Bly—Hass—Pinsky—Plumly—Stafford—C.Wright}

Breslin, James E., *From Modern to Contemporary: American Poetry 1945–1965* (U. of Chicago P., 1984) Ginsberg—Lowell—Levertov—Wright—O'Hara—{Ashbery—Bly—Creeley—Duncan—Olson—Rich—Roethke—Schwartz—Simpson—Wilbur}

Libby, Anthony, *Mythologies of Nothing: Mystical Death in American Poetry 1940–1970* (Urbana: U. of Illinois P., 1984) [Eliot-Williams-Stevens] Lowell—Roethke—Plath—Bly—Merwin

Mariani, Paul, *A Usable Past: Essays on Modern and Contemporary Poetry* (Amherst: U. of Massachussetts P., 1984) [Hopkins(5)-Williams(4)] Warren—[Tomlinson]—Creeley—[Montague]—Berryman—Peck—Merwin

Butterfield, R. W., ed., *Modern American Poetry* (NY: Barnes & Noble, 1984) [Whitman-Dickinson-Stevens-Williams-Pound-Jeffers-Moore-Crane]—Oppen—Olson—Cunningham—Lowell—Duncan—Dorn

Donoghue, Denis, *Connoisseurs of Chaos: Ideas of Order in Modern American Poetry* 2nd ed. (NY: Columbia U. P., 1984) [Whitman-Tuckerman-Melville-Dickinson-Frost-Stevens] Robinson/Cunningham/Lowell—Roethke—Bishop {added in this edition}

Williamson, Alan, *Introspection and Contemporary Poetry* (Cambridge: Harvard U. P., 1984) Plath—Ashbery—{Berryman—Bidart—Bly—Glück—Howard—Kinnell—Lowell—Merwin—Pinsky—Snyder—Strand—Tillinghast—Wakoski—Wright}

Trotter, David, *The Making of the Reader: Language and Subjectivity in Modern American, English, and Irish Poetry* (NY: St. Martin's, 1984) {misc. modern} [Larkin/Heaney-Hughes/Hill/Prynne] Ashbery/ O'Hara/Dorn

Martin, Wendy, *An American Triptych* (Chapel Hill: U. of North Carolina P., 1984) [Bradstreet-Dickinson] Rich

Bold, Alan, *The Longman Dictionary of Poets* (London: Longman, 1985) [alphabetical listing of global selection] Ammons—Ashbery—Baraka—Benedikt—Berryman—Bishop—Bly—Bowers—Brooks—Bukowski—Clark—Corso—Creeley—Dickey—Dorn—Dugan—Duncan—Eberhart—Ferlinghetti—Fitzgerald—Garrigue—Ginsberg—Haines—Hall—Hayden—Hecht—Ignatow—Jarrell—Jong—Junkins—Justice—Kennedy—Kinnell—Knight—Levertov—Levine—J. Logan—W. Logan—Lowell—Merrill—Merwin—Nemerov—O'Hara—Olson—Padgett—Plath—D. Randall—Rexroth—Reznikoff—Rich—Roethke—Rukeyser—Schwartz—Seidel—Sexton—Shange—Shapiro—Simpson—D. Smith—Snodgrass—Snyder—Stafford—Starbuck—Tarn—Tolson—R. P. Warren—Whittemore [mistakenly listed under Reed]—Wilbur—Woods—J. Wright—Zukofsky

*Smith, Dave, *Local Assays: On Contemporary American Poetry* (Urbana: U. of Illinois P., 1985) Warren(2)—Hugo—Wright—Swenson—Simpson—Plath—Dickey

North, Michael, *The Final Sculpture: Public Monuments and Modern Poets* (Ithaca: Cornell U. P., 1985) [Yeats—Pound]—[Stevens]/Berryman/Lowell

*Watten, Barrett, *Total Syntax* (Carbondale: Southern Illinois U. P., 1985) Olson—[Crane]/Eigner—{Coolidge—Silliman}

Stitt, Peter, *The World's Hieroglyphic Beauty: Five American Poets* (Athens: U. of Georgia P., 1985) Wilbur—Stafford—Simpson—Wright—Warren {interviews + essays on each} {Bly}

Hallberg, Robert von, *American Poetry and Culture, 1945–1980* (Cambridge: Harvard U. P., 1985) {topics} Creeley/Ashbery—Merrill—Lowell—Dorn—{Bishop—Bly—Duncan—Ginsberg—Hecht—Hollander—Olson—Pinsky—Rich—Wilbur}

Perloff, Marjorie, *The Dance of the Intellect* (NY: Cambridge U. P., 1985) Oppen—Cage—{Antin—Ashbery—Bernstein—Dorn—Hejinian—Silliman—Wright—Zukofsky}

Heller, Michael, *Conviction's Net of Branches: Essays on the Objectivist Poets and Poetry* (Carbondale: Southern Illinois U. P., 1985) Zukofsky(2)—Rakosi—Niedecker—Reznikoff—Oppen

Elder, John, *Imagining the Earth: Poetry and the Vision of Nature* (Urbana: U. of Illinois P., 1985) {topics} {Ammons—Berry—Everson—Levertov—Pack—Snyder}

Ross, Andrew, *The Failure of Modernism: Symptoms of American Poetry* (NY: Columbia U. P., 1986) [Eliot]—Olson—Ashbery

Paul, Sherman, *In Search of the Primitive* (Baton Rouge: LSU P., 1986) Antin—Rothenberg—Snyder

Bloom, Harold, ed., *Contemporary Poets* (NY: Chelsea House, 1986) Warren—R. Fitzgerald—Bishop—Brooks—Duncan—Swenson—Wilbur—Hecht—Dickey—Levertov—Koch—Ammons—Merrill—Ginsberg—Kinnell—Ashbery—Merwin—Wright—Feldman—Rich—Pack—Hollander—Feinman—Snyder—Strand—Baraka—C. Wright—Hine

Bauer, Bruce, *The Middle Generation* (Hamden, Ct.: Archon Books, 1986) Schwartz—Jarrell—Berryman—Lowell

Breslin, Paul, *The Psycho-Political Muse: American Poetry Since the Fifties* (U. of Chicago P., 1987) Ginsberg—Lowell—Plath—Merwin—Wright—Ashbery—{Berryman—Bly—Duncan—Kinnell—Levertov—Olson}

Blasing, Mutlu Konuk, *American Poetry: The Rhetoric of its Forms* (New Haven: Yale U. P., 1987) [Poe-Emerson-Whitman-Dickinson-Eliot-Stevens-Pound-Crane] Plath—Bishop—O'Hara—Ashbery

Parkinson, Thomas, *Poets, Poems, Movements* (Ann Arbor: UMI Research P., 1987) [Whitman-Pound-Williams-Stevens-British poets] {Beats}—[Crane]/Winters—Lowell(2)—Winters—Rexroth(2)—Duncan—Snyder—Ferlinghetti—Everson—Ginsberg

Keller, Lynn, *Re-making It New: Contemporary American Poetry and the Modernist Tradition* (NY: Cambridge U. P., 1987) [Stevens]/Ashbery(2)—[Moore]/Bishop(2)—[Williams]/Creeley(2)—[Auden]/Merrill(2)

Perkins, David, *A History of Modern Poetry: Modernism and After* (Cambridge: Harvard U. P., 1987) Ignatow/Zukofsky—Warren/Roethke/Bishop—Wilbur/Jarrell/Berryman—Lowell—Olson/Creeley/Levertov/Dorn/Blackburn/Duncan—O'Hara/Ginsberg—Bly/Wright/Kinnell/Merwin/Snyder—Plath/Sexton/Rich—[Tolson]/Hayden/Brooks/Baraka—Ashbery/Ammons—Merrill

Jackson, Richard, *The Dismantling of Time in Contemporary Poetry* (Tuscaloosa: U. of Alabama P., 1988) Warren—Hollander—Wright—Ashbery—Levertov—Simic

DesPres, Terence, *Praises and Dispraises: Poetry and Politics, the 20th Century* (NY: Viking, 1988) [Yeats—Brecht—Breytenbach]—McGrath—Rich

Bloom, Harold [ed. John Hollander], *Poetics of Influence* (NY: Henry R. Schwab, 1988) {topics + 19th c.} Warren—Bishop

Coniff, Brian, *The Lyric and Modern Poetry* (NY: Peter Lang, 1988) [Bunting]—Olson—Creeley

Finkelstein, Norman, *The Utopian Moment in Contemporary American Poetry* (Lewisburg, Pa.: Bucknell U. P., 1988)   O'Hara/Ashbery—{Adam—Bronk—Duncan—Johnson—Oppen—Spicer—Zukofsky}—[2nd ed. 1993: language poetry]

Vendler, Helen, *The Music of What Happens: Poems, Poets, Critics* (Cambridge: Harvard U. P., 1988)   {misc.} Ashbery/Glück—Ginsberg—Plath—Bishop—Sexton—Ammons—Merrill—Rich/Jared Carter/Levine—C. Wright—Smith—Clampitt—Bidart—Blumenthal—Glück/Dunn/Leithauser/Dove—Graham

Spiegelman, Willard, *The Didactic Muse: Scenes of Instruction in Contemporary American Poetry* (Princeton U. P., 1989)   [Auden] — Nemerov—Hecht/Ginsberg/Pinsky—Ammons—Rich—Merrill—{Ashbery—Bishop}

Ehrenpreis, Irvin, *Poetries of America: Essays on the Relation of Character to Style* (Charlottesville: U. of Virginia P., 1989)   [Whitman-Dickinson-Stevens-Pound-Eliot(3)]   Warren(2)—Bishop—Berryman(2)—Lowell(2)—Merrill—Ashbery/Justice—Oppen/[Hill]/Snyder—[Heaney]/Ammons/Strand—Plath

Gardner, Thomas, *Discovering Ourselves in Whitman: The Contemporary American Long Poem* (Urbana: U. of Illinois P., 1989)   Berryman—Kinnell—Roethke—Duncan—Ashbery—Merrill

McClatchy, J. D., *White Paper: On Contemporary American Poetry* (NY: Columbia U. P., 1989)   Warren—Lowell(3)—Bishop—Berryman—Plath—Snodgrass—Merrill—Howard—Hollander—Clampitt—Hecht

McCorkle, James, *The Still Performance: Writing, Self, and Interconnection in Five Postmodern American Poets* (Charlottesville: U. of Virginia P., 1989)   Bishop—Ashbery—Rich—Merwin—C. Wright

Kalaidjian, Walter B., *Languages of Liberation: The Social Text in Contemporary American Poetry* (NY: Columbia U. P., 1989) Merwin/Wright—Olson—Merrill—Bly—Rich—Brooks

Kerkhoff, Ingrid, *Poetiken und lyrischer Discurs im Kontext gesellschaftlicher Dynamik: USA: "The Sixties"* (Frankfurt am Main: Peter Lang, 1989)   {topics +} Lowell/Berryman/Plath—Olson/Creeley/Duncan/Levertov—O'Hara/Koch/Ashbery—Bly—Dickey—Ginsberg/Snyder/McClure—Bukowski/Levy—Baraka/Sanchez/Madhubuti—Alurista/de Hoyos/Salinas—Ortiz—Rich/Piercy/Giovanni

Bartlett, Lee, *The Sun is But a Morning Star: Studies in West Coast Poetry and Poetics* (Albuquerque: U. of New Mexico P., 1989) Rexroth—Everson—Duncan—Snyder—McClure—Gunn/Tarn—Palmer/Silliman

*Davidson, Michael, *The San Francisco Renaissance: Poetics and Community at Mid-Century* (NY: Cambridge U. P., 1989) Duncan—Spicer—Snyder/Whalen—{Adam—Everson—Ginsberg—Grahn—Hass—Hejinian—Kyger—McClure—Olson—Rexroth}

Hartley, George, *Textual Politics and the Language Poets* (Bloomington: Indiana U. P., 1989) {Andrews—Bernstein—[McCaffery]—Perelman—Silliman—Watten}

Paul, Sherman, *Hewing to Experience: Essays and Reviews on Recent American Poetry and Poetics, Nature and Culture* (Iowa City: U. of Iowa P., 1989) [misc. topics-Emerson-Williams-H. D.-Crane] Olson(6)—Creeley(2)—Snyder(2)—Berry

Walker, Jeffrey, *Bardic Ethos and the American Epic Poem* (Baton Rouge: LSU P., 1989) [Whitman-Pound-Crane-Williams] Olson

Byers, Thomas B., *What I Cannot Say: Self, Word and World in Whitman, Stevens, and Merwin* (Urbana: U. of Illinois P., 1989) [Whitman-Stevens] Merwin

Merrin, Jeredith, *An Enabling Humility: Marianne Moore, Elizabeth Bishop, and the Uses of Tradition* (New Brunswick, NJ: Rutgers U. P., 1990) [Moore] Bishop

Prunty, Wyatt, *"Fallen from the Symboled World": Precedents for the New Formalism* (NY: Oxford U. P., 1990) {topics, +} Nemerov—Justice/Hecht/Van Duyn/Bishop/Wilbur/Hollander/Pack/Pinsky—{Ammons—Creeley—Lowell—Stafford}

Trawick, Leonard, ed., *World, Self, Poem: Essays on Contemporary Poetry from the "Jubilation of Poets"* [Kent State festival, October 1986] (Kent State U.P., 1990) Dorn—Glück—Stern—Rich—Ashbery—Snyder/Berry—Levertov/Rich—Stafford—Duncan

Perloff, Marjorie, *Poetic License: Essays on Modernist and Postmodernist Lyric* (Evanston, Ill.: Northwestern U. P., 1990) {misc. + topics} [Pound-Stein] Plath—Ginsberg—Merwin—Blackburn—Ashbery—Howe—[McCaffery]—{Cage—Coolidge—[Creeley]—[Duncan]—Lowell—Niedecker—O'Hara—Olson—[Oppen]—Rothenberg—Zukofsky}

*Bly, Robert, *American Poetry: Wildness and Domesticity* (NY: Harper & Row, 1990) Wright—Ignatow—Knight—Levertov—Merwin—McGrath—Lowell—Simpson—Dickey—Kinnell—Hall—Logan

Diehl, Joanne Feit, *Women Poets and the American Sublime* (Bloomington: Indiana U. P., 1990) [Emerson/Whitman-Dickinson-Moore] Bishop—Plath—Rich

Fredman, Stephen, *Poet's Prose: The Crisis in American Verse* 2nd ed. (NY: Cambridge U. P., 1990[1983]) [Williams] Creeley—Ashbery—Antin—Bromige/Silliman/Davidson—{Duncan—Olson—Zukofsky}

Gray, Richard, *American Poetry of the Twentieth Century* (London: Longman, 1990) {prewar + regionalism includes: Zukofsky/Oppen/Reznikoff/Niedecker—Warren/Berry/Dickey/Eberhart/Cunningham/Winters—Rexroth/Hayden/Miles/Rukeyser}—Bishop/Roethke/Lowell/Berryman/Plath—Olson/J.Williams/ Levertov/Blackburn/Wieners/Creeley/Dorn/Duncan /Ferlinghetti /Everson/ Spicer/Lamantia/Whalen/McClure/Snyder/Ginsberg/Corso/Bukowski/Baraka/Kaufman/Joans/ Evans/Sanchez/Giovanni/Lee/Karenga/Nelson/O'Hara/Guest/Schuyler/Berrigan/Koch/Ashbery/Merrill

Gilbert, Roger, *Walks in the World: Representation and Experience in Modern American Poetry* (Princeton U. P., 1991) [Frost-Stevens-Williams] Roethke/Bishop—O'Hara/Snyder—Ammons/ Ashbery

Conte, Joseph M., *Unending Design: The Forms of Postmodern Poetry* (Ithaca: Cornell U. P., 1991) Duncan/Blackburn/Creeley—Spicer/Oppen/Zukofsky/Niedecker—Ashbery/Zukofsky—Kees/Creeley/Zukofsky—Mathews/Bronk/Creeley—Mathews/Cage

Myers, Jack, & David Wojahn, eds., *A Profile of Twentieth-Century American Poetry* (Carbondale: Southern Illinois U. P., 1991) {Ashbery—Berryman—Bishop—Brooks—Creeley—Jarrell—Lowell—O'Hara—Rich—Roethke—Rukeyser—Schwartz—Wilbur}

Rotella, Guy, *Reading Writing Nature* (Boston: Northeastern U. P., 1991) [Frost-Stevens-Moore] Bishop

Hartman, Charles O., *Jazz Text: Voice and Improvisation in Poetry, Jazz, and Song* (Princeton U. P., 1991) Creeley—Antin—MacLow—{Ai—Levine}

Baker, Peter, *Obdurate Brilliance: Exteriority and the Modern Long Poem* (Gainesville: U. of Florida P., 1991) [Perse-Char-Pound] Olson—[Stein]/Zukofsky—Ashbery—Coolidge/Palmer/Mayer—{Bernstein}

Perloff, Marjorie, *Radical Artifice: Writing Poetry in the Age of Media* (U. of Chicago P., 1991) {Ashbery—Bernstein—Cage—Coolidge—Drucker—Hejinian—Howe—[McCaffery]—Oppen—Silliman—Zukofsky}

Rosenthal, M. L., *Our Life in Poetry: Selected Essays and Reviews* (NY: Persea, 1991) {many modern and foreign} Ciardi/Wilbur—Wilbur —Jarrell(3)—Rukeyser—Ginsberg(2)—Kunitz/Ferlinghetti— Roethke—Roethke/Berryman—Lowell(2)—Lowell/Plath—Plath— Snodgrass/Duncan—Warren—Schwartz—Baraka—Brooks— Olson(2)—Winters/Blackburn/Zukofsky—Kinnell—Plumly/ Ammons/Kennedy—Creeley—Blackburn—Zukofsky—Simpson

Quartermain, Peter, *Disjunctive Poetics: From Gertrude Stein and Louis Zukofsky to Susan Howe* (NY: Cambridge U. P., 1992) Zukofsky(5)—Reznikoff—Creeley—Duncan—Howe—Davenport

Reinfeld, Linda, *Language Poetry: Writing as Rescue* (Baton Rouge: LSU P., 1992) Palmer—Howe—Bernstein—{Melnick—Silliman}

Beach, Christopher, *The ABC of Influence: Ezra Pound and the Remaking of American Poetic Tradition* (Berkeley: U. of California P., 1992) Zukofsky—Olson(2)—Duncan(2)—Levertov/Snyder—Dorn—Bernstein

*Lehman, David, *The Line Forms Here* (Ann Arbor: U. of Michigan P., 1992) Bishop—Merrill—Ammons—Hollander—Ashbery

*Taylor, Henry, *Compulsory Figures: Essays on Recent American Poets* (Baton Rouge: LSU, 1992) Wheelock—Garrett—Meredith—Chappell—Robert Watson—Ghiselin—Stafford—W. J. Smith—J. Wright— Slavitt—Mac Low—Sarton—G. Brooks—Simpson—Woods—Cunningham—Hecht

McGann, Jerome, *Black Riders: The Visible Language of Modernism* (Princeton U. P., 1993) {Bernstein—Howe—Silliman—Spicer}

Shetley, Vernon, *After the Death of Poetry: Poet and Audience in Contemporary America* (Durham: Duke U. P., 1993) Bishop—Merrill—Ashbery—{Language writing/New Formalism}

Scott, Nathan A. Jr., *Visions of Presence in Modern American Poetry* (Baltimore: Johns Hopkins U.P., 1993) [Stevens—Auden]—Roethke— Bishop—R. P. Warren—Wilbur—Ammons—J. Wright—Nemerov

Kinzie, Mary, *The Cure of Poetry in an Age of Prose: Moral Essays on the Poet's Calling* (U. of Chicago P., 1993) Roethke/Lowell/Sexton— Jarrell/Bishop—Nemerov—{Ammons/Strand/Glück/Pinsky/[Hughes]}—[Heaney]—Ashbery

Cushman, Stephen, *Fictions of Form in American Poetry* (Princeton U. P., 1993) [Whitman-Dickinson-Pound] Bishop—Ammons

Damon, Maria, *The Dark End of the Street: Margins in American Vanguard Poetry* (Minneapolis: U. of Minnesota P., 1993) Kaufman—{Lowell}—Spicer/Duncan

Fredman, Stephen, *The Grounding of American Poetry: Charles Olson and the Emersonian Tradition* (NY: Cambridge U. P., 1993) Olson(3)—Duncan—Creeley

Ward, Geoff, *Statutes of Liberty: The New York School of Poets* (London: Macmillan, 1993) Schuyler—O'Hara—Ashbery—{Language poetry}

*Mackey, Nathaniel, *Discrepant Engagement: Dissonance, Cross-Culturality, and Experimental Writing* (NY: Cambridge U. P., 1993) Baraka—Major—Duncan(2)—Creeley—Olson—[Brathwaite—Wilson Harris]

APPENDIX 10: INTERVIEWS/COLLECTIONS OF POETS' ESSAYS

Ossman, David, ed., *The Sullen Art: Interviews* (NY: Corinth, 1963) Rexroth—Carroll—Blackburn—Rothenberg—Kelly—Bly—J. Logan—Sorrentino—Creeley—Merwin—Levertov—Baraka—Dorn—Ginsberg

Ostroff, Anthony, ed., *The Contemporary Poet as Artist and Critic* (Boston: Little, Brown, 1964) Wilbur—Roethke—Kunitz—Lowell—[Ransom—Auden]—Eberhart—Shapiro—{critics: Eberhart—Horan—Swenson—Kunitz—Miles—Lowell—Wilbur—Nims—Berryman—Snodgrass—Booth—Stafford—Shapiro—Rich—Justice—Dickey—[Ransom— Deutsch—Elliott—L. Adams—Bogan—Beloof]}

Nemerov, Howard, ed., *Poets on Poetry* (NY: Basic Books, 1966) Aiken—Belitt—Berryman—Brinnin—Corso—Cunningham—Dickey—Duncan—Eberhart—Gilbert—Howes—V. Miller—Moore—Nemerov—Smith—Swenson—Weiss—Whittemore—Wilbur

Meltzer, David, ed., *The San Francisco Poets* (NY: Ballantine, 1971) Rexroth—Everson—Ferlinghetti—Welch—McClure—Brautigan

Perkins, George, ed., *American Poetic Theory* (NY: Holt, Rinehart and Winston, 1972) [19th–20th c.] Roethke—Jarrell—Lowell—Olson—Ginsberg—Creeley—Bly—J. Dickey

Dembo, L. S., & Cyrena Pondrom, eds., *The Contemporary Writer: Interviews* (Madison: U. of Wisconsin P., 1972) Merrill—Rexroth—Oppen—Rakosi—Reznikoff—Zukofsky—Brooks

Allen, Donald, & Warren Tallman, eds., *Poetics of the New American Poetry* (NY: Grove Press, 1973) [moderns] Zukofsky—Olson—Duncan—Spicer—Blaser—Creeley—Dorn—Levertov—Ginsberg—Wieners—O'Hara—Baraka—MacLow—Snyder—McClure—Ferlinghetti—Kandel—Whalen

Packard, William, ed., *The Craft of Poetry: Interviews from* The New York
Quarterly (NY: Doubleday, 1974) Blackburn—Sexton—Kunitz—
Rothenberg—Ginsberg—Levertov—Kinnell—Ashbery—J. Dickey—
Rukeyser—Wilbur—Creeley—MacLow—Moss—Jong—Wakoski

Boyers, Robert, ed., *Contemporary Poetry in America: Essays and Interviews*
(NY: Schocken, 1974) {interviews: Kunitz—Snodgrass—Kinnell}

Turner, Alberta T., ed., *50 Contemporary Poets: The Creative Process* (NY:
Longman, 1977) Amorosi—Anderson—Bell—Benedikt—Booth—
Carruth—Chester—Dubie—Eberhart—Edson—Everwine—Francis—
Friebert—Gildner—Glück—Haines—Hall—J. B. Hall—Harper—
Hey—Justice—Kaufman—Kennedy—Klappert—Kumin—Levertov—
Lipsitz—C. Macdonald—McPherson—Matthews—Mazzaro—V.
Miller—Minty—Pastan—Ray—Reiss—Schmitz—Shelton—Simic—
Simpson—Stafford—Stanford—Swift—Tate—Wallace—Wilbur—
Willard—Woods—C. Wright—D. Young

Faas, Ekbert, *Towards a New American Poetics: Essays and Interviews*
(Santa Barbara, CA: Black Sparrow, 1978) {interviews: Duncan—
Snyder—Creeley—Bly—Ginsberg} {essay: Olson}

Gibbons, Reginald, ed., *The Poet's Work: 29 Masters of 20th Century Poetry
on the Origins and Practice of Their Art* (Boston: Houghton Mifflin,
1979) {European, etc.} Schwartz—Shapiro—Berry—Jarrell—Levertov—Duncan—Snyder

Waldman, Anne, & Marilyn Webb, eds., *Talking Poetics from the Naropa
Institute,* 2 vols. (Boulder: Shambhala, 1979) Duncan—DiPrima—
T. Berrigan—Burroughs—Dorn—McClure—Padgett—Coolidge—
MacLow—Cage—Brownstein—Whalen—Rothenberg—Waldman—
Algarin—MacAdams—Sanders—Ginsberg

Hall, Donald, ed., *Claims for Poetry* (Ann Arbor: U. of Michigan P., 1982)
Ammons—Bell—Berry—Bly—Carruth—Creeley—Duncan—
Edson—Gallagher—S. Gilbert—Haines—Hall—Hass—Higgins—Hol-
lander—Hugo—Ignatow—Justice—Kennedy—Kern—Kinnell—
Kostelanetz—Levertov—J. Logan—Lorde—McGrath—MacLow—
Merwin—O'Hara—Ostriker—Padgett—Pinsky—Rich—Ryan—Silli-
man—Simic—Simpson—Snodgrass—Snyder—Stafford—Strand—
A. Walker—Wilbur

Palmer, Michael, ed., *Code of Signals: Recent Writings in Poetics* (Berkeley:
North Atlantic Books, 1983) Mackey—Taggart—Burnside—F.
Howe—Stein—Strauss—Gaynor—D. Shapiro—Bromige—Davidson—Ward—Corbett—Mayer—Coolidge—Shurin—S. Howe—Perelman—Palmer—Lansing—Barone—Bernstein—Ashbery—[McCaf-
fery-Hocquard-Chamberlain-Clifford-Grossinger]

Jackson, Richard, ed., *Acts of Mind: Conversations With Contemporary Poets* (Tuscaloosa: U. of Alabama P., 1983) [interviews from *Poetry Miscellany*] Plumly—M. Williams—Strand—Simic—Valentine—Ammons—Muske—Merwin—R. Warren—Bell—Ashbery—St. John—Booth—McHugh—Pack—Merwin—Kunitz—Daniel Mark Epstein—Stafford—Wier—Wilbur—Finkel—Chappell—Pastan—Creeley—Ignatow—Piercy—Harper—Hall—Hollander

Bellamy, Joe David, ed., *American Poetry Observed: Poets on Their Work* (Urbana: U. of Illinois P., 1984) Ai—Ashbery—Bell—Benedikt—Bishop—Bly—J. Dickey—Harper—Hugo—Justice—Kinnell—Kunitz—Levertov—Merwin—Miles—Rich—Sarton—Simic—Snodgrass—Stafford—Strand—Tate—Wagoner—Wakoski—Wilbur—J. Wright

Jones, Richard, ed., *Poetry and Politics: An Anthology of Essays* (NY: Quill, 1985) [Eliot—Auden—Spender—Hamburger]—Rukeyser—Snyder—Kunitz—Bly—Rich—Nemerov—Levertov—Baraka—J. Jordan—Hampl—Berry—Forché—Hyde—Carruth—Kinnell—{Kinnell/Baraka/J. Cooper/Ignatow/J. Jordan/Knight/Kunitz/Levertov/Levine/Miles/Ortiz}

Perelman, Bob, ed., *Writing/Talks* (Carbondale: Southern Illinois U. P., 1985) R. Glück—Bernstein—Armantrout—K. Robinson—Perelman—Boone—Davies—Dahlen—Harryman—Watten—Silliman—F. Howe—Palmer—Grenier—Bernheimer—Hejinian

Bartlett, Lee, ed., *Talking Poetry: Conversations in the Workshop with Contemporary Poets* (Albuquerque: U. of New Mexico P., 1987) Coolidge—Enslin—Eshleman—Everson—Gunn—Irby—Palmer—Raworth—Reed—Rodefer—Tarn—Wakoski—Waldman

Frank, Robert, & Henry Sayre, eds., *The Line in Postmodern Poetry* (Urbana: U. of Illinois P., 1988) [Perloff-Caws-Henderson-Hubert] Holden—S. Gilbert—Hongo—Scully—K. Fraser—Andrews—Bernstein—Benson—Drucker—Grenier—Hejinian—Howe—Inman—[McCaffery]—Mandel—Silliman—Weiner

McClatchy, J. D., ed., *Poets on Painters: Essays on the Art of Painting by Twentieth-Century Poets* (Berkeley: U. of California P., 1988) [modern British and American] Bishop—Rexroth—Nemerov—Jarrell—O'Hara—Creeley—Duncan—Davenport—Ashbery—Schuyler—[Tomlinson-Hughes]—Merrill—Howard—Strand—Hollander

Ingersoll, Earl G., Judith Kitchen, & Stan Rubin, eds., *The Post-Confessionals: Conversations with American Poets of the Eighties* (Rutherford, N.J.: Fairleigh Dickinson U. P., 1989) C. Wright—W. Matthews—Harper—Orr—Dove—Mueller—Plumly—Dennis—Willard—Hirsch—Pastan—Holden—P. Schultz—R. Morgan—Dunn—Pollitt—Waters—B. Bennett—Zimmer

Bernstein, Charles, ed., *The Politics of Poetic Form: Poetry and Public Policy*
(NY: Roof, 1990)   Rothenberg—Andrews—R. Waldrop—[Brossard-
McGann]—Mackey—Silliman—S. Howe—Hunt—MacLow—Bern-
stein—Inman/Weiner/Sherry/Piombino

McCorkle, James, ed., *Conversant Essays: Contemporary Poets on Poetry*
(Detroit: Wayne State U. P., 1990)   Anzaldúa—Bell—Bernstein—
Christensen—Clampitt—C. Clarke—Corn—Crase—Davidson—
DuPlessis—Eshleman—Fulton—Galassi—S. Gilbert—Gioia—
Grahn—Grosholz—Hacker—Hadas—Hamill—Harjo—Hartman—
Heller—Hirsch—Jensen—Klepfisz—Lauterbach—Lehman—Lei-
thauser—Levertov—Levis—W. Logan—Mackey—McClatchy—
McDowell—McKean—Ostriker—Peacock—Plumly—M. Randall—
Retallack—Rothenberg—Rudman—Schulman—Silliman—Snyder—
Steele—Stern—St. John—Swander—Taggart—Umpierre—R. War-
ren—C. K. Williams—Wormser

BIBLIOGRAPHY

Abrams, M. H. "Art-as-Such: The Sociology of Modern Aesthetics." *Bulletin of The American Academy of Arts and Sciences* 38.6 (1985): 8–33.

Adorno, Theodor. *Aesthetic Theory*. Trans. C. Lenhardt. Ed. Gretel Adorno and Rolf Tiedemann. London: Routledge, 1984.

———. *The Culture Industry: Selected Essays on Mass Culture*. Ed. J. M. Bernstein. New York: Routledge, 1991.

———. *Notes to Literature*, vol. 1. Trans. Shierry Nicholsen. Ed. Rolf Tiedemann. New York: Columbia UP, 1991.

———. *Prisms*. Trans. Samuel and Shierry Weber. Cambridge: MIT, 1981.

Agger, Ben. *Fast Capitalism: A Critical Theory of Significance*. Urbana: U of Illinois P, 1989.

Ahmad, Aijaz. *In Theory: Classes, Nations, Literatures*. London: Verso, 1992.

Aiken, Conrad. *Selected Letters*. Ed. Joseph Killorin. New Haven: Yale UP, 1978.

Allen, Donald M., ed. *The New American Poetry*. New York: Grove, 1960.

Allen, Donald M. and Warren Tallman, eds. *Poetics of The New American Poetry*. New York: Grove, 1973.

Altick, Richard D. *The Shows of London*. Cambridge, MA: Harvard UP, 1978.

Altieri, Charles. *Self and Sensibility in Contemporary American Poetry*. New York: Cambridge UP, 1984.

———. "Without Consequence Is No Politics: A Response to Jerome McGann." *Politics and Poetic Value*. Ed. Robert von Hallberg. Chicago: U of Chicago P, 1987. 301–08.

577

Altman, Rick. "Television/Sound." *Studies in Entertainment: Critical Approaches to Mass Culture.* Ed. Tania Modleski. Bloomington: Indiana UP, 1986. 39–54.

Alvarez, A. "The Limits of Analysis." *The American Scholar* 28.3 (1959): 367–75.

Anderson, Benedict. *Imagined Communities: Reflections on the Origin and Spread of Nationalism.* London: Verso, 1983.

Andrews, Bruce. Response to "Is There, Currently, An American Poetry? A Symposium." *American Poetry* 4.2 (1987): 2–4.

———. "Writing Social Work & Political Practice." *The L=A=N=G=U=A=G=E Book.* Andrews and Bernstein 133–36.

Andrews, Bruce and Charles Bernstein, eds. *The L=A=N=G=U=A=G=E Book.* Carbondale: Southern Illinois UP, 1984.

Antin, David. "Fine Furs." *Critical Inquiry* 19.1 (1992): 151–63.

———. "Modernism and Postmodernism: Approaching the Present in American Poetry." *Boundary 2* 1 (1972): 98–133.

Arendt, Hannah. *The Origins of Totalitarianism.* New ed. New York: Harcourt Brace, 1973.

Arnold, Matthew. *Selected Prose.* Ed. P. J. Keating. Harmondsworth: Penguin, 1970.

Aronowitz, Stanley. *False Promises: The Shaping of American Working-Class Consciousness.* New York: McGraw-Hill, 1973.

Arrowsmith, William. "*Partisan Review* and American Writing." *The Hudson Review* 1.4 (1949): 526–36.

Ashbery, John. *Houseboat Days.* New York: Viking, 1977.

———. Interview. *American Poetry Observed.* Bellamy 9–20.

———. Interview.*Writers at Work: Paris Review Interviews 7.* Ed. George Plimpton. New York: Viking, 1986. 178–205.

———. *A Wave.* New York: Viking, 1984.

Atlas, James. *Delmore Schwartz: The Life of an American Poet.* New York: Avon, 1978.

Auden, W.H. *Collected Poems.* Ed. Edward Mendelson. New York: Random House, 1976.

Avens, Robert. "Reflections on Wolfgang Giegerich's *The Burial of the Soul in Technological Civilization*." *Sulfur* 20 (1987): 34–54.

Baker, Peter. *Obdurate Brilliance: Exteriority and the Modern Long Poem.* Gainesville: University of Florida Press, 1991.

Balibar, Etienne. "The Nation Form: History and Ideology." *Race, Nation, Class: Ambiguous Identities.* Ed. Etienne Balibar and Immanuel Wallerstein. Trans. Chris Turner. London: Verso, 1991. 86–106.

Baraka, Amiri (LeRoi Jones). "Cultural Revolution and the Literary Canon."*Callaloo* 14.1 (1991): 150–56.

———. *Home: Social Essays.* New York: Morrow, 1966.

———. *Selected Plays and Prose of Amiri Baraka/LeRoi Jones.* New York: Morrow, 1979.

———. *Selected Poetry of Amiri Baraka/LeRoi Jones.* New York: Morrow, 1979.

Baraka, Amiri, et al. "Poets Against the End of the World." *Poetry and Politics: An Anthology of Essays.* Ed. Richard Jones. New York: Morrow, 1985. 300–16.

Barthes, Roland. *The Pleasure of the Text.* Trans. Richard Miller. New York: Hill & Wang, 1975.

Bartlett, Lee. *Talking Poetry: Conversations in the Workshop with Contemporary Poets.* Albuquerque: U of New Mexico P, 1987.

Baudrillard, Jean. *America.* Trans. Chris Turner. London: Verso, 1988.

———. *Cool Memories.* Trans. Chris Turner. London: Verso, 1990.

———. *Simulations.* Trans. Paul Foss, Paul Patton, and Philip Beitchman. New York: Semiotext(e), 1983.

Beach, Christopher. *ABC of Influence: Ezra Pound and the Remaking of American Poetic Tradition.* Berkeley: U of California P, 1992.

Beaver, Harold. "Despondency and Madness." *Parnassus* 12.1 (1984): 123–31.

Bedient, Calvin. "Illegible Lowell (The Late Volumes)." *Robert Lowell: Essays on the Poetry.* Ed. Steven Gould Axelrod and Helen Deese. New York: Cambridge UP, 1986. 139–55.

Bellamy, Joe David, ed. *American Poetry Observed: Poets on Their Work.* Urbana: U of Illinois P, 1984.

Benjamin, Walter. "Central Park." Trans. Lloyd Spencer, with Mark Harrington. *New German Critique* 34 (1985): 32–55.

———. *Illuminations.* Trans. Harry Zohn. Ed. Hannah Arendt. New York: Schocken, 1969.

Bennett, Tony. "The Exhibitionary Complex." *Culture/Power/History: A Reader in Contemporary Social Theory.* Ed. Nicholas B. Dirks, Geoff Eley, and Sherry B. Ortner. Princeton: Princeton UP, 1994. 123–54.

Benson, Steve. "For *Change.*" *In the American Tree.* Silliman 486–87.

Berman, Russell A. *Modern Culture and Critical Theory: Art, Politics, and the Legacy of the Frankfurt School.* Madison: U of Wisconsin P, 1989.

Bernstein, Charles. *Artifice of Absorption.* Philadelphia: Singing Horse/ Paper Air, 1987.

———. "The Conspiracy of 'Us,'" *The L=A=N=G=U=A=G=E Book.* Andrews and Bernstein 185–88.

———. Response to "Is There, Currently, An American Poetry? A Symposium." *American Poetry* 4.2 (1987): 7–9.

———. *A Poetics.* Cambridge: Harvard UP, 1992.

———. "Stray Straws and Straw Men." *The L=A=N=G=U=A=G=E Book.* Andrews and Bernstein 39–45.

———. "Writing and Method." *In the American Tree.* Silliman 583–98.

Bernstein, Charles, ed. *The Politics of Poetic Form: Poetry and Public Policy.* New York: Roof, 1990.

Berryman, John. *The Freedom of the Poet.* New York: Farrar Straus, 1976.

———. "From the Middle and Senior Generations." *The American Scholar* 28, no. 3 (1959): 384–89.

———. Response to "The State of American Writing, 1948: Seven Questions." *Partisan Review* 15.8 (1948): 856–60.

Berthoff, Warner. *A Literature Without Qualities: American Writing Since 1945.* Berkeley: U of California P, 1979.

Bertholf, Robert. "An Elegant Inconclusion." *Caterpillar* 20 (1973): 121–34.

Bérubé, Michael. *Marginal Forces/Cultural Centers: Tolson, Pynchon, and the Politics of the Canon.* Ithaca: Cornell UP, 1992.

Beverley, John. *Against Literature.* Minneapolis: U of Minnesota P, 1993.

Biggs, Mary. *A Gift That Cannot Be Refused: The Writing and Publishing of Contemporary American Poetry.* Westport, CT: Greenwood, 1990.

Blackburn, Paul. "The International Word." *The Nation* 194 (April 21, 1962): 357–60.

Blackmur, R. P. *The Lion and the Honeycomb: Essays in Solicitude and Critique.* London: Methuen, 1956.

————. Response to "The State of American Writing, 1948: Seven Questions." *Partisan Review* 15.8 (1948): 861–65.

Blaser, Robin. "Poetry and Positivisms: High Huck-a-Muck or 'Spiritual Ketchup.'" *Silence, the Word, and the Sacred.* Ed. E. D. Blodgett and H. G. Coward. Waterloo: Wilfrid Laurier UP/The Calgary Institute for the Humanities, 1989. 21–50.

————. "The Practice of Outside." Jack Spicer. *The Collected Books.* Ed. Robin Blaser. Los Angeles: Black Sparrow, 1975. 269–329.

Bloom, Harold. *Agon: Towards a Theory of Revisionism.* New York: Oxford UP, 1982.

Bly, Robert. *American Poetry: Wildness and Domesticity.* New York: Harper & Row, 1990.

————. *Selected Poems.* New York: Harper & Row, 1986.

————. *Talking All Morning.* Ann Arbor: U of Michigan P, 1980.

Bode, Carl. *The Half-World of American Culture: A Miscellany.* Carbondale: Southern Illinois UP, 1965.

Bogan, Louise. *Poet's Alphabet: Reflections on the Literary Art and Vocation.* Ed. Robert Phelps and Ruth Limmer. New York: McGraw-Hill, 1970.

————. *What the Woman Lived: Selected Letters of Louise Bogan 1920–1970.* Ed. Ruth Limmer. New York: Harcourt Brace, 1973.

Bolter, J. David. *Turing's Man: Western Culture in the Computer Age.* Chapel Hill: U of North Carolina P, 1984.

Bookchin, Murray. *The Modern Crisis.* Philadelphia: New Society Publishers, 1986.

Borges, Jorge Luis. *Other Inquisitions, 1937–1952.* Trans. Ruth L. C. Simms. New York: Washington Square, 1966.

Bourdieu, Pierre. "The Forms of Capital." *Handbook of Theory and Research for the Sociology of Education.* Ed. John G. Richardson. Westport, CT: Greenwood, 1986. 241–58.

Brantlinger, Patrick. *Bread and Circuses: Theories of Mass Culture as Social Decay.* Ithaca: Cornell UP, 1983.

Brecht, Bertolt. "Binocular Vision in the Theatre: The Alienation Effect." *Sociology of Literature and Drama.* Ed. Elizabeth and Tom Turns. Harmondsworth: Penguin Education, 1974. 36–74.

————. *Brecht on Theatre: The Development of an Aesthetic.* Trans. and ed. John Willett. New York: Hill and Wang, 1964.

Breslin, James E. B. *From Modern to Contemporary: American Poetry, 1945–1965.* Chicago: U of Chicago P, 1984.

———. "Poetry." *Columbia Literary History of the United States.* Ed. Emory Elliott. New York: Columbia UP, 1987. 1079–1100.

Brodhead, Richard. "After the Opening: Problems and Prospects for a Reformed American Literature." *The Yale Journal of Criticism* 5.2 (1992): 59–71.

Brookeman, Christopher. *American Culture and Society Since the 1930s.* New York: Shocken, 1984.

Brooks, Cleanth. "The Quick and the Dead: A Comment on Humanistic Studies." *The Humanities: An Appraisal.* Harris 1–21.

Brooks, Cleanth and Robert Penn Warren. *Understanding Poetry.* 4th ed. New York: Holt, Rinehart, and Winston, 1976.

Bukatman, Scott. *Terminal Identity: The Virtual Subject in Postmodern Science Fiction.* Durham, NC: Duke UP, 1993.

Burke, Kenneth. *A Grammar of Motives.* Berkeley: U of California P, 1969.

Burroughs, William. "Deposition: Testimony Concerning a Sickness." *The Portable Beat Reader.* Charters 136–44.

Bush, Douglas. "The New Criticism: Some Old-Fashioned Queries." *PMLA* 64, supplement, pt. 2 (1949): 13–21.

Byrd, Don. "Learned Ignorance and Other Defenses." *Sulfur* 11 (1984): 168–77.

———. "Meter-Making Argument." *Epoch* 29.2 (1980): 178–83.

———. *The Poetics of the Common Knowledge.* Albany, NY: SUNY, 1994.

Cain, William. *The Crisis in Criticism: Theory, Literature, and Reform in English Studies.* Baltimore: Johns Hopkins UP, 1984.

Calder, Alex. "*Notebook 1967–1968:* Writing the Process Poem." *Robert Lowell: Essays on the Poetry.* Ed. Steven Gould Axelrod and Helen Deese. New York: Cambridge UP, 1986. 117–38.

Cambon, Glauco. *Recent American Poetry.* Minneapolis: U of Minnesota P, 1962.

Carafiol, Peter. *The American Ideal: Literary History as a Worldly Activity.* New York: Oxford UP, 1991.

Carpenter, Humphrey. *A Serious Character: The Life of Ezra Pound.* Boston: Houghton Mifflin, 1988.

———. *W. H. Auden, A Biography.* Boston: Houghton Mifflin, 1981.

Casillo, Robert. *The Genealogy of Demons: Anti-Semitism, Fascism, and the Myths of Ezra Pound.* Evanston: Northwestern UP, 1988.

Certeau, Michel de. *Heterologies: Discourse on the Other.* Trans. Brian Massumi. Minneapolis: U of Minnesota P, 1986.

———. *Practice of Everyday Life.* Trans. Steven Rendall. Berkeley: U of California P, 1984.

———. *The Writing of History.* Trans. Tom Conley. New York: Columbia UP, 1988.

Chapin, Katherine Garrison. "Fifteen Years of New Writing." *New Republic* 144 (January 9, 1961): 25–26.

Charters, Ann, ed. *The Portable Beat Reader.* New York: Penguin, 1992.

Chermayeff, Serge. "The Social Aspects of Art." *The Humanities: An Appraisal.* Harris 140–42.

Chow, Rey. "Benjamin's Love Affair with Death." *New German Critique* 48 (1989): 63–86.

Christensen, Paul. "'Malignant Innocence.'" *Parnassus* 12.1 (1984): 154–82.

———. "Struggling to be a Courtier: The Poetry of Richard Wilbur." *Sulfur* 27 (1990): 60–67.

Ciardi, John. *Dialogue With an Audience.* Philadelphia: Lippincott, 1963.

Ciardi, John, ed. *Mid-Century American Poetry.* Boston: Twayne, 1950.

Clark, Tom. *Charles Olson: The Allegory of a Poet's Life.* New York: Norton, 1991.

Clifford, James. *The Predicament of Culture: Twentieth-Century Ethnography, Literature, and Art.* Cambridge: Harvard UP, 1988.

Collins, Billy. "Literary Reputation and the Thrown Voice." *A Gift of Tongues: Critical Challenges in Contemporary American Poetry.* Ed. Marie Harris and Kathleen Aguero. Athens: U of Georgia P, 1987. 295–306.

Collins, Jim. *Uncommon Cultures: Popular Culture and Post-Modernism.* New York: Routledge, 1989.

Collins, Wilkie. *My Miscellanies,* vol. 1. London: Sampson Low, 1863.

Cooney, Terry. *The Rise of the New York Intellectuals: Partisan Review and Its Circle.* Madison: U of Wisconsin P, 1986.

Corso, Gregory. "Variations on a Generation." *Casebook on the Beat.* Ed. Thomas Parkinson. New York: Crowell, 1961. 88–97.

Cottrell, Leonard. *Madame Tussaud.* London: Evans, 1951.

Crary, Jonathan. "Eclipse of the Spectacle." *Art After Modernism: Rethinking Representation.* Ed. Brian Wallis. New York: New Museum of Contemporary Art/Boston: Godine, 1984. 283–94.

Crawford, Robert. *Devolving English Literature.* Oxford: Clarendon, 1992.

Creeley, Robert. *The Collected Essays.* Berkeley: U of California P, 1989.

——. *The Collected Poems of Robert Creeley, 1945–1975.* Berkeley: U of California P, 1982.

——. *Contexts of Poetry: Interviews 1961–1971.* Ed. Donald Allen. Bolinas: Four Seasons, 1973.

cummings, e.e. *i: six non-lectures.* New York: Atheneum, 1962.

——. *Complete Poems.* 2 vols. London: MacGibbon & Kee, 1968.

Damon, Maria. *The Dark End of the Street: Margins in American Vanguard Poetry.* Minneapolis: U of Minnesota P, 1993.

Daniels, Guy. "Post-Mortem on San Francisco." *The Nation* 187 (August 2, 1958): 53–55.

Dasenbrock, Reed Way. "What to Teach When the Canon Closes Down: Toward a New Essentialism." *Reorientations.* Henricksen and Morgan 63–76.

Davenport, Guy. *The Geography of the Imagination.* San Francisco: North Point, 1981.

Davidson, Michael. *The San Francisco Renaissance: Poetics and Community at Mid-century.* New York: Cambridge UP, 1989.

Davie, Donald. *The Poet in the Imaginary Museum: Essays of Two Decades.* Ed. Barry Alpert. New York: Persea, 1977.

Davis, Robert Gorham. "The Question of the Pound Award." *Partisan Review* 16.5 (1949): 513–15.

——. Response to "The State of American Writing, 1948: Seven Questions." *Partisan Review* 15.8 (1948): 866–70.

De Landa, Manuel. *War in the Age of Intelligent Machines.* New York: Zone, 1991.

Defert, Daniel. "The Collection of the World: Accounts of Voyages from the Sixteenth to the Eighteenth Centuries." Trans. Marie Diamond. *Dialectical Anthropology* 7 (1982): 11–20.

Deleuze, Gilles. "Postscript on the Societies of Control." *October* 59 (1992): 3–7.

Deleuze, Gilles, and Felix Guattari. *Kafka: Toward a Minor Literature.* Trans. Dana Polan. Minneapolis: U of Minnesota P, 1986.

———. *A Thousand Plateaus: Capitalism and Schizophrenia.* Trans. Brian Massumi. Minneapolis: U of Minnesota P, 1987.

Deleuze, Gilles and Claire Parnet. *Dialogues.* Trans. Hugh Tomlinson and Barbara Habberjam. New York: Columbia UP, 1987.

Derrida, Jacques. "Canons and Metonymies: An Interview with Jacques Derrida." *Logomachia: The Conflict of the Faculties.* Ed. Richard Rand. Lincoln: U of Nebraska P, 1992. 195–218.

Dickey, James. *Babel to Byzantium: Poets and Poetry Now.* New York: Farrar Straus, 1968.

———. *Poems 1957–1967.* New York: Collier, 1968.

Didi-Huberman, Georges. "The Figurative Incarnation of the Sentence (Notes on the 'Autographic' Skin)." Trans. Caryn Davidson. *Journal: A Contemporary Art Magazine* 47.5 (1987): 67–70.

Diggins, John Patrick. *The Proud Decades: America in War and Peace, 1941–1960.* New York: Norton, 1988.

Di Piero, W. S. *Memory and Enthusiasm.* Princeton: Princeton UP, 1989.

Docherty, Thomas. "Postmodernism: An Introduction." *Postmodernism: A Reader.* Ed. Thomas Docherty. New York: Columbia UP, 1993. 1–31.

Donaldson, Scott. *Poet in America: Winfield Townley Scott.* Austin: U of Texas P, 1972.

Donoghue, Denis. *Reading America: Essays on American Literature.* New York: Knopf, 1987.

Dooley, David. "The Contemporary Workshop Aesthetic." *The Hudson Review* 43.2 (1990): 259–80.

Doreski, Carole. "The Harvard Book of Contemporary American Poetry." *American Poetry* 3.3 (1986): 85–90.

Dorn, Edward. *Hello, La Jolla.* Berkeley: Wingbow, 1978.

———. *Gunslinger.* Durham, NC: Duke UP, 1989.

Doty, Mark. "The 'Forbidden Planet' of Character: The Revolutions of the 1950s." *A Profile of Twentieth-Century American Poetry.* Ed. Jack Myers and David Wojahn. Carbondale: Southern Illinois UP, 1991. 131–57.

Duncan, Robert. *Fictive Certainties.* New York: New Directions, 1985.

————. *The First Decade: Selected Poems 1940–1950*. London: Fulcrum, 1968.

————. *Ground Work: Before the War*. New York: New Directions, 1984.

————. *Ground Work II: In the Dark*. New York: New Directions, 1987.

————. "The Homosexual in Society (1944, 1959)." *Jimmy & Lucy's House of "K"* 3 (1985): 51–69.

————. "An Interview with Robert Duncan." *Contemporary Literature* 21.4 (1980): 511–48.

DuPlessis, Rachel Blau. "On the Davidson/Weinberger Exchange." *Sulfur* 22 (1988): 188–93.

Dussel, Enrique. *Philosophy of Liberation*. Trans. Aquilina Martinez and Christine Morkovsky. Maryknoll, NY: Orbis, 1985.

Eagleton, Terry. *Literary Theory: An Introduction*. Minneapolis: U of Minnesota P, 1983.

Easthope, Antony. *Poetry as Discourse*. London: Methuen, 1983.

Easthope, Antony and John O. Thompson, eds. *Contemporary Poetry Meets Modern Theory*. London: Harvester Wheatsheaf, 1991.

Eberhart, Richard. *Of Poetry and Poets*. Urbana: U of Illinois P, 1979.

Eco, Umberto. *Travels in Hyper-Reality*. Trans. William Weaver. New York: Harcourt Brace, 1987.

Ehrenreich, Barbara and John. "The Professional-Managerial Class." *Between Labor and Capital*. Ed. Pat Walker. Boston: South End, 1979. 5–45.

Eliot, T. S. *Selected Essays*. London: Faber & Faber, 1951.

Elton, William. *A Guide to the New Criticism*. Revised edition. Chicago: The Modern Poetry Association, 1951.

Emerson, Ralph Waldo. *Essays and Lectures*. New York: Library of America, 1983.

Engell, James. *Forming the Critical Mind*. Cambridge: Harvard UP, 1989.

Enzensberger, Hans Magnus. *The Consciousness Industry: On Literature, Politics and the Media*. Ed. Michael Roloff. New York: Seabury, 1974.

Eshleman, Clayton. *Antiphonal Swing: Selected Prose, 1962–1987*. Ed. Caryl Eshleman. Kingston, NY: McPherson & Co., 1989.

————. *Hades in Manganese*. Santa Barbara: Black Sparrow, 1981.

Faas, Ekbert. *Young Robert Duncan: Portrait of the Poet as Homosexual in Society.* Santa Barbara: Black Sparrow, 1983.

Faas, Ekbert, ed. *Towards a New American Poetics: Essays and Interviews.* Santa Barbara: Black Sparrow, 1978.

Fabian, Johannes. *Time and the Other: How Anthropology Makes Its Object.* New York: Columbia UP, 1983.

Fawcett, Brian. "Agent of Language." *The L=A=N=G=U=A=G=E Book.* Andrews and Bernstein 151–54.

———. *Cambodia: A book for people who find television too slow.* Vancouver: Talonbooks, 1986.

Fekete, John. *The Critical Twilight: Explorations in the Ideology of Anglo-American Literary Theory from Eliot to McLuhan.* London: Routledge & Kegan Paul, 1978.

Fellows in American Letters of the Library of Congress. *The Case Against the* Saturday Review of Literature. Chicago: Modern Poetry Association, 1949.

Fiedler, Leslie. Response to "The State of American Writing, 1948: Seven Questions." *Partisan Review* 15.8 (1948): 870–75.

Fish, Stanley. *Doing What Comes Naturally: Change, Rhetoric, and the Practice of Theory in Literary and Legal Studies.* Durham, NC: Duke UP, 1989.

———. *There's No Such Thing As Free Speech, and It's a Good Thing Too.* New York: Oxford UP, 1994.

Fisher, Philip. *Making and Effacing Art: Modern American Art in a Culture of Museums.* New York: Oxford UP, 1991.

Foerster, Heinz von, Margaret Mead, and Hans Teuber. "A Note by the Editors." *Cybernetics: Circular Causal and Feedback Mechanisms in Biological and Social Systems.* Ed. Heinz von Foerster et al. New York: Josiah Macy Jr. Foundation, 1952. xi–xx.

Foerster, Norman. "The Esthetic Judgment and the Ethical Judgment." *The Intent of the Critic.* Ed. Donald Stauffer. Princeton: Princeton University Press, 1941. 65–88.

Foerster, Norman, et al. *Literary Scholarship: Its Aims and Methods.* Chapel Hill: U of North Carolina P, 1941.

Forché, Carolyn. *The Angel of History.* New York: HarperCollins, 1994.

———. "Sensibility and Responsibility." *The Writer and Human Rights.* Ed. Toronto Arts Group for Human Rights. Toronto: Lester & Orpen Dennys, 1983. 23–25.

Forché, Carolyn, ed. *Against Forgetting: Twentieth-Century Poetry of Witness*. New York: Norton, 1993.

Foster, Hal. "Armor Fou." *October* 56 (1991): 65–97.

Foucault, Michel. *Discipline and Punish: The Birth of the Prison*. Trans. Alan Sheridan. New York: Pantheon, 1977.

———. *The Order of Things: An Archaeology of the Human Sciences*. New York: Pantheon, 1970.

Fraser, Russell. *A Mingled Yarn: The Life of R. P. Blackmur*. New York: Harcourt Brace, 1981.

Fredman, Stephen. *The Grounding of American Poetry: Charles Olson and the Emersonian Tradition*. New York: Cambridge UP, 1993.

Freedman, Jonathan. "Autocanonization: Tropes of Self-Legitimation in 'Popular Culture.'" *Yale Journal of Criticism* 1.1 (1987): 203–17.

Freud, Sigmund. "The 'Uncanny.'"*Collected Papers*. Trans. Alix Strachey. Vol. IV. London: Hogarth Press, 1925. 368–407.

Frost, Robert. "Maturity No Object." *The New Poets of England and America*. Hall, Pack, and Simpson 10–12.

———. *Poetry and Prose*. Ed. Edward C. Lathem and Lawrance Thompson. New York: Holt, Rinehart and Winston, 1972.

Garrett, George. "Against the Grain: Poets Writing Today." *American Poetry*. Ed. Irvin Ehrenpreis. London: Edward Arnold, 1965. 221–39.

———. "The Future of Creative Writing Programs." *Creative Writing in America*. Moxley 47–62.

Gates, Henry Louis Jr. *Loose Canons*. New York: Oxford UP, 1992.

Gelpi, Albert. "The Genealogy of Postmodernism: Contemporary American Poetry." *The Southern Review* 26 (1990): 517–41.

Gilbert, Jack. "The Landscape of American Poetry in 1964." *Poets on Poetry*. Ed. Howard Nemerov. New York: Basic Books, 1966. 104–13.

Gilroy, Paul. *The Black Atlantic: Modernity and Double Consciousness*. Cambridge, MA: Harvard UP, 1993.

Ginsberg, Allen. *Howl*. San Francisco: City Lights, 1956.

———. "Prose Contribution to Cuban Revolution." *The Poetics of The New American Poetry*. Allen and Tallman 334–44.

Gioia, Dana. "Can Poetry Matter?" *The Atlantic* (May 1991): 94–106.

Glück, Louise. "Disruption, Hesitation, Silence." *American Poetry Review* 22.5 (1993): 30–32.

Goldbarth, Albert. *Popular Culture.* Columbus: Ohio State UP, 1990.

———. *A Sympathy of Souls: Essays.* Minneapolis: Coffee House, 1990.

Golding, Alan. "A History of American Poetry Anthologies." *Canons.* Hallberg 279–307.

Gooch, Brad. *City Poet: The Life and Times of Frank O'Hara.* New York: Knopf, 1993.

Gorak, Jan. *The Making of the Modern Canon: Genesis and Crisis of a Literary Idea.* London: Athlone, 1991.

Graff, Gerald. "The Future of Theory in the Teaching of Literature." *The Future of Literary Theory.* Ed. Ralph Cohen. New York: Routledge, 1989. 250–67.

———. *Poetic Statement and Critical Dogma.* Evanston: Northwestern UP, 1970.

———. *Professing Literature: An Institutional History.* Chicago: U of Chicago P, 1987.

———. "What Should We Be Teaching—When There's No 'We'?" *Yale Journal of Criticism* 1.2 (1988): 189–211.

Greenberg, Clement. Response to "The State of American Writing, 1948: Seven Questions." *Partisan Review* 15.8 (1948): 876–79.

Greer, Michael. "Ideology and Theory in Recent Experimental Writing, or, the Naming of 'Language Poetry.'" *Boundary 2* 16.2/3 (1989): 335–55.

Gregory, Horace. "The Postwar Generation in Arts and Letters: Poetry." *Saturday Review* 30 (March 14, 1953): 13–14, 64–65.

Guilbaut, Serge. *How New York Stole the Idea of Modern Art: Abstract Expressionism, Freedom, and the Cold War.* Trans. Arthur Goldhammer. Chicago: U of Chicago P, 1983.

Guillory, John. "The Ideology of Canon Formation: T. S. Eliot and Cleanth Brooks." *Canons.* Hallberg 337–62.

———. *Cultural Capital: The Problem of Literary Canon Formation.* Chicago: U of Chicago P, 1993.

Gwynn, R. S. "No Biz Like Po' Biz." *Sewanee Review* 100.2 (1992): 311–23.

Hacking, Ian. "Biopower and the Avalanche of Printed Numbers." *Humanities in Society* 5.3/4 (1982): 279–95.

Hall, Donald. "Ah, Love, Let Us Be True: Domesticity and History in Contemporary Poetry." *The American Scholar* 28.3 (1959): 310–19.

———. "The Battle of the Bards." *Horizon* 4.1 (1961): 116–21.

———. *Goatfoot Milktongue Twinbird: Interviews, Essays, and Notes on
Poetry, 1970–1976.* Ann Arbor: U of Michigan P, 1978.

———. "'There Are Eyes in This Water.'" *The Nation* (June 3, 1961): 484–85.

Hall, Donald, ed. *Contemporary American Poetry.* 2nd ed. Baltimore: Penguin, 1972.

Hall, Donald, with Robert Pack and Louis Simpson, eds. *The New Poets of
England and America.* New York: Meridien, 1957.

Hall, Lesley A. *Hidden Anxieties: Male Sexuality, 1900–1950.* London: Polity, 1991.

Hallberg, Robert von. *American Poetry and Culture 1945–1980.* Cambridge,
MA: Harvard UP, 1985.

Hallberg, Robert von, ed.*Canons.* Chicago: U of Chicago P, 1984.

Hamilton, Ian. *Robert Lowell, A Biography.* New York: Random House, 1982.

Hammer, Langdon. *Hart Crane and Allen Tate: Janus-Faced Modernism.*
Princeton UP, 1993.

Haraway, Donna. "Teddy Bear Patriarchy: Taxidermy in the Garden of Eden,
New York City, 1908–1936." *Social Text* 11 (1984/85): 20–64.

Harmon, William. "The Lightweight Contender's New Clothes." *Parnassus*
15.1 (1989): 99–124.

Harpham, Geoffrey Galt. *The Ascetic Imperative in Culture and Criticism.*
Chicago: U of Chicago P, 1987.

Harris, Julian, ed. *The Humanities: An Appraisal.* Madison: U of Wisconsin
P, 1950.

Harris, Neil. *Cultural Excursions: Marketing Appetites and Cultural Tastes
in Modern America.* Chicago: U of Chicago P, 1990.

Hartman, Geoffrey. *Criticism in the Wilderness: The Study of Literature
Today.* New Haven: Yale UP, 1980.

———. "English as Something Else." *English Inside and Out: The Place of
Literary Criticism.* Ed. Susan Gubar and Jonathan Kamholtz. New
York: Routledge, 1993. 37–46.

Haydn, Hiram, with William Barrett, Kenneth Burke, Malcolm Cowley,
Robert Gorham Davis, and Allen Tate. "The New Criticism: American Scholar Forum." *The American Scholar* 20.1 (1950/51): 86–104,
and 20.2 (1951): 218–31.

Hecht, Anthony. *Collected Earlier Poems*. New York: Knopf, 1990.

Heller, Michael. Response to "Is There, Currently, An American Poetry? A Symposium." *American Poetry* 4.2 (1987): 21–24.

Hemley, Cecil. "Within a Budding Grove." *Hudson Review* 13.4 (1960/61): 626–30.

Henricksen, Bruce, and Thaïs E. Morgan, eds. *Reorientations: Critical Theories and Pedagogies*. Urbana: U of Illinois P, 1990.

Hillman, James. "Senex and Puer." Hillman et al. *Puer Papers*. Irving, TX: Spring, 1979. 3–53.

Hillyer, Robert. *In Pursuit of Poetry*. New York: McGraw-Hill, 1960.

Hobsbawm, Eric. "Mass-Producing Traditions: Europe, 1870–1914." *The Invention of Tradition*. Ed. Eric Hobsbawm and Terence Ranger. New York: Cambridge UP, 1983. 263–307.

Hodgen, Margaret T. *Early Anthropology in the Sixteenth and Seventeenth Centuries*. Philadelphia: U of Pennsylvania P, 1964.

Hoffman, Daniel. "Arrivals and Rebirths." *Sewanee Review* 68 (1960): 118–37.

———. "Poetry." *Literary History of the U.S.: History*. Ed. Robert Spiller et al. 4th ed. New York: Macmillan, 1974. 1426–46.

Hoffman, Daniel, ed. *The Harvard Guide to Contemporary American Writing*. Cambridge: Harvard UP, 1979.

Holden, Jonathan. *The Fate of American Poetry*. Athens: U of Georgia P, 1991.

hooks, bell. "Marginality as Site of Resistance." *Out There: Marginalization and Contemporary Cultures*. Ed. Russell Ferguson et al. Cambridge, MA: MIT, 1990.

Hooper-Greenhill, Eilean. *Museums and the Shaping of Knowledge*. London: Routledge, 1992.

Hubbell, Jay B. *Who Are the Major American Writers? A Study of the Changing Literary Canon*. Durham, NC: Duke UP, 1972.

Huet, Marie-Hélène. *Monstrous Imagination*. Cambridge: Harvard UP, 1993.

Humphries, Rolfe. *Poets, Poetics, and Politics: America's Literary Community Viewed from the Letters of Rolfe Humphries, 1910–1969*. Ed. Richard Gillman and Michael Novak. Lawrence: UP of Kansas, 1992.

Hutchins, Robert M. "Preface." *The Great Conversation. The Great Books of the Western World*. Vol. 1. Chicago: Encyclopedia Britannica, 1952.

Iser, Wolfgang. *Prospecting: From Reader Response to Literary Anthropology*. Baltimore: Johns Hopkins UP, 1989.

Jacoby, Russell. *The Last Intellectuals: American Culture in the Age of Academe*. New York: Basic Books, 1987.

James, Henry. *The American Scene*. Ed. W. H. Auden. New York: Scribner's, 1946.

———. "The Real Thing." *The Complete Tales*. Ed. Leon Edel. Vol. 8. Philadelphia: J. B. Lippincott, 1963. 229–58.

Jameson, Fredric. *The Political Unconscious*. Ithaca: Cornell UP, 1981.

———. *Postmodernism: Or, The Cultural Logic of Late Capitalism*. Durham, NC: Duke UP, 1991.

———. "Reflections in Conclusion." Ernst Bloch et al. *Aesthetics and Politics*. London: NLB, 1977. 196–213.

Janssen, Marian. *The Kenyon Review 1939–1970: A Critical History*. Baton Rouge: LSU, 1990.

Janssens, G. A. M. *The American Literary Review: A Critical History 1920–1950*. The Hague: Mouton, 1968.

Jarrell, Randall. *Kipling, Auden, & Co.: Essays and Reviews 1935–1964*. New York: Farrar Straus, 1980.

———. *Poetry and the Age*. New York: Knopf, 1953.

———. "Poets, Critics and Readers." *The American Scholar*. 28.3 (1959): 277–92.

———. *Randall Jarrell's Letters: An Autobiographical and Literary Selection*. Ed. Mary Jarrell. London: Faber, 1985.

Jezer, Marty. *The Dark Ages: Life in the United States 1945–1960*. Boston: South End, 1982.

Johnson, Glen M. "The Teaching Anthology and the Canon of American Literature: Some Notes on Theory in Practice." *The Hospitable Canon*. Nemoianu and Royal 111–36.

Jones, David. *The Dying Gaul and Other Writings*. Ed. Harman Grisewood. London: Faber & Faber, 1978.

Jordanova, Ludmilla. "Objects of Knowledge: A Historical Perspective on Museums." *The New Museology*. Ed. Peter Vergo. London: Reaktion, 1989. 22–40.

Kalaidjian, Walter. *Languages of Liberation: The Social Text in Contemporary American Poetry*. New York: Columbia UP, 1989.

Kaminer, Wendy. *I'm Dysfunctional, You're Dysfunctional: The Recovery Movement and Other Self-Help Fashions.* Reading, MA: Addison-Wesley, 1992.

Kaplan, Justin. *Walt Whitman, A Life.* New York: Simon and Schuster, 1980.

Katz, Alfred H. *Self-Help in America: A Social Movement Perspective.* New York: Twayne, 1993.

Kerkhoff, Ingrid. *Poetiken und lyrischer Diskurs im Kontext gesellschaftlicher Dynamik, USA: "The Sixties."* Frankfurt am Main: Peter Lang, 1989.

Kermode, Frank. *The Classic.* London: Faber & Faber, 1975.

Kinnell, Galway. *Walking Down the Stairs: Selections from Interviews.* Ann Arbor: U of Michigan P, 1978.

Kinzie, Mary. *The Cure of Poetry in an Age of Prose: Moral Essays on the Poet's Calling.* Chicago: U of Chicago P, 1993.

Kirshenblatt-Gimblett, Barbara. "Objects of Ethnography." *Exhibiting Cultures: The Poetics and Politics of Museum Display.* Ed. Ivan Karp and Steven D. Lavine. Washington, DC: Smithsonian, 1991. 386–443.

Kittler, Friedrich A. *Discourse Networks 1800/1900.* Trans. Michael Metteer and Chris Cullens. Stanford: Stanford UP, 1990.

Kizer, Carolyn. "Poetry of the 'Fifties: in America." *International Literary Annual No. 1.* Ed. John Wain. London: John Calder, 1958. 60–96.

Knight, Arthur and Kit, eds. *The Beat Vision: A Primary Sourcebook.* New York: Paragon House, 1987.

Koethe, John. "Contrary Impulses: The Tension between Poetry and Theory." *Critical Inquiry* 18.1 (1991): 64–75.

Kolb, Harold H., Jr. "Defining the Canon." *Redefining American Literary History.* Ed. LaVonne Brown Ruoff and Jerry W. Ward, Jr. New York: Modern Language Association, 1990. 35–51.

Kozloff, Sarah. *Invisible Storytellers: Voice-Over Narration in American Fiction Film.* Berkeley: U of California P, 1988.

Kuberski, Philip. "Charles Olson and the American Thing: The Ideology of Literary Revolution." *Criticism* 27.2 (1985): 175–93.

Kunitz, Stanley. "American Poetry's Silver Age." *Harper's* October 1959: 173–79.

———. "Process and Thing: A Year of Poetry." *Harper's* September 1960: 96–104.

———. "The Sense of a Life." *Robert Lowell: Interviews and Memoirs.* Ed. Jeffrey Meyers. Ann Arbor: U of Michigan P, 1988. 230–35.

Langbaum, Robert. "The New Nature Poetry." *The American Scholar* 28.3 (1959): 323–40.

Larson, Magali S. *The Rise of Professionalism: A Sociological Analysis.* Berkeley: U of California P, 1977.

Latour, Bruno. "Give Me a Laboratory and I Will Raise the World." *Science Observed: Perspectives on the Social Study of Science.* Ed. Karin Knorr-Cetina and Michael Mulkay. Los Angeles: Sage, 1983. 141–70.

———. *Science in Action: How to Follow Scientists and Engineers through Society.* Cambridge: Harvard UP, 1987.

Lauretis, Teresa de. *Alice Doesn't: Feminism, Semiotics, Cinema.* Bloomington: Indiana UP, 1984.

Lawrence, Amy. *Echo and Narcissus: Women's Voices in Classical Hollywood Cinema.* Berkeley: U of California P, 1991.

Lazer, Hank. "Poetry Readings and the Contemporary Canon." *American Poetry* 7.2 (1990): 64–72.

———. "The Politics of Form and Poetry's Other Subjects: Reading Contemporary American Poetry." *American Literary History* 2.3 (1990): 503–27.

Lears, T. Jackson. "A Matter of Taste: Corporate Cultural Hegemony in a Mass-Consumption Society." *Recasting America: Culture and Politics in the Age of Cold War.* Ed. Larry May. Chicago: U of Chicago P, 1989. 38–57.

Lefebvre, Henri. *Everyday Life in the Modern World.* Trans. Sacha Rabinovitch. New Brunswick, NJ: Transaction, 1984.

Leitch, Vincent B. *American Literary Criticism From the 30s to the 80s.* New York: Columbia UP, 1988.

Lentricchia, Frank. *Modernist Quartet.* New York: Cambridge UP, 1994.

Levis, Larry. "Eden and My Generation." *Conversant Essays.* McCorkle 466–78.

Lewis, Wyndham. *The Apes of God.* Harmondsworth: Penguin, 1965.

———. *The Childermass.* London: John Calder, 1965.

Lhamon, W. T., Jr. *Deliberate Speed: The Origins of a Cultural Style in the American 1950s.* Washington, DC: Smithsonian, 1990.

Liu, Alan. "Local Transcendence: Cultural Criticism, Postmodernism, and the Romanticism of Detail." *Representations* 32 (1990): 75–113.

Loftus, Beverly J. G. "Ezra Pound and the Bollingen Prize: The Controversy in Periodicals." *Journalism Quarterly* 39 (1962): 347–54, 394.

Lowell, Robert. *Collected Prose*. Ed. Robert Giroux. New York: Farrar, Straus, Giroux, 1987.

———. *Day by Day*. New York: Farrar, Straus, Giroux, 1977.

———. *The Dolphin*. New York: Farrar, Straus, Giroux, 1973.

———. *For the Union Dead*. New York: Farrar, Straus, Giroux, 1964.

———. *History*. London: Faber & Faber, 1973.

———. *Life Studies*. New York: Farrar, Straus, Giroux, 1959.

Lyotard, Jean-François. *The Inhuman: Reflections on Time*. Stanford: Stanford UP, 1991.

MacCannell, Dean. *Empty Meeting Grounds: The Tourist Papers*. New York: Routledge, 1992.

Macdonald, Dwight. *Against the American Grain: Essays on the Effects of Mass Culture*. New York: Vintage, 1962.

Mackey, Nathaniel. *Discrepant Engagement: Dissonance, Cross-Culturality, and Experimental Writing*. New York: Cambridge UP, 1993.

MacLeish, Archibald. *New and Collected Poems 1917–1976*. Boston: Houghton Mifflin, 1976.

———. *Poetry and Opinion: The Pisan Cantos of Ezra Pound, a Dialogue on the Role of Poetry*. Urbana: U of Illinois P, 1950.

———. *Reflections*. Ed. Bernard A. Drabeck and Helen E. Ellis. Amherst: U of Massachusetts P, 1986.

———. *A Time to Speak: The Selected Prose of Archibald MacLeish*. Boston: Houghton Mifflin, 1941.

Mac Low, Jackson. "'Language-Centered.'" *In the American Tree*. Silliman 491–95.

Mailer, Norman. *The Armies of the Night: History as a Novel, the Novel as History*. New York: Signet, 1968.

Malraux, André. *The Voices of Silence*. Trans. Stuart Gilbert. London: Secker & Warburg, 1954.

Manicas, Peter T. *A History and Philosophy of the Social Sciences*. Oxford: Blackwell, 1987.

Marcuse, Herbert. *Negations: Essays in Critical Theory.* Boston: Beacon, 1968.

Mariani, Paul. *Dream Song: The Life of John Berryman.* New York: Morrow, 1990.

Matthews, William. *Curiosities.* Ann Arbor: U of Michigan P, 1989.

Maturana, Humberto R. and Francisco J. Varela. *Autopoiesis and Cognition: The Realization of the Living.* Dordrecht: D. Reidel, 1980.

McCaffery, Steve. *North of Intention: Critical Writings 1973–1986.* New York: Roof/Toronto: Nightwood, 1986.

McClatchy, J. D., ed. *The Vintage Book of Contemporary American Poetry.* New York: Vintage, 1990.

McClure, Michael. *Scratching the Beat Surface.* San Francisco: North Point, 1982.

McCorkle, James, ed. *Conversant Essays: Contemporary Poets on Poetry.* Detroit: Wayne State UP, 1990.

McGann, Jerome. *Black Riders: The Visible Language of Modernism.* Princeton: Princeton UP, 1993.

———. "The *Cantos* of Ezra Pound, the Truth in Contradiction." *Critical Inquiry* 15.1 (1988): 1–25.

———. "Contemporary Poetry, Alternate Routes." *Politics and Poetic Value.* Ed. Robert von Hallberg. Chicago: U of Chicago P, 1987. 253–76.

McGuire, William. *Bollingen: An Adventure in Collecting the Past.* Princeton: Princeton UP, 1982.

McKay, Anne. "Speaking Up: Voice Amplification and Women's Struggle for Public Expression." *Technology and Women's Voices: Keeping in Touch.* Ed. Cheris Kramarae. New York: Routledge, 1988. 187–206.

Melville, Herman. *Journey of a Visit to Europe and the Levant, October 11, 1856–May 6, 1857.* Ed. Howard A. Horsford. Princeton: Princeton UP, 1955.

———. *Pierre, Israel Potter, The Piazza Tales, The Confidence-Man, Uncollected Prose, Billy Budd, Sailor.* New York: Library of America, 1984.

Merrill, James. *The Changing Light at Sandover.* New York: Atheneum, 1982.

———. Interview. *The Contemporary Writer.* Ed. L. S. Dembo and Cyrena Pondrom. Madison: U of Wisconsin P, 1972. 139–52.

——. *Late Settings.* New York: Atheneum, 1985.

——. *Recitative: Prose by James Merrill.* Ed. J. D. McClatchy. San Francisco: North Point, 1986.

Merwin, W. S. "The Art of Poetry." Interview. *Paris Review* 102 (1987): 56–81.

——. *The Lice.* New York: Atheneum, 1967.

——. "W. S. Merwin." Interview. *American Poetry Observed.* Bellamy 168–80.

——. *Writings to an Unfinished Accompaniment.* New York: Atheneum, 1973.

Meyer, Donald. *The Positive Thinkers: Religion as Pop Psychology.* New York: Pantheon, 1980.

Meyers, Jeffrey. *Manic Power: Robert Lowell and His Circle.* New York: Arbor House, 1987.

Michaels, Walter Benn. "*Walden*'s False Bottoms." *Glyph* 1. Baltimore: Johns Hopkins UP, 1977. 132–49.

Monson, Ingrid. "Doubleness and Jazz Improvisation: Irony, Parody, and Ethnomusicology." *Critical Inquiry* 20.2 (1994): 283–313.

Moore, Geoffrey, ed. *The Penguin Book of Modern American Verse.* Harmondsworth: Penguin, 1954.

Moore, Rosalie. "The Beat and the Unbeat." *Poetry* 93.2 (1958): 104–07.

Moxley, Joseph M., ed. *Creative Writing in America: Theory and Pedagogy.* Urbana: National Council of Teachers of English, 1989.

Mullaney, Steven. *The Place of the Stage: License, Play, and Power in Renaissance England.* Chicago: U of Chicago P, 1988.

Myers, D. G. "The Rise of Creative Writing." *Journal of the History of Ideas* 54.2 (1993): 277–97.

National Poetry Festival, Washington, D.C., 1962: Proceedings. Washington, DC: Library of Congress, 1964.

Nealon, Jeffrey. *Double Reading: Postmodernism after Deconstruction.* Ithaca: Cornell UP, 1993.

Nelson, Cary. *Repression and Recovery: Modern American Poetry and the Politics of Cultural Memory, 1910–1945.* Madison: U of Wisconsin P, 1989.

Nemoianu, Virgil. "Literary Canons and Social Value Options." *The Hospitable Canon.* Nemoianu and Royal 215–47.

Nemoianu, Virgil, and Robert Royal, eds. *The Hospitable Canon: Essays on Literary Play, Scholarly Choice, and Popular Pressures.* Philadelphia: John Benjamins, 1991.

Ohmann, Richard. *Politics of Letters.* Middletown: Wesleyan UP, 1987.

Olson, Charles. *Charles Olson and Ezra Pound: An Encounter at St. Elizabeth's.* Ed. Catherine Seelye. New York: Grossman, 1975.

———. *The Collected Poems.* Ed. George Butterick. Berkeley: U of California P, 1987.

———. *The Maximus Poems.* Ed. George Butterick. Berkeley: U of California P, 1983.

———. *Selected Writings.* Ed. Robert Creeley. New York: New Directions, 1966.

———. *The Special View of History.* Ed. Ann Charters. Berkeley: Oyez, 1970.

O'Neill, John. *Five Bodies: The Human Shape of Modern Society.* Ithaca: Cornell UP, 1985.

Palmer, Michael. *First Figure.* San Francisco: North Point, 1984.

———. "An Interview with Michael Palmer, Conducted by Keith Tuma." *Contemporary Literature* 30.1 (1989): 1–12.

———. "Michael Palmer: 'The man by contrast is fixed symmetrically.'" Interview. *Talking Poetry.* Bartlett 125–47.

———. *Sun.* San Francisco: North Point, 1988.

Parini, Jay, ed. *The Columbia History of American Poetry.* New York: Columbia UP, 1993.

Parkinson, Thomas, ed. *A Casebook on the Beat.* New York: Crowell, 1961.

———. "Phenomenon or Generation." *Casebook on the Beat.* Parkinson 276–90.

———. *Poets, Poems, Movements.* Ann Arbor: UMI Research, 1987.

Parsegian, V. I. *This Cybernetic World of Men, Machines, and Earth Systems.* Garden City: Doubleday, 1972.

Pecora, Vincent P. "Adversarial Culture and the Fate of Dialectics." *Cultural Critique* 8 (1987/88): 197–216.

Perelman, Bob. *Captive Audience.* Great Barrington, MA: The Figures, 1988.

———. *The First World.* Great Barrington, MA: The Figures, 1986.

———. "The Marginalization of Poetry." *Essays in Postmodern Culture.* Ed. Eyal Amiran and John Unsworth. New York: Oxford UP, 1993. 229–38.

Perkins, David. *A History of Modern Poetry: Modernism and After.* Cambridge, MA: Harvard UP, 1987.

Perloff, Marjorie. *The Dance of the Intellect: Studies in the Poetry of the Pound Tradition.* New York: Cambridge UP, 1985.

———. "Fascism, Anti-Semitism, Isolationism: Contextualizing the 'Case of EP.'" *Paideuma* 16.3 (1987): 7–21.

———. *Radical Artifice: Writing Poetry in the Age of Media.* Chicago: U of Chicago P, 1991.

Pfeil, Fred. *Another Tale to Tell: Politics and Narrative in Postmodern Culture.* London: Verso, 1990.

Pinsky, Robert. *Poetry and the World.* New York: Ecco Press, 1988.

———. *The Situation of Poetry.* Princeton: Princeton UP, 1976.

Plath, Sylvia. *The Collected Poems.* Ed. Ted Hughes. New York: Harper and Row, 1981.

Podhoretz, Norman. "The Know-Nothing Bohemians." *Casebook on the Beat.* Parkinson 201–12.

Postman, Neil. *Technopoly: The Surrender of Culture to Technology.* New York: Knopf, 1992.

Pound, Ezra. *The Cantos.* New York: New Directions, 1972.

Procopiow, Norma. *Robert Lowell: The Poet and His Critics.* Chicago: American Library Association, 1984.

Prunty, Wyatt. *"Fallen from the Symboled World": Precedents for the New Formalism.* New York: Oxford UP, 1990.

Pynchon, Thomas. *Gravity's Rainbow.* New York: Viking, 1973.

Raban, Jonathan. *The Society of the Poem.* London: Harrap, 1971.

Rabinow, Paul. "Masked I Go Forward: Reflections on the Modern Subject." *A Crack in the Mirror: Reflexive Perspectives in Anthropology.* Ed. Jay Ruby. Philadelphia: U of Pennsylvania P, 1982. 173–85.

Rajchman, John. *Philosophical Events: Essays of the '80s.* New York: Columbia UP, 1991.

Ransom, John Crowe. "On the 'Brooks-MacLeish Thesis.'" *Partisan Review* 9.1 (1942): 40–41.

———. *Poems and Essays.* New York: Vintage, 1955.

———. *Selected Essays.* Ed. Thomas D. Young and John Hindle. Baton Rouge: LSU, 1984.

——. *Selected Letters*. Ed. Thomas D. Young and George Core. Baton Rouge: LSU, 1985.

——. "Strategy for English Studies." *The Southern Review* 6.2 (1940): 226–35.

Rasula, Jed. "The Catastrophe of Charm." *Sulfur* 20 (1987): 169–76.

——. "The Compost Library." *Sagetrieb* 1.2 (1982): 190–219.

——. "Exfoliating Cosmos." *Sagetrieb* 2.1 (1983): 35–71.

——. "Nietzsche in the Nursery: Naive Classics and Surrogate Parents in Postwar Cultural Debates." *Representations* 29 (1990): 50–77.

——. "Part of Nature, Part of—'Us'? The Role of Critics and the Emperor's New Clothes in American Poetry." *Sulfur* 9 (1984): 149–67.

——. "*Selected Poems* by Robert Bly." *Sulfur* 19 (1987): 129–34.

Reiss, Timothy J. *The Meaning of Literature*. Ithaca: Cornell UP, 1992.

Renza, Louis. *"A White Heron" and the Question of Minor Literature*. Madison: U of Wisconsin P, 1984.

Rexroth, Kenneth. *American Poetry in the Twentieth Century*. New York: Seabury, 1973.

——. "Disengagement: The Art of the Beat Generation." *Casebook on the Beat*. Parkinson. 179–193.

——. *Kenneth Rexroth and James Laughlin: Selected Letters*. Ed. Lee Bartlett. New York: Norton, 1991.

Reznikoff, Charles. *Testimony, Volume 1: The United States (1885–1915) Recitative*. Santa Barbara: Black Sparrow, 1978.

Rich, Adrienne.*What Is Found There: Notebooks on Poetry and Politics*. New York: Norton, 1993.

——. *Your Native Land, Your Life*. New York: Norton, 1986.

Riding [Jackson], Laura. *The Poems of Laura Riding*. New York: Persea, 1980.

Robbins, Bruce. "Comparative Cosmopolitanism." *Social Text* 10.2/3 (1992): 169–86.

——. *Secular Vocations: Intellectuals, Professionalism, Culture*. London: Verso, 1993.

Rodefer, Stephen. "Stephen Rodefer: 'I inhabit the language the world heaps upon me.'" Interview. *Talking Poetry*. Bartlett 184–207.

Roethke, Theodore. *Collected Poems*. New York: Doubleday, 1966.

————. *Selected Letters.* Ed. Ralph J. Mills, Jr. Seattle: U of Washington P, 1968.

Rogin, Michael Paul. *Ronald Reagan, the Movie, and Other Episodes in Political Demonology.* Berkeley: U of California P, 1987.

Rorty, Richard. "Two Cheers for the Cultural Left." *South Atlantic Quarterly* 89.1 (1990): 227–34.

Rosenthal, M. L. *Our Life in Poetry: Selected Essays and Reviews.* New York: Persea, 1991.

Ross, Andrew. "The New Sentence and the Commodity Form: Recent American Writing." *Marxism and the Interpretation of Culture.* Ed. Cary Nelson and Lawrence Grossberg. Urbana: U of Illinois P, 1988. 361–80.

————. *No Respect: Intellectuals and Popular Culture.* New York: Routledge, 1989.

Rothenberg, Jerome. *Pre-Faces and Other Writings.* New York: New Directions, 1981.

Rothenberg, Jerome, and George Quasha, eds. *America a Prophecy.* New York: Random House, 1973.

Roussel, Raymond. *Locus Solus.* Trans. Rupert Cuningham. London: Calder & Boyars, 1970.

Rukeyser, Muriel. *The Life of Poetry.* New York: Current Books, 1949.

Russo, John Paul. "The Tranquilized Poem: The Crisis of New Criticism in the 1950s." *Texas Studies in Literature and Language* 30.2 (1988): 198–229.

Ryan, Paul. *Video Mind, Earth Mind: Art, Communications, and Ecology.* New York: Peter Lang, 1993.

Said, Edward. "The Horizon of R. P. Blackmur." *Raritan* 6.2 (1986): 29–50.

————. *The World, the Text, and the Critic.* Cambridge: Harvard UP, 1983.

Schiller, Herbert I. *Culture Inc.: The Corporate Takeover of Public Expression.* New York: Oxford UP, 1989.

Scholes, Robert. "Toward a Curriculum in Textual Studies." *Reorientations.* Henricksen and Morgan 95–112.

Schumacher, Michael. *Dharma Lion: A Critical Biography of Allen Ginsberg.* New York: St. Martin's, 1992.

Schwartz, Delmore. *Delmore Schwartz and James Laughlin: Selected Letters.* Ed. Robert Phillips. New York: Norton, 1993.

———. *Selected Essays*. Ed. Donald A. Dike and David H. Zucker. Chicago: U of Chicago P, 1970.

Seager, Allan. *The Glass House: The Life of Theodore Roethke*. New York: McGraw-Hill, 1968.

Seltzer, Mark. *Bodies and Machines*. New York: Routledge, 1992.

Sexton, Anne. *The Complete Poems*. Boston: Houghton Mifflin, 1981.

Shapiro, Alan. *In Praise of the Impure: Poetry and the Ethical Imagination: Essays, 1980–1991*. Evanston: Triquarterly/ Northwestern UP, 1993.

Shapiro, Karl. Contribution to "The Careful Young Men: Tomorrow's Leaders Analyzed by Today's Teachers." *The Nation* 30 (March 9, 1957): 208.

———. "The Case of Ezra Pound." *Partisan Review* 16.5 (1949): 518–20.

———. *In Defense of Ignorance and Other Essays*. New York: Random House, 1960.

———. "Poetry in 1956." *Prairie Schooner* 31 (1957): 11.

———. "Poets of the Silent Generation." *Prairie Schooner* 31 (1957): 298–99.

———. *Reports of My Death*. Chapel Hill: Algonquin Books, 1990.

———. *To Abolish Children, and Other Essays*. Chicago: Quadrangle, 1968.

———. *Trial of a Poet and Other Poems*. New York: Reynal & Hitchcock, 1947.

———. "W. H. Auden: A Leave-Taking." *Prairie Schooner* 31 (1957): 164–67.

Shell, Marc. *Children of the Earth: Literature, Politics and Nationhood*. New York: Oxford UP, 1993.

Shelnutt, Eve. "Notes from a Cell: Creative Writing Programs in Isolation." *Creative Writing in America*. Moxley 3–24.

Shetley, Vernon. *After the Death of Poetry: Poet and Audience in Contemporary America*. Durham, NC: Duke UP, 1993.

Showalter, Elaine. "The Other Bostonians: Gender and Literary Study." *The Yale Journal of Criticism* 1.2 (1988): 179–87.

Silliman, Ron. *The Age of Huts*. New York: Roof, 1986.

———. "Canons and Institutions: New Hope for the Disappeared." *The Politics of Poetic Form*. Bernstein 149–74.

———. "If by 'Writing' We Mean Literature...." *The L=A=N=G=U=A=G=E Book*. Andrews and Bernstein 167–68.

————. *Ketjak*. San Francisco: This, 1978.

————. "Negative Solidarity: Revisionism and 'New American' Poetics." *Sulfur* 22 (1988): 169–76.

————. "The Political Economy of Poetry." *Open Letter* 5.1 (1982): 52–65.

————. *Tjanting*. Berkeley: The Figures, 1981.

Silliman, Ron, ed. *In the American Tree*. Orono, ME: National Poetry Foundation, 1986.

Silverman, Deborah. *Selling Culture: Bloomingdale's, Diana Vreeland, and the New Aristocracy of Taste in Reagan's America*. New York: Pantheon, 1986.

Simpson, Eileen. *Poets in Their Youth: A Memoir*. New York: Random House, 1982.

Simpson, Louis. *Air with Armed Men*. London: London Magazine Editions, 1972.

————. *A Company of Poets*. Ann Arbor: U of Michigan P, 1981.

Smith, Anthony. *The Shadow in the Cave: The Broadcaster, His Audience, and the State*. Urbana: U of Illinois P, 1973.

Smith, Dave, and David Bottoms, eds. *The Morrow Anthology of Younger American Poets*. New York: Morrow, 1985.

Söderlind, Sylvia. *Margin/Alias: Language and Colonization in Canadian and Quebeçois Fiction*. Toronto: U of Toronto P, 1991.

Spender, Stephen. *Love-Hate Relations: A Study of Anglo-American Sensibilities*. London: Hamilton, 1974.

Spicer, Jack. *The Collected Books*. Ed. Robin Blaser. Los Angeles: Black Sparrow, 1975.

Spigal, Lynn. *Make Room for TV: Television and the Family Ideal in Postwar America*. Chicago: U of Chicago P, 1992.

Spitzer, Leo. "History of Ideas Versus Reading of Poetry." *Southern Review* 6.3 (Winter 1941): 584–609.

Spivak, Gayatri. *Outside in the Teaching Machine*. New York: Routledge, 1993.

Stafford, William. *Writing the Australian Crawl: Views on the Writer's Vocation*. Ann Arbor: U of Michigan P, 1978.

Stein, Charles. "Modalities of Identity." *The Little Magazine* 20 (1994): 21–36.

Steiner, George. *On Difficulty and Other Essays*. New York: Oxford UP, 1978.

Stern, Richard G. "American Poetry of the Fifties: Preface." *The Western Review* 21.3 (1957): 167–68.

Stevens, Wallace. *The Necessary Angel.* New York: Knopf, 1951.

———. *The Palm at the End of the Mind.* Ed. Holly Stevens. New York: Knopf, 1971.

———. Response to "The State of American Writing, 1948: Seven Questions." *Partisan Review* 15.8 (1948): 884–86.

Stewart, Susan. *On Longing: Narratives of the Miniature, the Gigantic, the Souvenir, the Collection.* Baltimore: Johns Hopkins UP, 1984.

Stimpson, Catharine R. "Reading for Love: Canons, Paracanons, and Whistling Jo March." *New Literary History* 21 (1990): 957–76.

Swingewood, Alan. *A Short History of Sociological Thought.* London: Macmillan, 1984.

Szacki, Jerzy. *History of Sociological Thought.* Westport, CT: Greenwood, 1979.

Tate, Allen. *Collected Essays.* Denver: Alan Swallow, 1959.

———. "Further Remarks on the Pound Award." *Partisan Review* 16.6 (1949): 666–68.

———. "Introduction to American Poetry, 1900–1950." *Modern Verse in English.* Ed. David Cecil and Allen Tate. London: Eyre & Spottiswoode, 1958. 39–48.

———. "Poetry Modern and Unmodern." *The Hudson Review* 21.2 (1968): 251–62.

———. *Sixty American Poets 1896–1944.* Washington, DC: Library of Congress, 1944; reissued 1954.

Thoreau, Henry David. *Walden, and Civil Disobedience.* Ed. Owen Thomas. New York: Norton, 1966.

Tompkins, Jane. *Sensational Designs: The Cultural Work of American Fiction, 1790–1860.* New York: Oxford UP, 1985.

Torrey, E. Fuller. *The Roots of Treason: Ezra Pound and the Secret of St. Elizabeth's.* New York: McGraw-Hill, 1984.

Trilling, Lionel. *The Liberal Imagination: Essays on Literature and Society.* New York: Viking, 1950.

———. Response to "The State of American Writing, 1948: Seven Questions." *Partisan Review* 15.8 (1948): 886–93.

Turner, Frederick. *Natural Classicism: Essays on Literature and Science.* New York: Paragon House, 1985.

Twitchell, James B. *Carnival Culture: The Trashing of Taste in America.* New York: Columbia UP, 1992.

Untermeyer, Louis. *American Poetry Since 1900.* New York: Holt, 1923.

———. "Modern American Poetry: A Selected List for the Medium Size Library." *Library Journal* 87 (June 1, 1962): 2084–85.

Valéry, Paul. "The Problem of Museums." *Degas, Manet, Morisot.* Trans. David Paul. The Collected Works in English. Vol. 12. New York: Pantheon/ Bollingen Series, 1960. 202–06.

Vendler, Helen. "Ha—mine soul—I say 'alas' and I say 'alas' and 'alas' and 'alas'!" *The New York Times Book Review* Dec. 30, 1973: 7–8.

———. "Presidential Address 1980." *PMLA* 96.3 (1981): 344–50.

Vendler, Helen, ed. *The Harvard Book of Contemporary American Poetry.* Cambridge: Harvard UP, 1985.

Vidler, Anthony. *The Architectural Uncanny: Essays in the Modern Unhomely.* Cambridge: MIT, 1992.

Viereck, Peter. "Anti-Form or Neo: A Curse on Both Houses." *Parnassus* 17.2/18.1 (1993): 306–21.

———. *Archer in the Marrow: The Applewood Cycles of 1968–1984.* New York: Norton, 1987.

———. *Dream and Responsibility: Four Test Cases of the Tension Between Poetry and Society.* Washington, DC: The University Press, 1953.

———. *The Unadjusted Man: A New Hero for Modern America.* New York: Capricorn, 1962.

Vincent, Stephen. "Poetry Readings/Reading Poetry: San Francisco Bay Area, 1958–1980." *The Poetry Reading: A Contemporary Compendium on Language and Performance.* Ed. Stephen Vincent and Ellen Zweig. San Francisco: Momo's Press, 1981. 19–54.

Virilio, Paul and Sylvère Lotringer. *Pure War.* Trans. Mark Polizotti. New York: Semiotext(e), 1983.

Vogler, Thomas A. "Introduction." *Books as Objects.* Portland: Comus Gallery, 1993.

Wagner-Martin, Linda. Response to "Is There, Currently, an American Poetry?" *American Poetry* 4.2 (1987).

Wakoski, Diane. "The New Conservatism in American Poetry." *New Letters* (Fall 1989): 17–38.

———. *Toward a New Poetry*. Ann Arbor: U of Michigan P, 1980.

Waldrop, Rosmarie. *The Reproduction of Profiles*. New York: New Directions, 1987.

Walker, Peter. "Arnold's Legacy: Religious Rhetoric of Critics on the Literary Canon." *The Hospitable Canon*. Nemoianu and Royal 181–98.

Wallerstein, Immanuel. *Geopolitics and Geoculture: Essays on the Changing World-System*. New York: Cambridge UP, 1991.

Ward, Geoff. *Statutes of Liberty: The New York School of Poets*. London: Macmillan, 1993.

Ward, J. P. *Poetry and the Sociological Idea*. Sussex: Harvester, 1981.

Watten, Barrett. "For *Change*." *In the American Tree*. Silliman 485–86.

———. "Note." *The L=A=N=G=U=A=G=E Book*. Andrews and Bernstein 17–18.

———. *Total Syntax*. Carbondale: Southern Illinois UP, 1985.

———. "The XYZ of Reading: Negativity (&)." *Poetics Journal* 6 (1986): 3–5.

Webster, Grant. *The Republic of Letters: A History of Postwar American Literary Opinion*. Baltimore: Johns Hopkins UP, 1979.

Weinberger, Eliot. "Davidson and Weinberger on Language Poetry." *Sulfur* 22 (1988): 177–88.

———. "A Final Response." *Sulfur* 22 (1988): 199–202.

———. "To the Editors." *American Poetry Review* 23.4 (1994): 43–44.

Weinberger, Eliot, ed. *American Poetry Since 1950: Innovators and Outsiders*. New York: Marsilio, 1993.

Wellek, René. *A History of Modern Criticism: 1750–1950*. Vol. 6. New Haven: Yale UP, 1986.

Wells, Henry W. "The Usable Past in Poetry." *American Quarterly* 1.3 (1949): 235–46.

Wesling, Donald. *The Chances of Rhyme: Device and Modernity*. Berkeley: U of California P, 1980.

West, Cornel. "Minority Discourse and the Pitfalls of Canon Formation." *Yale Journal of Criticism* 1.1 (1987): 193–201.

Wharton, Edith. *The Age of Innocence*. New York: Macmillan, 1986.

Whiteside, Thomas. *The Blockbuster Complex*. Middletown, CT: Wesleyan UP, 1981.

Whitman, Walt. *Leaves of Grass and Selected Prose*. Ed. Lawrence Buell. New York: Modern Library, 1981.

Whittemore, Reed. "Aesthetics in the Sonnet Shop." *The American Scholar* 28.3 (1959): 344–53.

Wilbur, Richard. "Craft Interview." *The Craft of Poetry: Interviews from The New York Quarterly*. Ed. William Packard. New York: Doubleday, 1974. 177–94.

———. *The Poems of Richard Wilbur*. New York: Harcourt, Brace & World, 1963.

Williams, Martin. *The Jazz Tradition*. Revised ed. New York: Oxford UP, 1983.

Williams, Raymond. *Problems in Materialism and Culture*. London: Verso, 1980.

Williams, William Carlos. *The Autobiography of William Carlos Williams*. New York: New Directions, 1967.

———. *The Embodiment of Knowledge*. Ed. Ron Loewinsohn. New York: New Directions, 1974.

———. *Imaginations*. Ed. Webster Schott. New York: New Directions, 1970.

———. *Paterson*. New York: New Directions, 1948.

Wordsworth, William. *The Prelude*. Ed. Ernest de Selincourt. Corrected by Stephen Gill. London: Oxford UP, 1970.

Wright, James. *Collected Prose*. Ed. Anne Wright. Ann Arbor: U of Michigan P, 1982.

Yau, John. "Neither Us Nor Them." *American Poetry Review* 23.2 (1994): 45–54.

Jed Rasula teaches English at Queen's University in Kingston, Ontario. He holds a Ph.D. in the History of Consciousness from the University of California at Santa Cruz, and taught previously at Pomona College in California. He is co-editor of *Imagining Language, An Anthology* (forthcoming, MIT Press), and co-author, with Don Byrd, of *Tactics of Attention*, a collection of essays on the poetry scene in America from 1975 to 1995 (forthcoming). He worked for a number of years in radio and television in Hollywood, including a stint as researcher for the ABC television series "Ripley's Believe It Or Not." He lives in Kingston with his wife and two daughters.